1001 All-Time Best-Selling Home Plans

HOME PLANNERS, LLC
Wholly owned by Hanley-Wood, LLC

Table of Contents

Editor's Note

Because of the volume of plans in this book, browsing can be quite a daunting task. We suggest you take your time and look throughout the book—there may be styles of homes you may never have considered, but which would fit your needs completely.

Besides house plans, we also offer many helpful additional products and services. For instance, our Quote One® pricing system will help you determine the cost of building a particular home in your area—before you build. Look for homes that are part of the Quote One® system that display this symbol:

QUOTE ONE®

Cost to build? See page 684
to order complete cost estimate
to build this house in your area!

For additional information about Quote One®, see page 684. We also offer finishing touches for your home—landscape and deck plans to help dress up the exterior. Plans that have corresponding landscape and deck plans will have these symbols:

See pages 686 and 687 for more information about these outdoor plans. Many of the homes in this book are also customizable. See page 701 for more information about this program. For a description of other products to make your home building experience easy and understandable, see pages 684-685.

HOME PLANNERS, LLC
Wholly owned by Hanley-Wood, LLC

Published by Home Planners, LLC
Wholly owned by Hanley-Wood, LLC

Editorial and Corporate Offices:
3275 West Ina Road, Suite 110
Tucson, Arizona 85741

Distribution Center:
29333 Lori Lane
Wixom, Michigan 48393

Rickard D. Bailey, *CEO and Publisher*
Cindy Coatsworth Lewis, *Director of Publishing*
Jan Prideaux, *Executive Editor*
Paulette Mulvin, *Editor*
Jeanine Newsom, *Proofreader*
Brenda McClary, *Publications Assistant*
Jennifer Skiffington, *Editorial Assistant*
Morenci Wodraska, *Editorial Assistant*
Alan Mitchell, *Editorial Assistant*
Sara Lisa Rappaport, *Manufacturing Coordinator*
Jay C. Walsh, *Graphic Designer*
Robert D. Caldwell, *Production Artist*
Peter Zullo, *Production Artist*

Photo Credits

Front Cover:
Design A126 (main image), page 315.
Photo by Robert Starling / Orlando

Design F146 (inset), page 183.
Photo by Roger Hart

10 9 8 7 6 5 4 3 2 1

Printed in the United States of America

Library of Congress Catalog Card Number:
99-80139

ISBN: 1-881955-67-2

The home, as shown in the photograph, may differ from the actual blueprints.
For more detailed information, please check the floor plans carefully.

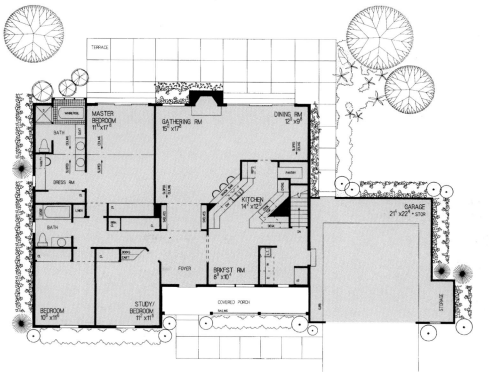

Quote One®

Cost to build? See page 684
to order complete cost estimate
to build this house in your area!

Design by
© Home Planners

Width 75'-0"
Depth 43'-5"

This charming one-story traditional home greets visitors with a covered porch. A galley-style kitchen shares a snack bar with the spacious gathering room where a fireplace is the focal point.

An ample master suite includes a luxury bath with a whirlpool tub and a separate dressing room. Two additional bedrooms, one that could double as a study, are located at the front of the home.

DESIGN 2947
Square Footage: 1,830
L D

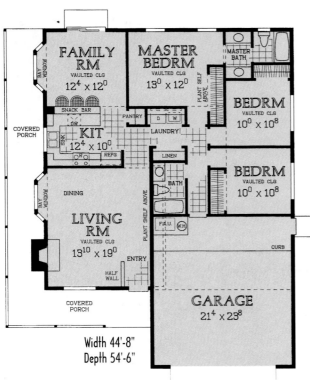

FAMILY RM
VAULTED CLG
12⁴ x 12⁰

MASTER BEDRM
VAULTED CLG
13⁰ x 12⁰

MASTER BATH

PLANT SHELF ABOVE

BEDRM
VAULTED CLG
10⁰ x 10⁸

SNACK BAR

PANTRY

KIT
12⁴ x 10⁰

LAUNDRY

D W

DW

SINK

REFG

LINEN

DINING

BATH

BEDRM
VAULTED CLG
10⁰ x 10⁸

COVERED PORCH

BAY WINDOW

BAY WINDOW

PLANT SHELF ABOVE

LIVING RM
VAULTED CLG
13¹⁰ x 19⁰

F.A.U.

W.H.

CURB

ENTRY

HALF WALL

COVERED PORCH

GARAGE
21⁴ x 23⁸

Width 44'-8"
Depth 54'-6"

DESIGN 3460
Square Footage: 1,389
L

A double dose of charm, this special farmhouse plan offers two elevations in its blueprint package. Though rooflines and porch options are different, the floor plan is basically the same and very livable. A formal living room has a warming fireplace and a delightful bay window. The kitchen separates this area from the more casual family room. Three bedrooms include two family bedrooms served by a full, shared bath and a lovely master suite with its own private bath. Each room has a vaulted ceiling and large windows to let the outdoors in beautifully. A two-car garage sits to the front.

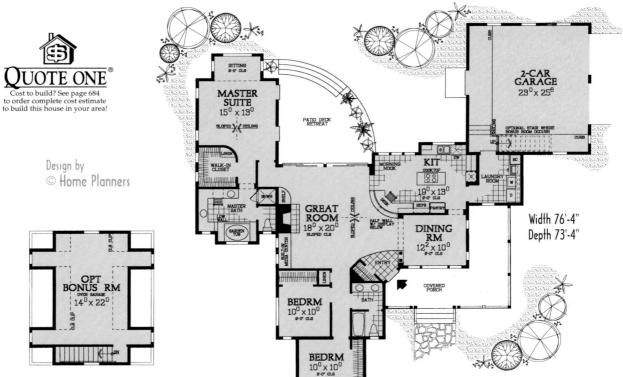

QUOTE ONE®
Cost to build? See page 684
to order complete cost estimate
to build this house in your area!

Design by
© Home Planners

OPT BONUS RM
over garage
14⁰ x 22⁰

SITTING
9'-0" CLG

MASTER SUITE
15⁰ x 19⁰
SLOPED CEILING

LINEN

WALK-IN CLOSET

MASTER BATH
LOW WALL

SHELF

SHWR

GARDEN TUB

GREAT ROOM
18⁰ x 20⁰
SLOPED CLG

BUILT-IN MEDIA CENTER

LINEN

BEDRM
10⁰ x 10⁰
9'-0" CLG

BEDRM
10⁰ x 10⁰
9'-0" CLG

BATH

PATIO DECK RETREAT

MORNING NOOK

KIT
19⁰ x 13⁰
9'-0" CLG

COOKTOP

LAUNDRY ROOM

PANTRY

REFG

HALF WALL W/ DISPLAY BELOW

DINING RM
12² x 10⁰
9'-0" CLG

ENTRY

COVERED PORCH

2-CAR GARAGE
23⁰ x 25⁶

OPTIONAL STAIR WHERE BONUS ROOM OCCURS

Width 76'-4"
Depth 73'-4"

The dining room of this flowing, three-bedroom design looks onto the covered porch for relaxing dining. The tiled entry foyer leads directly to the great room, with its built-in media center, corner shelves, and access to the rear patio deck. A country kitchen with island cooktop, morning nook and built-in desk is open to the great room over a half wall. The master suite, with sloped ceiling, features an extended sitting area with windows on three sides. The walk-in closet provides built-in linen shelves, and the master bath has dual vanities, a separate shower and a garden tub.

DESIGN 3662
Square Footage: 1,937
Bonus Room: 414 square feet

BEST-SELLING HOMES IN COLOR

©1992 Donald A. Gardner Architects, Inc.

SCREENED PORCH
40-0 × 10-6
skylights skylights

DECK

seat

spa

Design by
Donald A. Gardner
Architects, Inc.

MASTER BED RM.
12-8 × 17-2

walk-in closet

master bath

GREAT RM.
15-4 × 24-0
fireplace
balcony above

BRKFST.
10-4 × 8-8

UTILITY
9-6 × 9-8
w d
cl

storage storage

GARAGE
23-4 × 21-8

covered breezeway

bath
lin.
cl

BED RM./ STUDY
12-8 × 11-0
cl
cl
up

KITCHEN
12-8 × 14-6

FOYER
15-4 × 9-8

DINING
14-8 × 12-8

© 1992 Donald A. Gardner Architects, Inc.

PORCH
40-0 × 8-0

Width 93'-10"
Depth 62'-0"

Quote One®
Cost to build? See page 684
to order complete cost estimate
to build this house in your area!

clerestory with arched window

(cathedral ceiling)
great room below

railing

skylight skylight

BED RM.
12-8 × 11-6

LOFT
11-10 × 7-8

BED RM.
12-8 × 11-6

down

foyer below

clerestory with palladian window

**DESIGN
9712**
First Floor: 1,766 square feet
Second Floor: 670 square feet
Total: 2,436 square feet

With an elegant but casual exterior, this four-bedroom farmhouse celebrates sunlight from a Palladian window and triple dormers, a skylit screened porch and a rear arched window. The clerestory window in the two-story foyer throws natural light across the loft to the great room, with a fireplace and a cathedral ceiling. The center island kitchen and the break- fast area open to the great room through an elegant colonnade. The first-floor master suite is a calm retreat with its own access to the screened porch through a bay area—and a luxurious bath awaits with a garden tub, dual lavatories and a separate shower. Upstairs, two family bedrooms offer plush amenities: a sky- light, private bath and dormer window in each room.

© 1991 Donald A. Gardner Architects, Inc.

Design by
Donald A. Gardner
Architects, Inc.

Width 56'-8"
Depth 54'-4"

© 1991 Donald A. Gardner Architects, Inc.

DECK 42-0 x 14-0

seat   seat

spa

skylights   skylights

GREAT RM. 15-4 x 21-0

BRKFST. 10-4 x 10-2

UTILITY 7-6 x 7-10

walk-in closet

MASTER BED RM. 12-8 x 19-6

fireplace

master bath

balcony above

KITCHEN 12-8 x 13-0

lin.

bath

BED RM./ STUDY 12-8 x 11-0

sto.   cl

up

FOYER 15-4 x 5-4

DINING 12-8 x 12-8

walk-in closet

PORCH

clerestory with arched window

(cathedral ceiling)
great room below

storage   storage

railing

BED RM. 12-8 x 12-0

balcony

BED RM. 12-8 x 12-0

down

cl   cl   bath   cl   cl

foyer below

clerestory with palladian window

QUOTE ONE®
Cost to build? See page 684
to order complete cost estimate
to build this house in your area!

A wraparound covered porch at the front and sides of this house and an open deck at the back provide plenty of outside living area. The spacious great room features a fireplace, cathedral ceiling and clerestory with an arched window. The island kitchen has an attached, skylit breakfast room complete with a bay window. The first-floor master bedroom contains a generous closet and a master bath with garden tub, double-bowl vanity and shower. The second floor sports two bedrooms and a full bath with double-bowl vanity. An elegant balcony overlooks the great room. Look for a spa on the rear deck. A basement or crawlspace foundation is available.

DESIGN 9632
First Floor: 1,756 square feet
Second Floor: 565 square feet
Total: 2,321 square feet

BEST-SELLING HOMES IN COLOR

The home, as shown in the photograph, may differ from the actual blueprints.
For more detailed information, please check the floor plans carefully.

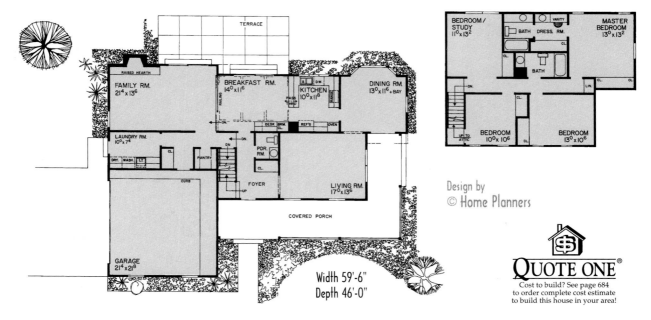

TERRACE

RAISED HEARTH

FAMILY RM.
21⁴ x 13⁶

BREAKFAST RM.
14⁰ x 11⁶

KITCHEN
10⁰ x 11⁸

DINING RM.
13⁰ x 11⁶ + BAY

LAUNDRY RM.
10⁰ x 7⁶

DRY. WASH.

CL.

PANTRY

DESK BRM.
CL.

REF'G OVEN

PASS
THRU

RANGE

D.W.

FOYER

PDR.
RM.

CL.

UP

DN.

DN.

CURB

GARAGE
21⁴ x 21⁸

COVERED PORCH

LIVING RM.
17⁰ x 13⁶

Width 59'-6"
Depth 46'-0"

BEDROOM /
STUDY
11⁰ x 13²

BATH

DRESS. RM.

VANITY

MASTER
BEDROOM
13⁰ x 13²

CL.

CL.

CL.

BATH

LIN.

CL.

CL.

DN.

UP TO
ATTIC

BEDROOM
10⁰ x 10⁶

BEDROOM
13⁰ x 10⁶

Design by
© Home Planners

QUOTE ONE®
Cost to build? See page 684
to order complete cost estimate
to build this house in your area!

BEST-SELLING HOMES IN COLOR

DESIGN
2774
First Floor: 1,366 square feet
Second Floor: 969 square feet
Total: 2,335 square feet
Bonus Room: 969 square feet

L D

Here's a great farmhouse adaptation with all the most up-to-date features. There is the quiet corner living room with an opening to the sizable dining room. This room will enjoy plenty of natural light from the delightful bay window overlooking the rear yard and is conveniently located near the efficient U-shaped kitchen. The kitchen features many built-ins and a pass-through to the beam-ceilinged nook. Sliding glass doors to the terrace are found in both the family room and nook. The service entrance to the garage is flanked by a clothes closet and a large, walk-in pantry. Recreational activities and hobbies can be pursued in the basement. Four bedrooms and two baths are located on the second floor. The master bedroom has a dressing room and double vanity.

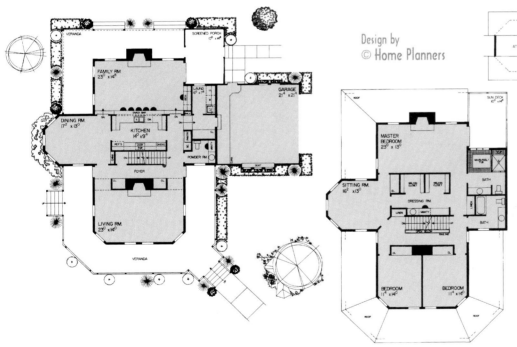

Design by
© Home Planners

Width 67'-0"
Depth 66'-0"

QUOTE ONE®

Cost to build? See page 684
to order complete cost estimate
to build this house in your area!

This charming Victorian home features a covered outdoor living area on all four sides! It even ends at a screened porch that features a sun deck above. This interesting plan offers three floors of livability. There are formal and informal living facilities to go along with the potential of five bedrooms. The master suite is just fantastic. It is adjacent to a wonderful sitting room and offers a sun deck and lavish bath/personal care facilities. The third floor will make a wonderful haven for the family's student members.

DESIGN 2970

First Floor: 1,538 square feet
Second level: 1,526 square feet
Third Level: 658 square feet
Total: 3,722 square feet

L

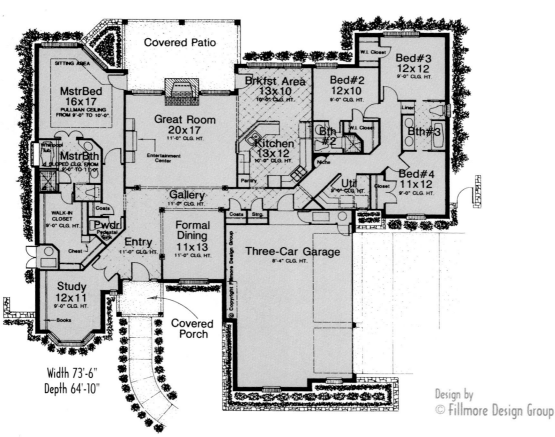

Covered Patio

SITTING AREA

MstrBed
16x17
PULLMAN CEILING
FROM 9'-0" TO 10'-0"

Great Room
20x17
11'-0" CLG. HT.

Brkfst Area
13x10
10'-0" CLG. HT.

Bed#2
12x10
9'-0" CLG. HT.

W.I. Closet

Bed#3
12x12
9'-0" CLG. HT.

Whirlpool
Tub

MstrBth
SLOPED CLG. FROM
9'-0" TO 11'-0"

Entertainment
Center

Kitchen
13x12
10'-0" CLG. HT.

Bth
#2

W.I. Closet

Niche

Linen

Bth#3

WALK-IN
CLOSET
9'-0" CLG. HT.

Coats

Pantry

Bed#4
11x12
9'-0" CLG. HT.

Pwdr
Pedestal
Sink

Gallery
11'-0" CLG. HT.

Util
9'-0" CLG. HT.

Closet

Chest

Entry
11'-0" CLG. HT.

Coats

Strg

Formal
Dining
11x13
11'-0" CLG. HT.

Three-Car Garage
8'-4" CLG. HT.

© Copyright Fillmore Design Group

Study
12x11
9'-0" CLG. HT.

Books

Covered
Porch

Width 73'-6"
Depth 64'-10"

Design by
© Fillmore Design Group

DESIGN M131
Square Footage: 2,590

With a solid exterior of rough cedar and stone, this new country French design will stand the test of time. A wood-paneled study on the front features a large bay window. The heart of the house is found in a large, open great room with a built-in entertainment center. The spacious master bedroom features a corner reading area and access to an adjacent covered patio. A three-car garage and three additional bedrooms complete this generous family home.

The home, as shown in the photograph, may differ from the actual blueprints. For more detailed information, please check the floor plans carefully.

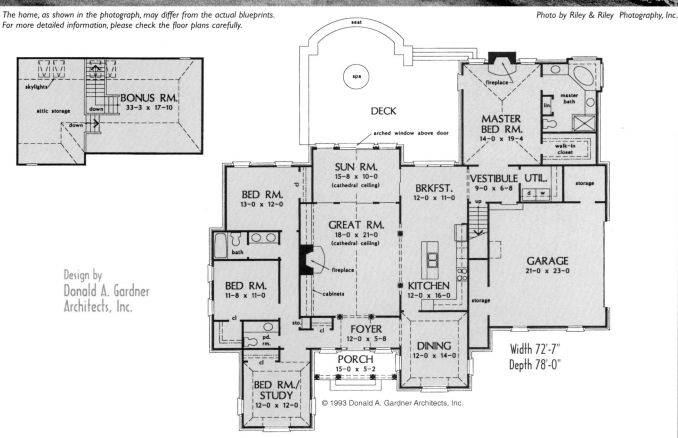

BONUS RM. 33-3 x 17-10

skylights
attic storage
down
down

seat
spa
DECK
arched window above door

Design by
Donald A. Gardner
Architects, Inc.

BED RM. 13-0 x 12-0

SUN RM. 15-8 x 10-0 (cathedral ceiling)

BRKFST. 12-0 x 11-0

fireplace

MASTER BED RM. 14-0 x 19-4

master bath

lin

walk-in closet

VESTIBULE UTIL. 9-0 x 6-8

storage

d w

GREAT RM. 18-0 x 21-0 (cathedral ceiling)

bath

fireplace

BED RM. 11-8 x 11-0

cabinets

KITCHEN 12-0 x 16-0

up

GARAGE 21-0 x 23-0

cl

pd. rm.

sto.

cl

FOYER 12-0 x 5-8

storage

DINING 12-0 x 14-0

Width 72'-7"
Depth 78'-0"

BED RM./ STUDY 12-0 x 12-0

cl

PORCH 15-0 x 5-2

© 1993 Donald A. Gardner Architects, Inc.

This home features large arched windows, round columns, a covered porch and brick veneer siding. The arched window in the clerestory above the entrance provides natural light to the interior. The great room boasts a cathedral ceiling, a fireplace, built-in cabinets and bookshelves. Sliding glass doors lead to the sun room. The L-shaped kitchen serves the dining room, the breakfast area and the great room. The master bedroom suite, with a fireplace, uses a private passage to the deck and its spa. Three additional bedrooms—one could serve as a study—are at the other end of the house for privacy

BEST-SELLING HOMES IN COLOR

DESIGN 9709
Square Footage: 2,663
Bonus Room: 653 square feet

Design by
© Home Planners

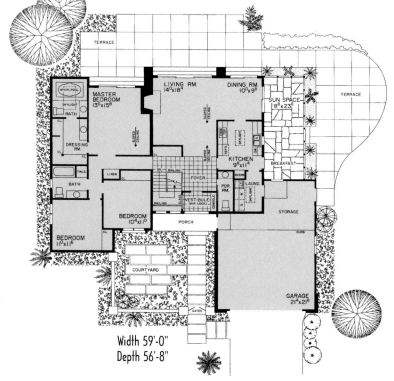

Width 59'-0"
Depth 56'-8"

QUOTE ONE®

Cost to build? See page 684
to order complete cost estimate
to build this house in your area!

DESIGN
2902
Square Footage: 1,632
Bonus Room: 216 square feet

L

A sun space highlights this passive solar design. It features access from the kitchen, the dining room and the garage. It will be a great place to enjoy meals because of its location. Three skylights highlight the interior—in the kitchen, laundry and master bath. An air-locked vestibule helps this design's energy efficiency. Interior livability is excellent. The living/dining room rises with a sloped ceiling and enjoys a fireplace and two sets of sliding glass doors to the terrace. Three bedrooms are in the sleeping wing. The master bedroom will delight with its private bath that has a luxurious whirlpool tub.

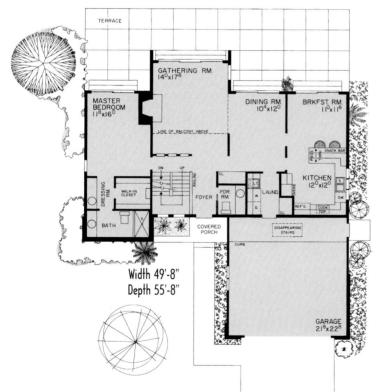

Width 49'-8"
Depth 55'-8"

Design by
© Home Planners

All of the livability in this plan is in the back! With this sort of configuration, this home makes a perfect lakefront or beachfront home. Each first-floor room, except the kitchen, maintains access to the rear terrace via sliding glass doors. However, the kitchen is open to the breakfast room and thus takes advantage of the view. The master bedroom delights with its private bath and walk-in closet. Two secondary bedrooms comprise the second floor. One utilizes a walk-in closet while both make use of a full hall bath. A lounge overlooks the foyer as well as the gathering room below.

DESIGN 2905
First Floor: 1,342 square feet
Second Floor: 619 square feet
Total: 1,961 square feet
L D

Design by
© Home Planners

Width 75'-6"
Depth 62'-6"

QUOTE ONE®
Cost to build? See page 684
to order complete cost estimate
to build this house in your area!

DESIGN 3639
First Floor: 2,137 square feet
Second Floor: 671 square feet
Total: 2,808 square feet

L

f first impressions really make the most important statements, this home makes it in grand style. The two-story entry-way and double doors to the reception foyer make a first impression that can't be beat. Inside, formal living areas grab your attention with a dining room and an elegant living room that opens to a covered entertainment area outside. The family room—with a fire-place—features open views to the kitchen and breakfast nook. The nearby "recipe corner" includes a built-in desk. The laundry room is fully functional with a laundry tub and a broom closet. On the left side of the plan, the master bedroom suite has a full, private bath and a lanai perfect for a spa. A large den could easily double as a study. Two bedrooms and a full bath are located upstairs.

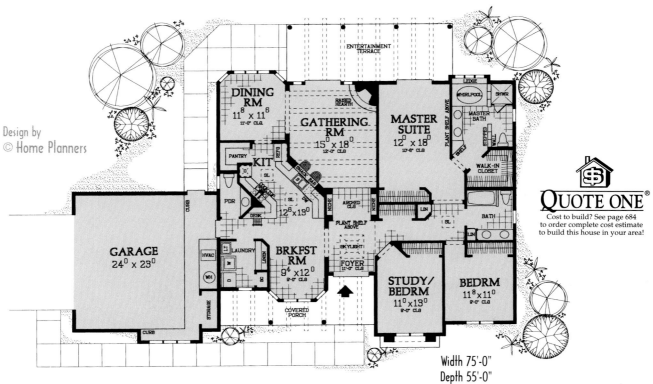

Design by
© Home Planners

Quote One®
Cost to build? See page 684
to order complete cost estimate
to build this house in your area!

Width 75'-0"
Depth 55'-0"

BEST-SELLING HOMES IN COLOR

This classic stucco design provides a cool retreat in any climate. From the covered porch, enter the skylit foyer to find an arched ceiling leading to the central gathering room with its raised-hearth fireplace and terrace access. A connecting corner dining room is conveniently located near the amenity-filled kitchen that features an abundant pantry, a snack bar and a separate breakfast area. The large master bedroom includes terrace access and a master bath with a whirlpool tub, separate shower and plenty of closet space. A second bedroom and a study that can be converted to a bedroom complete this wonderful plan.

DESIGN
3486
Square Footage: 2,000

The home, as shown in the photograph, may differ from the actual blueprints. For more detailed information, please check the floor plans carefully.

Photo by Bob Greenspan

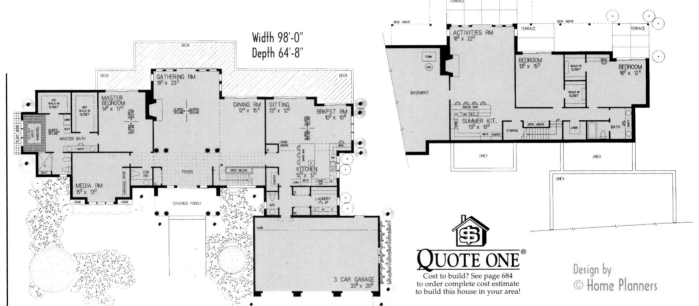

Width 98'-0"
Depth 64'-8"

QUOTE ONE®
Cost to build? See page 684 to order complete cost estimate to build this house in your area!

Design by
© Home Planners

DESIGN 3311
Main Level: 2,662 square feet
Lower Level: 1,548 square feet
Total: 4,210 square feet
L D

Here's a hillside haven for family living with plenty of room to entertain in style. Enter the main level from a dramatic columned portico that leads to a large entry hall. The gathering room, graced by a fireplace and sliding glass doors to the rear deck, is straight back and adjoins a formal dining area. A true gourmet kitchen with plenty of room for casual eating and conversation is nearby. The abundantly appointed master suite on this level is complemented by a luxurious bath complete with His and Hers walk-in closets, a whirlpool tub in a bumped-out bay and a separate shower. Note the media room to the front of the house. On the lower level are two more bedrooms—each with access to the rear terrace—a full bath, a large activity area with fireplace and a convenient summer kitchen. A three-car garage connects at the laundry room.

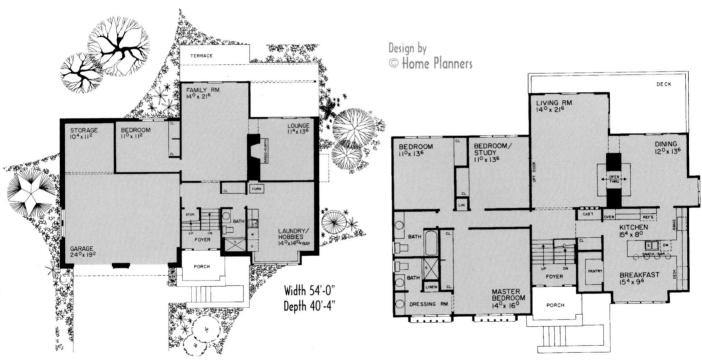

Design by
© Home Planners

Width 54'-0"
Depth 40'-4"

Spanish-style bi-level? Why not? This one has lots going for it upstairs and down. Up top, note the living room and formal dining room; they share a fireplace, and each leads to a comfy deck out back. In addition, the kitchen and breakfast area are centers of attention; the latter has a won-

derful, over-sized pantry. Zoned to the left of the entry are three bedrooms (two if you make one a study). Down below is a potpourri of space: family room, lounge with raised-hearth fireplace, large laundry room (note the bay window), another bedroom, full bath and plenty of storage in the garage.

DESIGN 2843
Main Level: 1,861 square feet
Lower Level: 1,181 square feet
Total: 3,042 square feet
L

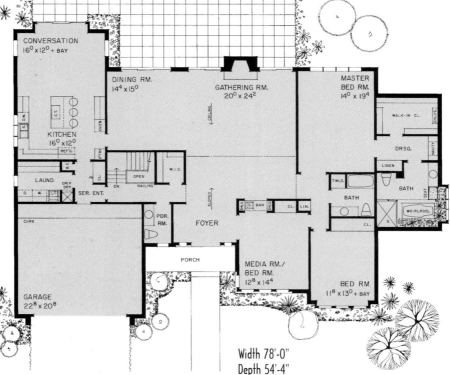

CONVERSATION
16⁰ x 12⁰ + BAY

DINING RM.
14⁴ x 15⁰

GATHERING RM.
20⁰ x 24²

MASTER
BED RM.
14⁰ x 19⁴

WALK-IN CL.

SHLVS.

Design by
© Home Planners

KITCHEN
16⁰ x 12⁰

DRSG.

VANITY

LINEN

OVEN

REFG.

LAUND.

DRIP DRY

SER. ENT.

W.I.C.

OPEN

DN

RAILING

BAR

CL.

LIN.

TWLS.

BATH

BATH

SEAT

WHIRLPOOL

CL.

CURB

PDR.
RM.

FOYER

SLOPED

QUOTE ONE®

Cost to build? See page 684
to order complete cost estimate
to build this house in your area!

PORCH

MEDIA RM./
BED RM.
12⁸ x 14⁴

BED RM.
11⁸ x 13⁰ + BAY

GARAGE
22⁸ x 20⁸

Width 78'-0"
Depth 54'-4"

DESIGN
3368
Square Footage: 2,722
L D

Rooflines are the key to the interesting exterior of this design. Their configuration allows for sloped ceilings in the gathering room and large foyer. Both the gathering room and the dining room offer access to the rear terrace via sliding glass doors. The master

bedroom suite has a huge walk-in closet, garden whirlpool tub and separate shower. Two family bedrooms share a full bath. One of these bedrooms could be used as a media room with pass-through wet bar. Note the large kitchen with conversation bay and the wide terrace to the rear.

The home, as shown in the photograph, may differ from the actual blueprints. For more detailed information, please check the floor plans carefully.

Photo by Bob Greenspan

Width 97'-0"
Depth 102'-8"

Design by
© Home Planners

REAR VIEW

Quote One®
Cost to build? See page 684
to order complete cost estimate
to build this house in your area!

Cost to build? See page 684

This contemporary design has a great deal to offer. A fireplace opens up to both the living room and country kitchen. The kitchen is a gourmet's delight, with a huge walk-in pantry, a deluxe work island that includes a snack bar, and easy access to the formal dining room. A media room has plenty of storage and offers access to the rear terrace. Privacy is the key word when describing the sleeping areas. The first-floor master bedroom is away from the traffic of the house and features a dressing/exercise room, a whirlpool tub and shower and a spacious walk-in closet. Two more bedrooms and a full bath are on the second floor. The three-car garage is arranged so that the owners have use of a double-garage with an attached single on reserve for guests. The cheerful sun room adds 296 square feet to the total. Don't miss the clutter room just off the kitchen.

DESIGN 2920
First Floor: 3,067 square feet
Second Floor: 648 square feet
Total: 3,715 square feet
Bonus Room: 296 square feet
L D

BEST-SELLING HOMES IN COLOR

Design by
© Design Basics, Inc.

ALTERNATE FRONT VIEW

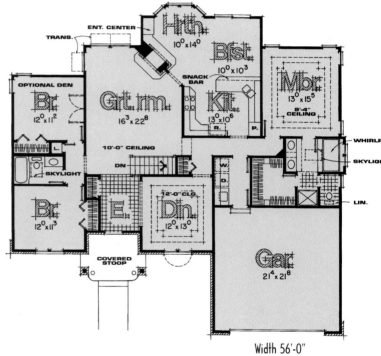

Width 56'-0"
Depth 58'-0"

QUOTE ONE®

Cost to build? See page 684
to order complete cost estimate
to build this house in your area!

BEST-SELLING HOMES IN COLOR

**DESIGN
9204**
Square Footage: 1,911

This sophisticated ranch design shows off its facade with fanlights and elegant arches. Grace pervades the interior, starting with the formal dining room with a twelve-foot coffered ceiling and an arched window. An extensive great room shares a through-fireplace with a bayed hearth room. The well-planned kitchen features a spacious work area and a snack-bar pass-through to the breakfast area. The secluded master suite offers a coffered ceiling, corner windows, a whirlpool bath and a skylight. On the opposite side of the plan, two family bedrooms, or one and a den, share a hall bath that has a skylight. An alternate elevation is available at no extra cost. A two-car garage protects the master suite from street noise.

Design by
© Stephen Fuller,
American Home Gallery

BATH

BEDROOM NO. 3
11'-6" X 11'-0"

BEDROOM NO. 2
11'-4" X 11'-0"

SUN ROOM
12'-0" X 13'-9"

PORCH

MASTER BATH

W.I.C.

MASTER BEDROOM
13'-4" X 15'-8"

BREAKFAST
10'-0" X 9'-0"

FAMILY ROOM
18'-0" X 14'-0"

LAUNDRY

KITCHEN
12'-0" X 13'-9"

DN.

BATH

DINING ROOM
10'-6" X 13'-6"

FOYER

DEN
11'-4" X 12'-6"

TWO CAR GARAGE
20'-4" X 20'-8"

STOOP

Width 62'-0"
Depth 62'-6"

QUOTE ONE®
Cost to build? See page 684
to order complete cost estimate
to build this house in your area!

Arched-top windows act as graceful accents for this wonderful design. Inside, the floor plan is compact but commodious. A central family room serves as the center of activity. It has a fireplace and connects to a lovely sun room with rear-porch access. The formal dining room to the front of the plan is open to the entry foyer. A private den also

opens off the foyer with double doors. It has its own private, cozy fireplace. The kitchen area opens to the sun room, and it contains an island work counter. Bedrooms are split, with the master suite to the right side of the design and family bedrooms to the left. There are also three full baths in this plan. This home is designed with a basement foundation.

DESIGN T080
Square Footage: 2,120

BEST-SELLING HOMES IN COLOR

The home, as shown in the photograph, may differ from the actual blueprints. For more detailed information, please check the floor plans carefully.

Photo by Andrew D. Lautman

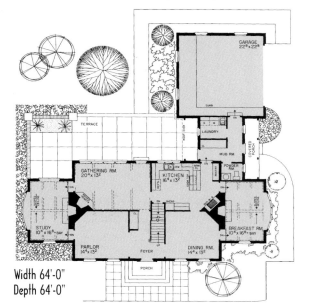

Width 64'-0"
Depth 64'-0"

Design by
© Home Planners

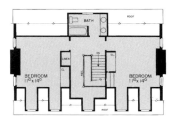

QUOTE ONE®

Cost to build? See page 684
to order complete cost estimate
to build this house in your area!

DESIGN 2662

First Floor: 1,735 square feet
Second Floor: 1,075 square feet
Third Floor: 746 square feet
Total: 3,556 square feet

L

Three floors of livability are available in this stately brick Federal design. From the two chimney stacks to the five dormer windows, the appeal is pure Americana. First-floor features include fireplaces in the gathering room, breakfast room and study, as well as a built-in barbecue in the gourmet kitchen. A handy mudroom with a powder room connects the kitchen to the laundry and the garage beyond. The second floor is dominated by a sumptuous master suite and two family bedrooms that share a full bath. A third floor holds two additional bedrooms that might serve well as guest rooms or as a studio or study space. A full bath with a double vanity finishes this floor.

The home, as shown in the photograph, may differ from the actual blueprints.
For more detailed information, please check the floor plans carefully.

Photo by Laszlo Regos

Design by
© Home Planners

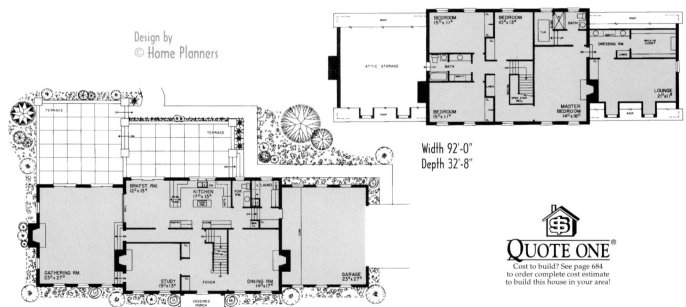

Width 92'-0"
Depth 32'-8"

Quote One®
Cost to build? See page 684
to order complete cost estimate
to build this house in your area!

This dignified brick home is reminiscent of Tulip Hill, an 18th-Century manor in Arundel County, Maryland. It features the symmetrical facade and classical details of the Georgian era. The two-story center section is complemented by the 1½-story wings, one of which is filled by the elegant step-down gathering room.

Flanking the foyer are a study and the formal dining room, each warmed by a fireplace. The breakfast room and the kitchen are drenched in sunlight from the sliding glass door and the triple window above the sink. Sleeping quarters include three family bedrooms and a master suite with a fireplace, pampering bath and spacious lounge.

DESIGN 2683
First Floor: 2,126 square feet
Second Floor: 1,882 square feet
Total: 4,008 square feet

L D

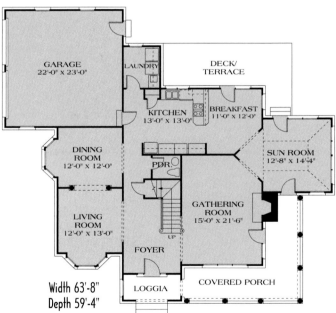

Design by
© Living Concepts Home Planning

GARAGE 22'-0" x 23'-0"

LAUNDRY

DECK/ TERRACE

KITCHEN 13'-0" x 13'-0"

BREAKFAST 11'-0" x 12'-0"

DINING ROOM 12'-0" x 12'-0"

PDR.

SUN ROOM 12'-8" x 14'-4"

LIVING ROOM 12'-0" x 13'-0"

GATHERING ROOM 15'-0" x 21'-6"

FOYER

UP

Width 63'-8"
Depth 59'-4"

LOGGIA

COVERED PORCH

W.I.C.

W.I.C.

SUITE 3 12'-0" x 12'-6"

SUITE 2 12'-0" x 11'-0"

MASTER BATH

BATH

W.I.C.

W.I.C.

SUITE 4 12'-0" x 12'-6"

DN

MASTER SUITE 15'-0" x 18'-0"

SITTING AREA

BALCONY

DESIGN A122
First Floor: 1,583 square feet
Second Floor: 1,431 square feet
Total: 3,014 square feet

A wraparound porch offers additional outside living while giving this design, oriented for front and side views, a great informal feel. Inside is an economical layout featuring a spacious gathering room and open living and dining room. The full kitchen is easily accessible from both the dining room and breakfast room. A vaulted ceiling gives added dimension to the large sun room. The upstairs master suite offers a spacious bedroom with a tray ceiling and His and Hers walk-in closets. Outside the master suite are a sitting area and balcony. There are three additional suites upstairs, including a suite with a private bath.

Width 61'-0"
Depth 70'-6"

DECK

BREAKFAST
13'-6" X 8'-6"

KITCHEN
14'-6" X 14'-2"

TWO STORY
GREAT ROOM
19'-8" X 14'-0"

MASTER BEDROOM
13'-4" X 20'-2"

W.I.C.

POWDER

LAUNDRY
9'-6" X 9'-10"

MASTER BATH
10'-0" X 15'-0"

DINING ROOM
13'-10" X 12'-6"

FOYER
7'-0" X 13'-2"

LIVING ROOM
13'-10" X 12'-6"

PORCH

BREEZEWAY

STOOP

TWO CAR GARAGE
21'-6" X 21'-6"

Design by
© Stephen Fuller,
American Home Gallery

BEDROOM NO. 2
14'-6" X 11'-0"

OPEN TO BELOW

UNFIN. STORAGE
7'-10" X 12'-2"

BATH

BATH

BEDROOM NO. 3
13'-10" X 12'-2"

BEDROOM NO. 4
13'-10" X 12'-6"

Copyright 1990 Stephen S. Fuller, Inc.

BONUS ROOM
10'-0" X 21'-4"

QUOTE ONE®
Cost to build? See page 684
to order complete cost estimate
to build this house in your area!

Cost to build? See page 684

Traditionalists will appreciate the classic styling of this Colonial home. The foyer opens to both a banquet-sized dining room and formal living room with fireplace. Just beyond is the two-story great room. The entire right side of the main level is taken up by the master suite. The other side of the main level includes a large kitchen and breakfast room just steps away from the detached garage. Upstairs, each bedroom features ample closet space and direct access to bathrooms. The detached garage features an unfinished office or studio on its second level. This home is designed with a basement foundation.

DESIGN T023
First Floor: 1,960 square feet
Second Floor: 905 square feet
Total: 2,865 square feet
Bonus Room: 297 square feet

BEST-SELLING HOMES IN COLOR

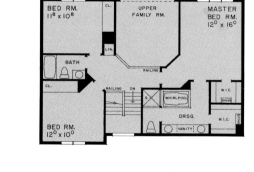

BED RM.
11⁸ x 10⁸

UPPER
FAMILY RM.

SLOPED CEILING

MASTER
BED RM.
12⁰ x 16⁰

BATH

WHIRLPOOL

DRSG.

VANITY

W.I.C.

BED RM.
12⁰ x 10⁰

LIVING RM.
12⁴ x 15⁰

ALCOVE

FAMILY RM.
13⁴ x 15⁰ + ALCOVE

DINING RM.
11⁴ x 12⁰

Width 40'-0"
Depth 54'-0"

PDR. RM.

FOYER

DESK

KITCHEN
14⁰ x 15⁰

SER.
ENT.

PORCH

GARAGE
19⁴ x 19⁸

Design by
© Home Planners

QUOTE ONE®
Cost to build? See page 684
to order complete cost estimate
to build this house in your area!

DESIGN 3562
First Floor: 1,182 square feet
Second Floor: 927 square feet
Total: 2,109 square feet
L D

Interesting detailing marks the exterior of this home as a beauty. Double doors on the left open to a large foyer with a handy coat closet and a powder room with a curved wall. Living areas of the home are open and well planned. The formal living room shares a through-fireplace with the large family room, which is enhanced by a cabinet-lined alcove. The adjoining dining room has a pass-through counter to the efficient L-shaped kitchen. Each of the three main rooms on this floor has sliding glass doors to the rear terrace. Upstairs, the master bath offers a whirlpool tub, double vanities, a separate shower, two walk-in closets and a good-sized dressing area. Two family bedrooms share a full bath.

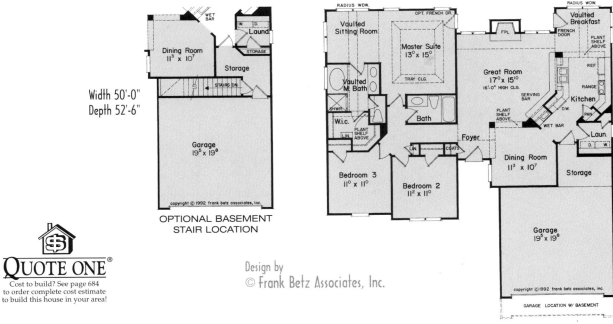

Width 50'-0"
Depth 52'-6"

OPTIONAL BASEMENT
STAIR LOCATION

QUOTE ONE®
Cost to build? See page 684
to order complete cost estimate
to build this house in your area!

Design by
© Frank Betz Associates, Inc.

**DESIGN
P128**
Square Footage: 1,575

This impressive home will be the envy of the neighborhood during holiday parties. The massive great room, with its fireplace flanked by windowed views to the rear yard, will become entertainment central. A serving bar connects it to the amenity-filled kitchen, which flows into the formal dining room or into the vaulted breakfast nook. The sleeping wing on the left side of the plan features a luxurious master suite with a tray ceiling, separate sitting room (big enough for an office) and vaulted master bath with dual sinks and a walk-in closet. Two family bedrooms and a full hall bath complete this stunning plan. Please specify basement or crawlspace foundation when ordering.

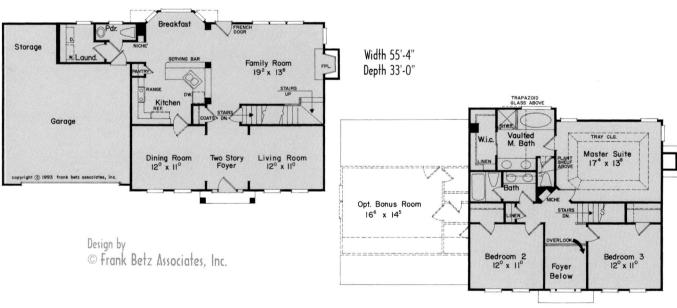

Storage

D.
W. Laund.

Pdr.
NICHE'
Breakfast
FRENCH DOOR

Garage

SERVING BAR

PANTRY

RANGE
REF.
Kitchen
DW.
Family Room
19² x 13⁸
FPL.

STAIRS UP

COATS
STAIRS DN.
STAIRS

Dining Room
12⁰ x 11⁰
Two Story Foyer
Living Room
12⁰ x 11⁰

copyright © 1993 frank betz associates, inc.

Design by
© Frank Betz Associates, Inc.

Width 55'-4"
Depth 33'-0"

TRAPAZOID GLASS ABOVE
SHWR
Vaulted M. Bath
W.i.c.
LINEN
PLANT SHELF ABOVE
TRAY CLG.
Master Suite
17⁴ x 13⁶

Bath
LINEN
NICHE
STAIRS DN.

Opt. Bonus Room
16⁶ x 14⁵

OVERLOOK

Bedroom 2
12⁰ x 11⁰
Foyer Below
Bedroom 3
12⁰ x 11⁰

DESIGN P131
First Floor: 1,028 square feet
Second Floor: 878 square feet
Total: 1,906 square feet
Bonus Room: 315 square feet

Colonial symmetry is the key to the good looks of this fine design. It is complemented by a center-hall floor plan that features a formal dining room and living room flanking the two-story foyer. The family room sits to the rear and is warmed by a large central fireplace. The nearby kitchen has a serving bar that separates it from the breakfast nook and the family room. Bedrooms are found on the second floor: two family bedrooms and a master suite. The master bedroom enjoys a tray ceiling and luxury bath with a vaulted ceiling, walk-in closet and whirlpool tub. An optional bonus room may be developed into additional sleeping space later. Extra storage space in the two-car garage will come in handy. Please specify basement, crawlspace or slab foundation when ordering.

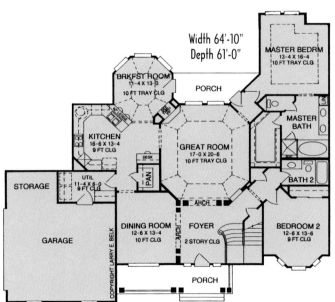

Width 64'-10"
Depth 61'-0"

BRKFST ROOM
11-4 X 13-0
10 FT TRAY CLG

MASTER BEDRM
13-4 X 16-4
10 FT TRAY CLG

PORCH

KITCHEN
16-6 X 13-4
9 FT CLG

GREAT ROOM
17-0 X 20-6
10 FT TRAY CLG

MASTER
BATH

DESK

PAN

BATH 2

STORAGE

UTIL
11-4 X 6-0
9 FT CLG

DINING ROOM
12-6 X 13-4
10 FT CLG

FOYER
2 STORY CLG

ARCH

BEDROOM 2
12-6 X 13-6
9 FT CLG

GARAGE

COPYRIGHT LARRY E. BELK

PORCH

Design by
© Larry E. Belk Designs

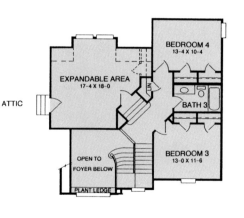

EXPANDABLE AREA
17-4 X 18-0

BEDROOM 4
13-4 X 10-4

ATTIC

BATH 3

OPEN TO
FOYER BELOW

PLANT LEDGE

BEDROOM 3
13-0 X 11-6

D ouble columns and an arch-top clerestory create an inviting entry to this fresh interpretation of traditional style. The two-story foyer features a decorative ledge perfect for displaying a tapestry. Decorative columns and arches open to the formal dining room and to the octagonal great room, which has a ten-foot tray ceiling. The U-shaped kitchen looks over an angled counter to a sweet breakfast bay, which brings in the outdoors and shares a through-fireplace with the great room. A sitting area and a lavish bath set off the secluded master suite. A nearby secondary bedroom with its own bath could be used as a guest suite, while upstairs, two family bedrooms share a full bath and a hall that leads to an expandable area. The two-car garage has extra storage space. Please specify basement, crawlspace or slab foundation when ordering.

**DESIGN
8161**
First Floor: 2,028 square feet
Second Floor: 558 square feet
Total: 2,586 square feet
Bonus Room: 272 square feet

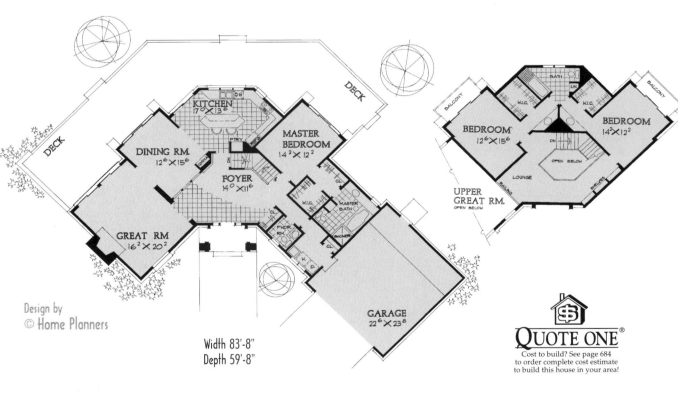

Design by
© Home Planners

Width 83'-8"
Depth 59'-8"

QUOTE ONE®
Cost to build? See page 684
to order complete cost estimate
to build this house in your area!

**DESIGN
3310**
First Floor: 1,668 square feet
Second Floor: 905 square feet
Total: 2,573 square feet
L D

If you're looking for a different angle on a new home, try this enchanting transitional house. The open foyer creates a rich atmosphere. To the left you'll find a great room with raised-brick hearth and sliding glass doors that lead out to a wraparound deck. The kitchen enhances the first floor with a snack bar and deck access. The master bedroom, with a balcony and a bath that has a whirlpool tub, is located on the first floor for privacy. Upstairs, two family bedrooms, both with balconies and walk-in closets, share a full bath. Don't overlook the lounge and elliptical window that give the second floor added charisma.

The home, as shown in the photograph, may differ from the actual blueprints. For more detailed information, please check the floor plans carefully.

Photo by Dave Dawson

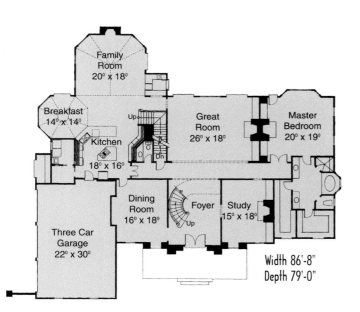

Width 86'-8"
Depth 79'-0"

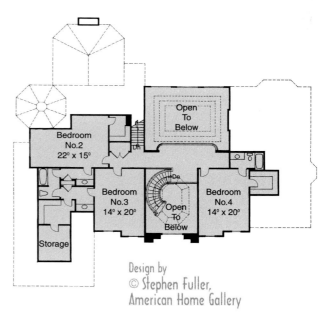

Design by
© Stephen Fuller,
American Home Gallery

The ornamental stucco detailing on this home creates an Old World Mediterranean charm and complements its strength and prominence. The two-story foyer with a sweeping curved stair opens to the large formal dining room and study. The master suite, offering convenient access to the study, is complete with a fireplace, His and Hers walk-in closets, a bath with twin vanities and a separate shower and tub. The two-story great room overlooks the rear patio. A large kitchen with an island workstation opens to an octagonal shaped breakfast room and the family room. A staircase located off the family room provides additional access to the three second-floor bedrooms that offer walk-in closets and plenty of storage. This home is designed with a basement foundation.

DESIGN T124
First Floor: 3,568 square feet
Second Floor: 1,667 square feet
Total: 5,235 square feet

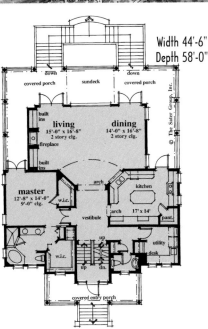

Width 44'-6"
Depth 58'-0"

covered porch   **sundeck**   **covered porch**

down   down

built ins

living
15'-0" x 16'-8"
2 story clg.

dining
14'-0" x 16'-8"
2 story clg.

fireplace

built ins

master
12'-8" x 14'-0"
9'-0" clg.

arch

w.i.c.

kitchen

vestibule

arch   17' x 14'

pant.

w.i.c.

up

utility

desk

up   dn.

covered entry porch

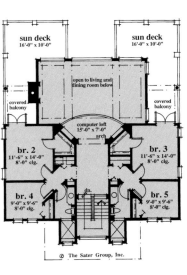

sun deck
16'-0" x 10'-0"

sun deck
16'-0" x 10'-0"

open to living and
dining room below

covered
balcony

computer loft
15'-0" x 7'-0"

arch

covered
balcony

br. 2
11'-6" x 14'-0"
8'-0" clg.

br. 3
11'-6" x 14'-0"
8'-0" clg.

dn.

br. 4
9'-0" x 9'-6"
8'-0" clg.

br. 5
9'-0" x 9'-6"
8'-0" clg.

© The Sater Group, Inc.

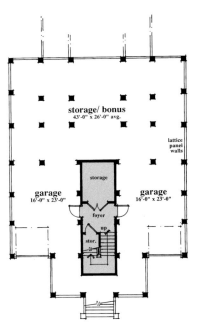

storage/ bonus
43'-0" x 26'-0" avg.

lattice
panel
walls

garage
16'-0" x 23'-0"

storage

garage
16'-0" x 23'-0"

foyer

up

stor.

Design by
© The Sater Design Collection

**DESIGN
6689**

First Floor: 1,642 square feet
Second Floor: 1,165 square feet
Lower Level: 150 square feet
Total: 2,957 square feet

Prevailing summer breezes find their way through many joyful rooms in this Neoclassical Revival design. Inspired by 19th-Century Key West houses, the exterior is heart-stoppingly beautiful with Doric columns, lattice and fretwork, and a glass-paneled, arched entry. The mid-level foyer eases the trip from ground level to living and dining areas, which offer flexible space for planned events or cozy gatherings. Two sets of French doors lead out to the gallery and sun deck, and a two-story picture window invites in natural light.

Design by
© Design Basics, Inc.

QUOTE ONE®
Cost to build? See page 684
to order complete cost estimate
to build this house in your area!

WHIRLPOOL   LIN.   COVERED PORCH   **Gath. rm.** 17⁴ x 15⁷
                     SKYLIGHTS
                     TRANSOMS   10'-0" CLG.

Mbr. 15¹ x 17³
10'-0" CEILING   **Grt. rm.** 20⁰ x 16⁰   ENT. CENTER
                      10'-0" CEILING   SNACK BAR   DESK
                                    WET BAR   **Kit.** 13⁰ x 16⁴

Br. 3 14¹ x 11⁰
OPTIONAL DEN   DISPLAY
                                    Din. 12⁴ x 15⁴
                      DN   E.   10'-0" CEILING
Br. 2 12⁸ x 11⁸
10'-0" CEILING   P.   P.

                      TRANSOMS
                      COVERED PORCH

                                    Gar. 21⁴ x 35⁰

© design basics inc. 1992

Width 66'-0"
Depth 68'-0"

REAR VIEW

Tapered columns accent a grand entry, topped off by an arched pediment, a keystone and a glittering arched transom. Inside, the great room offers wide open spaces and cozy niches, a fireplace and wet bar, ten-foot ceilings and floor-to-ceiling windows set off by transoms that really let in the light. Twin sets of French doors accent the master suite—one leading to the skylit covered porch and one leading to a lavish bath with a luxurious whirlpool tub. Two secondary bedrooms share a compartmented bath.

DESIGN
9375
Square Footage: 2,456

DESIGN
9257
Square Footage: 1,735

A covered porch at the entry to this home welcomes family and guests alike. The formal dining room sits between the kitchen area and the great room. Three bedrooms include two family bedrooms, with a shared bath, and master bedroom suite. An open staircase in the entry allows for the possibility of a finished basement area in the future.

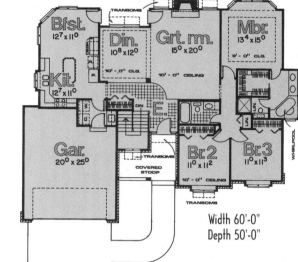

Design by
© Design Basics, Inc.

Width 60'-0"
Depth 50'-0"

DESIGN
9237
Square Footage 1,697

This volume-look home gives the impression of size and scope in just under 1,700 square feet. The large great room with fireplace is perfect for entertaining. Its proximity to the kitchen, with breakfast room, and to the formal dining room ensures easy clean-up and serving. Besides a large walk-in closet, other features in the master bath include a whirlpool tub and a double vanity. Two family bedrooms share a full bath with skylight.

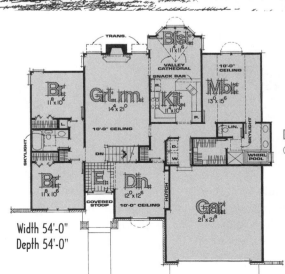

Design by
© Design Basics, Inc.

Width 54'-0"
Depth 54'-0"

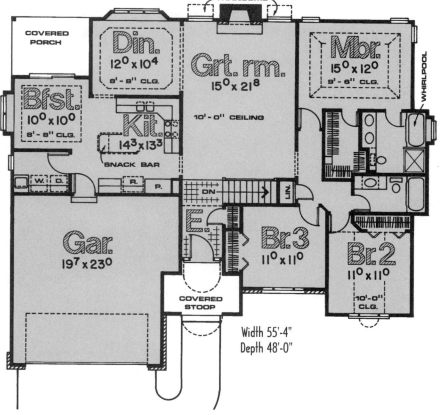

COVERED PORCH

Din.
12⁰ x 10⁴
8' - 8" CLG.

Bfst.
10⁰ x 10⁰
8' - 8" CLG.

Kit.
14³ x 13³

SNACK BAR

TRANSOMS

Grt. rm.
15⁰ x 21⁸
10' - 0" CEILING

Mbr.
15⁰ x 12⁰
9' - 6" CLG.

WHIRLPOOL

Design by
© Design Basics, Inc.

W. D. R. P.

DN LIN.

Gar.
19⁷ x 23⁰

Br.3
11⁰ x 11⁰

Br.2
11⁰ x 11⁰
10' - 0" CLG.

COVERED STOOP

Width 55'-4"
Depth 48'-0"

The delightfully updated European plan has brick and stucco on the dramatic front elevation, showcased by sleek lines and decorative windows. An inviting entry has a view into the great room and is enhanced by an arched window and plant shelves above. The great room's fireplace is framed by sunny windows with transoms above. The bay-windowed dining room is nestled between the great room and the superb eat-in kitchen. The secluded master suite has a roomy walk-in closet and a luxurious bath with dual lavatories and whirlpool tub. Two additional bedrooms share a hall bath.

DESIGN 9361
Square Footage: 1,666

DESIGN 9347

Square Footage: 2,149

Beautiful and accommodating, this ranch home features open entry views into formal rooms plus volume ceilings in major living spaces. The family room has a beamed ceiling and cozy fireplace. The kitchen is equipped with a snack bar open to the breakfast area, a built-in desk and a pantry. Sleeping areas are comprised of three bedrooms, including a master suite with walk-in closet, double vanity and whirlpool tub. Two additional family bedrooms share a private bath. Bedroom 3 may be used as a den with French doors to the hall.

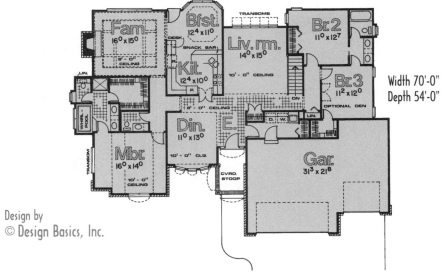

Design by
© Design Basics, Inc.

Width 70'-0"
Depth 54'-0"

DESIGN 9362

Square Footage: 2,172

This one-story home with grand rooflines holds a most convenient floor plan. The great room to the rear complements a front-facing living room. The formal dining room sits just across the hall from the living room and is also easily accessible from the kitchen. A bedroom at this end of the house works fine as an office or guest bedroom since a full bath is close by. Two additional bedrooms are to the right of the plan: a master suite with a grand bath and one additional secondary bedroom.

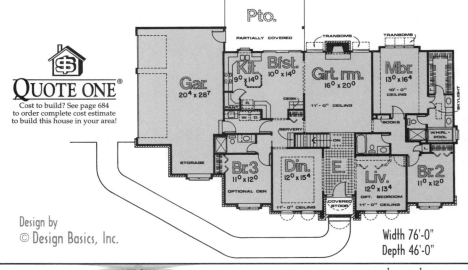

QUOTE ONE®
Cost to build? See page 684
to order complete cost estimate
to build this house in your area!

Design by
© Design Basics, Inc.

Width 76'-0"
Depth 46'-0"

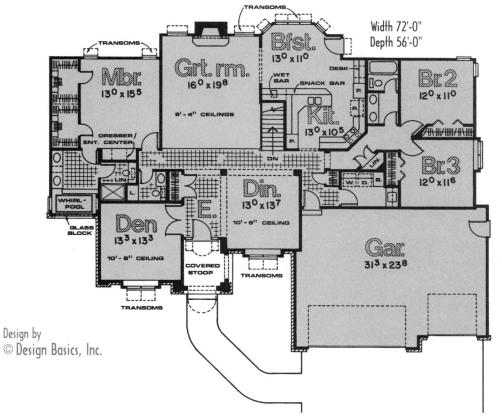

TRANSOMS

Mbr.
13⁰ x 15⁵

Grt. rm.
16⁰ x 19⁸

9'-4" CEILINGS

Bfst.
13⁰ x 11⁰

Width 72'-0"
Depth 56'-0"

WET BAR

SNACK BAR

DESK

Br. 2
12⁰ x 11⁰

DRESSER / ENT. CENTER

Kit.
13⁰ x 10⁵

P.

P.

Br. 3
12⁰ x 11⁶

WHIRL-POOL

GLASS BLOCK

LIN.

L.

DN

Din.
13⁰ x 13⁷

10'-8" CEILING

W.D.

LIN.

Den
13³ x 13³

10'-8" CEILING

E.

COVERED STOOP

TRANSOMS

Gar.
31³ x 23⁸

TRANSOMS

Design by
© Design Basics, Inc.

ONE-STORY TRADITIONAL HOMES

D rama and harmony are expressed by utilizing a variety of elegant exterior materials. An expansive entry views the private den with French doors and an open dining room (both rooms have extra-high ceilings). The great room with a window-framed fireplace is conveniently located next to the eat-in kitchen with bayed breakfast area. Special amenities include a wet bar/servery, two pantries, planning desk and snack bar. Two secluded secondary bedrooms enjoy easy access to a compartmented bath with a twin vanity. His and Hers closets and a built-in armoire that could be an entertainment center or a dresser grace the master bedroom. A luxurious master bath features glass blocks over the whirlpool tub, double sinks and an extra linen storage cabinet. An alternate elevation is provided at no extra cost.

DESIGN
9323
Square Footage: 2,276

DESIGN
M135
Square Footage: 1,664

Soaring round-top windows lend excitement to the brick exterior of this traditional design. A spacious living room opens to the kitchen and dining areas on the right and an appealing covered patio on the left. The large split master suite features a double-vanity bath and an oversized walk-in closet. The utility area has direct access to the garage and a large walk-in pantry.

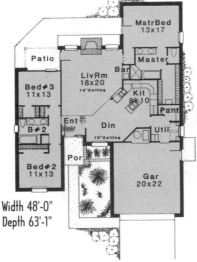

Width 48'-0"
Depth 63'-1"

Design by
© Fillmore Design Group

ALTERNATE VIEW

DESIGN
Q387
Square Footage: 2,094

Abold arched entry with decorative columns and a half-round transom window opens to a skylit foyer. A quiet den sits immediately to the right of the foyer. A sunken living room with fireplace and a vaulted dining room with skylit patio beyond are ideal for formal entertaining. The gourmet kitchen, with pantry storage area, breakfast room and counter bar, is open to the family room. The master bedroom is split from the two family bedrooms for privacy. Plans include details for both a basement and a crawlspace foundation.

Design by
© Select Home Designs

Width 58'-4"
Depth 71'-10"

Design by
© Stephen Fuller,
American Home Gallery

Keeping Room 16⁴ x 11²

Breakfast 14⁶ x 13⁸

Covered Porch

Master Bedroom 18⁰ x 15⁴

Kitchen

One Car Garage 17⁴ x 12⁵

Dining Room 17⁴ x 12⁵

Great Room 17⁴ x 15³

Master Bath

17⁴ x 12⁵

Two Car Garage 21⁴ x 21⁴

Bedroom #3 12⁸ x 13⁸

Bedroom #2 14⁰ x 11⁴

Bath

Width 75'-0"
Depth 70'-0"

This home has a rather unique floor plan—and for those who like to entertain in style, it works well. Enter through double doors and find a bedroom or study immediately to the right. Straight ahead is a large, open area defined by columns that holds the formal dining room and the great room—a fireplace and built-in bookshelves are amenities here. Views here are stunning, past the covered porch and on to the backyard. The kitchen separates this area from the breakfast nook and keeping room—perfect for more casual pursuits. Each bedroom has a private bath and walk-in closet. The master suite offers porch access and a lovely tray ceiling. Notice the two separate garages—one a two-car garage and the other a one-car garage. This home is designed with a basement foundation.

DESIGN T240
Square Footage: 2,973

DESIGN P111
Square Footage: 1,553

This traditional split floor plan is quite manageable in size while featuring amenities found in much larger homes. Decorative columns frame the entrances to the dining room and the expansive family room, which features a vaulted ceiling and a French door to the rear yard. The step-saving kitchen has a planning desk, breakfast area and pass-through to the family room. A tray ceiling crowns the bedroom of the master suite. Two family bedrooms share a hall bath. Please specify basement, crawlspace or slab foundation when ordering.

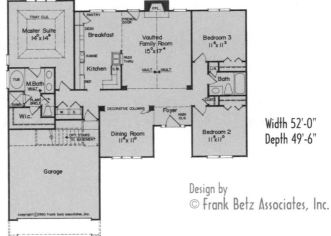

Width 52'-0"
Depth 49'-6"

Design by
© Frank Betz Associates, Inc.

DESIGN 9328
Square Footage: 1,496

Sleek rooflines, lap siding and brick accents highlight the exterior of this three-bedroom ranch home. The spacious great room features a sloping cathedral ceiling and a window-framed fireplace. Note the strategic location of the dining room with nine-foot boxed ceiling and wet bar/servery. Well-segregated sleeping quarters add to the flexibility of this modern floor plan. Bedroom 3 is easily converted to a den or home office. With the nine-foot boxed ceiling, walk-in closet, sunlit whirlpool tub and double vanities, the master suite is soothing and luxurious.

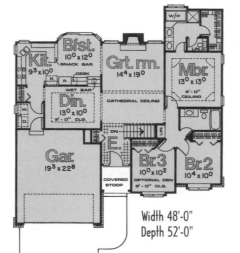

Design by
© Design Basics, Inc.

OPTIONAL DEN

Width 48'-0"
Depth 52'-0"

8'-8" CEILING

Mbr
13⁰ x 14⁰

SKYLIGHT

W/P

Br
10⁸ x 10³

Grt. rm.
15⁰ x 20⁰

CATHEDRAL CEILING

WET BAR

L.

DN

Br
11⁰ x 10⁰

COVERED STOOP

Bfst.
9¹⁰ x 12⁷

DESK

P.

9'-0" CEILING

Dn.
13⁰ x 11⁰

HUTCH

Kit.
9⁶ x 10⁷

W.
D.

Gar
19⁴ x 23⁰

Width 48'-8"
Depth 48'-0"

ONE-STORY TRADITIONAL HOMES

ALTERNATE VIEW

Design by
© Design Basics, Inc.

QUOTE ONE®
Cost to build? See page 684
to order complete cost estimate
to build this house in your area!

T houghtful arrangement makes this uncomplicated three-bedroom plan comfortable. The living and working areas are grouped together for convenience—a great room with cathedral ceiling, dining room with wet-bar pass-through and kitchen with breakfast room. The sleeping area features a spacious mas- ter suite with a skylight, double sinks and whirlpool tub in the bath, and a walk-in closet. Two smaller bedrooms accommo- date guests graciously. A convenient serv- ice entrance leads from the garage, through the laundry room and into the kitchen. An alternate elevation is available at no extra cost.

DESIGN 9200
Square Footage: 1,604

© American Home Gallery, Ltd.

KEEPING ROOM
13'-0" X 15'-0"

PORCH

MASTER BEDROOM
17'-4" X 15'-0"

W.I.C.

BREAKFAST
11'-4" X 10'-0"

DINING ROOM
11'-6" X 13'-0"

GREAT ROOM
16'-0" X 15'-0"

MASTER BATH

PANTRY

KITCHEN
14'-0" X 11'-0"

LAUNDRY
8'-0" X 5'-4"

PWDR.

FOYER
8'-0" X 13'-0"

BEDROOM NO. 3
11'-0" X 12'-0"

BEDROOM NO. 2/
STUDY
11'-0" X 12'-0"

BATH

TWO CAR GARAGE
21'-4" X 21'-8"

STOOP

Width 64'-0"
Depth 64'-4"

PORCH ABOVE

EXTERIOR STORAGE
13'-0" X 10'-0"

STORAGE
14'-6" X 35'-0"

FUTURE RECREATION ROOM
27'-6" X 15'-0"

FUTURE FAMILY ROOM
19'-0" X 15'-0"

UP

MECHANICAL
18'-8" X 5'-4"

STORAGE
8'-0" X 9'-4"

FUTURE W.I.C.

FUTURE BATH

FUTURE BEDROOM
11'-8" X 12'-0"

STOOP ABOVE

SLAB ON GRADE

Design by
© Stephen Fuller,
American Home Gallery

DESIGN T030
Square Footage: 2,150

This home draws its inspiration from both French and English country homes. From the foyer and across the spacious great room, French doors give a generous view of the covered rear porch. The dining room is subtly defined by columns and a large triple window. The kitchen has a generous work island and breakfast area and joins the inviting keeping room. Warmed by a fireplace, the keeping room occupies one bay while the master bedroom occupies the opposite bay. Look for a walk-in closet and luxury bath here. Two family bedrooms share a private bath. This home is designed with a basement foundation.

© American Home Gallery, Ltd.

Flared eaves, multi-pane windows and graceful arches decorate the country European facade of this traditional home. The elegant foyer opens to the formal rooms and leads to casual living space. The bayed breakfast nook brings in the outdoors and opens to a spacious kitchen with a peninsula cooktop counter. Sleeping quarters include a master suite with twin vanities and a garden tub, and two family bedrooms that share a full bath with separate vanities. This home is designed with a basement foundation.

Design by
© Stephen Fuller,
American Home Gallery

Width 65'-0"
Depth 55'-11"

QUOTE ONE®
Cost to build? See page 684
to order complete cost estimate
to build this house in your area!

© American Home Gallery, Ltd.

One-story living takes a lovely traditional turn in this brick one-story home. The foyer opens to the dining room through columned arches and to the great room, creating an extensive living area. To the right of the plan, this area opens to a second, more casual, living area through double doors. Gourmet cooks will fully appreciate the well-appointed kitchen and the adjacent keeping room. To the left of the plan, two family bedrooms and a full bath share a central hall, which leads to a sizable master suite with a sumptuous bath. This home is designed with a basement foundation.

Design by
© Stephen Fuller,
American Home Gallery

QUOTE ONE®
Cost to build? See page 684
to order complete cost estimate
to build this house in your area!

Width 69'-0"
Depth 49'-6"

ONE-STORY TRADITIONAL HOMES

DESIGN Q345
Square Footage: 1,204

This attractive siding-and-brick home is not only beautiful, but economical to build as well. The sunken entry steps up to the living room, warmed by a fireplace. An open railing defines the basement stairway and enhances spaciousness. A gourmet kitchen offers a walk-in pantry and a center preparation island. Sliding glass doors in the breakfast nook lead to a rear patio. The master bedroom has a separate full bath. Two secondary bedrooms share a bath with soaking tub. A two-car garage sits to the front of the plan, creating privacy and quiet for the bedrooms.

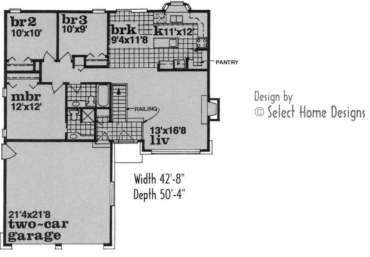

Design by
© Select Home Designs

Width 42'-8"
Depth 50'-4"

DESIGN Q323
Square Footage: 1,936

Choose from one of two exteriors for this lovely home—details for both are included in the blueprints. A transom window over the entry accentuates the vaulted ceiling, which stretches throughout the home. A glass-walled fireplace shares space with both the living room and the breakfast room. The L-shaped kitchen features a pantry and island cooktop. Bedrooms include a master suite with a sitting bay, deck access and a well-appointed bath. Two family bedrooms and a full bath are to the front of the home.

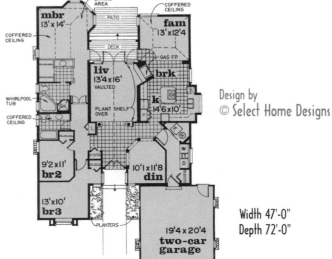

Design by
© Select Home Designs

Width 47'-0"
Depth 72'-0"

DESIGN Q365
Square Footage: 1,624

This affordable ranch home offers a choice of exteriors—a contemporary California stucco or a traditional version with horizontal siding and brick detailing. The entry is graced by light-giving transom windows. The living room has a vaulted ceiling, fireplace and rear-yard access. The formal dining room is also vaulted with tall, arched windows at the front. The master bedroom boasts French-door access to the patio and features a walk-in closet and a bath with a whirlpool tub. Two additional bedrooms share a main bath. A large laundry area leads to a two-car garage.

OPTIONAL
BASEMENT STAIR
LOCATION

Design by
© Select Home Designs

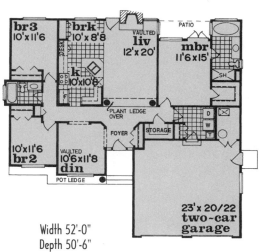

Width 52'-0"
Depth 50'-6"

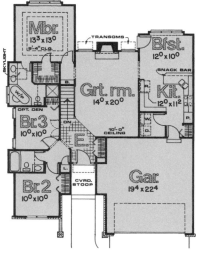

DESIGN 9256
Square Footage: 1,347

From the high ceiling in the entry and great room to the snack bar in the open kitchen, there's a great deal to enjoy in this home. One of the bedrooms could serve as a den with French doors off the entry. The main suite has a boxed window and tiered ceiling; the deluxe bath offers a corner whirlpool tub and dual vanities naturally lit by an overhead skylight. Two family bedrooms share a hall bath.

Design by
© Design Basics, Inc.

Width 42'-0"
Depth 54'-0"

DESIGN M148
Square Footage: 2,194

Decorative gables enhance the roofline of this lovely traditional four-bedroom, one-story home. A recessed porch opens to the entry foyer and center gallery. An angled kitchen is the hub for this home, with a breakfast room, family room with fireplace, formal living room and formal dining room radiating out from it. A spacious patio is accessed from the breakfast room as well as the family room and master bedroom. Three secondary bedrooms share a full hall bath. A two-car garage easily shelters the family fleet.

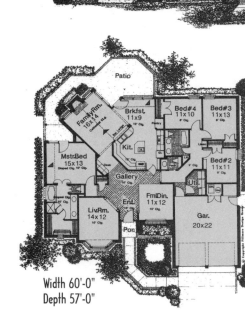

Width 60'-0"
Depth 57'-0"

ALTERNATE VIEW

Design by
© Fillmore Design Group

DESIGN Y007
Square Footage: 2,444

Multiple rooflines combine with the stonework to give this home plenty of curb appeal. Copper-topped, shuttered and arch-top windows add a graceful sense of variety to the combination also. Inside, the foyer is flanked by a formal dining room and a cozy study. Here, double doors welcome you and a private patio offers a peaceful getaway. The spacious great room flows into the nearby family room and also has access to the rear covered porch. Three bedrooms include a lavish master suite with private bath. Please specify crawlspace or slab foundation when ordering.

Width 67'-0"
Depth 66'-0"

Design by
© Michael E. Nelson,
Nelson Design Group, LLC

© American Home Gallery, Ltd.

Design by
© Stephen Fuller,
American Home Gallery

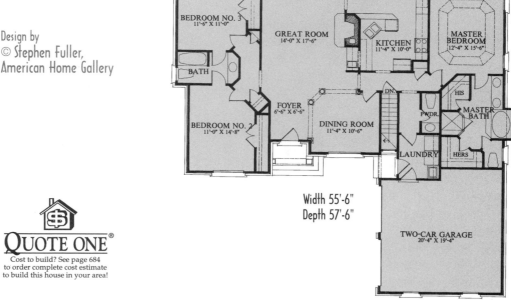

DECK

BREAKFAST
11'-4" X 8'-6"

BEDROOM NO. 3
11'-6" X 11'-0"

GREAT ROOM
14'-0" X 17'-6"

KITCHEN
11'-4" X 10'-0"

MASTER BEDROOM
12'-4" X 15'-6"

BATH

FOYER
6'-6" X 6'-6"

DN

HIS

MASTER BATH

BEDROOM NO. 2
11'-0" X 14'-8"

DINING ROOM
11'-4" X 10'-6"

PWDR

HERS

LAUNDRY

Width 55'-6"
Depth 57'-6"

TWO-CAR GARAGE
20'-4" X 19'-4"

Quote One®
Cost to build? See page 684
to order complete cost estimate
to build this house in your area!

Delightfully different, this brick one-story home has everything for the active family. The foyer opens to a formal dining room accented with decorative columns, and to a great room with warming fireplace and lovely French doors to the rear deck. The efficient kitchen adjoins a light-filled breakfast nook. A split-bedroom plan offers a secluded master suite with coffered ceiling, His and Hers walk-in closets, double vanity and garden tub. Two family bedrooms, or one and a study, have separate access to a full bath on the left side of the plan. This home is designed with a basement foundation.

DESIGN T090
Square Footage: 1,733

DESIGN
P100
Square Footage: 1,945

Corner quoins and keystones above graceful window treatments have long been a hallmark of elegant European-style exteriors. The foyer is beautifully framed by columns in the dining room and entrance to the vaulted great room. The left wing holds three secondary bedrooms—one doubles as a study—and a full bath. To the right of the combined kitchen and vaulted breakfast room you will find the master suite. A relaxing master bath and a large walk-in closet complete this splendid retreat. Please specify basement or crawlspace foundation when ordering.

QUOTE ONE®
Cost to build? See page 684
to order complete cost estimate
to build this house in your area!

Width 56'-6"
Depth 52'-6"

Design by
© Frank Betz Associates, Inc.

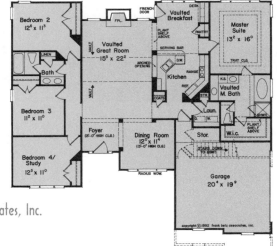

DESIGN
P126
Square Footage: 2,236

The master suite of this one-story traditional plan will be a haven for any homeowner. The vaulted master bath includes a three-sided mirror, corner whirlpool tub, His and Hers sinks and walk-in closet with built-in linen storage. Radius windows highlight the central living room, arches create a dramatic entrance to the dining room and the open kitchen area includes a serving bar to the vaulted family room with its cozy fireplace. Two bedrooms and a full bath with dual basins complete this amenity-filled design. Please specify basement or crawlspace foundation when ordering.

Width 63'-0"
Depth 67'-0"

Design by
© Frank Betz Associates, Inc.

ONE-STORY TRADITIONAL HOMES

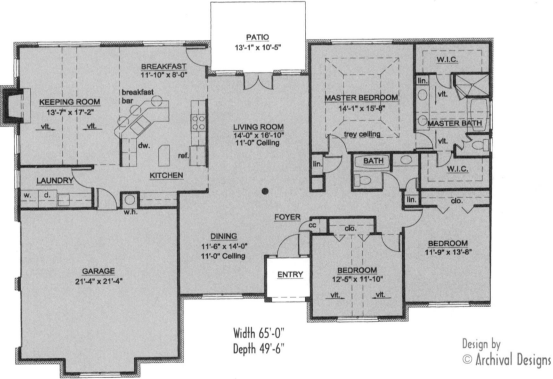

PATIO
13'-1" x 10'-5"

BREAKFAST
11'-10" x 8'-0"

KEEPING ROOM
13'-7" x 17'-2"
vlt.   vlt.

breakfast
bar

W.I.C.

lin.   vlt.

MASTER BEDROOM
14'-1" x 15'-8"

MASTER BATH

vlt.

trey ceiling

LIVING ROOM
14'-0" x 16'-10"
11'-0" Ceiling

dw.

ref.

lin.

BATH

lin.

W.I.C.

LAUNDRY
w.   d.

KITCHEN

clo.

lin.

w.h.

FOYER

cc   clo.

BEDROOM
11'-9" x 13'-8"

DINING
11'-6" x 14'-0"
11'-0" Ceiling

ENTRY

BEDROOM
12'-5" x 11'-10"
vlt.   vlt.

GARAGE
21'-4" x 21'-4"

Width 65'-0"
Depth 49'-6"

Design by
© Archival Designs

DESIGN
S129
Square Footage: 2,054

efined by an elegant column, the covered entrance to this three-bedroom home welcomes friends and family. Inside, a formal dining room and formal living room, also defined by a graceful column, are open to one another, providing a wonderful entertaining area. The kitchen, enhanced by angles, features a work island and a breakfast bar. The nearby keeping room offers a vaulted ceiling and a warming fireplace. Two secondary bedrooms share a hall bath, while the master bedroom is complete with many amenities. Here, a tray ceiling, two walk-in closets and a vaulted bath are sure to please.

DESIGN 7667

Square Footage: 2,014
Bonus Room: 377 square feet

Octagonal porches front and back (the latter screened), an octagonal breakfast room and a bay-windowed bedroom enhance this brick exterior. Columns, turrets and unusual windows add interest. The foyer connects through columns with the dining room and the great room. Separated from family bedrooms for privacy, the master suite provides a great retreat. Two family bedrooms share a bath but have separate dressing areas, each with a vanity and a toilet. A bonus room completes the plan.

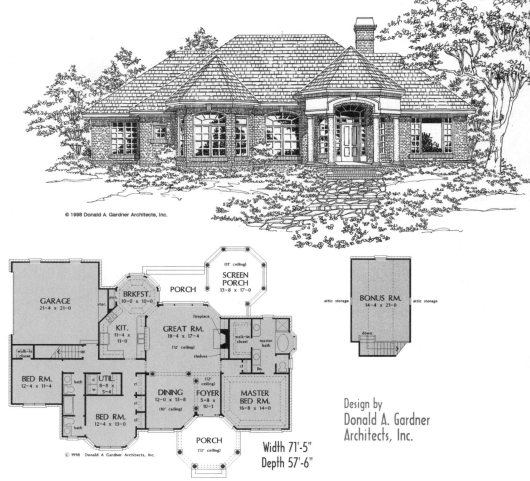

© 1998 Donald A. Gardner Architects, Inc.

Design by
Donald A. Gardner
Architects, Inc.

Width 71'-5"
Depth 57'-6"

DESIGN Y013

Square Footage: 2,392

Brickwork accented by corner quoins and gabled rooflines enhance an attractive four-bedroom home. Inside, the foyer presents a formal dining room directly to the right, with a spacious great room just ahead. A work island features a snack bar, and the adjacent breakfast room makes the kitchen a gourmet's dream. The lavish master suite enjoys two walk-in closets and a luxurious bath. On the other side of the house, three family bedrooms—or make one a study—share a full hall bath. Please specify crawlspace or slab foundation when ordering.

Design by
© Michael E. Nelson,
Nelson Design Group, LLC

Width 67'-2"
Depth 71'-8"

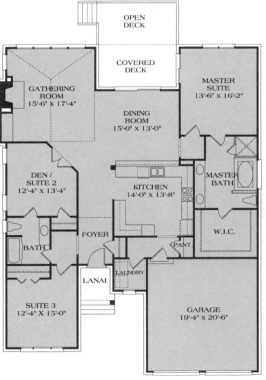

Width 46'-10"
Depth 61'-0"

OPEN DECK

COVERED DECK

GATHERING ROOM
15'-6" X 17'-4"

MASTER SUITE
13'-6" X 16'-2"

DINING ROOM
15'-0" X 13'-0"

DEN / SUITE 2
12'-4" X 13'-4"

MASTER BATH

KITCHEN
14'-0" X 13'-8"

W.I.C.

FOYER

BATH

PANT.

LANAI

LAUNDRY

SUITE 3
12'-4" X 15'-0"

GARAGE
19'-4" X 20'-6"

Design by
© Living Concepts Home Planning

T his traditional home begins with a stylish columned lanai, which leads to a spacious foyer and hall that opens to all areas. The kitchen overlooks a central formal dining room with views and access to the rear deck. An open, spacious gathering room shares the glow of an extended-hearth fireplace with the dining area and kitchen. The master suite opens from a private vestibule and offers a deluxe bath with a garden tub, separate shower and U-shaped walk-in closet. Two additional suites share a full bath on the other side of the plan. One of these rooms could serve as a den or study. A service entrance from the two-car garage leads to a pantry area and the laundry.

DESIGN A246
Square Footage: 1,913

ONE-STORY TRADITIONAL HOMES

DESIGN 8000
Square Footage: 2,540
L

A gabled stucco entry with oversized columns emphasizes the arched glass entry of this winsome one-story brick home. An arched passage, flanked by twin bookcases and a plant ledge, provides focal interest to the living room. Bedroom 4 may also be a study, and can be entered from double French doors off the living room. A large, efficient kitchen shares space with an octagonal breakfast area and family room with fireplace. The master bedroom features a cathedral ceiling. Please specify crawlspace or slab foundation when ordering.

Design by
© Larry E. Belk Designs

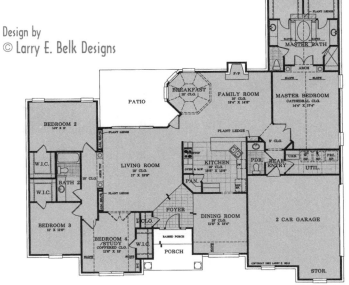

Width 70'-0"
Depth 65'-0"

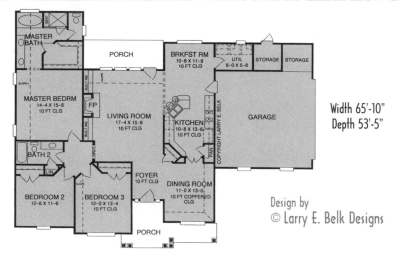

DESIGN 8183
Square Footage: 1,890

This classic home exudes elegance and style. Ten-foot ceilings throughout the plan lend an aura of spacious hospitality. A generous living room, with a sloped ceiling, built-in bookcases and a centerpiece fireplace, offers views and access to the rear yard. The nearby breakfast room shares an eating counter with the ample kitchen, which serves the coffered-ceiling dining room. Three bedrooms include a sumptuous master suite with a windowed whirlpool tub and walk-in closet, and two family bedrooms that share a full bath. Please specify slab or crawlspace foundation when ordering.

Width 65'-10"
Depth 53'-5"

Design by
© Larry E. Belk Designs

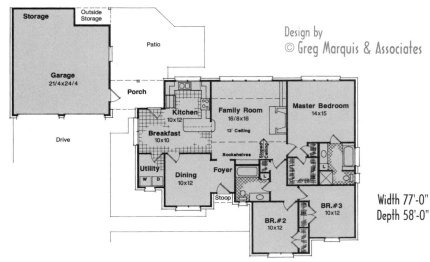

Design by
© Greg Marquis & Associates

Storage

Outside Storage

Patio

Garage
21/4 x 24/4

Porch

Drive

Kitchen
10x12

Family Room
16/8 x 18
13' Ceiling

Master Bedroom
14x15

Bookshelves

Sloped Ceiling

Breakfast
10x10

Utility
W D

Dining
10x12

Foyer

Stoop

BR.#2
10x12

BR.#3
10x12

Width 77'-0"
Depth 58'-0"

This house has real curb appeal, and the inside's just as pleasing! The large family room with warming fireplace vaults to thirteen feet for added drama. The open kitchen and breakfast area with eat-in bar make casual meals a breeze. The nearby formal dining room easily accommodates dinner parties. In the sleeping zone, two family bedrooms have access to a full hall bath, while the master bedroom pampers with a private bath and a large walk-in closet. The detached garage connects via a covered walk and accommodates the family fleet.

© 1998 Donald A. Gardner Architects, Inc.

An arched entry provides a touch of class to the exterior of this plan. The foyer leads to all areas of the home, minimizing corridor space. The dining room displays decorative columns, while the great room boasts a cathedral ceiling, a fireplace and access to the screened porch. The master suite has two walk-in closets and a lavish bath. Two large family bedrooms share a bath on the opposite side of the plan.

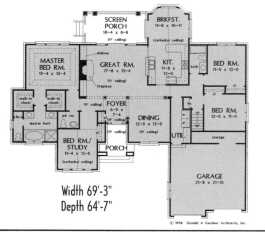

SCREEN PORCH
18-4 x 8-8
(11' ceiling)

BRKFST.
11-8 x 10-11
(cathedral ceiling)

shelves

MASTER BED RM.
15-4 x 13-4
(11' ceiling)

GREAT RM.
17-8 x 15-4
(11' ceiling)

fireplace

KIT.
11-8 x 12-0

bath

BED RM.
11-0 x 12-0

walk-in closet

walk-in closet

master bath

FOYER
6-0 x 7-4
(11' ceiling)

pd. rm.

DINING
12-0 x 13-0
(11' ceiling)

BED RM.
12-0 x 11-0

BED RM./STUDY
11-4 x 12-0
(cathedral ceiling)

PORCH

UTIL.

storage

GARAGE
21-8 x 21-10

down

skylights

BONUS RM.
12-4 x 20-0

attic storage

attic storage

Width 69'-3"
Depth 64'-7"

© 1996 Donald A. Gardner Architects, Inc.

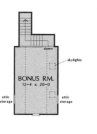

Design by
Donald A. Gardner
Architects, Inc.

ONE-STORY TRADITIONAL HOMES

DESIGN 7657
Square Footage: 2,198
Bonus Room: 325 square feet

If you find that the great livability in this one-story home is not quite enough, you can develop the bonus room into a home office, guest suite or hobby room. In the meantime, you'll find that the floor plan holds superior spaces: formal dining room, great room, gourmet-style kitchen with attached breakfast room, and three bedrooms with two full baths. The wraparound porch at the rear of the plan extends its invitation to the master suite, great room and breakfast room.

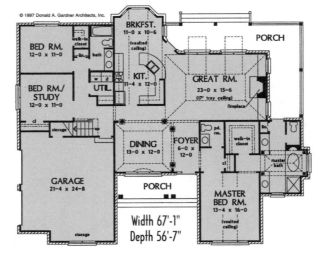

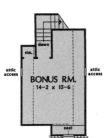

Width 67'-1"
Depth 56'-7"

Design by
Donald A. Gardner
Architects, Inc.

DESIGN 7692
Square Footage: 1,488
Bonus Room: 338 square feet

There's not a bit of wasted space in this cozy, well-designed home. The foyer opens to a spacious great room with a cathedral ceiling, fireplace and access to the rear porch. The formal dining room features a bay window that offers wide views of the property. Split sleeping quarters include a master suite with a walk-in closet, oversized shower and garden tub, as well as two secondary bedrooms that share a full bath.

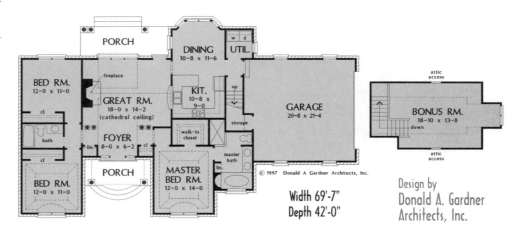

Width 69'-7"
Depth 42'-0"

Design by
Donald A. Gardner
Architects, Inc.

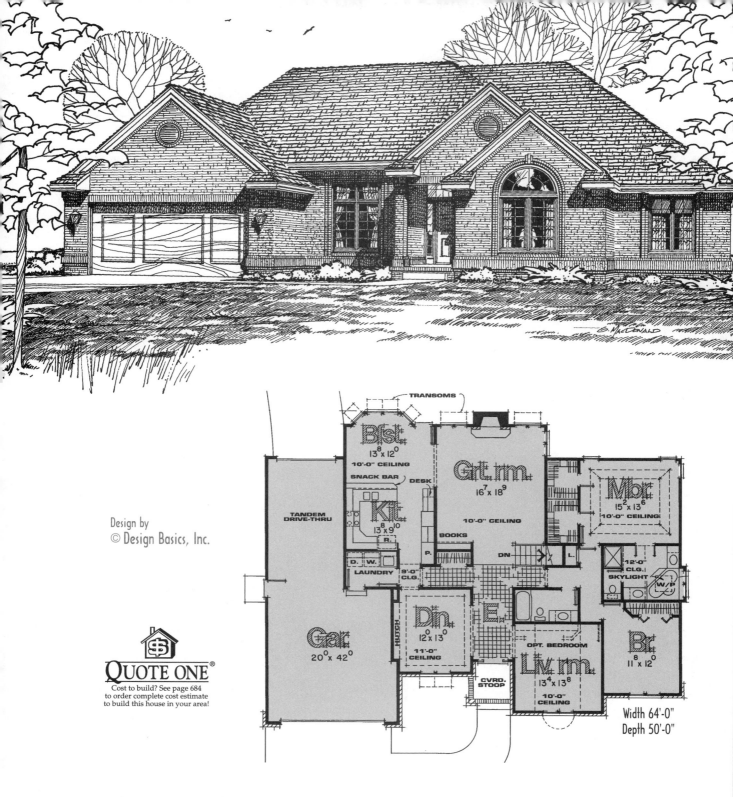

Design by
© Design Basics, Inc.

QUOTE ONE®
Cost to build? See page 684
to order complete cost estimate
to build this house in your area!

Width 64'-0"
Depth 50'-0"

Cost to build? See page 684 to order complete cost estimate to build this house in your area!

ONE-STORY TRADITIONAL HOMES

P ractical, yet equipped with a variety of popular amenities, this pleasant traditional home is an excellent choice for empty-nesters or small families. The front living room can become a third bedroom if you choose. The great room with dramatic fireplace serves as the main living area. A luxurious master suite features a ten-foot tray ceiling and a large bath with whirlpool tub, skylight, plant ledge and twin vanities. The kitchen with breakfast room serves both the dining and great rooms. A snack bar separates the kitchen and breakfast room. A tandem drive-through garage holds space for a third car or extra storage. Please specify basement or slab foundation when ordering.

DESIGN 9201
Square Footage: 1,996

DESIGN 7232
Square Footage: 2,512

Repeating arches and striking brick detail complement this superb ranch-style home. Impressive tapered columns define the formal dining room and add to its ten-foot ceiling, while, in the entry, a domed ceiling lies above the curved stairway. French doors open to the den—or convert the den into a third bedroom. Arched windows and a through-fireplace define the central great room. The great room's fireplace is shared with the open hearth room, island kitchen and gazebo-shaped breakfast nook. The master bedroom delights with a skylit walk-in closet and a sumptuous bath.

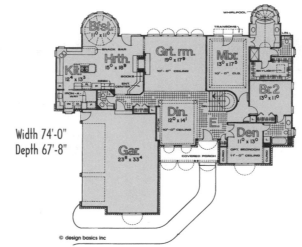

Width 74'-0"
Depth 67'-8"

© design basics inc

Design by
© Design Basics, Inc.

OPTIONAL BEDROOM

QUOTE ONE®
Cost to build? See page 684 to order complete cost estimate to build this house in your area!

DESIGN 9660
Square Footage: 2,108

Multi-pane windows, dormers, copper-covered bay windows, a covered porch with round columns and brick siding help to emphasize the sophisticated appearance of this three-bedroom home. The great room features a fireplace, cathedral ceiling and sliding glass doors with arched window above. The spacious master bedroom contains a walk-in closet and a bath with double-bowl vanity, shower and garden tub. Two family bedrooms are located at the opposite end of the house for privacy.

© 1990 Donald A. Gardner Architects, Inc.

Design by
Donald A. Gardner Architects, Inc.

Width 68'-9"
Depth 68'-7"

© 1990 Donald A. Gardner Architects, Inc.

© 1994 Donald A. Gardner Architects, Inc.

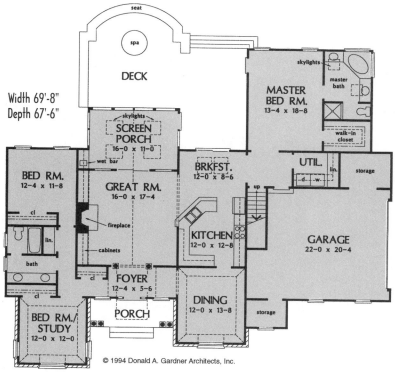

Width 69'-8"
Depth 67'-6"

seat
spa
DECK

skylights
SCREEN
PORCH
16-0 x 11-0

wet bar

BED RM.
12-4 x 11-8

cl

GREAT RM.
16-0 x 17-4

fireplace

cabinets

bath

lin.

cl

BRKFST.
12-0 x 8-6

KITCHEN
12-0 x 12-8

up

MASTER
BED RM.
13-4 x 18-8

skylights
master
bath

walk-in
closet

UTIL.
d w

lin.

storage

GARAGE
22-0 x 20-4

FOYER
12-4 x 5-6

cl

BED RM./
STUDY
12-0 x 12-0

PORCH

DINING
12-0 x 13-8

storage

© 1994 Donald A. Gardner Architects, Inc.

Design by
Donald A. Gardner
Architects, Inc.

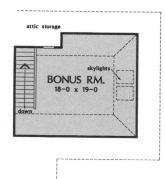

attic storage

BONUS RM.
18-0 x 19-0

skylights

down

Quote One®
Cost to build? See page 684
to order complete cost estimate
to build this house in your area!

DESIGN
9734

Square Footage: 1,977
Bonus Room: 430 square feet

A two-story foyer with a Palladian window above sets the tone for this sunlit home. Columns mark the passage from the foyer to the great room, where a centered fireplace and built-in cabinets are found. A screened porch with four skylights above and a wet bar provides a pleasant place to start the day or wind down after work. The kitchen is flanked by the formal dining room and the breakfast room with sliding glass doors to the large, rear deck. Hidden quietly in the rear, the master suite includes a bath with dual vanities and skylights. Two family bedrooms (one an optional study) share a bath that has twin sinks. A basement or crawlspace foundation is available.

ONE-STORY TRADITIONAL HOMES

DESIGN
C154
Square Footage: 1,443

An interesting floor plan is the key to great livability in this cozy one-story home. A vaulted foyer leads to the roomy great room with a fireplace or down a hallway to the bedrooms. A study, or formal dining room, opens through double doors just at the entry. The kitchen, with a vaulted ceiling, has an attached casual dining area with bay window and sliding glass doors. The master bedroom and Bedroom 2 also have vaulted ceilings.

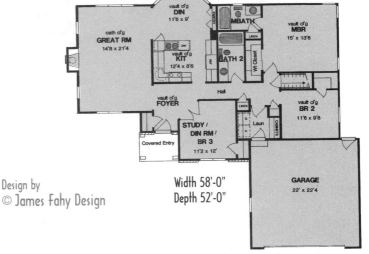

Design by
© James Fahy Design

Width 58'-0"
Depth 52'-0"

DESIGN
C153
Square Footage: 1,286

Brick paves the way to a solidly traditional one-story home. A volume ceiling, adding appeal on the exterior, allows for vaulted ceilings in the foyer, dining room, kitchen and great room. Because Bedroom 3 opens directly to the foyer as well as to the hallway, it may easily be used as a study or den. It shares a full bath with Bedroom 2. The master suite includes its own bath and a large walk-in closet. Separating the kitchen from living spaces is an angled island counter.

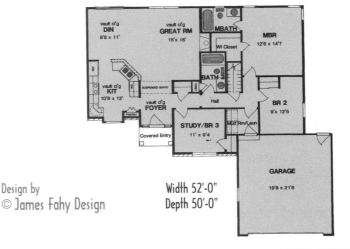

Design by
© James Fahy Design

Width 52'-0"
Depth 50'-0"

© 1996 Donald A. Gardner Architects, Inc.

B. NATHAN

Design by
Donald A. Gardner
Architects, Inc.

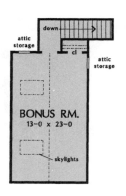

attic storage

down

attic storage

BONUS RM.
13-0 x 23-0

skylights

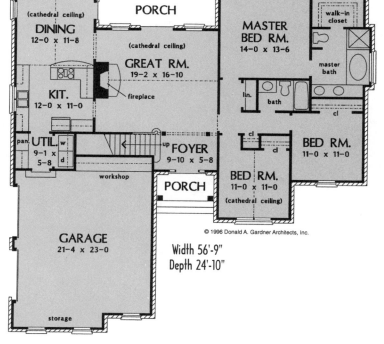

(cathedral ceiling)

PORCH

DINING
12-0 x 11-8

(cathedral ceiling)

GREAT RM.
19-2 x 16-10

fireplace

KIT.
12-0 x 11-0

pan.

UTIL
9-1 x 5-8

w
d

workshop

up **FOYER**
9-10 x 5-8

PORCH

GARAGE
21-4 x 23-0

storage

MASTER BED RM.
14-0 x 13-6

walk-in closet

master bath

lin.

bath

cl

cl

cl

BED RM.
11-0 x 11-0

BED RM.
11-0 x 11-0

(cathedral ceiling)

© 1996 Donald A. Gardner Architects, Inc.

Width 56'-9"
Depth 24'-10"

This lovely traditional plan says "welcome home" to modern homeowners. Inside, cathedral ceilings add an aura of hospitality, while flexible bonus space over the garage invites future development. A luxurious master suite boasts a windowed whirlpool tub, a sizable walk-in closet and twin vanities. The spacious dining room works well for both casual family meals and formal events, with elegant touches such as a cathedral ceiling and a wall of windows. The kitchen is designed for easy meal preparation and service. A two-car garage has a designated workshop area plus separate space for storage.

DESIGN 7639
Square Footage: 1,666
Bonus Room: 335 square feet

ONE-STORY TRADITIONAL HOMES

DESIGN S128

Square Footage: 2,588

Mediterranean mansion or an Italian villa—these are the influences on the exterior of this grand one-story home. The parlor and dining room flank the elegant entry foyer. The family room is introduced by columns and is further enhanced by a fireplace and double doors to the rear yard. The kitchen area is magnified by a breakfast room full of light. A guest bedroom, or private suite, is down the hall behind the garage and has a private bath. Two family bedrooms at the other end of the hall share a full bath. The master suite may be accessed through a private foyer, either at the hall or from the parlor.

Design by
© Archival Designs

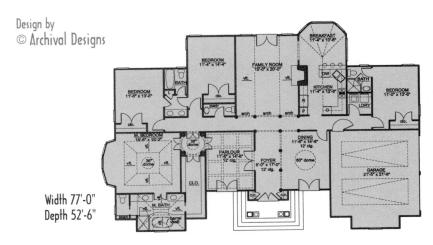

Width 77'-0"
Depth 52'-6"

DESIGN S132

Square Footage: 3,823
Bonus Space: 1,017 square feet

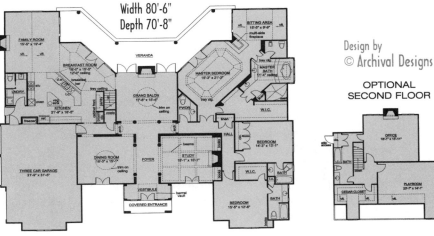

This Neo-Classical home has plenty to offer! The elegant entrance is flanked by a formal dining room on the left and a beam-ceilinged study—complete with a fireplace—on the right. An angled kitchen is sure to please with a work island, plenty of counter and cabinet space and a snack counter that it shares with the sunny breakfast room. A family room with a second fireplace is nearby. The lavish master bedroom suite features many amenities, including a huge walk-in closet, three-sided fireplace and lavish bath. Two secondary bedrooms each have private baths.

Width 80'-6"
Depth 70'-8"

Design by
© Archival Designs

OPTIONAL
SECOND FLOOR

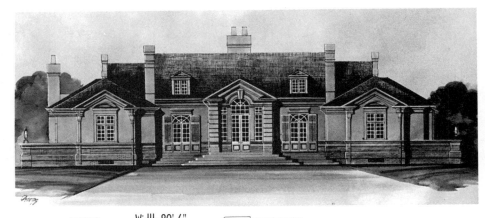

© 1990 Donald A. Gardner Architects, Inc.

REAR VIEW

Design by
Donald A. Gardner
Architects, Inc.

Width 68'-4"
Depth 68'-7"

© 1990 Donald A. Gardner Architects, Inc.

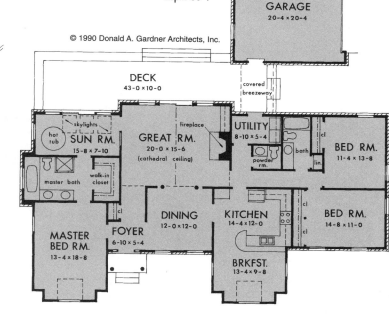

GARAGE
20-4 x 20-4

DECK
43-0 x 10-0

covered breezeway

SUN RM.
15-8 x 7-10

GREAT RM.
20-0 x 15-6
(cathedral ceiling)

fireplace

UTILITY
8-10 x 5-4

powder rm.

bath

lin.

cl

BED RM.
11-4 x 13-8

hot tub

skylights

master bath

walk-in closet

cl

FOYER
6-10 x 5-4

DINING
12-0 x 12-0

KITCHEN
14-4 x 12-0

cl

cl

BED RM.
14-8 x 11-0

MASTER BED RM.
13-4 x 18-8

BRKFST.
13-4 x 9-8

ONE-STORY TRADITIONAL HOMES

By putting the garage to the rear of this plan, nothing is taken away from the beautiful stone and stucco facade. Access from the garage is enhanced by a covered breezeway that passes the rear covered porch and connects to the home at the utility room. A great room with cathedral ceiling and fireplace has sliding glass doors to the rear deck and access to the skylit sun room, which also opens to the deck. The master bath connects to the sun room as well. It is the perfect complement to the private master bedroom. Choose two styles of dining: the formal dining room with columned entrance to the great room, or the sunny breakfast room, attached to the U-shaped kitchen. Two additional bedrooms are at the right side of the plan and share a full bath.

DESIGN 9656
Square Footage: 2,099

DESIGN T009
Square Footage: 2,902

Arches, transoms and sweeping rooflines blend artfully to highlight this French exterior. The interior starts with a great room that features a tray ceiling, wet bar and French doors to the outside. Adjoining the kitchen and breakfast room, the spacious keeping room provides a fireplace and lots of windows. The master suite offers a sitting room and a sumptuous bath, while two family bedrooms share a connecting bath. This home is designed with a basement foundation.

Width 71'-3"
Depth 66'-3"

Design by
© Stephen Fuller,
American Home Gallery

QUOTE ONE®
Cost to build? See page 684
to order complete cost estimate
to build this house in your area!

DESIGN A150
Square Footage: 1,947
Bonus Room: 255 square feet

Twin columns frame the arched entry to this three-bedroom home. Three additional columns define the formal dining room to the right of the entry foyer. The large gathering room, with fireplace and built-in bookshelves, is open to the breakfast area (note the bay window), which has access to the rear deck/terrace. The master suite features a sloped ceiling, oval garden tub and His and Hers walk-in closets. The two additional bedrooms share an adjoining bath with dual vanity.

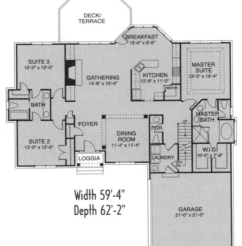

Width 59'-4"
Depth 62'-2"

Design by
© Living Concepts Home Planning

ONE-STORY TRADITIONAL HOMES

Quote One®

Cost to build? See page 684
to order complete cost estimate
to build this house in your area!

Design by
© Frank Betz Associates, Inc.

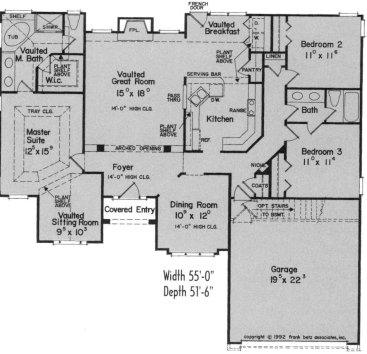

Width 55'-0"
Depth 51'-6"

DESIGN
P123

Square Footage: 1,715

A grand double bank of windows looking in on the formal dining room mirrors the lofty elegance of the extra-tall vaulted ceiling inside. From the foyer, an arched entrance to the great room visually frames the fireplace on the back wall. The wraparound kitchen has plenty of counter and cabinet space, along with a handy serving bar. The luxurious master suite features a front sitting room for quiet times and a large spa-style bath. Two family bedrooms are split from the master suite for privacy and share a hall bath. Please specify basement, crawlspace or slab foundation when ordering.

DESIGN
M147
Square Footage: 2,354

The sweeping expanse of gables, arched window trim and decorative round windows makes this four-bedroom plan deserve a second look. The entry gallery leads to the center of the home with a tiled kitchen and breakfast bay open to a covered patio. An outstanding arrangement of bedrooms in this single-level design provides privacy for family or guests. The generous master suite features a large walk-in closet and double basins in the vanity. A formal living room and dining room plus family room offer many entertainment options.

ALTERNATE VIEW

Width 81'-0"
Depth 64'-7"

Design by
© Fillmore Design Group

DESIGN
U257
Square Footage: 1,868

A large living area opens off of a vaulted foyer through a doorway with soffit. At one end is a warming hearth; at the other, another soffitted opening to the dining area and island kitchen. The dining area is enhanced by a bay window with sliding glass doors to the outdoors. The bedrooms at the opposite end of the plan include two family bedrooms and a master suite. Accents in the master suite include a sliding glass door to the rear yard, corner shower, whirlpool tub and walk-in closet.

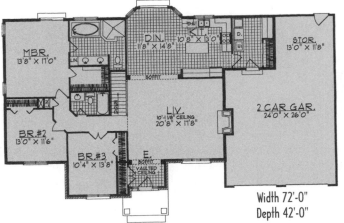

Design by
© Ahmann Design, Inc.

Width 72'-0"
Depth 42'-0"

www.homeplanners.com

The home, as shown in the photograph, may differ from the actual blueprints.
For more detailed information, please check the floor plans carefully.

Photo by Ahmann Design

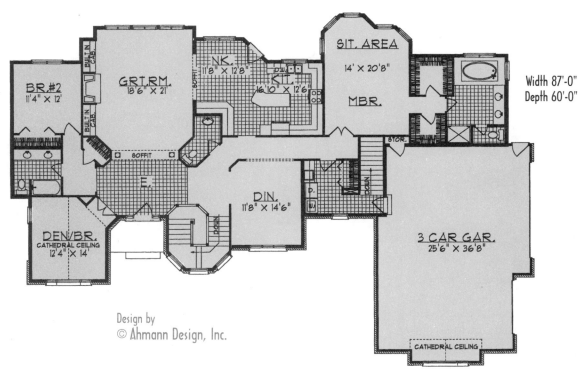

Width 87'-0"
Depth 60'-0"

Design by
© Ahmann Design, Inc.

ONE-STORY TRADITIONAL HOMES

Varied rooflines, shutters and multi-pane windows all combine to give this home plenty of curb appeal. A tiled entry presents a grand view of the spacious great room, which is complete with a warming fireplace and built-in cabinets. A den opens off the foyer through double doors and can be used as a guest bedroom when needed. The island in the kitchen provides plenty of workspace to an already well-equiped area. With direct access to both the formal dining room as well as the sunny nook, the kitchen is sure to please. A sumptuous master bedroom suite is located off to the right, and features a bayed sitting area, two walk-in closets and a lavish bath. The three-car garage will efficiently shelter the family fleet.

DESIGN U112
Square Footage: 2,600

DESIGN
7274
Square Footage: 2,399

Interesting window treatments and a charming porch extend the attention-getting nature of this brick ranch home. Beyond the covered porch, the entry showcases the formal dining room to the right and the multi-windowed living room straight ahead. The L-shaped kitchen features an island cooktop and blends with the bay-windowed breakfast room and welcoming family room to create a comfortable area. The master suite includes a huge walk-in closet. The amenity-filled master bath contains twin vanities and an oval whirlpool tub. Two secondary bedrooms share a full bath.

DESIGN
9258
Square Footage: 2,498

Elegant arches at the covered entry of this home give way to beautiful views of the formal dining and living rooms inside. Ceilings in the main living areas and the master bedroom are vaulted. The gazebo dinette is open to the family room and to the gourmet kitchen, which includes an island cooktop and snack bar. One of these could become a sitting area for the master suite, if desired. A luxurious master bath provides twin vanities, a large walk-in closet and an oval whirlpool tub.

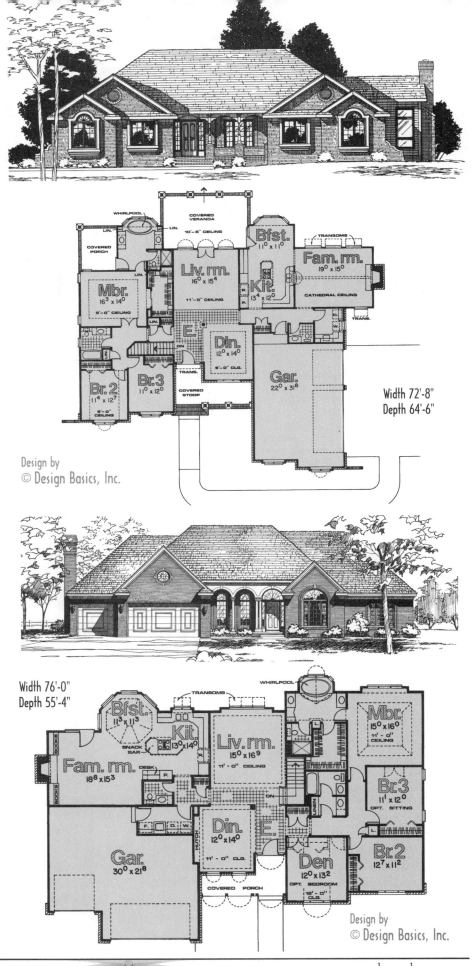

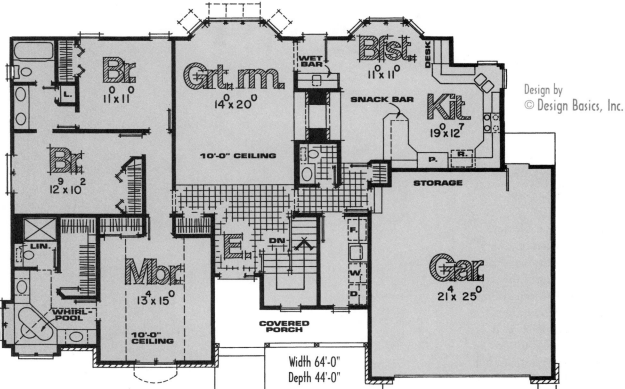

TRANSOMS

Br.
11 x 11

Grt. rm.
14⁰ x 20⁰

WET BAR

Bfst.
11⁰ x 11⁰

DESK

Design by
© Design Basics, Inc.

SNACK BAR

Kit.
19⁰ x 12⁷

10'-0" CEILING

Br.
12 x 10⁹²

P.   **R.**

STORAGE

LIN.

Mbr
13⁴ x 15⁰

F.

DN

W.
D.

Gar.
21⁴ x 25⁰

WHIRL-POOL

10'-0" CEILING

COVERED PORCH

Width 64'-0"
Depth 44'-0"

Discriminating buyers will love the refined yet inviting look of this three-bedroom ranch plan. A tiled entry with ten-foot ceilings leads into the spacious great room with large bay window. An open-hearth fireplace warms both the great room and kitchen. The sleeping area features a large master suite with a dramatic arched window and a bath with whirlpool, His and Hers vanities and a walk-in closet. Don't miss the storage space in the oversized garage.

DESIGN 9202
Square Footage: 1,808

DESIGN
F131
Square Footage: 2,529

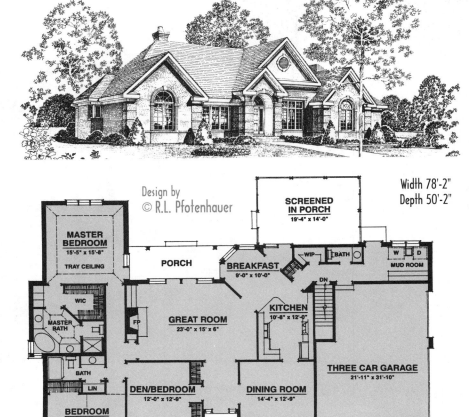

This charming home grabs attention with a beautiful facade. The floor plan holds great livability. A central great room connects to the breakfast room and galley-style kitchen. A formal dining room, just off the foyer, has a huge wall of windows for elegant dining. A complementary room to the left of the foyer serves as a den or guest bedroom as needed. The master bedroom features a tray ceiling and wonderfully appointed bath. A family bedroom to the front of the plan has a vaulted ceiling.

Design by
© R.L. Pfotenhauer

Width 78'-2"
Depth 50'-2"

SCREENED IN PORCH
19'-4" x 14'-0"

MASTER BEDROOM
15'-5" x 15'-8"
TRAY CEILING

PORCH

BREAKFAST
9'-0" x 10'-0"

WIP   BATH   W D
MUD ROOM

WIC

MASTER BATH

FP

GREAT ROOM
23'-0" x 15' x 6"

KITCHEN
10'-6" x 12'-0"

DN

THREE CAR GARAGE
21'-11" x 31'-10"

BATH

LIN

DEN/BEDROOM
12'-0" x 12'-9"

DINING ROOM
14'-4" x 12'-9"

BEDROOM
15'-5" x 10' x 6"
VAULTED CEILING

DESIGN
M136
Square Footage: 2,858

Multiple front gables, eyebrow windows and an recessed entry make up the front exterior of this attractive home. Ten-foot ceilings are featured throughout the sprawling main living areas. A massive fireplace and built-in bookshelves or entertainment units make up one wall of the 16' x 17' family room. The open kitchen and breakfast room has a large bay window facing the patio. The master bedroom suite features a luxurious bath and walk-in closet, plus an adjacent wood-paneled study.

Design by
© Fillmore Design Group

3-Car-Gar
24x32

Patio Area

BrkfstRm
13x10
10'Clg

Patio Area

FamilyRm
16x17
10'Clg

Util
8'Clg

MstrBed
17x14

LivRm
17x15
10'Clg

Kit
13x14
10'Clg

Ent/Gallery
11'Clg

Bed#4
12x12
8'Clg

Study
11x11

FmlDin
12x13
11'Clg

Bed#3
12x12
10'Clg

Bed#2
14x11

Width 89'-7"
Depth 68'-4"

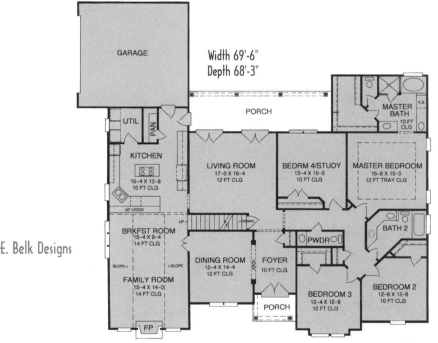

GARAGE

Width 69'-6"
Depth 68'-3"

PORCH

UTIL | PAN

MASTER
BATH
10 FT
CLG

K.S.

KITCHEN
15-4 X 13-6
10 FT CLG

LIVING ROOM
17-0 X 16-4
12 FT CLG

BEDRM 4/STUDY
13-4 X 15-0
10 FT CLG

MASTER BEDROOM
15-6 X 15-0
12 FT TRAY CLG

42" LEDGE

UP | DOWN

BATH 2

Design by
© Larry E. Belk Designs

BRKFST ROOM
15-4 X 9-4
14 FT CLG

PWDR

SLOPE | SLOPE

DINING ROOM
12-4 X 14-4
12 FT CLG

FOYER
10 FT CLG

FAMILY ROOM
15-4 X 14-0
14 FT CLG

PORCH

BEDROOM 3
12-4 X 12-8
10 FT CLG

BEDROOM 2
12-6 X 12-8
10 FT CLG

FP

ONE-STORY TRADITIONAL HOMES

Country French appointments give this home an elegant Old World look. The foyer opens to the well-proportioned dining room, with twelve-foot ceiling. A stair is conveniently located in the home to provide access to the basement below and the attic above. Double French doors with transoms open off the living room to the rear porch. The kitchen, breakfast room and family room are open to one another. The fireplace is visible from all these areas and provides a lovely focal point for the room. All bedrooms are conveniently grouped. The master bedroom features a tray ceiling and a luxury master bath. Please specify basement, crawlspace or slab foundation when ordering.

**DESIGN
8266**
Square Footage: 2,757

DESIGN M121
Square Footage: 2,061

This one-living-area plan is perfect for the contemporary family with a taste for classic design. The great room is open to the kitchen and dinette. Full-view doors lead to a large covered patio. Off the entry is a home office/study with plenty of built-ins. The master bedroom features a sloped ceiling from eight feet to eleven feet. The master bath completes this plan with an eleven-foot ceiling and a huge walk-in closet.

Width 60'-0"
Depth 57'-0"

Design by
© Fillmore Design Group

DESIGN M104
Square Footage: 2,696

A brick archway covers the front porch of this European-style home, creating a truly grand entrance. Situated beyond the entry, the living room features a fireplace flanked by tall windows that overlook the backyard. To the right is a bayed eating area and an efficient kitchen. Steps away is the formal dining room. If you wish, combine the master suite with the study, using it as a private retreat and Bedroom 2 as a nursery, creating a private wing. Completing this plan are two family bedrooms—each with a walk-in closet.

Design by
© Fillmore Design Group

Width 80'-0"
Depth 64'-1"

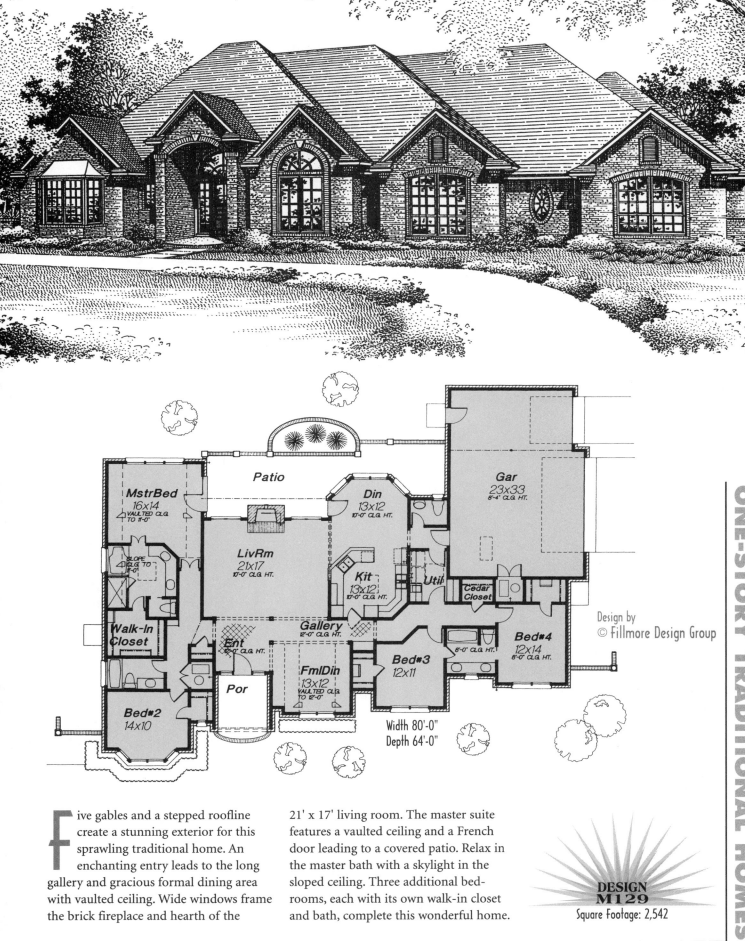

Patio

MstrBed
16x14
VAULTED CLG
TO 11'-0"

Din
13x12
10'-0" CLG. HT.

Gar
23x33
8'-4" CLG. HT.

LivRm
21x17
10'-0" CLG. HT.

Kit
13x12
10'-0" CLG. HT.

Util

Cedar Closet

Walk-In Closet

Gallery
12'-0" CLG. HT.

Bed#4
12x14
8'-0" CLG. HT.

Design by
© Fillmore Design Group

Ent
12'-0" CLG. HT.

FmlDin
13x12
VAULTED CLG
TO 12'-0"

Bed#3
12x11

8'-0" CLG. HT.

Por

Bed#2
14x10

Width 80'-0"
Depth 64'-0"

F ive gables and a stepped roofline create a stunning exterior for this sprawling traditional home. An enchanting entry leads to the long gallery and gracious formal dining area with vaulted ceiling. Wide windows frame the brick fireplace and hearth of the 21' x 17' living room. The master suite features a vaulted ceiling and a French door leading to a covered patio. Relax in the master bath with a skylight in the sloped ceiling. Three additional bedrooms, each with its own walk-in closet and bath, complete this wonderful home.

DESIGN M129
Square Footage: 2,542

ONE-STORY TRADITIONAL HOMES

DESIGN 9236
Square Footage: 1,271

This charmingly snug three-bedroom home offers all the features you've been looking for in a family home. The great room has a lovely cathedral ceiling and a fireplace surrounded by windows. Nearby is the dining area and efficient kitchen with a window box, planning desk, and snack-bar counter. Intriguing ceiling treatment dominates the master bedroom where you'll also find corner windows, a dressing area with large vanity and a walk-in closet. Two family bedrooms share a full bath and are located near the laundry room.

Width 50'-0"
Depth 46'-0"

Design by
© Design Basics, Inc.

DESIGN Q369
Square Footage: 1,760

This brick one-story home offers a covered, rail porch that provides a weather-protected entry to the home. The vaulted foyer carries its ceiling detail into the living room where there is a fireplace and double-door access to the rear patio. The dining room has a tray ceiling and is found to the right of the entry. The master bedroom boasts a tray ceiling and full bath with whirlpool spa, separate shower and double vanity. Family bedrooms share a full bath that separates them. An open rail stairway leads to a basement that could be expanded in the future.

Width 68'-0"
Depth 46'-0"

REAR VIEW

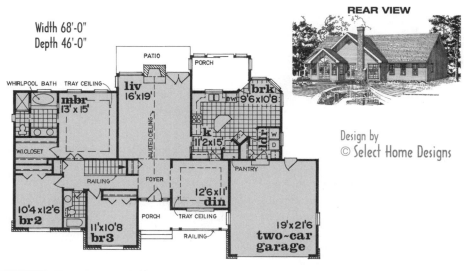

Design by
© Select Home Designs

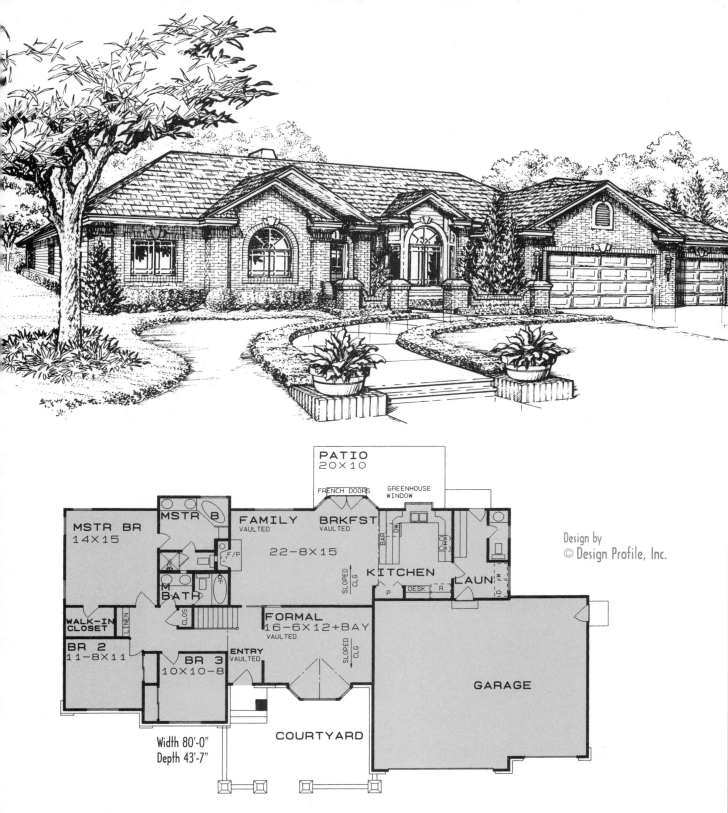

PATIO
20×10

FRENCH DOORS   GREENHOUSE WINDOW

MSTR BR
14×15

MSTR B

FAMILY   BRKFST
VAULTED   VAULTED

22-8×15

KITCHEN

LAUN

Design by
© Design Profile, Inc.

BAR   DW

F/P

SLOPED CLG

M BATH

LINEN

CLOS

P   DESK   R

WALK-IN CLOSET

FORMAL
16-6×12+BAY
VAULTED

BR 2
11-8×11

BR 3
10×10-8

ENTRY
VAULTED

SLOPED CLG

GARAGE

Width 80'-0"
Depth 43'-7"

COURTYARD

Τhis three-bedroom, two-bath home features an open kitchen-family plan, ideal for family entertainment. The conveniently located laundry can also serve as a mudroom for small children with easy access to the half bath and rear yard. The vaulted ceilings in the formal, family and breakfast areas add to the feeling of spaciousness. The formal room can be used as a living, dining, music or game room or a home office. The unfinished basement has a large recreation room, three more bedrooms and plenty of storage to accommodate a growing family. A three-car garage sits to the front of the plan.

**DESIGN
K100**
Square Footage: 1,817
Unfinished Basement: 1,784 square feet

DESIGN 9634
Square Footage: 2,099

This enchanting design incorporates the best in floor planning all on one level. The central great room, the hub of the plan, is highlighted with a fireplace and cathedral ceiling. Nearby is a skylit sun room with sliding glass doors to the rear deck and a built-in wet bar. The galley-style kitchen adjoins an attached breakfast room that also connects to the sun room. The master suite offers access to the rear deck. Its bathroom contains a walk-in closet and double vanity. Family bedrooms share a full bath also with double vanity. A basement or crawlspace foundation is available.

© 1990 Donald A. Gardner Architects, Inc.

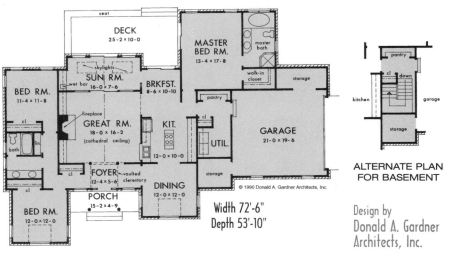

Width 72'-6"
Depth 53'-10"

© 1990 Donald A. Gardner Architects, Inc.

ALTERNATE PLAN FOR BASEMENT

Design by
Donald A. Gardner
Architects, Inc.

ONE-STORY TRADITIONAL HOMES

DESIGN 7623
Square Footage: 2,602
Bonus Room: 399 square feet

Classic brick-and-siding dress up this traditional home and introduce a well-cultivated interior. The foyer opens to an expansive great room with a centered fireplace flanked by built-in cabinets. The secluded master suite nestles to the rear of the plan and boasts a vaulted ceiling and a skylit master bath with an angled spa tub and two vanities. Three additional bedrooms—or make one a study—share a full bath and a convenient powder room on the opposite side of the plan.

© 1996 Donald A. Gardner Architects, Inc.

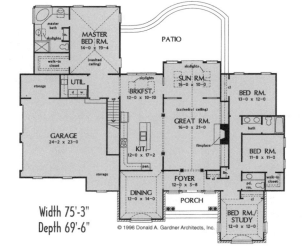

Width 75'-3"
Depth 69'-6"

© 1996 Donald A. Gardner Architects, Inc.

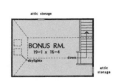

BONUS RM.
19-1 x 16-4

Design by
Donald A. Gardner
Architects, Inc.

Floor Plan

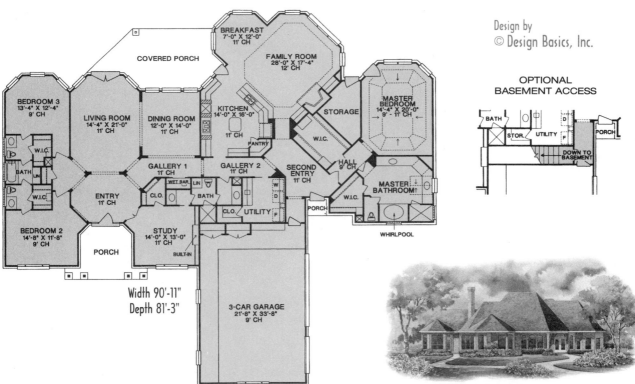

BREAKFAST
7'-0" X 12'-0"
11' CH

COVERED PORCH

FAMILY ROOM
28'-0" X 17'-4"
12' CH

BEDROOM 3
13'-4" X 12'-4"
9' CH

LIVING ROOM
14'-4" X 21'-0"
11' CH

DINING ROOM
12'-0" X 14'-0"
11' CH

KITCHEN
14'-0" X 16'-0"
11' CH

STORAGE

MASTER BEDROOM
14'-4" X 20'-0"
9' - 11' CH

W.I.C.

W.I.C.

BATH

LN

PANTRY

W.I.C.

GALLERY 1
11' CH

GALLERY 2
11' CH

SECOND ENTRY
11' CH

HALL
9' CH

MASTER BATHROOM

W.I.C.

WET BAR

LIN

CLO.

BATH

W
D

WHIRLPOOL

ENTRY
11' CH

CLO.

UTILITY

F

PORCH

BEDROOM 2
14'-8" X 11'-8"
9' CH

STUDY
14'-0" X 13'-0"
11' CH

BUILT-IN

PORCH

Width 90'-11"
Depth 81'-3"

3-CAR GARAGE
21'-8" X 33'-8"
9' CH

Design by
© Design Basics, Inc.

OPTIONAL BASEMENT ACCESS

BATH

STOR.

UTILITY

F

D

PORCH

DOWN TO BASEMENT

REAR VIEW

Hipped rooflines, fine brick detailing and twin sets of square columns flanking the entrance all combine to give this home a touch of grandeur. Inside, the octagonal foyer leads to the formal living and dining rooms as well as to a noise-free study and two family bedrooms. The large island kitchen easily services the bayed breakfast room and the spacious family room, which is enhanced by a warming fireplace. A lavish master suite has two walk-in closets, a bay window and a whirlpool tub. Please specify basement or slab foundation when ordering.

**DESIGN
7388**
Square Footage: 3,312

DESIGN 9728
Square Footage: 1,576

© 1993 Donald A. Gardner Architects, Inc.

S. NATHAN.

This stately, three-bedroom, one-story home exhibits sheer elegance with its large, arched windows, round columns, covered porch and brick veneer. In the great room, a dramatic cathedral ceiling and a fireplace set the mood. Through gracious, round col-umns, the kitchen and breakfast room open up. For sleeping, turn to the master bedroom. Here, a large, walk-in closet and a well-planned master bath with a double-bowl vanity, a garden tub, and a shower will pamper. Two additional bedrooms are located at the opposite end of the house for privacy.

Design by
Donald A. Gardner
Architects, Inc.

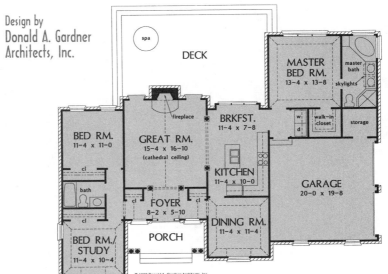

Width 60'-6"
Depth 50'-9"

© 1993 Donald A. Gardner Architects, Inc.

DESIGN 9760
Square Footage: 1,475

© 1994 Donald A. Gardner Architects, Inc.

B. NATHAN.

The front porch of this timeless design leads to the columned foyer. A cathedral ceiling in the great room lends height and a feeling of openness. A fireplace here is framed by doors leading to a rear deck. The kitchen easily serves the dining room while remaining open to the great room. The quiet master bedroom is accented with a tiered ceiling, a private bath and a walk-in closet. Two secondary bedrooms share a full hall bath. The two-car garage is located out of sight, at the rear of the plan.

Width 59'-6"
Depth 54'-7"

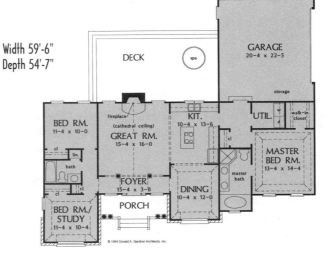

Design by
Donald A. Gardner
Architects, Inc.

© 1994 Donald A. Gardner Architects, Inc.

www.homeplanners.com

B. NATHAN

© 1995 Donald A. Gardner Architects, Inc.

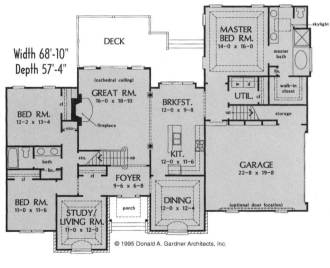

Width 68'-10"
Depth 57'-4"

DECK

(cathedral ceiling)

GREAT RM.
16-0 x 18-10

fireplace

BED RM.
12-2 x 13-4

sto.

bath

lin.

BED RM.
11-0 x 11-6

STUDY/
LIVING RM.
11-0 x 12-0

porch

FOYER
9-6 x 6-8

DINING
12-0 x 12-4

BRKFST.
12-0 x 9-8

KIT.
12-0 x 11-6

up

MASTER
BED RM.
14-0 x 16-0

skylight

master
bath

UTIL.

walk-in
closet

storage

GARAGE
22-8 x 19-8

(optional door location)

© 1995 Donald A. Gardner Architects, Inc.

Design by
Donald A. Gardner
Architects, Inc.

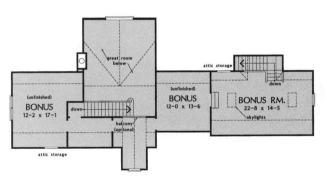

great room
below

attic storage

(unfinished)
BONUS
12-2 x 17-1

down

balcony
(optional)

(unfinished)
BONUS
12-0 x 13-6

BONUS RM.
22-8 x 14-5

skylights

down

attic storage

Brick accents and bright, arch-topped windows highlight the facade of this appealing home. The foyer introduces a clever interior design, starting with stylish formal living and dining rooms flanking the entry, each with a coffered ceiling and an arched, multi-pane window. The elegance continues with a cathedral ceiling in the great room, which features a warming fireplace as well as rear-deck access and opens to a sunny breakfast room through a columned archway. A convenient kitchen with food preparation island easily serves casual and formal dining areas. The dramatic master suite is carefully positioned to the rear of the plan for privacy and offers a coffered ceiling and access to the rear deck. A skylit bath with twin lavs, garden tub, separate shower and walk-in closet completes this lavish retreat. The second story offers 615 square feet of bonus space and a balcony overlook to the great room below.

**DESIGN
9799**
Square Footage: 2,170
Bonus Room: 615 square feet

DESIGN
T241
Square Footage: 2,077

This American classic begins with a recessed entry that announces a modern interior designed for entertaining and relaxed gatherings. The foyer leads to the living room, which opens through French doors to the back property, and to a dining room defined by a splendid colonnade. The spacious kitchen offers a work island and a sunlit breakfast area. French doors open to the master suite, which features a bay window and a lavish bath. Two family bedrooms share a bath that includes dual vanities. This home is designed with a basement foundation.

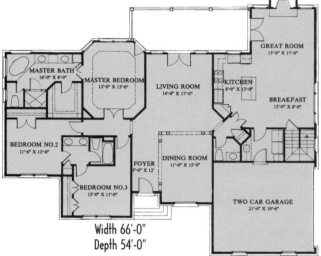

Design by
© Stephen Fuller,
American Home Gallery

Width 66'-0"
Depth 54'-0"

DESIGN
M101
Square Footage: 2,065

Brick, shutters and corner quoins provide European ambience, or gables and horizontal wood siding offer a more traditional facade—the elevation choice is yours. With an eleven-foot ceiling, views of the rear property, a fireplace and built-in bookcases, the great room will be the family's favorite room. Split bedrooms offer privacy, with three family bedrooms and a full bath on the left side. The master bedroom on the right features two walk-in closets and a compartmented bath with a relaxing tub, separate shower and double-bowl vanity.

Design by
© Fillmore Design Group

Width 60'-0"
Depth 65'-10"

ALTERNATE VIEW

WHIRLPOOL

GLASS
BLOCK

BUILT-IN
DRESSERS

Mbr.
13⁰ x 20⁴
9'-0" CEILING

LN

TRANSOMS

Din.
16⁰ x 13⁰
12'-0" CEILING

Bfst.
12⁴ x 12⁰
9'-0" CLG.

SNACK BAR

Kit.
14⁰ x 14⁸

SHELVES

P.

Fam. rm.
19⁰ x 17⁴

CATHEDRAL
CEILING

COVERED
PORCH

P.

DN

Br. 2
13⁰ x 11⁰
OPTIONAL DEN
10'-0" CEILING

E.

Liv. rm.
13⁴ x 16⁰
10'-0" CEILING

Gar.
22⁴ x 31⁴

Br. 3
11⁰ x 13⁰

TRANSOMS

COVERED
PORCH

TRANSOMS

Design by
© Design Basics, Inc.

Width 68'-8"
Depth 64'-8"

The grand front porch gives this home a unique style and majestic curb appeal. Inside, the entry centers on the stately dining room with bowed window. Both the living room and the second bedroom, which can be converted into a den, have ten-foot ceilings. The island kitchen features abundant pantries, a lazy Susan and a snack bar. A sun-filled breakfast area opens to the large family room, with its cathedral ceiling and central fireplace. The private bedroom wing offers two secondary bedrooms and a luxurious master suite featuring a spacious walk-in closet with built-in dressers and private access to the backyard. It also includes a vaulted ceiling, corner whirlpool tub and His and Hers vanities in the master bath. A three-car garage has extra storage space.

**DESIGN
7233**
Square Footage: 2,538

ONE-STORY TRADITIONAL HOMES

DESIGN
M132
Square Footage: 2,026

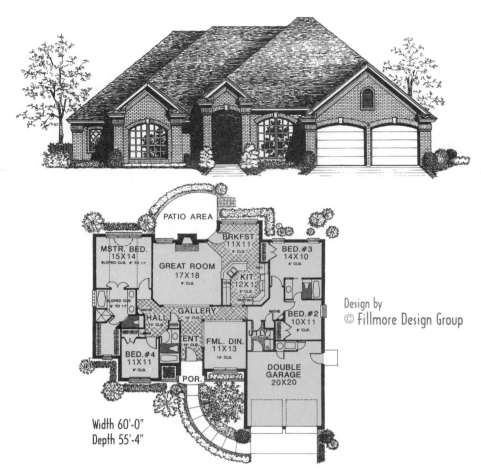

The graceful high roofline, brick gables and arch-top windows give balance to this outstanding traditional home. A colonnaded formal dining room and gallery add an atmosphere of luxury. The great room features a wide brick fireplace and flanking full-height windows, which look out to a private patio surrounded by brick seating. The master suite contains a high sloped ceiling, a Palladian-influenced window and a generous walk-in closet. Three additional bedrooms provide space for family and guests.

Design by
© Fillmore Design Group

Width 60'-0"
Depth 55'-4"

DESIGN
M171
Square Footage: 2,526

Interesting angles and creative detailing characterize the exterior of this brick cottage. The centrally located island kitchen opens to an informal dining area with overlooks to two covered patios. An angled peninsula with a double sink separates the kitchen from the family room, which boasts a cathedral ceiling, fireplace and French door to a patio. Family sleeping quarters include two bedrooms to the right of the plan and another bedroom, which could be used as a study, on the left. The master suite enjoys a vaulted ceiling, walk-in closet, whirlpool tub and dual vanities.

Width 64'-0"
Depth 81"-7"

Design by
© Fillmore Design Group

ALTERNATE VIEW

Design by
© Fillmore Design Group

LANAI

MSTR. BATH
CATHL. CLG.

MSTR. BDRM.
18X16
PULLMAN CLG.
8' TO 10'

COVERED PATIO

BRKFT.
13X12
10" CLG.

UTLY
W/D

BDRM. #3
15X12
CATHL. CLG.

FAMILY RM.
22X16
CATHL. CLG.

KIT
12X12
CATHL. CLG.

BDRM. #2
12X13
8' CLG.

GALLERY
10" CLG.

ENT
10" CLG.

FML. DIN.
13X14
10" CLG.

BDRM. #4
12X12
8' CLG.

LIVING ROOM
14X17
SLOPED CLG. 10" TO 12'

POR.

3 CAR GARAGE
22X30

Width 68'-6"
Depth 78'-1"

© Copyright Fillmore Design Group

Alternate exteriors—both European style! Stone quoins and shutters give one elevation the appearance of a French country cottage. The other, with a keystone window treatment and a copper roof over the bay window, creates the impression of a stately French chateau. From the entry, graceful columned openings access formal living areas—living room to the left and dining room to the right. Straight ahead, the comfortable family room awaits with its fireplace and cathedral ceiling, offering room to relax and enjoy casual gatherings. The private master suite features a pullman ceiling, a luxurious bath and twin walk-in closets. The master bath offers access to a private lanai. Located nearby, Bedroom 2 serves nicely as a guest room, nursery or study. Two family bedrooms, a connecting bath, a handy kitchen and breakfast room, and a utility room complete the floor plan. A three-car garage sits to the back.

DESIGN M102
Square Footage: 2,888

DESIGN U208
Square Footage: 2,991

Solid-looking stone adds its appeal to the facade of this spacious one-story plan. The recessed entry opens to a foyer with a barrel-vaulted ceiling. The massive great room beyond, also accented with a barrel-vaulted ceiling, includes arched doorways at the hallway and connects to the nook. The kitchen features an island work counter and a planning desk. The den opens through double doors, while inside are built-in shelves, a window seat and a door opening to the porch. The master bedroom sits protected behind the three-car garage.

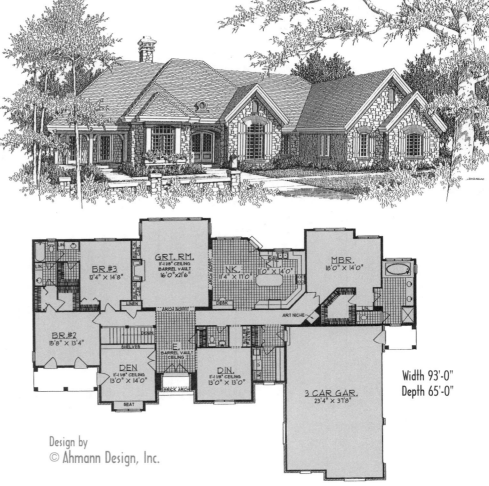

Width 93'-0"
Depth 65'-0"

Design by
© Ahmann Design, Inc.

DESIGN U207
Square Footage: 2,896

Elegance in design with details that demand attention— these are the pluses of this grand one-story home. A stone facade, mini-cupola and covered, double-door entry add to the charm. Directly opposite the entry is the main living area: a great room with fireplace accessed through a columned opening. An open den is to the right of the entry; a more private study with built-ins is to the left. Family bedrooms share a bath and are split from the master suite. Two walk-in closets and a bath with separate shower and tub and dual vanities grace the master bedroom.

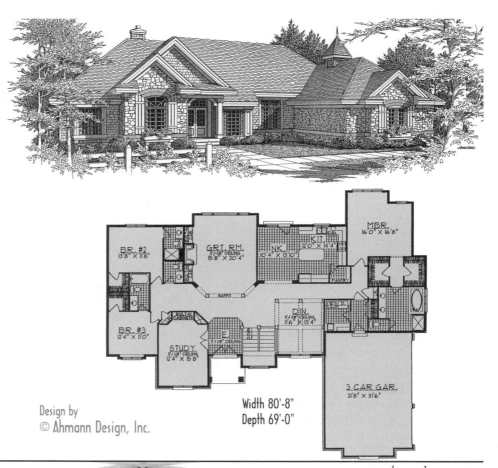

Design by
© Ahmann Design, Inc.

Width 80'-8"
Depth 69'-0"

www.homeplanners.com

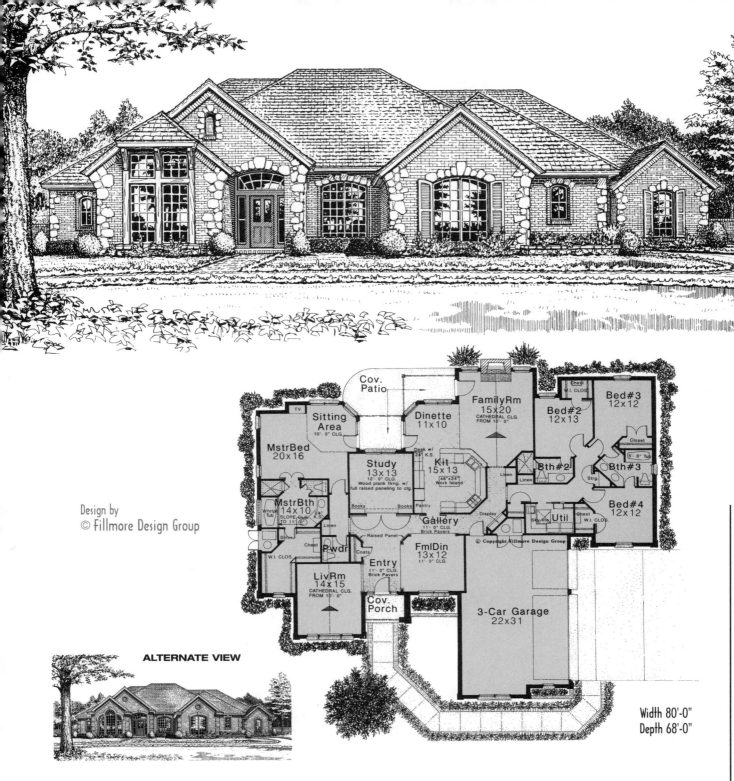

Design by
© Fillmore Design Group

ALTERNATE VIEW

Width 80'-0"
Depth 68'-0"

Varying rooflines, a stately brick exterior and classic window treatment accentuate the beauty of this traditional one-story home. Inside, formal living areas flank the entry—living room to the left and dining room to the right—presenting a fine introduction. Double French doors provide an elegant entrance to the centrally located study. To the right you will find the casual living areas: a U-shaped kitchen, dinette and large family room with cathedral ceiling. Three secondary bedrooms and two full baths complete this side of the plan. Tucked behind the living room is the master suite. Amenities enhancing this private getaway include a sitting area with built-in space for a television, a huge walk-in closet, and a master bath with a whirlpool tub and separate shower.

DESIGN M103
Square Footage: 2,985

DESIGN 7619
Square Footage: 1,912
Bonus Room: 398 square feet

An appealing blend of stone, siding and stucco announces a 21st-Century floor plan. A formal dining area defined by decorative columns opens to a grand great room with a centered hearth. The gourmet kitchen overlooks the great room, and enjoys natural light brought in by the bayed breakfast nook. The sleeping wing, to the right of the plan, includes a sumptuous master suite with a tray ceiling and a skylit bath with twin vanities. A secluded study near a family bedroom shares its bath.

© 1996 Donald A. Gardner Architects, Inc.

Width 67'-7"
Depth 56'-7"

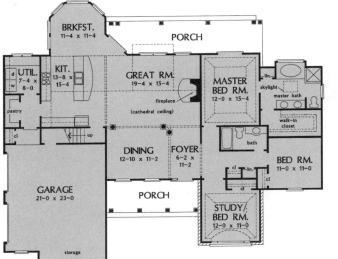

BRKFST.
11-4 x 11-4

PORCH

UTIL.
7-4 x 8-0

KIT.
13-8 x 15-4

GREAT RM.
19-4 x 15-4

MASTER BED RM.
12-0 x 15-4

master bath

walk-in closet

pantry

fireplace
(cathedral ceiling)

DINING
12-10 x 11-2

FOYER
6-2 x 11-2

bath

BED RM.
11-0 x 11-0

GARAGE
21-0 x 23-0

PORCH

STUDY/
BED RM.
12-0 x 11-0

storage

© 1996 Donald A. Gardner Architects, Inc.

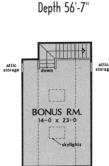

attic storage

down

attic storage

BONUS RM.
14-0 x 23-0

skylights

Design by
Donald A. Gardner
Architects, Inc.

DESIGN P275
Square Footage: 1,980
Bonus Room: 226 square feet

A variety of shapes, textures and window treatments gives this home instant curb appeal. Inside, decorative columns define the formal dining room, while a vaulted family room offers the warmth of a fireplace. The efficient kitchen features a walk-in pantry. Two family bedrooms—one with a bay window—share a full hall bath, while the master suite offers an octagonal sitting room, tray ceiling, vaulted bath filled with amenities and walk-in closet. Please specify basement or crawlspace foundation when ordering.

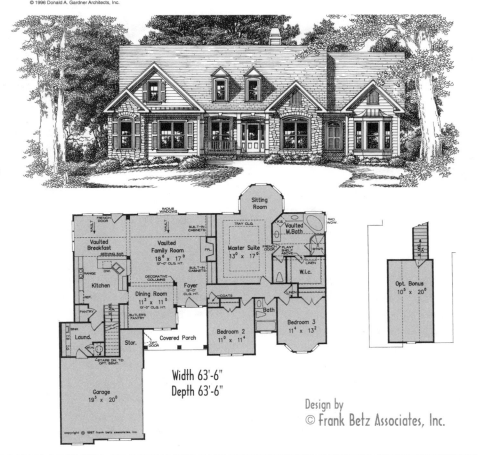

Sitting Room

Vaulted Breakfast

Vaulted Family Room
18⁶ x 17⁰

Master Suite
13⁰ x 17⁰

Vaulted M.Bath

W.i.c.

Kitchen

Dining Room
11³ x 11⁰

Foyer

Bath

Bedroom 3
11⁴ x 13²

Laund.

pantry

Bedroom 2
11⁰ x 11⁴

Garage
19³ x 20⁰

Covered Porch

Stor.

Width 63'-6"
Depth 63'-6"

Opt. Bonus
10⁵ x 20⁰

Design by
© Frank Betz Associates, Inc.

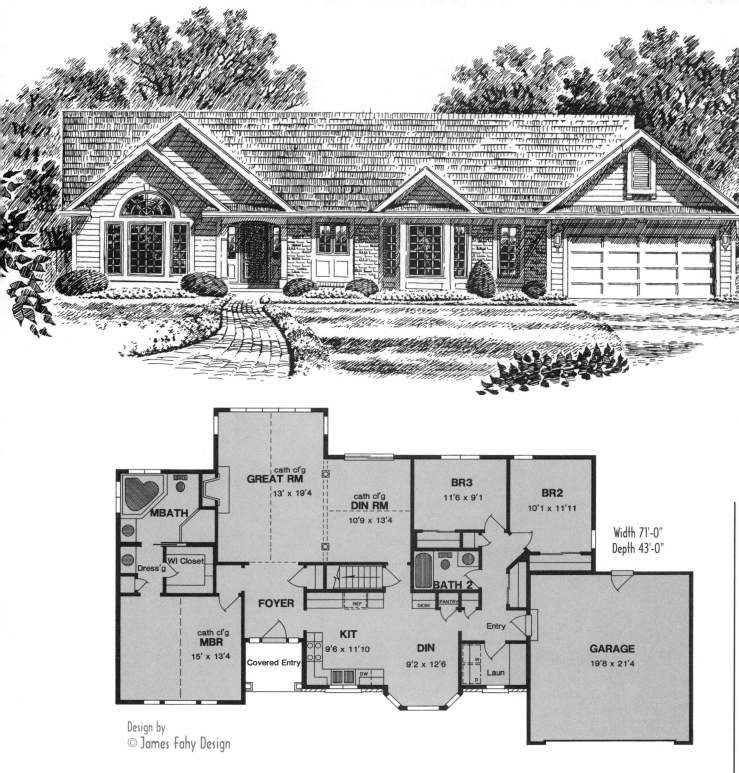

GREAT RM
cath cl'g
13' x 19'4

MBATH

DIN RM
cath cl'g
10'9 x 13'4

BR3
11'6 x 9'1

BR2
10'1 x 11'11

Width 71'-0"
Depth 43'-0"

WI Closet

Dress'g

FOYER

REF

BATH 2

DESK

PANTRY

Entry

MBR
cath cl'g
15' x 13'4

Covered Entry

KIT
9'6 x 11'10

DIN
9'2 x 12'6

DW

W
D

Laun

GARAGE
19'8 x 21'4

Design by
© James Fahy Design

ONE-STORY TRADITIONAL HOMES

G ables along the roofline enhance this traditional ranch home. Inside, the foyer opens to the spacious great room and formal dining room soaring with cathedral ceilings and lots of glass, creating a dramatic impact. The front kitchen and dinette are conveniently located for your family's living needs while the formal entertaining areas are located at the rear of the home. Your guests will dine with warmth from the fireplace. Natural light is abundant throughout the entire house. The master bedroom features a cathedral ceiling and is tucked away to the left of the foyer. Every amenity, from a corner whirlpool tub, glass corner shower, and His and Hers vanities, is found in the adjoining master bath. Family bedrooms share a full bath on the right side of the plan.

**DESIGN
C101**
Square Footage: 1,724

Design by
© Home Planners

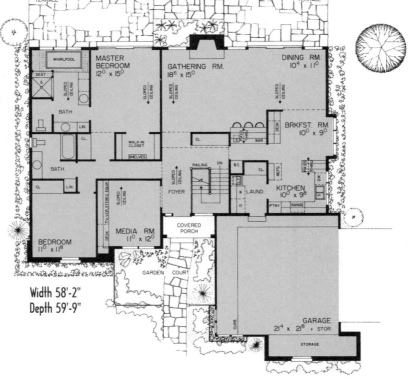

Width 58'-2"
Depth 59'-9"

DESIGN
2941
Square Footage: 1,842
D

This Early American exterior is charming with its horizontal siding, stone accents and window boxes. The covered entrance opens to a spacious foyer with a dramatic open staircase to the basement recreation area. Sloped ceilings dominate the living areas and the master suite. Notice also the abundance of windows and window walls that allow sunbursts of natural light to warm the home. The media room contains a full wall of built-ins, the gathering room features its own fireplace, and the master suite pampers with a luxurious whirlpool tub, separate shower, compartmented toilet and dual sinks. A garden court in the front and a terrace to the rear enhance outdoor livability. The garage contains a large storage area that could also allow room for a workshop.

DESIGN 2805

Width 58'-0"
Depth 51'-5"

Design by
© Home Planners

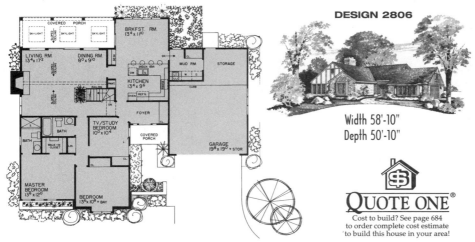

DESIGN 2806

Width 58'-10"
Depth 50'-10"

QUOTE ONE®
Cost to build? See page 684
to order complete cost estimate
to build this house in your area!

DESIGN 2805
Square Footage: 1,547
L D

DESIGN 2806
Square Footage: 1,584
L D

Choose which elevation you want—design 2805 is an appealing stone home, while design 2806 offers a Tudor facade. Both include the same practical floor plan. The living/dining room features a sloped ceiling and direct access to the covered porch. The master bedroom enjoys a private bath and a walk-in closet. The front bedroom has a bay window, while a third bedroom may serve as a study. Quote One available for design 2805 only.

DESIGN 2707
Square Footage: 1,267
L D

Here is a charming Early American adaptation that will serve both young families and empty-nesters equally well. The raised-hearth fireplace highlights the spacious living area. The kitchen features eating space and easy access to the garage and basement. The dining room, adjacent to the kitchen, provides views of the rear yard. The bedroom wing offers three bedrooms and two full baths. Don't miss the sliding doors to the terrace from the living room and the master bedroom.

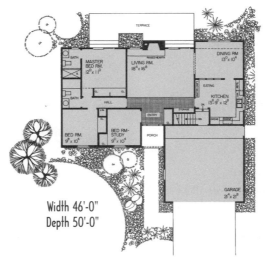

Design by
© Home Planners

Quote One®
Cost to build? See page 684
to order complete cost estimate
to build this house in your area!

Width 46'-0"
Depth 50'-0"

Special touches add so much to the exterior of this home: fan detailing, a barrel-vaulted covered porch, graceful columns and shuttered windows. The floor plan offers extras of its own to appreciate. Columned entries define both the formal living and dining rooms. The family room includes a focal-point fireplace and sliding glass doors leading to the rear yard. The casual dining area is delightfully shaped with windows all around and a tray ceiling. Three bedrooms are to the left of the plan. The master suite provides a bath with whirlpool tub, walk-in closet and double sinks.

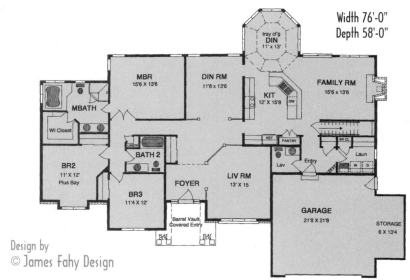

Width 76'-0"
Depth 58'-0"

Design by
© James Fahy Design

DESIGN T053
Square Footage: 2,770

This English cottage features board-and-batten siding and shingles in an attractively proportioned exterior. Finishing touches include flower boxes and shuttered windows. The foyer opens to both the dining room and great room beyond, with French doors opening to the deck. Convenient to a sun-filled breakfast area, the U-shaped kitchen offers abundant counterspace. The spacious master bedroom features a sitting room and walk-in closets on both sides of the entrance to the grand master bath. Two family bedrooms share a full bath. This home is designed with a basement foundation.

Design by
© Stephen Fuller,
American Home Gallery

Width 73'-6"
Depth 78'-0"

Screened Porch

sliding French doors

French doors

Breakfast
10' x 10'
13' ceiling

French doors

display niche

Bath

linen

Living Area
16' x 20'

Kitchen
12' x 12'

Bedroom 2
12'-8" x 14'-4"

Bath

Master Bedroom
13' x 18'
10' stepped ceiling

Bedroom 3
14'-4" x 12'

Gallery
10' clg.

books

Foyer
10' clg.

Bath

books

Dining
12' x 14'
13' clg.

Util.

Storage
10' x 5'

Study/Br 4
11'-4" x 13'
10' ceiling

2-Car Garage
21'-4" x 19'

Width 62'-0"
Depth 67'-10"

QUOTE ONE®
Cost to build? See page 684
to order complete cost estimate
to build this house in your area!

Design by
© Larry W. Garnett & Associates, Inc.

The combination of finely detailed brick and shingle siding recalls some of the distinctive architecture of the East Coast during the early part of this century. The foyer and gallery provide for a functional traffic pattern. Columns outline the formal dining room, which features a thirteen-foot ceiling. The extensive living area offers a corner fireplace and French doors to the screened porch. It surrounds the breakfast room and is an ideal entertainment area. The master suite features two spacious closets and a bath with a garden tub and an oversized shower. The two family bedrooms to the right of the plan both include private access to a shared bath. Bedroom 4 can serve as a study, nursery, guest room or home office.

**DESIGN
8923**
Square Footage: 2,361
Bonus Room: 214 square feet

ONE-STORY TRADITIONAL HOMES

Dual chimneys (one a false chimney created to enhance the aesthetic effect) and a double stairway to the covered entry of this home create a balanced architectural statement. The sunlit foyer leads straight into the spacious great room, which features a tray ceiling and fireplace, bordered by twin bookcases. A great view is offered from the kitchen with breakfast bar and work island. The master suite provides a large balanced bath, spacious closet and sitting area with access to the veranda. This home is designed with a basement foundation.

Width 65'-3"
Depth 67'-3"

QUOTE ONE®
Cost to build? See page 684 to order complete cost estimate to build this house in your area!

Design by
© Stephen Fuller,
American Home Gallery

Volume rooflines and a covered front porch are just two of the many reasons this home is sure to please. The highly efficient floor plan is another, with the spacious great room attracting attention with its fireplace and built-ins. An L-shaped kitchen provides a snack bar into the sunny breakfast room, while also serving the formal dining room easily. The secluded master suite features a huge walk-in closet, whirlpool tub and separate vanities. Three bedrooms—or make one a study—share a full hall bath. Please specify crawlspace or slab foundation when ordering.

Width 72'-10"
Depth 67'-0"

Design by
© Michael E. Nelson
Nelson Design Group, LLC

QUOTE ONE®

Cost to build? See page 684
to order complete cost estimate
to build this house in your area!

Design by
© Frank Betz Associates, Inc.

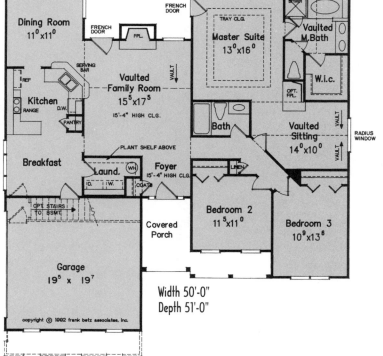

Dining Room 11⁰x11⁰

FRENCH DOOR

FRENCH DOOR

FPL.

SERVING BAR

REF

Kitchen

RANGE

D.W.

PANTRY

Vaulted Family Room 15⁵x17⁵

15'-4" HIGH CLG.

VAULT

TRAY CLG.

Master Suite 13⁰x16⁰

SHWR

Vaulted M.Bath

W.i.c.

OPT. FPL.

Bath

Vaulted Sitting 14⁰x10⁰

VAULT

RADIUS WINDOW

Breakfast

PLANT SHELF ABOVE

Laund.

WH

Foyer 15'-4" HIGH CLG.

COATS

LINEN

OPT. STAIRS TO BSMT.

Covered Porch

Bedroom 2 11⁵x11⁰

Bedroom 3 10⁹x13⁶

Garage 19⁵ x 19⁷

copyright © 1992 frank betz associates, inc.

Width 50'-0"
Depth 51'-0"

ONE-STORY TRADITIONAL HOMES

Asymmetrical gables, a columned porch and an abundance of windows brighten the exterior of this compact home. An efficient kitchen boasts a pantry and a serving bar that it shares with the formal dining room and the vaulted family room. A sunny breakfast room and nearby laundry room complete the living zone. Be sure to notice extras such as the focal-point fireplace in the family room and a plant shelf in the laundry room. The sumptuous master suite offers a door to the backyard, a vaulted sitting area and a pampering bath with whirlpool tub and separate shower. Two family bedrooms share a hall bath. Please specify basement, crawlspace or slab foundation when ordering.

DESIGN P233
Square Footage: 1,671

DESIGN
P115
Square Footage: 1,856

Southern charm is written all over this country home. Formal living and dining rooms frame an open foyer, both bright with windows. Decorative columns announce an expansive family room set off by a focal-point fireplace. The well-appointed kitchen shares a serving bar with the breakfast area, which provides a French door to the rear property. A lavish master suite features a vaulted bath with a radius window and a plant shelf. Two family bedrooms on the opposite side of the plan share a full bath. Please specify basement, slab or crawlspace foundation when ordering.

Width 59'-0"
Depth 54'-6"

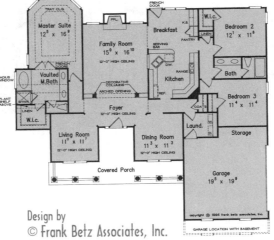

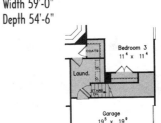

OPTIONAL BASEMENT ACCESS

Design by
© Frank Betz Associates, Inc.

QUOTE ONE®
Cost to build? See page 684
to order complete cost estimate
to build this house in your area!

ONE-STORY TRADITIONAL HOMES

DESIGN
8143
Square Footage: 2,648
Bonus Room: 266 square feet

This Southern raised elevation looks cozy but lives large. Twelve-foot ceilings and graceful columns and arches lend hospitality to the formal rooms and the family living space. Double doors open to the gourmet kitchen, which offers a built-in desk, a snack counter and a breakfast room with a picture window. The secluded master suite features His and Hers walk-in closets, a whirlpool tub and a knee-space vanity. Both family bedrooms enjoy separate access to a shared bath and a private vanity. Please specify basement, crawlspace or slab foundation when ordering.

Width 68'-10"
Depth 77'-10"

Design by
© Larry E. Belk Designs

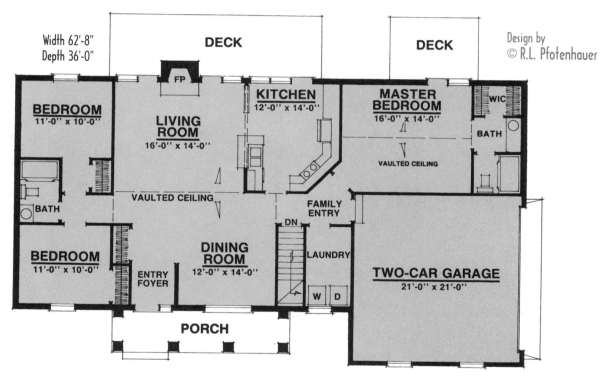

Width 62'-8"
Depth 36'-0"

DECK

DECK

Design by
© R.L. Pfotenhauer

BEDROOM
11'-0" x 10'-0"

LIVING
ROOM
16'-0" x 14'-0"

FP

KITCHEN
12'-0" x 14'-0"

MASTER
BEDROOM
16'-0" x 14'-0"

WIC

BATH

VAULTED CEILING

BATH

VAULTED CEILING

FAMILY
ENTRY

BEDROOM
11'-0" x 10'-0"

DINING
ROOM
12'-0" x 14'-0"

DN

LAUNDRY

TWO-CAR GARAGE
21'-0" x 21'-0"

ENTRY
FOYER

W D

PORCH

ONE-STORY TRADITIONAL HOMES

A handsome porch dressed up with Greek Revival details greets visitors warmly into this one-story Early American home. From the entry, one is struck by the volume of space provided by the vaulted ceiling in the dining and living rooms, and also extends to the kitchen with eating space. The secluded master bedroom also sports a vaulted ceil-ing and is graced with a dressing area, a private bath and walk-in closet. Two decks located at the rear of the plan are conveniently accessed by the master bedroom, kitchen and living room. A full bath serves the two family bedrooms and is readily accessible by guests. Adjacent to the two-car garage is a laundry room that handily accommodates all family members.

DESIGN
F117
Square Footage: 1,550

**DESIGN
7365**
Square Footage: 1,729

Simple, single-level designs need not be plain or ordinary, as this lovely plan proves. The accommodating floor plan provides well-defined living and sleeping areas. A large great room with ten-foot ceiling dominates the center of the plan, with a dining room, a light-filled breakfast room and a U-shaped kitchen falling to the right. On the left are two family bedrooms with a full bath. The master suite stands alone and is graced by a walk-in closet, separate shower and tub and dual lavatories. A two-car garage completes the plan.

Design by
© Design Basics, Inc.

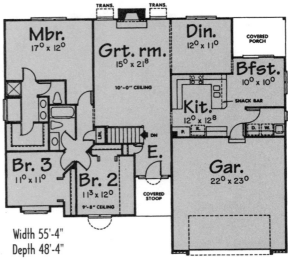

Width 55'-4"
Depth 48'-4"

**DESIGN
3327**
Square Footage: 2,881

L D

The high, massive hip roof of this home creates an impressive facade. A central foyer leads to the various zones of the house. A built-in china cabinet and planter unit are fine decor features, while the angular kitchen includes a high ceiling and efficient work space. The conversation room may act as a multi-purpose room. Sleeping quarters start with the spacious master bedroom, which features a tray ceiling and sliding doors outside. Two sizable bedrooms accommodate family or guests.

Width 77'-11"
Depth 73'-11"

Quote One®
Cost to build? See page 684 to order complete cost estimate to build this house in your area!

Design by
© Home Planners

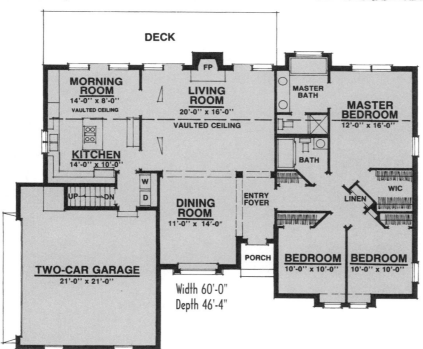

DECK

MORNING ROOM
14'-0'' x 8'-0''
VAULTED CEILING

LIVING ROOM
20'-0'' x 16'-0''
VAULTED CEILING

FP

MASTER BATH

MASTER BEDROOM
12'-0'' x 16'-0''

KITCHEN
14'-0'' x 10'-0''

BATH

W
D

UP   DN

DINING ROOM
11'-0'' x 14'-0''

ENTRY FOYER

LINEN   WIC

TWO-CAR GARAGE
21'-0'' x 21'-0''

PORCH

BEDROOM
10'-0'' x 10'-0''

BEDROOM
10'-0'' x 10'-0''

Width 60'-0''
Depth 46'-4''

Design by
© R.L. Pfotenhauer

This cozy one-story plan features a volume roofline that allows vaulted ceilings in the living room, morning room and master bedroom. The dining room opens, through gracious columns, to the foyer and the living room. Special features in the living areas include a fireplace in the living room and doors leading to the rear yard from the living room and morning room. The kitchen is designed with the gourmet cook in mind. It contains an island cook-top, over-the-sink window and loads of counter space. Family bedrooms share a hall bath and include box windows perfect for window seats. The master suite is appointed with all the expected amenities, including a garden whirlpool tub, separate shower and double sinks. A hall linen closet provides plenty of storage space, as does the two-car garage. A laundry alcove resides in the service entrance.

DESIGN
F148
Square Footage: 1,732

DESIGN
P235
Square Footage: 1,070

Here is a plan that packs a lot of house into just over 1,000 square feet. The front door, protected by a covered porch, opens directly into the vaulted family room with its enticing corner fireplace and sliding glass doors to the rear property. A coat closet and hall bath are near the entrance for the convenience of guests. A folding door hides the washer and dryer from the galley kitchen, which enjoys the natural light from a sunny breakfast area. The master suite boasts many of the amenities found in much larger homes. Please specify basement, crawlspace or slab foundation when ordering.

Width 48'-0"
Depth 36'-0"

Design by
© Frank Betz Associates, Inc.

copyright © 1990 frank betz associates, inc.

DESIGN
3708
Square Footage: 1,298

Traditional charm with an outstanding layout describes this low-cost one-story ranch home. A covered front porch welcomes visitors. Three bedrooms or two bedrooms and a study are accompanied by two full baths. Livability may be enhanced by completion of an optional standard or double-size deck, a fireplace in the living room and a two-car garage. The blueprints show how to build both the basic, low-cost version and the enhanced, upgraded version.

ENHANCED PLAN

Design by
© Home Planners

BASIC PLAN

Width 52'-0"
Depth 44'-5"

The home, as shown in the photograph, may differ from the actual blueprints.
For more detailed information, please check the floor plans carefully.

Photo by Andrew D. Lautman

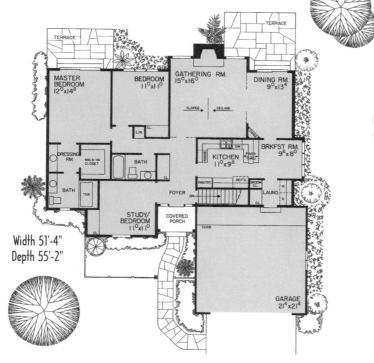

Width 51'-4"
Depth 55'-2"

Design by
© Home Planners

QUOTE ONE®
Cost to build? See page 684
to order complete cost estimate
to build this house in your area!

This charming one-story traditional design offers plenty of livability in a compact size. Thoughtful zoning puts all sleeping areas to one side of the house away from household activity in the living and service areas. The home includes a spacious gathering room with a sloped ceiling, in addition to a formal dining room and a separate breakfast room. There's also a handy pass-through between the breakfast room and the large, efficient kitchen. The laundry is strategically located adjacent to the garage and the breakfast/kitchen areas for handy access. A master bedroom enjoys a private bath and a walk-in closet. A third bedroom can double as a sizable study just off the foyer.

DESIGN
2878
Square Footage: 1,530
L D

DESIGN 7709

Square Footage: 1,629
Bonus Room: 316 square feet

© 1998 Donald A. Gardner Architects, Inc.

A columned, arched entrance and windows provide classic style to the exterior of this plan. The foyer leads to the great room warmed by an extended-hearth fireplace. A bay windowed dining room has views to the rear property and the rear deck with built-in seat. One of two family bedrooms is highlighted by a vaulted ceiling; the master suite boasts cathedral dimensions and a roomy walk-in closet. An upstairs bonus room offers space for future expansion.

Width 58'-6"
Depth 49'-8"

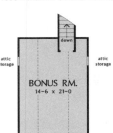

Design by
Donald A. Gardner
Architects, Inc.

© 1998 Donald A Gardner, Inc.

DESIGN Q470

Square Footage: 1,392

Traditional corner columns add prestige to this three-bedroom ranch house. The vaulted living room features a gas fireplace and a built-in media center. An open kitchen with work island adjoins the dining room, which contains a large bay window and double French doors leading to the rear deck. An abundance of natural light from the skylights in the main hallways adds dramatic effect. The master suite is appointed with His and Hers wall closets and a private bath. Plans include details for both a crawlspace and a basement foundation.

Width 44'-0"
Depth 52'-6"

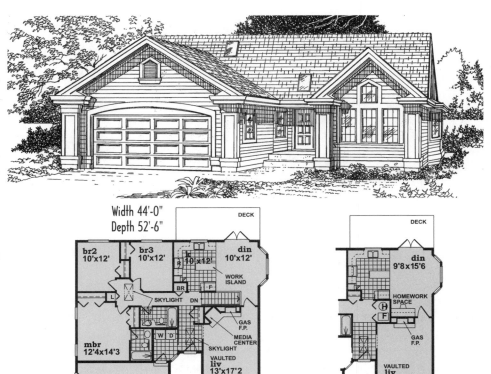

Design by
© Select Home Designs

ALTERNATE LAYOUT
FOR CRAWLSPACE

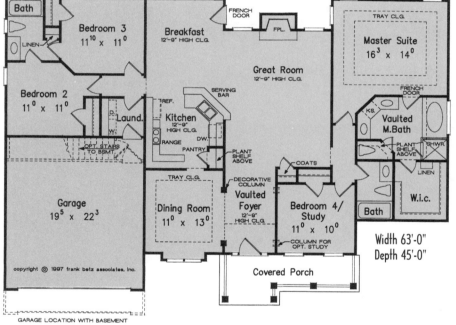

Bath

Bedroom 3
11^{10} x 11^{0}

LINEN

Bedroom 2
11^{0} x 11^{0}

Laund.
D. W.

OPT. STAIRS TO BSMT.

Garage
19^{5} x 22^{3}

copyright © 1997 frank betz associates, inc.

GARAGE LOCATION WITH BASEMENT

Breakfast
12'-9" HIGH CLG.

FRENCH DOOR

FPL.

Great Room
12'-9" HIGH CLG.

SERVING BAR

REF.

Kitchen
12'-9" HIGH CLG.

RANGE

DW.

PANTRY

PLANT SHELF ABOVE

TRAY CLG.

Dining Room
11^{0} x 13^{0}

DECORATIVE COLUMN

Vaulted Foyer
12'-9" HIGH CLG.

COATS

COLUMN FOR OPT. STUDY

Bedroom 4/ Study
11^{0} x 10^{0}

Covered Porch

TRAY CLG.

Master Suite
16^{3} x 14^{0}

FRENCH DOOR

KS

Vaulted M.Bath

PLANT SHELF ABOVE

SHWR.

LINEN

W.i.c.

Bath

Design by
© Frank Betz Associates, Inc.

Width 63'-0"
Depth 45'-0"

DESIGN P296
Square Footage: 1,932

Special architectural aspects turn this quaint home into much more than just another one-story ranch design. It is enhanced by a covered, columned front porch, large window areas, a dormer and horizontal wood siding. The floor plan is equally thoughtful in design. A central great room acts as the hub of the plan and is graced by a fireplace flanked on either side by windows. This room is separated from the kitchen by a convenient serving bar. Formal din-ing is accomplished to the front of the plan in a room with a tray ceiling. Casual dining takes place in the breakfast room with its full wall of glass. Two bedrooms to the left share a full bath. The master suite and one additional bedroom are to the right. Bedroom 4 would make the perfect study, with the option of a door-way opening directly to the foyer. A two-car garage shields family bedrooms from noise. Please specify basement or crawl-space foundation when ordering.

ALTERNATE VIEWS

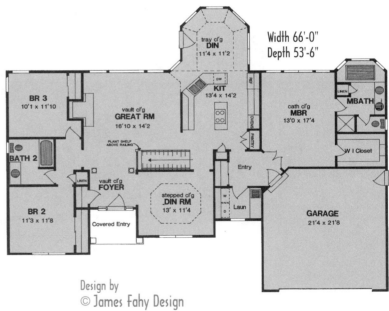

Width 66'-0"
Depth 53'-6"

tray cl'g
DIN
11'4 x 11'2

KIT
13'4 x 14'2

BR 3
10'1 x 11'10

vault cl'g
GREAT RM
16'10 x 14'2

cath cl'g
MBR
13'0 x 17'4

MBATH

LINEN

BATH 2

PLANT SHELF
ABOVE RAILING

PANTRY

W I Closet

Entry

LINEN

vault cl'g
FOYER

stepped cl'g
DIN RM
13' x 11'4

BR 2
11'3 x 11'8

Laun

GARAGE
21'4 x 21'8

Covered Entry

Design by
© James Fahy Design

**DESIGN
C146**
Square Footage: 1,838

Y ou'll love the ceiling treatments in
the special rooms of this home.
They are made possible by a volume roofline that adds appeal to
the exterior as well. Both the foyer and the
great room feature vaulted ceilings, while
the formal dining room has a step ceiling
and the casual dining area has a tray ceiling. The master bedroom is graced by a

cathedral ceiling, just one of many details
that make it luxurious. Family bedrooms
are split away from the master suite for
privacy and share a hall bath. The two-car
garage connects conveniently to the main
house via a service entry that also leads to
the laundry area and the island kitchen.
Double doors at this point lead to the
master suite and keep it private.

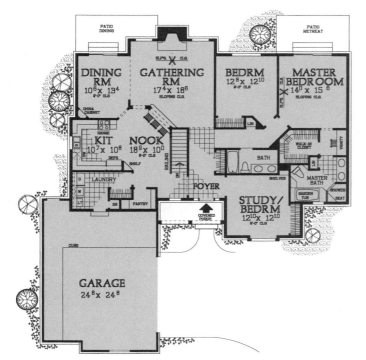

Design by
© Home Planners

Width 64'-0"
Depth 69'-8"

Cost to build? See page 684
to order complete cost estimate
to build this house in your area!

This is a fine home for a young family or for empty-nesters. The versatile bedroom/study offers room for growth or a quiet haven for reading. The U-shaped kitchen includes a handy nook with a snack bar and easy accessibility to the dining room or the gathering room—perfect for entertaining. The master bedroom includes its own private outdoor retreat, a walk-in closet and an amenity-filled bathroom with double sinks, vanity area and garden tub. An additional bedroom, a large laundry room with an adjacent, walk-in pantry, and a two-car garage with storage space complete the plan.

DESIGN
3491
Square Footage: 2,098
L D

ONE-STORY TRADITIONAL HOMES

**DESIGN
N120**
Square Footage: 1,926

A crisp, contemporary exterior combines with great interior elements to produce a home that accommodates today's active lifestyles. Inside, a skylit foyer opens to a large great room. The country kitchen, adjacent to the columned dining room, features an island counter, multi-windowed eating area and fireplace with wood storage. The master bedroom features twin walk-in closets and a pampering bath with a whirlpool tub. Two family bedrooms—each with a bumped-out window—share a full bath. Please specify basement or slab foundation when ordering.

Design by
© Perfect Home Plans, Inc.

Width 77'-2"
Depth 39'-5"

**DESIGN
N123**
Square Footage: 1,686

The warmth of New England charm dresses up this traditional one-story home. Planned for efficiency, each portion of the home is defined by its function: formal, informal, sleeping and service. The two-car garage opens to the mudroom and powder room, which in turn leads to the informal living space. Here, a step-saving kitchen easily serves both formal and informal living areas. Bedrooms grouped to the right of the plan include a master suite with a private bath and walk-in closet, two family bedrooms, and a full bath. Please specify basement or slab foundation when ordering.

Design by
© Perfect Home Plans, Inc.

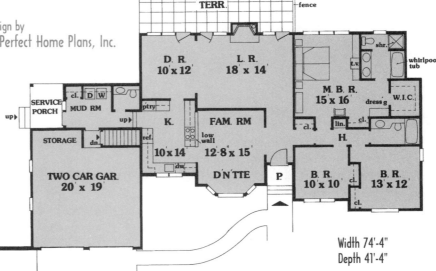

Width 74'-4"
Depth 41'-4"

MASTER
BEDRM
17⁴ x 14⁰

LIVING
RM
17⁰ x 15⁴

DINING
RM
10⁰ x 12⁶

BEDRM
14⁴ x 12⁰

PATIO

WALK-IN
CLOSET

LINEN

LINEN

BATH

MASTER
BATH

SNACK BAR

PANTRY

FOYER

KIT
19⁰ x 11²

BEDRM
14⁴ x 14⁴

SHOWER

GARDEN
TUB

LAUNDRY

COVERED
PORCH

RAILING

GARAGE
21⁴ x 20⁴

Width 64'-8"
Depth 54'-7"

Design by
© Home Planners

QUOTE ONE®

Cost to build? See page 684
to order complete cost estimate
to build this house in your area!

S mall, but so livable, this charming ranch home is great for starters or empty-nesters. The cozy covered porch opens to a tiled foyer, which then leads into the huge kitchen on the right. The kitchen connects to the living room/dining room area via a snack bar and enjoys views to the front covered porch. Look for a warming fireplace in the living room and a sunny patio through sliding glass doors in the dining room. Bedrooms are split with two family bedrooms and a full bath on the right and the master suite on the left. A handy laundry room connects the home to a two-car garage.

DESIGN 3652
Square Footage: 2,076
L D

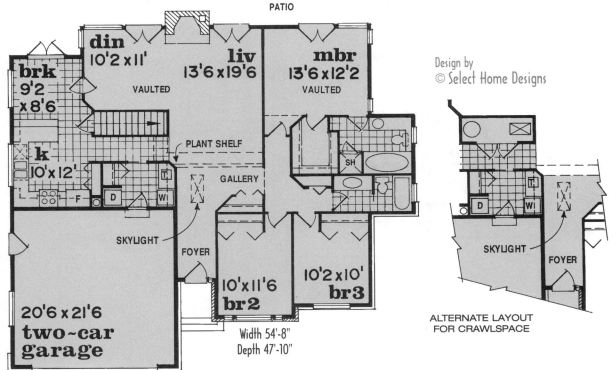

ONE-STORY TRADITIONAL HOMES

PATIO

din
10'2 x 11'

brk
9'2
x 8'6

VAULTED

liv
13'6 x 19'6

mbr
13'6 x 12'2

VAULTED

Design by
© Select Home Designs

k
10' x 12'

PLANT SHELF

GALLERY

SH

SKYLIGHT

FOYER

F   D   W

10' x 11'6
br2

10'2 x 10'
br3

Width 54'-8"
Depth 47'-10"

20'6 x 21'6
**two-car
garage**

D   W

SKYLIGHT

FOYER

**ALTERNATE LAYOUT
FOR CRAWLSPACE**

**DESIGN
Q367**
Square Footage: 1,647

This floor plan is designed for a home that captures a view to the rear of the lot. French doors in the dining room, living room, master bedroom and breakfast room all lead out to the foyer in the back. In the front, a skylit patio is visually zoned from the living room by a plant shelf. Both the living and dining rooms have vaulted ceilings and

enjoy a warming fireplace set between them. A U-shaped kitchen has a breakfast bar to serve the sunny breakfast room. The bedrooms to the right include two family bedrooms sharing a full bath. The vaulted master suite has a walk-in closet and private bath with separate tub and shower. Plans include details for both a basement and a crawlspace foundation.

www.homeplanners.com

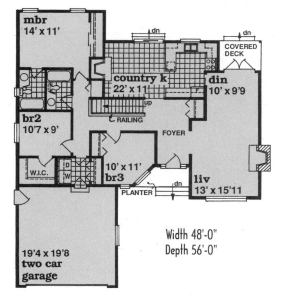

Design by
© Select Home Designs

mbr
14' x 11'

br2
10'7 x 9'

W.I.C.

br3
10' x 11'

PLANTER

COVERED
DECK

country k
22' x 11

din
10' x 9'9

FOYER

RAILING

liv
13' x 15'11

19'4 x 19'8
two car
garage

Width 48'-0"
Depth 56'-0"

DESIGN
Q362
Square Footage: 1,493

A weather-protected entrance, with garden planter and decorative wood trim, adorn the exterior of this compact family home. The foyer opens into the living room/dining room combination on the right. Special features here include a fireplace and double doors to a covered deck at the back. A step-saving, U-shaped country kitchen, with sliding glass door to the garden, is warmed by a masonry fireplace—a cozy gathering spot for the family. The master suite boasts a full wall closet and private bath while two family bedrooms share a hall bath. The third bedroom could easily double as a guest room, office or den.

Design by
© Select Home Designs

mbr
15' x 12'

br2
11'8 x 9'

br3
10'x 9'

PATIO

SKYLIGHT OVER
PLANTER SHELF

fam/brk
17'2 X 14'& 12'

W.I. CLOSET

SKYLIGHT
OVER

k
9'x 10'

REF

din
12'x 9'6

OPEN RAILING

16' X 13'
liv

two-car
garage
21'6 x21'10

OPTIONAL BAY WINDOW
FOR ELEVATION 'B'

Width 48'-0"
Depth 58'-10"

DESIGN
Q240
Square Footage: 1,608

The recessed entry of this one-story home opens to a skylit, tiled foyer. The sunken living room enjoys a bay window and focal-point fireplace. Adjoining is the formal dining room, separated from the living room by an open railing. The kitchen takes on a modified U-shape and has a bright window box over the sink. The connecting breakfast bay and family room have a corner fireplace and sliding glass door to the patio. Bedrooms are positioned away from traffic areas and include a master suite with full bath (note the plant shelf and skylight). Two family bedrooms and a shared bath are nearby.

ONE-STORY TRADITIONAL HOMES

DESIGN 3705
Square Footage: 1,200

This three-bedroom ranch home contains many spacious features. It includes a full-size bath in the master bedroom and a shared bath for the secondary bedrooms. The dining room and living room combine to create a spacious formal or informal gathering area. A two-car garage, a standard deck, decorative louvers and a centrally located fireplace are optional. The blueprints for this home show how to build both the basic version and the enhanced, upgraded version.

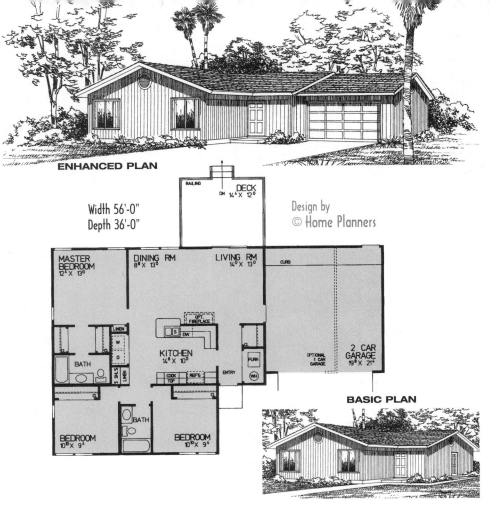

ENHANCED PLAN

Width 56'-0"
Depth 36'-0"

Design by
© Home Planners

BASIC PLAN

DESIGN 3701
Square Footage: 1,130

Traditional charm is an apt description for this economical ranch home. The kitchen is designed to serve as an eat-in kitchen for this efficient home. The master bedroom offers a full bath plus ample closet space. A full-sized bath adjoins the other two bedrooms. Options include a one- or two-car garage, a front porch, a rear deck with railing, a box-bay window and a fireplace. The blueprints for this house show how to build both a basic, low-cost version and an enhanced, upgraded version.

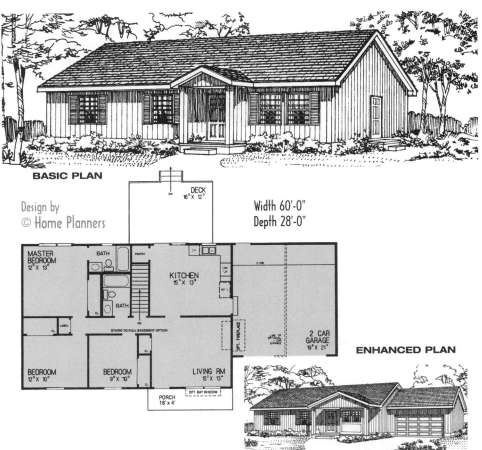

BASIC PLAN

Design by
© Home Planners

Width 60'-0"
Depth 28'-0"

ENHANCED PLAN

QUOTE ONE®
Cost to build? See page 684
to order complete cost estimate
to build this house in your area!

Design by
© Home Planners

Width 49'-8"
Depth 52'-0"

Projecting the garage to the front of a house is very economical in two ways. One, it reduces the required lot size for building, and two, it will protect the interior from street noise. Many other characteristics of this design deserve mention, too. The foyer leads to a central hall with a galley kitchen on the left and the gathering room ahead. The gathering room has a sloped ceiling and fireplace flanked by windows overlooking the rear terrace. A small dining space in the left corner allows access to the terrace. The light-filled breakfast room holds a planning desk. Two or three bedrooms sit to the right of the hall—use one as a study if you wish. The master suite contains a dressing room, terrace access and bath with spa tub and skylight. The study also has terrace access.

DESIGN 2864
Square Footage: 1,387
L D

**DESIGN
C102**

Square Footage: 1,546

This charming traditional-style home with its covered porch and railing offers lots of curb appeal. The openness of the main living areas produces a spacious, livable floor plan enhanced by half walls with wood caps. A garden window above the kitchen sink provides plenty of natural light. The raised snack bar creates a nice separation from the dinette. Double doors lead to the restful master bedroom, which is secluded from the two family bedrooms at the opposite end of the home. A spacious mudroom/laundry area with ample closet space completes the plan.

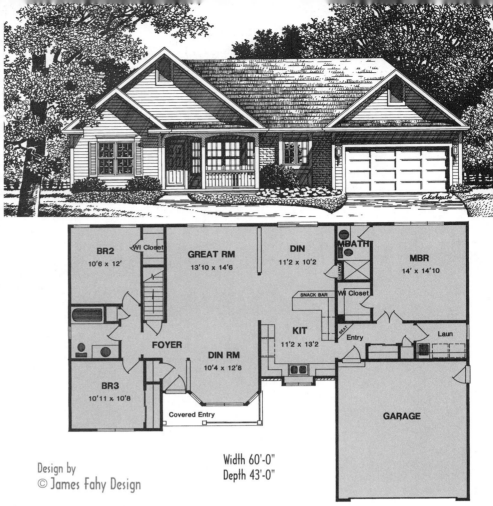

Design by
© James Fahy Design

Width 60'-0"
Depth 43'-0"

**DESIGN
F147**

Square Footage: 1,550

If you like the rustic appeal of ranch-style homes, you'll love this version. The entry opens to a huge open living/dining room combination. A fireplace in the living area is flanked by windows and doors to one of two rear decks. A vaulted ceiling runs the width of this area. The kitchen also accesses the deck and features counter space galore. Look for a private deck behind the master suite. A vaulted ceiling graces the master bedroom. Two family bedrooms have good closet space and share a full bath at the opposite end of the hall.

Design by
© R.L. Pfotenhauer

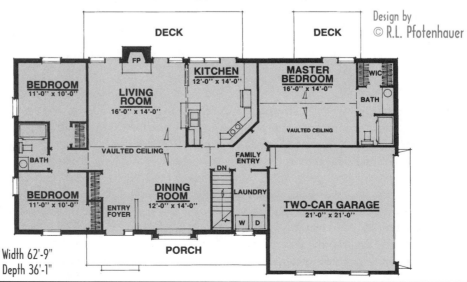

Width 62'-9"
Depth 36'-1"

www.homeplanners.com

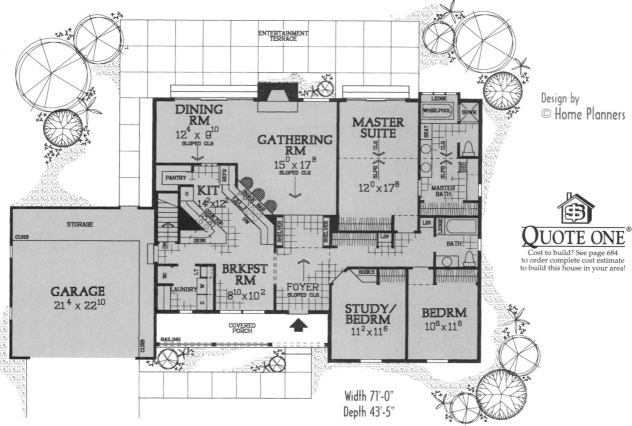

ENTERTAINMENT
TERRACE

DINING
RM
12⁴ x 9¹⁰
SLOPED CLG

GATHERING
RM
15⁰ x 17⁸
SLOPED CLG

MASTER
SUITE

12⁰ x 17⁸

LEDGE
WHIRLPOOL
SHWR
SEAT
CL⁸
MASTER
BATH

PANTRY
REF/B
KIT
14²x12²

SNACK BAR

DESK

LIN

LIN
LEDGE

BATH

STORAGE

GARAGE
21⁴ x 22¹⁰

CURB

LAUNDRY

BRKFST
RM
8¹⁰ x 10²

FOYER
SLOPED CLG

BOOKS

STUDY/
BEDRM
11² x 11⁶

BEDRM
10⁶ x 11⁶

SHELVES

SHELVES

COVERED
PORCH

RAILING

CURB

Width 71'-0"
Depth 43'-5"

Design by
© Home Planners

Quote One®
Cost to build? See page 684
to order complete cost estimate
to build this house in your area!

ONE-STORY TRADITIONAL HOMES

ountry comfort is the focus of this charming plan, ready for any region. A cozy covered porch offers a warm introduction to the tiled foyer, which leads to the living areas and opens to the breakfast room and kitchen. The expansive gathering room features an extended-hearth fireplace and adjoins the formal dining room, served by the kitchen. The entertainment terrace enjoys access from the dining room as well as the master suite. A sumptuous master bath provides a relaxing retreat for the home-owner, with a windowed whirlpool tub, separate shower, two vanities and a sloped ceiling. A study at the front of the plan could be used as a bedroom. A two-car garage connects at a service entry.

**DESIGN
3487**
Square Footage: 1,835

L

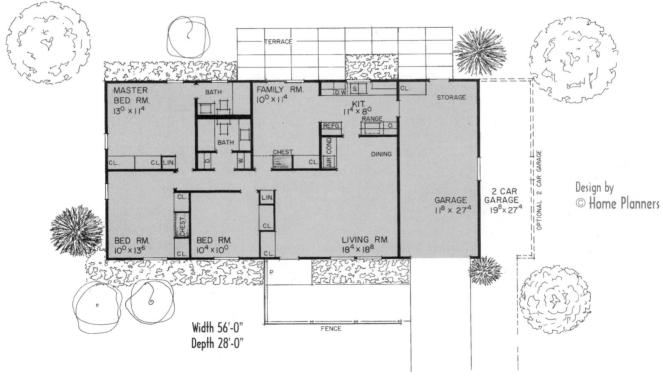

Design by
© Home Planners

Width 56'-0"
Depth 28'-0"

**DESIGN
1191**
Square Footage: 1,232
L D

A careful study of the floor plan for this cozy traditional home reveals a fine combination of features. For instance, notice the wardrobe and storage facilities in the bedroom area—a built-in chest in one bedroom and also one in the family room. The master suite has a private bath, while the family bedrooms share the use of the main bath. Note the laundry alcove at the entrance to the main bath. The spacious living room contains space for a dining area, plus a handy coat closet. The kitchen is designed for efficiency and features a window over the sink. A rear terrace can be reached through sliding glass doors in the family room and also from the single-car garage, which may be expanded to a two-car garage if needed. Extra storage space is found in the garage.

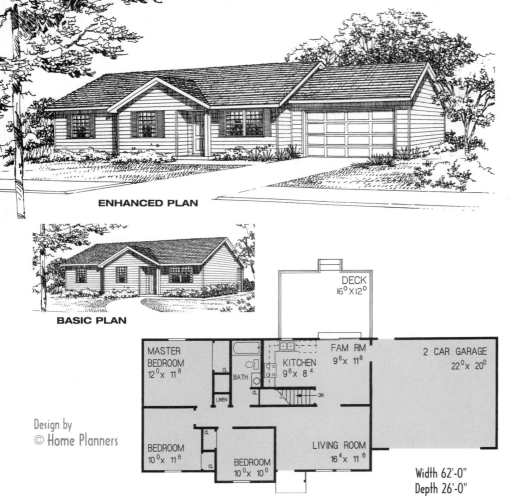

ENHANCED PLAN

BASIC PLAN

Design by
© Home Planners

DECK
16⁰ X 12⁰

MASTER
BEDROOM
12⁰ x 11⁸

BATH

KITCHEN
9⁶ x 8⁴

FAM RM
9⁶ x 11⁸

2 CAR GARAGE
22⁰ x 20⁰

LINEN

DN

BEDROOM
10⁰ x 11⁶

BEDROOM
10⁰ x 10⁰

LIVING ROOM
16⁴ x 11⁶

Width 62'-0"
Depth 26'-0"

DESIGN 3725
Square Footage: 982

Here is an affordable ranch home with optional enhancements. Both options include three bedrooms and one full bath with room for a washer and dryer, while the basement option adds two linen closets. The kitchen is located next to the family room to help serve gatherings. The front living room accommodates more formal occasions. The sliding glass door, a two-car garage and rear deck are all optional. The blueprints for this house show how to build both the basic, low-cost version, and the enhanced, upgraded version.

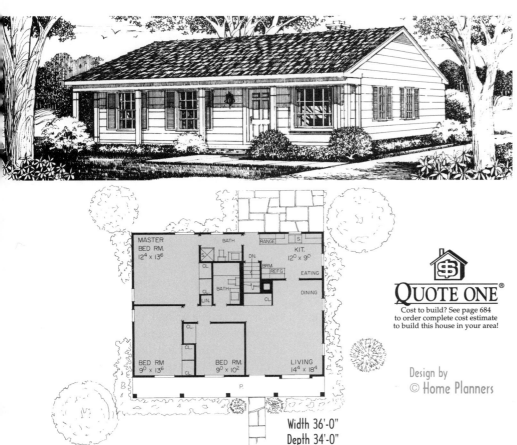

MASTER
BED RM.
12⁴ x 13⁶

BATH

RANGE

S

KIT.
12⁰ x 9⁰

BRM
REFG

EATING

BATH

LIN.

DINING

BED RM.
9⁰ x 13⁶

BED RM.
9⁰ x 10²

LIVING
14⁴ x 18⁴

P.

Width 36'-0"
Depth 34'-0"

QUOTE ONE®
Cost to build? See page 684
to order complete cost estimate
to build this house in your area!

Design by
© Home Planners

DESIGN 1113
Square Footage: 1,080
L D

A cozy plan, but just right for a small family or empty-nesters. A covered front porch shelters visitors from inclement weather. An ample living room/dining room area leads the way to a rear kitchen overlooking a terrace. Two full baths serve three bedrooms—one a master suite. The kitchen includes informal eating space. Stairs lead to a full basement that may be developed as desired. Multi-lite windows with quaint shutters add a touch of charm to this design.

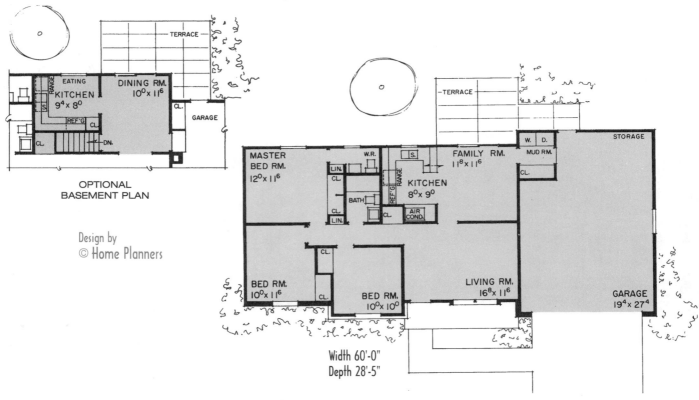

TERRACE

EATING
KITCHEN
9⁴ x 8⁰

DINING RM.
10⁰ x 11⁶

GARAGE

REF'G   CL.

CL.   DN.

CL.

**OPTIONAL
BASEMENT PLAN**

Design by
© Home Planners

TERRACE

MASTER
BED RM.
12⁰ x 11⁶

W.R.

LIN.
CL.

BATH

LIN.
CL.

CL.

S.

RANGE

REF'G

AIR
COND.

KITCHEN
8⁰ x 9⁰

FAMILY RM.
11⁸ x 11⁶

MUD RM.

W.   D.

STORAGE

CL.

CL.

BED RM.
10⁰ x 11⁶

CL.

CL.

BED RM.
10⁰ x 10⁰

LIVING RM.
16⁸ x 11⁶

GARAGE
19⁴ x 27⁴

Width 60'-0"
Depth 28'-5"

**DESIGN
1311**
Square Footage: 1,050
Ⓛ

Delightful design and effective, flexible planning come in small packages, too! This fine traditional exterior, with its covered front entrance, features an alternate basement plan. Note how the non-basement layout provides a family room and mudroom, while the basement option shows a kitchen eating area and a dining room. In both versions, sliding glass doors lead from the dining or family room space to a rear terrace. The U-shaped kitchen features a sink with a window overlooking the rear yard. Three bedrooms include two front-facing family bedrooms sharing a full bath and a master bedroom with a half bath. The garage has extra storage space and connects to the main house through a service entrance with a mudroom.

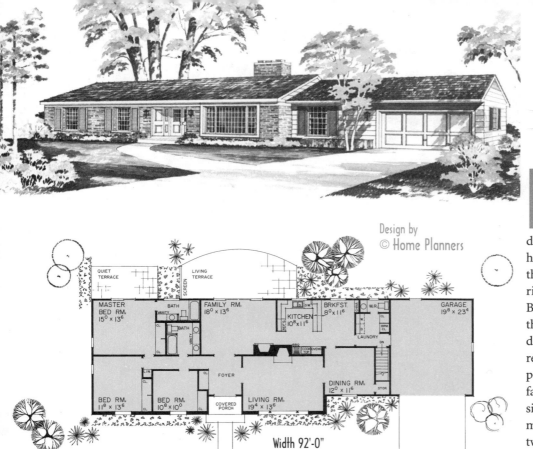

Design by
© Home Planners

DESIGN 1325

Square Footage: 1,942

L D

Brick veneer, multi-paned windows and quaint shutters come together in a classic one-story rendition. Double doors introduce the large entry hall, which permits direct access to the formal living room on the right and the family room ahead. Both living spaces boast fireplaces; the family room has sliding glass doors to the living terrace at the rear. The U-shaped kitchen has a pass-through counter to the breakfast room. Bedrooms at the opposite end of the house include a master suite with private bath and two family bedrooms sharing a full bath.

Width 92'-0"
Depth 28'-0"

Width 60'-10"
Depth 28'-10"

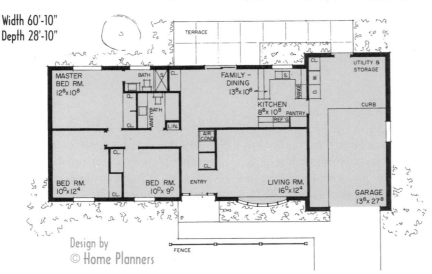

DESIGN 1364

Square Footage: 1,142

D

The family working within the confines of a restricted building budget will find this eye-catching traditional ranch home the solution to their housing needs. The living room is free of cross-room traffic and features a large bow window. The family/dining room is easily served by an efficient kitchen with a pass-through counter, and offers access to a terrace for outdoor living. The kitchen leads to a garage service entrance and laundry with closet. The master bedroom has its own private bath, while two family bedrooms share a full bath with long vanity and linen closet.

Design by
© Home Planners

ONE-STORY TRADITIONAL HOMES

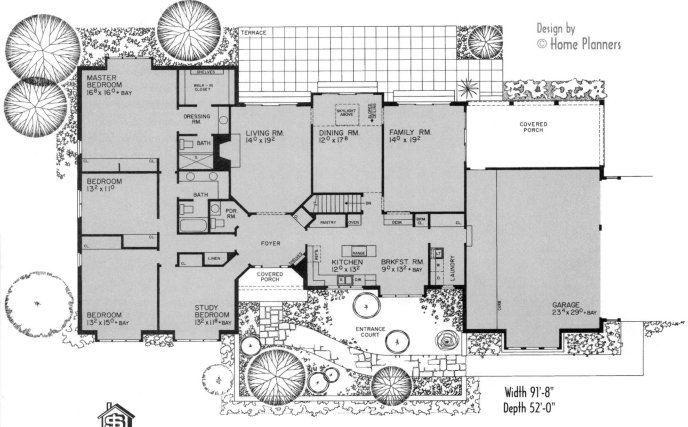

TERRACE

MASTER BEDROOM
16⁸ x 16⁰ + BAY

SHELVES

WALK-IN CLOSET

DRESSING RM.

BATH

S

LIVING RM.
14⁰ x 19²

SKYLIGHT ABOVE

SLOPED CEILING

DINING RM.
12⁰ x 17⁸

FAMILY RM.
14⁰ x 19²

Design by
© Home Planners

COVERED PORCH

BEDROOM
13² x 11⁰

CL.

CL.

BATH

PDR. RM.

PANTRY

OVEN

DN

DESK

BRM. CL.

CL.

CL.

CL.

FOYER

LINEN

SHELVES

REF'G.

KITCHEN
12⁰ x 13²

RANGE

BRKFST. RM.
9⁰ x 13² + BAY

LT.

W.

D.

LAUNDRY

CURB

GARAGE
23⁴ x 29⁰ + BAY

S.

D.W.

BEDROOM
13² x 15⁰ + BAY

STUDY BEDROOM
13² x 11⁸ + BAY

COVERED PORCH

ENTRANCE COURT

Width 91'-8"
Depth 52'-0"

QUOTE ONE®
Cost to build? See page 684
to order complete cost estimate
to build this house in your area!

**DESIGN
2851**
Square Footage: 2,739
L

This spacious one-story home has a classic country French hip roof. Beyond the covered porch is an octagonal foyer. All of the living areas overlook the rear yard. Features include a fireplace in the living room, a skylight in the dining room and a second set of sliding glass doors in the family room leading to a covered porch. An island cooktop and other built-ins are featured in the roomy kitchen. Adjacent is the breakfast room, which can be used for informal dining. The four bedrooms and the baths are clustered in one wing. Box-bay windows brighten the master bedroom, the breakfast room and the three-car garage.

ONE-STORY TRADITIONAL HOMES

www.homeplanners.com

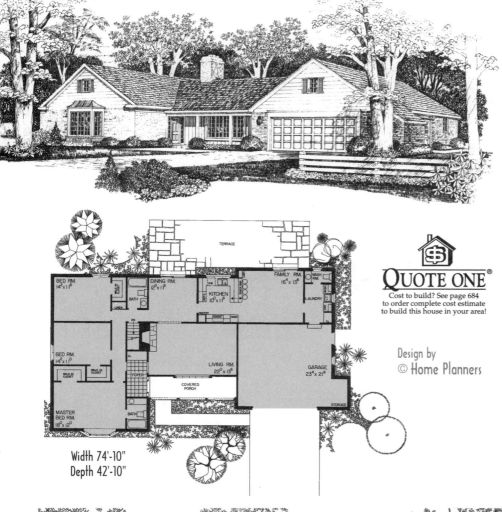

DESIGN
2603
Square Footage: 1,949

L D

I t would be difficult to beat the appeal of this traditional one-story home. Its slightly modified U-shape with two front-facing gables, bay window, covered front porch and the interesting use of exterior materials all add to its charm. In addition, there are three large bedrooms served by two full baths and three walk-in closets. The formal dining room and the informal family room flank the excellent kitchen. A pantry, built-in oven and pass-through snack bar further enhance the livability of this area. A formal living room with a warming fireplace rounds out this design.

QUOTE ONE
Cost to build? See page 684
to order complete cost estimate
to build this house in your area!

Design by
© Home Planners

Width 74'-10"
Depth 42'-10"

DESIGN
3332
Square Footage: 2,203

L

N othing completes a traditional-style home quite as well as a country kitchen with fireplace and built-in wood box. Notice also the second fireplace (with raised hearth) and the sloped ceiling in the living room. The nearby dining room has an attached porch and separate dining terrace. Besides two family bedrooms with a shared full bath, there is also a marvelous master suite with rear-terrace access, walk-in closet, whirlpool tub and double vanities. A handy washroom is near the laundry, just off the two-car garage.

Width 77'-2"
Depth 46'-6"

Design by
© Home Planners

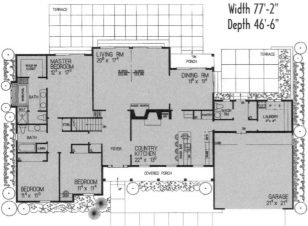

QUOTE ONE
Cost to build? See page 684
to order complete cost estimate
to build this house in your area!

ONE-STORY TRADITIONAL HOMES

DESIGN 1892
Square Footage: 2,036
L D

The romance of French Provincial architecture is captured here by the hip roofs, the window detailing, the brick quoins, the delicate dentil work at the cornices, the massive centered chimney and the recessed double front doors. The highlight of the interior will be the sunken living room. The family room, with its beam ceiling, will not be far behind in popularity. The separate dining room, mudroom and efficient kitchen complete the livability.

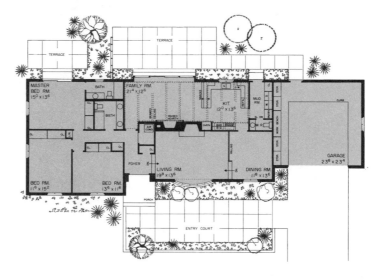

Width 90'-10"
Depth 32'-10"

OPTIONAL BASEMENT

Design by
© Home Planners

DESIGN 1896
Square Footage: 1,690

This design has a truly delightful traditional exterior. The fine layout inside features a center entrance hall with a storage closet in addition to the coat closet. Then, there is the formal living room and the adjacent dining room. The U-shaped kitchen has plenty of counter and cupboard space; there is even a pantry. The family room functions with the kitchen and is but a step away from the outdoor terrace. The mudroom has space for storage and laundry equipment. The large family will find those four bedrooms and two full baths just the answer for sleeping and bath accommodations.

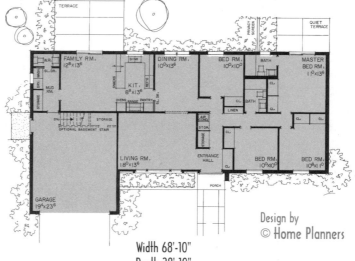

Design by
© Home Planners

Width 68'-10"
Depth 38'-10"

ONE-STORY TRADITIONAL HOMES

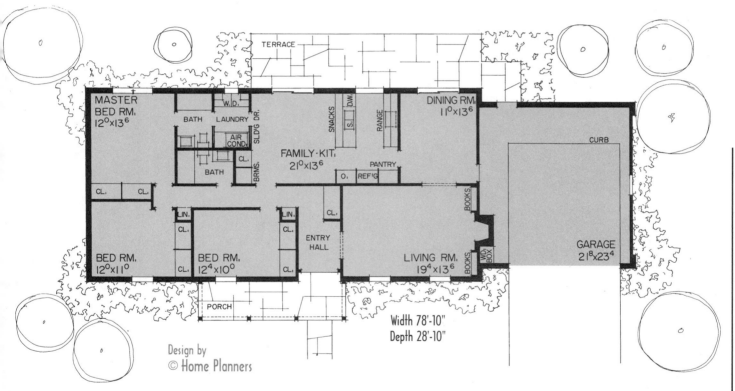

Width 78'-10"
Depth 28'-10"

Design by
© Home Planners

MASTER BED RM. 12⁰x13⁶
BATH
LAUNDRY
W.D.
SLD'G DR.
AIR COND.
BATH
CL.
BRMS.
CL.
CL.
BED RM. 12⁰x11⁰
LIN.
CL.
BED RM. 12⁴x10⁰
LIN.
CL.
CL.
PORCH
ENTRY HALL
CL.
FAMILY-KIT. 21⁰x13⁶
SNACKS
S.I.
D.W.
RANGE
PANTRY
REF'G
O.
BOOKS
WD. BOX
BOOKS
LIVING RM. 19⁴x13⁶
DINING RM. 11⁰x13⁶
TERRACE
CURB
GARAGE 21⁸x23⁴

The pedimented gable and columns at the front porch set the tone for this modestly sized traditional home. The pleasant symmetry of the windows and the double front doors complete the picture. Inside, each square foot is wisely planned for efficient livability. Note the formal living room with a fireplace flanked by built-in bookshelves. The attached formal dining room accesses the rear terrace through sliding glass doors. The family room area of the kitchen also has sliding glass doors to the terrace and gives way to the laundry area and shared bath with the master bedroom. Two family bedrooms share a full bath in the hallway. Note the two linen closets, the utility and broom closets and the coat closet.

DESIGN 1890
Square Footage: 1,628

Design by
© **Home Planners**

MASTER SUITE 13⁸ x 10⁴ SLOPED CLG
BEDRM 11⁰ x 10⁴ SLOPED CLG
COVERED PATIO
ULTRA TUB
MASTER BATH
LIVING RM 15⁰ x 14⁰ SLOPED CLG
BEDRM 9⁰ x 9⁸ SLOPED CLG
LINEN
BATH
REFG
HVAC WH
D W
KITCHEN 8⁰ x 14⁶
FOYER
3-SIDED FP SLVS
CURB
COVERED ENTRY
DINING RM 9¹⁰ x 9⁴ COFFERED CLG
COURTYARD
BATH
BRICK PLANTER
SLPNG CLG
OFFICE/ GUEST 13² x 11¹⁰
BRICK WING WALLS W/POST

Width 44'-8"
Depth 52'-4"

DESIGN 3655

MASTER SUITE 15¹⁰ x 12⁸ SLOPED CLG
COVERED PATIO
WALK-IN CLOSET
SHOWER
MASTER BATH
ULTRA TUB
LIVING RM 15⁰ x 14⁰ SLOPED CLG
BEDRM 9⁰ x 9⁸ SLOPED CLG
LINEN
BATH
REFG
HVAC WH
D W
KITCHEN 8⁰ x 14⁶
FOYER
3-SIDED FP SLVS
CURB
COVERED ENTRY
DINING RM 9¹⁰ x 9⁴ COFFERED CLG
COURTYARD
BATH
BRICK PLANTER
SLPNG CLG
OFFICE/ GUEST 13² x 11¹⁰
BRICK WING WALLS W/POST

Width 44'-8"
Depth 54'-4"

DESIGN 3656

GARAGE 19⁴ x 22¹⁰

QUOTE ONE®
Cost to build? See page 684
to order complete cost estimate
to build this house in your area!

DESIGN 3656
Square Footage: 1,414
L

DESIGN 3655
Square Footage: 1,418
L

This cozy cottage offers the choice of a three- (Design 3656) or four-bedroom (Design 3655) plan. Both designs feature a front-facing office/guest suite that provides privacy for the entry courtyard. With its separate entrance, it offers the perfect haven for an in-home office or for those with live-in parents. The remainder of the house is designed with the same level of efficiency. It contains a large living area with access to a covered patio and a three-sided fireplace that shares its warmth with a dining room featuring built-ins. A unique kitchen provides garage access. The bedrooms include a comfortable master suite with a whirlpool tub, double-bowl vanity and twin closets.

DESIGN
A101
Square Footage: 1,383

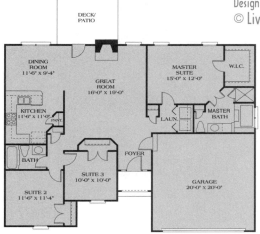

Design by
© Living Concepts Home Planning

DECK/
PATIO

DINING ROOM
11'-6" x 9'-4"

GREAT ROOM
16'-0" x 19'-0"

KITCHEN
11'-6" x 11'-0"

PANT.

MASTER SUITE
15'-0" x 12'-0"

W.I.C.

MASTER BATH

LAUN.

BATH

FOYER

SUITE 3
10'-0" x 10'-0"

SUITE 2
11'-6" x 11'-4"

GARAGE
20'-0" x 20'-0"

Width 50'-0"
Depth 39'-0"

First-time homebuyers and retirees alike will take pleasure in this modest-yet-handsome one-story home, which can be constructed in brick or frame. A vaulted ceiling in the great room and high glass windows on the rear wall combine to create an open, spacious feel. Off the great room is an open dining room. The ample kitchen layout features a built-in pantry. A generous walk-in closet is found in the master suite. Please specify basement, slab or crawlspace foundation when ordering.

DESIGN
3355
Square Footage: 1,387
L D

Though modest in size, this fetching one-story home offers a great deal of livability with three bedrooms (or two with a study) and a spacious gathering room with fireplace and sloped ceiling. The galley kitchen, designed to save steps, provides a pass-through snack bar, planning desk and attached breakfast room. In addition to two secondary bedrooms with a full bath, there's a private master bedroom that enjoys views and access to the backyard. The master bath features a large dressing area, corner vanity and raised whirlpool tub.

QUOTE ONE®
Cost to build? See page 684
to order complete cost estimate
to build this house in your area!

TERRACE

DINING
8'0" X 11'0"

GATHERING RM
15'6" X 14'4"

STUDY/
BEDROOM
9'0" X 11'0"

MASTER BEDROOM
13'8" X 11'0"

BRKFST RM
9'2" X 8'4"

SLOPED CEILING

SLOPED CEILING

SNACK BAR

KITCHEN
12'0" X 9'0"

BATH

MASTER BATH

LAUNDRY

DESK

FOYER

BEDROOM
10'0" X 10'0"

WHIRLPOOL

STORAGE

GARAGE
19'4" X 21'8"

COVERED PORCH

COURTYARD

Design by
© Home Planners

Width 54'-0"
Depth 52'-0"

DESIGN 2810
Square Footage: 1,536
L D

This design is particularly energy efficient. All exterior walls employ 2x6 studs to permit the installation of thick insulation. The high cornice design also allows for more ceiling insulation. Efficiency begins right at the front door where the vestibule acts as an airlock restricting the flow of cold air to the interior. Economy is also embodied in such features as back-to-back plumbing, a centrally located furnace, minimal window and door openings and, most important of all, size.

Width 72'-0"
Depth 36'-0"

Design by
© Home Planners

OPTIONAL
CRAWLSPACE PLAN

OPTIONAL FRONT
ENTRANCE GARAGE

QUOTE ONE®
Cost to build? See page 684
to order complete cost estimate
to build this house in your area!

DESIGN 1829
Square Footage: 1,800
L D

The charm of traditional heritage is apparent in this one-story home with its narrow, horizontal siding, delightful window treatment and high-pitched roof. Inside, the living potential is outstanding. The sleeping wing is self-contained and has four bedrooms and two baths. Formal and informal living areas are well-designed with the living and dining room to the fore, and the family room and the kitchen to the rear.

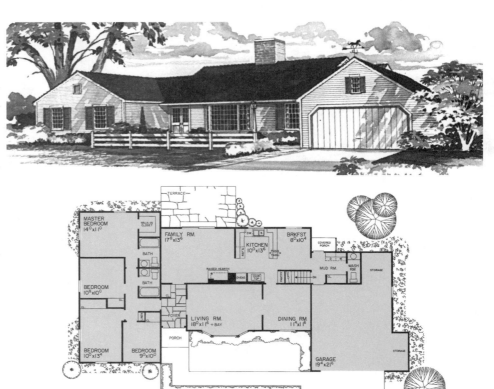

Design by
© Home Planners

Width 80'-0"
Depth 40'-0"

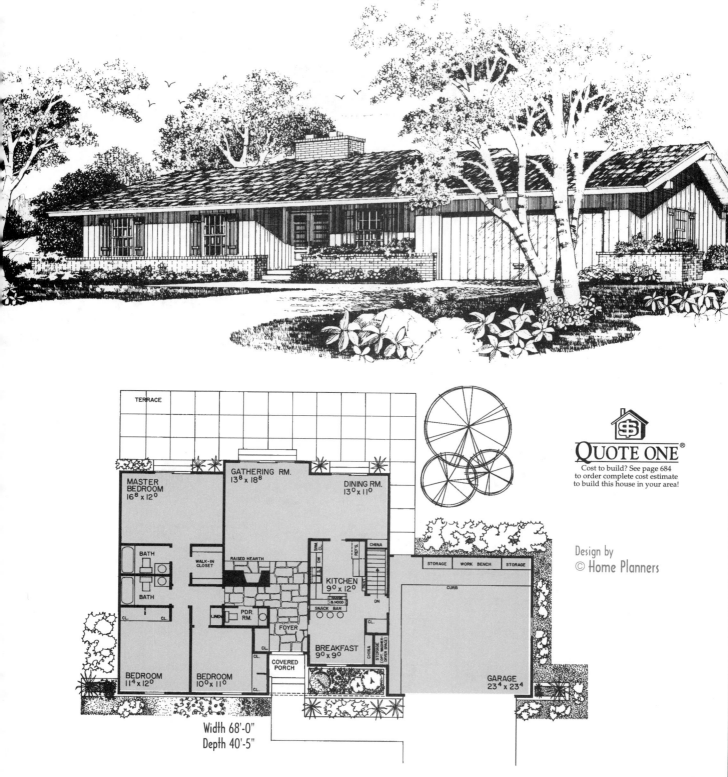

TERRACE

MASTER BEDROOM
16⁸ x 12⁰

GATHERING RM.
13⁸ x 18⁸

DINING RM.
13⁰ x 11⁰

BATH

WALK-IN CLOSET

RAISED HEARTH

BATH

CL.   CL.

CHINA

KITCHEN
9⁰ x 12⁰

PDR. RM.

FOYER

BREAKFAST
9⁰ x 9⁰

BEDROOM
11⁴ x 12⁰

BEDROOM
10⁰ x 11⁰

COVERED PORCH

CHINA

STORAGE   WORK BENCH   STORAGE

CURB

GARAGE
23⁴ x 23⁴

Width 68'-0"
Depth 40'-5"

Design by
© Home Planners

ONE-STORY TRADITIONAL HOMES

The rustic exterior of this one-story home features vertical wood siding. The entry foyer is floored with flagstone and leads to the three areas of the plan: the sleeping, living and work zones. The sleeping area features three bedrooms. The master bedroom utilizes sliding glass doors to the rear terrace. The living area, consisting of gathering and dining rooms, also enjoys access to the terrace. The work center is efficiently planned. It houses the kitchen with a snack bar, the breakfast room with a built-in china cabinet and stairs to the basement. This is a very livable plan. Special amenities include a walk-in closet in the master bedroom and a raised-hearth fireplace.

DESIGN
2671
Square Footage: 1,589
L D

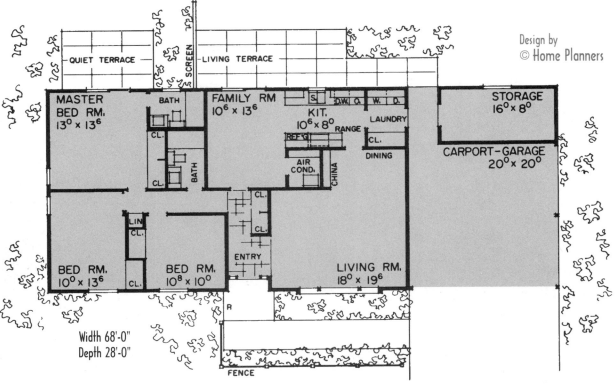

QUIET TERRACE

SCREEN

LIVING TERRACE

MASTER
BED RM.
13⁰ x 13⁶

BATH

FAMILY RM.
10⁶ x 13⁶

S

D.W. O. W. D.

STORAGE
16⁰ x 8⁰

CL.

KIT.
10⁶ x 8⁰

RANGE

LAUNDRY

CL.

REF'G

BATH

DINING

CARPORT-GARAGE
20⁰ x 20⁰

AIR
COND.

CHINA

CL.

LIN
CL.

CL.

BED RM.
10⁰ x 13⁶

BED RM.
10⁸ x 10⁰

CL.

ENTRY

LIVING RM.
18⁰ x 19⁶

R

Width 68'-0"
Depth 28'-0"

FENCE

ONE-STORY TRADITIONAL HOMES

**DESIGN
1323**
Square Footage: 1,344
L D

ncorporated into the set of blueprints for this design are details for building each of the three charming, traditional exteriors. Each of the three alternate exteriors is distinguished in its own way. A study of the floor plan reveals fine livability. There are two full baths, a fine family room, an efficient work center, a formal dining area, bulk storage facilities and sliding glass doors to the quiet and living terraces. The laundry room is strategically located near the kitchen. Three bedrooms include a master bedroom with double closets and a full, private bath. Two secondary bedrooms share a full hall bath.

QUOTE ONE®

Cost to build? See page 684
to order complete cost estimate
to build this house in your area!

ONE-STORY TRADITIONAL HOMES

**DESIGN
Q441**
Square Footage: 1,265

Detailing on the outside of this compact, country home includes a covered porch and shuttered windows. The front entry opens directly into the vaulted great room, which features a three-sided fireplace that it shares with the country kitchen. A deck just beyond the kitchen will serve as an outdoor dining spot. A laundry area holds the basement stairway and access to the two-car garage with storage space. Three bedrooms include two family bedrooms and a full bath, plus a master bedroom with private bath. Plans include details for both a basement and a crawlspace foundation.

Design by
© Select Home Designs

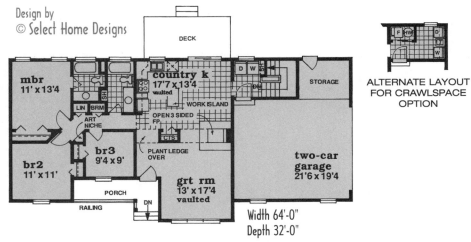

ALTERNATE LAYOUT
FOR CRAWLSPACE
OPTION

Width 64'-0"
Depth 32'-0"

**DESIGN
3700**
Square Footage: 1,317

All the charm of a traditional country home is wrapped up in this efficient, economical ranch design. The time-honored, three-bedroom plan can also serve as two bedrooms plus a study or playroom. The formal living room provides a warm welcome to guests, while the open kitchen and family room offer plenty of space for active family gatherings. A one- or two-car garage may be attached. Other options include a front porch with railing, a bay window and a fireplace.

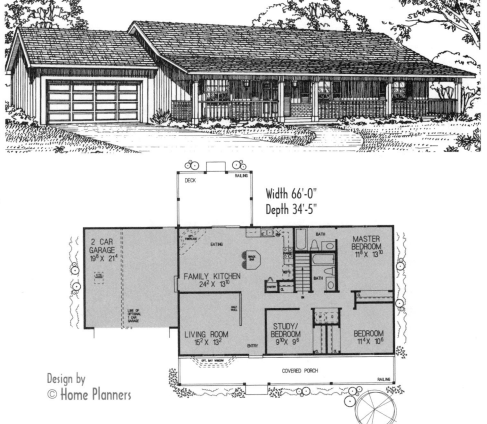

Width 66'-0"
Depth 34'-5"

Design by
© Home Planners

© 1998 Donald A. Gardner Architects, Inc.

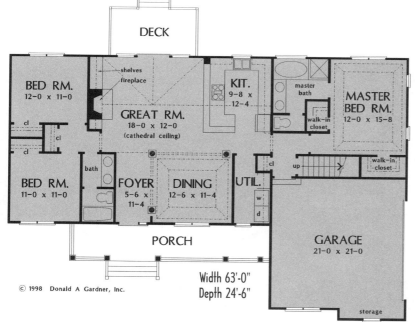

DECK

shelves
fireplace

BED RM.
12-0 x 11-0

cl
cl
cl

GREAT RM.
18-0 x 12-0
(cathedral ceiling)

KIT.
9-8 x
12-4

master
bath

walk-in
closet

MASTER BED RM.
12-0 x 15-8

BED RM.
11-0 x 11-0

bath

FOYER
5-6 x
11-4

DINING
12-6 x 11-4

UTIL.

cl

up

w
d

walk-in
closet

PORCH

GARAGE
21-0 x 21-0

storage

© 1998 Donald A Gardner, Inc.

Width 63'-0"
Depth 24'-6"

down

BONUS RM.
10-6 x 21-0

attic storage   attic storage

Design by
**Donald A. Gardner
Architects, Inc.**

DESIGN 7673
Square Footage: 1,544
Bonus Room: 320 square feet

A covered front porch, fine stick-work and detailed windows give this home a fine Craftsman-style feeling. The foyer opens to a formal dining room on the right, defined by pillars, and a spacious great room directly ahead. Here, a cathedral ceiling, built-in shelves, a warming fireplace and access to the rear deck enhance the welcome of this house. The kitchen is sure to please with plenty of counter and cabinet space. Two family bedrooms occupy the left side of the home and share a full hall bath. A lavish master suite offers two walk-in closets and a pampering bath with a separate tub and shower. Note the bonus room over the garage, perfect for storage or future expansion.

DESIGN W008

Square Footage: 1,512
Bonus Room: 555 square feet

Perfectly symmetrical on the outside, this appealing home has an equally classic floor plan. The spacious great room is open to the dining room and U-shaped kitchen for convenience and gracious entertaining. The master bedroom lies to the front with a view of the covered porch. Its bath features a whirlpool tub, separate shower and dual sinks. A room-sized walk-in closet is an added amenity. Two family bedrooms reside to the back. Please specify basement or crawl-space foundation when ordering.

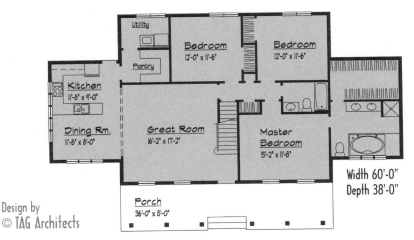

Design by
© TAG Architects

Width 60'-0"
Depth 38'-0"

DESIGN 3659

Square Footage: 1,118

L

Compact and perfect for starters or empty-nesters, this is a wonderful single-level home. Just to the left of the entry is a roomy kitchen with bright windows and convenient storage. The octagonal dining room shares a three-sided fireplace with the living room. A covered patio to the rear enhances outdoor living. A fine master suite with a grand bath is complemented by a secondary bedroom and bath.

Quote One®

Cost to build? See page 684
to order complete cost estimate
to build this house in your area!

Design by
© Home Planners

Width 44'-4"
Depth 47'-4"

ONE-STORY TRADITIONAL HOMES

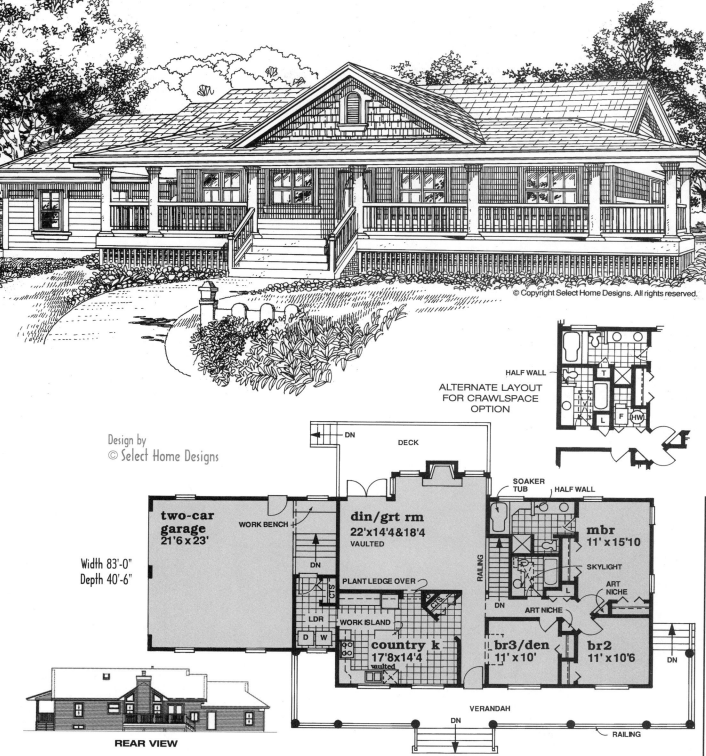

HALF WALL

ALTERNATE LAYOUT
FOR CRAWLSPACE
OPTION

Design by
© Select Home Designs

DN

DECK

two-car
garage
21'6 x 23'

WORK BENCH

din/grt rm
22'x14'4 & 18'4
VAULTED

SOAKER
TUB

HALF WALL

mbr
11' x 15'10

DN

SKYLIGHT

RAILING

Width 83'-0"
Depth 40'-6"

DN

PLANT LEDGE OVER

ART
NICHE

CT'S

DN

ART NICHE

LDR

WORK ISLAND

D   W

country k
17'8x14'4
vaulted

br3/den
11' x 10'

br2
11' x 10'6

DN

VERANDAH

RAILING

DN

REAR VIEW

ONE-STORY TRADITIONAL HOMES

With a graceful pediment above and a sturdy, columned veranda below, this quaint home was made for country living. The veranda wraps slightly around on two sides of the facade and permits access to a central foyer with a den (or third bedroom) on the right and the country kitchen on the left. Look for an island work space in the kitchen. A fireplace warms the great room and is flanked by windows overlooking the rear deck. A casually defined dining space has double-door access to this same deck. Bedrooms are clustered on the right side of the plan. The master suite offers an art niche at its entry and a bath with separate tub and shower. Family bedrooms share a skylit bath. Plans include details for both a basement and a crawlspace foundation.

DESIGN
Q449
Square Footage: 1,578

© 1998 Donald A. Gardner Architects, Inc.

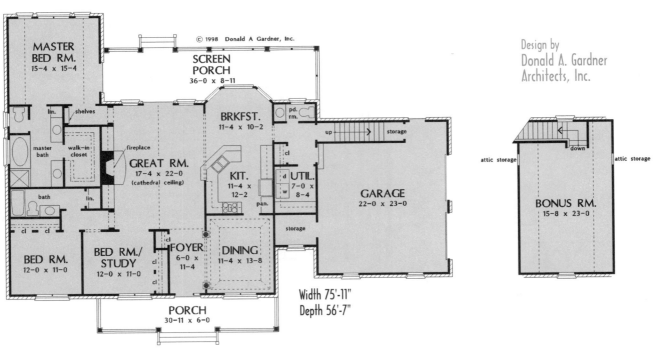

© 1998 Donald A Gardner, Inc.

MASTER BED RM.
15-4 x 15-4

SCREEN PORCH
36-0 x 8-11

lin. shelves

master bath

walk-in closet

fireplace

GREAT RM.
17-4 x 22-0
(cathedral ceiling)

BRKFST.
11-4 x 10-2

pd. rm.

up storage

cl

KIT.
11-4 x 12-2

d **UTIL.**
7-0 x 8-4

w pan.

GARAGE
22-0 x 23-0

bath

lin.

cl cl

BED RM.
12-0 x 11-0

BED RM./ STUDY
12-0 x 11-0

cl

FOYER
6-0 x 11-4

cl

DINING
11-4 x 13-8

storage

PORCH
30-11 x 6-0

Width 75'-11"
Depth 56'-7"

Design by
Donald A. Gardner
Architects, Inc.

attic storage

up

down

attic storage

BONUS RM.
15-8 x 23-0

ONE-STORY TRADITIONAL HOMES

DESIGN 7669
Square Footage: 2,042
Bonus Room: 475 square feet

A pleasing mixture of styles, this home combines a traditional brick veneer with an otherwise country home appearance. Built-ins flank the fireplace in the great room, while a soaring cathedral ceiling expands the room visually. The kitchen's angled counter opens the room to both the breakfast bay and great room. A large screened porch, with access from both the great room and the master suite, serves as a casual area for family relaxation. The master suite enjoys a deluxe private bath, while two family bedrooms (or one and a study) share a full hall bath. The bonus room above the garage can serve as storage space or an addition later on. The two-car garage is side-facing.

B. NATHAN

© 1996 Donald A. Gardner Architects, Inc.

Design by
Donald A. Gardner
Architects, Inc.

BONUS RM.
22-8 x 13-0

attic access

3' wall

down

DECK

MASTER BED RM.
14-0 x 16-0

skylight

master bath

BED RM.
12-0 x 13-0

GREAT RM.
16-8 x 19-6
(cathedral ceiling)
fireplace

BRKFST.
12-0 x 9-8

UTILITY
7-0 x 6-4

down

d w

up

lin.

walk-in closet

storage

cl

bath

lin.

KIT.
12-0 x 12-2

GARAGE
22-8 x 19-8

FOYER
8-2 x 6-8

cl   cl

BED RM./
STUDY
12-0 x 11-4

PORCH

DINING
12-0 x 12-4

(optional door location)

Width 65'-8"
Depth 55'-2"

© 1996 Donald A Gardner Architects, Inc.

Square columns with chamfered corners set off classic clapboard siding and complement a country-style dormer and twin pediments. The vaulted great room has a focal-point fireplace and access to the rear deck. The well-appointed kitchen opens to a bright breakfast area and enjoys its natural light.

The dining room, front bedroom/study and master bedroom feature tray ceilings. The private master suite also includes a bath with skylight, double vanities and separate tub and shower. Two family bedrooms—or make it one and a study—share a full bath with dual vanities.

DESIGN
7637
Square Footage: 1,959
Bonus Room: 385 square feet

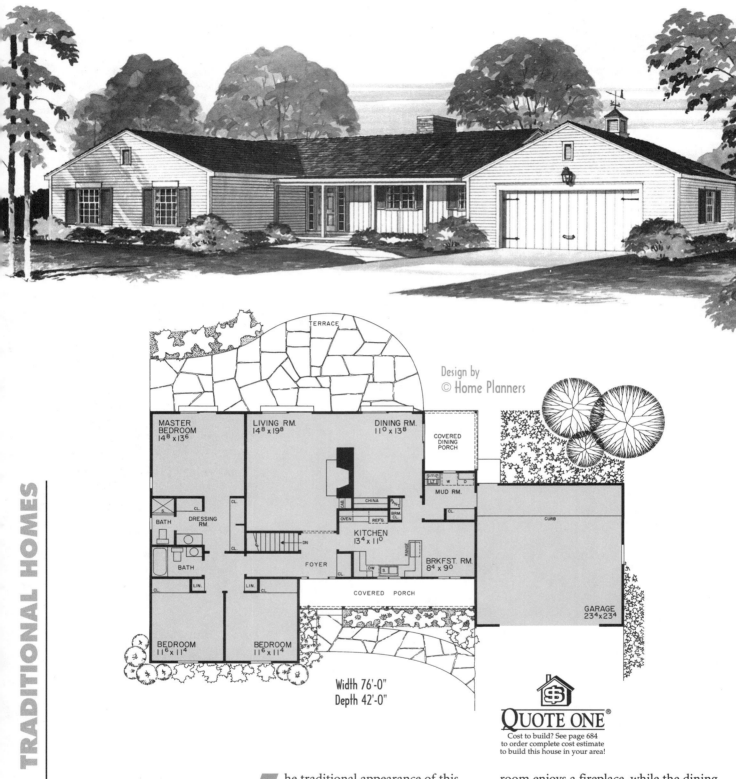

Design by
© Home Planners

MASTER
BEDROOM
14⁸ x 13⁶

LIVING RM.
14⁸ x 19⁸

DINING RM.
11⁰ x 13⁸

COVERED
DINING
PORCH

TERRACE

BATH

DRESSING
RM.

CHINA

CAB.

OVEN

REF'G.

PAN.

BRM.
CL.

MUD RM.

CURB

BATH

KITCHEN
13⁴ x 11⁰

FOYER

RANGE

DW

BRKFST. RM.
8⁴ x 9⁰

GARAGE
23⁴ x 23⁴

BEDROOM
11⁶ x 11⁴

BEDROOM
11⁶ x 11⁴

COVERED PORCH

Width 76'-0"
Depth 42'-0"

QUOTE ONE®
Cost to build? See page 684
to order complete cost estimate
to build this house in your area!

DESIGN
2672
Square Footage: 1,717
L D

The traditional appearance of this one-story home is emphasized by its covered porch, multi-paned windows, narrow clapboard and vertical wood siding. Not only is the exterior eye-appealing but the interior has an efficient floor plan and is very livable. The front U-shaped kitchen will work with the breakfast room and mudroom. The living room enjoys a fireplace, while the dining room leads directly to a covered dining porch for meals on pleasant summer evenings. Sleeping facilities consist of three bedrooms and two full baths. The master suite offers His and Hers closets and a dressing area. Note the three sets of sliding glass doors leading to the terrace. The garage connects to the mudroom.

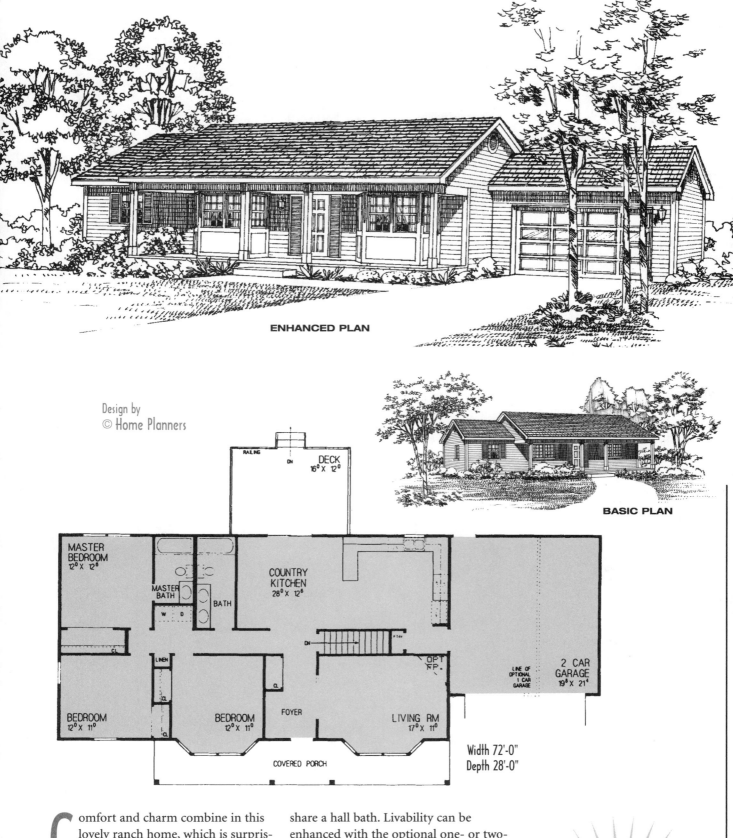

ENHANCED PLAN

Design by
© Home Planners

BASIC PLAN

DECK
16⁰ X 12⁰

MASTER BEDROOM
12⁰ X 12⁸

MASTER BATH

BATH

COUNTRY KITCHEN
28⁰ X 12⁸

2 CAR GARAGE
19⁸ X 21⁴

LINE OF OPTIONAL 1 CAR GARAGE

BEDROOM
12⁰ X 11⁰

LINEN

BEDROOM
12⁰ X 11⁰

FOYER

OPT FP.

LIVING RM
17⁰ X 11⁰

COVERED PORCH

Width 72'-0"
Depth 28'-0"

ONE-STORY TRADITIONAL HOMES

Comfort and charm combine in this lovely ranch home, which is surprisingly affordable. The old-fashioned porch welcomes all visitors. Inside, a large dining area with deck door joins the oversized kitchen. A master bedroom has a private bath; two additional bedrooms share a hall bath. Livability can be enhanced with the optional one- or two-car garage, rear deck with a railing, two angle-bay windows and a fireplace. The blueprints for this house show how to build both a basic, low-cost version and an enhanced, upgraded version.

DESIGN 3704
Square Footage: 1,492

**DESIGN
3688**

Square Footage: 1,646

L

From its wraparound covered porch to its two bay windows, this design has plenty of amenities. The foyer opens directly into the attractive living room, which is enhanced by a warming fireplace, a vaulted ceiling and one of the two bay windows. A U-shaped kitchen works well with both the dining area and the sunny family room, offering a snack bar to this room. Two secondary bedrooms share a full bath and easily accommodate family or friends. At the back of the plan, a master suite waits to pamper the homeowner with a walk-in closet and luxurious bath.

Width 64'-0"
Depth 44'-8"

Design by
© Home Planners

Quote One®

Cost to build? See page 684
to order complete cost estimate
to build this house in your area!

**DESIGN
5507**

Square Footage: 1,676

The ease of everything-on-one-floor and the covered porch that wraps halfway around the house increase the possibilities of enjoying a relaxed lifestyle in this three-bedroom home. The living room presents two special attractions: a bay window and a fireplace. A second bay window graces the family room. A snack bar separates the family room and U-shaped kitchen, which features a walk-in pantry and a window sink. The laundry room and linen closet are conveniently located near the bedrooms. The master suite includes a garden tub, separate shower, double-bowl vanity and its own linen closet.

Width 45'-0"
Depth 64'-0"

Design by
© Home Planners

Quote One®

Cost to build? See page 684
to order complete cost estimate
to build this house in your area!

www.homeplanners.com

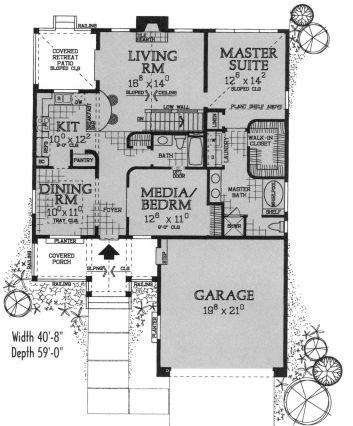

Width 40'-8"
Depth 59'-0"

QUOTE ONE®
Cost to build? See page 684
to order complete cost estimate
to build this house in your area!

Design by
© Home Planners

**DESIGN
3442**
Square Footage: 1,273
L D

For those just starting out, or for the empty-nester, this unique one-story plan is sure to delight. A covered porch introduces a dining room with a coffered ceiling and views out two sides of the house. The kitchen is just off this room and is most efficient with a double sink, dishwasher and pantry. The living room gains attention with a volume ceiling, fireplace and access to a covered patio. The master bedroom also features a volume ceiling while enjoying the luxury of a private bath. A walk-in closet, washer/dryer, double-bowl vanity, garden tub, separate shower and compartmented toilet comprise the amenities here. Not to be overlooked, a second bedroom may easily convert to a media room and study—the choice is yours. The garage shields the bedrooms from noise.

DESIGN 7601
Square Footage: 1,787
Bonus Room: 326 square feet

A neighborly porch wraps around this charming country home. Inside, cathedral ceilings add spaciousness. To the left of the foyer, the great room is enhanced with a fireplace and built-in bookshelves. A uniquely shaped formal dining room separates the kitchen and breakfast area. The secluded master suite features a walk-in closet and luxurious bath. Two additional bedrooms, one with a walk-in closet, share a skylit bath. A basement or crawlspace foundation is available.

The home, as shown in the photograph, may differ from the actual blueprints. For more detailed information, please check the floor plans carefully.

Photo by Riley & Riley Photography, Inc.

Design by
Donald A. Gardner Architects, Inc.

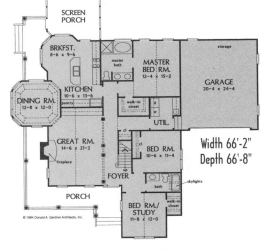

Width 66'-2"
Depth 66'-8"

DESIGN Z047
Square Footage: 1,667

Two gables adorn the front of this fine duplex, while inside, matching units offer a place to call home. The foyer opens directly into the living area where there is space for both a living room and a dining area. The open kitchen offers a cheerful pass-through to the dining area. Here, sliding glass doors access the side yard, letting natural light flood the area. Two bedrooms share a full hall bath, which features both a shower as well as a tub. The one-car garage offers storage space. This home is designed with a basement foundation.

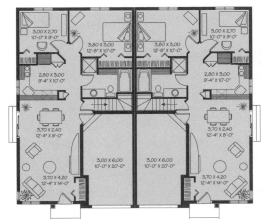

Width 48'-0"
Depth 44'-0"

Design by
© Drummond Designs, Inc.

ONE-STORY TRADITIONAL HOMES

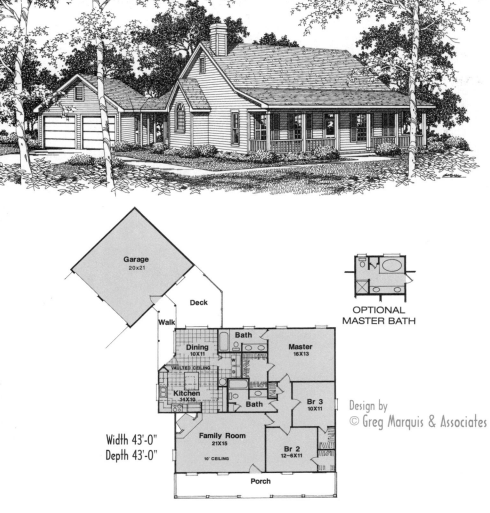

DESIGN
B107
Square Footage: 1,475

Garage
20x21

Deck

Walk

OPTIONAL
MASTER BATH

Dining
10X11

VAULTED CEILING

Bath

Master
16X13

Kitchen
14X10

Bath

Br 3
10X11

Design by
© Greg Marquis & Associates

Width 43'-0"
Depth 43'-0"

Family Room
21X15

10' CEILING

Br 2
12-6X11

Porch

This home features a welcoming front porch across it's entire length. Once you enter, you'll be greeted by ten-foot ceilings and an angled fireplace in the large family room. The vaulted eat-in kitchen with its popular L-shape and work island includes an ample pantry and a laundry room. Note the large master bedroom with a walk-in closet. Each of the other two bedrooms also have walk-in closets. Out back, a covered walk runs next to the deck and connects the angled two-car garage with the living space in a charming way.

© 1996 Donald A. Gardner Architects, Inc.

DESIGN
7603
Square Footage: 1,864
Bonus Room: 319 square feet

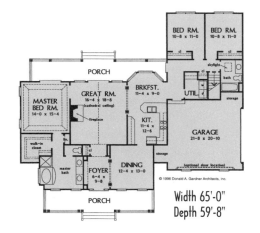

PORCH

BED RM.
10-8 x 11-0

BED RM.
10-8 x 11-0

MASTER
BED RM.
14-0 x 15-4

GREAT RM.
16-4 x 18-8
(cathedral ceiling)

fireplace

BRKFST.
11-4 x 9-0

UTIL.

skylight

bath

walk-in closet

KIT.
11-4 x 12-6

master bath

FOYER
6-4 x 9-8

DINING
12-4 x 13-0

GARAGE
21-8 x 20-10

storage

(optional door location)

© 1996 Donald A. Gardner, Inc.

PORCH

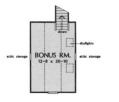

BONUS RM.
12-8 x 20-10

attic storage

attic storage

skylights

down

Design by
Donald A. Gardner
Architects, Inc.

Width 65'-0"
Depth 59'-8"

Two covered porches, three dormers and multi-pane windows combine to give this three-bedroom home plenty of curb appeal. Inside, directly beyond the foyer, the spacious great room offers a cathedral ceiling, a fireplace and access to the rear porch. The U-shaped kitchen works well with both the dining room and the bayed breakfast room. The two family bedrooms on the right side share a skylit bath. The deluxe master suite, with its tray ceiling, large walk-in closet and pampering bathroom, is on the left side of the plan.

DESIGN 9655

© 1990 Donald A. Gardner Architects, Inc.

B. NATHAN

DESIGN 9619

© 1985 Donald A. Gardner Architects, Inc.

B. NATHAN

DESIGN 9655
Square Footage: 2,032

DESIGN 9619
Square Footage: 2,021

Two separate facades with the same floor plan, these two designs offer great variety. Design 9655 is sided in stucco with corner quoins, while multi-pane windows, dormers, bay windows and a delightful covered porch provide a neighborly welcome into Design 9619. The great room contains a fireplace, cathedral ceiling and sliding glass doors with an arched window above to allow for natural illumination. A sun room with a hot tub leads to an adjacent deck. This space can also be reached from the master bath. The generous master suite is filled with amenities that include a walk-in closet and a spacious bath with a double-bowl vanity, shower and garden tub. Two additional bedrooms are located at the other end of the house for privacy. The garage is connected to the house by a breezeway. A basement or crawlspace foundation is available.

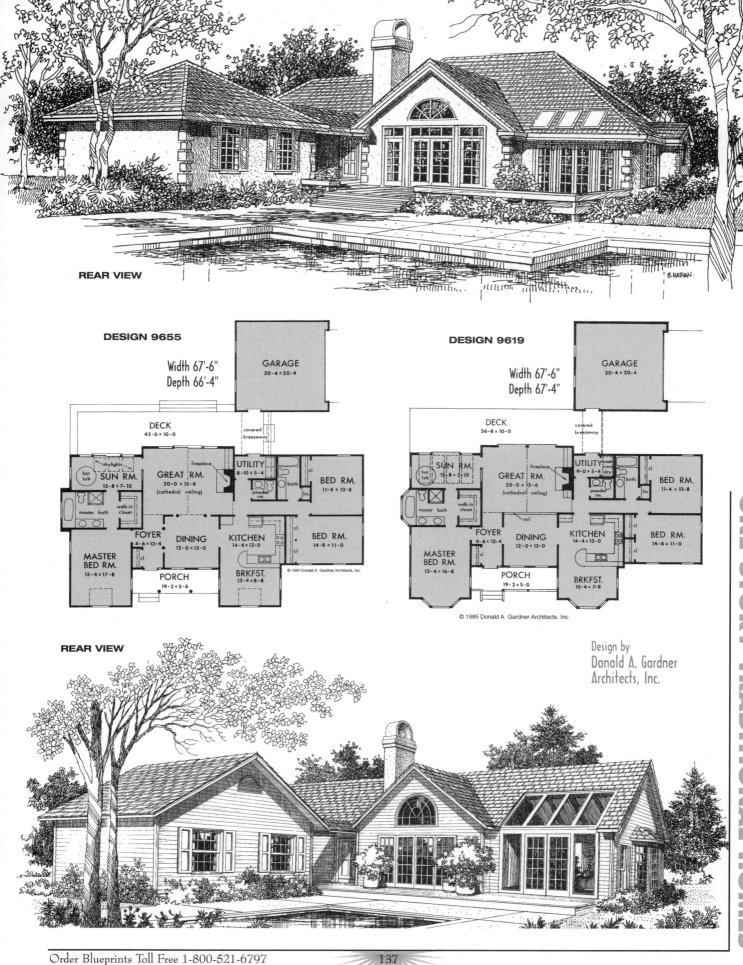

REAR VIEW

DESIGN 9655

Width 67'-6"
Depth 66'-4"

GARAGE
20-4 × 20-4

DECK
43-0 × 10-0

covered breezeway

skylights

hot tub

SUN RM.
15-8 × 7-10

GREAT RM.
20-0 × 15-6
(cathedral ceiling)

fireplace

UTILITY
8-10 × 5-4

bath

powder rm.

lin.

BED RM.
11-4 × 13-8

master bath

walk-in closet

FOYER
4-6 × 12-4

DINING
12-0 × 12-0

KITCHEN
14-4 × 12-0

cl

BED RM.
14-8 × 11-0

MASTER BED RM.
13-4 × 17-8

cl

PORCH
19-2 × 5-6

BRKFST.
13-4 × 8-8

© 1990 Donald A. Gardner Architects, Inc.

DESIGN 9619

Width 67'-6"
Depth 67'-4"

GARAGE
20-4 × 20-4

DECK
36-8 × 10-0

covered breezeway

hot tub

SUN RM.
15-8 × 7-10

GREAT RM.
20-0 × 15-6
(cathedral ceiling)

fireplace

UTILITY
9-0 × 5-4

wash dry

bath

powder rm.

lin.

BED RM.
11-4 × 13-8

master bath

walk-in closet

rail

FOYER
4-6 × 12-4

DINING
12-0 × 12-0

KITCHEN
14-4 × 12-0

cl

BED RM.
14-8 × 11-0

MASTER BED RM.
13-4 × 16-8

cl

PORCH
19-2 × 5-0

BRKFST.
13-4 × 7-8

© 1985 Donald A. Gardner Architects, Inc.

REAR VIEW

Design by
Donald A. Gardner
Architects, Inc.

ONE-STORY TRADITIONAL HOMES

Design by
© Greg Marquis & Associates

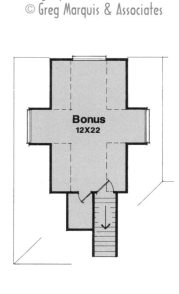

Bonus
12X22

**DESIGN
B112**
Square Footage: 2,215
Bonus Room: 253 square feet

Garage
22x22

Drive

Storage

Porch

D   W

Porch

Master
16x14

Family
20x17
12' CLG

Breakfast
14x10

Br.#3
11x12

Width 63'-0"
Depth 61'-0"

Dining
12X15
10'CLG

10'CLG

Br.#2
11x12

Kitchen
10x13
10'CLG

Foyer

Living/Br.#4
12x12

This symmetrical design offers single-story convenience with an optional bonus room over the garage—great for a home office! A formal living room could also be used as a fourth bedroom. The columned dining room opens into a spacious family room with a fireplace and built-in shelves, plus a nice view

of the rear porch through a series of French doors. The master suite also accesses the porch and features a tray ceiling, twin walk-in closets and separate lavatories. Two family bedrooms share a full hall bath. A large laundry room with a built-in sink makes chores easier. And there's even extra storage in the garage.

www.homeplanners.com

DESIGN 3569

Square Footage: 1,981

L D

Width 58'-0"
Depth 56'-4"

An impressive arched entry graces this transitional one-story design. An elegant foyer introduces an open gathering room/dining room combination. A front-facing study with sloped ceiling could easily be converted into a guest room with a full bath. In the kitchen, such features as an island cooktop and a built-in desk add convenience. The master suite sports a whirlpool bath and walk-in closet, and also offers access to the rear terrace. Other special features of the plan include multi-pane windows, a warming fireplace, a cozy covered dining porch and a two-car garage.

DESIGN 3559

Square Footage: 2,916

L D

Circle and half-circle window detailing and multi-pane windows create a distinctive exterior on this home. A formal living room/dining room area offers access to the terrace and opens to a sunny conversation bay perfect for informal gatherings. The kitchen includes an angled snack-bar counter. A media room just off the foyer could be a den or even a library. The master suite features a coffered ceiling and access to the rear terrace. A private dressing area complements His and Hers walk-in closets, twin vanities, a step-down shower and whirlpool tub.

Width 77'-10"
Depth 73'-10"

ONE-STORY TRADITIONAL HOMES

© American Home Gallery, Ltd.

DESIGN T011
Square Footage: 2,770

The European-inspired excitement of this stucco home can be seen in its use of large, abundant windows. Inside, the spacious foyer leads directly to a large great room with a massive fireplace. The banquet-sized dining room receives the brilliant light of the triple window and features a dramatic, vaulted ceiling. The kitchen and breakfast room provide openness. The master suite features a separate sitting area with a cathedral ceiling and access to the patio. The two additional bedrooms each have a vanity within a shared bath. This home is designed with a basement foundation.

Width 74'-0"
Depth 79'-0"

Design by
© Stephen Fuller,
American Home Gallery

QUOTE ONE®
Cost to build? See page 684
to order complete cost estimate
to build this house in your area!

© American Home Gallery, Ltd.

DESIGN T045
Square Footage: 2,295

The abundance of details in this plan make it the finest in one-story living. The great room and formal dining room are defined by a simple column at the entry foyer—allowing for an open, dramatic sense of space. The kitchen, with preparation island, shares the right side of the plan with a bayed breakfast area and a keeping room with fireplace. Sleeping accommodations to the left of the plan include a master suite with sitting area, double closet and separate tub and shower. Two family bedrooms share a full bath. This home is designed with a basement foundation.

Design by
© Stephen Fuller,
American Home Gallery

QUOTE ONE®
Cost to build? See page 684
to order complete cost estimate
to build this house in your area!

Width 69'-0"
Depth 49'-6"

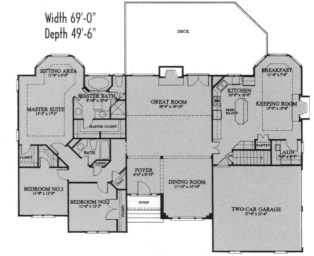

QUOTE ONE®
Cost to build? See page 684 to order complete cost estimate to build this house in your area!

Design by
© Stephen Fuller,
American Home Gallery

DECK

BEDROOM NO. 3
11'-6" X 11'-0"

GREAT ROOM
14'-0" X 17'-6"

BREAKFAST
11'-4" X 8'-0"

KITCHEN
11'-4" X 10'-0"

MASTER BEDROOM
12'-4" X 15'-6"

BATH

BEDROOM NO. 2
11'-0" X 12'-2"

FOYER
6'-6" X 5'-0"

DINING ROOM
11'-4" X 10'-6"

STOOP

DN

PWDR

HIS

MASTER BATH

LAUNDRY

HERS

Width 55'-6"
Depth 57'-6"

TWO-CAR GARAGE
20'-4" X 19'-4"

Charmingly compact, this one-story home is as beautiful as it is practical. The impressive arch over the double front door is repeated with an arched window in the formal dining room. This room opens to a spacious great room with fireplace and is near the kitchen and bayed breakfast area. Split sleeping arrangements put the master suite with His and Hers walk-in closets at the right of the plan and two family bedrooms at the left. Additional space in the basement can later be developed as the family grows. This home is designed with a basement foundation.

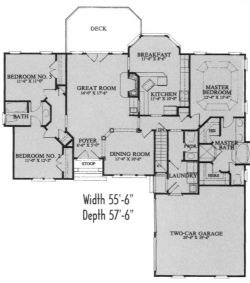

Bedroom #3
11'6" x 11'0"

Sun Room
12'0" x 13'0"

Porch

Bedroom #2
11'3" x 11'0"

Porch

Breakfast
10'6" x 9'0"

Kitchen
12'6" x 13'3"

Great Room
18'0" x 14'0"

Master Bedroom
13'3" x 15'0"

Dining Room
10'7" x 10'7"

Den/Guest Room
13'4" x 14'8"

Two Car Garage
20' x 21'0"

Design by
© Stephen Fuller,
American Home Gallery

Width 62'-0"
Depth 60'-6"

Imagine the luxurious living you'll enjoy in this beautiful home! The natural beauty of stone combined with sophisticated window detailing represent the good taste you'll find carried throughout the design. Common living areas occupy the center of the plan and include a great room with fireplace, sun room and breakfast area, plus rear and side porches. A second fireplace is located in the front den. The master suite features private access to the rear porch and a wonderfully planned bath. This home is designed with a basement foundation.

ONE-STORY TRADITIONAL HOMES

DESIGN
A131
Square Footage: 2,765
Bonus Room: 367 square feet

Molded window facades join with triple gables to decorate the exterior of this three-bedroom plan. Entertain in the formal dining room, the grand room or the gracious gathering room with wrap-around windows and fireplace. Breakfast in the bay-windowed breakfast nook that faces the covered lanai. The master bedroom suite stretches along the left wing of the house and features His and Hers walk-in closets, toilet compartment and garden tub. Two additional bedrooms on the other side of the house share a full bath.

Width 66'-0"
Depth 82'-9"

Design by
© Living Concepts Home Planning

DESIGN
P374
Square Footage: 2,279

Spacious quarters for a large family occur on one floor in this four-bedroom, traditional design with country French accents. The master suite occupies the left side of the plan, while the right side contains family bedrooms and a vaulted living room. The hub of this home is the vaulted great room with a fireplace. The kitchen, breakfast nook and dining room are nearby. Please specify basement or crawlspace foundation when ordering.

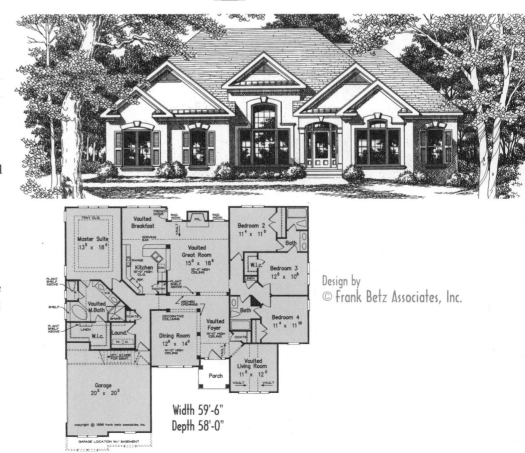

Design by
© Frank Betz Associates, Inc.

Width 59'-6"
Depth 58'-0"

The home, as shown in the photograph, may differ from the actual blueprints. For more detailed information, please check the floor plans carefully.

Photo by Living Concepts Home Planning

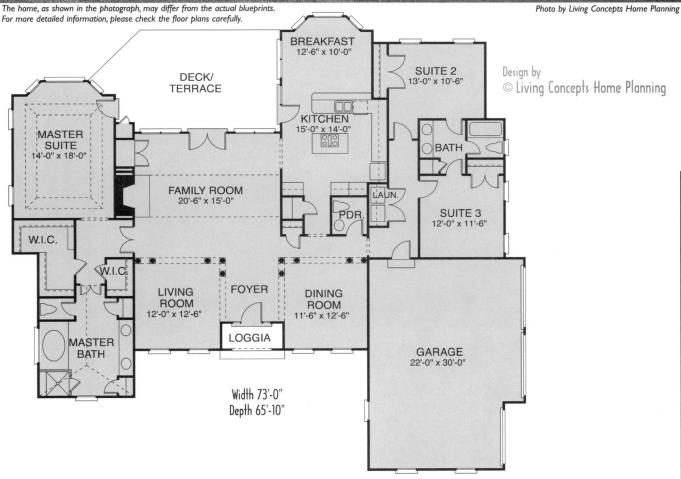

DECK/ TERRACE

BREAKFAST
12'-6" x 10'-0"

SUITE 2
13'-0" x 10'-6"

Design by
© Living Concepts Home Planning

KITCHEN
15'-0" x 14'-0"

MASTER SUITE
14'-0" x 18'-0"

BATH

FAMILY ROOM
20'-6" x 15'-0"

LAUN.

PDR.

SUITE 3
12'-0" x 11'-6"

W.I.C.

W.I.C

LIVING ROOM
12'-0" x 12'-6"

FOYER

DINING ROOM
11'-6" x 12'-6"

LOGGIA

GARAGE
22'-0" x 30'-0"

MASTER BATH

Width 73'-0"
Depth 65'-10"

Triple dormers highlight the roofline of this distinctive single-level French country design. Double doors enhance the covered entryway leading to a grand open area with graceful columns outlining the dimensions of the formal living room and dining room. The large family room with fireplace opens through double doors to the rear terrace. An L-shaped island kitchen opens to a breakfast area with a bay window. The master suite fills one wing and features a bay window, vaulted ceilings and access to the terrace. Two additional bedrooms on the opposite side of the house share a full bath.

DESIGN
A157
Square Footage: 2,500

DESIGN A163

Square Footage: 2,677
Bonus Room: 319 square feet

A beautiful cove entry with double doors opens to a foyer with unobstructed views to the grand room. A formal dining room with tray ceiling is to the right and the master suite fills the wing to the left. A sitting area with bay window and an entrance to the deck highlight the master bedroom. A breakfast nook occupies another bay window just off the U-shaped kitchen. The island cooktop borders the keeping den, which offers a sloped ceiling and fireplace. Two additional bedrooms each have their own bath.

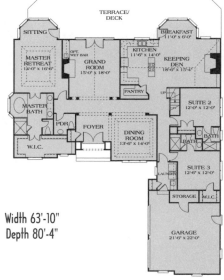

Width 63'-10"
Depth 80'-4"

Design by
© Living Concepts Home Planning

DESIGN A106

Square Footage: 2,585
Bonus Room: 519 square feet

While designed to take full advantage of panoramic rear vistas, this house possesses some great visual effects of its own. Its unusual and creative space plan, including an angled gathering room, expansive grand room and continuous covered lanai, is perfect for entertaining. The pentagonal shape of the open dining room is reflected in its tray ceiling. The master retreat features a sitting area and a bath including both His and Hers vanities and walk-in closets. Please specify basement or crawlspace foundation when ordering.

Width 62'-6"
Depth 83'-10"

Design by
© Living Concepts Home Planning

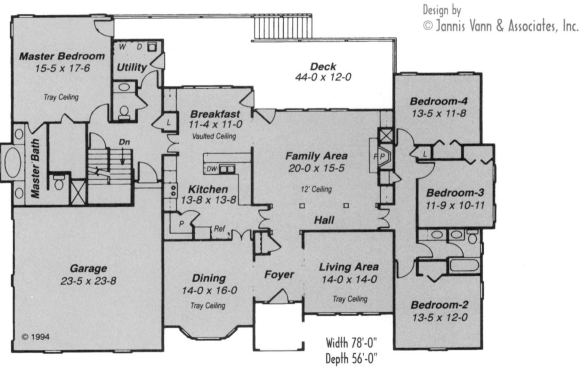

Master Bedroom
15-5 x 17-6

Tray Ceiling

Utility

W D

Master Bath

Dn

Breakfast
11-4 x 11-0
Vaulted Ceiling

DW

Kitchen
13-8 x 13-8

P   Ref

Garage
23-5 x 23-8

© 1994

Dining
14-0 x 16-0
Tray Ceiling

Foyer

Deck
44-0 x 12-0

Family Area
20-0 x 15-5

12' Ceiling

Hall

FP

Living Area
14-0 x 14-0
Tray Ceiling

Bedroom-4
13-5 x 11-8

Bedroom-3
11-9 x 10-11

Bedroom-2
13-5 x 12-0

Width 78'-0"
Depth 56'-0"

Design by
© Jannis Vann & Associates, Inc.

ONE-STORY TRADITIONAL HOMES

A grand entry enhances the exterior of this stylish stucco home. Inside, elegant columns separate front-facing formal living and dining areas from rear-facing informal living areas. The family room features a twelve-foot ceiling, fireplace and a door leading to an expansive deck. The kitchen, breakfast room and leisure room flow together for entertaining ease. Bedrooms are split for privacy. The secondary bedrooms share a full bath. The secluded master suite features a tray ceiling, large walk-in closet and bumped-out tub with dual vanities. The two-car garage is reached via a service entry near the laundry.

**DESIGN
X033**
Square Footage: 2,720

Master Bedroom
volume ceiling
24⁴ • 14⁸

Bath

Covered Patio
vaulted ceiling

Breakfast

Family Room
volume ceiling
17⁰ • 16⁸
fireplace

shelf

shelf

summer kitchen

Kitchen

Living Room
vaulted ceiling
15⁸ • 14⁸

dw

ref

Bedroom 3
volume ceiling
12² • 11⁸

w.i.c.   w.i.c.

pantry

lin   Bath

Bath
volume ceiling

Den Study
volume ceiling
11⁴ • 10⁴

Foyer

Dining
volume ceiling
15¹⁰ • 11⁰

Utility

w
d

Bedroom 2
volume ceiling
13² • 12²

ac

wh

Entry

Garage

Width 70'-8"
Depth 83'-0"

Design by
© Home Design Services, Inc.

**DESIGN
8666**
Square Footage: 2,931

The brick French-door entrance, corner quoins and keystone windows are just a few of this home's beautiful finishing touches. Inside, rich tile flows throughout for a beautiful decorating accent that starts from the ground up. The foyer opens to a large living room with a vaulted ceiling. The wonderfully equipped kitchen, with a walk-in pantry, opens up to the windowed breakfast area and an immense family room with built-in shelves and a fireplace. The large covered patio with a summer kitchen is perfect for cookouts and entertaining and is accessible through the breakfast area, living room or master suite. His and Hers walk-in closets, twin sinks, a compartmented toilet and a windowed tub make the master suite a study in elegance. Two family bedrooms share a bath.

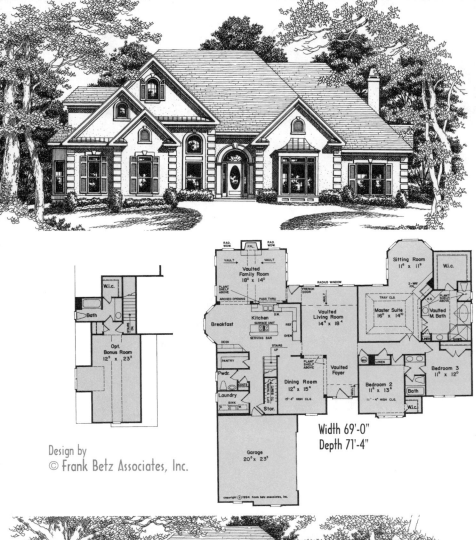

Design by
© Frank Betz Associates, Inc.

Width 69'-0"
Depth 71'-4"

DESIGN P234
Square Footage: 2,622
Bonus Room: 478 square feet

Multiple gables, corner quoins and a variety of window treatments decorate the facade of this stucco home. Inside, high ceilings in the foyer, dining room and living room add to the spaciousness. The L-shaped kitchen includes an island work area and serving bar, walk-in pantry, pass-through to the family room and a light-filled breakfast bay with built-in desk. An elegant master suite offers a bright sitting room and luxurious bath. Please specify basement or crawlspace foundation when ordering.

Design by
© Frank Betz Associates, Inc.

Width 55'-6"
Depth 64'-0"

DESIGN P261
Square Footage: 1,927
Bonus Room: 424 square feet

Stone and stucco complement stately gables on this lovely European-style facade. Beautiful amenities abound inside, starting with the foyer, which opens to the formal dining room and to the vaulted great room. A gourmet kitchen is filled with natural light from a vaulted breakfast bay with a French door to the back property. The master suite features a sitting bay with its own French door. A radius window, plant shelf, garden tub and walk-in closet highlight the master bath. Please specify basement or crawlspace foundation when ordering.

ONE-STORY TRADITIONAL HOMES

DESIGN 3638

Square Footage: 2,861

L

Double columns and an arched entry create a grand entrance to this elegant one-story home. Inside, arched colonnades add grace and definition to the formal living and dining rooms as well as the family room. The master suite occupies a separate wing and features a master bath, which includes a bumped-out whirlpool tub, separate shower and twin vanities. A snack bar separates the island kitchen from the bay-windowed morning room. Two family bedrooms share a full hall bath with dual vanities. The central guest bedroom has an adjacent full bath.

Design by
© Home Planners

Width 93'-4"
Depth 66'-6"

QUOTE ONE®
Cost to build? See page 684
to order complete cost estimate
to build this house in your area!

DESIGN 3612

Square Footage: 2,946

L

This home's varying hipped-roof planes make a strong statement. Inside, the extremely functional floor plan fosters flexible living patterns. The central foyer, with its high ceiling, leads to interesting traffic patterns. The formal and informal living areas are well defined by the living and family rooms. The sunken family room is wonderfully spacious with its high, sloping ceiling. It has a complete media-center wall and a fireplace flanked by doors to the entertainment patio. Occupying the isolated end of the floor plan is the master suite and its adjacent office/den.

Design by
© Home Planners

Width 94'-1"
Depth 67'-4"

QUOTE ONE®
Cost to build? See page 684
to order complete cost estimate
to build this house in your area!

www.homeplanners.com

Design by
© Home Planners

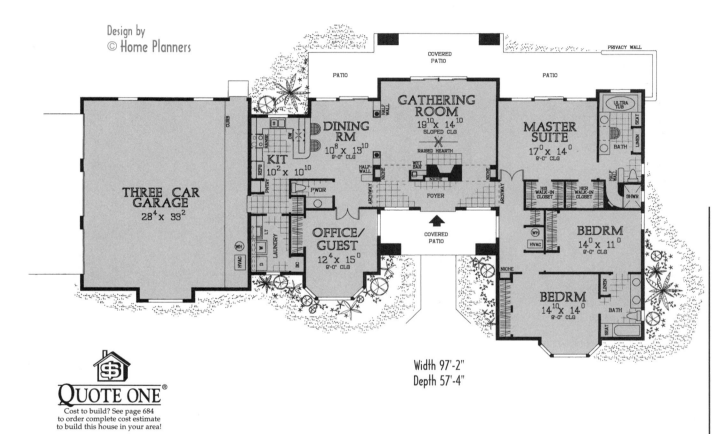

Width 97'-2"
Depth 57'-4"

THREE CAR GARAGE 28⁴ x 33²

KIT 10² x 10¹⁰

DINING RM 10⁸ x 13¹⁰ 9'-0" CLG

GATHERING ROOM 19¹⁰ x 14¹⁰ SLOPED CLG

MASTER SUITE 17⁰ x 14⁰ 9'-0" CLG

OFFICE/ GUEST 12⁴ x 15⁰ 9'-0" CLG

BEDRM 14⁰ x 11⁰ 9'-0" CLG

BEDRM 14¹⁰ x 14⁰ 9'-0" CLG

DESIGN 3657
Square Footage: 2,319

Covered patios front and back enhance sun-country living for this elegant mission-style design. On chilly evenings, warm up in front of the raised hearth in the huge gathering room. Both the gathering room and dining room open with sliding doors to the patio. A snack bar separates the U-shaped kitchen from the dining room. The efficient arrangement includes a large laundry room off the kitchen and a half bath between the home office and dining room. The home office could double as a guest room. Two family bedrooms on the right of the plan share a bath that includes a double-bowl vanity and a linen closet. The master suite blends luxury and function with two walk-in closets, access to the rear patio, and a bath with twin vanities and separate tub and shower. A three-car garage opens to the side and connects at the service entry.

ONE-STORY TRADITIONAL HOMES

DESIGN P189
Square Footage: 1,502

This plan masterfully combines stylish architectural elements in a smaller square footage. The great room is fashioned with a fireplace and provides an open view into the breakfast room and serving bar. The modified galley kitchen offers a convenient rear entry to the formal dining room. Two family bedrooms and a full bath are neatly tucked behind the breakfast nook. The master suite includes a cozy sitting room accented with a vaulted ceiling and sunny windows. Please specify basement or crawlspace foundation when ordering.

Width 51'-0"
Depth 50'-6"

BEDROOM OPTION

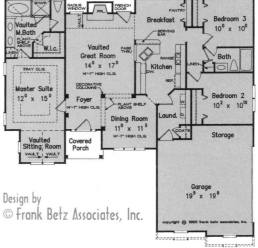

Design by
© Frank Betz Associates, Inc.

ONE-STORY TRADITIONAL HOMES

DESIGN P127
Square Footage: 2,322

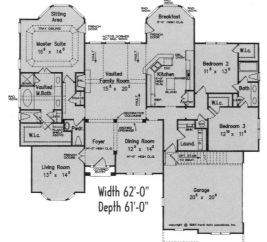

An eclectic mix of building materials—stone, stucco and siding—complement the European charm of this one-story home. Decorative columns set off the formal dining room and foyer from the vaulted family room, while the formal living room is quietly tucked behind French doors. The gourmet kitchen contains an angled snack bar and a sunny breakfast room. Two family bedrooms each have a walk-in closets and private access to a shared bath. The master suite has a lush master bath. Please specify basement, crawlspace or slab foundation when ordering.

Width 62'-0"
Depth 61'-0"

Design by
© Frank Betz Associates, Inc.

QUOTE ONE®
Cost to build? See page 684
to order complete cost estimate
to build this house in your area!

www.homeplanners.com

Master Suite
14⁰ x 17⁰
TRAY CEILING

Breakfast

Vaulted
Living Room
15⁶ x 20²
13'- 8" HIGH CEILING

Bedroom 2
11² x 11⁰

Kitchen

Vaulted
M.Bath

Bath

Bedroom 3
11² x 11⁸

Foyer
13'- 8" HIGH CEILING

W.i.c.

Pwdr.

Dining Room
11³ x 12⁰
13'- 8" HIGH CEILING

Covered Porch

Laund.

Stor.

Garage
23⁰ x 19⁵

Width: 56'-0"
Depth: 60'-0"

copyright © 1994 frank betz associates, inc.

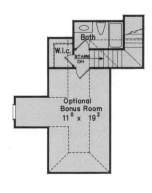

Bath

W.i.c.

Optional
Bonus Room
11⁰ x 19²

Design by
© Frank Betz Associates, Inc.

QUOTE ONE®
Cost to build? See page 684
to order complete cost estimate
to build this house in your area!

The stucco exterior and combination rooflines give a stately appearance to this traditional home. Inside, the well-lit foyer leads to an elegant living room with a vaulted ceiling, fireplace, radius window and a French door leading to the rear yard. Two family bedrooms share a full bath on the right side of the home, while an impressive master suite is located on the left side for privacy. The master suite includes a tray ceiling and a vaulted master bath with dual sinks, separate tub and shower and a walk-in closet. A formal dining room and an open kitchen area with plenty of counter space and a serving bar complete this plan. An optional bonus room with a full bath, perfect for a college student, could be added later. Please specify basement or crawlspace foundation when ordering.

DESIGN
P129
Square Footage: 1,845
Bonus Room: 409 square feet

DESIGN
P109
Square Footage: 1,670

A grand front window display illuminates the formal dining room and the great room of this country French charmer. Open planning allows for easy access between the formal dining room, great room, vaulted breakfast nook and kitchen. Extra amenities include a decorative column, fireplace and an optional bay window in the breakfast nook. The elegant master suite is fashioned with a tray ceiling in the bedroom, a vaulted master bath and a walk-in closet. Two family bedrooms share a large hall bath. Please specify basement, crawlspace or slab foundation when ordering.

Quote One®
Cost to build? See page 684
to order complete cost estimate
to build this house in your area!

OPTIONAL BASEMENT
STAIR LOCATION

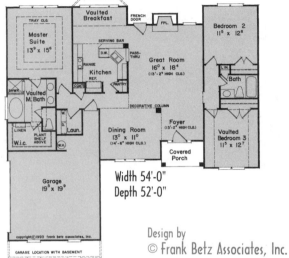

Width 54'-0"
Depth 52'-0"

Design by
© Frank Betz Associates, Inc.

DESIGN
P110
Square Footage: 1,429

This home's gracious exterior is indicative of the elegant, yet extremely livable, floor plan inside. Stately columns set off the formal dining room from the foyer and vaulted family room. The spacious family room includes a corner fireplace, rear-yard access and serving bar. A breakfast bay flanks the kitchen on one end while a wet bar/serving pantry lead to the dining room on the other. The split bedroom plan allows the amenity-rich master suite maximum privacy. A pocket door leads to the hall housing the two family bedrooms and a full bath. Please specify basement, crawlspace or slab foundation when ordering.

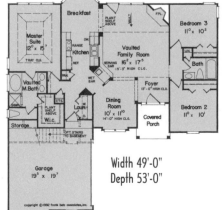

Width 49'-0"
Depth 53'-0"

Design by
© Frank Betz Associates, Inc.

Quote One®
Cost to build? See page 684
to order complete cost estimate
to build this house in your area!

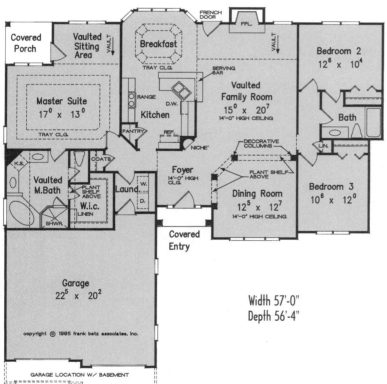

Covered Porch

Vaulted Sitting Area

Breakfast
TRAY CLG.

FRENCH DOOR

FPL.

Master Suite
17⁰ x 13⁰
TRAY CLG.

SERVING BAR

RANGE

D.W.

Kitchen

PANTRY

REF.

NICHE

Vaulted Family Room
15⁰ x 20⁷
14'-0" HIGH CEILING

Bedroom 2
12⁶ x 10⁴

Bath

LIN.

K.S.

Vaulted M.Bath

PLANT SHELF ABOVE

W.i.c.

LINEN

SHWR.

COATS

Laund.

W.

D.

Foyer
14'-0" HIGH CLG.

DECORATIVE COLUMNS

PLANT SHELF ABOVE

Dining Room
12⁵ x 12⁷
14'-0" HIGH CEILING

Bedroom 3
10⁶ x 12⁰

Covered Entry

Garage
22⁵ x 20²

copyright © 1995 frank betz associates, inc.

Width 57'-0"
Depth 56'-4"

GARAGE LOCATION W/ BASEMENT

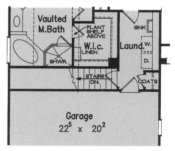

Vaulted M.Bath

PLANT SHELF ABOVE

SHWR.

W.i.c.

LINEN

STAIRS DN.

SINK

Laund.

W.

D.

COATS

Garage
22⁵ x 20²

OPTIONAL BASEMENT
STAIR LOCATION

Design by
© Frank Betz Associates, Inc.

E uropean style shines from this home's facade in the form of its stucco detailing, hipped rooflines, fancy windows and elegant entryway. Inside, the formal dining room is defined by decorative columns and a plant shelf, and works well with the vaulted family room. The efficient kitchen offers a serving bar to both the family room and the deluxe breakfast room. Located apart from the family bedrooms for privacy, the master suite is sure to please with its many amenities, including a vaulted sitting area and a private covered porch. The two secondary bedrooms share a full hall bath. Please specify basement or crawlspace foundation when ordering.

DESIGN
P191
Square Footage: 1,779

ONE-STORY TRADITIONAL HOMES

DESIGN P176

Square Footage: 2,403
Bonus Room: 285 square feet

Arch-top windows accent a European-style exterior. Inside, a spider-beam ceiling and a centered fireplace framed by shelves redraw the open space of the family room to cozy dimensions. The vaulted breakfast nook enjoys a radius window and a French door that leads outside. Split sleeping quarters lend privacy to the master suite, which offers a windowed whirlpool tub, two walk-in closets and a columned vestibule that leads to a sitting room (or formal living room). Please specify basement or crawlspace foundation when ordering.

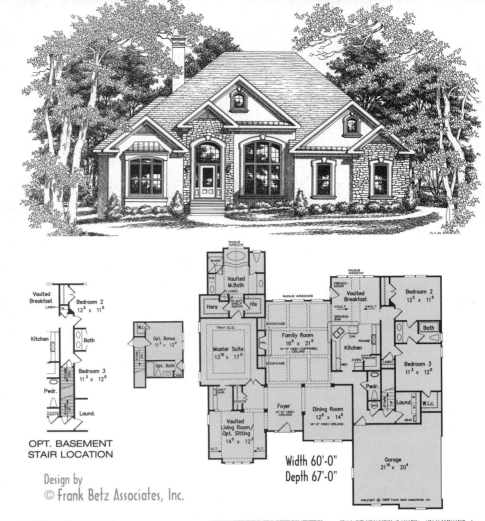

OPT. BASEMENT
STAIR LOCATION

Width 60'-0"
Depth 67'-0"

Design by
© Frank Betz Associates, Inc.

DESIGN P125

Square Footage: 1,875

An oversized picture window gives a cheerful first impression to this home. Boxed columns frame the formal dining room. A living room or den is to the other side. A lovely fireplace flanked by windows and a wraparound serving bar make the family room the heart of family gatherings. The kitchen has all the amenities, including a sunny breakfast nook. The secluded master suite features a lush compartmented bath and walk-in closet. Two family bedrooms, a hall bath and laundry room complete this favorite plan. Please specify basement, crawlspace or slab foundation when ordering.

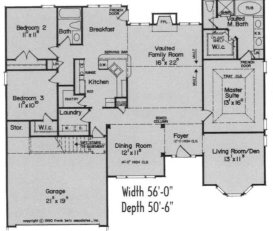

Design by
© Frank Betz Associates, Inc.

Width 56'-0"
Depth 50'-6"

© American Home Gallery, Ltd.

Design by
© Stephen Fuller,
American Home Gallery

Width 72'-0"
Depth 73'-0"

2-CAR GARAGE
21'-3" x 26'-0"

M. BATH

SITTING

LAUN.

BREAKFAST
11'-6" x 12'-0"

MASTER SUITE
15'-6" x 23'-3"

MASTER
CLOSET

KITCHEN
14'-0" x 16'-6"

DN

GREAT ROOM
16'-0" x 20'-6"

PAN.

BEDROOM No.3
12'-0" x 13'-6"

Quote One®

Cost to build? See page 684
to order complete cost estimate
to build this house in your area!

DINING ROOM
13'-0" x 13'-6"

FOYER

STUDY/
BEDROOM No.2
13'-0" x 13'-6"

GUEST ROOM/
CHILDRENS
DEN
13'-6" x 16'-9"

The balance and symmetry of this European home have an inviting quality. An entry foyer allowing a grand view out of the back of the house leads directly to the great room. Just off the great room are a convenient and functional gourmet kitchen and a bright adjoining bay-windowed breakfast room. The master suite enjoys privacy in its position at the rear of the home. Three other bedrooms, one that might serve as a guest room or children's den and one that might work well as a study, round out the sleeping accommodations. A two-car garage is at the back of the plan and has a side entry. This home is designed with a basement foundation.

DESIGN
T008
Square Footage: 2,785

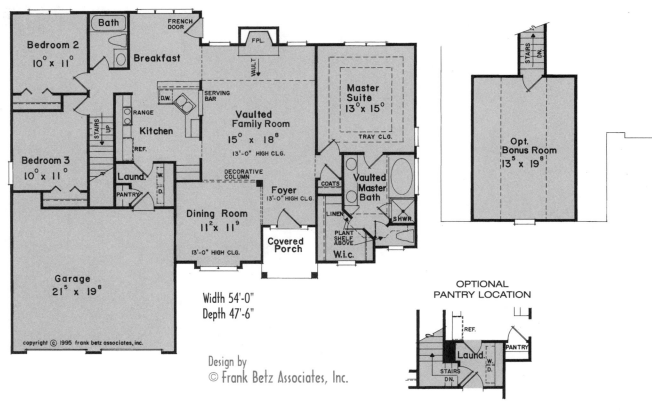

Bath

FRENCH DOOR

Bedroom 2
10⁰ x 11⁰

Breakfast

FPL.

VAULT

Master Suite
13⁰ x 15⁰

D.W.

SERVING BAR

Vaulted Family Room
15⁰ x 18⁸
13'-0" HIGH CLG.

TRAY CLG.

RANGE

Kitchen

STAIRS UP

REF.

Bedroom 3
10⁰ x 11⁰

DECORATIVE COLUMN

Laund.

W. D.

PANTRY

Foyer
13'-0" HIGH CLG.

COATS

Vaulted Master Bath

LINEN

SHWR.

Dining Room
11² x 11⁹

13'-0" HIGH CLG.

Covered Porch

PLANT SHELF ABOVE

W.i.c.

Garage
21⁵ x 19⁸

copyright © 1995 frank betz associates, inc.

STAIRS DN.

Opt. Bonus Room
13⁵ x 19⁸

Width 54'-0"
Depth 47'-6"

Design by
© Frank Betz Associates, Inc.

OPTIONAL PANTRY LOCATION

REF.

Laund.

W. D.

PANTRY

STAIRS DN.

DESIGN P232
Square Footage: 1,544
Bonus Room: 284 square feet

A steep front gable and a delightful arch framing the entry porch give this stately European home a distinctive look. Openness abounds in the spacious family room and formal dining room—tall ceilings and decorative touches like a column and fireplace set them apart. The efficient kitchen has wraparound counters and a cozy breakfast nook. Two family bedrooms and a full bath are split from the master suite for privacy. The master suite offers a vaulted master bath, tray ceiling and a large walk-in closet. Please specify basement or crawlspace foundation when ordering.

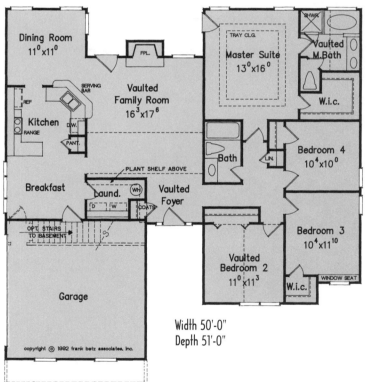

Dining Room
11⁰x11⁰

Vaulted Family Room
16³x17⁶

SERVING BAR

REF

Kitchen

RANGE DW
PANT.

Breakfast

OPT STAIRS TO BASEMENT

Laund.
D W WH
COATS

Vaulted Foyer

PLANT SHELF ABOVE

FPL

Garage

copyright © 1992 frank betz associates, inc.

Master Suite
13⁰x16⁰
TRAY CLG.

SHWR

Vaulted M.Bath

W.i.c.

Bath
LIN.

Bedroom 4
10⁴x10⁰

Bedroom 3
10⁴x11¹⁰

Vaulted Bedroom 2
11⁰x11³

W.i.c.

WINDOW SEAT

Width 50'-0"
Depth 51'-0"

Design by
© Frank Betz Associates, Inc.

DESIGN P205
Square Footage: 1,688

This deceptively small one-story home contains an enormous amount of living space and copious charming amenities. The sunken living room is the first clue that this home has been thoughtfully designed. Conveniently located nearby is the kitchen with its serving bar, preparation island, pantry, built-in desk and laundry-room access. A tray-ceilinged breakfast nook allows for sunlit and tranquil meals. An enormous master suite, as well as two bedrooms plus an optional fourth bedroom or sitting room, occupy the right side of the home. Please specify basement, crawlspace or slab foundation when ordering.

DESIGN 7634
Square Footage: 1,699
Bonus Room: 386 square feet

Keystone arches, asymmetrical gables and a stunning stucco exterior lend European sophistication to this great plan. The interior starts with an expansive great room, which features an extended-hearth fireplace and views to the outdoors. The U-shaped kitchen serves the dining room, which includes a bay window. A private master suite nestles to the rear of the plan and offers a tray ceiling and a lavish bath with a garden tub, twin vanities and separate shower. Two additional bedrooms share a full bath nearby, while upstairs bonus space is available for future development.

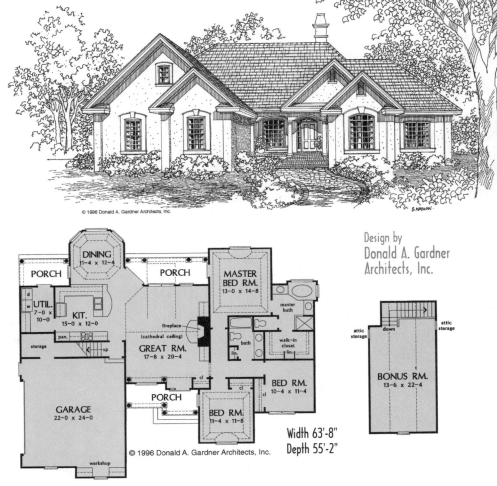

© 1996 Donald A. Gardner Architects, Inc.

Design by
Donald A. Gardner
Architects, Inc.

Width 63'-8"
Depth 55'-2"

DESIGN 7655
Square Footage: 1,782
Bonus Room: 229 square feet

Split sleeping arrangements and an open floor plan draw attention to this home. The great room, dining room and kitchen flow together, sharing the glow from the hearth and access to the screened porch. The master suite includes a walk-in closet and a compartmented bath with a double-bowl vanity and separate tub and shower. Two family bedrooms on the opposite side of the plan feature walk-in closets and share a full bath. Over the garage, there's a bonus room and attic storage.

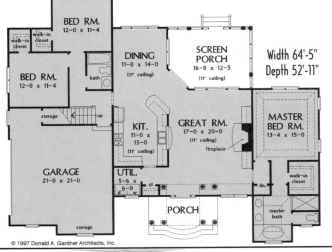

©1997 Donald A. Gardner Architects, Inc.

Design by
Donald A. Gardner
Architects, Inc.

Width 64'-5"
Depth 52'-11"

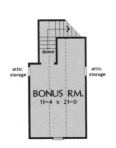

www.homeplanners.com

© 1997 Donald A. Gardner Architects, Inc.

Design by
Donald A. Gardner
Architects, Inc.

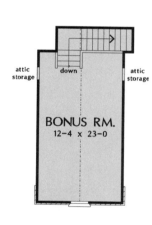

attic storage   down   attic storage

BONUS RM.
12-4 x 23-0

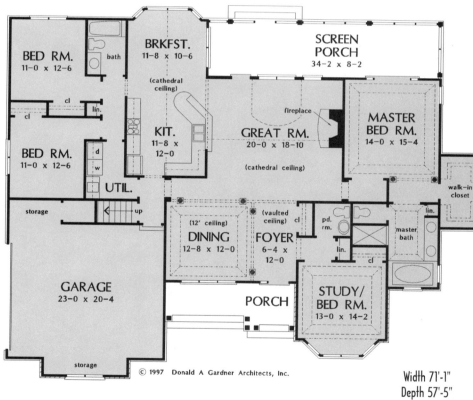

BED RM.
11-0 x 12-6
bath

cl
cl   lin.

BRKFST.
11-8 x 10-6

(cathedral ceiling)

SCREEN PORCH
34-2 x 8-2

fireplace

MASTER BED RM.
14-0 x 15-4

KIT.
11-8 x 12-0

GREAT RM.
20-0 x 18-10

(cathedral ceiling)

BED RM.
11-0 x 12-6
d
w

UTIL.

storage   up

walk-in closet

(12' ceiling)   (vaulted ceiling) cl
pd. rm.

lin.

master bath

DINING
12-8 x 12-0

FOYER
6-4 x 12-0

lin.   cl

GARAGE
23-0 x 20-4

PORCH

STUDY/ BED RM.
13-0 x 14-2

storage

© 1997 Donald A Gardner Architects, Inc.

Width 71'-1"
Depth 57'-5"

ONE-STORY TRADITIONAL HOMES

The combination of stone, stucco, and windows topped by keystone arches provides this home with Old World elements. The home has a sense of spaciousness, thanks to cathedral ceilings and a minimum of interior walls. Decorative columns separate the dining room from the great room, which offers a fireplace and access to the screened porch. The master suite with walk-in closet is split for privacy, with two family bedrooms located on the opposite side of the plan. The bonus room is available for future development.

DESIGN 7698
Square Footage: 2,282
Bonus Room: 354 square feet

DESIGN M146
Square Footage: 2,261

A wonderful combination of textures, trim and windows front this attractive single-story design. A large covered porch opens to an entry gallery flanked by a formal dining room and study. Ahead is a great room with vaulted ceiling, access to the patio and fieldstone fireplace. A U-shaped kitchen opens to a large breakfast room, which also opens to the patio. A fine master bedroom is tucked into the back corner of the house with a spacious bath and walk-in closet. Two additional bedrooms share a bath on the opposite side of the house.

Design by
© Fillmore Design Group

Width 82'-0"
Depth 54'-0"

DESIGN M117
Square Footage: 1,830

A cupola, shutters, arched transoms and an exterior of combined stone and lap siding give this one-story home its country identity. In the great room, a cathedral ceiling and a fireplace extend an invitation for family and friends alike to relax and enjoy themselves. Kitchen amenities include an island cooktop, built-in planning desk and pantry, while the multi-windowed dining room provides access to the covered veranda. A hall leads to sleeping quarters that include two secondary bedrooms and a luxurious master suite.

Design by
© Fillmore Design Group

Width 75'-0"
Depth 52'-3"

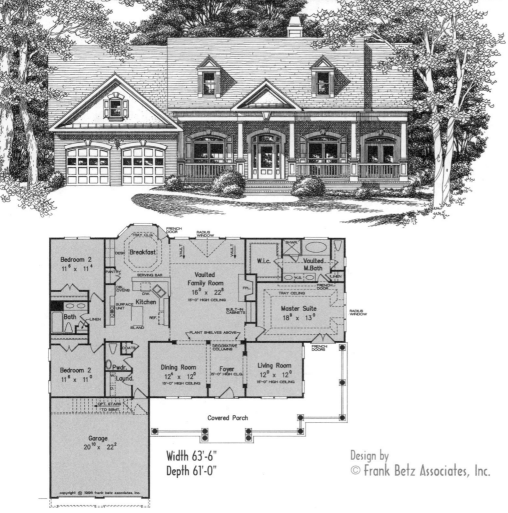

DESIGN
P242
Square Footage: 2,170

The covered front porch leads to a foyer flanked by formal living and dining rooms. The spacious family room opens to the breakfast bay. The well-positioned kitchen, with an island, easily serves the formal and informal areas. The master suite has a tray ceiling in the sleeping area and a vaulted ceiling in the bath. The other two bedrooms flank a full bath with a double-bowl vanity. Please specify basement or crawlspace foundation when ordering.

Width 63'-6"
Depth 61'-0"

Design by
© Frank Betz Associates, Inc.

DESIGN
M118
Square Footage: 2,078

In the interior of this Colonial farmhouse, double doors lead into a country dining room with a large island kitchen. The spacious great room features a centered fireplace flanked by large windows. The secluded master suite has a vaulted ceiling in the bedroom and a spacious bath and walk-in closet with two built-in chests. Three additional bedrooms and a three-car garage complete this plan.

Design by
© Fillmore Design Group

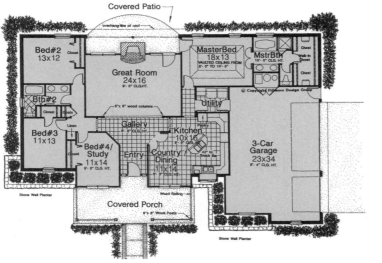

Width 75'-0"
Depth 47'-10"

DESIGN X012

Square Footage: 1,716

A superb blend of textures, trim and windows front this attractive single-story design. A recessed columned porch opens into an entry foyer with convenient coat closet nearby. Ahead is an open living area that flows well into a bay-windowed dining room with access to a deck. A U-shaped kitchen opens to a large breakfast room, which also opens to the patio. A luxurious master suite is tucked into the back corner of the house with a bumped-out bath and walk-in closet. Three additional bedrooms share a hall bath.

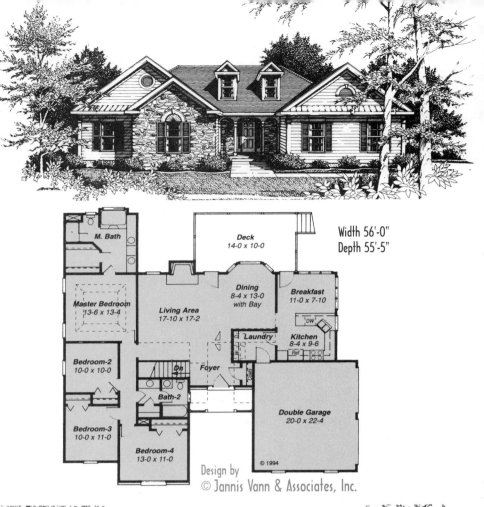

Width 56'-0"
Depth 55'-5"

M. Bath

Deck
14-0 x 10-0

Master Bedroom
13-6 x 13-4

Living Area
17-10 x 17-2

Dining
8-4 x 13-0
with Bay

Breakfast
11-0 x 7-10

Laundry

Kitchen
8-4 x 9-6

Foyer

Bedroom-2
10-0 x 10-0

Bath-2

Double Garage
20-0 x 22-4

Bedroom-3
10-0 x 11-0

Bedroom-4
13-0 x 11-0

© 1994

Design by
© Jannis Vann & Associates, Inc.

DESIGN 2777

Square Footage: 2,006

L D

M any years of delightful living will surely be enjoyed in this one-story traditional. Easy living centers around the large gathering room with a raised-hearth fireplace and sliding doors to the rear terrace. The dining room can accommodate more formal dinners. The kitchen amenities include a cooktop island, an abundance of cabinet and counter space and an adjoining utility room. The master bedroom enjoys private patio access, a large walk-in closet and compartmented bath. A study, a secondary bedroom and a full hall bath complete the plan.

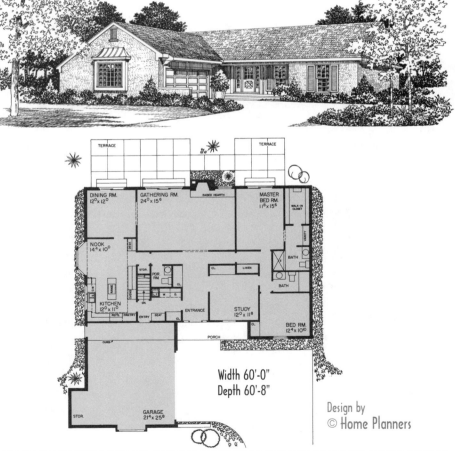

TERRACE

TERRACE

DINING RM.
12⁰ x 12⁰

GATHERING RM.
24⁰ x 15⁶

RAISED HEARTH

MASTER BED RM.
11⁸ x 15⁶

WALK-IN CLOSET

NOOK
14⁴ x 10⁰

VANITY

BATH

LINEN

CL.

BATH

KITCHEN
12⁰ x 11⁰

PDR. RM.

STUDY
12⁰ x 11⁶

PANTRY

ENTRY

ENTRANCE

BED RM.
12⁴ x 10¹⁰

CURB

PORCH

STOR.

GARAGE
21⁴ x 25⁸

Width 60'-0"
Depth 60'-8"

Design by
© Home Planners

©1996 Donald A. Gardner Architects, Inc.

B. NATHAN.

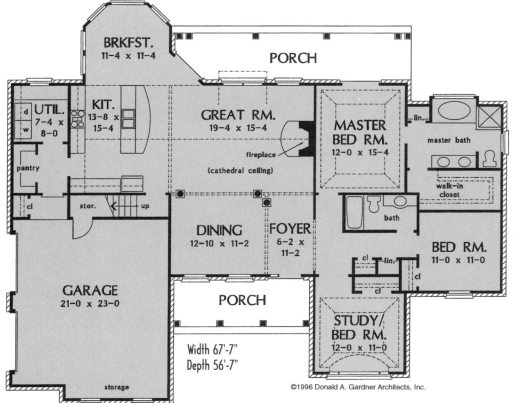

BRKFST.
11-4 x 11-4

PORCH

d
w

UTIL.
7-4 x
8-0

KIT.
13-8 x
15-4

GREAT RM.
19-4 x 15-4

MASTER
BED RM.
12-0 x 15-4

lin.

master bath

pantry

fireplace

(cathedral ceiling)

walk-in
closet

cl

stor.

up

bath

DINING
12-10 x 11-2

FOYER
6-2 x
11-2

GARAGE
21-0 x 23-0

PORCH

storage

cl   lin.

cl

BED RM.
11-0 x 11-0

STUDY/
BED RM.
12-0 x 11-0

Width 67'-7"
Depth 56'-7"

©1996 Donald A. Gardner Architects, Inc.

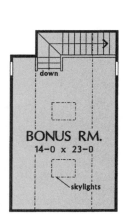

down

BONUS RM.
14-0 x 23-0

skylights

Design by
Donald A. Gardner
Architects, Inc.

ONE-STORY TRADITIONAL HOMES

This delightful country-cottage elevation gives way to a modern floor
plan that excels in livability. The formal dining room greets the foyer
and is set off from the expansive great
room with decorative columns. The
cathedral ceiling topping the great room
extends through to the presentation
kitchen. Amenities here include an abundance of counter and cabinet space, a bi-
level island with a snack bar, and a gazebo
breakfast nook. The master bedroom is
detailed with a tray ceiling and features a
lush master bath with a large walk-in
closet. Two additional bedrooms share a
full hall bath. A bonus room over the
garage can be finished as extra living
space.

**DESIGN
7618**
Square Footage: 1,972
Bonus Room: 398 square feet

DESIGN T061
Square Footage: 2,170

This classic cottage features a stone and wooden exterior with an arch-detailed porch and a box-bay window. From the foyer, double doors open to the den with built-ins and a fireplace. The family room's hearth is framed by windows overlooking the rear porch. The master bedroom and sun room also open to the rear porch. The master bath, with a large walk-in closet, double vanities, corner tub and separate shower completes the master suite. Two secondary bedrooms share a full bath. This home is designed with a basement foundation.

© American Home Gallery, Ltd.

Design by
© Stephen Fuller,
American Home Gallery

Cost to build? See page 684
to order complete cost estimate
to build this house in your area!

Width 62'-4"
Depth 62'-2"

DESIGN 3314
Square Footage: 1,959
L

Formal living areas in this plan are joined by a three-bedroom sleeping wing. One bedroom, with foyer access, could function as a study. Two verandas and a screened porch enlarge the plan and enhance indoor/outdoor livability. Notice the abundant storage space, walkin pantry, built-in planning desk, whirlpool tub and pass-through snack bar. The sloped ceiling in the gathering room gives this area an open, airy quality. The breakfast room, with its wealth of windows, will be a cheerful and bright spot to enjoy the morning.

Design by
© Home Planners

Cost to build? See page 684
to order complete cost estimate
to build this house in your area!

Width 56'-0"
Depth 48'-8"

www.homeplanners.com

© American Home Gallery, Ltd.

QUOTE ONE®

Cost to build? See page 684
to order complete cost estimate
to build this house in your area!

MASTER
BATH

MASTER BEDRDOOM
16'-4" X 13'-6"

PORCH

BREAKFAST
13'-4" X 9'-0"

BEDROOM/
OFFICE
10'-4" X 11'-0"

GREAT ROOM
17'-0" X 17'-8"

BEDROOM NO. 2
10'-4" X 12'-0"

KITCHEN
13'-4" X 10'-6"

BATH

LAUNDRY

BATH

DINING ROOM
11'-4" X 12'-10"

FOYER
5'-4" X
12'-10"

BEDROOM/
STUDY
11'-2" X 12'-0"

TWO CAR GARAGE
20'-6" X 19'-6"

PORCH

Width 61'-0"
Depth 70'-6"

ONE-STORY TRADITIONAL HOMES

This traditional home features board-and-batten and cedar shingles in an attractively proportioned exterior. Finishing touches include a covered entrance and porch with column detailing, an arched transom, flower boxes and shuttered windows. The foyer opens to both the dining room and great room beyond, which offers French-door access to the porch. Through the double doors to the right of the foyer is the combination bedroom/study. A short hallway leads to a full bath and a secondary bedroom with ample closet space. The master bedroom is spacious, with walk-in closets on both sides of the entrance to the master bath. With separate vanities, a shower and toilet, the master bath forms a private retreat at the rear of the home. Convenient to both the great room and dining room, the kitchen opens to an attractive breakfast area featuring a bay window. An additional room is remotely located off the kitchen, providing a retreat for today's at-home office or guest. This home is designed with a basement foundation.

DESIGN
T052
Square Footage: 2,090

DESIGN
S126
Square Footage: 1,751

This raised-porch farmhouse holds all the charisma of others of its style, but boasts a one-story floor plan. A huge living area features a vaulted ceiling, built-ins and a warming fireplace. The formal dining room across the hall is open to the foyer and the living area. Casual dining takes place in a light-filled breakfast room, attached to the designer kitchen. A spectacular master suite sits behind the two-car garage. It has a tray ceiling, enormous walk-in closet and well-appointed bath. Family bedrooms share a bath with separate vanity area.

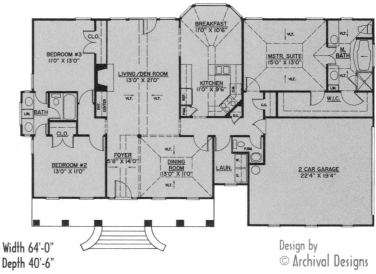

Width 64'-0"
Depth 40'-6"

Design by
© Archival Designs

DESIGN
P107
Square Footage: 1,373

Columns add style as well as support to the covered porch that dresses up this classic one-story home. The foyer opens to a family room that combines with the dining room to accommodate every occasion. The adjacent kitchen is designed for efficiency, uniting with the breakfast room for casual meals. Sleeping quarters include two secondary bedrooms that share a full bath and convenient laundry-room access. The master suite enjoys a private bath with a relaxing tub, separate shower and walk-in closet with linen storage and plant shelf. Please specify basement or crawl-space foundation when ordering.

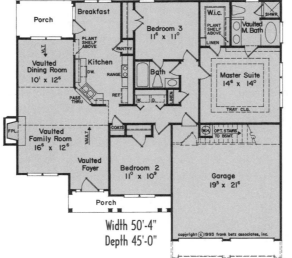

Width 50'-4"
Depth 45'-0"

Quote One®
Cost to build? See page 684
to order complete cost estimate
to build this house in your area!

Design by
© Frank Betz Associates, Inc.

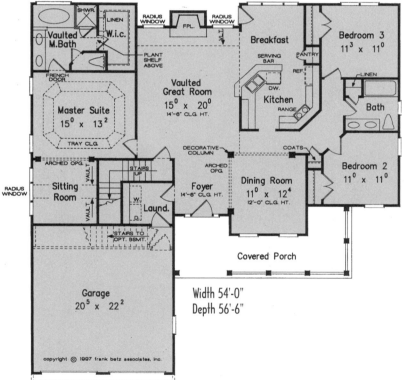

Vaulted M.Bath

SHWR.

LINEN

W.i.c.

RADIUS WINDOW

FPL.

RADIUS WINDOW

Breakfast

Bedroom 3
11³ x 11⁰

SERVING BAR

PANTRY

DW.

REF.

LINEN

FRENCH DOOR.

PLANT SHELF ABOVE

Vaulted Great Room
15⁰ x 20⁰
14'-6" CLG. HT.

Kitchen

RANGE

Bath

Master Suite
15⁰ x 13²

TRAY CLG.

DECORATIVE COLUMN

COATS

Design by
© Frank Betz Associates, Inc.

ARCHED OPG.

ARCHED OPG.

Foyer
14'-6" CLG. HT.

Dining Room
11⁰ x 12⁴
12'-0" CLG. HT.

Bedroom 2
11⁰ x 11⁰

RADIUS WINDOW

VAULT

VAULT

Sitting Room

STAIRS UP

W.
D.

Laund.

STAIRS TO OPT. BSMT.

Garage
20⁵ x 22²

Covered Porch

Width 54'-0"
Depth 56'-6"

copyright © 1997 frank betz associates, inc.

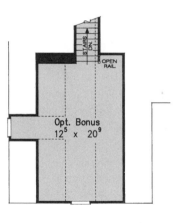

STAIRS DN.

OPEN RAIL

Opt. Bonus
12⁵ x 20⁹

ONE-STORY TRADITIONAL HOMES

The wraparound covered porch of this delightful design evokes memories of sipping lemonade on a warm afternoon or stargazing on a balmy night. The interior is equally enchanting. The vaulted great room is warmed by a cozy fireplace flanked by radius windows. A central kitchen easily serves the breakfast room and the front-facing formal dining room. The master suite is lavish in its appointments with special features such as a private sitting room, tray ceiling, vaulted master bath and walk-in closet. The two-car garage shields the master suite from street noise. Two family bedrooms sharing a hall bath occupy the right side of the plan. Please specify basement or crawlspace foundation when ordering.

DESIGN
P328
Square Footage: 1,692

DESIGN
F114
Square Footage: 1,890

It's easy to imagine this charming one-story home nestled in the picturesque countryside of France. However, this amenity-filled plan—designed to fit handily on a narrow lot—is at home wherever you live. Efficient floor planning places the kitchen and morning room to the left of the foyer, allowing the formal dining room, the great room and the master bedroom to take advantage of rear views. From the garage—cleverly disguised as a barn—there is a laundry room adjoining two secondary bedrooms and a bath. The master bedroom is highlighted by a dressing area with a walk-in closet and a master bath with a whirlpool tub, double-bowl vanity and separate shower. A stairway leads to a large attic storage area that can be modified for future development if needed.

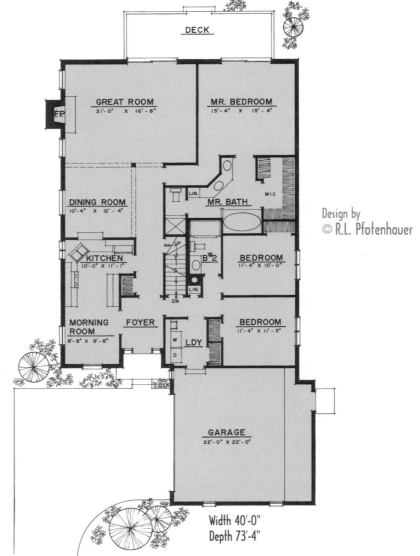

Design by
© R.L. Pfotenhauer

Width 40'-0"
Depth 73'-4"

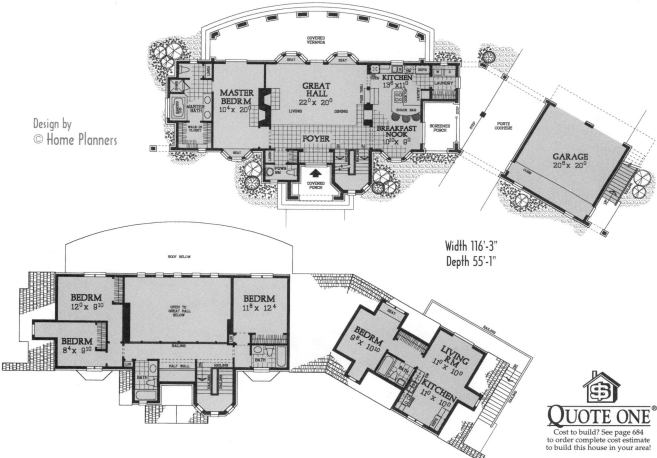

Design by
© Home Planners

Width 116'-3"
Depth 55'-1"

DESIGN
3622
First Floor: 1,566 square feet
Second Floor: 837 square feet
Total: 2,403 square feet
Bonus Room: 506 square feet

L

Be the master of your own country estate—this two-story home gives the look and feel of grand-style living without the expense of large square footage. The entry leads to a massive foyer and great hall, worthy of your estate lifestyle. There's space enough here for living and dining areas and two window seats overlooking the rear veranda. One fireplace warms the living area, while another looks through the dining room to the kitchen and breakfast nook. A screened porch offers casual dining space for warm weather. The master suite has another fireplace and window seat and adjoins a luxurious master bath with separate tub and shower. The second floor contains three family bedrooms and two full baths. Over the garage is a separate apartment, with its own living room, kitchen and bedroom. This space can be developed later.

TWO-STORY TRADITIONAL HOMES

DESIGN 2995

First Floor: 2,465 square feet
Second Floor: 617 square feet
Total: 3,082 square feet

L D

This New England Colonial home delivers beautiful proportions and great livability on 1½ levels. The main area of the house, the first floor, holds a living room, library, family room, dining room and gourmet kitchen. The master bedroom, also on this floor, features a sumptuous master bath with a whirlpool tub and sloped ceiling. A long rear terrace stretches the full width of the house. Two bedrooms on the second floor share a full bath; each has a built-in desk.

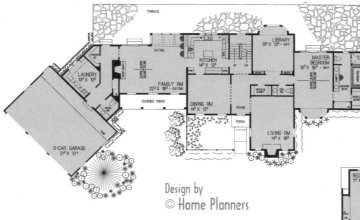

Width 120'-11"
Depth 52'-6"

Design by
© Home Planners

DESIGN 2699

First Floor: 2,188 square feet
Second Floor: 858 square feet
Total: 3,046 square feet

L

Luxury is evident throughout this design, beginning with the elegantly proportioned dining and living rooms. The spacious U-shaped country kitchen includes a work area, an island cooktop, an eating area and built-ins, while a fireplace provides the central focus. In the secluded master bedroom curl up with a good book in the lounge or pamper yourself in the whirlpool tub. A handy laundry room, a washroom and a mud area are near the three-car garage. Two second-floor bedrooms each enjoy a private bath and share a lounge area.

Width 106'-8"
Depth 32'-0"

Design by
© Home Planners

Design by
© Home Planners

Width 90'-8"
Depth 80'-4"

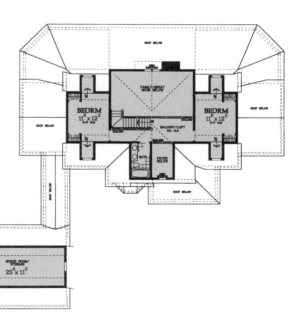

QUOTE ONE®
Cost to build? See page 684
to order complete cost estimate
to build this house in your area!

Varying roof planes, gables and dormers help create the unique character of this house. Inside, the family/great room gains attention with its high ceiling, fireplace/media center wall, view of the upstairs balcony and French doors to the sun room. In the U-shaped kitchen, an island work surface, planning desk and pantry are added conveniences. The spacious master suite can function with the home office, library or private sitting room. Its direct access to the huge raised veranda provides an ideal outdoor private haven for relaxation. The second floor highlights a balcony/loft area, plus two bedrooms and a bath. Extra space can be found in the garage, with its workshop area and stairway to a bonus second-floor storage or multi-purpose room.

**DESIGN
3606**
First Floor: 1,969 square feet
Second Floor: 660 square feet
Total: 2,629 square feet
Bonus Room: 360 square feet

L D

TWO-STORY TRADITIONAL HOMES

DESIGN 2563

First Floor: 1,500 square feet
Second Floor: 690 square feet
Total: 2,190 square feet

L D

This charming Cape Cod will capture your heart with its warm appeal. From the large living room with a fireplace and adjacent dining room to the farm kitchen with an additional fireplace, the plan works toward livability. The first-floor master bedroom is highlighted by a luxurious bath and sliding glass doors to the rear terrace. A front study might be used as a guest bedroom or library. Upstairs, two bedrooms and a sitting room plus a full bath accommodate the needs of family members. A three-car garage includes storage space.

The home, as shown in the photograph, may differ from the actual blueprints. For more detailed information, please check the floor plans carefully.

Photo by Laszlo Regos

Design by
© Home Planners

QUOTE ONE®
Cost to build? See page 684 to order complete cost estimate to build this house in your area!

Width 80'-0"
Depth 32'-0"

DESIGN 2921

First Floor: 3,215 square feet
Second Floor: 711 square feet
Total: 3,926 square feet
Bonus Room: 296 square feet

L D

This traditional design makes for a comfortable home. Quiet areas of the house include a media room and master suite, with a fitness area, spacious closet and bath, as well as a lounge. Informal living areas include a sun room, country kitchen and food-prep island. Formal living areas include a living area and formal dining room. The second floor holds two bedrooms and a lounge. Service areas include a room just off the garage for laundry, sewing or hobbies.

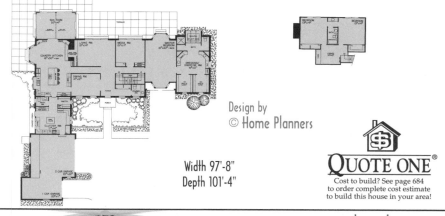

The home, as shown in the photograph, may differ from the actual blueprints. For more detailed information, please check the floor plans carefully.

Photo by Laszlo Regos

Design by
© Home Planners

Width 97'-8"
Depth 101'-4"

QUOTE ONE®
Cost to build? See page 684 to order complete cost estimate to build this house in your area!

Design by
© Home Planners

Cost to build? See page 684
to order complete cost estimate
to build this house in your area!

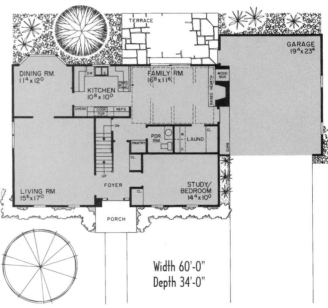

Width 60'-0"
Depth 34'-0"

Cape Cod homes are among the most popular designs of all time. This moderately sized 1½-story plan is symmetrically beautiful. The traditional central foyer leads to a formal living area on the left and a study (or additional bedroom) on the right. A bay windowed dining room is located between the spacious kitchen and the living room.

A family room with a beam ceiling and raised-hearth fireplace offers access to the rear terrace through sliding glass doors. Dormer windows grace two of the three bedrooms on the second floor. The family bedrooms share a full bath. The master bedroom contains a private bath with a dressing area. The garage offers storage or workshop space.

DESIGN
1791
First Floor: 1,157 square feet
Second Floor: 875 square feet
Total: 2,032 square feet

The home, as shown in the photograph, may differ from the actual blueprints. For more detailed information, please check the floor plans carefully.

Photo by Andrew D. Lautman

Design by
© Home Planners

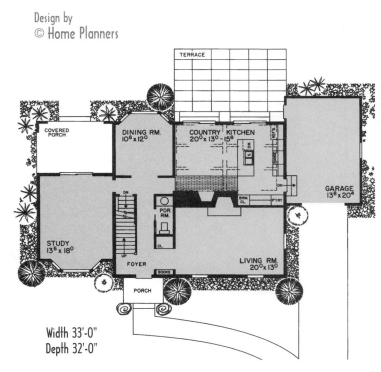

Width 33'-0"
Depth 32'-0"

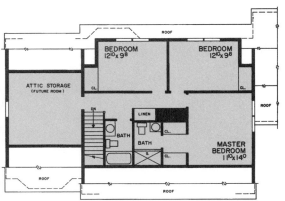

Cost to build? See page 684
to order complete cost estimate
to build this house in your area!

DESIGN 2682
First Floor: 1,016 square feet
Second Floor: 766 square feet
Total: 1,782 square feet

Here is an expandable Colonial home with a full measure of Cape Cod charm. For those who wish to build the basic house, there is an abundance of low-budget livability. Twin fireplaces serve the formal living room and the informal country kitchen. Note the spaciousness of both areas. A dining room and a powder room are also on the first floor of this basic plan. The expanded version adds a study wing, as well as an attached garage with a service entrance to the kitchen. Both versions include three second-floor bedrooms, including a master bedroom with a private bath. A linen closet is tucked in the hall.

www.homeplanners.com

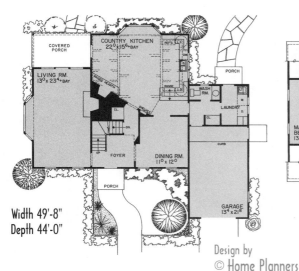

Width 49'-8"
Depth 44'-0"

Design by
© Home Planners

Quote One®
Cost to build? See page 684
to order complete cost estimate
to build this house in your area!

See page 684 to order complete cost estimate

DESIGN 2657

First Floor: 1,217 square feet
Second Floor: 868 square feet
Total: 2,085 square feet

L

This home is packed with all-American charm and no small number of features. On either side of the large entry foyer are a formal dining room and a living room with a gigantic bay window, fireplace and access to a covered porch overlooking the backyard. Dominating the back of the first floor is a U-shaped country kitchen with a number of amenities. A washroom and a laundry are close by. The cozy second floor holds three bedrooms and two full baths. Cleverly designed window seats in the dormer windows hide small storage areas.

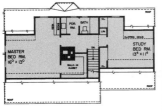

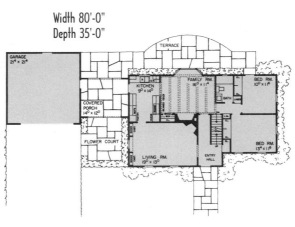

Width 80'-0"
Depth 35'-0"

Design by
© Home Planners

DESIGN 2146

First Floor: 1,182 square feet
Second Floor: 708 square feet
Total: 1,890 square feet

L D

Historically referred to as a "half house," this authentic adaptation has its roots in the heritage of New England. With completion of the second floor, the growing family doubles its sleeping capacity. Notice that both the family and living rooms have fireplaces. Don't overlook the many built-in units featured throughout the plan.

TWO-STORY TRADITIONAL HOMES

QUOTE ONE®
Cost to build? See page 684
to order complete cost estimate
to build this house in your area!

Design by
© Home Planners

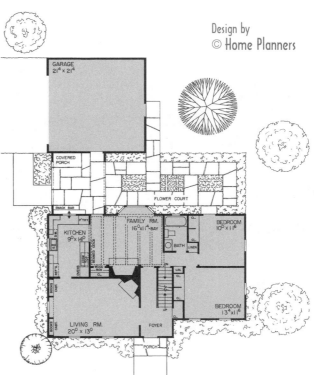

Width 44'-0"
Depth 64'-0"

DESIGN 2145

First Floor: 1,182 square feet
Second Floor: 708 square feet
Total: 1,890 square feet

L

This authentic adaptation is a "half house" similar to the one on the previous page. With completion of the second floor, the growing family doubles their sleeping capacity. A fireplace warms the living room while a large hearth dominates the beam-ceilinged family room. A deluxe master bedroom located upstairs offers built-ins and a walk-in closet. Take note of the covered porch leading to the garage and the flower court.

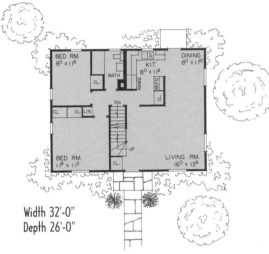

DESIGN 1394

First Floor: 832 square feet
Second Floor: 512 square feet
Total: 1,344 square feet

L D

The growing family with a smaller building budget will find this to be a great investment. The floor plan is efficient, yet includes four bedrooms and two full baths. On the first floor, the living room connects to a dining area and L-shaped kitchen. A full bath on this floor is shared by two bedrooms. The second floor, which may be finished at a later date, holds two bedrooms and a full bath as well. One of the bedrooms has a convenient dressing room.

Width 32'-0"
Depth 26'-0"

Design by
© Home Planners

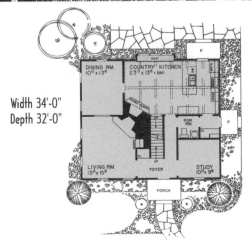

DESIGN 2661

First Floor: 1,100 square feet
Second Floor: 808 square feet
Total: 1,908 square feet

L D

It would be difficult to find a starter or retirement home with more charm than this. Inside, it contains a very livable floor plan. An outstanding first floor centers around the huge country kitchen, which includes a beam ceiling, raised-hearth fireplace, window seat and rear-yard access. The living room, with its warming corner fireplace, and a private study are to the front of the plan. Upstairs are three bedrooms and two full baths. Built-in shelves and a linen closet in the second-floor hallway provide excellent storage.

Width 34'-0"
Depth 32'-0"

Design by
© Home Planners

QUOTE ONE®
Cost to build? See page 684 to order complete cost estimate to build this house in your area!

DESIGN 2596

First Floor: 1,489 square feet
Second Floor: 982 square feet
Total: 2,471 square feet

L D

Captivating as a New England village! From the weather-vane atop the garage to the roofed side entry and multi-lite windows, this home is perfectly detailed. Inside, there is a lot of living space. An exceptionally large family room includes a dining area and features a raised-hearth fireplace. The adjoining kitchen has a laundry just steps away. The formal living and dining rooms are in the front. Upstairs, the master bedroom offers a roomy bath with a walk-in closet and a dressing area. Two family bedrooms share a compartmented bath.

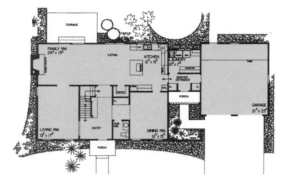

Design by
© Home Planners

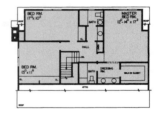

Width 76'-0"
Depth 32'-0"

DESIGN 2684

First Floor: 1,600 square feet
Second Floor: 1,145 square feet
Total: 2,745 square feet
Bonus Room: 353 square feet

L D

Dormers and a columned entry are nicely offset by multi-paned shuttered windows on the outside of this delightful home. Inside, the spacious country kitchen features an island cooktop and casual living/dining space with sliding glass doors and a fireplace. It complements the formal living and dining rooms (note the fireplace in the living room) and a study (with another fireplace). Bedrooms on the second floor include a master suite with dressing area and full bath.

Design by
© Home Planners

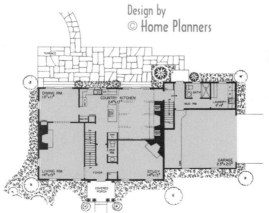

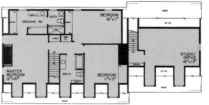

Width 66'-0"
Depth 34'-0"

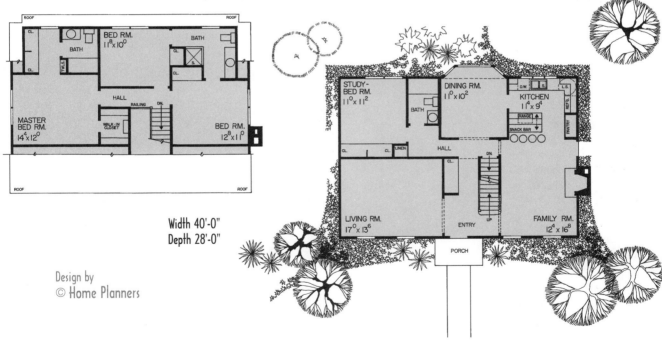

Width 40'-0"
Depth 28'-0"

Design by
© Home Planners

This cozy Cape Cod home has an efficient plan that's long on style and comfort. Multi-pane windows and mock shutters lend a welcoming appeal to the charming exterior. Inside, to the right of the foyer, the comfortable family room features a fireplace and snack bar. The separate dining room has a gorgeous bay window and is just steps from the efficient kitchen. The formal living room and study/bedroom, with nearby full bath, round out the first floor. Upstairs, the master suite has a walk-in closet and large bath. Two spacious family bedrooms share a full bath that has separate entrances.

DESIGN 2571
First Floor: 1,137 square feet
Second Floor: 795 square feet
Total: 1,932 square feet

DESIGN 7497

First Floor: 1,198 square feet
Second Floor: 673 square feet
Total: 1,871 square feet

This petite bungalow would be perfect for either empty-nesters or those just starting out. The charm of the exterior is echoed inside, where a comfortable floor plan is very accommodating. A G-shaped kitchen serves the dining room with a pass-through. The spacious great room features a corner fireplace and sliding glass doors to the rear yard. The vaulted master bedroom, on the first floor, offers a walk-in closet and private bath. Upstairs, three secondary bedrooms share a full hall bath and a large linen closet.

Design by
© Alan Mascord
Design Associates, Inc.

Width 40'-0"
Depth 47'-0"

DESIGN 3316

First Floor: 1,111 square feet
Second Floor: 886 square feet
Total: 1,997 square feet

L

Don't be fooled by the small-looking exterior. This plan offers three bedrooms and plenty of living space. Notice that the screened porch leads to a rear terrace with access to the breakfast room. A living room/dining room combination adds spaciousness to the floor plan. Other welcome amenities include: boxed windows in the breakfast room and dining room, a fireplace in the living room, a planning desk and pass-through snack bar in the kitchen, a whirlpool tub in the master bath and a two-story foyer.

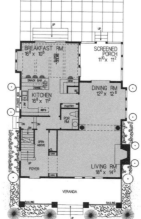

Width 34'-1"
Depth 50'-0"

Design by
© Home Planners

QUOTE ONE®

Cost to build? See page 684 to order complete cost estimate to build this house in your area!

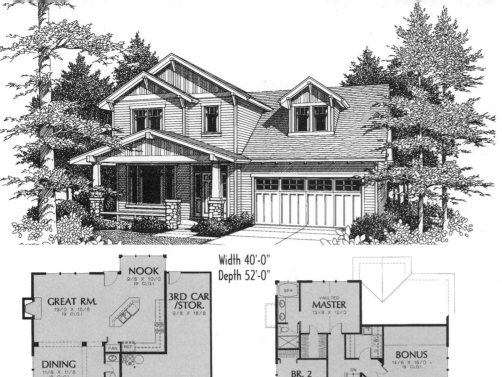

DESIGN 7470

First Floor: 1,082 square feet
Second Floor: 864 square feet
Total: 1,946 square feet
Bonus Room: 358 square feet

From the covered front porch to the trio of gables, this design has a lot of appeal. The L-shaped kitchen is open to the nook and great room, and offers easy access to the formal dining area. Upstairs, two family bedrooms share a full bath and access to both a laundry room and a large bonus room. Complete with a walk-in closet and a pampering bath, the vaulted master suite will be heaven to come home to.

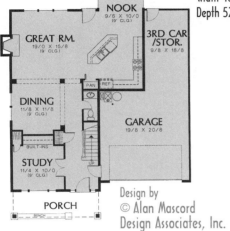

Width 40'-0"
Depth 52'-0"

GREAT RM. 19/0 X 15/8 (9' CLG.)
NOOK 9/6 X 10/0 (9' CLG.)
3RD CAR /STOR. 9/8 X 18/8
DINING 11/8 X 11/8 (9' CLG.)
GARAGE 19/8 X 20/8
STUDY 11/4 X 10/0 (9' CLG.)
BUILT-INS
PAN REF
PORCH
BENCH

SPA
MASTER VAULTED 13/8 X 12/0
BONUS 14/6 X 18/0 + (9' CLG.)
BR. 2 11/4 X 10/0
DN
BR. 3 11/4 X 11/0

Design by
© Alan Mascord
Design Associates, Inc.

DESIGN 7521

First Floor: 1,097 square feet
Second Floor: 807 square feet
Total: 1,904 square feet

The combination of rafter tails, stone-and-siding and gabled rooflines give this home plenty of curb appeal. Inside, enter a cozy vaulted den through double doors, just to the left of the foyer. A spacious, vaulted great room features a fireplace and is right near the formal dining room. The kitchen offers an octagonal island, a corner sink with window and a pantry. Upstairs, two secondary bedrooms share a hall bath, while the master suite is enhanced with a private bath and a walk-in closet.

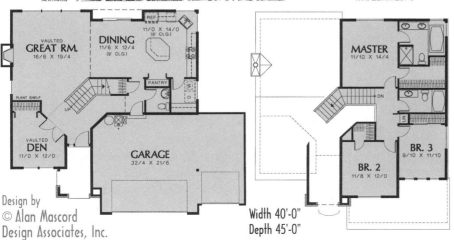

GREAT RM. VAULTED 16/6 X 19/4
DINING 11/6 X 12/4 (9' CLG.)
11/0 X 14/0 (9' CLG.)
REF
PLANT SHELF
UP
PANTRY
DEN VAULTED 11/0 X 12/0
GARAGE 32/4 X 21/6

MASTER 11/10 X 14/4
DN
LIN
BR. 3 9/10 X 11/10
BR. 2 11/8 X 12/0

Design by
© Alan Mascord
Design Associates, Inc.

Width 40'-0"
Depth 45'-0"

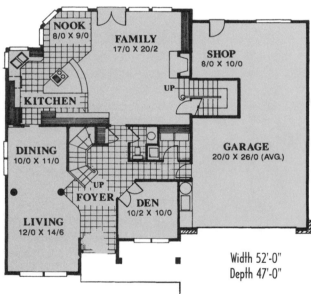

Design by
© Mark Stewart & Associates, Inc.

NOOK
8/0 X 9/0

FAMILY
17/0 X 20/2

SHOP
8/0 X 10/0

KITCHEN

UP

DINING
10/0 X 11/0

GARAGE
20/0 X 26/0 (AVG.)

UP

FOYER

DEN
10/2 X 10/0

LIVING
12/0 X 14/6

Width 52'-0"
Depth 47'-0"

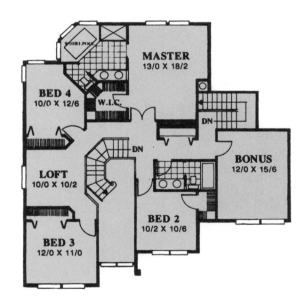

WHIRLPOOL

MASTER
13/0 X 18/2

BED 4
10/0 X 12/6

W.I.C.

DN

LOFT
10/0 X 10/2

DN

BONUS
12/0 X 15/6

BED 2
10/2 X 10/6

BED 3
12/0 X 11/0

DESIGN J138

First Floor: 1,383 square feet
Second Floor: 1,181 square feet
Total: 2,564 square feet
Bonus Room: 200 square feet

The columned living room and second-floor bedrooms are just the first of many attractive features you'll notice in this home. There are abundant windows and two staircases, one of them angular. The kitchen is compact but complete, with a triangular cooking island providing a snack bar for the family room. The garage is extra long, making space for a workshop. Upstairs you'll find the master suite with its huge walk-in closet and whirlpool bath, three other bedrooms, a loft and a bonus room. Family bedrooms share a full bath. Please specify basement or crawlspace foundation when ordering.

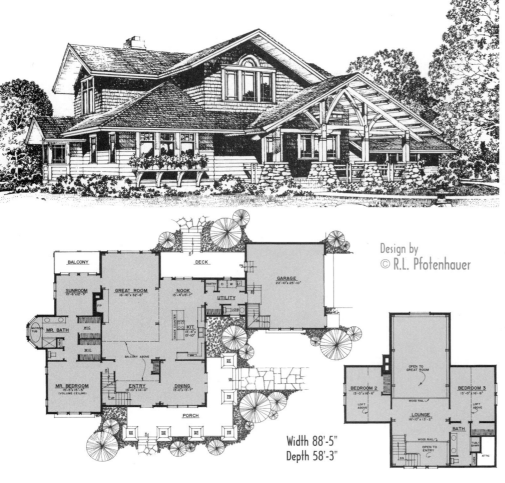

Design by
© R.L. Pfotenhauer

Width 88'-5"
Depth 58'-3"

Upon entering this Craftsman-style house, guests are greeted with a cathedral-ceilinged great room with fireplace. The kitchen has a snack-counter island with breakfast nook that opens out to a deck, which can be used for alfresco dining. Located on the first floor for privacy, the master suite contains plenty of windows, two walk-in closets and a whirlpool tub with views out a bayed window. Two bedrooms share a lounge area on the second level.

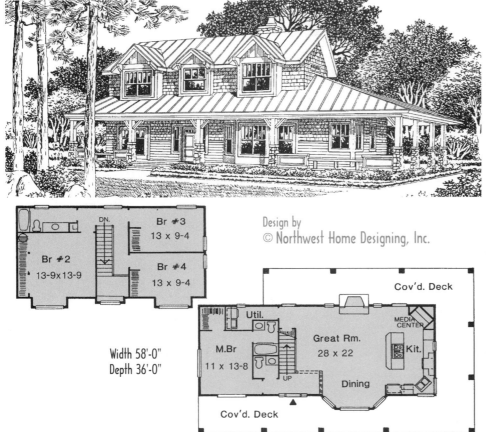

Design by
© Northwest Home Designing, Inc.

Width 58'-0"
Depth 36'-0"

A metal-seamed roof, a trio of gables and a wraparound, covered porch combine with shingles and siding to create a home with a ton of charm. The floor plan is a real charmer, too, with a bayed dining area, a fireplace in the great room and an efficient kitchen with a large work island and plenty of counter and cabinet space. The first-floor master suite is sure to please with a walk-in closet and a private bath. Upstairs, the sleeping zone consists of three family bedrooms, all sharing a hall bath and linen closet.

TWO-STORY TRADITIONAL HOMES

© 1996 Donald A. Gardner Architects, Inc.

DESIGN 7610

First Floor: 1,585 square feet
Second Floor: 439 square feet
Total: 2,024 square feet
Bonus Room: 333 square feet

Elegant family living is comfortably achieved in this delightful, traditional home. The formal dining room and breakfast room, both topped with vaulted ceilings, flank the spacious kitchen in a welcome design of efficiency. The magnificent great room provides a cathedral ceiling, views of the open staircase, a central fireplace and doors to the rear porch. The vaulted master suite enjoys a private bath complete with a walk-in closet. Upstairs, two family bedrooms share a full hall bath.

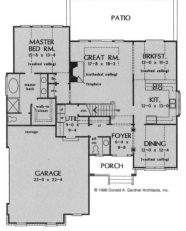

Design by
Donald A. Gardner
Architects, Inc.

Width 49'-4"
Depth 58'-5"

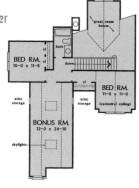

© 1996 Donald A. Gardner Architects, Inc.

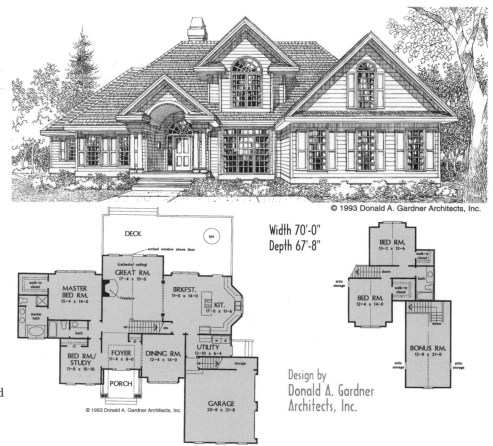

© 1993 Donald A. Gardner Architects, Inc.

DESIGN 9736

First Floor: 1,839 square feet
Second Floor: 527 square feet
Total: 2,366 square feet
Bonus Room: 344 square feet

An arched entrance and windows combine with round columns to give a touch of class to the exterior of this four-bedroom plan. The large, open kitchen with an island cooktop is convenient to the breakfast and dining rooms. The master suite has plenty of walk-in closet space and a well-planned master bath. A nearby bedroom would make an excellent guest room or study. The second level offers two bedrooms, with sloped ceilings and walk-in closets, and a full bath.

Width 70'-0"
Depth 67'-8"

Design by
Donald A. Gardner
Architects, Inc.

© 1993 Donald A. Gardner Architects, Inc.

TWO-STORY TRADITIONAL HOMES

© 1991 Donald A. Gardner Architects, Inc.

DESIGN 9661

First Floor: 1,416 square feet
Second Floor: 445 square feet
Total: 1,861 square feet
Bonus Room: 284 square feet

An arched entrance and windows provide class to the exterior of this plan. The dining room displays round columns at the entrance while the great room boasts a cathedral ceiling, fireplace and arched window over exterior doors to the deck. The large kitchen is open to the breakfast nook and sliding glass doors present a second access to the deck. In the master suite is a walk-in closet and lavish bath. On the second level are two bedrooms and a full bath. A basement or crawlspace foundation is available.

QUOTE ONE®
Cost to build? See page 684 to order complete cost estimate to build this house in your area!

Width 58'-3"
Depth 68'-9"

© 1991 Donald A. Gardner Architects, Inc.

Design by
Donald A. Gardner
Architects, Inc.

DESIGN 9790

First Floor: 1,799 square feet
Second Floor: 730 square feet
Total: 2,529 square feet
Bonus Room: 328 square feet

With its Palladian window and covered front porch, this plan is one everyone will call home. From the formal living room and formal dining room at the front of the plan, to the breakfast area and family room at the back, every need is met. Secluded on the first floor, the master suite is lavish with amenities, including a huge walk-in closet, a separate shower and tub and a dual-bowl vanity. Upstairs, three secondary bedrooms share a full bath. A basement or crawlspace foundation is available.

© 1996 Donald A. Gardner Architects, Inc.

Width 55'-4"
Depth 61'-4"

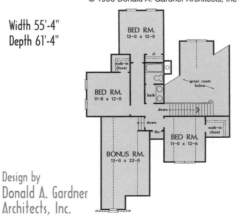

Design by
Donald A. Gardner
Architects, Inc.

© 1996 Donald A. Gardner Architects, Inc.

TWO-STORY TRADITIONAL HOMES

DESIGN 9209

First Floor: 1,963 square feet
Second Floor: 778 square feet
Total: 2,741 square feet

Gracious family living is the hallmark of this plan. The roomy first floor features space for any activity. There's a formal dining room with bay window off the entry. A cozy corner den with built-in bookshelves provides a quiet refuge while the spacious great room can accommodate large gatherings. A through-fireplace warms both the great room and the kitchen. The three-bedroom second floor will sleep quite a crew.

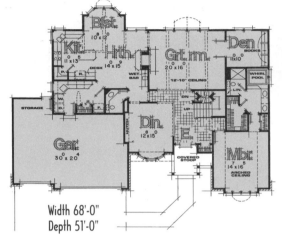

Width 68'-0"
Depth 51'-0"

Design by
© Design Basics, Inc.

DESIGN 9247

First Floor: 1,297 square feet
Second Floor: 558 square feet
Total: 1,855 square feet

The covered front porch of this home opens to a great floor plan. From the entry, go left to reach the formal dining room with boxed window. Straight back is the great room with handsome fireplace and tall windows. A snack bar, pantry and planning desk in the kitchen make it convenient and appealing. The breakfast room has sliding glass doors to the rear yard. The first-floor master bedroom has a luxurious bath with skylit whirlpool. Upstairs are three more bedrooms and a full bath.

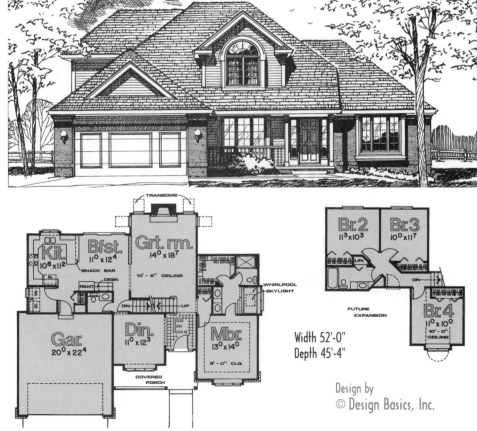

Width 52'-0"
Depth 45'-4"

Design by
© Design Basics, Inc.

QUOTE ONE®

Cost to build? See page 684
to order complete cost estimate
to build this house in your area!

Width 52'-0"
Depth 45'-4"

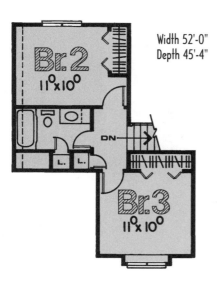

Br.2
11⁰x10⁰

DN

Br.3
11⁰x10⁰

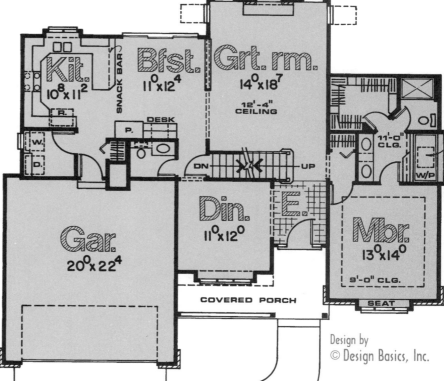

TRANSOMS

Kit.
10⁸x11²

Bfst.
11⁰x12⁴

Grt. rm.
14⁰x18⁷

12'-4"
CEILING

SNACK BAR

DESK

P.

W.
D.

DN   UP

11'-0"
CLG.

W/P

Gar.
20⁰x22⁴

Din.
11⁰x12⁰

E.

Mbr.
13⁰x14⁰

9'-0" CLG.

COVERED PORCH

SEAT

Design by
© Design Basics, Inc.

TWO-STORY TRADITIONAL HOMES

A lovely covered porch welcomes family and guests to this delightful 1½-story home. The entry opens to the formal dining room with a box-bay window and leads back to the great room, which offers an extended-hearth fireplace. An open kitchen/breakfast area features a pantry, planning desk and snack-bar counter. The elegant master suite is appointed with formal ceiling detail and a window seat. The skylight above the whirlpool and the double lavatories dress up the master bath. Secondary bedrooms on the second floor share a centrally located bath. A two-car garage is attached at the service entry.

DESIGN
9265

First Floor: 1,297 square feet
Second Floor: 388 square feet
Total: 1,685 square feet

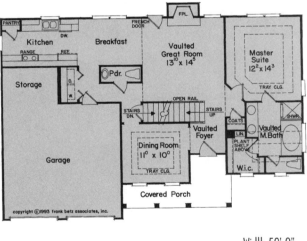

Design by
© Frank Betz Associates, Inc.

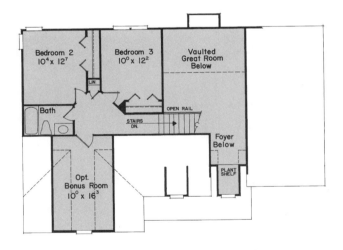

Width 50'-0"
Depth 37'-4"

DESIGN P142

First Floor: 1,065 square feet
Second Floor: 435 square feet
Total: 1,500 square feet
Bonus Room: 175 square feet

Although this home would work well on a narrow lot, it would fit just as comfortably on a lot surrounded by land available for a garden or for the kids to have plenty of running room. The front covered porch leads to a vaulted foyer and a formal dining room with a tray ceiling. A vaulted great room with a fireplace and rear-yard access will be ideal for family gatherings. The master suite, located on the first floor for privacy, features a vaulted bath with a walk-in closet and a separate tub and shower. Two bedrooms and a full bath are available upstairs, as well as an optional bonus room that can be developed later as needed. Please specify basement or crawlspace foundation when ordering.

www.homeplanners.com

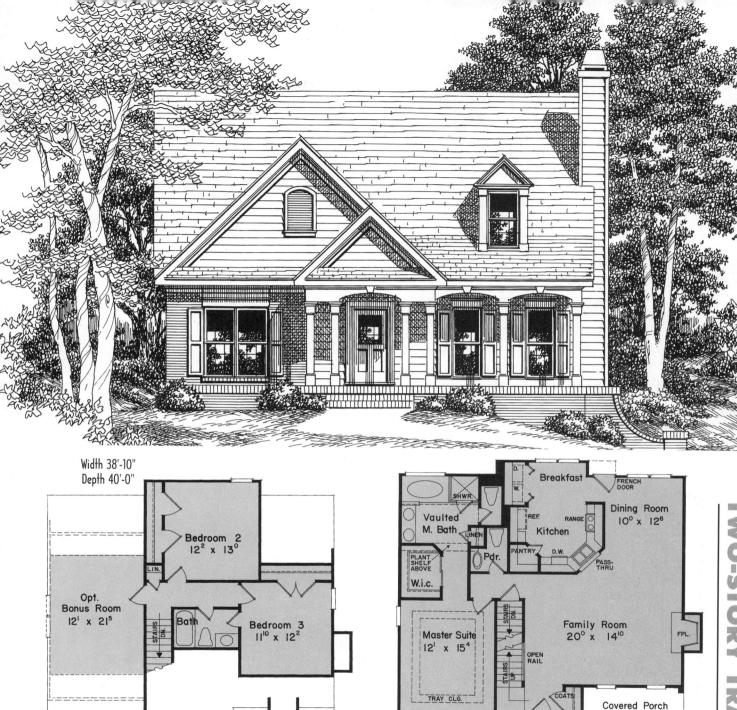

Width 38'-10"
Depth 40'-0"

Bedroom 2
12² x 13⁰

Opt.
Bonus Room
12¹ x 21⁵

STAIRS DN.

Bath

LIN.

Bedroom 3
11¹⁰ x 12²

D. W.

SHWR.

Vaulted
M. Bath

LINEN

Breakfast

FRENCH
DOOR

REF

RANGE

Dining Room
10⁰ x 12⁸

Kitchen

PANTRY

D.W.

PASS-
THRU

PLANT
SHELF
ABOVE

Pdr.

W.i.c.

Master Suite
12¹ x 15⁴

STAIRS DN.

OPEN
RAIL

STAIRS UP

Family Room
20⁰ x 14¹⁰

FPL.

TRAY CLG.

COATS

Covered Porch

Design by
© Frank Betz Associates, Inc.

Graceful columns and gabled rooflines combine with a welcoming covered porch to give this home plenty of curb appeal. Inside, the foyer opens directly into a spacious family room enhanced by a warming fireplace. This room expands into the dining room, providing a perfect area for entertaining.

The efficient kitchen offers a walk-in pantry and a nearby breakfast nook. Located for privacy, the first-floor master suite is designed to pamper, with a tray ceiling, large walk-in closet and sumptuous bath. Upstairs, two family bedrooms share a full bath. Note the optional bonus room for future expansion.

**DESIGN
P188**

First Floor: 1,142 square feet
Second Floor: 470 square feet
Total: 1,612 square feet
Bonus Room: 271 square feet

Two-Story Traditional Homes

Order Blueprints Toll Free 1-800-521-6797

DESIGN J136

First Floor: 1,278 square feet
Second Floor: 1,175 square feet
Total: 2,453 square feet
Bonus Room: 415 square feet

This three-bedroom is a natural for a young family. The den and formal living room flank the tiled foyer, which leads to the island kitchen with a corner sink, breakfast nook and access to the rear patio and formal dining room. The family room with fireplace and built-in bookcases is open to the second floor and flooded with light. Upstairs, the master suite offers sloped ceilings and a bay-window reading nook. Two additional bedrooms with a bath share the remaining space with the bonus room.

Design by
© Mark Stewart & Associates, Inc.

Width 66'-0"
Depth 45'-0"

DESIGN E121

First Floor: 1,916 square feet
Second Floor: 617 square feet
Total: 2,533 square feet

This Southern cottage combines style with comfort and offers an ideal solution for those families needing additional space with an optional bedroom/study area. Nine-foot ceilings expand the plan throughout the first floor. The family chef will appreciate the large gourmet kitchen with an island cabinet, and there's room to relax with privacy in the spacious master suite. Upstairs, three family bedrooms enjoy private dressing areas. Please specify crawlspace or slab foundation when ordering.

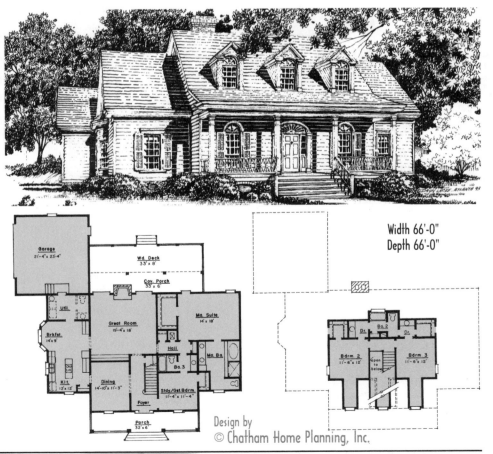

Width 66'-0"
Depth 66'-0"

Design by
© Chatham Home Planning, Inc.

Design by
© Chatham Home Planning, Inc.

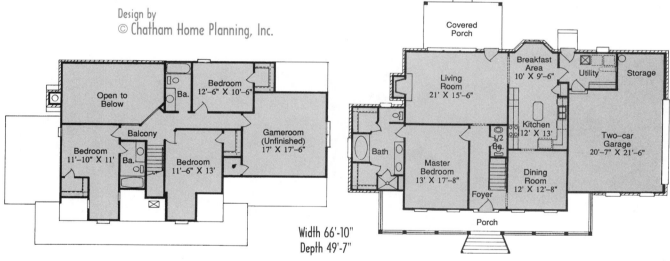

Width 66'-10"
Depth 49'-7"

This quintessential country exterior invites memories of lovely summer evenings spent sipping iced tea and sitting on the front porch swing—and this lovely home boasts two covered porches, front and rear. The roomy kitchen (with island cooktop cabinet) and its adjoining eating area provide plenty of room for casual dining and meal preparation. Formal dining space is at the front. The stunning master suite has it all—oversized tub, separate walk-in closets,

glass shower and compartmented toilet. Plenty of natural light and views to the rear yard show off the living area, warmed by a handsome fireplace. An upstairs balcony overlooks this spectacular living space and leads to three great family bedrooms and two full baths. An ample unfinished gameroom on this level offers additional storage, and there's a bonus storage area included with the two-car garage. Please specify crawlspace or slab foundation when ordering.

DESIGN E111
First Floor: 1,492 square feet
Second Floor: 865 square feet
Total: 2,357 square feet
Bonus Room: 285 square feet

TWO-STORY TRADITIONAL HOMES

DESIGN E102

First Floor: 1,576 square feet
Second Floor: 556 square feet
Total: 2,132 square feet

Design by
© Chatham Home Planning, Inc.

Width 62'-11"
Depth 58'-0"

This traditional cottage combines an easy-care brick exterior with a planned-to-perfection interior design. A dream master suite boasts amenities galore. The corner kitchen with sit-down bar is positioned to easily serve the formal dining area and the roomy breakfast area, which opens to a grand family room, complete with fireplace and views to the rear patio. The upstairs bedrooms feature dormers in each room along with attic access. Please specify crawlspace or slab foundation when ordering.

DESIGN T018

First Floor: 1,650 square feet
Second Floor: 1,060 square feet
Total: 2,710 square feet

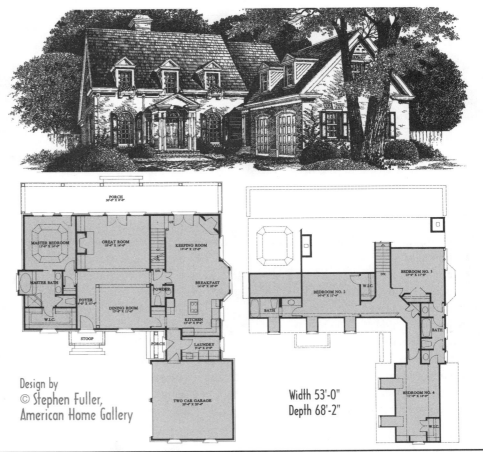

Design by
© Stephen Fuller,
American Home Gallery

Width 53'-0"
Depth 68'-2"

This home features brick jack arches that frame the arched front door. Inside, the foyer leads directly to the large great room with a fireplace. The kitchen and breakfast room offer a handy cooking island. Adjacent to the breakfast room is the keeping room, which includes a corner fireplace and French doors. Comfort and privacy describe the master suite. Upstairs, two additional bedrooms share access to a bath, while a fourth bedroom flaunts its own private bath. This home is designed with a basement foundation.

This fine brick, three-bedroom home is great for the growing family. Enter through a columned front porch to the foyer, which is flanked by a formal dining room and study. A huge master suite is located on the first floor for privacy and is complete with two walk-in closets and a sumptuous bath. Upstairs, two more bedrooms share a full hall bath. The island kitchen offers plenty of counter and cabinet space. Please specify basement, crawlspace or slab foundation when ordering.

Design by
© Michael E. Nelson
Nelson Design Group, LLC

Width 72'-4"
Depth 48'-4"

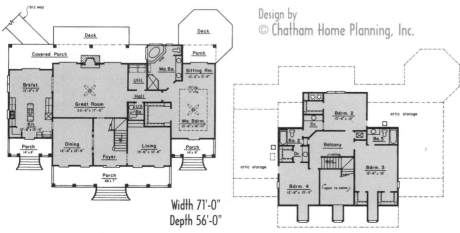

This large, Southern-style home offers luxury to spare, inside and out. Picture the central fireplace in the great room glowing between French doors, which open to a rear porch and deck. Luxury abounds in the opulent master suite, complete with a sitting room, private rear porch and deck, a separate front porch and a master bath with a corner whirlpool tub. Upstairs, a hall balcony connects three family bedrooms and two full baths. Please specify crawlspace or slab foundation when ordering.

Design by
© Chatham Home Planning, Inc.

Width 71'-0"
Depth 56'-0"

TWO-STORY TRADITIONAL HOMES

DESIGN 9757

First Floor: 1,715 square feet
Second Floor: 620 square feet
Total: 2,335 square feet
Bonus Room: 265 square feet

With a decided European flavor, this two-story home features country living at its best. The foyer opens to a study or living room on the left. The dining room on the right offers large proportions and full windows. The family room remains open to the kitchen and breakfast room, which overlooks the rear yard. In the master suite, a bayed sitting area, walk-in closet and pampering bath are sure to please. Upstairs, two bedrooms flank a loft or study area and a full hall bath.

© 1994 Donald A. Gardner Architects, Inc.

Width 58'-6"
Depth 50'-3"

Design by
Donald A. Gardner
Architects, Inc.

QUOTE ONE®
Cost to build? See page 684 to order complete cost estimate to build this house in your area!

DESIGN 7676

First Floor: 1,701 square feet
Second Floor: 534 square feet
Total: 2,235 square feet
Bonus Room: 274 square feet

Columns, gables, multi-pane windows and a stone-and-stucco exterior give this home its handsome appearance. The formal rooms are to the right and left of the foyer. The family room, with a cathedral ceiling, fireplace, built-ins and access to the rear patio, is open to the breakfast room through a pair of decorative columns. On the opposite side of the plan, the master suite offers two walk-in closets and a compartmented bath. Two family bedrooms on the second floor share a bath and a loft.

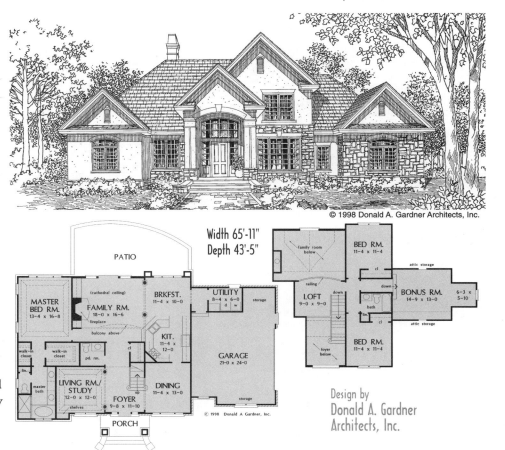

© 1998 Donald A. Gardner Architects, Inc.

Width 65'-11"
Depth 43'-5"

Design by
Donald A. Gardner
Architects, Inc.

© American Home Gallery, Ltd.

Design by
© Stephen Fuller,
American Home Gallery

Width 47'-0"
Depth 49'-6"

QUOTE ONE®
Cost to build? See page 684
to order complete cost estimate
to build this house in your area!

DESIGN T063

First Floor: 1,395 square feet
Second Floor: 1,210 square feet
Total: 2,605 square feet
Bonus Room: 225 square feet

The well-balanced use of stucco and stone makes this English country home especially inviting. The two-story foyer opens on the right to formal living and dining rooms. A spacious U-shaped kitchen adjoins a breakfast nook. This area flows nicely into the two-story great room, which offers a through-fireplace to the media room. Generous walk-in closet space and a bath with garden tub highlight the master suite. Two family bedrooms share a full bath and a balcony hall. This home is designed with a basement foundation.

DESIGN T014

First Floor: 1,724 square feet
Second Floor: 700 square feet
Total: 2,424 square feet

All the charm of gables, stonework and multi-level rooflines combine to create this cozy English cottage. To the left of the foyer you will see the dining room. In the gourmet kitchen is a work island, oversized pantry and a breakfast room with gazebo ceiling. The great room features a pass-through wet bar, fireplace and bookcases. The master suite enjoys privacy at the rear of the home. An open-rail loft above the foyer leads to additional bedrooms with walk-in closets. This home is designed with a basement foundation.

QUOTE ONE®
Cost to build? See page 684
to order complete cost estimate
to build this house in your area!

Design by
© Stephen Fuller,
American Home Gallery

Width 47'-10"
Depth 63'-10"

DESIGN 7608

First Floor: 1,784 square feet
Second Floor: 657 square feet
Total: 2,441 square feet

This traditional, family home allows you the option of a more formal plan by converting the master bedroom study into a front living room, complete with a fireplace. A cathedral ceiling, along with a fireplace, lets the family room be a welcoming gathering room for activities. The large, island kitchen has a sunny breakfast nook. The master bedroom holds a compartmented bath and large walk-in closet. Three family bedrooms, a full hall bath and a bonus room round out the second floor.

© 1996 Donald A. Gardner Architects, Inc.

Width 56'-8"
Depth 55'-5"

Design by
Donald A. Gardner
Architects, Inc.

DESIGN T021

First Floor: 2,070 square feet
Second Floor: 790 square feet
Total: 2,860 square feet

The striking combination of wood frame, shingles and glass create the exterior of this classic cottage. To the left of the foyer is a study with a warming hearth and a vaulted ceiling. To the right is the formal dining room. A great room with an attached breakfast area is near the kitchen. The master suite provides an expansive tray ceiling, a glass sitting area and easy passage to the outside deck. Upstairs, two bedrooms are accompanied by a sunken loft for a quiet getaway. This home is designed with a basement foundation.

Width 58'-4"
Depth 54'-10"

Design by
© Stephen Fuller,
American Home Gallery

Quote One®
Cost to build? See page 684
to order complete cost estimate
to build this house in your area!

www.homeplanners.com

A wide bay window and a large front porch welcome visitors to this stately country home. The bay window and a fireplace grace the private study on the left, while a formal dining room opens to the right. Straight ahead lies a massive great room, featuring a second fireplace and opening to the breakfast area and the efficient kitchen. A luxurious master suite with rear-deck access and an amenity-filled bath is located behind the study. On the upper level, two bedrooms share a full bath. This home is designed with a basement foundation.

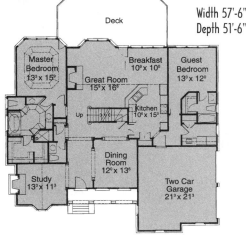

Width 57'-6"
Depth 51'-6"

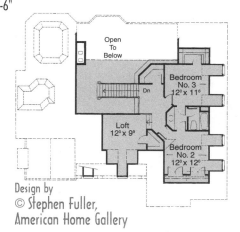

Design by
© Stephen Fuller,
American Home Gallery

© 1993 Donald A. Gardner Architects, Inc.

This attractive three-bedroom house offers a touch of country with its covered front porch. The foyer, flanked by the dining room and the bedroom/study, leads to the spacious great room. The dining room and breakfast room have cathedral ceilings with arched windows, filling the house with natural light. The master bedroom boasts a cathedral ceiling and bath with whirlpool tub, shower and double-bowl vanity. Two family bedrooms reside upstairs. A basement or crawlspace foundation is available.

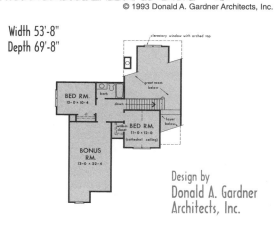

Width 53'-8"
Depth 69'-8"

Design by
Donald A. Gardner
Architects, Inc.

TWO-STORY TRADITIONAL HOMES

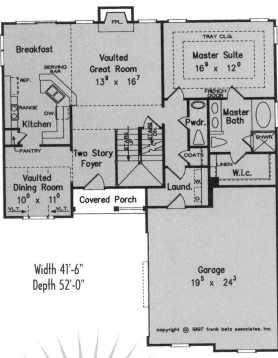

Breakfast

Vaulted Great Room
13^9 x 16^7

Master Suite
16^9 x 12^0

TRAY CLG.

SERVING BAR

REF.

RANGE

DW.

Kitchen

PANTRY

Pwdr.

Master Bath

FRENCH DOOR

STAIRS UP

STAIRS DN

COATS

SHWR

LINEN

W.i.c.

Two Story Foyer

Vaulted Dining Room
10^0 x 11^0

VLT.

VLT.

Covered Porch

Laund.

W. D.

Width 41'-6"
Depth 52'-0"

Garage
19^5 x 24^3

copyright © 1997 frank betz associates, inc.

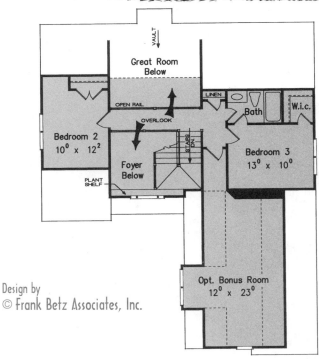

VAULT

Great Room Below

OPEN RAIL

OVERLOOK

LINEN

Bath

W.i.c.

Bedroom 2
10^0 x 12^2

Foyer Below

STAIRS DN

Bedroom 3
13^0 x 10^0

PLANT SHELF

Opt. Bonus Room
12^0 x 23^0

Design by
© Frank Betz Associates, Inc.

DESIGN P357
First Floor: 1,179 square feet
Second Floor: 460 square feet
Total: 1,639 square feet
Bonus Room: 350 square feet

With vaulted ceilings in the dining room and great room, as well as a tray ceiling in the master suite and a two-story foyer filled with natural light, this inviting design offers a wealth of sunlight and space. An optional bonus room adds 350 square feet. The counter-filled kitchen opens to a large breakfast area with rear-yard access. Each bedroom is separated enough to offer privacy to every occupant. Bedroom 3 and the master suite have walk-in closets. Please specify basement or crawlspace foundation when ordering.

© 1996 Donald A. Gardner Architects, Inc.

Width 65'-3"
Depth 43'-8"

PATIO

GREAT RM.
18-2 x 21-4
(cathedral ceiling)
fireplace

MASTER
BED RM.
13-0 x 14-4

BRKFST.
11-4 x 8-10

UTIL.
d 8-6 x
w 9-0

storage

walk-in
closet

balcony above

KIT.
11-4 x 12-6

master bath

pd. rm.

FOYER
10-7 x 5-2

DINING
11-4 x 12-10

GARAGE
21-0 x 23-8

PORCH

© 1996 Donald A. Gardner Architects, Inc.

great room
below

BED RM.
11-4 x 12-4

cl

attic storage

attic storage

railing

down

bath

lin.

cl

attic storage

BED RM.
11-4 x 14-0
(cathedral ceiling)

foyer below

skylights

BONUS RM.
12-2 x 27-4

Design by
Donald A. Gardner
Architects, Inc.

Doric columns and an arch-top pediment announce a home designed with a casually elegant style. A quiet foyer with an L-shaped staircase leads to a formal dining room and to casual living space, which offers a cathedral ceiling and a rounded-hearth fireplace. The great room opens to the outdoors and lets in the views through three windows, while the cozy breakfast nook enjoys a columned, private entry to the rear patio. Sleeping quarters include a lavish first-floor master suite and two family bedrooms upstairs.

© 1998 Donald A. Gardner Architects, Inc.

Design by
Donald A. Gardner
Architects, Inc.

PORCH

BRKFST.
11-8 x 10-0

MASTER
BED RM.
14-0 x 16-0

fireplace

GREAT RM.
20-0 x 16-0
(two story ceiling)

KIT.
11-8 x 12-8

GARAGE
21-0 x 21-0

walk-in
closet

walk-in
closet

bath

cl

railing

up

UTIL.
6-0 x
9-0
w

storage

FOYER
8-0 x 10-4
(two story ceiling)

DINING
12-0 x 13-0

master bath

shelves

lin.

PORCH

© 1998 Donald A Gardner, Inc.

Width 69'-3"
Depth 45'-10"

great room
below

BED RM.
11-8 x 13-0

cl

cl

cl

bath

attic storage

BONUS RM.
16-6 x 12-0

linen

down

foyer
below

BED RM.
12-0 x 13-0

walk-in
closet

attic storage

attic storage

© 1998 Donald A Gardner, Inc.

A brick portico with keystone accent introduces you to this fine traditional brick home. To the right of the two-story foyer, a formal dining room will handle traditional gatherings, while the rear-facing great room offers a crackling fireplace for intimate coziness. The master suite features dual walk-in closets and a master bath with garden tub and built-in shelves. Two second-floor family bedrooms share a full bath.

TWO-STORY TRADITIONAL HOMES

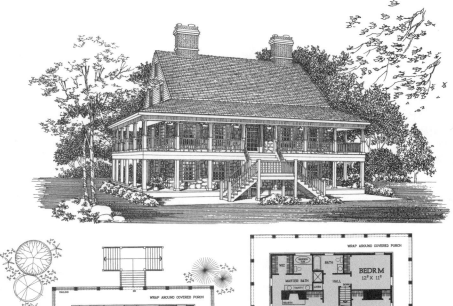

DESIGN 3521

Main Floor: 1,120 square feet
Lower Floor: 1,120 square feet
Total: 2,240 square feet
Bonus Room: 590 square feet

L

This rural Colonial design calls up the charm of simpler times. Wraparound covered porches on both the lower and upper levels invite outdoor living. The foyer leads up to a formal living room as well as to casual areas. A through-hearth warms the living areas, while the den enjoys its own fireplace and built-in cabinetry. The lower floor offers a spacious master suite. Two additional bedrooms share a full bath.

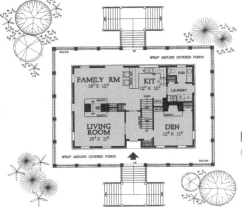

Design by
© Home Planners

Width 52'-0"
Depth 40'-0"

Quote One®
Cost to build? See page 684 to order complete cost estimate to build this house in your area!

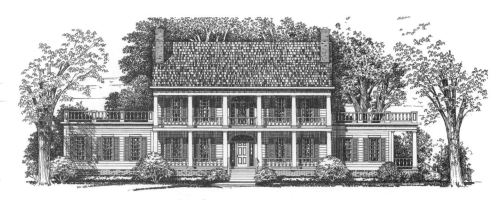

DESIGN 3508

First Floor: 2,098 square feet
Second Floor: 1,735 square feet
Total: 3,833 square feet

L

Make history with this modern version of Louisiana's "Rosedown House." The dining and living rooms flank the foyer—each is highlighted by a fireplace. A library or music room offers a corner fireplace and access to a covered porch. A breakfast area is open to the family room and kitchen. Sleeping quarters upstairs include a master suite with two walk-in closets and private bath, a guest room with a private bath, and a family bedroom and study with a nearby hall bath.

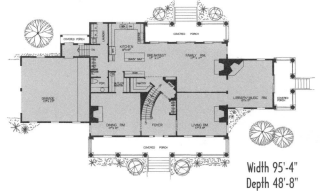

Quote One®
Cost to build? See page 684 to order complete cost estimate to build this house in your area!

Width 95'-4"
Depth 48'-8"

Design by
© Home Planners

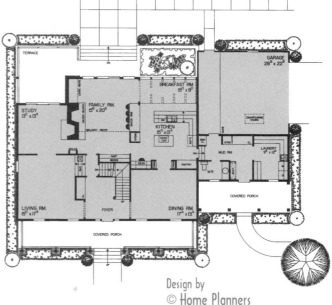

Width 72'-0"
Depth 57'-0"

REAR VIEW

Design by
© Home Planners

This formal two-story home recalls a Louisiana plantation house, Land's End, built in 1857. The Ionic columns of the front porch and the pediment gable echo Greek Revival style. Highlighting the interior is the bright and cheerful spaciousness of the informal family room area. It features a wall of glass stretching to the second-story sloping ceiling. Enhancing the drama of this area is the adjacent glass area of the breakfast room. A huge mudroom and laundry have access to a covered porch. Note the His and Hers areas of the master bedroom. Two second-floor family bedrooms and a hall bath complete the plan.

DESIGN 2981
First Floor: 2,104 square feet
Second Floor: 2,015 square feet
Total: 4,119 square feet

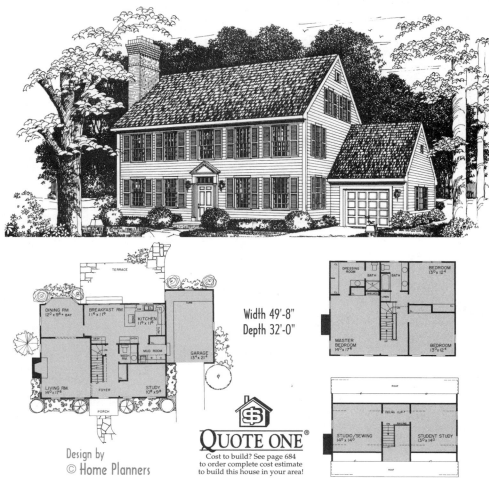

DESIGN 2659

First Floor: 1,023 square feet
Second Floor: 1,008 square feet
Third Floor: 476 square feet
Total: 2,507 square feet

L D

The facade of this three-story, pitch-roofed house has a symmetrical placement of windows and a restrained but elegant central entrance. The central hall expands midway through the house to a family kitchen. Off the foyer are two rooms, a living room with a fireplace and a study. The windowed third-floor attic can be used as a study and a studio. Three bedrooms housed on the second floor include a deluxe master suite with a pampering bath.

Width 49'-8"
Depth 32'-0"

Design by
© Home Planners

QUOTE ONE®
Cost to build? See page 684
to order complete cost estimate
to build this house in your area!

DESIGN 9239

First Floor: 998 square feet
Second Floor: 1,206 square feet
Total: 2,204 square feet

The bright entry of this two-story home opens to the formal living and dining space. To the back is the more informal family room with a fireplace and built-in bookshelves. An island kitchen features a corner sink, pantry and convenient planning desk. Upstairs, the master bedroom has a vaulted ceiling and a sumptuous master bath with a skylit dressing area, whirlpool tub and walk-in closet. Three family bedrooms and a full bath round out sleeping accommodations.

Design by
© Design Basics, Inc.

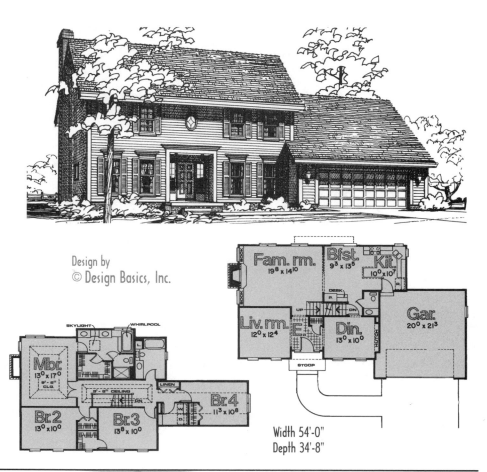

Width 54'-0"
Depth 34'-8"

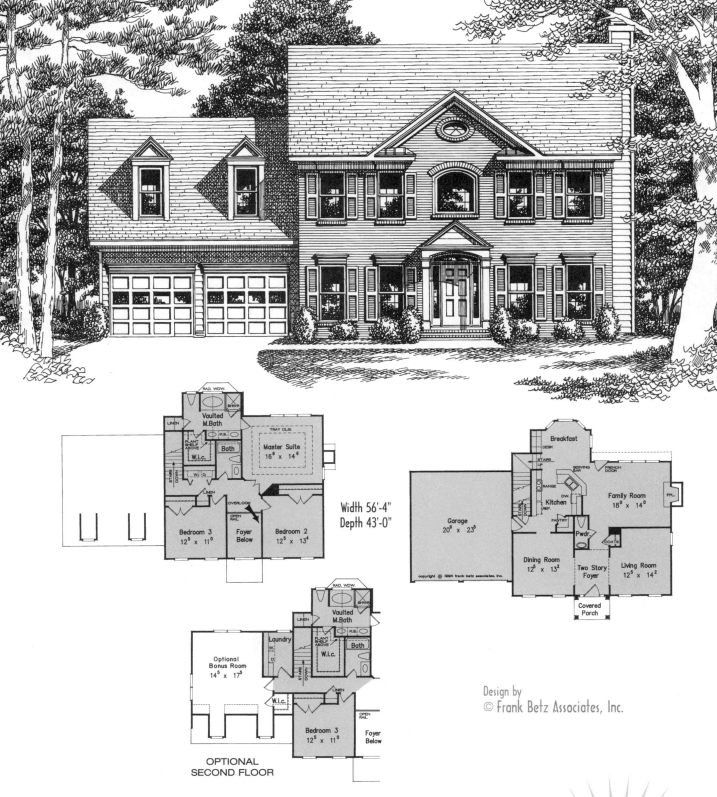

Width 56'-4"
Depth 43'-0"

Master Suite 16⁶ x 14⁶

Bedroom 3 12⁵ x 11⁰

Bedroom 2 12⁵ x 13⁴

Garage 20⁹ x 23⁵

Breakfast

Family Room 18⁰ x 14⁰

Dining Room 12⁵ x 13²

Living Room 12⁵ x 14²

Two Story Foyer

Covered Porch

Optional Bonus Room 14⁵ x 17⁵

Bedroom 3 12⁵ x 11⁰

OPTIONAL SECOND FLOOR

Design by
© Frank Betz Associates, Inc.

TWO-STORY TRADITIONAL HOMES

Two upper-level floor-plan options are included with this delightful design. Both options include space for two family bedrooms, a full bath and a master suite with a tray ceiling and a lavish master bath with a bay-windowed tub. The second option adds an upper-level laundry room and a bonus room with a walk-in closet. Downstairs, the large family room, bayed breakfast room and efficient kitchen cater to comfort. A formal dining room and a formal living room complete this plan. The two-car garage connects to the main house at the service entry. Please specify basement or crawlspace foundation when ordering.

DESIGN P134
First Floor: 1,068 square feet
Second Floor: 977 square feet
Total: 2,045 square feet
Bonus Room: 412 square feet

© American Home Gallery, Ltd.

DESIGN T082

First Floor: 1,165 square feet
Second Floor: 1,050 square feet
Total: 2,215 square feet

Classic design knows no boundaries in this gracious two-story home. From the formal living and dining areas to the more casual family room, it handles any occasion with ease. A central fireplace provides a focal point in the family room. Of special note on the first floor are the L-shaped kitchen with attached breakfast area and the guest-pampering half bath. Upstairs are three bedrooms, including a master suite with a fine bath and a walk-in closet. This home is designed with a basement foundation.

Design by
© Stephen Fuller,
American Home Gallery

Width 58'-0"
Depth 36'-0"

QUOTE ONE®
Cost to build? See page 684
to order complete cost estimate
to build this house in your area!

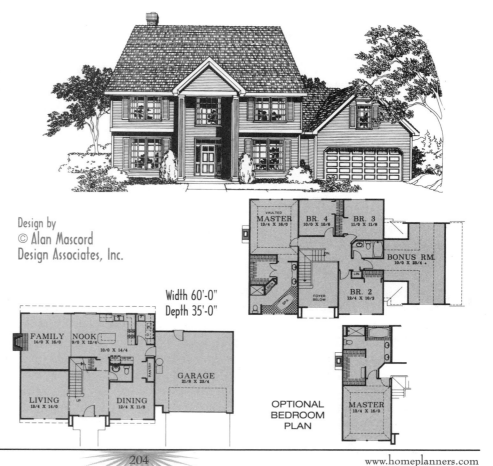

DESIGN 7528

First Floor: 1,167 square feet
Second Floor: 1,080 square feet
Total: 2,247 square feet
Bonus Room: 358 square feet

A two-story pillared portico provides a dramatic entrance to this Colonial-style home. Formal rooms flank the two-story foyer, which leads to informal space at the rear of the plan: a family room with an extended-hearth fireplace, breakfast nook and kitchen with preparation island. Three family bedrooms and a luxurious master suite complete the upper level. Note the alternative layout for the master bedroom.

Design by
© Alan Mascord
Design Associates, Inc.

Width 60'-0"
Depth 35'-0"

OPTIONAL BEDROOM PLAN

TWO-STORY TRADITIONAL HOMES

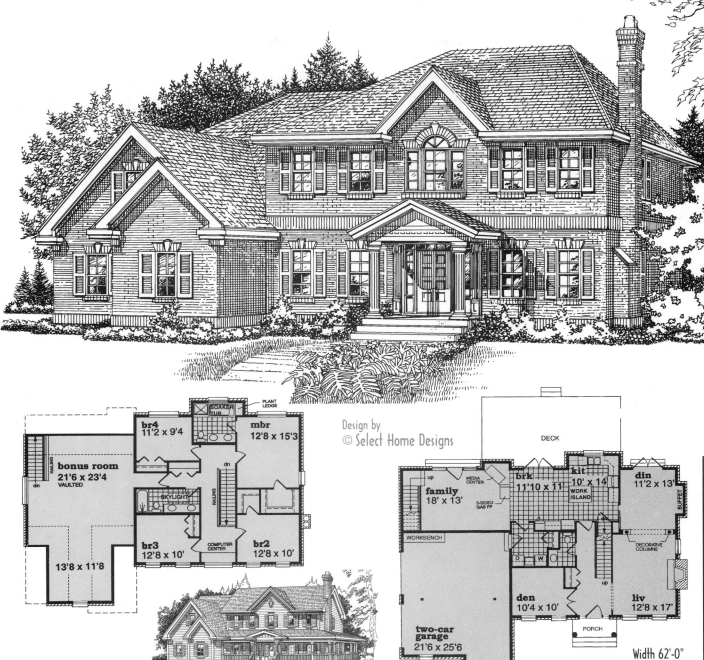

Design by
© Select Home Designs

ALTERNATE FRONT VIEW

Width 62'-0"
Depth 48'-0"

Build this home as a wood-sided farmhouse with wrapping veranda, or as a stately brick traditional home. Plans include details for both facades. Enter the foyer and you'll be greeted by double doors opening to the den on the left and a spacious living room with fireplace on the right. The dining room is separated from the living room by a plant bridge and pair of columns, and has double-door access to the rear yard. The kitchen includes entertainment-sized space with a center work island and an abundance of counter space. The sunny breakfast room provides double doors to the rear deck. The full-sized family room features a three-sided fireplace. A staircase from the family room leads to bonus space over the garage. Four bedrooms on the second floor cluster around a center hall. The master suite and one family bedroom have walk-in closets. Plans include details for both a basement and a crawlspace foundation.

**DESIGN
Q452**
First Floor: 1,452 square feet
Second Floor: 1,100 square feet
Total: 2,552 square feet
Bonus Room: 687 square feet

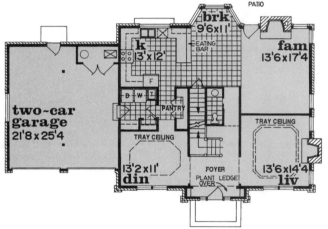

PATIO

brk 9'6"x11'

k 13'x12'

EATING BAR

fam 13'6"x17'4"

two-car garage 21'8 x 25'4

F

D W

PANTRY

TRAY CEILING

TRAY CEILING

13'2"x11' **din**

FOYER PLANT LEDGE OVER

13'6"x14'4" **liv**

Width 60'-8"
Depth 39'-8"

Design by
© Select Home Designs

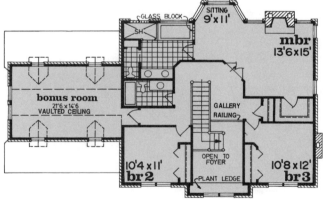

GLASS BLOCK

SITTING 9'x11'

SH

mbr 13'6"x15'

bonus room 21'6 x 14'6 VAULTED CEILING

GALLERY RAILING

OPEN TO FOYER

10'4"x11' **br2**

PLANT LEDGE

10'8"x12' **br3**

**DESIGN
Q410**
First Floor: 1,308 square feet
Second Floor: 1,187 square feet
Total: 2,495 square feet
Bonus Room: 366 square feet

This traditional three-bedroom estate clearly defines formal and informal living areas. Tray ceilings add architectural interest to the dining room and living room. The living room and family room feature fireplaces. The open kitchen design contains a U-shaped workspace with a snack bar and a breakfast bay overlooking the rear patio. On the second floor, a gallery offers access to the bedrooms and a bonus room with vaulted ceiling. Develop the bonus space later, if you wish, to provide more bedrooms or a private office. The master suite is filled with natural light from the full wall of glass, interrupted only by a wood-burning fireplace. Glass-block detailing adds light to the master bath over the whirlpool tub. The family bedrooms share a bath and have large wall closets.

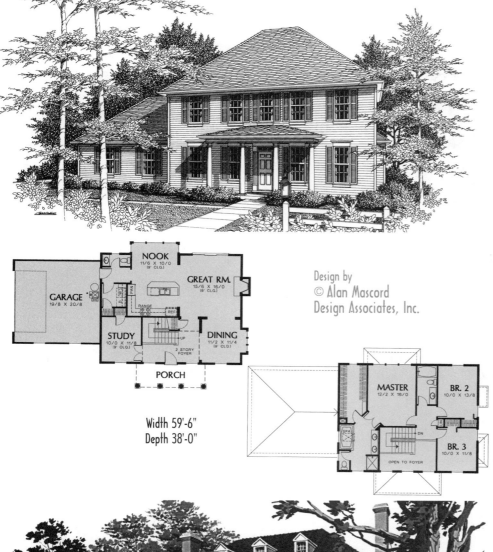

DESIGN 7524

First Floor: 1,102 square feet
Second Floor: 888 square feet
Total: 1,990 square feet

The beautiful Georgian facade of this design is typically called "five over four and a door," describing the arrangement of windows. An elegant porch supported by columns leads to the front door and an entry flanked by the formal dining room and a study. Casual living takes place directly ahead in the spacious great room with fireplace, the rear-facing breakfast nook and roomy kitchen. Upstairs, a lavish main suite includes an extra large walk-in closet and a sumptuous bath. Two family bedrooms share a full hall bath.

Design by
© Alan Mascord
Design Associates, Inc.

Width 59'-6"
Depth 38'-0"

DESIGN 2192

First Floor: 1,884 square feet
Second Floor: 1,521 square feet
Total: 3,405 square feet
Bonus Room: 808 square feet

L D

This is surely a fine adaptation from the 18th Century, when formality and elegance were bywords. Inside, the formal living room features a corner fireplace. A second fireplace is found in the family room. Built-in amenities include a wall of bookshelves and cabinets in the library, corner china cabinets in the formal dining room and cabinets in both passages to the family room. Two family bedrooms share a hall bath on the second floor while the master bedroom offers a private bath.

Design by
© Home Planners

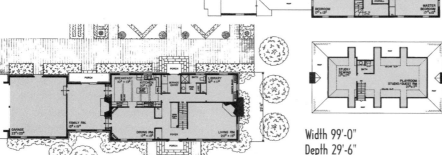

Width 99'-0"
Depth 29'-6"

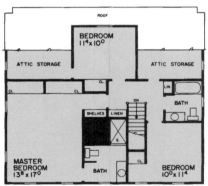

Design by
© Home Planners

REAR VIEW

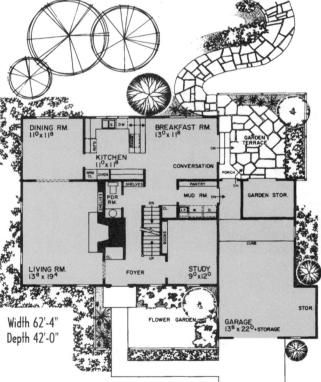

Width 62'-4"
Depth 42'-0"

DESIGN 2654

First Floor: 1,152 square feet
Second Floor: 844 square feet
Total: 1,996 square feet

This is certainly an authentic traditional saltbox. It features a symmetrical design with a center fireplace, a wide, paneled doorway and multi-paned, double-hung windows. Tucked behind the one-car garage is a garden shed that provides work and storage space. The breakfast room features French doors that open to a flagstone terrace. The U-shaped kitchen has built-in counters that make efficient use of space. The second floor plan houses three bedrooms.

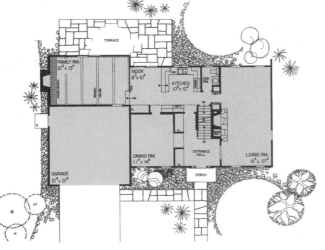

Width 59'-8"
Depth 36'-0"

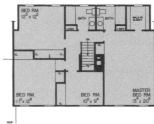

Design by
© Home Planners

DESIGN 2623

First Floor: 1,368 square feet
Second Floor: 1,046 square feet
Total: 2,414 square feet

L D

A center-hall Colonial, this gracious home is enhanced by a saltbox roofline, multi-pane windows and sidelights at the front door. Inside, the main hall leads to a grand-sized living room on the right and formal dining room on the left. The living room has a fireplace with wood box and lots of natural light. The kitchen attaches to a breakfast nook, which then leads to a sunken family room with a fireplace. The second floor holds three family bedrooms and a master suite with a walk-in closet and full bath.

Width 71'-0"
Depth 34'-0"

Design by
© Home Planners

DESIGN 2538

First Floor: 1,503 square feet
Second Floor: 1,095 square feet
Total: 2,598 square feet

L D

This Saltbox provides great livability for the growing family. The spacious entry opens to the second-floor balcony. Living areas include a formal living room and dining room, a private study and family room with raised-hearth fireplace. The grand kitchen offers an island range and attached nook with sliding glass doors to the terrace. The second-floor master suite contains its own fireplace and a large walk-in closet in the dressing area. Three more bedrooms share a full bath.

TWO-STORY TRADITIONAL HOMES

DESIGN 2639

First Floor: 1,556 square feet
Second Floor: 1,428 square feet
Total: 2,984 square feet

L D

Here is a New England Georgian adaptation with an elevated doorway highlighted by pilasters and a pediment. It gives way to a second-story Palladian window, capped by a pediment projecting from the hipped roof. Inside, both the formal living room and the formal dining room are warmed by fireplaces. Openness is the key to the layout of the U-shaped kitchen, breakfast nook and family room. Upstairs, three family bedrooms share a full hall bath, while the master suite has its own bath.

Design by
© Home Planners

Width 74'-0"
Depth 34'-0"

DESIGN 2979

First Floor: 1,440 square feet
Second Floor: 1,394 square feet
Total: 2,834 square feet

Perfect for a narrow site, this historic adaptation is in "temple form"—the gable end of the house faces the street, as in a Greek temple. Three chimneys support four fireplaces—in the living room, study, kitchen and master bedroom. Family members and guests will love the huge country kitchen, with room for relaxing, a snack bar for quick meals and access to the terrace. The master suite offers a deluxe bath and a private balcony. Three bedrooms and two full baths complete the plan.

Design by
© Home Planners

Width 38'-0"
Depth 62'-0"

Design by
© Home Planners

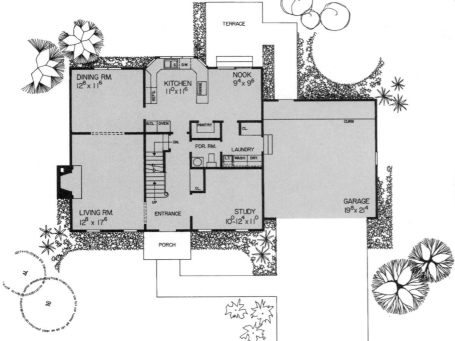

Width 54'-0"
Depth 30'-0"

Affordable style is the hallmark of this Colonial design. The U-shaped kitchen with large pantry and adjacent breakfast nook is the very heart of the plan. Placed conveniently nearby is a formal dining room. The living room with fireplace, first-floor study and efficient service area round out the ground level. The second floor features a sizable master suite complete with twin vanities and roomy walk-in closet. Family bedrooms share a full bath.

DESIGN
2731
First Floor: 1,039 square feet
Second Floor: 973 square feet
Total: 2,012 square feet

DESIGN 9344

First Floor: 1,000 square feet
Second Floor: 1,345 square feet
Total: 2,345 square feet

An arched entry, shutters and a brick facade highlight the exterior of this modern, two-story Colonial home. Living and dining rooms at the front of the plan accommodate formal occasions. The rear of the plan is designed for informal gatherings, with a generous family room, a bright breakfast area and a well-equipped U-shaped kitchen with snack bar. Bright windows and French doors add appeal to the living room. Upstairs, a U-shaped balcony hall overlooks the entry below and connects four bedrooms, including the master suite.

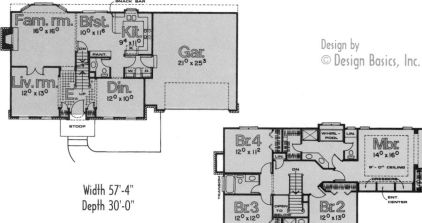

Width 57'-4"
Depth 30'-0"

Design by
© Design Basics, Inc.

DESIGN 9343

First Floor: 1,000 square feet
Second Floor: 993 square feet
Total: 1,993 square feet

At less than 2,000 square feet, this plan captures the heritage and romance of an authentic Colonial home with many modern amenities. A central hall leads to the formal rooms at the front where showpiece furnishings can be displayed. A bookcase and large linen cabinet are thoughtful touches upstairs. Further evidence of tasteful design is shown in the master suite. A volume ceiling, large walk-in closet and whirlpool tub await the fortunate homeowner. Each secondary bedroom has bright windows to add natural lighting and comfort.

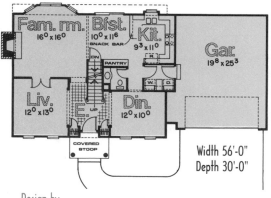

Width 56'-0"
Depth 30'-0"

Design by
© Design Basics, Inc.

Quote One®
Cost to build? See page 684
to order complete cost estimate
to build this house in your area!

www.homeplanners.com

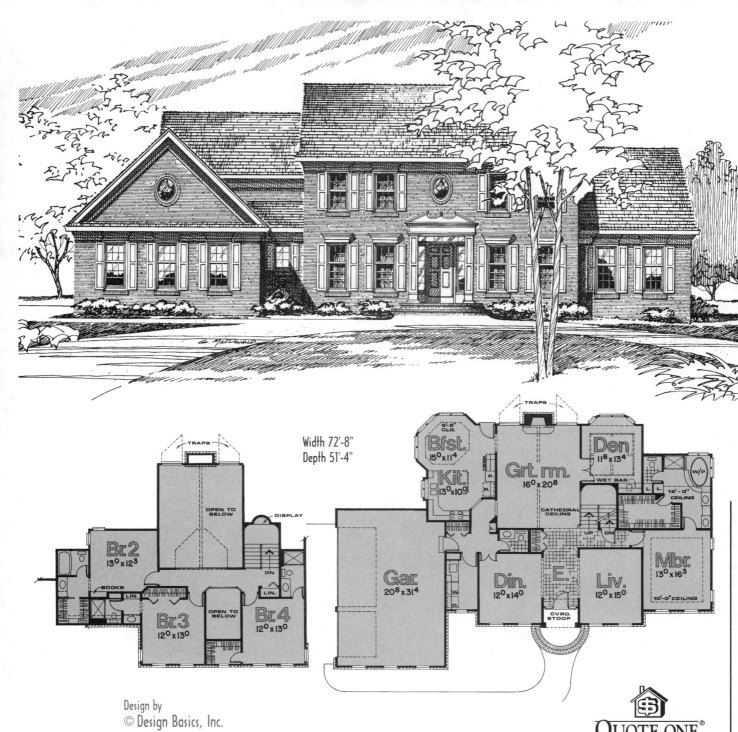

Width 72'-8"
Depth 51'-4"

Design by
© Design Basics, Inc.

An elegant brick elevation and rows of shuttered windows lend timeless beauty to this two-story Colonial design. The volume entry opens to the formal dining and living rooms and the magnificent great room. Sparkling floor-to-ceiling windows flank the fireplace in the great room, which offers a cathedral ceiling. French doors, bayed windows and a decorative ceiling, plus a wet bar highlight the private den. Special lifestyle amenities in the kitchen and bayed breakfast area include a built-in desk, wrapping counters and island. A boxed ceiling adds elegance to the master suite. In the master bath/dressing area, note the large walk-in closet, built-in dresser, His and Hers vanities, oval whirlpool tub and plant shelves. Each secondary bedroom upstairs has a roomy closet and private bath. A three-car garage sits to the side of the plan.

DESIGN 9299

First Floor: 2,063 square feet
Second Floor: 894 square feet
Total: 2,957 square feet

TWO-STORY TRADITIONAL HOMES

Width 56'-4"
Depth 30'-0"

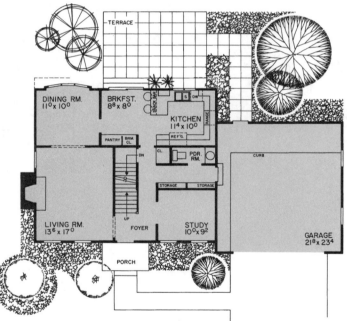

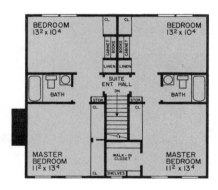

Design by
© Home Planners

DESIGN 2870
First Floor: 900 square feet
Second Floor: 960 square feet
Total: 1,860 square feet

This Colonial home was designed to provide comfortable living space for two families. The first floor is the common living space. To the left of the foyer, a spacious living room with a cheery fireplace offers a warm welcome. The adjacent dining room is drenched in sunlight from bowed windows. Thoughtful planning makes its way to the breakfast area, combined with an efficient kitchen featuring a window above the sink and a snack bar. A handy powder room and a quiet study complete this floor. Upstairs—with areas that could split into two "suites"—four bedrooms include two that could serve as master bedrooms. The remaining two bedrooms feature built-ins, and two full baths assure convenience. A two-car garage connects at the service entrance.

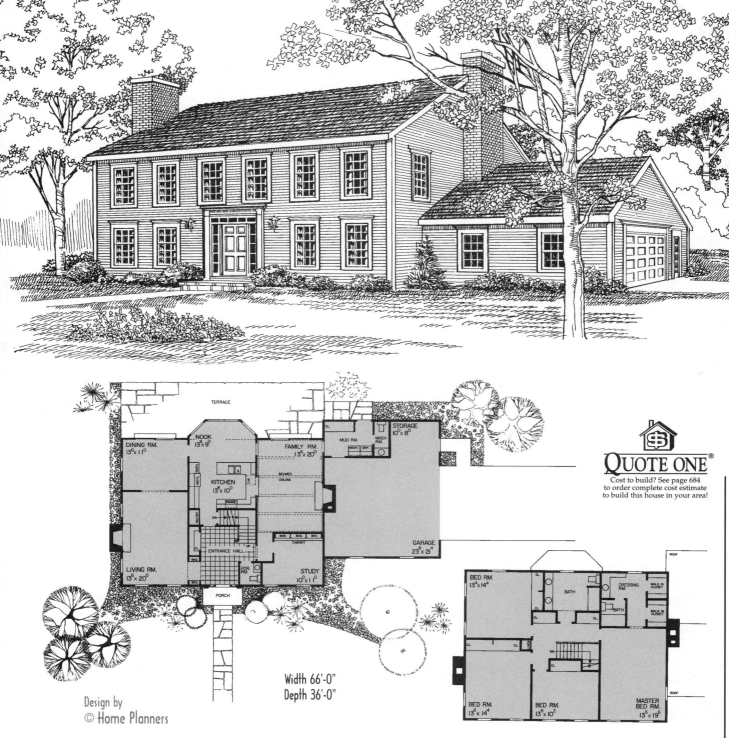

Width 66'-0"
Depth 36'-0"

Design by
© Home Planners

TWO-STORY TRADITIONAL HOMES

This full, two-story traditional home will be noteworthy wherever it is built. The front entrance detail is inviting. The narrow horizontal siding and the corner boards are appealing as are the two massive chimneys. The center entrance hall provides a handy powder room nearby. The study contains built-in bookshelves and offers a full measure of privacy. The interior kitchen has a pass-through to the family room and enjoys natural light from the bay-windowed nook. A beam ceiling, fireplace and sliding glass doors are features of the family room. The mudroom highlights a closet, laundry equipment and an extra washroom. Study the upstairs with those four bedrooms, two baths and plenty of closet space. The master suite has a private bath with dressing area.

DESIGN 2610
First Floor: 1,505 square feet
Second Floor: 1,344 square feet
Total: 2,849 square feet
L D

DESIGN Q232

First Floor: 1,146 square feet
Second Floor: 1,117 square feet
Total: 2,263 square feet

Twin bay windows adorn the living and dining rooms of this stately brick design. Enter through double doors into a skylit foyer that boasts a sweeping, curved staircase. To the rear of the plan, the spacious family room features an imposing fireplace with a raised hearth and log storage. Upstairs, the master bedroom is highlighted by a dressing room and private bath. Three family bedrooms share the main bathroom, which boasts a luxurious raised whirlpool spa and twin vanity.

Width 50'-0"
Depth 32'-8"

Design by
© Select Home Designs

DESIGN P119

First Floor: 1,424 square feet
Second Floor: 1,256 square feet
Total: 2,680 square feet

An elegant arch-top clerestory and a box-bay window set off this understated European adaptation, and introduce an interior assigned with a wealth of amenities. Formal rooms enjoy boxed columns with shelves for curios and books, while the family room boasts a vaulted ceiling and an extended-hearth fireplace. An elegant master suite shares the second floor with three family bedrooms and a convenient laundry. Please specify basement or crawlspace foundation when ordering.

Design by
© Frank Betz Associates, Inc.

Width 57'-0"
Depth 41'-0"

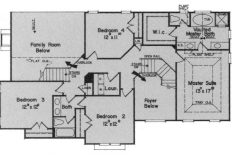

QUOTE ONE®
Cost to build? See page 684 to order complete cost estimate to build this house in your area!

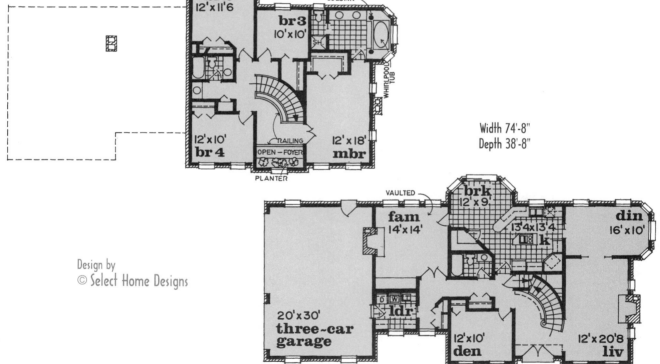

br2
12' x 11'6"

DECORATIVE COLUMN

br3
10' x 10'

WHIRLPOOL TUB

12' x 10'
br4

RAILING

OPEN - FOYER

12' x 18'
mbr

PLANTER

Width 74'-8"
Depth 38'-8"

Design by
© Select Home Designs

VAULTED

brk
12' x 9'

fam
14' x 14'

13'4" x 13'4"

k

din
16' x 10'

20' x 30'
three-car garage

ldr

D W

12' x 10'
den

12' x 20'8"
liv

T his stately design features classic exterior details: circle-head windows, an arched entry, shutters, corner quoins and brick veneer. The living room contains a fireplace and pocket doors that lead to the formal dining room. The den is to the front of the plan, across from a full bath. The vaulted family room offers a fireplace and an audio-visual center. The kitchen is styled for gourmets with a walk-in pantry, center cooking island and peninsular counter separating the kitchen and the breakfast bay. Four second-floor bedrooms include three family bedrooms with a shared full bath. The master suite features a walk-in closet and a bath with a separate shower, double-bowl vanity and whirlpool tub accented by columns. Plans include details for both a basement and crawlspace foundation.

DESIGN Q301
First Floor: 1,580 square feet
Second Floor: 1,232 square feet
Total: 2,812 square feet

TWO-STORY TRADITIONAL HOMES

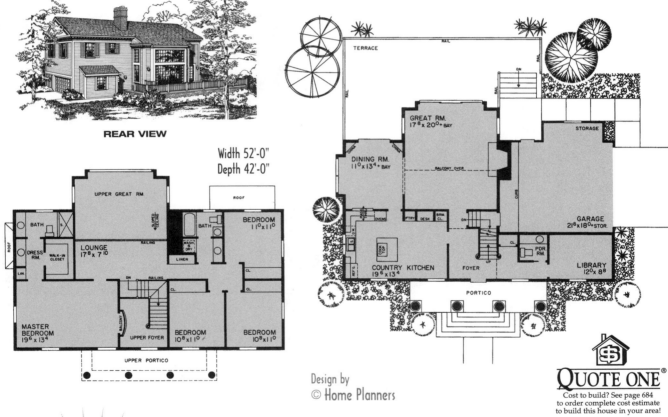

REAR VIEW

Width 52'-0"
Depth 42'-0"

Design by
© Home Planners

Quote One®
Cost to build? See page 684
to order complete cost estimate
to build this house in your area!

DESIGN 2668
First Floor: 1,206 square feet
Second Floor: 1,254 square feet
Total: 2,460 square feet

L

This elegant exterior houses a very livable plan. Every bit of space has been put to good use. The front country kitchen is a good place to begin. It is efficiently planned with its island cooktop, pantry, desk and pass-through to the dining room. The large great room will be the center of all family activities. It features a fireplace and sliding glass doors to a terrace. Quiet times can be enjoyed in the front library. The second floor contains the sleeping zone made up of three family bedrooms and a grand master suite with a balcony over the foyer.

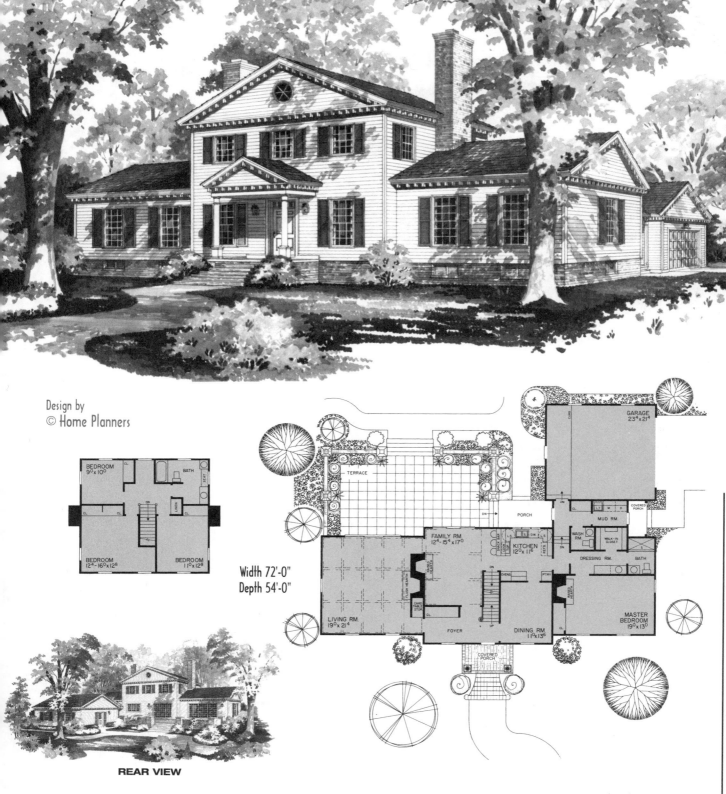

Design by
© Home Planners

Width 72'-0"
Depth 54'-0"

REAR VIEW

Two one-story wings flank the two-story center section of this design, which echoes the architectural forms of 18th-Century Tidewater Virginia. The left wing is a huge living room; the right, the master bedroom suite, service area and garage. The kitchen, dining room and family room are centrally located on the first floor. Special touches here include a raised-hearth fireplace in the family room, a convenient coat closet in the foyer, and stacked ovens, two lazy Susans and a snack bar in the kitchen. Upstairs, three family bedrooms share a full hall bath that has twin vanities and a window seat.

DESIGN 2667
First Floor: 1,827 square feet
Second Floor: 697 square feet
Total: 2,524 square feet

L

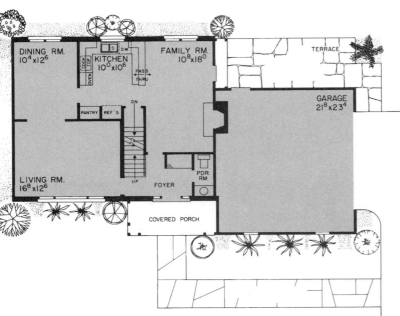

TERRACE

DINING RM.
10⁴x12⁶

KITCHEN
10⁰x10⁶

FAMILY RM.
10⁸x18⁰

PASS THRU

GARAGE
21⁸x23⁴

PANTRY   REF'G

DN

LIVING RM.
16⁸x12⁶

CL.

PDR. RM.

UP   FOYER

COVERED PORCH

Width 54'-0"
Depth 32'-5"

BEDROOM
10⁰x11⁰

BEDROOM
8⁶x10⁰

BEDROOM
10⁰x10⁰

ROOF

CL

LINEN   CL

BATH

MASTER BEDROOM
11⁴x13¹⁰

DN

BEDROOM
10⁸x12⁴

BATH

ROOF

Design by
© Home Planners

DESIGN 1318

First Floor: 854 square feet
Second Floor: 896 square feet
Total: 1,750 square feet

Multi-pane windows, shutters and a covered porch combine to give this warm Colonial a welcoming appeal. The foyer offers a coat closet and a powder room. The huge formal living room just off the foyer connects to the formal dining room for ease in entertaining. The U-shaped kitchen, with pantry and window sink, works well with the large family room via a pass-through. The family room also has a warming fireplace and access to the large flagstone terrace in the rear of the plan. Upstairs, four family bedrooms share a full hall bath and a linen closet. The master suite offers its own bath for privacy. A two-car garage loads from the side to keep the facade true to its Colonial heritage.

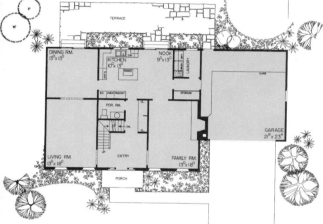

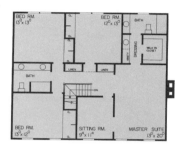

Width 62'-0"
Depth 32'-4"

Design by
© Home Planners

DESIGN 2540

First Floor: 1,306 square feet
Second Floor: 1,360 square feet
Total: 2,666 square feet

L D

This comfortable Colonial home puts a good foot forward in family living. The wide entry hall graciously receives guests. Flanking it are the family room with fireplace and the formal living room. A dining room leads directly to the L-shaped kitchen with island range. A handy utility area features washer/dryer space and storage and has an exterior door to the two-car garage. Upstairs are four bedrooms with two full baths. The master bedroom holds a sitting room, dressing area, walk-in closet and bath with dual vanities.

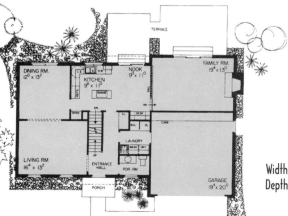

Width 54'-0"
Depth 33'-0"

Design by
© Home Planners

DESIGN 2733

First Floor: 1,177 square feet
Second Floor: 1,003 square feet
Total: 2,180 square feet

L D

This four-bedroom Colonial home is both charming and livable. The first floor holds living and working areas—both formal and informal. The kitchen features an island range and other built-ins. All will enjoy the sunken family room with its fireplace and sliding glass doors leading to the terrace. A basement provides room for recreational activities while the laundry remains on the first floor for extra convenience. Second-floor bedrooms include a master suite with double-bowl vanity, and three family bedrooms share a full bath.

QUOTE ONE®
Cost to build? See page 684
to order complete cost estimate
to build this house in your area!

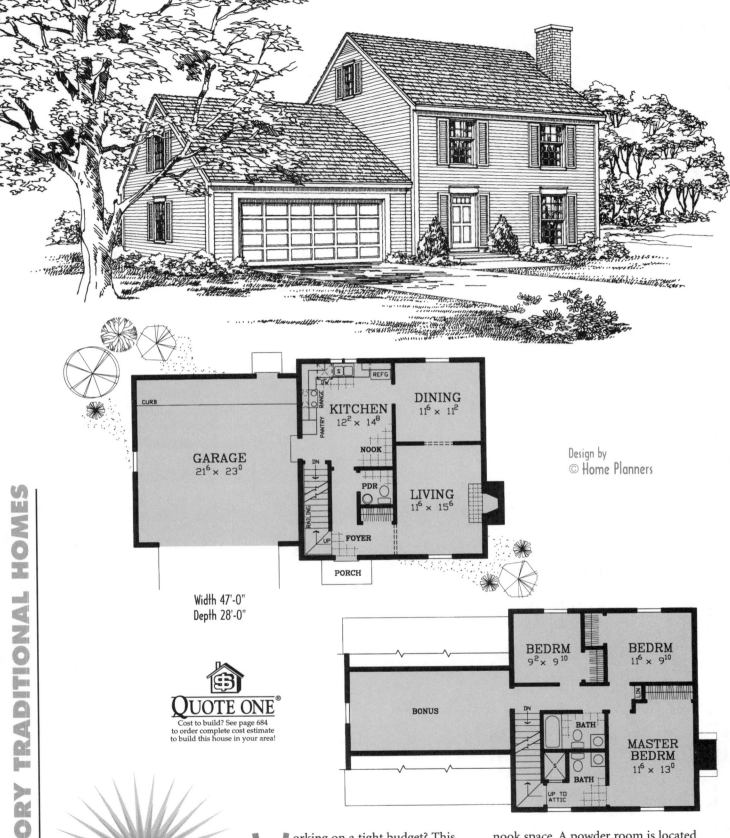

GARAGE
21⁶ × 23⁰

CURB

KITCHEN
12² × 14⁸

DINING
11⁶ × 11²

PANTRY

RANGE

DW

REFG

S

NOOK

PDR

LIVING
11⁶ × 15⁶

DN

RAILING

UP

FOYER

PORCH

Design by
© Home Planners

Width 47'-0"
Depth 28'-0"

BEDRM
9² × 9¹⁰

BEDRM
11⁶ × 9¹⁰

BONUS

DN

BATH

LIN

MASTER BEDRM
11⁶ × 13⁰

BATH

S

UP TO ATTIC

QUOTE ONE®
Cost to build? See page 684
to order complete cost estimate
to build this house in your area!

DESIGN 2622
First Floor: 700 square feet
Second Floor: 700 square feet
Total: 1,400 square feet
Bonus Room: 268 square feet

L D

Working on a tight budget? This Colonial adaptation provides a functional design that allows for expansion in the future. Note the cozy fireplace in the living room and roomy L-shaped kitchen with breakfast-nook space. A powder room is located conveniently nearby. The second-floor holds two bedrooms, a full bath and master bedroom with attached bath. A large storage area over the two-car garage can become a bedroom with attached bath.

Width 50'-0"
Depth 34'-10"

Design by
© Home Planners

QUOTE ONE®
Cost to build? See page 684
to order complete cost estimate
to build this house in your area!

ALTERNATE VIEWS

When you order blueprints for this design you will receive details for the construction of each of the three charming exteriors pictured. Whichever exterior you finally decide to build, the floor plan will be essentially the same except for the location of the windows. The first floor contains a living room, dining room and U-shaped kitchen with breakfast area. A beamed ceiling and a fireplace highlight the family room. There are four bedrooms and two full baths upstairs.

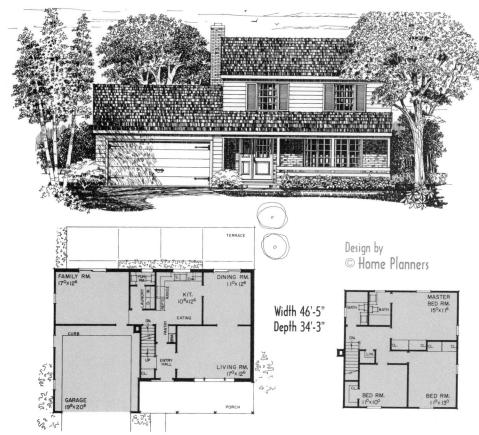

Design by
© Home Planners

Width 46'-5"
Depth 34'-3"

DESIGN 1361

First Floor: 965 square feet
Second Floor: 740 square feet
Total: 1,705 square feet

L D

An abundance of livability is offered by this charming, traditional adaptation. The entry hall gives way to a central, L-shaped kitchen. The formal dining room opens to the right. The spacious living room affords many different furniture arrangements. In the family room, casual living takes off with direct access to the rear terrace. Note the first-floor laundry conveniently located near the kitchen. Upstairs, three bedrooms include a master bedroom with a private bath. One of the secondary bedrooms features a walk-in closet.

TWO-STORY TRADITIONAL HOMES

DESIGN 1868

First Floor: 1,190 square feet
Second Floor: 1,300 square feet
Total: 2,490 square feet

A five-bedroom farmhouse adaptation is truly a home for family living. The formal living room flanks the foyer and opens to the formal dining room. The sunken family room contains a fireplace to warm casual gatherings and sliding glass doors for outdoor livability. The U-shaped kitchen serves both the formal dining room and the breakfast room with ease. Four family bedrooms on the second floor include one with its own bath. Note the grand master bedroom suite.

Width 54'-5"
Depth 34'-10"

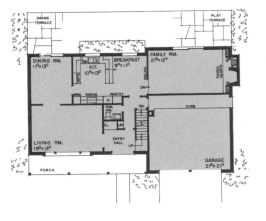

Design by
© Home Planners

DESIGN 5541

First Floor: 1,179 square feet
Second Floor: 1,120 square feet
Total: 2,299 square feet

A covered porch and multi-paned windows draw attention to this four-bedroom farmhouse. The foyer leads to the media room or straight ahead to the kitchen. The breakfast nook, with a snack bar, opens to the rear patio. Laundry facilities are on the second floor, where three family bedrooms—two of them with window seats—share a bath that offers a double-bowl vanity. The master suite provides a walk-in closet and a private bath that has a corner tub and separate vanities.

Design by
© Home Planners

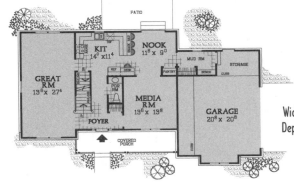

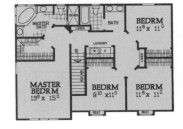

Width 61'-8"
Depth 35'-8"

QUOTE ONE®
Cost to build? See page 684
to order complete cost estimate
to build this house in your area!

www.homeplanners.com

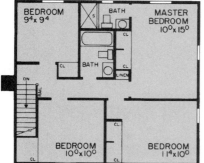

BEDROOM
9⁴ x 9⁴
BATH
MASTER BEDROOM
10⁰ x 15⁰
BEDROOM
10⁰ x 10⁰
BEDROOM
11⁴ x 10⁰

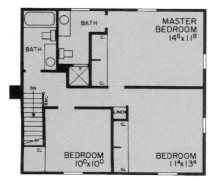

BATH
MASTER BEDROOM
14⁸ x 11⁸
BEDROOM
10⁰ x 10⁰
BEDROOM
11⁴ x 13⁴

**OPTIONAL
THREE-BEDROOM LAYOUT**

TERRACE

FAMILY RM.
19⁴ x 12⁰

BRKFST.
7⁶ x 11²

KITCHEN
9⁶ x 11²

DINING RM.
10⁰ x 11²

PDR RM

LIVING RM.
16⁰ x 13²

FOYER

GARAGE
19⁴ x 21⁰

COVERED PORCH

Width 48'-0"
Depth 34'-10"

Design by
© Home Planners

Simple, functional and loaded with Colonial appeal, this versatile two-story plan features the finest in family floor plans. The entry foyer offers a powder room for guests and a staircase to the second floor. A large formal living room connects to the dining room, allowing adequate space for entertaining in style. The U-shaped kitchen features a pass-through counter to the breakfast room. The sunken family room is enhanced by a beam ceiling, raised-hearth fireplace and built-in bookshelves. Two plans are available for the second floor: one with three bedrooms and one with four. Either option allows for a master bedroom with a private bath and family bedrooms with shared bath. Other highlights of the plan include a full-length rear terrace and extra storage space.

**DESIGN
1956**
First Floor: 990 square feet
Second Floor: 728 square feet
Total: 1,718 square feet

D

Width 54'-0"
Depth 42'-0"

Fam. rm.
15⁰ x 19⁶

Bfst.
11⁶ x 13⁶

Kit.
10⁰ x 13⁴

DESK   SNACK BAR

P.   R.

SALAD SINK

DN

Liv. rm.
12⁸ x 15²

UP

Dn.
12⁰ x 13⁰

HUTCH

STORAGE

Gar.
19⁴ x 26⁰

COVERED PORCH

WHIRL-POOL

LIN.

Br.
11⁰ x 11⁶

Br.
12⁰ x 11⁶

DN

Mbr.
12⁸ x 15¹⁰

11'-0"
CEILING

PLANTS
OPEN
TO
BELOW

Br.
11⁰ x 11

Design by
© Design Basics, Inc.

DESIGN
9230
First Floor: 1,303 square feet
Second Floor: 1,084 square feet
Total: 2,387 square feet

It's hard to get beyond the covered front porch of this home, but doing so reveals a bright two-story entry open to the central hall. Just to the left, an enticing bay window enlivens the living room featuring French doors that connect to the family room. The efficient kitchen with snack bar and pantry is open to the bay-windowed breakfast area with planning desk. The salad sink and counter space double as a service for the formal dining room. The second-floor master bedroom features a raised ceiling and arched window. Its adjoining bath contains a walk-through closet/transition area and a corner whirlpool tub. Three family bedrooms and a hall bath complete this level.

www.homeplanners.com

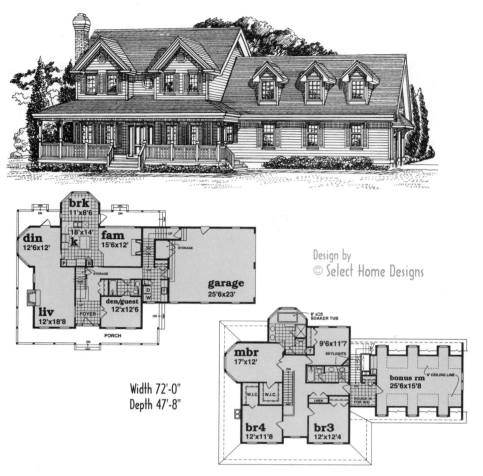

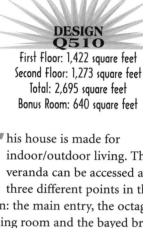

DESIGN Q510

First Floor: 1,422 square feet
Second Floor: 1,273 square feet
Total: 2,695 square feet
Bonus Room: 640 square feet

This house is made for indoor/outdoor living. The veranda can be accessed at three different points in the plan: the main entry, the octagonal dining room and the bayed breakfast room. Both the living room and the family room are warmed by hearths; the den has access to a full bath so it can easily double as a guest room. Four bedrooms on the second floor include a master suite with a lavish bath. Both the master bedroom and Bedroom 4 have walk-in closets. Plans include details for both a basement and a crawlspace foundation.

Design by
© Select Home Designs

Width 72'-0"
Depth 47'-8"

DESIGN T049

First Floor: 2,078 square feet
Second Floor: 896 square feet
Total: 2,974 square feet

This Georgian country-style home displays an impressive appearance. Columns frame both the living and dining rooms, while the living room features its own fireplace. The foyer opens onto the two-story great room with built-in cabinetry, a fireplace and a large bay window overlooking the rear deck. A dramatic tray ceiling, a wall of glass and access to the rear deck complete the master bedroom. Each of three upstairs bedrooms features direct access to a bathroom. This home is designed with a basement foundation.

Width 69'-9"
Depth 65'-0"

Design by
© Stephen Fuller,
American Home Gallery

Quote One®
Cost to build? See page 684
to order complete cost estimate
to build this house in your area!

Two-Story Traditional Homes

DESIGN C108

First Floor: 1,360 square feet
Second Floor: 1,310 square feet
Total: 2,670 square feet
Bonus Room: 349 square feet

American tradition and styling welcome you to this beautiful home with round porch columns, louvered vents and double-hung windows. Inside, an open floor plan is perfect for today's way of life. The family room, kitchen and dinette join to form a huge living area. Columns and a bay window accent the formal living room. The second floor boasts four large bedrooms including the deluxe master suite, which features an octagonal sitting nook.

Design by
© James Fahy Design

Width 62'-0"
Depth 44'-4"

DESIGN P267

First Floor: 1,428 square feet
Second Floor: 1,000 square feet
Total: 2,428 square feet

Clapboard siding enjoys a partnership with classic brick accents on this new traditional design. The foyer opens to the formal rooms and leads to an expansive, two-story family room made cozy by an extended-hearth fireplace. The second-floor master suite holds a box-bay window with a seat, and an interior French door that leads to a lavish vaulted bath. A balcony hall overlooks the family room and the foyer. Please specify crawlspace or basement foundation when ordering.

Design by
© Frank Betz Associates, Inc.

Width 61'-0"
Depth 41'-0"

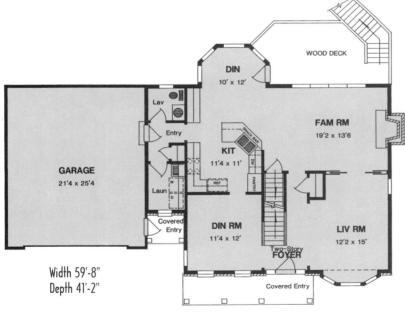

DIN
10' x 12'

WOOD DECK

Lav

Entry

FAM RM
19'2 x 13'6

KIT
11'4 x 11'

GARAGE
21'4 x 25'4

Laun
W
D
REF

DIN RM
11'4 x 12'

LIV RM
12'2 x 15'

Covered Entry

Two-Story
FOYER

Covered Entry

Width 59'-8"
Depth 41'-2"

Design by
© James Fahy Design

BR3
10' x 11'8

BR4
10'2 x 10'4

MBATH

BATH 2

Balcony

W/Closet

BR2
11' 6 x 10'11

Foyer Below

MBR
12'2 x 14'2

PLANT SHELF

Traditional elements invite you to feel right at home in this charming two-story home. Stately porch columns, wood shutters and third-floor dormers help make up its appeal. Once inside, you'll enjoy the bay window lighting the living room and the fireplace and deck access in the family room. The large family room also opens to the kitchen with snack bar and octagonal dinette, perfect for today's family. The second floor offers four bedrooms and two full baths. A plant shelf and window highlight the two-story foyer. The two-car garage, the laundry area and a nearby powder room complete the plan.

DESIGN C113

First Floor: 1,160 square feet
Second Floor: 997 square feet
Total: 2,157 square feet

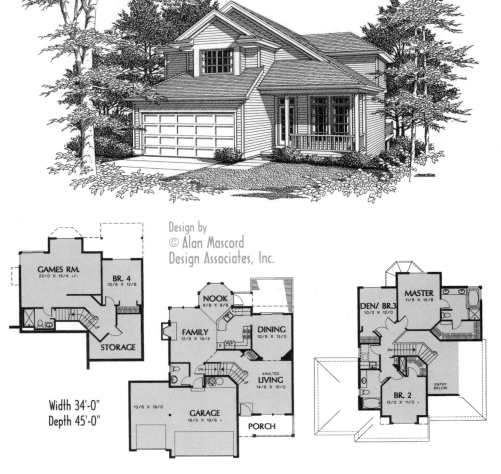

DESIGN 7435

First Floor: 920 square feet
Second Floor: 923 square feet
Basement: 730 square feet
Total: 2,573 square feet

Traditional elements get a stylish update in this design, while the floor plan provides abundant, thoughtfully arranged living space. High, multipane windows spill light from the covered front porch into the living room with vaulted ceiling. Pass through the angled hallway to find a rear wall comprised almost entirely of windows, giving light to the family room and bayed breakfast nook. Three roomy bedrooms upstairs include the master suite. The basement offers even more living space and a storage room.

Design by
© Alan Mascord
Design Associates, Inc.

Width 34'-0"
Depth 45'-0"

DESIGN 5538

First Floor: 802 square feet
Second Floor: 757 square feet
Total: 1,559 square feet

Offering a smaller space while still providing today's necessary amenities, this two-story traditional home would be ideal for smaller or corner lots. The combination living/dining room features a large fireplace and access to the rear patio. The corner kitchen includes plenty of counter space and a pass-through to the breakfast nook with a sunny bay window. Upstairs, two family bedrooms share a full hall bath while the master bedroom features its own bath with dual sinks.

Design by
© Home Planners

Width 47'-0"
Depth 38'-6"

Quote One®
Cost to build? See page 684
to order complete cost estimate
to build this house in your area!

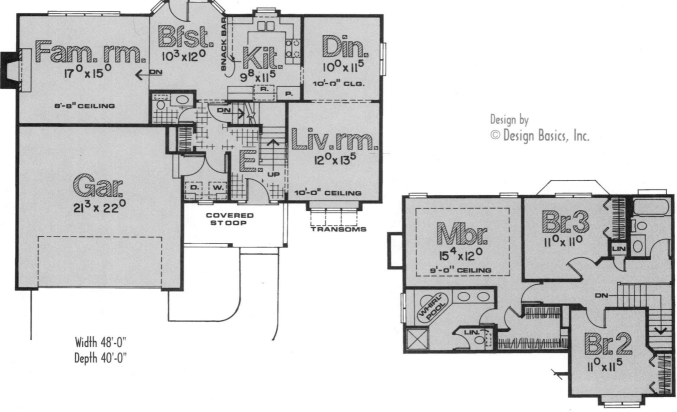

Fam. rm.
17⁰ x 15⁰
8'-8" CEILING

Bfst.
10³ x 12⁰

Kit.
9⁸ x 11⁵

Din.
10⁰ x 11⁵
10'-0" CLG.

SNACK BAR

DN

Gar.
21³ x 22⁰

Liv. rm.
12⁰ x 13⁵
10'-0" CEILING

DN

UP

D. W.

COVERED STOOP

TRANSOMS

Width 48'-0"
Depth 40'-0"

Design by
© Design Basics, Inc.

Mbr.
15⁴ x 12⁰
9'-0" CEILING

Br. 3
11⁰ x 11⁰

LIN

WHIRL-POOL

LIN.

DN

Br. 2
11⁰ x 11⁵

At 1,845 square feet, this classic two-story home is perfect for a variety of lifestyles. Upon entry from the covered front porch, the thoughtful floor plan is immediately evident. To the right of the entry is a formal living room with ten-foot ceiling. Nearby is the formal dining room with a bright window. Serving the dining room and bright bayed dinette, the kitchen features a pantry, lazy Susan and window sink. Off the breakfast area, step down into the family room with a handsome fireplace and wall of windows. Upstairs, two secondary bedrooms share a hall bath. The private master bedroom enjoys a boxed ceiling, walk-in closet and a pampering dressing area with double vanity and whirlpool tub.

DESIGN 9282
First Floor: 1,042 square feet
Second Floor: 803 square feet
Total: 1,845 square feet

TWO-STORY TRADITIONAL HOMES

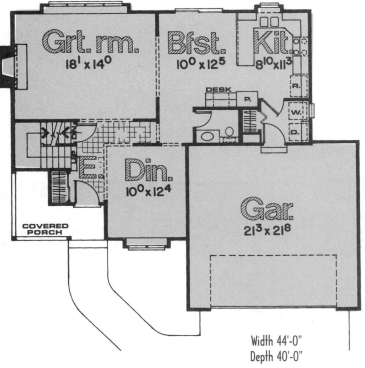

Grt. rm.
18¹ x 14⁰

Bfst.
10⁰ x 12⁵

Kit.
8¹⁰ x 11³

DESK

P.

R.

W.

D.

Din.
10⁰ x 12⁴

Gar.
21³ x 21⁸

COVERED
PORCH

Width 44'-0"
Depth 40'-0"

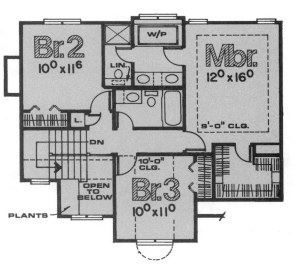

Br. 2
10⁰ x 11⁶

W/P

LIN.

Mbr.
12⁰ x 16⁰

9'-0" CLG.

L.

DN

10'-0"
CLG.

OPEN
TO
BELOW

Br. 3
10⁰ x 11⁰

PLANTS

TWO-STORY TRADITIONAL HOMES

**DESIGN
9260**

First Floor: 891 square feet
Second Floor: 759 square feet
Total: 1,650 square feet

This modest-sized home provides a quaint covered front porch that opens to a two-story foyer. The formal dining room features a boxed window that can be seen from the entry. A fireplace in the great room adds warmth and coziness to the attached breakfast room and the well-planned kitchen. Sliding glass doors lead from the breakfast room to the rear yard. In a near-by utility room, a washer and dryer reside and a closet provides ample storage. A powder room is provided nearby for guests. Three bedrooms are on the second floor; one of these includes an arched window under a vaulted ceiling. The deluxe master suite provides a large walk-in closet and a dressing area with double vanity, whirlpool tub, separate shower, linen closet and compartmented toilet.

www.homeplanners.com

DESIGN P382

First Floor: 760 square feet
Second Floor: 854 square feet
Total: 1,614 square feet

Exterior detailing is the first attraction to this home: shingles, a gabled roof and a classic covered porch. Inside, a two-story family room is warmed by a fireplace with a French door leading outside. The kitchen easily serves the formal dining room and breakfast bay and is highlighted by a corner sink overlooking the rear yard. On the upper level, two family bedrooms share a full bath and a roomy master suite contains a vaulted master bath and walk-in closet. Please specify basement or crawlspace foundation when ordering.

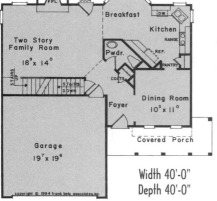

Width 40'-0"
Depth 40'-0"

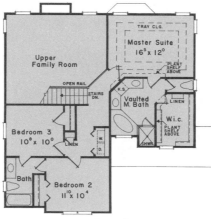

Design by
© Frank Betz Associates, Inc.

DESIGN P144

First Floor: 1,426 square feet
Second Floor: 1,408 square feet
Total: 2,834 square feet

An island country kitchen with an adjacent breakfast room will be one of many highlights of this two-story traditional home. The formal dining room is accessible via an arched opening from the two-story foyer. The central family room includes a fireplace flanked by windows. The master suite enjoys a luxurious bath with a walk-in closet and a corner whirlpool tub. Please specify basement or crawlspace foundation when ordering.

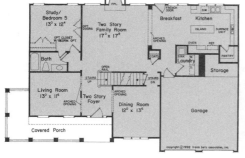

Width 60'-0"
Depth 41'-4"

Design by
© Frank Betz Associates, Inc.

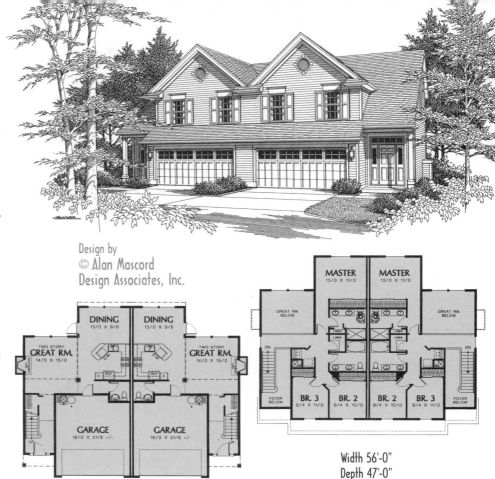

DESIGN 7459

First Floor: 704 square feet
Second Floor: 782 square feet
Total: 1,486 square feet

Seeing double? No! You're just looking at the smart design of an efficient and comfortable two-story duplex. Inside each unit, a two-story great room offers a warming fireplace for those cool winter evenings. The dining room accesses the rear yard, while also having easy access to the C-shaped kitchen. A powder room completes this level. Upstairs, the sleeping zone is made up of two secondary bedrooms sharing a full hall bath that has a dual-bowl vanity and a walk-in linen closet, and a master suite with a private bath.

Design by
© Alan Mascord
Design Associates, Inc.

Width 56'-0"
Depth 47'-0"

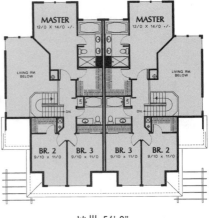

DESIGN 7458

First Floor: 785 square feet
Second Floor: 902 square feet
Total: 1,687 square feet

With shingles and stone-work, a trellis-covered front walk and twin gables, this fine two-story duplex is sure to please. Inside, the two-story living room offers a fireplace and built-in media center for cozy get-togethers. The C-shaped kitchen features a window over the sink, plenty of counter and cabinet space and a serving counter into the dining room. Upstairs two secondary bedrooms—one with a walk-in closet—share a full hall bath. The master suite offers a large walk-in closet and a pampering private bath.

Design by
© Alan Mascord
Design Associates, Inc.

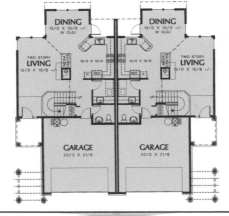

Width 56'-0"
Depth 56'-0"

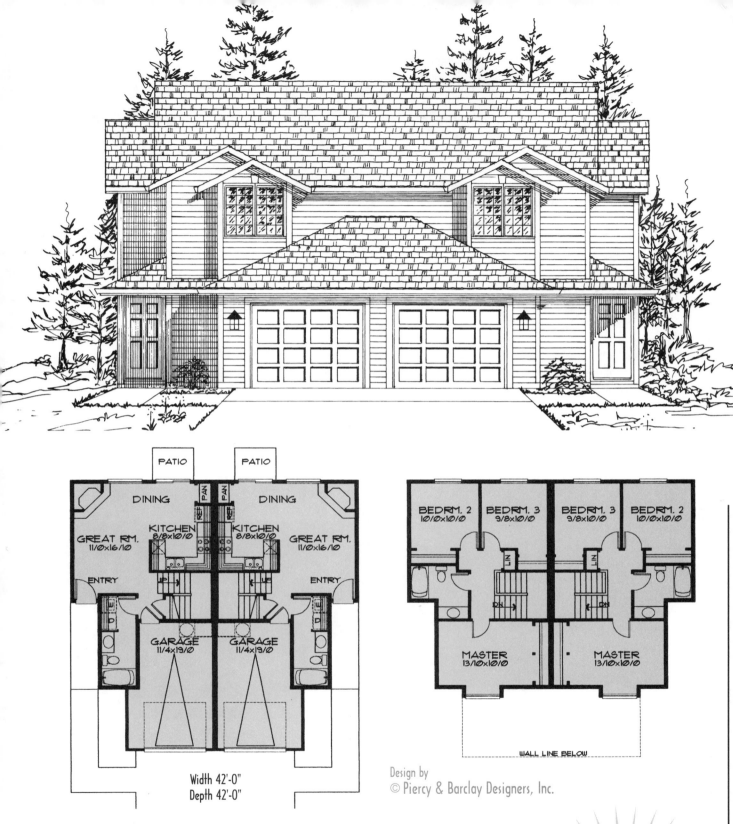

PATIO   PATIO

DINING   DINING

KITCHEN 8/8x10/0   KITCHEN 8/8x10/0

GREAT RM. 11/0x16/10   GREAT RM. 11/0x16/10

ENTRY   ENTRY

GARAGE 11/4x19/0   GARAGE 11/4x19/0

Width 42'-0"
Depth 42'-0"

BEDRM. 2 10/0x10/0   BEDRM. 3 9/8x10/0   BEDRM. 3 9/8x10/0   BEDRM. 2 10/0x10/0

LIN   LIN

DN   DN

MASTER 13/10x10/0   MASTER 13/10x10/0

WALL LINE BELOW

Design by
© Piercy & Barclay Designers, Inc.

Two-Story Traditional Homes

With gabled rooflines and two-story convenience, this fine duplex is sure to please. Inside, the units are mirror images of each other. The entry opens to the great room, where a corner fireplace waits to warm cool winter evenings. The L-shaped kitchen is con-venient to the dining area, which features access to a patio. A full bath and a wash-er/dryer area complete this level. Upstairs, three bedrooms—one a spacious master bedroom—share a second full bath and a linen closet. The garages shield the units from street noise.

DESIGN C504
First Floor: 996 square feet
Second Floor: 1,140 square feet
Total: 2,136 square feet

DESIGN T068

First Floor: 1,475 square feet
Second Floor: 1,460 square feet
Total: 2,935 square feet

Quaint keystones and shutters offer charming accents to this stately English country home. The two-story foyer opens through decorative columns to the formal living room, which offers a wet bar. The nearby media room shares a through-fireplace with the two-story great room. A bumped-out bay holds a breakfast area that shares its light with an expansive gourmet kitchen. One wing of the second floor is dedicated to the rambling master suite. This home is designed with a basement foundation.

Design by
© Stephen Fuller,
American Home Gallery

Width 57'-6"
Depth 46'-6"

Quote One®
Cost to build? See page 684
to order complete cost estimate
to build this house in your area!

DESIGN T088

First Floor: 1,205 square feet
Second Floor: 1,160 square feet
Total: 2,365 square feet

This charming exterior conceals a perfect family plan. The formal dining and living rooms are located to either side of the foyer. At the rear of the home is a family room with a fireplace and access to a deck and a side veranda. The modern kitchen features a sunlit breakfast area. The second floor provides room for four bedrooms, one of which may be finished at a later date and used as a guest suite. The master bedroom includes a pampering bath and a walk-in closet. This home is designed with a basement foundation.

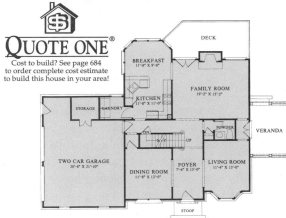

Design by
© Stephen Fuller,
American Home Gallery

Width 52'-6"
Depth 43'-6"

Quote One®
Cost to build? See page 684
to order complete cost estimate
to build this house in your area!

Width 42'-0"
Depth 42'-0"

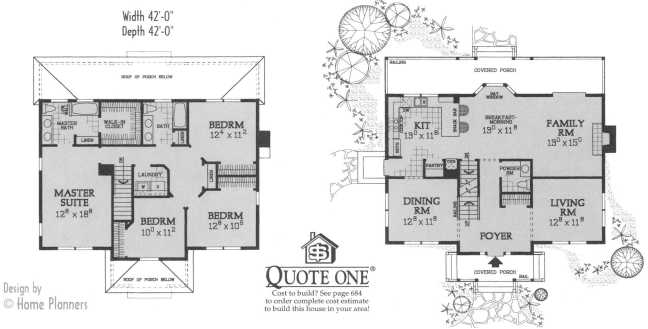

ROOF OF PORCH BELOW

MASTER BATH · WALK-IN CLOSET · BATH · LINEN

BEDRM
12⁴ x 11²

LINEN

LAUNDRY
W · D

LINEN

MASTER SUITE
12⁸ x 18⁸

BEDRM
10⁰ x 11²

BEDRM
12⁸ x 10⁶

ROOF OF PORCH BELOW

Design by
© Home Planners

RAILING

COVERED PORCH

BAY WINDOW

KIT
13⁰ x 11⁸

SNACK BAR

BREAKFAST-MORNING
13⁰ x 11⁸

FAMILY RM
13⁰ x 15⁰

DW · COOKTOP · REF/G

PANTRY · OVN

POWDER RM

DINING RM
12⁸ x 11⁸

RAILING · UP

LIVING RM
12⁸ x 11⁸

FOYER

COVERED PORCH · RAIL

QUOTE ONE®
Cost to build? See page 684
to order complete cost estimate
to build this house in your area!

A menities fill this two-story country home, beginning with a porch that offers access to the foyer. Formal living and dining rooms border the central foyer, each with windows to the front. At the rear of the first floor is an open family area with a U-shaped kitchen, bayed breakfast or morning area and a large family room with a fireplace and access to the

rear porch. Upstairs, three family bedrooms share a centrally located utility room and a full hall bath that has dual sinks. The master bedroom features a front-facing window and a master bath with separate sinks and a walk-in closet. An additional half bath on the first floor completes this exquisite design. Note the large pantry and snack bar in the kitchen.

DESIGN 5512
First Floor: 1,160 square feet
Second Floor: 1,111 square feet
Total: 2,271 square feet

TWO-STORY TRADITIONAL HOMES

DESIGN 7644

First Floor: 1,489 square feet
Second Floor: 534 square feet
Total: 2,023 square feet
Bonus Room: 393 square feet

A smart exterior and an economical use of interior space combine to create this spacious yet practical home. The grand foyer leads to a two-story great room with a centered fireplace, a wall of windows and access to the rear porch. The breakfast room, set off by decorative columns, has its own door to the porch and shares its natural light with the kitchen. Twin walk-in closets introduce a lavish private bath in the master suite. Additional bedrooms reside on the second floor and share a full bath.

© 1997 Donald A. Gardner Architects, Inc.

Width 59'-4"
Depth 58'-7"

© 1997 Donald A. Gardner Architects, Inc.

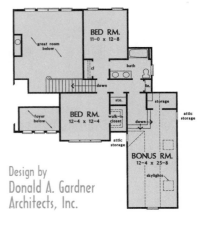

Design by
Donald A. Gardner
Architects, Inc.

DESIGN 7690

First Floor: 1,644 square feet
Second Floor: 606 square feet
Total: 2,250 square feet
Bonus Room: 548 square feet

Tradition abounds in this two-story home with transoms, keystone accents and multiple gables. An arched clerestory window casts light into the two-story foyer for a dramatic welcome. The two-story great room excites with its rear wall of windows. Columns define the open breakfast area where French doors lead to a screened porch. Double doors lead to the first-floor master suite with His and Hers walk-in closets and a bath with every amenity. Both bedrooms upstairs feature walk-in closets.

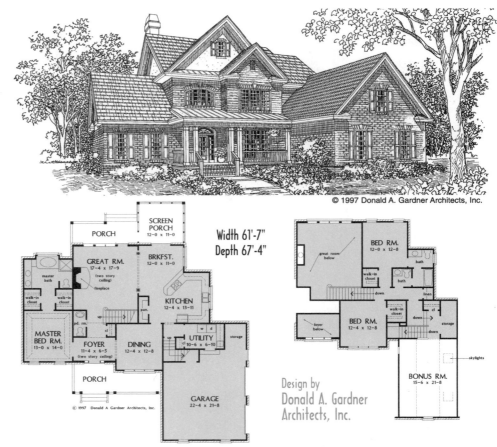

© 1997 Donald A. Gardner Architects, Inc.

Width 61'-7"
Depth 67'-4"

Design by
Donald A. Gardner
Architects, Inc.

© American Home Gallery, Ltd.

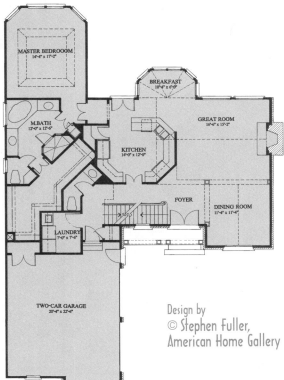

MASTER BEDROOOM
14'-4" x 17'-2"

BREAKFAST
10'-4" x 6'-0"

GREAT ROOM
16'-0" x 15'-2"

M.BATH
12'-0" x 12'-0"

KITCHEN
14'-0" x 12'-0"

FOYER

DINING ROOM
11'-4" x 11'-4"

LAUNDRY
7'-0" x 7'-6"

TWO-CAR GARAGE
20'-4" x 22'-6"

Design by
© Stephen Fuller,
American Home Gallery

BATH

BEDROOM No2
12'-2" x 13'-4"

BEDROOM No3
14'-4" x 12'-0"

FOYER

UNFINISHED
STORAGE

Width 48'-6"
Depth 70'-11"

QUOTE ONE®
Cost to build? See page 684
to order complete cost estimate
to build this house in your area!

This home is a true Southern original. Inside, the spacious foyer leads directly to a large vaulted great room with its handsome fireplace. The dining room, just off the foyer, features a dramatic vaulted ceiling. The spacious kitchen offers both storage and large work areas opening up to the breakfast room. At the rear of the home, you will find the master suite with its garden bath, His and Hers vanities and an oversized closet. The second floor provides two additional bedrooms with a shared bath and a balcony overlook to the foyer below. Each bedroom has a private lavatory in the bath. Storage space or a fourth bedroom may be placed over the garage area. This home is designed with a basement foundation.

DESIGN
T013
First Floor: 1,580 square feet
Second Floor: 595 square feet
Total: 2,175 square feet
Bonus Room: 290 square feet

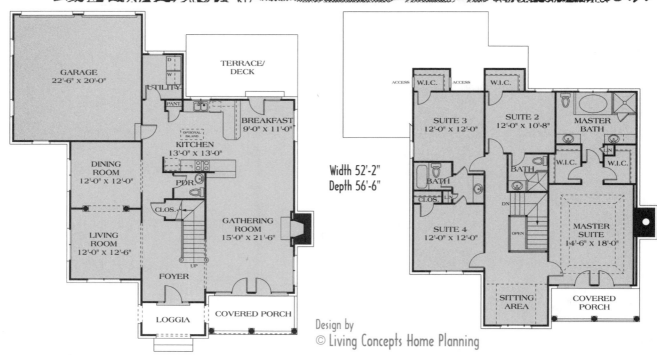

GARAGE
22'-6" x 20'-0"

UTILITY

TERRACE/
DECK

PANT.

OPTIONAL
ISLAND

BREAKFAST
9'-0" x 11'-0"

KITCHEN
13'-0" x 13'-0"

DINING
ROOM
12'-0" x 12'-0"

PDR.

CLOS.

LIVING
ROOM
12'-0" x 12'-6"

GATHERING
ROOM
15'-0" x 21'-6"

FOYER

UP

LOGGIA

COVERED PORCH

Width 52'-2"
Depth 56'-6"

ACCESS   W.I.C.   ACCESS   W.I.C.

SUITE 3
12'-0" x 12'-0"

SUITE 2
12'-0" x 10'-8"

MASTER
BATH

BATH

BATH

W.I.C.   W.I.C.

CLOS.   LN.

SUITE 4
12'-0" x 12'-0"

DN

OPEN

MASTER
SUITE
14'-6" x 18'-0"

SITTING
AREA

COVERED
PORCH

Design by
© Living Concepts Home Planning

DESIGN
A134
First Floor: 1,355 square feet
Second Floor: 1,442 square feet
Total: 2,797 square feet

This fresh Southern design offers a spacious gathering room, complete with an extended-hearth fireplace and lovely French doors. The gathering room is open to a sunny breakfast area, with its own French door to the back terrace and deck. A gourmet kitchen offers a food preparation island counter, wide wrapping counters and a sizable pantry. Upstairs, the master suite features a coffered ceiling, two walk-in closets and a lavish bath with separate vanities. Three family bedrooms, one with a private bath, share a hall that leads to a generous sitting area with space for chairs, books and computers.

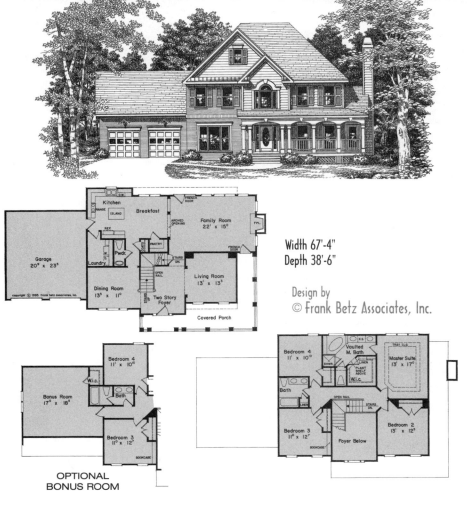

DESIGN P195

First Floor: 1,290 square feet
Second Floor: 1,108 square feet
Total: 2,398 square feet
Bonus Room: 399 square feet

Asymmetrical gables accent a comfortably elegant exterior. A centered fireplace framed by windows and a French door to the rear covered porch redraw the open space of the family room to cozy dimensions. Upstairs, the master suite offers a windowed whirlpool tub, twin lavatories with a knee-space vanity and a sizable walk-in closet. Three additional bedrooms share a central hall that has a balcony overlook to the foyer. Please specify basement or crawlspace foundation when ordering.

Width 67'-4"
Depth 38'-6"

Design by
© Frank Betz Associates, Inc.

OPTIONAL BONUS ROOM

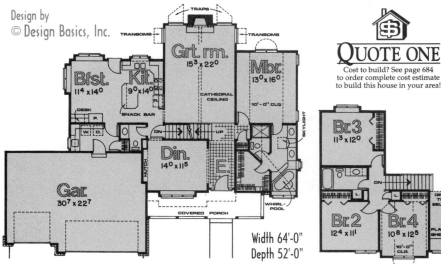

Design by
© Design Basics, Inc.

QUOTE ONE®
Cost to build? See page 684 to order complete cost estimate to build this house in your area!

Width 64'-0"
Depth 52'-0"

DESIGN 9310

First Floor: 1,505 square feet
Second Floor: 610 square feet
Total: 2,115 square feet

Windows, lap siding and a covered porch give this elevation a welcoming country flair. The formal dining room with hutch space is conveniently located near the island kitchen. Highlighting the spacious great room are a raised-hearth fireplace, cathedral ceiling and trapezoid windows. The master suite includes a large dressing area with a double vanity, skylight, step-up corner whirlpool tub and generous walk-in closet. Upstairs, the three secondary bedrooms share a hall bath.

DESIGN P184

First Floor: 1,583 square feet
Second Floor: 543 square feet
Total: 2,126 square feet
Bonus Room: 251 square feet

Here's a new country home with a fresh face and a dash of Victoriana. Inside, decorative columns help define an elegant dining room, but the heart of the home is the vaulted family room with a radius window and a French door to the rear property. The first-floor master suite features a private bath with a vaulted ceiling and a whirlpool tub. On the opposite side of the plan, an additional bedroom or guest suite offers its own full bath. Please specify basement, crawlspace or slab foundation when ordering.

Design by
© Frank Betz Associates, Inc.

Width 53'-0"
Depth 47'-0"

DESIGN P104

First Floor: 1,320 square feet
Second Floor: 554 square feet
Total: 1,874 square feet
Bonus Room: 155 square feet

Beyond the columned entrance of this 1½-story-home, the foyer introduces custom amenities that speak for themselves. Located on the first-floor, the master suite provides a luxurious bath and a walk-in closet. The vaulted family room with its warming fireplace opens to the breakfast room and island kitchen. The second floor holds three family bedrooms and a full bath. Please specify basement or crawlspace foundation when ordering.

Width 54'-6"
Depth 42'-4"

Design by
© Frank Betz Associates, Inc.

Width 54'-0"
Depth 43'-4"

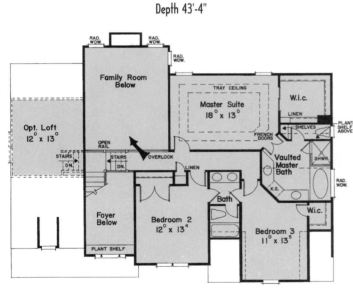

Opt. Loft
12⁰ x 13⁰

Family Room Below

RAD. WDW.   RAD. WDW.   RAD. WDW.

TRAY CEILING

Master Suite
18⁰ x 13⁰

W.i.c.

LINEN

FRENCH DOORS

PLANT SHELF ABOVE

SHELVES

OPEN RAIL

STAIRS DN.   STAIRS DN.   OVERLOOK

LINEN

Vaulted Master Bath

SHWR.

K.S.

RAD. WDW.

Foyer Below

Bedroom 2
12⁰ x 13⁴

Bath

Bedroom 3
11⁰ x 13⁵

W.i.c.

PLANT SHELF

FPL.

Den/Bedroom 4
12⁰ x 11²

Two Story Family Room
14⁰ x 18⁰

FRENCH DOOR

Laund.   W. D.

Breakfast

Kitchen

ISLAND   REF.

DW.

Bath   W.i.c.

STAIRS DN.

Pwdr.

SURFACE UNIT   DBL OVENS   PANTRY

Vaulted Living Room
12⁰ x 12⁰

COATS

Two Story Foyer

STAIRS UP

VLT.   VLT.

Dining Room
12⁰ x 13⁴

Garage
20⁵ x 22²

Covered Porch

copyright © 1995 frank betz associates, inc.

Design by
© Frank Betz Associates, Inc.

A covered porch leads into a two-story foyer in this four-bedroom plan. The foyer is flanked by the formal living room, which is designed to have no cross traffic, and the dining room, with a powder room nearby. The two-story family room features a fireplace and is open to the breakfast room. In the kitchen, a large pantry, adjacent laundry room and work island help ease chores. A den, or fourth bedroom, completes this level. Upstairs, two spacious bedrooms share a bath, while the master suite includes a walk-in closet, tray ceiling and a vaulted bath with a plant shelf. An optional loft can become a home office or additional bedroom. Please specify basement or crawlspace foundation when ordering.

DESIGN P257
First Floor: 1,415 square feet
Second Floor: 1,015 square feet
Total: 2,430 square feet
Bonus Room: 169 square feet

TWO-STORY TRADITIONAL HOMES

DESIGN P393

First Floor: 1,032 square feet
Second Floor: 988 square feet
Total: 2,020 square feet
Bonus Room: 337 square feet

A stunning blend of brick and horizontal siding complements a copper-seam roof on this country design. Formal rooms flank the two-story foyer, which leads to the family room to the rear of the plan. The fireplace here also warms the breakfast area and kitchen, which features a food-prep island and a serving bar. The dining room has a lovely triple window. The second floor includes a sizable master suite with a vaulted bath. Please specify basement or crawlspace foundation when ordering.

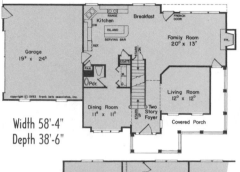

Width 58'-4"
Depth 38'-6"

OPTIONAL BONUS ROOM

Design by
© Frank Betz Associates, Inc.

DESIGN P305

First Floor: 1,107 square feet
Second Floor: 891 square feet
Total: 1,998 square feet

This charming farmhouse-style design features a grand, two-story family room with a centered fireplace and twin sets of windows that offer views to the back property. The two-story foyer opens to a formal dining room, which has access to the front porch through French doors. A vestibule leads to a secluded office or fourth bedroom and a full bath. Upstairs, a generous master suite offers a tray ceiling, vaulted bath and walk-in closet. Please specify basement or crawlspace foundation when ordering.

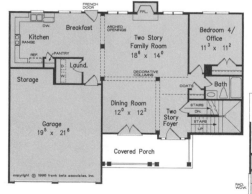

Width 50'-0"
Depth 38'-0"

Design by
© Frank Betz Associates, Inc.

Design by
© Frank Betz Associates, Inc.

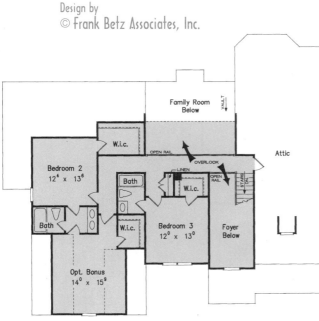

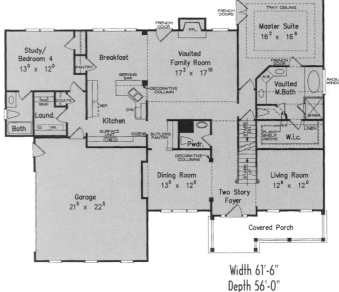

Width 61'-6"
Depth 56'-0"

An offset covered porch makes a fine country statement on this traditional two-story home. The floor plan is classic with formal areas flanking the foyer and a vaulted family room with fireplace to the back. The breakfast room and kitchen combine with the family room to form one large casual gathering space. The service entrance to the two-car garage also leads to a study (or fourth bedroom) and a laundry room. The master suite is on the first floor and features a sitting room and vaulted bath. Two bedrooms with two full baths join optional bonus space on the second floor. All bedrooms feature walk-in closets. Please specify basement, crawlspace or slab foundation when ordering.

DESIGN P278

First Floor: 2,026 square feet
Second Floor: 726 square feet
Total: 2,752 square feet
Bonus Room: 277 square feet

© 1996 Donald A. Gardner Architects, Inc.

Width 64'-11"
Depth 60'-6"

Design by
Donald A. Gardner
Architects, Inc.

PORCH

BRKFST.
13-0 x 11-9

(two story ceiling)

GREAT RM.
15-4 x 19-6

fireplace

KIT.
13-0 x 12-2

up

UTILITY
8-0 x 6-4

w d

storage

master bath

walk-in closet

walk-in closet

pd. rm.

up

pan.

cl

sto.

MASTER BED RM.
14-0 x 13-4

cl

FOYER
6-9 x 8-9

DINING
14-0 x 12-4

GARAGE
22-0 x 23-0

PORCH

storage

© 1996 Donald A. Gardner Architects, Inc.

great room below

BED RM.
13-0 x 12-0

walk-in closet

lin.

bath

down

down

foyer below

BED RM.
14-0 x 12-4

walk-in closet

(optional bedroom)
12-4 x 10-0

BONUS RM.
14-4 x 15-0

TWO-STORY TRADITIONAL HOMES

DESIGN 7638
First Floor: 1,710 square feet
Second Floor: 591 square feet
Total: 2,301 square feet
Bonus Room: 452 square feet

Traditional homes are known to be warm and inviting—this home is a perfect example. The stately brick exterior, set off with a finely detailed balustrade, beckons a welcome to all; the interior speaks of livability. The private master suite features a luxurious bath and dual walk-in closets. The expansive, vault-ed great room and the open kitchen with breakfast bay open to an inviting rear porch. Upstairs, two bedrooms, a bonus room and an optional fourth bedroom have easy access to all areas from the front and rear stairs. A two-car garage has volu-minous storage space and connects to the main house via the utility room.

www.homeplanners.com

DESIGN 3615

First Floor: 1,355 square feet
Second Floor: 582 square feet
Total: 1,937 square feet

L

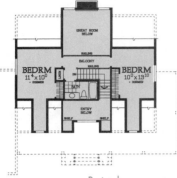

BEDRM 11⁴ x 10⁰

BEDRM 10⁰ x 19¹⁰

GREAT ROOM BELOW

BALCONY

Design by
© Home Planners

QUOTE ONE®
Cost to build? See page 684
to order complete cost estimate
to build this house in your area!

BRKFST 10⁸ x 9⁸

GREAT RM 19⁰ x 18⁰

KIT 12² x 10⁴

STORAGE ROOM

LAUNDRY ROOM

DINING RM 12² x 11⁴

FOYER

MASTER BEDRM 11⁸ x 14⁰

GARAGE 20⁰ x 22⁰

COVERED PORCH

Width 65'-0"
Depth 55'-8"

A portico makes a grand introduction to this country home. To the left of the foyer is the formal dining room. Close by, the tiled kitchen offers an angled snack bar and overlooks the great room. Casual living space provides a centered fireplace framed by doors to the entertainment deck. The master suite nestles to the right of the living area, and boasts a lavish walk-through bath with a door to a private area of the deck. Upstairs, two family bedrooms share a hall bath and a balcony overlook to the great room.

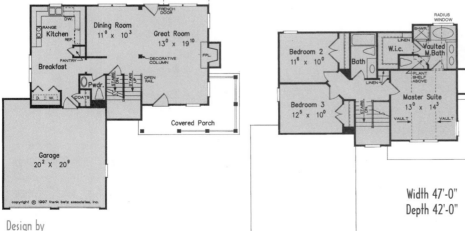

DESIGN P324

First Floor: 757 square feet
Second Floor: 735 square feet
Total: 1,492 square feet

The open foyer announces the living and dining areas, defined by decorative columns. A U-shaped kitchen serves both the breakfast area, which has two lovely windows, and the dining room. The great-room features a fireplace and opens to the rear property through a French door. Upstairs, the master suite provides a vaulted ceiling, garden tub with radius window, and walk-in closet with linen storage. Two additional bedrooms share a full bath. Please specify basement, slab or crawlspace foundation when ordering.

Kitchen

Dining Room 11⁰ x 10³

Great Room 13⁰ x 19¹⁰

Breakfast

Pantry

Pwdr.

Covered Porch

DECORATIVE COLUMN

OPEN RAIL

FPL

Garage 20² x 20⁹

copyright © 1997 frank betz associates, inc.

Bedroom 2 11⁶ x 10⁰

Bath

W.i.c.

Vaulted M.Bath

Bedroom 3 12⁵ x 10⁰

Master Suite 13⁰ x 14³

PLANT SHELF ABOVE

RADIUS WINDOW

VAULT

Width 47'-0"
Depth 42'-0"

Design by
© Frank Betz Associates, Inc.

TWO-STORY TRADITIONAL HOMES

Design by
© Drummond Designs, Inc.

Width 22'-0"
Depth 32'-0"

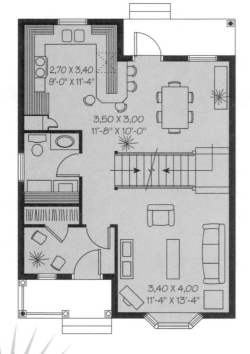

2,70 X 3,40
9'-0" X 11'-4"

3,50 X 3,00
11'-8" X 10'-0"

3,40 X 4,00
11'-4" X 13'-4"

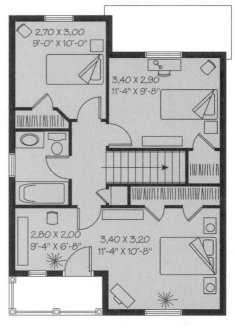

2,70 X 3,00
9'-0" X 10'-0"

3,40 X 2,90
11'-4" X 9'-8"

2,80 X 2,00
9'-4" X 6'-8"

3,40 X 3,20
11'-4" X 10'-8"

DESIGN Z023
First Floor: 620 square feet
Second Floor: 620 square feet
Total: 1,240 square feet

Down-home comfort enhances the uptown spirit of this traditional home. A charming bay window brightens the living room. A U-shaped kitchen serves a snack counter as well as the dining area. Upstairs, the second-floor master bedroom has a reading area and a private balcony. A full bath serves the second-floor sleeping quarters; a powder room serves the first floor. This home is designed with a basement foundation.

DESIGN
P402

First Floor: 842 square feet
Second Floor: 806 square feet
Total: 1,648 square feet
Bonus Room: 280 square feet

Open planning allows unrestrained living space in this stately design, which carefully blends elegance and informality. The warmth of the centered fireplace will be enjoyed from the breakfast area and even the kitchen. A pantry eases service to the formal dining room. Two family bedrooms and a master suite are on the second floor, along with bonus space for another bedroom. Please specify basement, crawlspace or slab foundation when ordering.

Design by
© Frank Betz Associates, Inc.

Width 53'-4"
Depth 32'-10"

Design by
© Frank Betz Associates, Inc.

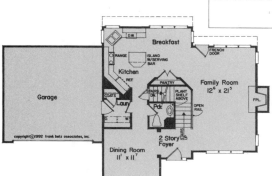

Width 52'-10"
Depth 34'-10"

DESIGN
P276

First Floor: 890 square feet
Second Floor: 739 square feet
Total: 1,629 square feet
Bonus Room: 379 square feet

Formal and casual space for living and entertaining dominate the first floor of this quaint plan. The spacious family room contains a fireplace and windows overlooking the backyard. The upper-level master suite has a tray ceiling, double-sink vanity and a separate shower and tub. Bonus space over the garage can add 379 square feet. Please specify basement or crawlspace foundation when ordering.

TWO-STORY TRADITIONAL HOMES

DESIGN C130

First Floor: 1,149 square feet
Second Floor: 847 square feet
Total: 1,996 square feet

Matching decorative trim spreads the drama of sunlight and shadow over the face of this four-bedroom design that has a three-bedroom option. An entry porch with mill-turned columns opens to a two-story foyer. A formal dining room is on the right and a great room with cathedral ceiling and fireplace fills the left wing. A dinette and an L-shaped kitchen stretch along the back. Upstairs, the master suite and three additional bedrooms and full bath cluster around the open balcony.

Design by
© James Fahy Design

Width 61'-4"
Depth 36'-0"

3-BEDROOM OPTION
FLOOR PLAN

DESIGN C141

First Floor: 1,861 square feet
Second Floor: 598 square feet
Total: 2,459 square feet

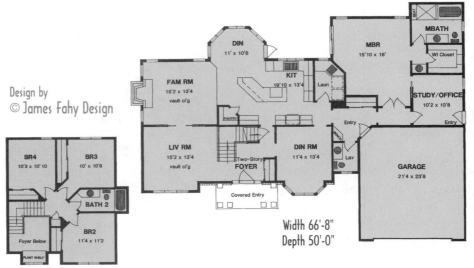

The balance created by double sets of square columns and rectangular windows is offset by asymmetrical gables, creating an interesting and sophisticated design. The lower-level living areas are well isolated from the master suite and office, providing secluded sleeping and working zones. Formal living and dining rooms are at the front of the plan, while casual living areas to the back offer many amenities, such as a windowed dining bay, fireplace, vaulted ceiling and large, angled island in the kitchen.

Design by
© James Fahy Design

Width 66'-8"
Depth 50'-0"

www.homeplanners.com

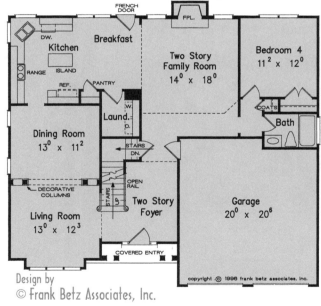

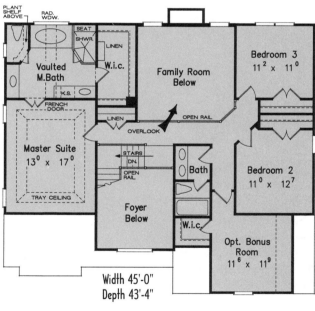

FRENCH DOOR

FPL.

Kitchen

Breakfast

DW.

Two Story
Family Room
14⁰ x 18⁰

Bedroom 4
11² x 12⁰

RANGE   ISLAND

PANTRY

REF.

Dining Room
13⁰ x 11²

Laund.

COATS

Bath

DECORATIVE
COLUMNS

STAIRS
DN.

Living Room
13⁰ x 12³

OPEN
RAIL

STAIRS

Two Story
Foyer

Garage
20⁰ x 20⁶

COVERED ENTRY

Design by
© Frank Betz Associates, Inc.

copyright © 1996 frank betz associates, inc.

PLANT
SHELF
ABOVE

RAD.
WDW.

SEAT

SHWR.

LINEN

Vaulted
M.Bath

W.i.c.

Family Room
Below

Bedroom 3
11² x 11⁰

K.S.

FRENCH
DOOR

LINEN

OPEN RAIL

OVERLOOK

Master Suite
13⁰ x 17⁰

Bath

STAIRS
DN.

OPEN
RAIL

Bedroom 2
11⁰ x 12⁷

Foyer
Below

W.i.c.

TRAY CEILING

Opt. Bonus
Room
11⁶ x 11⁹

Width 45'-0"
Depth 43'-4"

This casually elegant European country-style home offers more than just a slice of everything you've always wanted: this plan is designed with room to grow. Formal living and dining rooms are defined by decorative columns and open from a two-story foyer, which leads to casual living space. A two-story family room offers a fireplace and shares a French door to the rear property with the breakfast room. A gallery hall with a balcony overlook connects two sleeping wings upstairs. The master suite boasts a vaulted bath with compartmented toilet, dual sinks, a seated shower and a whirlpool tub. The family hall leads to bonus space. Please specify basement, crawlspace or slab foundation when ordering.

**DESIGN
P172**
First Floor: 1,290 square feet
Second Floor: 985 square feet
Total: 2,275 square feet
Bonus Room: 186 square feet

TWO-STORY TRADITIONAL HOMES

DESIGN
P101

First Floor: 882 square feet
Second Floor: 793 square feet
Total: 1,675 square feet
Bonus Room: 416 square feet

This fetching country home features a second-floor room-to-grow option. The first floor's living area locates formal living spaces to the front and casual living spaces grouped at the rear of the plan. Upstairs, the master suite is enhanced with a master bath that contains a walk-in closet. Two secondary bedrooms share a full bath. The second-floor plan includes a laundry room or an optional bonus room. Please specify basement, crawlspace or slab foundation when ordering.

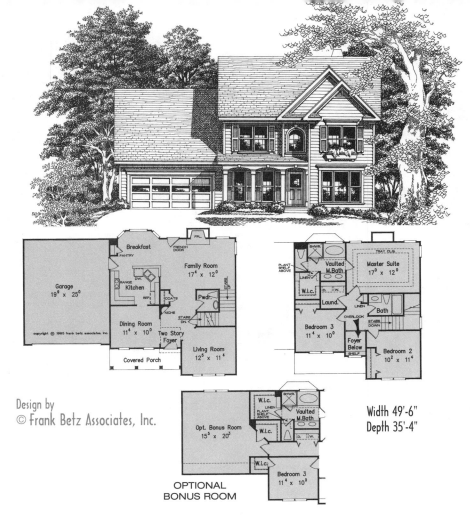

Design by
© Frank Betz Associates, Inc.

OPTIONAL
BONUS ROOM

Width 49'-6"
Depth 35'-4"

DESIGN
P160

First Floor: 844 square feet
Second Floor: 787 square feet
Total: 1,631 square feet
Bonus Room: 340 square feet

A brick and siding exterior, front gables and a covered front porch are clues to the amenities inside this home. The two-story foyer is flanked by a formal dining room and a formal living room. The spacious family room is highlighted by a fireplace and access to the outside. Upstairs, two family bedrooms share a full bath, while the master suite features a private vaulted bath. An alternate plan shows a finished bonus room. Please specify basement or crawlspace foundation when ordering.

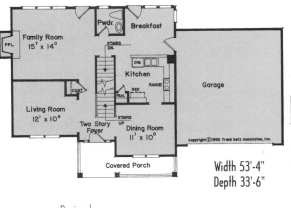

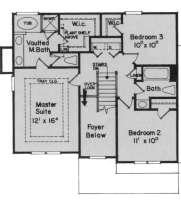

Design by
© Frank Betz Associates, Inc.

Width 53'-4"
Depth 33'-6"

Width 52'-0"
Depth 37'-6"

Decorative shutters, narrow-pane windows and a covered porch draw attention to this home. The two-story foyer displays a corner niche for collectibles and opens to the formal living and dining rooms. Extras in the kitchen include built-in corner shelves, a pantry and an angled work space that's open to the breakfast room and family room, where there's a corner fireplace. Upstairs, two family bedrooms share a hall bath. The lavish master suite offers a walk-in closet and a vaulted bath with a plant shelf. For convenience, the laundry room is upstairs. Note the extra storage space available in the two-car garage. Please specify basement, crawlspace or slab foundation when ordering.

DESIGN
P157
First Floor: 915 square feet
Second Floor: 963 square feet
Total: 1,878 square feet

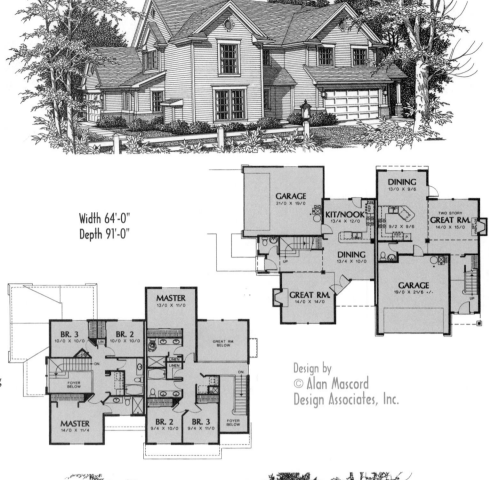

DESIGN 7457

First Floor: 723/708 square feet
Second Floor: 711/793 square feet
Total: 1,434/1,501 square feet

This farmhouse design combines two separate floor plans under one roof—a perfect arrangement for relatives or tenants. Each residence has a master suite, secondary bedrooms, formal dining room, great room and its own garage. The left plan has a centered fireplace in the great room and lovely views of the front property, while the second plan's great room looks to the backyard. Each plan has a well-organized kitchen, which serves both a dining room and a snack bar or nook.

Width 64'-0"
Depth 91'-0"

Design by
© Alan Mascord
Design Associates, Inc.

DESIGN X025

First Floor: 869 square feet
Second Floor: 963 square feet
Total: 1,832 square feet

A covered porch entrance creates an inviting front door on this country home. The openness of the rear rooms—living area, breakfast area and island kitchen—provide a feeling of spaciousness and flow. Upstairs, secondary bedrooms share a vanity area that opens to a private toilet and tub room. A rear sun deck, formal dining room and lavish master suite finish up a fine design.

Width 44'-0"
Depth 38'-0"

Design by
© Jannis Vann & Associates, Inc.

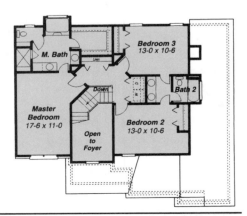

TWO-STORY TRADITIONAL HOMES

Bedroom 3
12^0 x 11^6

Family Room
Below

VAULT

LINEN

OPEN RAIL
STAIRS
DN.

OVERLOOK

Bath

Foyer
Below

Bedroom 2
11^7 x 12^0

W.i.c.

Opt. Bonus
12^0 x 23^6

Width 52'-4"
Depth 45'-10"

TRAY CEILING

Master Suite
13^0 x 16^0

FRENCH DOOR

FPL

FRENCH DOOR

Vaulted
Family Room
18^2 x 15^8

Breakfast

SERVING BAR

DW.

RADIUS WINDOW

Vltd.
M. Bath
9'-5"
CLG. HT

COATS

OPEN RAIL

STAIRS
UP

STAIRS
DN.

Kitchen

REF.

Laund.

RANGE

PANTRY

W. D.

SHWR

PLANT SHELF ABOVE

Pwdr.

Two
Story
Foyer

Dining Room
11^7 x 12^0

LINEN

W.i.c.

DECORATIVE COLUMNS

Garage
20^0 x 21^0

Covered Porch

copyright © 1997 frank betz associates, inc.

Design by
© Frank Betz Associates, Inc.

Variety in the facade is just a prelude to the charm to be found inside this attractive three-bedroom home. The two-story foyer opens on the right to a formal dining room, then leads back to a vaulted family room—complete with a warming fireplace. The efficient kitchen offers a breakfast bar and easy access to the breakfast area. A pantry, laundry area and plenty of cabinet and counter space further enhance this room. Located on the first floor for privacy, the main suite is lavish with its amenities. Included here is a huge walk-in closet, a separate tub and shower and a tray ceiling in the bedroom. Upstairs, two family bedrooms share a full hall bath. Bonus space over the garage can be developed later. Please specify basement or crawlspace foundation when ordering.

DESIGN P441

First Floor: 1,382 square feet
Second Floor: 436 square feet
Total: 1,818 square feet
Bonus Room: 298 square feet

DESIGN 5517

First Floor: 1,228 square feet
Second Floor: 1,080 square feet
Total: 2,308 square feet

A grand entrance graces this home, while spacious rooms and a flowing floor plan create a perfect setting for entertaining. The sunlit foyer opens to a combination living/dining room with corner shelves. Two glass doors let the outside in via the backyard and patio. Nearby, the island kitchen features a pantry, a writing desk and access to the utility room and a two-car garage. Three bedrooms, two full baths and a covered porch make up the second floor.

Design by
© Home Planners

Width 36'-8"
Depth 66'-2"

Quote One®
Cost to build? See page 684
to order complete cost estimate
to build this house in your area!

DESIGN 5503

First Floor: 1,185 square feet
Second Floor: 880 square feet
Total: 2,065 square feet

A stately brick exterior, interesting rooflines and classic window treatment will set this traditional home apart. The open foyer leads to the corner living room, the two-car garage or the gourmet kitchen with a pantry, desk, breakfast nook and plenty of counter space. The family room is at the rear of the home. Upstairs, two secondary bedrooms share a full bath. The master bedroom showcases a sumptuous master bath.

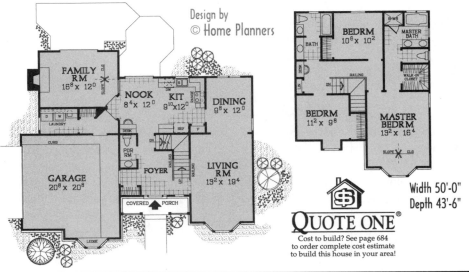

Design by
© Home Planners

Width 50'-0"
Depth 43'-6"

Quote One®
Cost to build? See page 684
to order complete cost estimate
to build this house in your area!

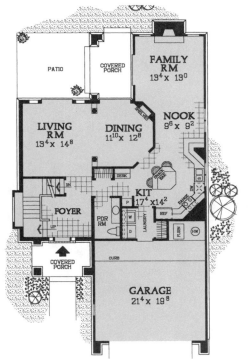

Design by
© Home Planners

Width 36'-8"
Depth 66'-2"

QUOTE ONE®
Cost to build? See page 684
to order complete cost estimate
to build this house in your area!

Spacious rooms and a flowing floor plan in this two-story traditional home create a perfect opportunity for entertaining family and friends. The sunlit foyer opens to a combination living/dining room separated by columns. Two glass doors let the outside in via the backyard and patio. Corner curio shelves in the dining area offer an excellent space for family heirlooms and/or conversation pieces. The spacious island kitchen features a pantry, writing desk and access to the utility room and two-car garage. Space between the kitchen and family room provides a great spot for the breakfast nook. Upstairs, two family bedrooms share a full hall bath that has dual sinks. The master bedroom features a central fireplace and a luxurious master bath with a corner whirlpool tub, separate basins and a walk-in closet. A deck provides views and completes the second floor.

**DESIGN
5519**
First Floor: 1,228 square feet
Second Floor: 1,080 square feet
Total: 2,308 square feet

TWO-STORY TRADITIONAL HOMES

DESIGN P193

First Floor: 1,589 square feet
Second Floor: 492 square feet
Total: 2,081 square feet
Bonus Room: 226 square feet

Gabled rooflines, copper roofs, and a covered front porch give this two-story home plenty of appeal. Inside, formal areas flank the two-story foyer. A curved staircase attractively separates the dining room from the vaulted family room. The efficient kitchen works well with the vaulted breakfast room. The first-floor master suite includes a vaulted ceiling, radius windows and a sumptuous master bath. Upstairs, two secondary bedrooms share a full bath. Please specify basement or crawlspace foundation when ordering.

Design by
© Frank Betz Associates, Inc.

Width 53'-0"
Depth 47'-8"

DESIGN P175

First Floor: 1,948 square feet
Second Floor: 544 square feet
Total: 2,492 square feet
Bonus Room: 400 square feet

High ceilings and big windows combine to produce openness and light. Arched openings outline the formal dining room and offer easy access from the kitchen to the vaulted family room. The master suite includes a sitting room, large walk-in closet and a compartmented bathroom with a garden tub. Two family bedrooms and bathrooms are upstairs, as well as an optional bonus room. Please specify basement, crawlspace or slab foundation when ordering.

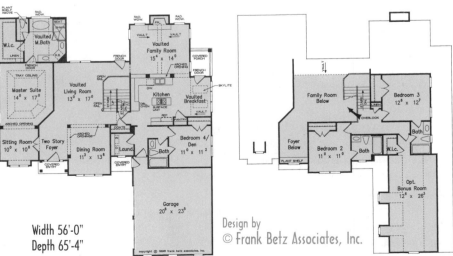

Width 56'-0"
Depth 65'-4"

Design by
© Frank Betz Associates, Inc.

www.homeplanners.com

Design by
© Frank Betz Associates, Inc.

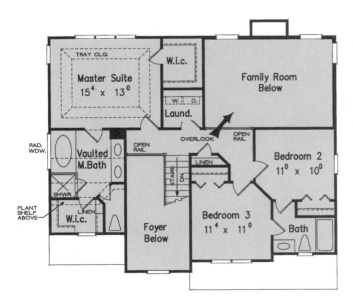

TRAY CLG.

W.i.c.

Master Suite
15⁴ x 13⁰

Family Room
Below

W. D.

Laund.

RAD.
WDW.

Vaulted
M.Bath

OPEN
RAIL

OVERLOOK

OPEN
RAIL

LINEN

STAIRS
DN

Bedroom 2
11⁰ x 10⁰

SHWR.

LINEN

PLANT
SHELF
ABOVE

W.i.c.

Foyer
Below

Bedroom 3
11⁴ x 11⁰

Bath

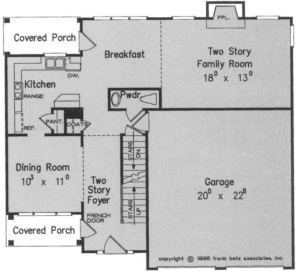

Covered Porch

Breakfast

Two Story
Family Room
18⁰ x 13⁰

FPL.

Kitchen

RANGE

DW.

Pwdr.

REF.

PANT.

COATS

Dining Room
10³ x 11⁰

Two
Story
Foyer

STAIRS
DN

Garage
20⁰ x 22⁸

Covered Porch

FRENCH
DOOR

STAIRS
UP

copyright © 1996 frank betz associates, inc.

Width 40'-0"
Depth 38'-10"

TWO-STORY TRADITIONAL HOMES

Elegant height, arches and distinguishing shutters draw attention to this stately home. An interior upper-level balcony overlooks the family room and its fireplace at the back of the home. The L-shaped kitchen adjoins the formal dining room and opens to the breakfast area, which has a door to the covered back porch. All three bedrooms are on the upper level. A tray ceiling highlights the master suite, which has two walk-in closets and a compartmented bath. Please specify basement or crawlspace foundation when ordering.

DESIGN P266
First Floor: 834 square feet
Second Floor: 872 square feet
Total: 1,706 square feet

**DESIGN
P132**

First Floor: 1,761 square feet
Second Floor: 580 square feet
Total: 2,341 square feet
Bonus Room: 276 square feet

Decorative arches and quoins give this home a wonderful curb appeal. The two-story foyer is bathed in natural light as it leads to the formal dining room, counter-filled kitchen and vaulted breakfast nook. A den, or possible fourth bedroom, includes a full bath. Located downstairs for privacy is a spacious master suite with a luxurious master bath. Two family bedrooms and a full bath are located on the second floor. Please specify basement or crawlspace foundation when ordering.

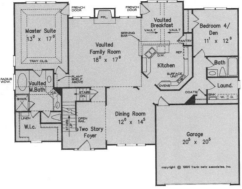

QUOTE ONE®

Cost to build? See page 684
to order complete cost estimate
to build this house in your area!

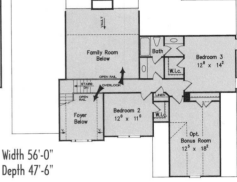

Design by
© Frank Betz Associates, Inc.

Width 56'-0"
Depth 47'-6"

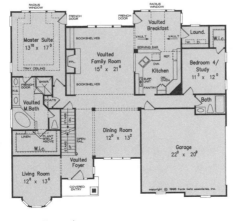

**DESIGN
P170**

First Floor: 2,015 square feet
Second Floor: 628 square feet
Total: 2,643 square feet
Bonus Room: 315 square feet

The offset entry in this plan leads to great livability inside. The formal living room opens directly off a vaulted foyer. An efficient kitchen serves the family room, vaulted breakfast room and the dining room. A secluded study can double as a guest suite. A full bath and two family bedrooms with walk-in closets are located on the upper level. An optional bonus room provides space for further expansion. Please specify crawlspace or basement foundation when ordering plans.

Design by
© Frank Betz Associates, Inc.

Width 56'-0"
Depth 52'-6"

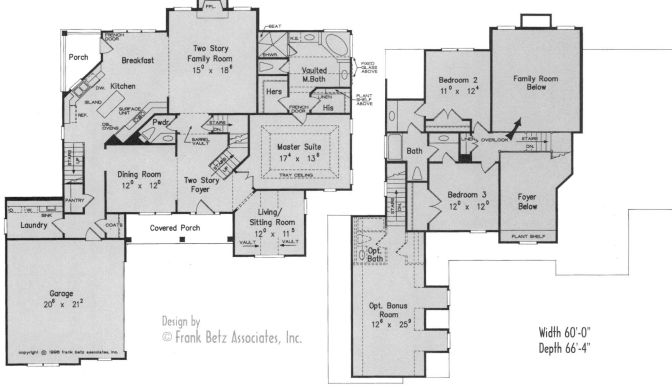

Porch

Breakfast

Two Story Family Room
15⁰ x 18⁶

FRENCH DOOR

FPL.

SEAT

K.S.

SHWR.

Vaulted M.Bath

FIXED GLASS ABOVE

Kitchen

DW.

ISLAND

REF.

SURFACE UNIT

DBL. OVENS

Hers

His

LINEN

FRENCH DOOR

PLANT SHELF ABOVE

Pwdr

STAIRS DN.

BARREL VAULT

Dining Room
12⁰ x 12⁰

Two Story Foyer

STAIRS UP

Master Suite
17⁴ x 13⁶

TRAY CEILING

STAIRS

PANTRY

Laundry

D. W. SINK

COATS

Covered Porch

Living/ Sitting Room
12⁰ x 11⁵

VAULT

VAULT

Garage
20⁶ x 21²

Design by
© Frank Betz Associates, Inc.

copyright © 1996 frank betz associates, inc.

Bedroom 2
11⁰ x 12⁴

Family Room Below

Bath

LINEN

OVERLOOK

STAIRS DN.

Bedroom 3
12⁰ x 12⁰

Foyer Below

PLANT SHELF

STAIRS DN.

Opt. Bath

Opt. Bonus Room
12⁶ x 25⁹

Width 60'-0"
Depth 66'-4"

Here is a truly elegant home with a striking exterior and an interior that uses diagonals to create comfort and space. The two-story foyer opens to the formal living/sitting room, which has a vaulted ceiling. The work areas of the kitchen, including an island, are at a 45-degree angle, making possible a triangular porch in that corner of the house. The two-car garage sits just beyond the laundry room and a coat closet. A secluded master suite offers two walk-in closets and a vaulted bath with an angled corner tub. The family room reaches to the second story, where two bedrooms and an optional bonus room complete the plan. Please specify basement or crawlspace foundation when ordering.

DESIGN P173
First Floor: 1,847 square feet
Second Floor: 548 square feet
Total: 2,395 square feet
Bonus Room: 395 square feet

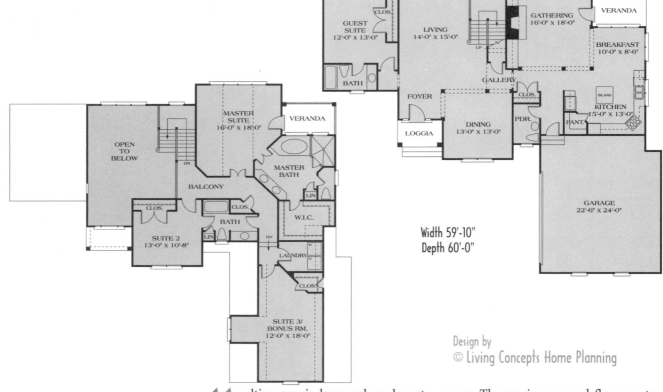

Width 59'-10"
Depth 60'-0"

GUEST SUITE 12'-0" x 13'-0"
LIVING 14'-0" x 15'-0"
GATHERING 16'-0" x 18'-0"
VERANDA
BREAKFAST 10'-0" x 8'-6"
CLOS.
BATH
UP
GALLERY
FOYER
CLOS.
ISLAND
KITCHEN 15'-0" x 13'-0"
LOGGIA
DINING 13'-0" x 13'-0"
PDR.
PANT.
GARAGE 22'-6" x 24'-0"

OPEN TO BELOW
MASTER SUITE 16'-0" x 18'-0"
VERANDA
MASTER BATH
DN
BALCONY
LIN
CLOS.
CLOS.
W.I.C.
BATH
SUITE 2 13'-0" x 10'-8"
LIN
DN
W D
LAUNDRY
CLOS.
SUITE 3/ BONUS RM. 12'-0" x 18'-0"

Design by
© Living Concepts Home Planning

DESIGN A161
First Floor: 1,644 square feet
Second Floor: 945 square feet
Total: 2,589 square feet
Bonus Room: 320 square feet

Multi-pane windows and an elegant two-story entrance add warmth to the exterior of this three-bed-room design with secluded guest suite on the first level. The living room and dining room share a large open area defined by columns. The large gathering room, with fireplace and built-in book-shelves, accesses the covered veranda and is open to the island kitchen and breakfast room. The spacious second-floor master bedroom suite features a sloped ceiling, private covered veranda, a bath with dual vanity and large walk-in closet. A second bedroom on this level shares a full bath with a generous bonus room over the garage. The laundry room is on the sec-ond floor near the bonus room for con-venience.

Design by
© Living Concepts Home Planning

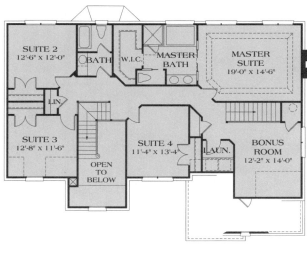

Width 57'-7"
Depth 44'-10"

DESIGN A164
First Floor: 1,426 square feet
Second Floor: 1,315 square feet
Total: 2,741 square feet
Bonus Room: 200 square feet

The handsome facade of this outstanding two-story contemporary home is equalled by its efficient interior design. A library with multi-pane windows is to the right of the entryway. The living room on the left adjoins a formal dining room with octagonal tray ceiling. The island kitchen fills a bay win-dow overlooking the rear deck. A large breakfast room is adjacent to the family room with fireplace and hearth. The master suite with cove ceiling, private bath and walk-in closet is on the second floor, along with three additional bedrooms and a full bath. A corner bonus room and laundry facilities are also on this level.

DESIGN M110

First Floor: 1,633 square feet
Second Floor: 629 square feet
Total: 2,262 square feet

High gables and corner quoins lend an extra dash of distinction to this fine traditional home. Columns grace the formal dining room, and straight ahead, the formal living room leads to the family room enhanced with a fireplace. The dinette, U-shaped kitchen and family room are all open to each other. A sloped ceiling and access to the backyard accent the master bedroom. A soothing tub, separate shower and large walk-in closet highlight the master bath. Upstairs, two family bedrooms share a full bath, with space allocated for an additional bath when needed.

Design by
© Fillmore Design Group

Width 55'-0"
Depth 55'-7"

DESIGN M133

First Floor: 1,815 square feet
Second Floor: 650 square feet
Total: 2,465 square feet

Towering brick gables create curb appeal in this traditional two-story design. A high-ceiling entry reveals an inviting formal dining room. A comfortable study contains full-wall bookshelves flanking an arch-top window. A wall of windows frames the spacious living room. The family room offers a high-vaulted ceiling, brick fireplace and hearth. The secluded master bedroom enjoys a high-sloped ceiling and atrium doors that open to a private patio. Upstairs, three additional bedrooms with full bath complete this marvelous home.

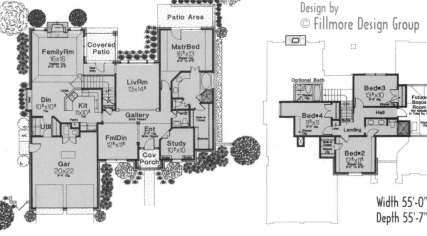

Design by
© Fillmore Design Group

Width 55'-0"
Depth 55'-7"

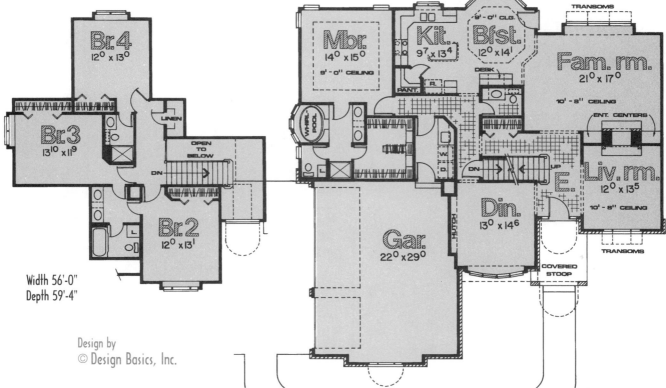

Mbr.
14⁰ x 15⁰
9'-0" CEILING

Kit.
9⁷ x 13⁴

Bfst.
12⁰ x 14¹
9'-0" CLG.

Fam. rm.
21⁰ x 17⁰
10'-8" CEILING

Br.4
12⁰ x 13⁰

Br.3
13¹⁰ x 11⁹

Br.2
12⁰ x 13¹

OPEN TO BELOW

LINEN

WHIRL POOL

PANT.

DESK

ENT. CENTERS

Liv. rm.
12⁰ x 13⁵
10'-8" CEILING

Gar.
22⁰ x 29⁰

Din.
13⁰ x 14⁶

HUTCH

COVERED STOOP

TRANSOMS

Width 56'-0"
Depth 59'-4"

Design by
© Design Basics, Inc.

The gorgeous entry of this traditional home opens to a formal dining room that offers hutch space, and a volume living room with through-fireplace to the spacious family room. Look for a tall ceiling and dual entertainment centers here. Adjacent is the bayed breakfast area and island kitchen with a wraparound counter and a walk-in pantry. The master suite is highlighted with a formal ceiling in the bedroom and a bath with a two-person whirlpool tub, bayed windows and a double vanity. Upstairs, two bedrooms share private access to a compartmented bath; another bedroom has a private bath. A three-car garage completes the plan.

DESIGN 9276
First Floor: 1,860 square feet
Second Floor: 848 square feet
Total: 2,708 square feet

Width 65'-11"
Depth 42'-5"

Design by
© James Fahy Design

DESIGN C135

First Floor: 1,445 square feet
Second Floor: 1,156 square feet
Total: 2,601 square feet
Bonus Room: 364 square feet

An offset covered entry porch and six charming gables accent the roofline of this delightful two-story traditional home. A well-lit study is tucked into the front-facing bay window. To the left of the foyer is the living room and formal dining room, defined by columns and a stepped ceiling. The L-shaped kitchen, dinette and family room with fireplace all flow together. A staircase outlining the two-story foyer leads to the master suite with a tray ceiling and corner tub. Three additional bedrooms on this level share a full bath. A bonus room over the garage offers an array of future options.

DESIGN K113

First Floor: 1,714 square feet
Second Floor: 723 square feet
Total: 2,437 square feet
Unfinished Basement: 1,698 square feet

This plan features a first-floor master suite with the secondary bedrooms upstairs. The family room rises a full two stories, creating a dramatic fireplace and window wall. Glass doors lead from the breakfast bay to the rear patio. The kitchen features a bar, pantry, pass-through window for easy cookouts and a phone desk. Three bedrooms on the second floor share a compartmented bath. The unfinished basement is designed for a future game room, bedrooms, a bath and storage.

Design by
© Design Profile, Inc.

Width 64'-0"
Depth 52'-0"

DESIGN K107

First Floor: 1,715 square feet
Second Floor: 1,257 square feet
Total: 2,972 square feet
Unfinished Basement: 1,811 square feet

Traditional elements from Federalist and Colonial styles combine to create a timeless look. A formal courtyard leads to the entry, which features a ceiling that rises above a curvilinear staircase. The oversized dining room is open to the living room. The dramatic two-story ceiling opens the family room to the loft above the wet bar. The spacious kitchen features a unique angular island. The master suite features a vaulted ceiling and a large glass bay window.

Width 62'-0"
Depth 63'-6"

Design by
© Design Profile, Inc.

TWO-STORY TRADITIONAL HOMES

DESIGN C109

First Floor: 1,577 square feet
Second Floor: 1,178 square feet
Total: 2,755 square feet

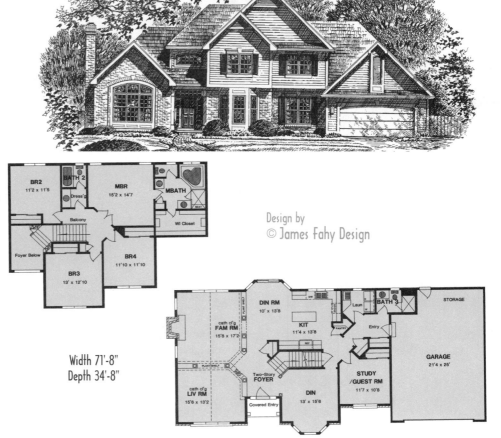

Design by
© James Fahy Design

A combination of brick and siding adds to the high style of this spacious home. The two-story foyer with a grand, angled staircase leads to the high volume of the living and family rooms. The gourmet kitchen features a center island work station and a walk-in pantry along with an adjoining dinette filled with natural light. Also found on the first floor is a private study that can double as a fifth bedroom. Double doors open to the second-floor master suite where an amenity-filled master bath provides a wealth of luxury.

Width 71'-8"
Depth 34'-8"

DESIGN C120

First Floor: 1,070 square feet
Second Floor: 789 square feet
Total: 1,859 square feet

Exterior appeal with elegant tradition is created by a detailed arched entry porch with Palladian window. The great room has an open and spacious atmosphere with its ten-foot walls and cathedral ceiling. Both the kitchen and dinette areas are filled with abundant natural light. The L-shaped stairs lead to a three-bedroom second floor with an angled balcony overlooking the foyer and great room. The master bedroom holds a large walk-in closet and a master bath featuring a corner glass shower and separate soaking tub.

Width 61'-4"
Depth 36'-0"

Design by
© James Fahy Design

Design by
© James Fahy Design

stepped cl'g
DIN
13' x 11'4
appx

KIT
11'6 x 12'6

Two-Story
Cl'g w/Vault
FAM RM
15' x 19'4

STUDY
10' x 11'4

Laun

D   W

Lav

Entry

DESK

LIV RM
13'6 x 11'4
plus bay

Two-Story
FOYER

DIN RM
12' x 16'2

GARAGE
21'8 x 22'8

Covered Entry

Width 60'-8"
Depth 49'-0"

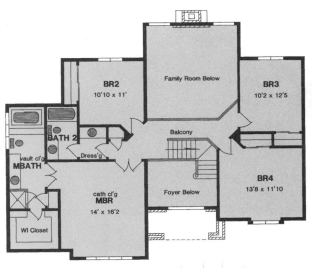

BR2
10'10 x 11'

Family Room Below

BR3
10'2 x 12'5

BATH 2

vault cl'g
MBATH

Dress'g

Balcony

cath cl'g
MBR
14' x 16'2

Foyer Below

BR4
13'8 x 11'10

WI Closet

TWO-STORY TRADITIONAL HOMES

T he graceful brick arch of the stepped cove entry is repeated in the window trim and the garage vent of this four-bedroom traditional home. The foyer is flanked by a formal dining room with bay window and offset living room with adjacent study. The family room with two-story vaulted ceiling features a center fireplace and windows on three sides. The island kitchen is open to a unique octagonal dinette with windows all around. Upstairs, a long balcony open to the family room below connects the master bedroom suite and three family bedrooms with shared hall bath. The master suite has a walk-in closet.

**DESIGN
C126**
First Floor: 1,422 square feet
Second Floor: 1,192 square feet
Total: 2,614 square feet

DESIGN 7023

First Floor: 1,979 square feet
Second Floor: 847 square feet
Total: 2,826 square feet

Here's a traditional home with an amenity-packed floor plan inside. The central great room has a centered fireplace framed by windows. A gourmet kitchen features an island cooktop counter, walk-in pantry and breakfast room. The sun room opens the morning area and kitchen to a sense of the outdoors. The private master suite provides an angled whirlpool tub, separate shower, double-bowl vanity and walk-in closet. Upstairs, each of three family bedrooms includes a walk-in closet.

Width 61'-0"
Depth 64'-4"

Design by
© Design Basics, Inc.

DESIGN 7261

First Floor: 1,093 square feet
Second Floor: 1,038 square feet
Total: 2,131 square feet

This beautifully proportioned design is complemented by a large covered porch framed with a wood railing. A bay window enhances the living room and French doors lead to the family room with its central fireplace. The dining room is just steps away from the open island kitchen and the breakfast bay. The four-bedroom sleeping zone is located on the second floor. The master bedroom contains a distinctive vaulted ceiling, plus a luxurious bath with a corner whirlpool tub and a massive walk-in closet.

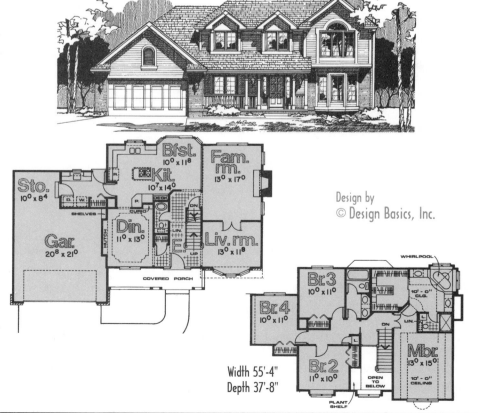

Design by
© Design Basics, Inc.

Width 55'-4"
Depth 37'-8"

www.homeplanners.com

Design by
© Design Basics, Inc.

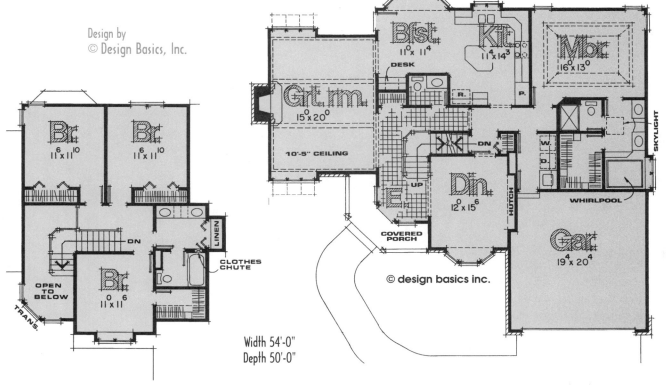

Width 54'-0"
Depth 50'-0"

© design basics inc.

This narrow-lot plan features a wrap-around porch at the two-story entry, which opens to the formal dining room with a beautiful bay window. The great room features a handsome fireplace and a ten-and-a-half foot ceiling. A well-equipped island kitchen with pantry and built-in desk is designed for the serious cook. The large master bedroom includes a vaulted ceiling and a luxury master bath. Upstairs, three secondary bedrooms with ample closet space share a compartmented bath. Note the large linen closet and clothes chute in the upstairs bath.

DESIGN 9232
First Floor: 1,551 square feet
Second Floor: 725 square feet
Total: 2,276 square feet

DESIGN 5527

First Floor: 1,228 square feet
Second Floor: 1,285 square feet
Total: 2,513 square feet

Amenities in this four-bedroom home include fireplaces in the family room and master bedroom, a covered porch that opens to the patio, and access from the master bedroom to an upper-level covered porch. From the tiled foyer, enter the open living/dining area or the kitchen with its planning desk and angled snack bar. Upstairs, the master suite includes a study area with a built-in desk and shelves, a walk-in closet and a luxurious bath with separate vanities. Three family bedrooms and a bath complete the second floor.

Design by
© Home Planners

Quote One®
Cost to build? See page 684
to order complete cost estimate
to build this house in your area!

Width 36'-8"
Depth 66'-2"

DESIGN 5555

First Floor: 1,356 square feet
Second Floor: 1,162 square feet
Total: 2,518 square feet

Four gables provide the facade of this home with elegant symmetry. The entry foyer leads to all rooms on both the first and second floors. A quiet study, or possible guest room, is tucked away at the front of the home. The U-shaped kitchen offers plenty of counter space, while the family room features French doors to the rear yard and a warming fireplace. On the upper level, the master bedroom includes a large walk-in closet and a secluded master bath. Three family bedrooms share a full hall bath.

Design by
© Home Planners

Quote One®
Cost to build? See page 684
to order complete cost estimate
to build this house in your area!

Width 58'-8"
Depth 44'-6"

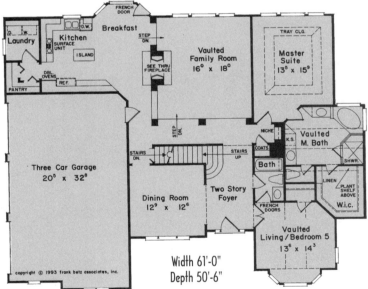

Width 61'-0"
Depth 50'-6"

copyright © 1993 frank betz associates, inc.

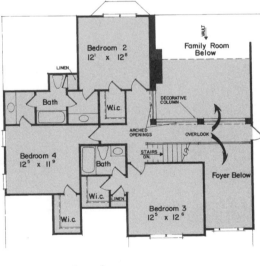

Design by
© Frank Betz Associates, Inc.

Brick and horizontal siding grace the facade of this super move-up two-story home. The square-footage, while being accommodating to any size family, is not excessive. The floor plan is thoroughly livable with main living areas and a master suite on the first floor and family bedrooms on the second floor. The vaulted family room can take care of both formal and informal gatherings and is complemented by both a bayed breakfast nook and a formal dining room. Or, if you prefer, make Bedroom 5 into a formal living room. The large kitchen features an island work station. The master suite holds all the luxury you expect: tray and vaulted ceilings, a walk-in closet, spa tub and double sinks. All three family bedrooms have walk-in closets; Bedroom 3 has a private bath. Please specify basement or crawlspace foundation when ordering.

DESIGN P388
First Floor: 1,870 square feet
Second Floor: 921 square feet
Total: 2,791 square feet

DESIGN T076

First Floor: 1,660 square feet
Second Floor: 665 square feet
Total: 2,325 square feet
Bonus Room: 240 square feet

This stately two-story Georgian home echoes tradition with the use of brick and jack-arch detailing. Inside, the foyer is flanked by a spacious dining room to the right and living room on the left. A two-story family room is accented by a warming fireplace. The secluded master bedroom with a tray ceiling includes a bath with His and Hers vanities, a garden tub and walk-in closet. Upstairs, three more bedrooms with roomy closets and two baths complete this home. This house is designed with a basement foundation.

Design by
© Stephen Fuller,
American Home Gallery

Width 64'-0"
Depth 48'-6"

Quote One®
Cost to build? See page 684 to order complete cost estimate to build this house in your area!

DESIGN 7240

First Floor: 1,800 square feet
Second Floor: 803 square feet
Total: 2,603 square feet

Columns and double doors create a majestic elevation. A two-story foyer opens to a bay-windowed den with spider beams and to a dining room that features built-in hutch space and French doors to the kitchen. Here, the adjoining breakfast room and gathering room share the warmth of a three-sided fireplace. The isolated master suite enjoys a private covered deck and a lavish bath with a whirlpool tub and walk-in closet. Upstairs, Bedroom 2 has a private bath while Bedrooms 3 and 4 share a compartmented bath.

Width 62'-0"
Depth 60'-8"

Design by
© Design Basics, Inc.

DESIGN 6721

First Floor: 3,010 square feet
Second Floor: 948 square feet
Total: 3,958 square feet

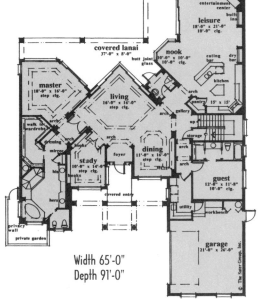

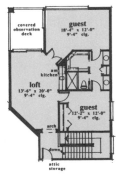

Width 65'-0"
Depth 91'-0"

Design by
© The Sater Design Collection

This elegant home has all the angles covered, from its varied roofline to its interesting interior spaces. As you enter this unique design, a gracious living room opens up before you with views through dramatic corner windows to the covered lanai and beyond. A study with built-in bookcases and a formal dining room with built-in server flank the front entrance. Built-in fixtures are also a feature of the large leisure area, kitchen and adjacent breakfast nook. A breathtaking master suite enjoys its own private garden.

DESIGN 6652

First Floor: 2,181 square feet
Second Floor: 710 square feet
Total: 2,891 square feet

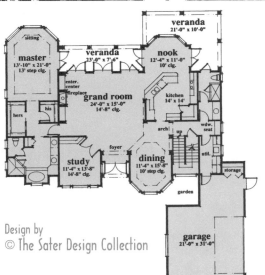

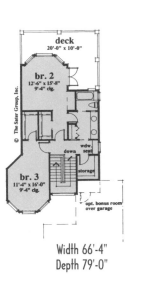

Design by
© The Sater Design Collection

Width 66'-4"
Depth 79'-0"

An arched, covered porch presents fine double doors leading to a spacious foyer in this decidedly European home. A two-story tower contains an elegant formal dining room on the first floor and a spacious bedroom on the second. The grand room contains a fireplace. The secluded master suite includes a sitting bay, rear-veranda access, His and Hers walk-in closets and a lavish bath. Upstairs, two bedrooms, both with walk-in closets, share a full hall bath with twin vanities. Please specify basement or slab foundation when ordering.

DESIGN 9369

First Floor: 1,369 square feet
Second Floor: 1,111 square feet
Total: 2,480 square feet

This delightful plan offers the best in transitional design. Combined dining and living areas provide abundant space for entertaining. Or if preferred, escape to the den for quiet time with a book—built-in bookshelves fill out one wall of this room. The kitchen makes use of the island counter space and breakfast nook. Take a step down into the large family room and enjoy the ambience of a cozy fireplace and beam ceiling. The master bedroom highlights the second floor. Three additional bedrooms and another full bath complete the design.

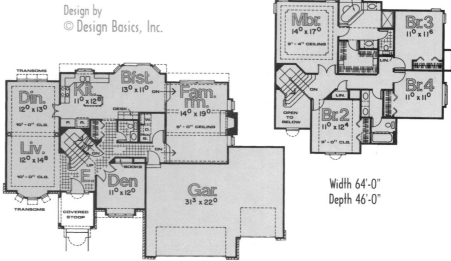

Design by
© Design Basics, Inc.

Width 64'-0"
Depth 46'-0"

DESIGN 9244

First Floor: 1,972 square feet
Second Floor: 893 square feet
Total: 2,865 square feet

Natural light from transom windows floods the entry of this home, traditionally flanked by the formal living room and dining room. The large great room to the rear of the plan features a cathedral ceiling and fireplace framed by windows. An island kitchen includes two pantries and a gazebo dinette. The sumptuous master suite has a bow window and tiered ceiling, plus a lush bath. Second-floor bedrooms include two with a Hollywood bath and one with its own three-quarter bath.

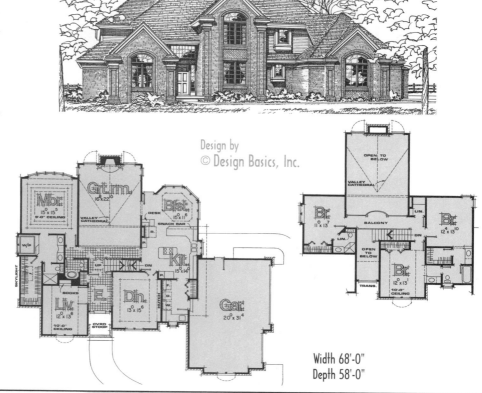

Design by
© Design Basics, Inc.

Width 68'-0"
Depth 58'-0"

www.homeplanners.com

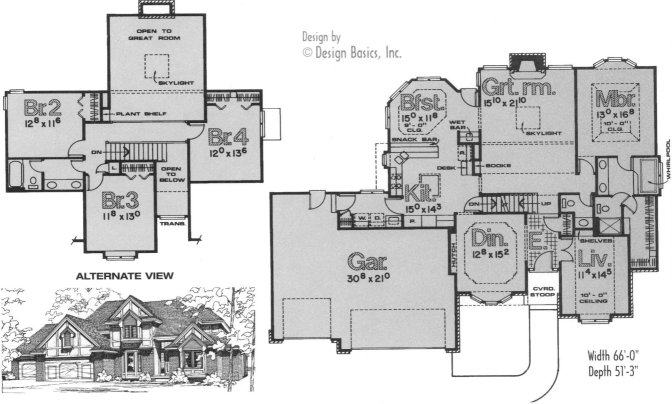

OPEN TO GREAT ROOM

SKYLIGHT

PLANT SHELF

Br.2
12⁸ x 11⁶

DN

Br.4
12⁰ x 13⁶

OPEN TO BELOW

Br.3
11⁸ x 13⁰

TRANS.

ALTERNATE VIEW

Design by
© Design Basics, Inc.

Bfst.
15⁰ x 11⁸
9'-0" CLG.

SNACK BAR

WET BAR

Grt. rm.
15¹⁰ x 21¹⁰

SKYLIGHT

Mbr.
13⁰ x 16⁸
10'-0" CLG.

WHIRLPOOL

DESK

BOOKS

Kit.
15⁰ x 14³

DN

UP

Gar.
30⁸ x 21⁰

P.

Din.
12⁸ x 15²

HUTCH

SHELVES

Liv.
11⁴ x 14⁵
10'-0" CEILING

CVRD. STOOP

Width 66'-0"
Depth 51'-3"

E nter this house to find a formal dining room graced with hutch space, special ceiling detail and a beautiful bayed window. Or, turn to the right and discover a formal living room with a bright boxed window. The great room contains a fireplace framed by windows, a sloped ceiling with a skylight, and a bookcase. The sunny breakfast area features a wet bar and is served by a snack bar in the island kitchen, which also includes a pantry and a planning desk. The three-car garage is just past the laundry at the service entry. The master bedroom, with a bay window, leads to a dressing/bath area featuring a walk-in closet and a whirlpool tub. Upstairs, three more bedrooms share a compartmented hall bath that has a double vanity. This plan comes with a choice of two exterior elevations.

TWO-STORY TRADITIONAL HOMES

DESIGN 9231
First Floor: 1,748 square feet
Second Floor: 834 square feet
Total: 2,582 square feet

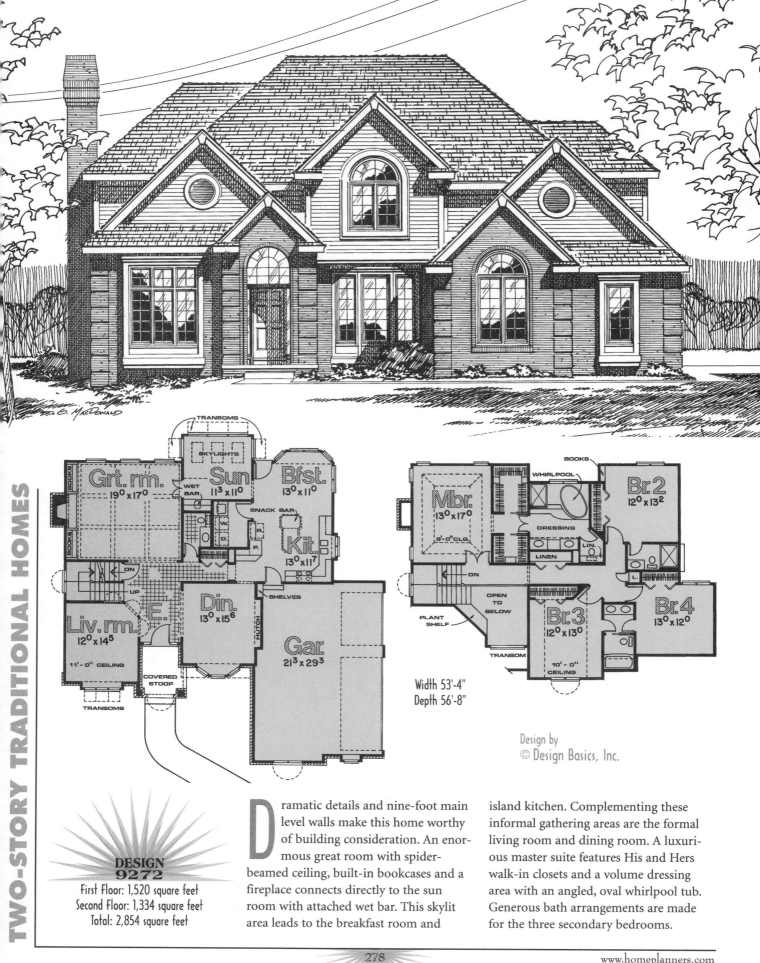

TRANSOMS

SKYLIGHTS

Grt. rm.
19⁰ x 17⁰

Sun
11³ x 11⁰

Bfst.
13⁰ x 11⁰

WET BAR

SNACK BAR

Kit.
13⁰ x 11⁷

Liv. rm.
12⁰ x 14⁵

11'-0" CEILING

Din.
13⁰ x 15⁶

SHELVES

HUTCH

Gar.
21³ x 29³

COVERED STOOP

TRANSOMS

DN
UP

BOOKS

WHIRLPOOL

Mbr.
13⁰ x 17⁰
9'-0" CLG.

Br. 2
12⁰ x 13²

DRESSING

LINEN

LIN.

DN

OPEN TO BELOW

PLANT SHELF

TRANSOM

Br. 3
12⁰ x 13⁰
10'-0" CEILING

Br. 4
13⁰ x 12⁰

BOOKS

Width 53'-4"
Depth 56'-8"

Design by
© Design Basics, Inc.

DESIGN 9272
First Floor: 1,520 square feet
Second Floor: 1,334 square feet
Total: 2,854 square feet

D ramatic details and nine-foot main level walls make this home worthy of building consideration. An enormous great room with spider-beamed ceiling, built-in bookcases and a fireplace connects directly to the sun room with attached wet bar. This skylit area leads to the breakfast room and island kitchen. Complementing these informal gathering areas are the formal living room and dining room. A luxurious master suite features His and Hers walk-in closets and a volume dressing area with an angled, oval whirlpool tub. Generous bath arrangements are made for the three secondary bedrooms.

DESIGN 9395

First Floor: 2,158 square feet
Second Floor: 821 square feet
Total: 2,979 square feet

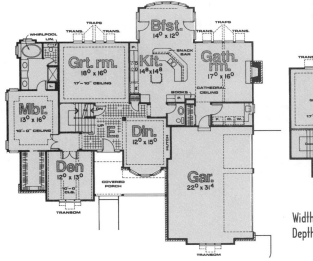

Design by
© Design Basics, Inc.

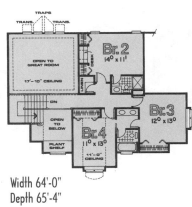

Width 64'-0"
Depth 65'-4"

The livability present in this design will delight even the most discerning homeowner. Upon entry, an elegant dining room with built-in hutch space commands attention. A two-story great room provides the perfect setting for entertaining. For quieter pursuits, a den is located at the front of the house. Family time is easily spent in the open kitchen, breakfast room and gathering room. Four bedrooms include a first-floor master suite with a private bath and a large, walk-in closet.

DESIGN 9504

First Floor: 1,465 square feet
Second Floor: 1,103 square feet
Total: 2,568 square feet
Bonus Room: 303 square feet

With a plan that boasts excellent traffic patterns, this home will accommodate the modern family well. Formal dining and living rooms remain to one side of the house. Highlights of the front den include a bay window and built-in bookshelves. The gourmet kitchen opens into a nook and a family room. Two second-floor family bedrooms share a large hall bath along with a bonus room. The spacious master suite has a walk-in closet and luxurious spa bath.

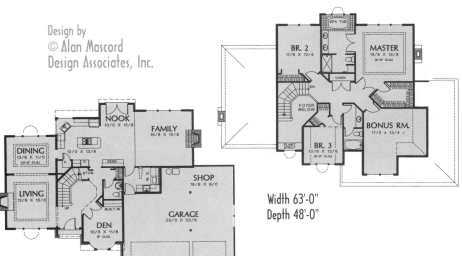

Design by
© Alan Mascord
Design Associates, Inc.

Width 63'-0"
Depth 48'-0"

DESIGN 9370

First Floor: 2,084 square feet
Second Floor: 848 square feet
Total: 2,932 square feet

The combination of brick, stucco and elegant detail provides this home with instant curb appeal. The entry is flanked by the formal dining room and the den with a fireplace. The great room offers a through-fireplace to the hearth room and French doors to a covered veranda. A sunny breakfast room and kitchen feature an island with snack bar, wrapping counters and a pantry. The first-floor master suite provides two closets, a whirlpool tub, His and Hers vanities and access to the covered veranda. Three second-floor bedrooms offer walk-in closets.

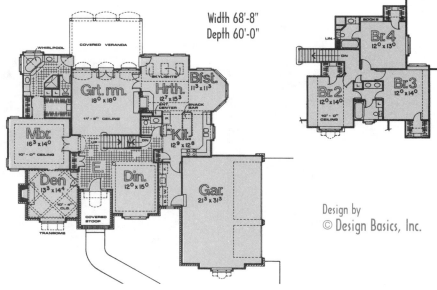

Width 68'-8"
Depth 60'-0"

Design by
© Design Basics, Inc.

DESIGN 9326

First Floor: 2,073 square feet
Second Floor: 741 square feet
Total: 2,814 square feet

From the curbside of this 1½-story home, brick and stucco accents command attention. Ten-foot ceilings enhance the living room and comfortable great room, which are separated by French doors. Special features in the gourmet kitchen and hearth room include a breakfast nook, snack bar and generous counter space. The main-floor master suite offers a tiered ceiling, huge walk-in closet, corner whirlpool tub and His and Hers vanities. Upstairs, three generous bedrooms share a compartmented bath.

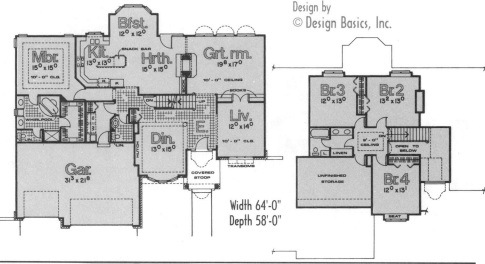

Design by
© Design Basics, Inc.

Width 64'-0"
Depth 58'-0"

Design by
© Design Basics, Inc.

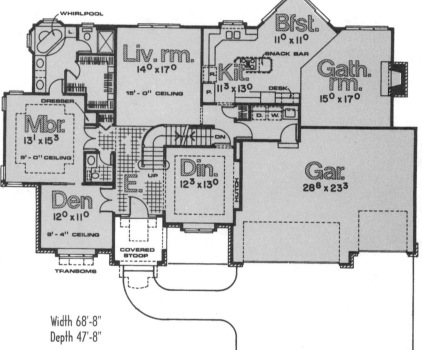

TRANSOMS

OPEN TO
LIVING ROOM

15'-0" CEILING

Br. 3
11⁰ x 12⁰

Br. 4
11⁰ x 12⁰

DN

UNFINISHED
STORAGE

OPEN
TO
BELOW

Br. 2
11³ x 13⁰

TRANSOMS

WHIRLPOOL

DRESSER

Mbr.
13¹ x 15³

9'-0" CEILING

Den
12⁰ x 11⁰

9'-4" CEILING

COVERED
STOOP

TRANSOMS

Liv. rm.
14⁰ x 17⁰

15'-0" CEILING

Bfst.
11⁰ x 11⁰

SNACK BAR

Kit.
11³ x 13⁰

P.

DESK

D. W.

**Gath.
rm.**
15⁰ x 17⁰

UP

Din.
12³ x 13⁰

HUTCH

DN

Gar.
28⁸ x 23³

Width 68'-8"
Depth 47'-8"

TWO-STORY TRADITIONAL HOMES

Elegant windows and trim details highlight the exterior of this traditional home. In the living room, transom windows let in plenty of light. The formal dining room features hutch space. Casual living is the focus in the heartwarming kitchen and gathering room. Long wrapping counters, a cooktop island with a snack bar and an angular breakfast nook nicely balance the large gathering room that's accented with a fireplace. The secluded master suite includes a nine-foot ceiling, pocket door to the den, corner whirlpool tub and huge walk-in closet. Three family bedrooms are on the second level.

**DESIGN
9325**
First Floor: 1,829 square feet
Second Floor: 657 square feet
Total: 2,486 square feet

DESIGN 9249

First Floor: 1,733 square feet
Second Floor: 672 square feet
Total: 2,405 square feet

Split-bedroom floor planning highlights this volume-look home. The first-floor master suite is completely private and perfectly pampering with a huge walk-in closet, double vanity and separate tub and shower. The great room and hearth room share a through-fireplace and are complemented by a breakfast area and island kitchen. Formal entertaining is enhanced by the dining room with hutch space and boxed window. A half bath just off the hearth room will be appreciated by visitors. Three family bedrooms upstairs share a full bath.

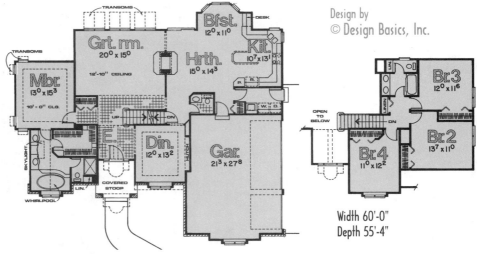

Design by
© Design Basics, Inc.

Width 60'-0"
Depth 55'-4"

DESIGN 9280

First Floor: 1,348 square feet
Second Floor: 603 square feet
Total: 1,951 square feet

Highlighting the elevation of this four-bedroom family home is a covered porch. Upon entering, a spacious great room gains attention. Cooks will enjoy the thoughtfully designed kitchen with a snack bar, pantry and window above the sink. A sunny breakfast room is open to this area. In the master suite, a tiered ceiling, double vanities, corner whirlpool tub and large walk-in closet are sure to please. Upstairs, three secondary bedrooms share a hall bath.

Width 54'-0"
Depth 48'-8"

Design by
© Design Basics, Inc.

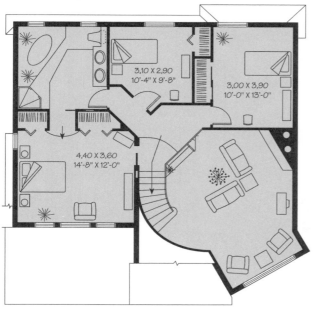

Design by
© Drummond Designs, Inc.

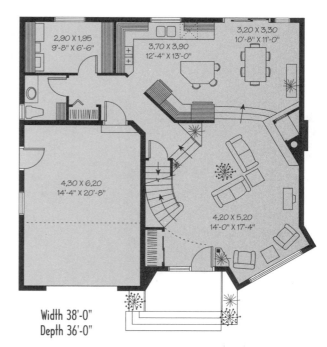

Width 38'-0"
Depth 36'-0"

A rch-top windows offer charming accents to this distinctive contemporary exterior. The entry leads to the living room, which has a fireplace and a cathedral ceiling. A gourmet kitchen serves the dining room, which opens to the outdoors. A laundry room and half bath complete the first floor. An angled whirlpool tub and a double vanity enhance the upstairs master suite. Two secondary bedrooms complete the upper level. A garage connects to the main house at a service entrance. This home is designed with a basement foundation.

DESIGN Z033

First Floor: 917 square feet
Second Floor: 742 square feet
Total: 1,659 square feet

Width 67'-10"
Depth 56'-4"

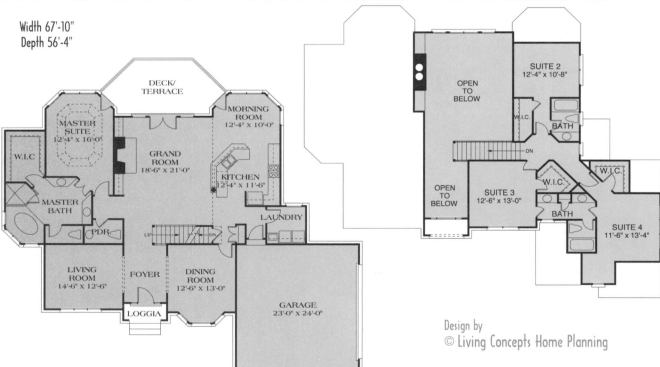

MASTER SUITE
12'-4" x 16'-0"

W.I.C

MASTER BATH

PDR.

DECK/TERRACE

GRAND ROOM
18'-6" x 21'-0"

MORNING ROOM
12'-4" x 10'-0"

KITCHEN
12'-4" x 11'-6"

LAUNDRY

UP DN

LIVING ROOM
14'-6" x 12'-6"

FOYER

DINING ROOM
12'-6" x 13'-0"

GARAGE
23'-0" x 24'-0"

LOGGIA

OPEN TO BELOW

SUITE 2
12'-4" x 10'-8"

W.I.C

BATH

DN

OPEN TO BELOW

SUITE 3
12'-6" x 13'-0"

W.I.C

W.I.C

BATH

SUITE 4
11'-6" x 13'-4"

Design by
© Living Concepts Home Planning

DESIGN A118
First Floor: 1,878 square feet
Second Floor: 886 square feet
Total: 2,764 square feet

This distinguished brick home with traditional stucco accents includes a spectacular, two-story foyer and grand room featuring a dramatic Palladian window. The grand room also opens to the kitchen and morning room. The master suite and morning room create matching bay wings to form a beautiful rear facade. A deck/terrace is accessible from both wings. The bay-windowed master suite features a tray ceiling in the bedroom, large walk-in closet and bath with dual vanities and garden tub. Upstairs are three additional suites and two baths. This design offers an optional basement plan that includes a guest suite and recreation area. It can be developed at a later time if desired.

DESIGN A117

First Floor: 1,737 square feet
Second Floor: 727 square feet
Total: 2,464 square feet
Bonus Room: 376 square feet

The beauty and warmth of a brick facade adds stately elegance to this traditional design. Its open floor plan is highlighted by a two-story living room and open dining room. A full kitchen, complete with a central cooking island, opens into a bright breakfast area. The master suite offers an ample walk-in closet/dressing area and a bath featuring an exquisite double vanity and a tub with corner windows. Please specify basement or crawlspace foundation when ordering.

Width 65'-6"
Depth 53'-0"

Design by
© Living Concepts Home Planning

DESIGN B138

First Floor: 1,520 square feet
Second Floor: 489 square feet
Total: 2,009 square feet

The multi-level hipped rooflines and right-angle garage create a cozy sense of enclosure in this spacious two-story home. The first floor centers around an enormous family room with a fireplace. The master suite comprises the left side of the plan with dual lavatories and separate shower and tub in the L-shaped bath. To the right of the plan, the large U-shaped kitchen is open to the breakfast area. The formal dining room features a built-in china cabinet. Two additional bedrooms upstairs adjoin a shared bath.

Width 57'-0"
Depth 61'-6"

Design by
© Greg Marquis & Associates

TWO-STORY TRADITIONAL HOMES

Width 62'-3"
Depth 51'-2"

Design by
© R.L. Pfotenhauer

DESIGN F153
First Floor: 1,407 square feet
Second Floor: 1,157 square feet
Total: 2,564 square feet

Although one of the massive chimneys on this French stucco home is decorative, fireplaces in the family, living and dining rooms will ensure that you have no trouble keeping warm. The front of the house appears symmetrical, but the front door is off center, adding a bit of eccentricity. The entrance opens to the formal rooms, then leads back to the kitchen, which opens to a breakfast area with French doors to the patio. The sunken family room also accesses the patio. Upstairs, skylights brighten two of the three bedrooms. One has a private bath and a walk-in closet. The others share a linen closet and a bath that has a dual-sink vanity. A garage with side load sits to the back of the plan.

DESIGN S102

First Floor: 1,375 square feet
Second Floor: 1,087 square feet
Total: 2,462 square feet
Bonus Room: 156 square feet

Design by
© Archival Designs

Width 59'-6"
Depth 39'-0"

Fanlight and oxeye windows over a casement door light the two-story foyer in this stately design. Columns decorate the formal dining hall, and the kitchen includes a butler's pantry, corner sink and bar. The morning room adjoins the two-story grand salon through an elegant archway. The second-floor master suite features double doors, an octagonal tray ceiling and closets in both the bedroom and the bath, which offers a corner tub, shower seat and twin vanities. Two additional bedrooms share a full bath that includes private vanities.

Design by
© Drummond Designs, Inc.

DESIGN Z012

First Floor: 924 square feet
Second Floor: 1,052 square feet
Total: 1,976 square feet

This magnificent European adaptation is highlighted by hip roofs, plenty of windows, cornice detailing and an elegant entrance door adjacent to an impressive two-story turret. Inside are a magnificent living/dining area, U-shaped kitchen, breakfast bar and comfortable family room. A gracious staircase leads upstairs to a deluxe master suite. A well-lit home office and two secondary bedrooms share this level with a full bath. This home is designed with a basement foundation.

Width 44'-8"
Depth 36'-0"

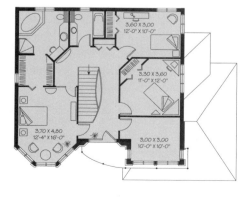

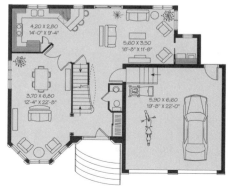

TWO-STORY TRADITIONAL HOMES

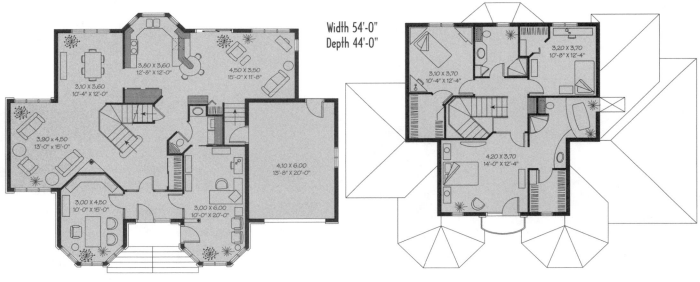

Width 54'-0"
Depth 44'-0"

3,80 x 3,60
12'-8" X 12'-0"

4,50 X 3,50
15'-0" X 11'-8"

3,10 X 3,60
10'-4" X 12'-0"

3,90 x 4,50
13'-0" X 15'-0"

4,10 X 6.00
13'-8" X 20'-0"

3,00 X 4,50
10'-0" X 15'-0"

3,00 X 6.00
10'-0" X 20'-0"

3,10 X 3,70
10'-4" X 12'-4"

3,20 x 3,70
10'-8" X 12'-4"

4,20 X 3,70
14'-0" X 12'-4"

Design by
© Drummond Designs, Inc.

DESIGN Z007
First Floor: 1,468 square feet
Second Floor: 936 square feet
Total: 2,404 square feet

The stately proportions and exquisite European detailing of this home are sure to please. Like so many European houses, interesting rooflines set the character of this design. Observe the delightful interplay of gable roof, hip roof and front turrets. A sturdy brick exterior is offset by delicate window detailing, railings and a romantic upstairs balcony above the front entry. Inside is a very livable plan. The kitchen features a circular breakfast counter for casual dining and an adjoining formal dining area. Two very large home offices are located in the front turrets with access to a private bathroom and private service door. A splendid staircase leads upstairs to the sleeping area containing a well-appointed master suite plus two family bedrooms that share a full bath. The garage opens into the family room. This home is designed with a basement foundation.

DESIGN Z016

First Floor: 916 square feet
Second Floor: 1,080 square feet
Total: 1,996 square feet

The entrance hall features a cathedral ceiling and an elegant stairway. Multiple windows in the turret provide natural light in the living room and master bedroom. The U-shaped kitchen counter ends with a snack bar shared with the family room. Three bedrooms, two full baths and the large laundry room are all on the second floor. This home is designed with a basement foundation.

Design by
© Drummond Designs, Inc.

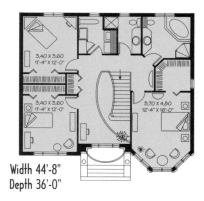

Width 44'-8"
Depth 36'-0"

DESIGN J133

First Floor: 1,357 square feet
Second Floor: 1,092 square feet
Total: 2,449 square feet
Bonus Room: 240 square feet

Two-story bay windows and decorative gables present an arresting exterior for this contemporary home. Double columns flank the covered entry foyer that leads to the formal dining room. An isolated den includes a separate balcony. The tiled kitchen features an angled cooktop counter facing the breakfast nook. A large family room accesses the rear deck. The master suite features sloped ceilings and an L-shaped walk-in closet. Please specify basement or crawlspace foundation when ordering.

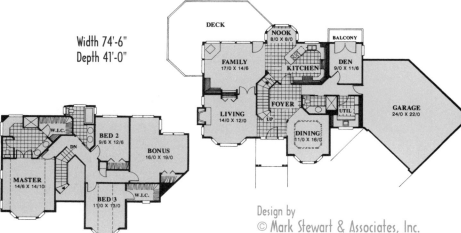

Width 74'-6"
Depth 41'-0"

Design by
© Mark Stewart & Associates, Inc.

DESIGN S120

First Floor: 1,920 square feet
Second Floor: 912 square feet
Total: 2,832 square feet

The impressive facade of this classic design previews an elegant floor plan. To the left of the large foyer, French doors open to a study filled with natural light. A single column defines the open dining room. The living room/den and kitchen provide space for family gatherings. A guest room features its own bath. The master suite offers a walk-in closet, luxurious bath and private access to the study. Upstairs, two bedrooms—each with a private compartmented vanity—share a bath.

Width 70'-0"
Depth 40'-0"

Design by
© Archival Designs

DESIGN S143

First Floor: 1,431 square feet
Second Floor: 1,519 square feet
Total: 2,950 square feet

Stunning stucco detailing and an elegant, arched entrance dress up this fine four-bedroom home. Inside columns separate the formal rooms. The spacious family room features a fireplace and rear-yard access. A solarium near the efficient kitchen provides a sunny place to relax. The keeping room is another gathering spot that will surely be a favorite of your family. The homeowner will have a hard time leaving the wonderful master suite. Two walk-in closets, a separate octagonal sitting room and a fabulous bath are sure to please.

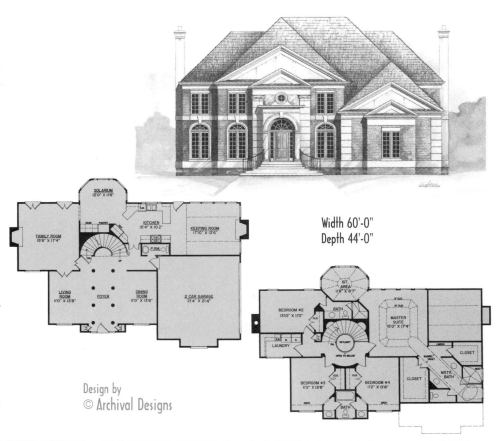

Width 60'-0"
Depth 44'-0"

Design by
© Archival Designs

Design by
© Design Basics, Inc.

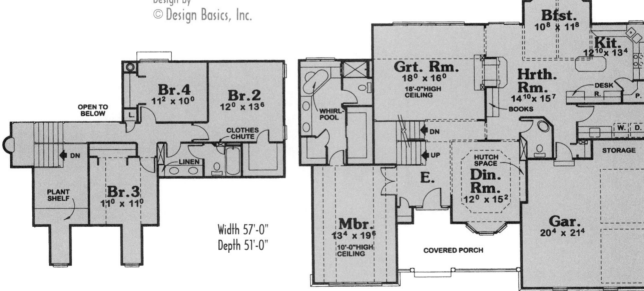

Br.4
11^2 x 10^0

Br.2
12^0 x 13^6

OPEN TO BELOW

CLOTHES CHUTE

LINEN

DN

PLANT SHELF

Br.3
11^0 x 11^0

Width 57'-0"
Depth 51'-0"

WHIRL-POOL

Grt. Rm.
18^0 x 16^0
18'-0"HIGH CEILING

Bfst.
10^8 x 11^8

Kit.
12^{10} x 13^4

Hrth. Rm.
14^{10} x 15^7
BOOKS

DESK
R.
P.

W.   D.

STORAGE

DN

UP

HUTCH SPACE

Din. Rm.
12^0 x 15^2

E.

Mbr.
13^4 x 19^6
10'-0"HIGH CEILING

Gar.
20^4 x 21^4

COVERED PORCH

TWO-STORY TRADITIONAL HOMES

T his stucco home features a volume roof, European detailing and a welcoming porch with columns and a balustrade. An elegant front door leads to a compact, open floor plan. Traffic flows easily from the entry to the dining room and the great room for formal entertaining, and around the hearth room, breakfast nook and kitchen for casual living. A through-fireplace warms both areas, while bay windows add a nice touch to the dining and breakfast rooms. The U-shaped kitchen includes a work island, corner windowed sink, walk-in pantry and built-in desk. The master suite fills the left side of the plan, and offers a corner tub and a compartmented toilet. Three family bedrooms are upstairs, sharing a bath that has a dual-bowl vanity and a clothes chute to the laundry.

DESIGN 7019
First Floor: 1,795 square feet
Second Floor: 717 square feet
Total: 2,512 square feet

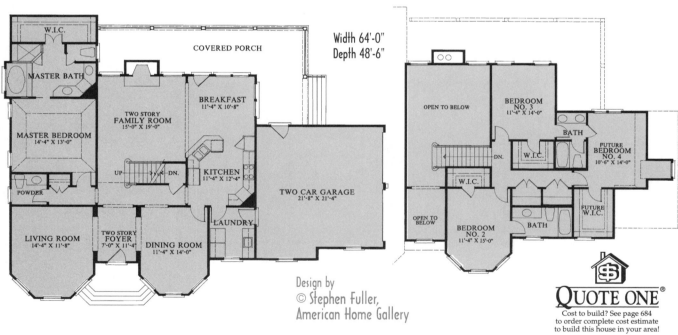

Width 64'-0"
Depth 48'-6"

COVERED PORCH

W.I.C.

MASTER BATH

MASTER BEDROOM
14'-4" X 13'-0"

POWDER

TWO STORY
FAMILY ROOM
15'-0" X 19'-0"

BREAKFAST
11'-4" X 10'-8"

UP   DN.

KITCHEN
11'-4" X 12'-4"

TWO CAR GARAGE
21'-8" X 21'-4"

LIVING ROOM
14'-4" X 11'-8"

TWO STORY
FOYER
7'-0" X 11'-4"

DINING ROOM
11'-4" X 14'-0"

LAUNDRY

OPEN TO BELOW

BEDROOM
NO. 3
11'-4" X 14'-0"

BATH

FUTURE
BEDROOM
NO. 4
10'-6" X 14'-0"

DN.

W.I.C.

W.I.C.

FUTURE
W.I.C.

OPEN TO
BELOW

BEDROOM
NO. 2
11'-4" X 15'-0"

BATH

Design by
© Stephen Fuller,
American Home Gallery

QUOTE ONE®
Cost to build? See page 684
to order complete cost estimate
to build this house in your area!

DESIGN T089
First Floor: 1,660 square feet
Second Floor: 665 square feet
Total: 2,325 square feet

This European design is filled with space for formal and informal occasions. Informal areas include an open kitchen, breakfast room and family room with fireplace. Formal rooms surround the foyer, with the living room on the left and dining room on the right. The master suite is conveniently placed on the first floor, with a gorgeous master bath and a walk-in closet. Each of the family bedrooms upstairs also features a sizable walk-in closet and access to a full bath. Additional storage space is found in the hallway. A fourth bedroom, not included in the square footage, is optional. Both the breakfast room and garage access the covered porch. This home is designed with a basement foundation.

The home, as shown in the photograph, may differ from the actual blueprints. For more detailed information, please check the floor plans carefully.

Photo by Bob Greenspan

Width 63'-0"
Depth 50'-0"

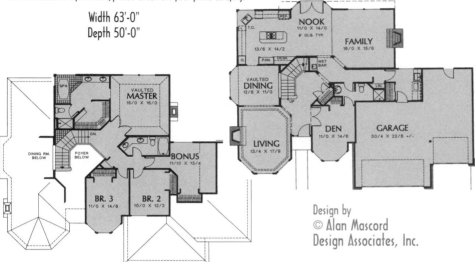

Design by
© Alan Mascord
Design Associates, Inc.

DESIGN 9478

First Floor: 1,586 square feet
Second Floor: 960 square feet
Total: 2,546 square feet

L

This country home offers a fresh face and plenty of personality. Inside, the foyer opens to a quiet den—the lower bay of the turret—through French doors. A formal living room with a tray ceiling leads to the vaulted dining room, which is served by a gourmet kitchen. A spacious family area offers its own fireplace with a tiled hearth. Upstairs, a secluded master suite boasts a corner tiled-rim spa tub and an angled walk-in closet. Two family bedrooms share a full hall bath and a sizable bonus room.

The home, as shown in the photograph, may differ from the actual blueprints. For more detailed information, please check the floor plans carefully.

Photo by Bob Greenspan

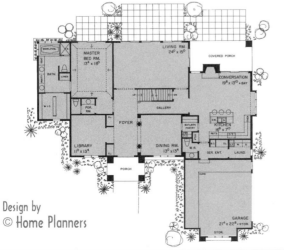

Design by
© Home Planners

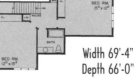

Width 69'-4"
Depth 66'-0"

Quote One®

Cost to build? See page 684 to order complete cost estimate to build this house in your area!

DESIGN 3558

First Floor: 2,328 square feet
Second Floor: 603 square feet
Total: 2,931 square feet

L D

This home will keep even the most active family from feeling cramped. A broad foyer opens to a living room that features sliding glass doors to a rear terrace and covered porch. Adjacent to the kitchen is a conversation area with additional access to the covered porch, a snack bar, fireplace and a window bay. Placed conveniently on the first floor, the master suite features a roomy bath with a huge walk-in closet and dual vanities. A library completes this level. Two large bedrooms are found on the second floor and share a full hall bath.

DESIGN X031

First Floor: 1,268 square feet
Second Floor: 1,333 square feet
Total: 2,601 square feet

Visual delight in this European-style home includes a high, hip roof, multi-pane windows and a glass entry with transom. Formal elegance is captured in the two-story living area featuring a warming fireplace and deck entry. The open space of the kitchen and breakfast area is accented by a bay window. One family bedroom with a full bath resides on the first floor; the remaining two bedrooms and luxurious master suite are located on the second floor.

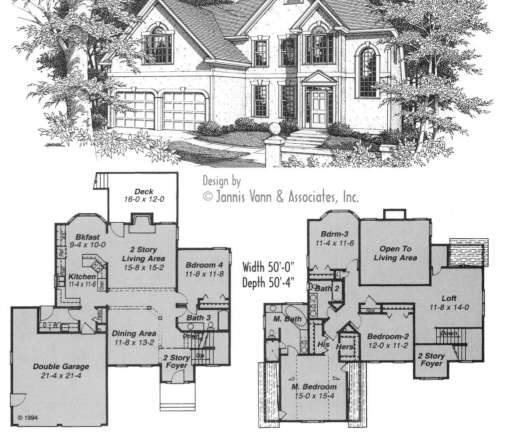

Design by
© Jannis Vann & Associates, Inc.

Width 50'-0"
Depth 50'-4"

DESIGN A112

First Floor: 2,167 square feet
Second Floor: 891 square feet
Total: 3,058 square feet
Bonus Room: 252 square feet

A key feature of this exciting plan is the den/guest suite on the main level. High-volume ceilings throughout and columns with half-walls in the dining and gathering rooms add special interest. A spacious recreation loft overlooks the breakfast area and great room. In addition to the large deck/terrace, there is a covered porch accessible from the den or breakfast area. The first-floor master suite features a tray ceiling, and its bath includes dual lavatories and an extra-large shower.

Width 64'-0"
Depth 73'-7"

Design by
© Living Concepts Home Planning

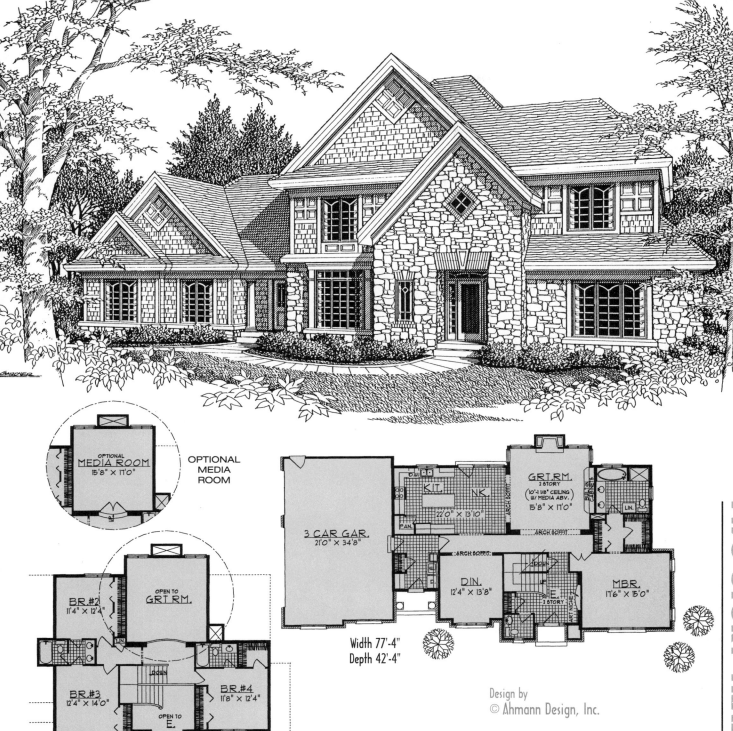

OPTIONAL
MEDIA
ROOM

OPTIONAL
MEDIA ROOM
15'8" X 17'0"

OPEN TO
GRT.RM.

BR. #2
11'4" X 12'4"

BR. #3
12'4" X 14'0"

BR. #4
11'8" X 12'4"

OPEN TO
E.

3 CAR GAR.
21'0" X 34'8"

KIT.
22'0" X 13'10"

NK

GRT.RM.
2 STORY
(10'4 1/8" CEILING
W/ MEDIA ABV.)
15'8" X 17'0"

DIN.
12'4" X 13'8"

E.
2 STORY

MBR.
17'6" X 15'0"

Width 77'-4"
Depth 42'-4"

Design by
© Ahmann Design, Inc.

Subtle, stylish details set this beautiful traditional home apart. Diamond-shaped windows and mouldings decorate the gables, sharply angled keystones adorn the portal and angled panes add grace to the windows. Rubble stonework and a varied roofline complete this stunning exterior. The splendor is carried indoors with a two-story entry and great room, arched thresholds and a U-shaped staircase with scrolled railing.

The lower-level master suite spans from front to rear and features a walk-through closet, garden tub, dual lavatory and separate shower. The spacious, U-shaped kitchen is equipped with an island for even more work space and is open to a roomy casual dining area. Upstairs, three bedrooms are arranged around a balcony overlooking the foyer and great room. Alternatively, a second-story media room may be built over the great room.

DESIGN
U104
First Floor: 1,793 square feet
Second Floor: 844 square feet
Total: 2,637 square feet
Bonus Room: 289 square feet

TWO-STORY TRADITIONAL HOMES

DESIGN P133

First Floor: 1,447 square feet
Second Floor: 1,325 square feet
Total: 2,772 square feet
Bonus Room: 301 square feet

Keystones, stucco arches and shutters add a gentle European flavor to this traditional home. Inside, formal rooms are defined by decorative columns and a lovely arched opening. An additional bedroom or den offers an adjacent bath. Open planning allows the breakfast area to enjoy the fireplace in the family room. The gourmet kitchen has a cooktop island counter and French door to the rear yard. On the second floor, a deluxe master suite has a vaulted bath. Please specify basement or crawlspace foundation when ordering.

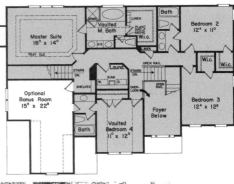

Width 56'-4"
Depth 41'-0"

Design by
© Frank Betz Associates, Inc.

DESIGN P174

First Floor: 2,384 square feet
Second Floor: 1,023 square feet
Total: 3,407 square feet
Bonus Room: 228 square feet

The covered front porch of this stucco home opens to a two-story foyer. Arched openings lead into both the formal dining room and the vaulted living room. The efficient kitchen features a snack bar. Nearby, the large breakfast area opens into the family room. Lavish with its amenities, the master suite offers a vaulted sitting room with a fireplace. Three bedrooms, optional bonus space and attic storage are found on the second floor. Please specify basement or crawlspace foundation when ordering.

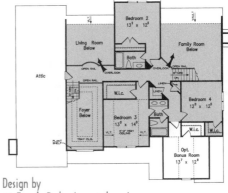

Width 63'-4"
Depth 57'-0"

Design by
© Frank Betz Associates, Inc.

Width 53'-6"
Depth 41'-4"

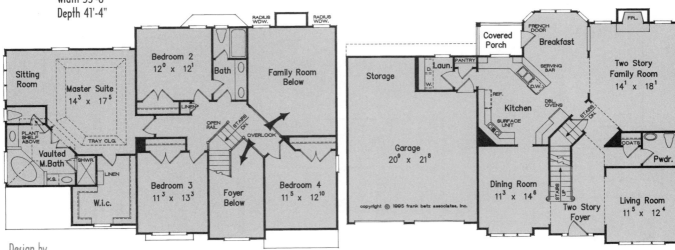

Design by
© Frank Betz Associates, Inc.

A taste of Europe is reflected in arched windows topped off by keystones in this traditional design. Formal rooms flank the foyer, which leads to a two-story family room with a focal-point fireplace. The sunny breakfast nook opens to a private covered porch through a French door. A spacious, well-organized kitchen features angled, wrapping counters, double ovens and a walk-in pantry. The garage offers a service entrance to the utility area and pantry. An angled staircase leads from the two-story foyer to sleeping quarters upstairs. Here, a gallery hall with a balcony overlooks the foyer and family room and connects family bedrooms. A private hall leads to the master bedroom. It boasts a well-lit sitting area, a walk-in closet with linen storage and a lavish bath with a vaulted ceiling, garden tub, double sinks, compartmented toilet and plant shelves. Please specify basement or crawlspace foundation when ordering.

DESIGN P147
First Floor: 1,205 square feet
Second Floor: 1,277 square feet
Total: 2,482 square feet

© 1997 Donald A. Gardner Architects, Inc.

Design by
Donald A. Gardner
Architects, Inc.

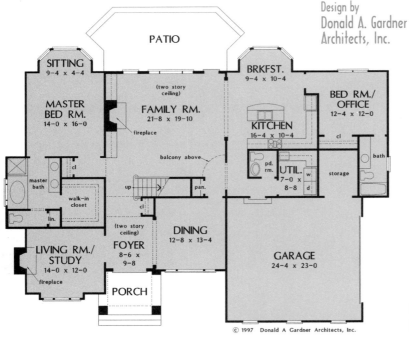

PATIO

SITTING
9-4 x 4-4

MASTER
BED RM.
14-0 x 16-0

FAMILY RM.
21-8 x 19-10

(two story ceiling)

fireplace

balcony above

master bath

walk-in closet

lin.

cl

up

pan.

cl

BRKFST.
9-4 x 10-4

KITCHEN
16-4 x 10-4

pd. rm.

UTIL.
7-0 x
8-8

w
d

storage

BED RM./
OFFICE
12-4 x 12-0

cl

bath

(two story ceiling)

LIVING RM./
STUDY
14-0 x 12-0

fireplace

FOYER
8-6 x
9-8

DINING
12-8 x 13-4

GARAGE
24-4 x 23-0

PORCH

© 1997 Donald A Gardner Architects, Inc.

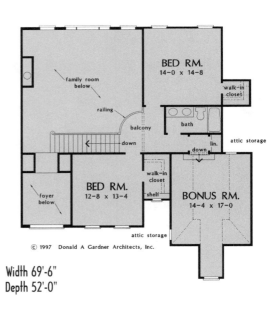

family room below

railing

balcony

down

foyer below

BED RM.
12-8 x 13-4

attic storage

BED RM.
14-0 x 14-8

walk-in closet

bath

lin.

attic storage

down

walk-in closet

shelf

BONUS RM.
14-4 x 17-0

© 1997 Donald A Gardner Architects, Inc.

Width 69'-6"
Depth 52'-0"

DESIGN 7696

First Floor: 2,249 square feet
Second Floor: 620 square feet
Total: 2,869 square feet
Bonus Room: 308 square feet

An impressive two-story entrance welcomes you to this stately home. Massive chimneys and pillars and varying rooflines add interest to the stucco exterior. The foyer, lighted by a clerestory window, opens to the formal living and dining rooms. The living room—which could also serve as a study—features a fireplace, as does the family room. The family room accesses the patio. The L-shaped island kitchen opens to a bay-windowed breakfast nook, which is echoed by the sitting area in the master suite. A room next to the kitchen could serve as a bedroom or a home office. The second floor contains two family bedrooms plus a bonus room for future expansion.

www.homeplanners.com

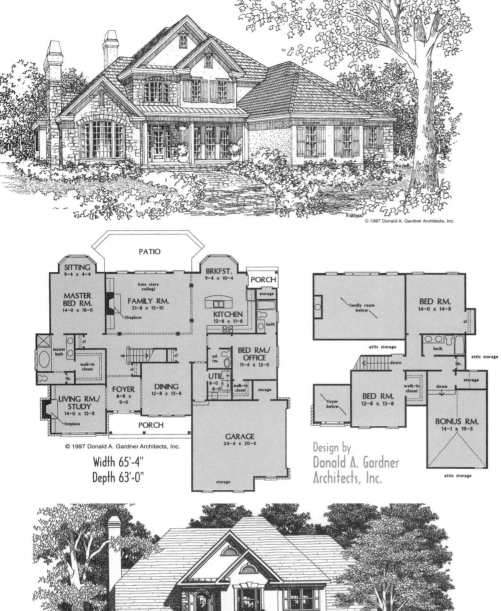

© 1997 Donald A. Gardner Architects, Inc.

© B. NATHAN
© 1997 Donald A. Gardner Architects, Inc.

Width 65'-4"
Depth 63'-0"

Design by
Donald A. Gardner
Architects, Inc.

Warmth personified, this stucco-and-stone beauty is like a breath of fresh air from the countryside of France. Space for formal occasions opens the plan—a living room (or make it a study) with fireplace and a formal dining room. The large family room opens to a rear patio. The master suite on the first floor is appointed with a sitting area and fine bath. An additional bedroom on this level makes a fine guest bedroom or a home office. The second floor holds two family bedrooms and a full bath.

Width 56'-4"
Depth 39'-6"

Design by
© Frank Betz Associates, Inc.

DESIGN P211

First Floor: 1,132 square feet
Second Floor: 1,208 square feet
Total: 2,340 square feet

A taste of Europe is reflected in arched windows topped off by capstones with this traditional design. Formal rooms flank the foyer, which leads to a family room with a focal-point fireplace. A spacious, well-organized kitchen features a food-preparation island, and serves the formal dining room through a butler's pantry. A gallery hall upstairs with a balcony overlook to the foyer connects family bedrooms. A private hall leads to the master retreat. Please specify basement, slab or crawlspace foundation when ordering.

TWO-STORY TRADITIONAL HOMES

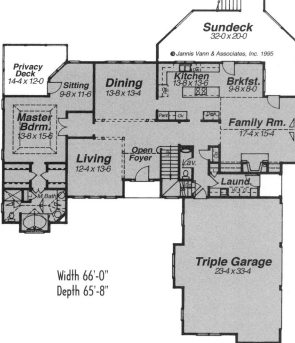

Privacy Deck 14-4 x 12-0

Sitting 9-8 x 11-6

Dining 13-8 x 13-4

Sundeck 32-0 x 20-0

© Jannis Vann & Associates, Inc. 1995

Kitchen 13-8 x 13-6

Brkfst. 9-8 x 8-0

Master Bdrm. 13-8 x 15-6

Living 12-4 x 13-6

Open Foyer

Family Rm. 17-4 x 15-4

Lav.

Laund.

M. Bath

Triple Garage 23-4 x 33-4

Width 66'-0"
Depth 65'-8"

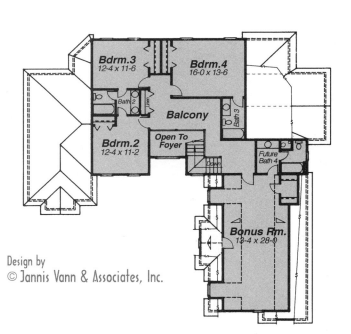

Bdrm.3 12-4 x 11-6

Bdrm.4 16-0 x 13-6

Bath 2

Balcony

Bath 3

Bdrm.2 12-4 x 11-2

Open To Foyer

Future Bath 4

Bonus Rm. 13-4 x 28-0

Design by
© Jannis Vann & Associates, Inc.

DESIGN XO41
First Floor: 1,967 square feet
Second Floor: 1,014 square feet
Total: 2,981 square feet
Bonus Room: 607 square feet

Arches and gables contrast and complement in a recurring theme on this impressive French exterior. Note particularly the clerestory window over the foyer. Formal living and dining rooms open off the foyer, providing a large area for entertaining. A sun deck expands outdoor living possibilities, with access from the breakfast room and the family room. A fireplace in the family room spreads cheer throughout the informal area. To the left of the plan, the master wing includes a deluxe bath, two walk-in closets and a sitting room with access to a privacy deck. The second floor offers three bedrooms, two baths and a bonus room for future use. A triple garage opens to the side for convenience.

Width 52'-0"
Depth 49'-0"

DECK

LAUNDRY
6'-8" X 8'-2"

TWO CAR GARAGE
21'-10" X 21'-10"

BREAKFAST
13'-0" X 11'-6"

KITCHEN
12'-4" X 11'-6"

DINING ROOM
14'-4" X 11'-10"

PWDR

FAMILY ROOM
15'-0" X 20'-0"

LIVING ROOM
14'-4" X 11'-4"

UP

FOYER
11'-10" X 13'-8"

STOOP

MASTER BATH
9'-0" X 12'-6"

W.I.C.

BEDROOM NO. 4
17'-10" X 11'-0"

BEDROOM NO. 3
12'-0" X 11'-6"

W.I.C.

BATH

BATH

MASTER BEDROOM
15'-0" X 19'-0"

OPEN TO
BELOW

DN.

BEDROOM NO. 2
12'-0" X 12'-0"

GALLERY

Design by
© Stephen Fuller,
American Home Gallery

DESIGN T033

First Floor: 1,360 square feet
Second Floor: 1,400 square feet
Total: 2,760 square feet

The appeal of this home is definitely European and its interior is open and inviting. Columns separate the formal living room and dining room. To the left of the foyer is the comfortable family room with a large fireplace and open-rail detailing, allowing access to the breakfast room and kitchen. The grand master suite includes a tray ceiling and a luxurious master bath. Two bedrooms with a connecting bath and a third bedroom with a private bath complete the plan. This home is designed with a basement foundation.

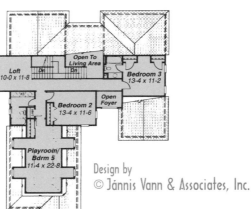

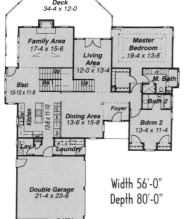

Deck
34-4 x 12-0

Family Area
17-4 x 15-6

Living
Area
12-0 x 13-4

Master
Bedroom
19-4 x 13-6

M. Bath

Bfast
10-10 x 11-8

Up

Dn

Dn

Bath 2

Kitchen
13-6 x 11-10

Dining Area
13-6 x 15-8

Foyer

Bdrm 2
13-4 x 11-4

Lav

Laundry

Double Garage
21-4 x 23-8

© 1994

Width 56'-0"
Depth 80'-0"

Loft
10-0 x 11-8

Dn
Dn

Open To
Living Area

Bedroom 3
13-4 x 11-2

Bedroom 2
13-4 x 11-6

Open
Foyer

Playroom/
Bdrm 5
11-4 x 22-8

Design by
© Jánnis Vann & Associates, Inc.

DESIGN X022

First Floor: 2,055 square feet
Second Floor: 898 square feet
Total: 2,953 square feet

An L-shaped plan and fine brick-and-siding detail present a home that is sure to please. The floor plan is designed to accommodate both formal and informal entertaining, with the formal dining and living rooms perfect for dinner parties. Toward the rear, a spacious family room offers a fireplace for cheery casual get-togethers. A guest suite is located to the right of the foyer, near the lavish master suite. The second floor consists of two bedrooms—one with its own bath—a loft and a huge playroom over the garage.

TWO-STORY TRADITIONAL HOMES

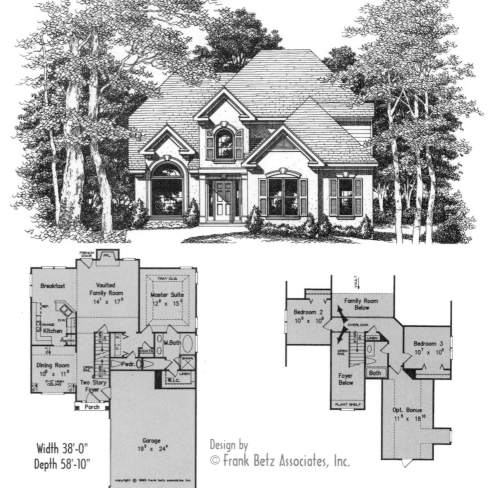

DESIGN P310

First Floor: 1,114 square feet
Second Floor: 427 square feet
Total: 1,541 square feet
Bonus Room: 258 square feet

This distinctive facade introduces a modern floor plan that's both comfortable and stylish. A two-story foyer opens to a lovely formal dining room, which is easily served by the adjacent kitchen. A fireplace warms the casual living space, while a French door brings in a sense of nature. The master suite occupies its own wing on the main floor. Upstairs, two additional bedrooms are connected by a hall that leads to bonus space.

Width 38'-0"
Depth 58'-10"

Design by
© Frank Betz Associates, Inc.

DESIGN P245

First Floor: 1,267 square feet
Second Floor: 1,568 square feet
Total: 2,835 square feet

Decorative cornices and capstones splash this New World home with a taste of Old World flavor. Inside, a two-story foyer opens to the formal dining room and the living room, which features French doors to the family room. The two-story breakfast room opens to the gourmet kitchen, which features a serving bar and a radius window above the double sink. A spacious sitting area, garden tub and walk-in closet make the master suite a relaxing retreat. Please specify basement, slab or crawlspace foundation when ordering.

Width 57'-6"
Depth 41'-0"

Design by
© Frank Betz Associates, Inc.

Width 58'-0"
Depth 33'-6"

Design by
© Frank Betz Associates, Inc.

S tately corner quoins and an exterior that's symmetrical in design reflect this home's functional yet elegant floor plan. The two-story foyer is framed by the formal living and dining rooms. The large family room has a fireplace flanked by windows and a French door to the rear yard. The efficient kitchen provides a serving bar and an abundance of counter and cabinet space. A stylish twin-entry staircase leads to the three family bedrooms and compartmented bath. The master suite holds an oversized bedroom, a sitting room that could double as an exercise area and a spa-style bath with a walk-in closet. Please specify basement or crawlspace foundation when ordering.

DESIGN P231
First Floor: 1,252 square feet
Second Floor: 1,348 square feet
Total: 2,600 square feet

DESIGN
P263

First Floor: 1,682 square feet
Second Floor: 516 square feet
Total: 2,198 square feet
Bonus Room: 301 square feet

A charming stone-and-stucco facade lends a European flavor to this country home. The two-story foyer opens to the formal rooms and leads to a vaulted family room made cozy by an extended-hearth fireplace and French doors to the rear property. The first-floor master suite has a bayed sitting area and a private bath with a windowed tub and separate shower. The kitchen shares a serving bar with the breakfast room. Please specify basement or crawlspace foundation when ordering.

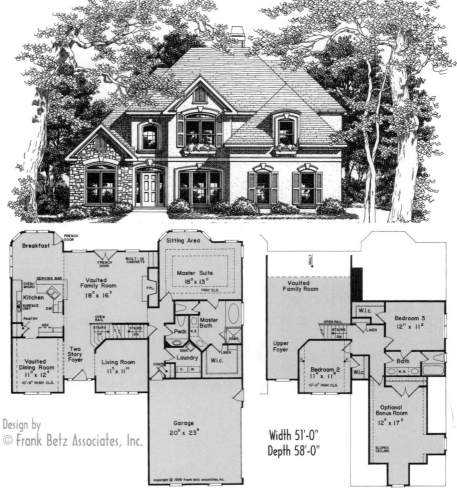

Design by
© Frank Betz Associates, Inc.

Width 51'-0"
Depth 58'-0"

DESIGN
P163

First Floor: 1,398 square feet
Second Floor: 515 square feet
Total: 1,913 square feet
Bonus Room: 282 square feet

Varied rooflines, keystones and arches set off a stucco exterior that's highlighted by a stone turret and a bay. Inside, the master suite enjoys a tray ceiling and floor-to-ceiling light from a sitting room. The formal dining room leads to a private covered porch. The central kitchen boasts an angled counter that overlooks the breakfast room. Two second-floor bedrooms share a balcony overlook and a full bath. Please specify basement, crawlspace or slab foundation when ordering.

Design by
© Frank Betz Associates, Inc.

Width 48'-0"
Depth 50'-10"

Floor plan labels (first floor):
- FRENCH DOOR
- Breakfast
- FRENCH DOOR
- STAIRS UP
- OPEN RAIL
- ISLAND
- OVENS
- SERVING BAR
- ARCHED OPENING
- Two Story Family Room 17⁰ x 19²
- FPL.
- Kitchen
- DW.
- SURFACE UNIT
- ARCHED OPENING
- Three Car Garage 20⁹ x 33⁵
- REF.
- ARCHED OPENING
- DECORATIVE COLUMNS
- STAIRS DN.
- PANTRY
- ARCHED OPENING
- COATS
- Pwdr.
- copyright © 1995 frank betz associates, inc.
- Dining Room 12⁰ x 14⁰
- OPEN RAIL
- Living Room 12⁴ x 11⁸
- STAIRS UP
- Two Story Foyer
- Width 58'-4"
- Depth 46'-6"
- Covered Porch

Floor plan labels (second floor):
- TRAY CEILING
- RADIUS WINDOW
- PLANT SHELF ABOVE
- SHWR.
- K.B.
- Vaulted M.Bath
- Master Suite 14⁰ x 18⁸
- PLANT SHELF
- W.i.c.
- DRESSING MIRROR
- LIN.
- Family Room Below
- W. D.
- Laun.
- Bedroom 4 12⁸ x 12⁰
- OPEN RAIL
- PLANT SHELF
- STAIRS DN.
- OVERLOOK
- W.i.c.
- STAIRS DN.
- OPEN RAIL
- Bath
- LINEN
- OVERLOOK
- Bath
- Bedroom 3 12⁰ x 12⁸
- Foyer Below
- Bedroom 2 12⁴ x 12²
- PLANT SHELF
- WINDOW SEAT

Design by
© Frank Betz Associates, Inc.

Two-Story Traditional Homes

From the covered front porch to the efficient floor plan, this house makes being at home pleasant. Formal areas are at the front of the home for convenience in entertaining. The large kitchen boasts a work island, walk-in pantry and a nearby breakfast area with attractive views from a large bay window and access to the three-car garage and rear yard. The two-story family room is defined by decorative columns and a fireplace. Upstairs, two family bedrooms share access to a full bath, while a third bedroom includes a private bath and a walk-in closet. The master suite is designed to pamper and includes a tray ceiling, bay window, vaulted bath and walk-in closet. A laundry is also on the second floor. Please specify basement or crawlspace foundation when ordering.

DESIGN P153
First Floor: 1,347 square feet
Second Floor: 1,493 square feet
Total: 2,840 square feet
Bonus Room: 243 square feet

DESIGN P121

First Floor: 1,457 square feet
Second Floor: 494 square feet
Total: 1,951 square feet
Bonus Room: 275 square feet

European details bring charm to this traditional home. Comfortable living space includes a vaulted family room with a centered fireplace. A sizable kitchen serves the dining room and overlooks the breakfast area with a serving bar. The master suite offers a tray ceiling and a vaulted sitting room, bright with windows. Two family bedrooms, a full bath and a bonus room are on the second floor. Please specify basement or crawlspace foundation when ordering.

Design by
© Frank Betz Associates, Inc.

Width 49'-0"
Depth 47'-10"

DESIGN P118

First Floor: 2,044 square feet
Second Floor: 896 square feet
Total: 2,940 square feet
Bonus Room: 197 square feet

Varied rooflines, keystones and arches set off a stucco exterior that's highlighted by a turret. Inside, the formal living room enjoys a tray ceiling and floor-to-ceiling light from the turret's windows. The formal dining room leads to a private covered porch. Sleeping quarters include a first-floor master suite with a vaulted bath and a sitting area, and three second-floor family bedrooms that share a balcony overlook. Please specify basement or crawlspace foundation when ordering.

Design by
© Frank Betz Associates, Inc.

Width 63'-0"
Depth 54'-0"

QUOTE ONE®
Cost to build? See page 684 to order complete cost estimate to build this house in your area!

TWO-STORY TRADITIONAL HOMES

www.homeplanners.com

Design by
© Frank Betz Associates, Inc.

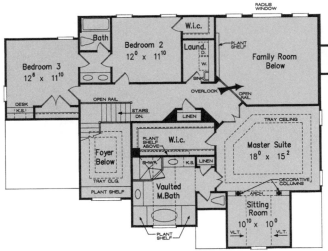

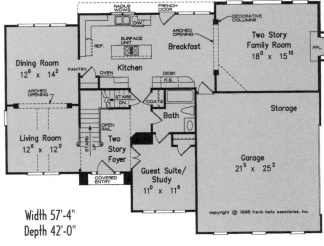

Width 57'-4"
Depth 42'-0"

Charming French accents create an inviting facade on this country home. An arched opening set off by decorative columns introduces a two-story family room with a fireplace and a radius window. The gourmet kitchen features an island cooktop counter, planning desk and a roomy breakfast area with a French door to the back property. The second-floor master suite offers a secluded sitting room, a tray ceiling in the bedroom and a lavish bath with an oversized corner shower. Two family bedrooms share a gallery hall that has a balcony overlook to the family room. A laundry room is also on the second floor for convenience. Please specify basement or crawlspace foundation when ordering.

DESIGN
P229
First Floor: 1,374 square feet
Second Floor: 1,311 square feet
Total: 2,685 square feet

DESIGN B128

First Floor: 1,395 square feet
Second Floor: 629 square feet
Total: 2,024 square feet

Arched window highlights detail the ornate stone-and-stucco exterior of this two-story, French modern design. A stepped covered entry with guest closet leads directly into the family room with high sloped ceiling and fireplace with fieldstone hearth. The master-bedroom wing features a vaulted ceiling, a full bath and lots of closet space. The large corner kitchen and breakfast area has a built-in desk and pantry. Three additional bedrooms with generous closets are upstairs and share a full bath.

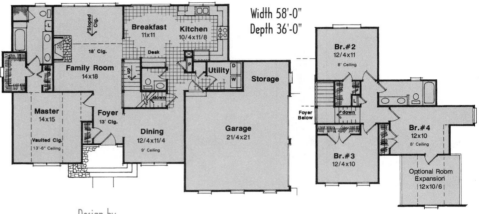

Width 58'-0"
Depth 36'-0"

Design by
© Greg Marquis & Associates

DESIGN P141

First Floor: 2,211 square feet
Second Floor: 719 square feet
Total: 2,930 square feet
Bonus Room: 331 square feet

Stucco, stone and intricate detailing give this home a pleasing facade. Inside, the two-story foyer leads to a family room with a welcoming fireplace. The kitchen shares open space with a sunlit, bayed breakfast room, which offers French-door access to the backyard. A luxurious master suite and a corner office complete the first floor. Upstairs, two bedrooms share a full bath, and a loft overlooks the family room. Please specify basement or crawlspace foundation when ordering.

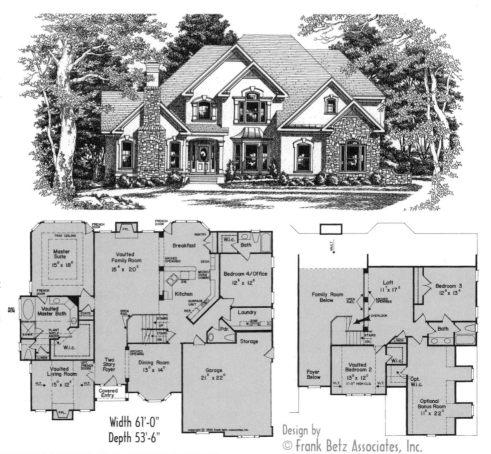

Width 61'-0"
Depth 53'-6"

Design by
© Frank Betz Associates, Inc.

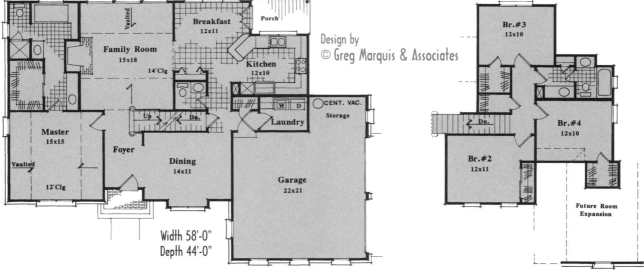

Design by
© Greg Marquis & Associates

Vaulted

Breakfast
12x11

Porch

Family Room
15x18

14'Clg

Kitchen
12x10

Master
15x15

Up · Dn.

CENT. VAC.
Storage

W D

Laundry

Vaulted

12'Clg

Foyer

Dining
14x11

Garage
22x21

Width 58'-0"
Depth 44'-0"

Br.#3
12x10

Dn.

Br.#2
12x11

Br.#4
12x10

**Future Room
Expansion**

A n understated asymmetry creates a look of updated elegance in this design. The hipped roof is aligned with gables on the sides, while a third gable is centered on the roofline. Varied multi-paned windows, accented by arches and shutters, augment the subtle contrasts at work on the exterior. Inside, vaulted ceilings and a comfortable floor plan complete the feeling of luxurious livability. The owner will enjoy an expansive master suite that features a twelve-foot vaulted ceiling. The master

bath includes a walk-in closet, garden tub and separate shower. The family room is accented by a fourteen-foot vaulted ceiling, brick fireplace and a wall of windows. The U-shaped kitchen provides an angled island and is open to the breakfast room, which accesses the porch through double doors. The formal dining room offers a full-height bay window and is comfortably isolated from the kitchen. Upstairs, three bedrooms have ample closet space and share a full bath. The two-car garage offers loads of storage space.

**DESIGN
B120**
First Floor: 1,441 square feet
Second Floor: 632 square feet
Total: 2,073 square feet

TWO-STORY TRADITIONAL HOMES

Design by
© Fillmore Design Group

Width 45'-0"
Depth 39'-5"

Patio Area

Patio Area

Kit
12x12

MstrBed
15x13
Cathedral Clg.

Din
10X12

Pwdr

Util

Gar
20x22

LivRm
14x17

Ent

UP

Por

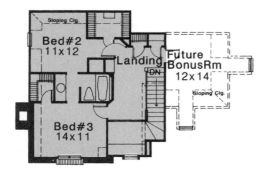

Sloping Clg.

Bed#2
11x12

Landing

Future
BonusRm
12x14

DN

Sloping Clg.

Bed#3
14x11

**DESIGN
M124**

First Floor: 1,149 square feet
Second Floor: 555 square feet
Total: 1,704 square feet
Bonus Room: 197 square feet

Native stone, brick, and stucco combine to provide the charming exterior for this 1½-story European
cottage design. An open staircase
leads from the entry area to a second-
floor reading hideaway. Downstairs, the
master suite with cathedral ceiling has
French doors that open to a secluded rear

patio area. The large master bath features
two separate vanities and a generous
walk-in closet. A dining room and living
room sit to the left of the kitchen. The
two upstairs bedrooms feature a connecting bath and separate walk-in closets.
Opposite the upstairs bedrooms is space
for a future bonus room above the garage.

www.homeplanners.com

DESIGN B121

First Floor: 1,317 square feet
Second Floor: 537 square feet
Total: 1,854 square feet
Bonus Room: 288 square feet

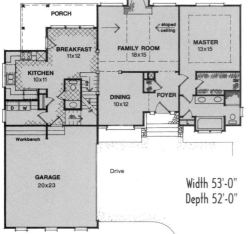

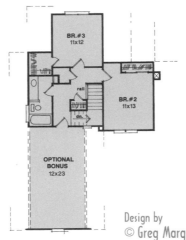

Width 53'-0"
Depth 52'-0"

Design by
© Greg Marquis & Associates

Interesting rooflines in this European-influenced stacked stone-and-stucco home are just one of the many architectural details that makes this home special. Note the flared copper roof over the extended bay window. The first-floor master suite, featuring a large walk-in closet, serves as a private retreat. Stairs are conveniently placed in the breakfast area. Check out the large laundry room, also wisely located near the garage entrance. The fireplace is a focal point in the vaulted family room.

DESIGN A158

First Floor: 2,183 square feet
Second Floor: 324 square feet
Total: 2,507 square feet

The unusual design of this three-bedroom, 1½-story design offers a variety of extras: a media room, a reading area in the master suite, a screened porch adjacent to the grand room, a workshop in the garage, and captain's quarters and an evening deck on the second level.

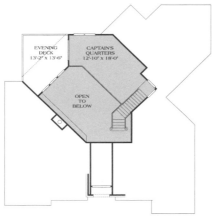

Width 59'-8"
Depth 62'-6"

Design by
© Living Concepts Home Planning

DESIGN B145

First Floor: 1,626 square feet
Second Floor: 522 square feet
Total: 2,148 square feet
Bonus Room: 336 square feet

Multiple rooflines and two dormers combine to give this home plenty of curb appeal. An elegant entrance leads to a foyer with a formal dining room to the left and a spacious family room directly ahead. The island kitchen is open to the sun room via a snack bar and to the adjacent breakfast room. The secluded master suite is designed to pamper with a walk-in closet and a sumptuous bath. Two secondary bedrooms, each with walk-in closets, share a large hall bathroom.

Width 54'-7"
Depth 62'-8"

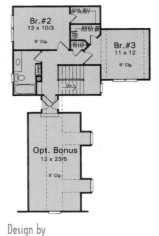

Design by
© Greg Marquis & Associates

DESIGN A120

First Floor: 1,706 square feet
Second Floor: 791 square feet
Total: 2,497 square feet
Bonus Room: 366 square feet

Extremely cost-effective to build, this house makes great use of interior space. The foyer opens into a two-story grand room that features a fireplace and an elegant Palladian window. A full kitchen connects the dining room and brightly lit morning room. The master suite overlooks the backyard through a bay window. A U-shaped staircase leads up to a loft and two additional suites that share a bath. Please specify basement or crawl-space foundation when ordering.

Width 53'-4"
Depth 63'-4"

Design by
© Living Concepts Home Planning

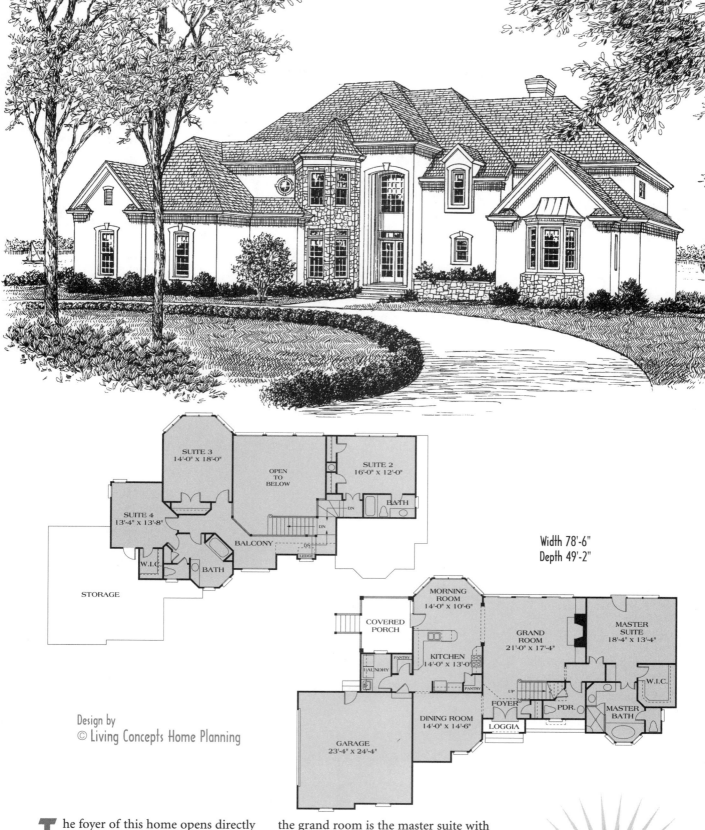

SUITE 3
14'-0" x 18'-0"

OPEN TO BELOW

SUITE 2
16'-0" x 12'-0"

BATH

SUITE 4
13'-4" x 13'-8"

DN

DN

BALCONY

LEDGE

W.I.C.

BATH

STORAGE

Width 78'-6"
Depth 49'-2"

MORNING ROOM
14'-0" x 10'-6"

COVERED PORCH

GRAND ROOM
21'-0" x 17'-4"

MASTER SUITE
18'-4" x 13'-4"

PANTRY

KITCHEN
14'-0" x 13'-0"

LAUNDRY

W.I.C.

PANTRY

UP

FOYER

PDR.

MASTER BATH

GARAGE
23'-4" x 24'-4"

DINING ROOM
14'-0" x 14'-6"

LOGGIA

Design by
© Living Concepts Home Planning

The foyer of this home opens directly to the grand room, which features a wall of windows and a fireplace. At the back of the house, a large bay window brightens the morning room and kitchen. A covered porch lies adjacent to the morning room. At the other side of the grand room is the master suite with shower, double vanity, whirlpool tub and walk-in closet. It also has its own entrance to the backyard. On the upper level, two secondary bedrooms share a bath; another bedroom has its own bath. A large storage space opens off of Suite 4.

TWO-STORY TRADITIONAL HOMES

DESIGN
A172

First Floor: 1,753 square feet
Second Floor: 1,233 square feet
Total: 2,986 square feet

DESIGN B119

First Floor: 1,670 square feet

Second Floor: 540 square feet

Total: 2,210 square feet

Bonus Room: 455 square feet

Shutters, multi-pane windows and corner quoins add to this great design. A separate dining room flows into the vaulted family room with a through-fireplace. The large vaulted kitchen/breakfast area with eat-in bar becomes a sun room overlooking a large deck. The vaulted master bedroom has a large angled closet. The convenient stair location allows upstairs traffic to flow down into the kitchen area. Upstairs, two family bedrooms share a hall bath that has a double-bowl vanity.

Design by
© Greg Marquis & Associates

Width 54'-0"
Depth 61'-0"

TWO-STORY TRADITIONAL HOMES

DESIGN A133

First Floor: 1,751 square feet

Second Floor: 1,043 square feet

Total: 2,794 square feet

Stately pilasters and a decorative balcony at a second-level window adorn this ornate four-bedroom design. Inside the recessed entryway, columns define the formal dining room. Ahead is a great room with fireplace, built-in bookshelves and access to the rear deck. A breakfast nook nestles in a bay window and joins an efficient island kitchen. The vaulted master suite features a walk-in closet and garden tub in the bath. Upstairs, a versatile loft, three additional bedrooms and two baths are connected by a hallway open to the great room below.

Width 45'-0"
Depth 69'-6"

Design by
© Living Concepts Home Planning

314

www.homeplanners.com

The home, as shown in the photograph, may differ from the actual blueprints.
For more detailed information, please check the floor plans carefully.

Photo by Robert Starling/Orlando

Design by
© Living Concepts Home Planning

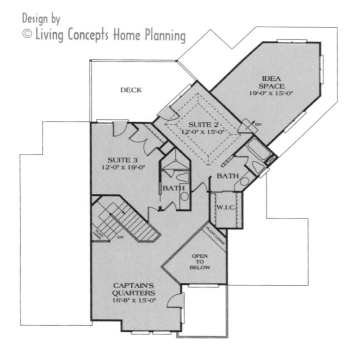

DECK

IDEA
SPACE
19'-0" x 15'-0"

SUITE 2
12'-0" x 15'-0"

DN

SUITE 3
12'-0" x 19'-0"

BATH

BATH

W.I.C.

DN

OPEN
TO
BELOW

CAPTAIN'S
QUARTERS
16'-8" x 15'-0"

VERANDA

SCREENED
ROOM
15'-8" x 12'-0"

LAUN.

GARAGE
21'-6" x 29'-0"

LOUNGE
9'-0" x 6'-6"

MORNING
ROOM
8'-8" x 10'-0"

GRAND
ROOM
16'-0" x 19'-0"

KITCHEN
14'-0" x 18'-0"

MASTER
SUITE
13'-0" x 16'-0"

OPT.
MORN.
KITCH.

DN TO
OPT. BSMT.

UP

PANT.

FOYER

DINING
ROOM
15'-0" x 12'-0"

MASTER
BATH

WARDROBE
ISLAND

PDR.

LOGGIA

SEAT

Width 60'-0"
Depth 60'-0"

A gently sloping, high-pitched roof complements keystones, arch-top windows and a delicate balcony balustrade, and calls up a sense of cozy elegance. The foyer opens to a grand room with a focal-point fireplace and access to a screened room that leads to the veranda. The gourmet kitchen offers a walk-in pantry, acres of counter space and a morning room with outdoor flow. An island wardrobe highlights the master suite, which boasts a secluded lounge with a door to a private area of the veranda. Upstairs, two secondary bedrooms enjoy a balcony overlook to the foyer, and each room has its own access to an outdoor deck. The captain's quarters area leads to a balcony and offers space for computers, books and quiet conversation. The two-car garage features extra space for storage.

DESIGN A126

First Floor: 1,862 square feet
Second Floor: 1,044 square feet
Total: 2,906 square feet
Bonus Room: 715 square feet

TWO-STORY TRADITIONAL HOMES

The home, as shown in the photograph, may differ from the actual blueprints.
For more detailed information, please check the floor plans carefully.

TWO-STORY TRADITIONAL HOMES

Design by
© Living Concepts Home Planning

Width 52'-4"
Depth 59'-10"

DESIGN A110

First Floor: 1,777 square feet
Second Floor: 657 square feet
Total: 2,434 square feet
Bonus Room: 340 square feet

The floor plan of this cottage beauty provides several living areas. An open keeping den/kitchen combination allows for close family communication. The two-story grand room features a fireplace and two sets of French doors opening to the outside. A covered side porch is located between the laundry and garage. The spacious master suite provides an impressive walk-in closet and dual vanities in the bath. Follow the dramatic, angled foyer staircase upstairs across a balcony that leads to two additional suites and an oversized bonus room. The two-car garage loads from the side to keep the facade style pure.

DESIGN A114

First Floor: 2,075 square feet
Second Floor: 859 square feet
Total: 2,934 square feet
Bonus Room: 262 square feet

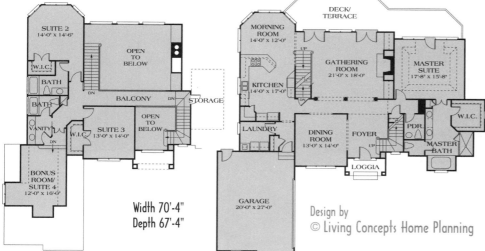

SUITE 2
14'-0" x 14'-6"

OPEN TO BELOW

W.I.C.

BATH

BATH

BALCONY

STORAGE

DN

VANITY

DN

W.I.C.

SUITE 3
13'-0" x 14'-0"

OPEN TO BELOW

BONUS ROOM/
SUITE 4
12'-0" x 16'-0"

Width 70'-4"
Depth 67'-4"

DECK/TERRACE

MORNING ROOM
14'-0" x 12'-0"

UP

GATHERING ROOM
21'-0" x 18'-0"

MASTER SUITE
17'-8" x 15'-8"

KITCHEN
14'-0" x 17'-0"

W.I.C.

LAUNDRY

DINING ROOM
13'-0" x 14'-0"

FOYER

PDR.

MASTER BATH

UP

LOGGIA

GARAGE
20'-0" x 27'-0"

Design by
© Living Concepts Home Planning

A European-style stone entrance graces the front elevation of this magnificent house. There is a columned entry into a two-story gathering room that includes a pair of spectacular arched windows and a fireplace. The dining room is just a step away from a very generous kitchen, which opens into a bay-windowed morning room. An immense master suite features a tray ceiling, walk-in closet and dual lavatories in the bath. A second-floor balcony overlooking the gathering room and foyer leads to two additional suites plus a bonus room.

DESIGN A121

First Floor: 2,398 square feet
Second Floor: 657 square feet
Total: 3,055 square feet
Bonus Room: 374 square feet

This home offers walls of windows in the living areas. The sun room opens from the breakfast nook and leads to a rear terrace or deck. Ten-foot ceilings throughout the main level provide interior vistas and add volume to the rooms. Classical columns divide the great room and dining room, which has a see-through wet bar. The deluxe master suite uses defining columns between the bedroom and the lavish bath and walk-in closet. Please specify basement or crawlspace foundation when ordering.

OPEN TO BELOW

SUITE 4
12'-6" x 12'-6"

BATH

W.I.C.

OPEN TO BELOW

BALCONY

DN

SUITE 3
15'-0" x 11'-0"

W.I.C.

BONUS ROOM
14'-0" x 20'-0"

Width 72'-8"
Depth 69'-1"

MASTER SUITE
15'-6" x 17'-6"

TERRACE/DECK

SUNROOM
14'-6" x 11'-6"

GREAT ROOM
19'-6" x 16'-6"

DINING ROOM
12'-0" x 14'-6"

BREAKFAST
14'-6" x 12'-6"

MASTER BATH

W.I.C.

BAR

PDR.

FOYER

UP

KITCHEN
14'-6" x 15'-6"

BATH

STUDY/GUEST/LIBRARY
12'-6" x 13'-6"

LOGGIA

LAUNDRY

PANT.

W.I.C.

GARAGE
23'-6" x 23'-6"

STOR.

Design by
© Living Concepts Home Planning

DESIGN
P220

First Floor: 922 square feet
Second Floor: 778 square feet
Total: 1,700 square feet

This home has all the modern conveniences plus lots of special amenities. A serving bar between the kitchen and the open breakfast area and family room makes casual dining a breeze. The spacious master bath contains a walk-in closet as well as a linen closet. An optional bonus room can be used as storage as well as providing a walk-in closet for Bedroom 2. Please specify basement or crawlspace foundation when ordering.

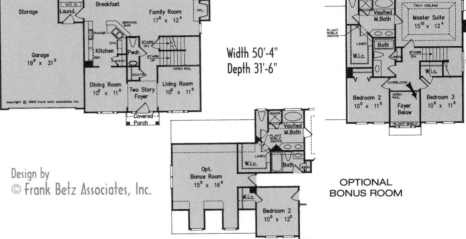

Width 50'-4"
Depth 31'-6"

Design by
© Frank Betz Associates, Inc.

OPTIONAL
BONUS ROOM

DESIGN
P253

First Floor: 1,192 square feet
Second Floor: 1,301 square feet
Total: 2,493 square feet

This home's facade is as big and bold as Colonial America, where it finds its roots. The two-story foyer includes a plant shelf above. Go left and you'll enter the formal living room. Go right to the formal dining room. A family room boasts a fireplace and a wall of windows. The kitchen has a serving bar that separates it from the breakfast nook. Special touches in the master suite include a tray ceiling, sitting room, room-sized walk-in closet and vaulted master bath. Please specify basement or crawlspace foundation when ordering.

Width 59'-10"
Depth 33'-0"

Design by
© Frank Betz Associates, Inc.

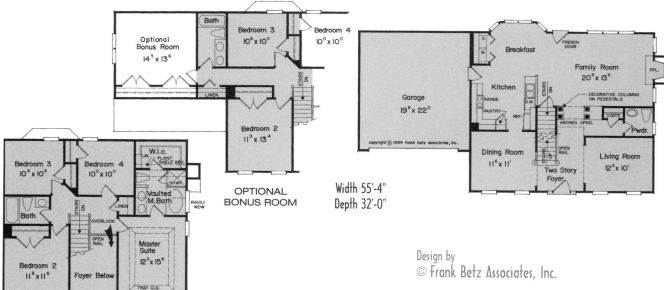

Optional
Bonus Room
14⁵ x 13⁶

Bath

Bedroom 3
10⁶ x 10⁰

Bedroom 4
10⁰ x 10⁰

LINEN

STAIRS DN.

Bedroom 2
11³ x 13⁴

OPTIONAL
BONUS ROOM

Bedroom 3
10⁶ x 10⁰

Bedroom 4
10⁰ x 10⁰

W.i.c.

LIN. PLANT SHELF ABV.

SHWR.

Bath

STAIRS DN.

OVERLOOK

OPEN RAIL

LINEN

Vaulted
M. Bath

RADIUS WDW.

Bedroom 2
11⁶ x 11⁶

Foyer Below

Master
Suite
12⁰ x 15⁶

TRAY CLG.

Width 55'-4"
Depth 32'-0"

Garage
19⁹ x 22⁰

Breakfast

FRENCH DOOR

Family Room
20⁸ x 13⁶

FPL.

Kitchen

RANGE

D.W.

STAIRS DN.

DECORATIVE COLUMNS ON PEDESTALS

PANTRY

REF.

ARCHED OPNG.

COATS

Pwdr.

Dining Room
11⁶ x 11¹

STAIRS UP

OPEN RAIL

Living Room
12⁰ x 10¹

Two Story
Foyer

copyright © 1994 frank betz associates, inc.

Design by
© Frank Betz Associates, Inc.

Colonial charm is highly evident in the facade of this four-bedroom home—from the gabled roof to the formal symmetry of the windows and the decorative details of the front door. Inside, the two-story foyer is flanked by the formal dining room to the left and the formal living room to the right. Casual living takes place directly ahead through an arched hallway. Spaciousness is the theme here, perpetu-ated by the large family room, the open bayed breakfast area and the roomy kitchen, which all flow together to make entertaining a breeze. Upstairs, a lavish master suite includes a tray ceiling, walk-in closet and sumptuous bath. Three family bedrooms share a full hall bath. An optional second-floor plan is included, adding a bonus room over the garage. Please specify basement or crawlspace foundation when ordering.

DESIGN
P206

First Floor: 1,007 square feet
Second Floor: 877 square feet
Total: 1,884 square feet
Bonus Room: 328 square feet

DESIGN T017

First Floor: 1,900 square feet
Second Floor: 800 square feet
Total: 2,700 square feet

Through the blending of stucco and stacked stone, this country French home represents a specific architectural motif. The foyer is flanked by the spacious dining room and vaulted study A great room with a full wall of glass brings the outdoors inside. The generous use of windows in the breakfast room make it feel more like a sun room extension for the spacious kitchen. The master suite provides the ultimate in convenience and privacy. The second-floor of this livable plan has three bedrooms, walk-in closets and a shared bath. This home is designed with a basement foundation.

Width 63'-0"
Depth 51'-0"

Design by
© Stephen Fuller,
American Home Gallery

Quote ONE®
Cost to build? See page 684
to order complete cost estimate
to build this house in your area!

DESIGN Q370

First Floor: 1,351 square feet
Second Floor: 504 square feet
Total: 1,855 square feet

This family home is well-suited to a narrow lot. The vaulted ceiling and full-height window enhance the sense of spaciousness in the living room. In the family room, the fire glow spreads to the kitchen and breakfast bay. Enter the master bedroom through French doors to find a window seat, walk-in closet, private bath and access to a private patio. Two additional bedrooms share a bath and a balcony that overlooks the foyer. Both bedrooms offer a window seat. Plans include details for a basement and a crawlspace foundation.

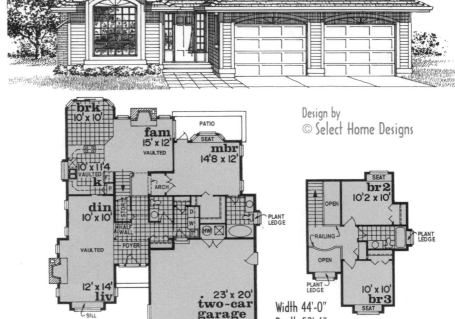

Design by
© Select Home Designs

Width 44'-0"
Depth 52'-6"

DECK

BREAKFAST
10'-0" x 7'-0"

Width 41'-0"
Depth 41'-0"

GREAT ROOM
18'-6" x 15'-6"

KITCHEN
12'-0" x 10'-10"

UP

DN

DINING
9'-6" x 12'-10"

FOYER

PDR

TWO-CAR GARAGE
20'-0" x 21'-0"

QUOTE ONE®
Cost to build? See page 684
to order complete cost estimate
to build this house in your area!

MASTER SUITE
14'-10" x 15'-8"

M. BATH

LAUN.
6'-0" x 5'-8"

W.I.C.

W.I.C.

BEDROOM No.2
11'-10" x 9'-6"

BEDROOM No.3
10'-0" x 12'-10"

BATH

W.I.C.

Design by
© Stephen Fuller,
American Home Gallery

TWO-STORY TRADITIONAL HOMES

DESIGN T048
First Floor: 780 square feet
Second Floor: 915 square feet
Total: 1,695 square feet

Columns, brickwork and uniquely shaped windows and shutters remind us of the best homes of turn-of-the-century America. Inside, contemporary priorities reign. To the left of the foyer is the powder room. Opposite is a formal dining room with passage to the kitchen, which is open to the breakfast area and great room. This area is particularly well-suited to entertaining both formally and informally, with an open, airy design. The large fire-place is framed by windows and is a love-ly focal point in the great room. The master suite's double-door entrance and tray ceiling are of special interest. The adjoin-ing master bath and walk-in closet com-plement this area well. The laundry room is found on this level, convenient to any of the bedrooms. Bedrooms 2 and 3 com-plete this level with a shared bath featur-ing private entrances. This home is designed with a basement foundation.

© American Home Gallery, Ltd.

DECK

BREAKFAST
12'-0" X 10'-0"

MASTER
BATH

MASTER BEDROOM
13'-0" X 15'-4"

TWO STORY
FAMILY ROOM
14'-6" X 15'-0"

KITCHEN
12'-0" X 14'-8"

POWDER

W.I.C.

DN.

STORAGE

LAUNDRY

DINING ROOM
13'-4" X 11'-8"

UP

TWO STORY
FOYER
9'-0" X 15'-0"

TWO CAR GARAGE
22'-4" X 20'-8"

LIVING ROOM
13'-4" X 11'-4"

STOOP

QUOTE ONE®
Cost to build? See page 684
to order complete cost estimate
to build this house in your area!

BEDROOM NO. 3
11'-10" X 12'-0"

OPEN TO BELOW

BATH

BALCONY

FUTURE
BEDROOM NO. 4
13'-6" X 12'-0"

DN.

BEDROOM
NO. 2
13'-0" X 12'-0"

FUTURE
BATH

OPEN TO
BELOW

FUTURE
STORAGE

Width 50'-0"
Depth 53'-6"

Design by
© Stephen Fuller,
American Home Gallery

DESIGN T075

First Floor: 1,720 square feet
Second Floor: 545 square feet
Total: 2,265 square feet

The foyer opens to the living and dining areas, providing a spectacular
entrance to this English country cottage. Just beyond the dining room is
a gourmet kitchen with work island and
food bar opening to the breakfast room.
Accented by a fireplace and built-in bookcases, the family room is an excellent setting for family gatherings. Remotely
located off the central hallway, the master

suite includes a rectangular ceiling detail
and access to the rear deck, while the
master bath features His and Hers vanities, a garden tub and a spacious walk-in
closet. The central staircase leads to the
balcony overlook and three bedrooms
with spacious closets and baths. Bedroom
4, with private bath and storage area, can
be completed later. This home is designed
with a basement foundation.

Design by
© Stephen Fuller,
American Home Gallery

Width 73'-6"
Depth 49'-0"

QUOTE ONE®
Cost to build? See page 684
to order complete cost estimate
to build this house in your area!

DESIGN T015

First Floor: 1,370 square feet
Second Floor: 1,673 square feet
Total: 3,043 square feet
Bonus Room: 339 square feet

This English Georgian home features a dramatic brick exterior. Enter into the two-story foyer—the unusually shaped staircase and balcony overlook create a tremendous first impression. Separated only by a classical colonnade detail, the living and dining rooms are perfect for entertaining. The great room features a fireplace and opens to the breakfast room and angled kitchen. Upstairs is a guest room, a children's den area, two family bedrooms and the master suite. This home is designed with a basement foundation.

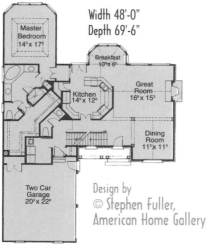

Width 48'-0"
Depth 69'-6"

Design by
© Stephen Fuller,
American Home Gallery

DESIGN T203

First Floor: 1,580 square feet
Second Floor: 595 square feet
Total: 2,175 square feet

Open planning of the dining room and the great room gives this plan a feeling of spaciousness. An octagonal kitchen works well with the bayed breakfast room. The secluded main-level master suite features a large walk-in closet and a private bath. Two family bedrooms and a full bath are on the upper level. Unfinished space above the garage is available for future expansion. This home is designed with a basement foundation.

TWO-STORY TRADITIONAL HOMES

DESIGN
TO41

First Floor: 1,053 square feet
Second Floor: 1,053 square feet
Total: 2,106 square feet
Bonus Room: 212 square feet

Brick takes a bold stand in grand traditional style in this treasured design. The front study has a nearby full bath, making it a handy guest bedroom. The family room with fireplace opens to a cozy breakfast area. The kitchen features a prep island and huge pantry. Upstairs, the master bedroom enjoys its own sitting room and a giant-sized closet. Two family bedrooms share a bath. This home is designed with a basement foundation.

Design by
© Stephen Fuller,
American Home Gallery

Width 52'-0"
Depth 34'-0"

QUOTE ONE®
Cost to build? See page 684 to order complete cost estimate to build this house in your area!

DESIGN
P255

First Floor: 955 square feet
Second Floor: 894 square feet
Total: 1,849 square feet
Bonus Room: 267 square feet

Fine brick detailing, attractive symmetry and an elegant entryway combine to give this two-story home plenty of curb appeal. From the formal dining room, guests can look across the hall to the formal living room. For more casual get-togethers, a spacious family room offers lots of room and a warming fireplace. The large kitchen offers an adjacent vaulted breakfast room. A master suite presents a sumptuous bath for pampering the fortunate homeowner. Please specify basement or crawlspace foundation when ordering.

Width 55'-10"
Depth 30'-0"

Design by
© Frank Betz Associates, Inc.

OPTIONAL BONUS ROOM

www.homeplanners.com

© Design Traditions

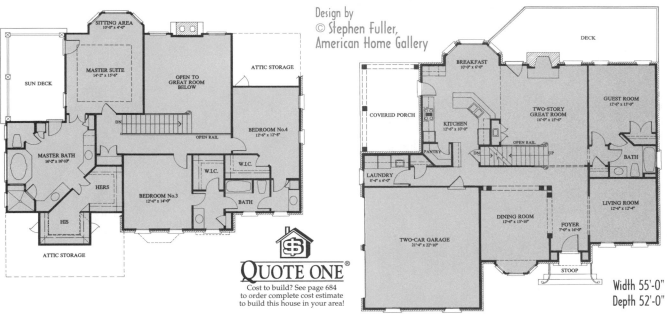

Design by
© Stephen Fuller,
American Home Gallery

SITTING AREA
10'-0" x 4'-0"

SUN DECK

MASTER SUITE
14'-2" x 15'-6"

OPEN TO GREAT ROOM BELOW

ATTIC STORAGE

DN

OPEN RAIL

BEDROOM No.4
12'-6" x 12'-8"

MASTER BATH
16'-2" x 16'-10"

HERS

W.I.C.

W.I.C.

BEDROOM No.3
12'-6" x 14'-0"

BATH

HIS

ATTIC STORAGE

BREAKFAST
10'-0" x 6'-0"

DECK

COVERED PORCH

KITCHEN
12'-6" x 10'-0"

TWO-STORY GREAT ROOM
16'-0" x 15'-0"

GUEST ROOM
12'-6" x 13'-0"

PANTRY

DN

OPEN RAIL

UP

BATH

LAUNDRY
8'-4" x 6'-0"

TWO-CAR GARAGE
21'-4" x 22'-10"

DINING ROOM
12'-4" x 15'-10"

FOYER
7'-0" x 16'-0"

LIVING ROOM
12'-6" x 12'-4"

STOOP

Width 55'-0"
Depth 52'-0"

Quote One®
Cost to build? See page 684
to order complete cost estimate
to build this house in your area!

Classical details and a stately brick exterior accentuate the grace and timeless elegance of this home. Inside, the foyer opens up to a large banquet-sized dining room and an adjacent formal living room. A central staircase, positioned for common access from all areas of the home, accents the foyer. Just beyond, the two-story great room awaits, featuring a wet bar and warming fireplace. To the left is the sunlit breakfast room and gourmet kitchen with breakfast bar. A large covered porch off the kitchen completes the family center. Upstairs, the master suite features an unusual bay-window design and private sun deck. The accompanying bath features His and Hers closets. Two bedrooms with a connecting bath complete the second floor. Each features a walk-in closet and a private dressing area with lavatory. This home is designed with a basement foundation.

DESIGN T028
First Floor: 1,581 square feet
Second Floor: 1,415 square feet
Total: 2,996 square feet

DESIGN A115

First Floor: 1,383 square feet
Second Floor: 546 square feet
Total: 1,929 square feet
Bonus Room: 320 square feet

This open, airy design is one that seems much larger than it actually is. A large, two-story great room, which can be viewed from the balcony above, opens into the dining room. The roomy master suite boasts a terrific walk-in closet and bath with dual lavatories. A breakfast area that opens onto a deck, and corner windows at the kitchen sink help bring the outdoors in. A bonus room can double as a fourth suite. Please specify slab or crawlspace foundation when ordering.

Width 50'-6"
Depth 42'-10"

Design by
© Living Concepts Home Planning

DECK/TERRACE

DINING ROOM 11'-0" x 12'-0"

BREAKFAST 8'-0" x 14'-6"

KITCHEN 10'-0" x 12'-0"

PANTRY

MASTER SUITE 15'-0" x 12'-0"

W.I.C.

MASTER BATH

LAUNDRY

GREAT ROOM 15'-0" x 19'-8"

UP

PDR.

LOGGIA

STOR.

GARAGE 20'-4" x 21'-0"

W.I.C.

SUITE 3/ OPT. LOFT 11'-0" x 12'-0"

W.I.C.

SUITE 2 12'-0" x 12'-0"

BALCONY

LEDGE

DN

OPEN TO BELOW

BATH

BONUS ROOM 16'-6" x 16'-0"

DESIGN P117

First Floor: 1,665 square feet
Second Floor: 1,554 square feet
Total: 3,219 square feet

Family living is the focus of this stately transitional home. The two-story family room features a lovely fireplace and windows to the rear yard. The remarkable kitchen provides wrap-around counters, a breakfast nook and a unique cooktop island that is angled to create a serving bar. A bedroom and full bath would make a comfortable guest suite or a quiet den. The master suite enjoys a sitting room with a through-fireplace to the vaulted bath. Please specify basement or crawlspace foundation when ordering.

Design by
© Frank Betz Associates, Inc.

Den/Bedroom 5 12² x 11⁰

Two Story Family Room 15³ x 21⁰

Breakfast

Kitchen

Bath

Living Room 12² x 14⁰

Two Story Foyer

Dining Room 12² x 13³

Garage

Laundry

copyright © 1993 frank betz associates, inc.

Bedroom 4 12² x 12²

Family Room Below

Master Suite 28⁶ x 14⁵

Sitting Room

W.i.c.

Bath

Bedroom 3 12² x 12²

Foyer Below

Bedroom 2 12² x 13³

Vaulted M. Bath

W.i.c.

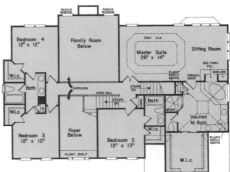

QUOTE ONE®

Cost to build? See page 684 to order complete cost estimate to build this house in your area!

Width 58'-6"
Depth 44'-10"

TWO-STORY TRADITIONAL HOMES

Home Office/
Bedroom 5
11⁶ x 12⁵

Bath

Pantry

Breakfast

FRENCH DOOR

Family Room
20⁰ x 14⁸

FPL.

W.i.c.

SERVING BAR

D.W.

Kitchen

RANGE

REF.

STAIRS DN.

STAIRS UP

COATS

Garage
19⁵ x 21⁹

Dining Room
11⁵ x 12⁰

Two-Story Foyer

Living Room
12⁰ x 12⁰

copyright © 1994 frank betz associates, inc.

Width 54'-4"
Depth 37'-6"

Quote One®
Cost to build? See page 684
to order complete cost estimate
to build this house in your area!

W.i.c.

LINEN

SHOWER

PLANT SHELF ABOVE

Vaulted M. Bath

FRENCH DOORS

TRAY CLG.

Master Suite
17⁰ x 14⁸

K.S.

Opt. Bonus/
Bedroom 4
13⁹ x 11⁵

W. D.
Laundry

Bath

STAIRS DN.

OPEN RAIL

W.i.c.

LINEN

OVERLOOK

W.i.c.

Bedroom 3
11⁵ x 12⁰

Foyer Below

Bedroom 2
12⁰ x 12⁰

Design by
© Frank Betz Associates, Inc.

Many extras make this home a stand-out. The home office includes a full bath, allowing it to also function as a guest suite. The two-story foyer is flanked by formal living and dining rooms. A large family room includes a fireplace and access to the rear yard. An efficient kitchen offers a serving bar into the breakfast room with a bay window. The upper-level bedrooms consist of a large master suite and two family bedrooms. An optional bonus room is available for future development. A laundry room is found on the second level, also. Please specify basement or crawl-space foundation when ordering.

DESIGN
P105

First Floor: 1,294 square feet
Second Floor: 1,067 square feet
Total: 2,361 square feet
Bonus Room: 168 square feet

Width 58'-10"
Depth 47'-0"

copyright © 1993 frank betz associates, inc.

Design by
© Frank Betz Associates, Inc.

**DESIGN
P254**
First Floor: 1,289 square feet
Second Floor: 1,375 square feet
Total: 2,664 square feet
Bonus Room: 115 square feet

Fine brick detailing, attractive symmetry and an elegantly covered entryway combine to give this two-story home plenty of curb appeal. Inside, this home is designed for entertaining. From the formal dining room, guests can migrate across the hall to the formal living room for after-dinner cocktails. For more casual get-togethers, a spacious family room offers lots of room to mingle as well as a warming fireplace. The large kitchen offers an adjacent vaulted breakfast room. The sleeping zone is located upstairs and includes three family bedrooms—each with a walk-in closet—sharing two full baths. A master suite completes this level and presents a sumptuous bath for pampering the fortunate homeowner. Please specify basement or crawlspace foundation when ordering.

www.homeplanners.com

Design by
© Design Basics, Inc.

COVERED DECK

LOUVERED OPENINGS IN ROOF

Grt. rm.
19⁰ x 19⁰

12'-0" CEILING
ARCHED CEILING

Bfst.
15⁰ x 12⁰

SNACK BAR

DESK

Kit.
10⁰ x 13⁰

PANTRY

Dn.
10⁸ x 15⁰
8'-8" CEILING

Mbr.
15⁰ x 13⁰
10'-0" CLG.

WHIRLPOOL

GLASS PANEL

LINEN

Br.
11⁰ x 14⁰

Br.
12⁴ x 11⁸

Gar.
27⁴ x 20⁴

STORAGE

© 1989 design basics inc.

COVERED STOOP

Width 74'-4"
Depth 58'-0"

The diagonal nature of this contemporary design makes it a versatile choice for a variety of lot arrangements. Inside, it is quite open visually. From the entry are exquisite views of the great room, with its fireplace flanked by windows, and of the stunning dining room. An island kitchen with a snack bar, planning desk and walk-in pantry adjoins the breakfast area. In the sleeping wing a romantic master suite accesses the yard and includes a ten-foot tiered ceiling and a bath with dual sinks, walk-in closet, separate shower and whirlpool tub. Two family bedrooms share a nearby full bath. The three-car garage holds extra storage space and allows access to the house through the mud/laundry room.

DESIGN 9250
Square Footage: 2,133

ONE-STORY CONTEMPORARY HOMES

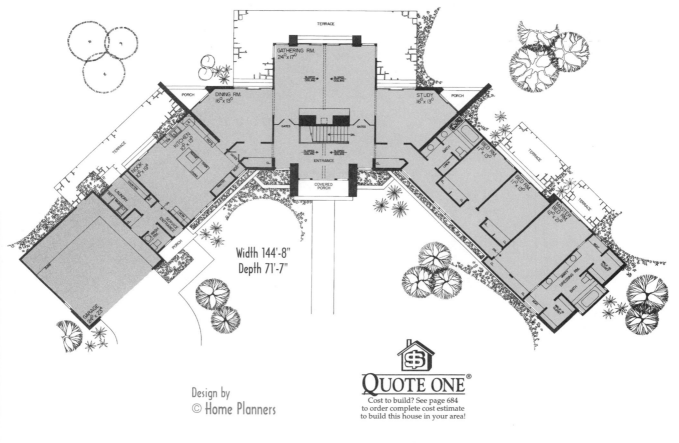

Width 144'-8"
Depth 71'-7"

Design by
© Home Planners

QUOTE ONE®
Cost to build? See page 684
to order complete cost estimate
to build this house in your area!

DESIGN 2534
Square Footage: 3,262

L

Using the best of Western design with in-line floor planning, this grand ranch house is made for open spaces. The wings effectively balance a truly dramatic front entrance. Massive masonry walls support the wide overhanging roof with its exposed beams. The patterned double front doors are surrounded by a delightful expanse of glass. The raised planter and the masses of quarried stone (or brick if you prefer) enhance the exterior appeal. Inside, a distinctive and practical floor plan emerges. The impressive entry leads through gates to the grand gathering room. The right wing holds the three bedrooms, each of which has terrace access. The master has three closets (two are walk-in!) and a dressing area in the bath. The left wing holds the kitchen, dining room and service area. Be sure to notice the many terraces and porches.

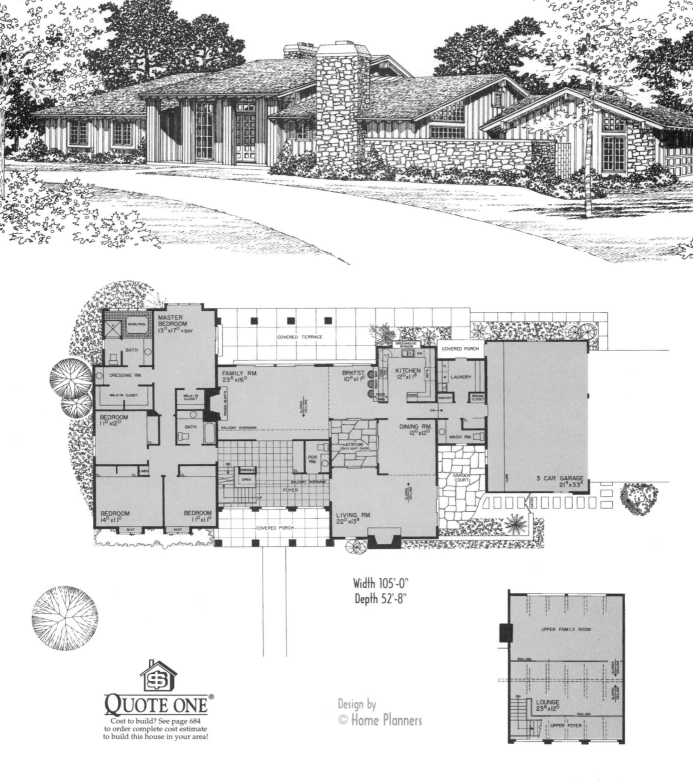

Width 105'-0"
Depth 52'-8"

QUOTE ONE®
Cost to build? See page 684
to order complete cost estimate
to build this house in your area!

Design by
© Home Planners

This lavish modern design has it all, including an upper lounge, family room and foyer. A front living room with its own fireplace looks out upon a side garden court and the centrally located atrium. A large, efficient kitchen with snack-bar service to the breakfast room also enjoys its own greenhouse window. The sleeping area is situated at one end of the house downstairs to ensure privacy and relaxation. Here, a deluxe master suite features a soothing whirlpool tub, a dressing area and an abundance of walk-in closets. Three secondary bedrooms, two with window seats, share a full bath.

DESIGN
2879
First Floor: 3,173 square feet
Second Floor: 267 square feet
Total: 3,440 square feet

DESIGN 2818

Square Footage: 1,566

L D

This outstanding contemporary design features a recessed front entry with a covered front porch. The rear gathering room offers a sloped ceiling, raised-hearth fireplace, sliding glass doors to the terrace and a snack bar with a pass-through to the U-shaped kitchen. The formal dining room is convenient to the kitchen and overlooks the planter court. Three bedrooms and two nearby baths are in the sleeping wing.

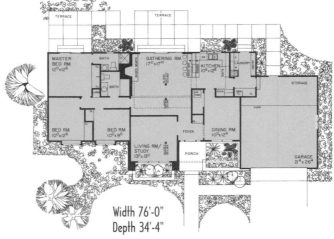

Width 76'-0"
Depth 34'-4"

Design by
© Home Planners

OPTIONAL
BASEMENT PLAN

Cost to build? See page 684
to order complete cost estimate
to build this house in your area!

DESIGN 3357

Square Footage: 2,913
Greenhouse: 147 square feet

L D

This plan opens with the formal living and dining rooms and a private media room that keeps noise at bay. The greenhouse offers access to the clutter room for gardening or hobby activities. The U-shaped kitchen includes two lazy Susans and a snack bar into the country kitchen with fireplace. At the opposite end of the house, the master bedroom, with a private bath, two family bedrooms and a shared bath make up the sleeping arrangements. A wealth of built-ins throughout the home make it especially inviting.

Width 82'-8"
Depth 74'-0"

Cost to build? See page 684
to order complete cost estimate
to build this house in your area!

Design by
© Home Planners

ONE-STORY CONTEMPORARY HOMES

www.homeplanners.com

DESIGN 2913
Square Footage: 1,835

D

This smart design features multi-gabled ends, varied rooflines and vertical windows. A covered porch leads through a foyer to a large, central gathering room with a fireplace, a sloped ceiling and its own special view of the rear terrace. A modern kitchen with a snack bar features a pass-through to the breakfast room with a view of the terrace. There's also an adjacent dining room. An isolated media room offers a quiet, private area for listening to stereos. A master bedroom suite includes its own whirlpool tub.

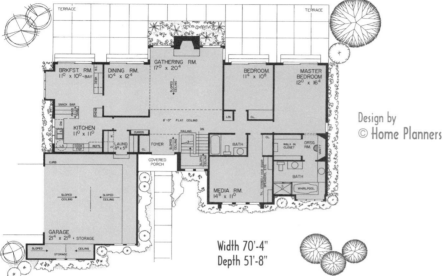

Design by
© Home Planners

Width 70'-4"
Depth 51'-8"

DESIGN 2915
Square Footage: 2,758
Greenhouse: 149 square feet

L D

What a grand plan! This well-zoned beauty has nearly everything going for it. Start with the country kitchen, which sports a fireplace, snack bar and greenhouse next door. Move to the media room, where there's a wall of built-ins, and then on to the combination living room/dining area (note the sloped ceiling, raised-hearth fireplace and doors leading to the terrace in back). Also check out both the master suite with His and Hers walk-in closets and whirlpool tub made for two, and all the extra storage space.

QUOTE ONE®
Cost to build? See page 684 to order complete cost estimate to build this house in your area!

Design by
© Home Planners

Width 81'-4"
Depth 78'-0"

DESIGN 2918

Square Footage: 1,693

D

Alternating use of stone and wood gives a textured look to this striking contemporary home with wide overhanging rooflines and a built-in planter box. The design is just as exciting on the inside, with two bedrooms, including a master suite, a study (or optional third bedroom), a rear gathering room with a fireplace and a sloped ceiling, a rear dining room and an efficient U-shaped kitchen with a pass-through to an adjoining breakfast room. A mudroom and washroom are located between the kitchen and the two-car garage.

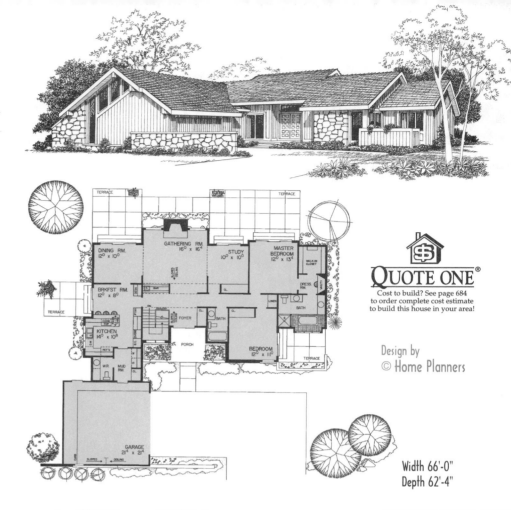

Cost to build? See page 684 to order complete cost estimate to build this house in your area!

Design by
© Home Planners

Width 66'-0"
Depth 62'-4"

DESIGN 2871

Square Footage: 1,824
Greenhouse: 81 square feet

D

A greenhouse area off the dining room and living room provides a cheerful focal point for this comfortable three-bedroom home. The spacious living room features a cozy fireplace and a sloped ceiling. In addition to the dining room, there's a breakfast room just off the modern kitchen. Both kitchen and breakfast areas look out to a front terrace. Stairs just off the foyer lead down to a basement recreation room. The master suite opens to a terrace. A mudroom and a washroom off the garage allow rear entry to the house.

Design by
© Home Planners

Cost to build? See page 684 to order complete cost estimate to build this house in your area!

Width 80'-4"
Depth 43'-0"

ONE-STORY CONTEMPORARY HOMES

334

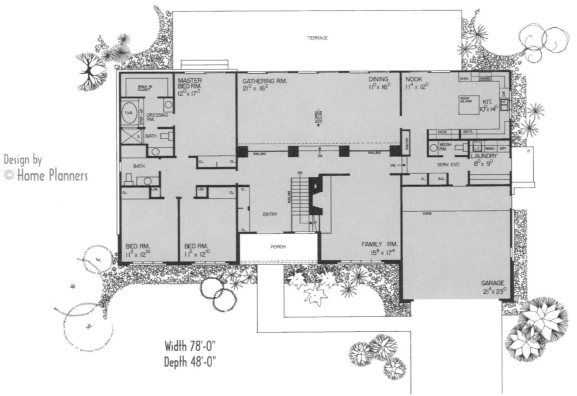

Design by
© Home Planners

Width 78'-0"
Depth 48'-0"

This impressive one-story design has numerous features that will assure the finest in contemporary living. For instance, the sunken gathering room and dining room share an impressive sloped ceiling; a series of three sliding glass doors provide access to the terrace. The family room, with a cozy fireplace, is ideal for informal entertaining. The kitchen features an efficient work island, pantry and built-in desk with a nearby sunny nook for morning coffee. The master bedroom opens to the rear terrace and its bath offers a step-up tub, a seperate shower, dual vanities, a compartmented toilet and a walk-in closet. Two additional bedrooms are located at the front of the home. The service entrance has a laundry area and washroom, plus access to the two-car garage.

DESIGN
2756
Square Footage: 2,652
L D

DESIGN 3454

Square Footage: 1,699

L D

Volume looks are achieved through the use of a high-pitched, hip roof on this design. An efficient, spacious interior comes through in this compact floor plan. Through a pair of columns, an open living and dining room creates a warm space for all sorts of living pursuits. Sliding glass doors guarantee a bright, cheerful interior while providing easy access to outdoor living. The L-shaped kitchen has an island work surface, practical planning desk and informal eating space. The master suite provides a tray ceiling and sliding glass doors to the yard.

Design by
© Home Planners

QUOTE ONE®
Cost to build? See page 684
to order complete cost estimate
to build this house in your area!

Width 52'-8"
Depth 49'-0"

DESIGN 3560

Square Footage: 2,189

L

Simplicity is the key to the stylish good looks of this home's facade. A walled garden entry and large window areas appeal to outdoor enthusiasts. Inside, the kitchen forms the hub of the plan. It opens directly off the foyer and features an island cooktop and a work counter with a snack bar. A sloped ceiling, a fireplace and sliding glass doors to the rear terrace are highlights in the living area. The master bedroom also sports sliding glass doors to the terrace, plus a dressing area enhanced with double walk-in closets.

QUOTE ONE®
Cost to build? See page 684
to order complete cost estimate
to build this house in your area!

Design by
© Home Planners

Width 56'-0"
Depth 72'-0"

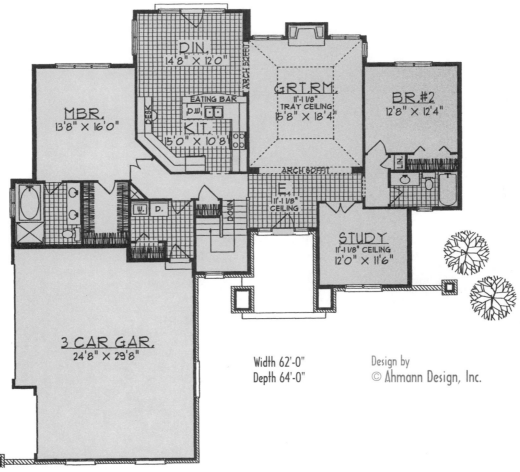

DIN.
14'8" X 12'0"

GRT. RM.
11'-1 1/8"
TRAY CEILING
15'8" X 18'4"

BR. #2
12'8" X 12'4"

MBR.
13'8" X 16'0"

EATING BAR

DESK

DW

KIT.
15'0" X 10'8"

ARCH SOFFIT

E.
11'-1 1/8"
CEILING

LIN.

W.   D.

DOWN

STUDY
11'-1 1/8" CEILING
12'0" X 11'6"

3 CAR GAR.
24'8" X 29'8"

Width 62'-0"
Depth 64'-0"

Design by
© Ahmann Design, Inc.

This beautiful contemporary ranch-style home offers interesting windows and varied siding textures. The tiled entry opens to the great room with a tray ceiling, arched thresholds and a fireplace. The casual dining area is open to the kitchen with a bar and built-in desk. The master suite is accented by double doors, a walk-in closet and a bath with oval tub and separate shower. A secondary bedroom is on the opposite side of the house, and a study to the front might also be used as a den or third bedroom. Note the three-car garage.

DESIGN
U107
Square Footage: 1,830

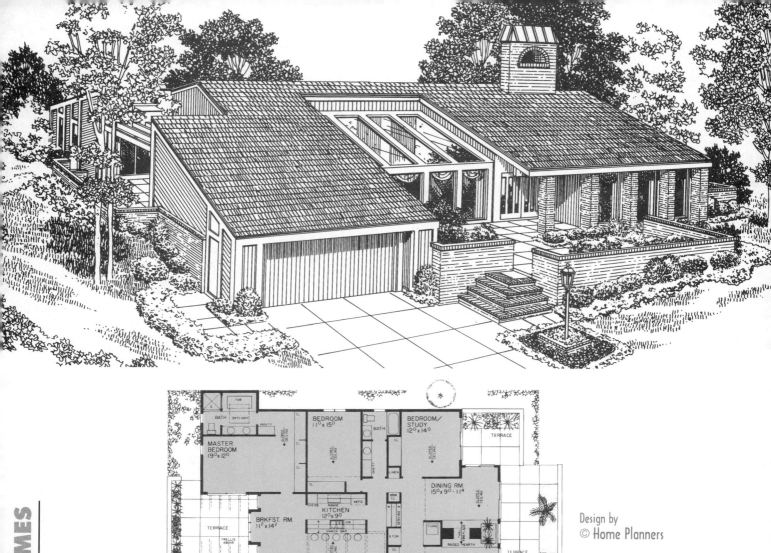

DESIGN 2858
Square Footage: 2,231

Width 62'-5"
Depth 62'-0"

Design by
© Home Planners

This sun-oriented design was created to face the south, allowing the morning sun to brighten the living and dining rooms and the adjacent terrace. During the winter, a glass roof and walls on the garden room will provide solar heat—and relief from high energy bills. Solar shades allow you to adjust the amount of light. The kitchen provides a snack bar and a serving counter to the dining room. The breakfast room with laundry area is also convenient to the kitchen. The master bath includes a four-foot-square skylight, a garden tub and a separate shower. Don't miss the private terrace outside the master bedroom. Two nearby family bedrooms share a full bath that includes double vanities.

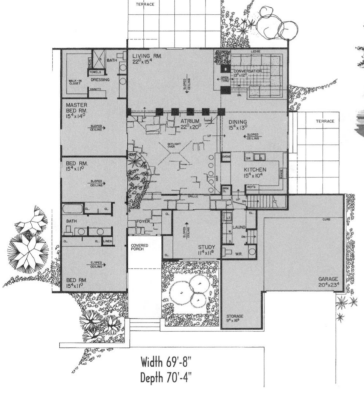

Width 69'-8"
Depth 70'-4"

REAR VIEW

Design by
© Home Planners

The advantage of passive solar heating is a significant highlight of this contemporary design. The huge skylight over the atrium shelters it during inclement weather, while permitting light to enter down below. The stone floor of this area absorbs an abundance of heat from the sun during the day and permits the circulation of warm air to other areas at night. Sloped ceilings highlight each of the major rooms: three bedrooms, formal living and dining areas and a study. Broad expanses of roof can accommodate solar panels, if desired, to complement this design. Note the terraces at the side and rear. The sunken conversation area with through-fireplace to the living room will really be something to talk about.

**DESIGN
2832**
Square Footage: 2,805
D

The home, as shown in the photograph, may differ from the actual blueprints. For more detailed information, please check the floor plans carefully.

Photo by Andrew D. Lautman

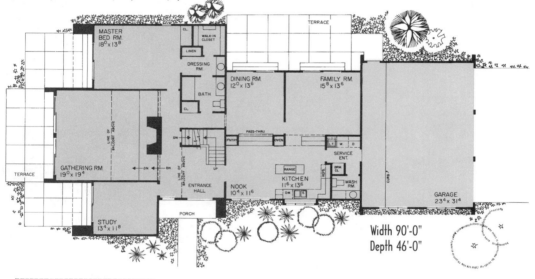

Width 90'-0"
Depth 46'-0"

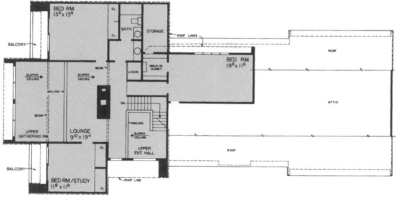

QUOTE ONE®
Cost to build? See page 684 to order complete cost estimate to build this house in your area!

Design by
© Home Planners

**DESIGN
2781**
First Floor: 2,132 square feet
Second Floor: 1,156 square feet
Total: 3,288 square feet
L D

This beautifully designed two-story home provides an eye-catching exterior. The floor plan is a perfect complement. The front kitchen features an island range, adjacent breakfast nook and pass-through to a formal dining room. The master suite offers a spacious walk-in closet and dressing room. The side terrace can be reached from the master suite, the gathering room and the study. The second floor contains three bedrooms and storage space galore. The center lounge offers a sloped ceiling and skylight.

www.homeplanners.com

The home, as shown in the photographs, may differ from the actual blueprints. For more detailed information, please check the floor plans carefully.

Photo by Andrew D. Lautman

REAR VIEW

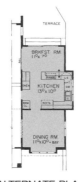

ALTERNATE PLAN

Width 49'-0"
Depth 54'-4"

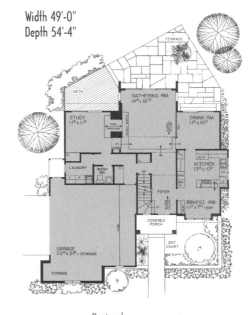

Design by
© Home Planners

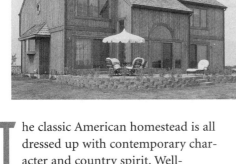

QUOTE ONE®
Cost to build? See page 684
to order complete cost estimate
to build this house in your area!

The classic American homestead is all dressed up with contemporary character and country spirit. Well-defined rooms, flowing spaces and the latest amenities blend the best of traditional and modern elements. The spacious gathering room offers terrace access and shares a through-fireplace with a secluded study. The second-floor master suite shares a balcony hallway, which overlooks the gathering room, with two family bedrooms. Dual vanities, built-in cabinets and shelves, and triple-window views highlight the master bedroom. In an alternate plan, the formal dining room and the breakfast room are switched, placing the dining room to the front of the plan.

DESIGN 2826
First Floor: 1,112 square feet
Second Floor: 881 square feet
Total: 1,993 square feet

DESIGN 2711

First Floor: 975 square feet
Second Floor: 1,024 square feet
Total: 1,999 square feet

L D

Sleek, modern lines define this two-story contemporary home. The formal dining area and informal eating counter, both easily served by the U-shaped kitchen, share the centered fireplace and generous views to the rear grounds from the gathering room. Amenities abound in the second-floor master suite, with a private balcony, walk-in closet, separate dressing area and knee-space vanity. Two secondary bedrooms and a full bath complete this floor.

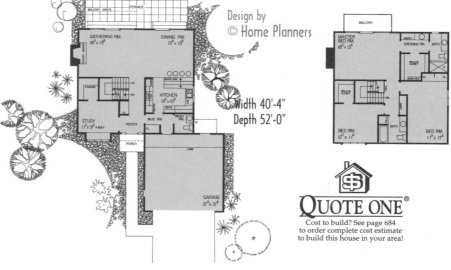

Design by
© Home Planners

Width 40'-4"
Depth 52'-0"

QUOTE ONE®
Cost to build? See page 684
to order complete cost estimate
to build this house in your area!

DESIGN 2925

First Floor: 1,128 square feet
Second Floor: 844 square feet
Total: 1,972 square feet

This two-story contemporary design features expansive overhanging roofs that make a distinctive design statement. The noteworthy front entry features panelled double doors below a large radial head window. To either side of the dining room are the kitchen and breakfast room and the grand gathering room. A through-fireplace connects the dining room and gathering room. A cozy media room has built-ins and a nearby powder room. Upstairs are two bedrooms—one a master suite with a fireplace and whirlpool tub.

Design by
© Home Planners

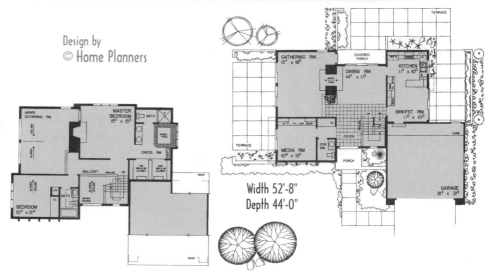

Width 52'-8"
Depth 44'-0"

www.homeplanners.com

QUOTE ONE®

Cost to build? See page 684
to order complete cost estimate
to build this house in your area!

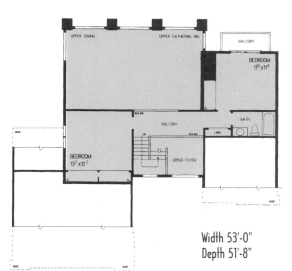

Width 53'-0"
Depth 51'-8"

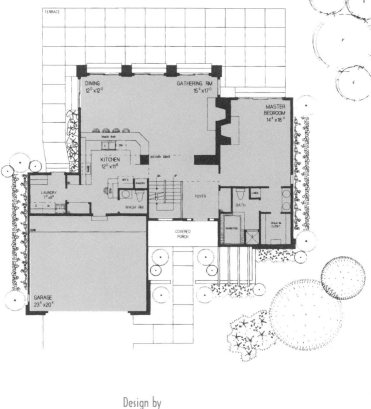

Design by
© Home Planners

Attractive, contemporary split-bedroom planning makes the most of this plan. The master suite pampers with a lavish bath and a fireplace. The living areas are open and have easy access to the rear terrace. Note, in particular, the convenient snack bar between the kitchen and the gathering room/dining room. A large laundry area and washroom separates the main house from the garage. A balcony overlook on the second floor allows views to the gathering room or to the entry foyer. One family bedroom has a private balcony.

**DESIGN
2490**
First Floor: 1,414 square feet
Second Floor: 620 square feet
Total: 2,034 square feet

Width 68'-0"
Depth 48'-0"

KITCHEN
9/0x10/0
DINING
GREAT RM.
24/0x17/6
GREAT RM.
24/0x17/6
DINING
KITCHEN
9/0x10/0
VAULTED
MORNING
ROOM
8/0x8/0
ENTRY
VAULTED
MORNING
ROOM
8/0x8/0
ENTRY
BREAKFAST PATIO
LINEN
UTILITY
UTILITY
LINEN
BREAKFAST PATIO
W D WH F
F WH D W
GARAGE
19/4x21/8
GARAGE
19/4x21/8

DEN/BEDRM. 3
19/0x10/2
STOR
LINEN
BEDRM. 2
9/6x10/2
BEDRM. 2
9/6x10/2
STOR
LINEN
DEN/BEDRM. 3
19/0x10/2
36" HIGH
WALL
OPEN TO
MORNING RM.
BELOW
DN
OPEN TO ENTRY
BELOW
BATH
BATH
BATH
BATH
DN
36" HIGH
WALL
OPEN TO
MORNING RM.
BELOW
OPEN TO
ENTRY
BELOW
DRESSING
DRESSING
MASTER
14/2x11/0
MASTER
14/2x11/0

Design by
© Piercy & Barclay Designers, Inc.

**DESIGN
C522**
First Floor: 750 square feet
Second Floor: 766 square feet
Total: 1,516 square feet
(each unit)

A s alike as two peas in a pod, the two wonderful units in this duplex make fine homes. Enter through a walled breakfast patio that is accessed from the entry and the vaulted morning room. Inside, the great room features a warming fireplace and rear-yard access. The L-shaped kitchen offers an angled work island and a pantry. A utility/bathroom and a linen closet complete this floor. Upstairs, the master bedroom suite is designed to pamper, with a walk-in closet, dressing area and private bath. A huge den—or make it a bedroom—has views down into the entry and morning room. A secondary bedroom accesses a full hall bath. Each unit has a two-car garage.

www.homeplanners.com

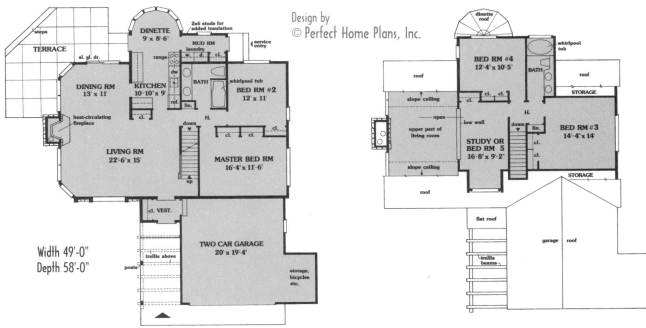

Design by
© Perfect Home Plans, Inc.

TERRACE
steps
sl. gl. dr.
DINING RM 13' x 11'
DINETTE 9' x 8'-6"
2x6 studs for added insulation
MUD RM laundry
service entry
KITCHEN 10'-10" x 9'
range
w. d. cl.
dw
BATH
BED RM #2 12' x 11'
whirlpool tub
heat-circulating fireplace
ref.
lin.
cl.
H.
LIVING RM 22'-6" x 15'
down
cl.
cl.
cl.
MASTER BED RM 16'-4" x 11'-6"
up
cl. **VEST.**
trellis above
posts
TWO CAR GARAGE 20' x 19'-4"
storage, bicycles etc.

Width 49'-0"
Depth 58'-0"

dinette roof
roof
BED RM #4 12'-4" x 10'-5"
BATH
whirlpool tub
roof
STORAGE
slope ceiling
cl. cl.
open
low wall
H.
down
lin.
cl.
upper part of living room
BED RM #3 14'-4" x 14'
STUDY OR BED RM 5 16'-8" x 9'-2"
slope ceiling
cl.
roof
STORAGE
flat roof
garage roof
trellis beams

TWO-STORY CONTEMPORARY HOMES

Creative design at its best is evident in this two-story contemporary home. A dramatic trellis-covered walkway leads into a vestibule with closet and on to the main living space. The combined living room and dining L has sixteen-foot ceilings, and a fieldstone, heat-circulating fireplace flanked by unique scalloped windows. A semi-circle of windows forms the dinette space, creating a flood of light into the adjoining well-equipped kitchen. Two large bedrooms and a full bath with dual vanities and oversized whirlpool tub share the first-floor sleeping wing. Two additional bedrooms are upstairs, plus an optional den open to the living room below. Stairs off the center hall lead to the full basement. A slab foundation is also available. Note the storage space in the garage.

DESIGN N105
First Floor: 1,345 square feet
Second Floor: 656 square feet
Total: 2,001 square feet

DESIGN 3563

First Floor: 1,023 square feet
Second Floor: 866 square feet
Total: 1,899 square feet

L D

This wonderful transitional plan's stucco exterior is enhanced by arched windows, a recessed arched entry and a lovely balcony off the second-floor master bedroom. A walled entry court extends the living room outside. The double front doors open to the foyer with a hall closet and powder room. The large living room adjoins directly to the dining room. The family features a sloped ceiling and fireplace. Sleeping quarters consist of two secondary bedrooms with a shared bath, and a generous master suite.

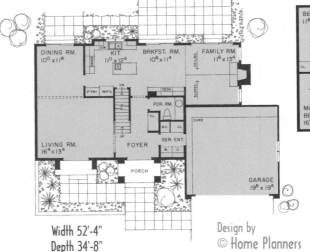

Width 52'-4"
Depth 34'-8"

Design by
© Home Planners

QUOTE ONE®
Cost to build? See page 684
to order complete cost estimate
to build this house in your area!

TWO-STORY CONTEMPORARY HOMES

DESIGN 2926

Main Level: 1,570 square feet
Upper Level: 598 square feet
Lower Level: 1,080 square feet
Total: 3,248 square feet

The dramatic use of balconies and overlooks in this ultra-modern design highlights the first-floor gathering room, the formal dining room and the kitchen. A goblet-shaped bedroom on this floor includes a balcony and full bath. Reached by a curved stair, the upper level is dominated by the master suite. A lower-level activities room with a bar and a fireplace, and an exercise room, with an attached sauna, hot tub and bath, overlook the lower terrace. Note the generous use of skylights throughout.

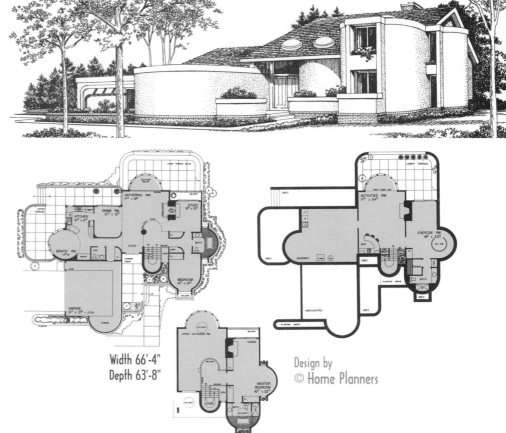

Width 66'-4"
Depth 63'-8"

Design by
© Home Planners

Width 60'-0"
Depth 43'-4"

Design by
© Drummond Designs, Inc.

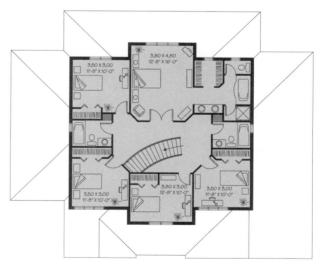

This contemporary design offers uncompromising livability. To the left of the foyer, the living room and adjoining dining room provide ample space for entertaining. The gourmet kitchen includes a breakfast bar and opens to the family room. A media room provides a cozy retreat for watching favorite movies. Two large master suites, one on both floors, each have a walk-in closet and a private bath. Four family bedrooms and two full bathrooms complete the plan. This home is designed with a basement foundation.

DESIGN ZO11

First Floor: 1700 square feet
Second Floor: 1,300 square feet
Total: 3,000 square feet

Design by
© Home Design Services, Inc.

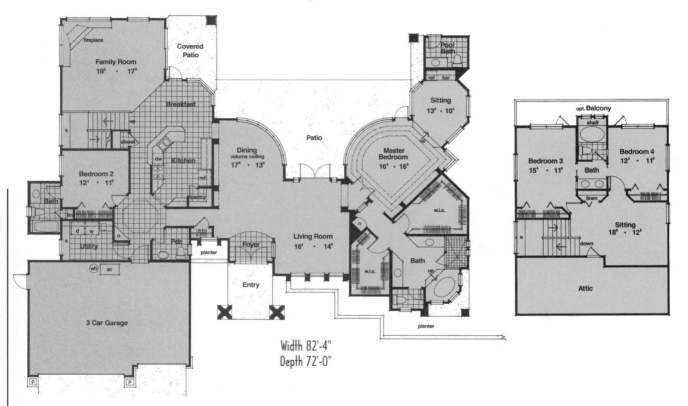

Width 82'-4"
Depth 72'-0"

TWO-STORY CONTEMPORARY HOMES

DESIGN 8679
First Floor: 2,531 square feet
Second Floor: 669 square feet
Total: 3,200 square feet

This exquisite brick and stucco contemporary home takes its cue from the tradition of Frank Lloyd Wright. The formal living and dining areas combine to provide a spectacular view of the rear grounds. Unique best describes the private master suite, highlighted by a mitered bow window, a raised sitting area complete with a wet bar, oversized His and Hers walk-in closets and a lavish master bath complete with a relaxing corner tub, separate shower and twin vanities. The family living area encompasses the left portion of the plan, featuring a spacious family room with a corner fireplace, access to the covered patio from the breakfast area and a step-saving kitchen. Bedroom 2 connects to a private bath. Upstairs, two bedrooms share a balcony, a sitting room and full bath.

QUOTE ONE®
Cost to build? See page 684
to order complete cost estimate
to build this house in your area!

Width 75'-10"
Depth 69'-4"

DESIGN 3636
Square Footage: 2,626

L

This adaptation reflects Frank Lloyd Wright's purest Prairie style complemented by a brick exterior, a multitude of windows and a low-slung hip roof. The foyer introduces a gallery wall while to the right, an archway leads to a formal dining room lined with a wall of windows. Centrally located, the two-story family/great room provides an ideal setting for gatherings. The left wing contains the sleeping quarters and an office/den. For a four-bedroom option, see Design 3637 below.

DESIGN 3637
Square Footage: 3,278

L

Form follows function in this Prairie adaptation, inspired by Frank Lloyd Wright. The great room offers a raised-hearth fireplace framed by built-in cabinetry and plant shelves. A lavish master suite harbors a sitting area with private access to the covered pergola. A spacious guest suite includes an angled whirlpool tub and twin lavatories. A fifth bedroom or home office provides access to the wraparound porch. For a three-bedroom option, see Design 3636 above. Plans for a detached garage with an optional guest suite are included with the blueprints.

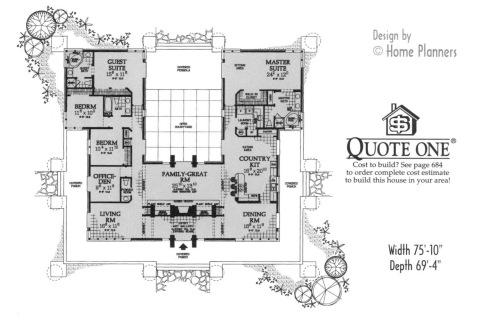

QUOTE ONE®
Cost to build? See page 684
to order complete cost estimate
to build this house in your area!

Width 75'-10"
Depth 69'-4"

TWO-STORY CONTEMPORARY HOMES

Design by
© Home Planners

TERRACE

TERRACE

GATHERING RM.
17⁴ x 19⁴

DINING RM.
11⁰ x 13⁶

NOOK
9⁴ x 8⁶

MASTER
BED RM.
11⁸ x 15¹⁰

RAISED HEARTH

SEAT

BATH

LINEN

UP   DN.

ENTRY
OPEN ABOVE

PDR.
RM.

CL.

RANGE

KITCHEN
10⁴ x 14¹⁰

TUB

DRESSING RM.

WALK-IN
CLOSET

PANTRY

LAUNDRY

VANITY

CL.

RAIL   OPEN

OPEN ABOVE

PORCH

CURB

DN.

GARAGE
21⁸ x 21⁴

STORAGE

BALCONY

BED RM.
11⁸ x 13⁶

SLOPED
CEILING

OPEN TO
GATHERING RM.
BELOW

OPEN

BED RM.
11⁰ x 13⁶

CL.

DRESS.
RM.

BATH

DN.

RAIL

OPEN TO
ENTRY BELOW

CL.

CL.

DRESS.
RM.

BATH

VANITY

RAIL

OPEN

Width 66'-8"
Depth 62'-4"

DESIGN
2729
First Floor: 1,590 square feet
Second Floor: 756 square feet
Total: 2,346 square feet

L

Entering this home through the sheltered walkway to the double front doors will be a pleasure. And the pleasure and beauty does not stop there. The entry hall and sunken gathering room are open to the second floor for added dimension. Three bedrooms include a lavish master suite. Both second-floor bedrooms feature private full baths with dressing areas. There are fine indoor/outdoor living relationships in this design. Note the private terrace, a living terraceand the balcony. The two-car garage has extra storage space.

DINING
11/0 X 11/0 +/-

DN.

PANTRY

TWO STORY
LIVING
13/0 X 14/4

FAMILY
13/6 X 17/6

DN.

UP

Design by
© Alan Mascord
Design Associates, Inc.

BR. 2
10/2 X 13/0

BR. 3
10/8 X 11/8

LIN.

DN.

TUB

LIVING RM.
BELOW

VAULTED
MASTER
13/6 X 12/6

Width 36'-0"
Depth 33'-0"

This house not only accommodates a narrow lot, but it also fits a sloping site. Notice how the two-car garage is tucked away under the first level of the house. The angled corner entry gives way to a two-story living room with a tiled hearth. The dining room shares an interesting angled space with this area and enjoys easy service from the efficient kitchen. A large pantry and an angled corner sink add character to this area. The family room offers double doors to a refreshing balcony. A powder room and a laundry room complete the main level. Upstairs, three bedrooms include a vaulted master suite with a private bath. Bedrooms 2 and 3 each take advantage of direct access to a full bath.

DESIGN 9509
First Floor: 1,022 square feet
Second Floor: 813 square feet
Total: 1,835 square feet

L

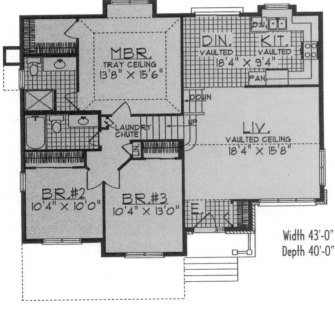

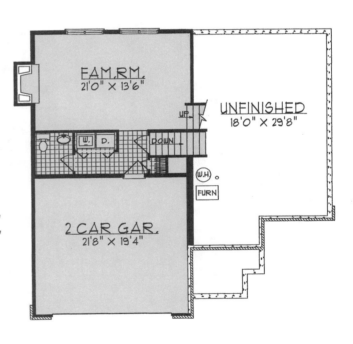

Width 43'-0"
Depth 40'-0"

Design by
© Ahmann Design, Inc.

DESIGN U109
Main Level: 1,289 square feet
Lower Level: 443 square feet
Total: 1,732 square feet

Enter this multi-level home through the front door or through the garage on the lower floor. The family room, laundry room, powder room and unfinished space are also on the lower floor. Stairs from this level lead up to the living room, which features a vaulted ceiling and wide corner windows. Step down a few steps to the master suite with its private bath, walk-in closet and box-bay window. Two family bedrooms share a bath and a laundry chute. The unfinished area can be basement or slab—please specify when ordering.

Width 38'-0"
Depth 31'-0"

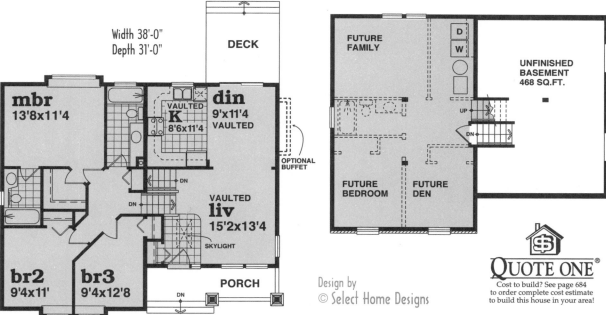

DECK

mbr
13'8x11'4

VAULTED
K
8'6x11'4

din
9'x11'4
VAULTED

OPTIONAL BUFFET

DN

DN

VAULTED
liv
15'2x13'4

SKYLIGHT

br2
9'4x11'

br3
9'4x12'8

DN

PORCH

FUTURE FAMILY

D
W

UNFINISHED BASEMENT
468 SQ.FT.

UP

DN

FUTURE BEDROOM

FUTURE DEN

Design by
© Select Home Designs

Quote One®
Cost to build? See page 684
to order complete cost estimate
to build this house in your area!

Craftsman styling and a welcoming porch create marvelous curb appeal for this design. A compact footprint allows economy in construction. A volume ceiling in the living and dining rooms and the kitchen make this home live larger than its modest square footage. The kitchen features generous cabinet space and flows directly into the dining room (note the optional buffet) to create a casual country feeling. The master bedroom offers a walk-in closet, full bath and a bumped-out window overlooking the rear yard. Two additional bedrooms also boast bumped-out windows and share a full bath. The lower level provides room for an additional bedroom, den, family room and full bath. Choose the unfinished basement or a crawlspace foundation under the living area.

DESIGN Q527
Square Footage: 1,108
Unfinished Lower Level: 620 square feet
Opt. Unfinished Basement: 468 square feet

DESIGN 2679

Main Level: 1,860 square feet
Lower Level: 1,323 square feet
Total: 3,183 square feet

This spacious contemporary home offers plenty of livability on many levels. The main level includes a breakfast room, a dining room and a sloped-ceilinged living room with raised hearth. The upper level features an isolated master suite with an adjoining study and balcony. The family level offers a long rectangular family room with terrace on one end and a bar with a washroom at the other end. Two lower-level bedrooms enjoy their own view of the terrace. A spacious basement is included.

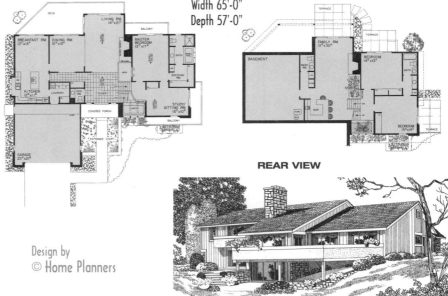

Width 65'-0"
Depth 57'-0"

REAR VIEW

Design by
© Home Planners

DESIGN 7518

Main Level: 1,362 square feet
Upper Level: 400 square feet
Lower Level: 538 square feet
Total: 2,300 square feet

This home, designed for lots that slope up from the street, features rafter tails, horizontal siding and stonework. The foyer opens on the lower level, giving access to a large den, full bath and laundry room. On the main level, a huge living/dining room awaits and features a fireplace, snack bar and built-in entertainment center. A built-in nook area provides space for casual meals. The lavish master suite offers many amenities. Two secondary bedrooms share a full bath on the upper floor.

Design by
© Alan Mascord
Design Associates, Inc.

Width 60'-0"
Depth 26'-0"

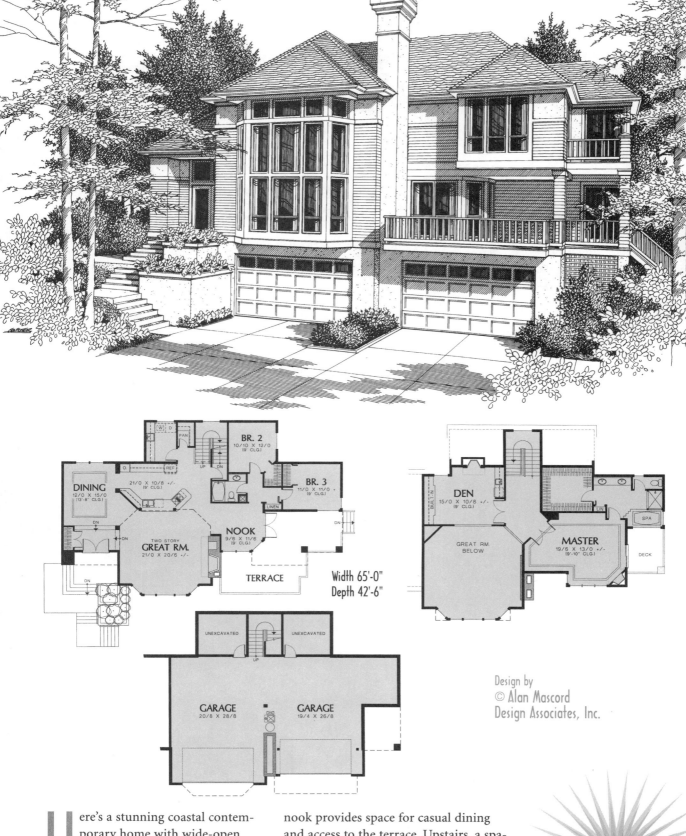

DINING
12/0 X 15/0
(13'-8" CLG.)

BR. 2
10/10 X 12/0
(9' CLG.)

21/0 X 10/8 +/-
(9' CLG.)

BR. 3
11/0 X 11/0
(9' CLG.)

LINEN

TWO STORY
GREAT RM.
21/0 X 20/6 +/-

NOOK
9/6 X 11/6
(9' CLG.)

TERRACE

Width 65'-0"
Depth 42'-6"

DEN
15/0 X 10/8 +/-
(9' CLG.)

GREAT RM.
BELOW

MASTER
19/6 X 13/0 +/-
(9'-10" CLG.)

SPA

DECK

UNEXCAVATED

UNEXCAVATED

UP

GARAGE
20/8 X 28/8

GARAGE
19/4 X 26/8

Design by
© Alan Mascord
Design Associates, Inc.

H ere's a stunning coastal contemporary home with wide-open views planned for the front of the home. The great room is thoughtfully positioned to benefit from the two-story windows and transoms. A nearby nook provides space for casual dining and access to the terrace. Upstairs, a spacious master suite has a plush bath and is near a secluded den with a fireplace. Note the four-car garage with generous storage space.

DESIGN 7507
First Floor: 1,765 square feet
Second Floor: 907 square feet
Total: 2,672 square feet

DESIGN Q488

Lower-Level Entry: 175 square feet
Main Level: 1,115 square feet
Total: 1,290 square feet
Unfinished Lower Level: 626 square feet

With the main living areas on the second floor, this plan makes a grand vacation retreat. The covered entry opens to a foyer and an open rail staircase leads to the living/dining room combination with fireplace and box window. Sliding glass doors in the dining room open to the wide sun deck that shades the patio below. The U-shaped kitchen provides a window over the sink. The master bedroom has a full bath and large wall closet. Family bedrooms have walk-in closets and share a full bath.

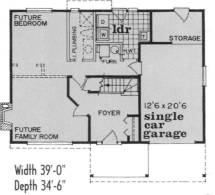

Width 39'-0"
Depth 34'-6"

Design by
© Select Home Designs

DESIGN 2511

Main Level: 1,043 square feet
Upper Level: 703 square feet
Lower Level: 794 square feet
Total: 2,540 square feet

L D

This outstanding multi-level home comes complete with outdoor deck and balconies. The entry level provides full living space: gathering room with fireplace, study (or optional bedroom) with bath, dining room and U-shaped kitchen. A bedroom and bunk room on the upper level are joined by a wide balcony area and full bath. Lower-level space includes a large activities room with fireplace, an additional bunk room and a full bath. Built-ins and open window areas abound throughout the plan.

Width 40'-4"
Depth 52'-0"

Design by
© Home Planners

QUOTE ONE®
Cost to build? See page 684
to order complete cost estimate
to build this house in your area!

Design by
© Ahmann Design, Inc.

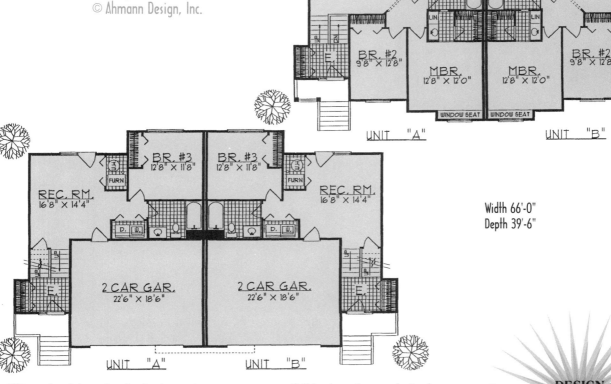

WOOD DECK
15'4" X 6'0"

DIN.
12'8" X 13'6"

KIT.

LIV.
16'8" X 16'0"

BR. #2
9'8" X 12'8"

MBR.
12'8" X 12'0"

WINDOW SEAT

UNIT "A"

WOOD DECK
15'4" X 6'0"

DIN.
12'8" X 13'6"

KIT.

LIV.
16'8" X 16'0"

BR. #2
9'8" X 12'8"

MBR.
12'8" X 12'0"

WINDOW SEAT

UNIT "B"

BR. #3
12'8" X 11'8"

REC. RM.
16'8" X 14'4"

FURN

2 CAR GAR.
22'6" X 18'6"

UNIT "A"

BR. #3
12'8" X 11'8"

REC. RM.
16'8" X 14'4"

FURN

2 CAR GAR.
22'6" X 18'6"

UNIT "B"

Width 66'-0"
Depth 39'-6"

**DESIGN
U188**

Main Level: 1,050 square feet
Lower Level: 528 square feet
Total: 1,578 square feet
(each unit)

Both of these lovely duplex units offer two bedrooms, an eat-in kitchen, a fireplace in the living room and a deck for star gazing—all on the main level, while a third bedroom, a full bath and a good-sized recreation room complete the lower level. The master bedroom enjoys a window seat and a walk-in closet. Both units offer a two-car garage.

MULTI-LEVEL & HILLSIDE HOMES

Width 56'-8"
Depth 36'-5"

Design by
© Home Planners

QUOTE ONE®
Cost to build? See page 684
to order complete cost estimate
to build this house in your area!

DESIGN 2608
Main Level: 728 square feet
Upper Level: 874 square feet
Lower Level: 310 square feet
Total: 1,912 square feet

L D

Tri-level living could hardly ask for more than this rustic design has to offer. Not only can you enjoy the three levels but there is also a fourth basement level for bulk storage and, perhaps, a shop area. The interior livability is outstanding. The main level provides an L-shaped formal living/dining area with a fireplace in the living room, sliding glass doors in the dining room leading to the upper terrace, a U-shaped kitchen and an informal eating area. Down a few steps to the lower level is the family room with another fireplace and sliding doors to the lower terrace, and a washroom and a laundry room. The upper level houses all of the sleeping facilities including three bedrooms, a bath and the master suite.

DESIGN 1850

Main Level: 1,456 square feet
Lower Level: 728 square feet
Total: 2,184 square feet

A perfect rectangle, this split-level home is comparatively inexpensive to build and very appealing to live in. It features a large upper-level living room with a fireplace, a formal dining room, three bedrooms (with two full baths nearby), and an outdoor deck. Another fireplace warms the family room on the lower level, which also has a full bath and room for a study or a fourth bedroom.

Design by
© Home Planners

Width 54'-8"
Depth 28'-0"

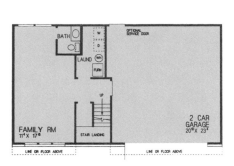

QUOTE ONE®

Cost to build? See page 684
to order complete cost estimate
to build this house in your area!

DESIGN 3713

Main Level: 1,028 square feet
Lower Level: 442 square feet
Total: 1,470 square feet

This home offers a living room, dining room, kitchen, two baths and three bedrooms. The lower level, with a two-car garage, can be finished in the future to include a family room, powder room and utility room. The basic plan may be enhanced with a fireplace in the living room, an exterior brick veneer, decorative louvers and a rear deck. The blueprints for this house show how to build both the basic, low-cost version and the enhanced, upgraded version.

Width 40'-0"
Depth 26'-0"

Design by
© Home Planners

MULTI-LEVEL & HILLSIDE HOMES

DESIGN P196
Square Footage: 2,193
Bonus Room: 400 square feet

From the hip and gabled roof to the gracious entryway, class is a common element in this home. Inside, the foyer is flanked by a formal living room and a formal dining room defined by columns. Directly ahead lies the spacious family room, offering a warming fireplace, radius windows and a pass-through to the efficient island kitchen. The split sleeping quarters include a deluxe master suite complete with a lavish bath. Please specify basement, crawl-space or slab foundation when ordering.

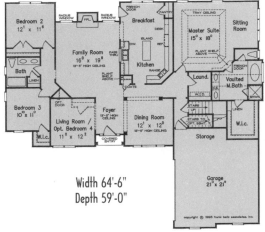

Design by
© Frank Betz Associates, Inc.

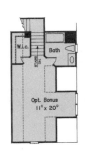

Width 64'-6"
Depth 59'-0"

DESIGN P194
Square Footage: 2,491
Bonus Room: 588 square feet

European details bring charm and a bit of *joie de vivre* to this traditional home, and a thoughtful floor plan warms up to a myriad of lifestyles. Comfortable living space includes a vaulted family room with a centered fireplace, and complements the formal dining room. A sizable gourmet kitchen offers a walk-in pantry and a center cooktop island counter. The master suite offers a tray ceiling and a private sitting room, bright with windows and a warming hearth. Please specify basement or crawlspace foundation when ordering.

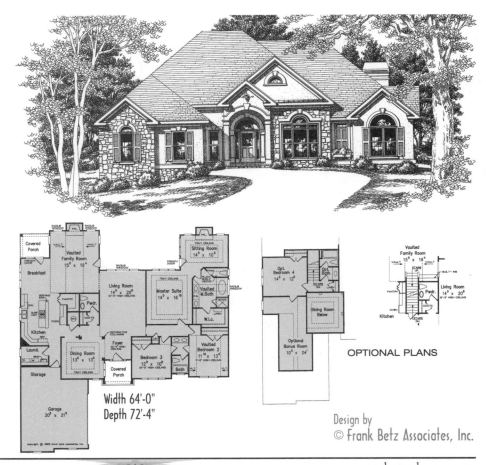

OPTIONAL PLANS

Width 64'-0"
Depth 72'-4"

Design by
© Frank Betz Associates, Inc.

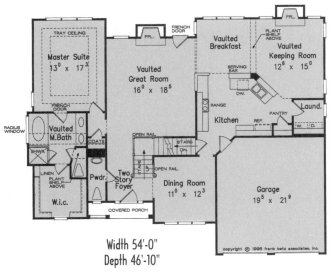

Width 54'-0"
Depth 46'-10"

copyright © 1998 frank betz associates, inc.

Design by
© Frank Betz Associates, Inc.

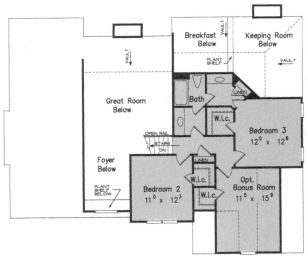

Multiple rooflines, charming stonework and a covered entry-way all combine to give this home plenty of curb appeal. Inside, the two-story foyer leads to either the formal dining room or the spacious, vaulted great room. Here, a fireplace waits to warm cool evenings and a French door gives access to the rear yard. An efficient kitchen offers an abundance of counter and cabinet space, plus a vaulted breakfast room and a nearby keeping room. Split sleeping quarters include a first-floor master suite and two secondary bedrooms sharing a full bath on the second floor. The master suite has a tray ceiling and a luxury bath. Please specify basement or crawlspace foundation when ordering.

DESIGN P199

First Floor: 1,628 square feet
Second Floor: 527 square feet
Total: 2,155 square feet
Bonus Room: 207 square feet

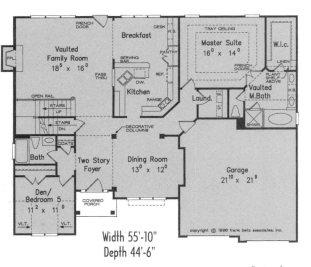

Width 55'-10"
Depth 44'-6"

copyright © 1996 frank betz associates, inc.

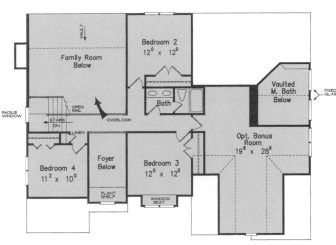

Design by
© Frank Betz Associates, Inc.

DESIGN P251

First Floor: 1,687 square feet
Second Floor: 694 square feet
Total: 2,381 square feet
Bonus Room: 407 square feet

Classic clapboard siding with brick accents that add splash complement asymmetrical gables and a quaint covered porch on this 21st-Century traditional design. A cultivated interior starts with a two-story foyer that leads to a vaulted family room with an extended-hearth fireplace. The kitchen boasts a serving bar and ample pantry and serves an elegant dining room with transom windows. An elegant master suite enjoys a private wing of the home and offers a vaulted bath with a whirlpool spa tub and a generous walk-in closet. Upstairs, three family bedrooms share a full bath and a hall that has a balcony overlook. Please specify basement or crawlspace foundation when ordering.

Design by
© Alan Mascord
Design Associates, Inc.

Width 40'-0"
Depth 54'-0"

This European-flavored contemporary home begins with a vaulted entry and a graceful curved staircase. An open formal living and dining room contains a fireplace and a tray ceiling. The U-shaped gourmet kitchen features a food-prep island and a morning nook.

A fireplace highlights the family room, which opens to a central hall. The quiet den provides an additional storage area and French doors to the hall. The media room can easily be converted to a fifth bedroom. Upstairs, the master suite enjoys a vaulted bath with a spa tub.

DESIGN
7503
First Floor: 1,747 square feet
Second Floor: 1,146 square feet
Total: 2,893 square feet

DESIGN
P217
Square Footage: 1,660

Decorative cornices and capstones splash this New World home with a taste of Old World flavor. Inside, columns define the formal dining room and open this area to the vaulted great room, highlighted by a centered fireplace flanked by windows. A serving bar integrates the breakfast room with the kitchen. A tray ceiling, garden tub and sizable walk-in closet make the master suite a relaxing retreat, while a full bath with twin lavatories serves two family bedrooms. The foyer adds 44 square feet to living space.

Design by
© Frank Betz Associates, Inc.

Width 53'-0"
Depth 35'-0"

DESIGN
P190
Square Footage: 1,677

This elegant home makes the most of the hillside lot by using the lower level for a two-car garage and expandable basement. A striking stair leads to the entry where another half flight continues up inside. The vaulted dining room's open rail overlooks the entry. A vaulted ceiling in the great room accents the fireplace. A modified galley kitchen has a snack bar and a breakfast nook. The master suite features a sitting room, compartmented bath and walk-in closet. Two family bedrooms share a full hall bath. The foyer adds 40 square feet to the living space.

Width 50'-0"
Depth 39'-4"

Design by
© Frank Betz Associates, Inc.

Vaulted Breakfast

Vaulted Family Room
16⁰ x 19⁴

RADIUS WINDOW — FPL. — RADIUS WINDOW

FRENCH DOOR

Kitchen
ISLAND

SURFACE UNIT

DW.

OVEN

PANTRY

REF.

LINEN
W.i.c.

SHWR.

Vaulted M.Bath

PLANT SHELF ABOVE

W.i.c.

Bath

WET BAR

COATS

Laund.
SINK
W. D.

Bedroom 4/ Study
11⁷ x 11⁰

Dining Room
11⁰ x 14⁰

OPEN RAIL

STAIRS

TRAY CLG.

Master Suite
13⁰ x 17⁰

Two Story Foyer

COVERED PORCH

OPT. DOORS

Living Room/ Opt. Sitting
13⁰ x 11⁴

Garage
21⁰ x 21⁰

copyright © 1998 frank betz associates, inc.

Width 54'-6"
Depth 56'-4"

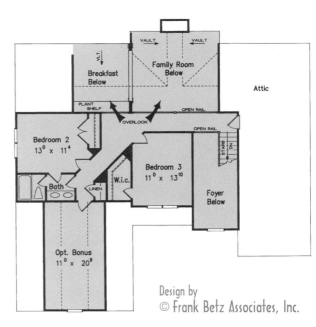

VAULT — VAULT

Breakfast Below

VLT.

Family Room Below

Attic

PLANT SHELF

OPEN RAIL

OVERLOOK

Bedroom 2
13⁰ x 11⁴

OPEN RAIL

Bedroom 3
11⁰ x 13¹⁰

STAIRS
DN.

Bath

LINEN

W.i.c.

Foyer Below

Opt. Bonus
11⁰ x 20⁹

Design by
© Frank Betz Associates, Inc.

Keystones, stucco arches and shutters add a French flavor to this traditional home. Inside, the formal dining room is defined by decorative columns. The gourmet kitchen has a worktop island and its own French door to the rear of the property. The secluded master suite fetaures a tray ceiling, an optional sitting room and a sumptuous master bath. Two additional bedrooms share a full bath on the upper level, where an optional bonus room provides space to grow. Please specify basement or crawlspace foundation when ordering.

DESIGN P331
First Floor: 1,860 square feet
Second Floor: 612 square feet
Total: 2,472 square feet
Bonus Room: 244 square feet

MULTI-LEVEL & HILLSIDE HOMES

DESIGN X003

Square Footage: 1,709
Bonus Room: 208 square feet

With a grand brick arch sheltering the entry, echoed by the arched window over the front door, this split-foyer home captures an elegant flair. The main level consists of a fine dining room, spacious living area with a fireplace and three bedrooms including a lavish master suite. The future playroom and bay along with a large storage area behind the garage give room for the expanding family.

Width 50'-0"
Depth 38'-0"

Design by
© Jannis Vann & Associates, Inc.

Sun Deck 18-4 x 12-0
Breakfast 9-6 x 11-6
Living Area 17-6 x 15-6
Master Bedroom 11-6 x 17-6
M. Bath
Kitchen 13-4 x 11-6
Ref P
Bath 2
Dining 13-4 x 11-6
Foyer
Bedroom-2 10-2 x 13-6
Bedroom-3 10-6 x 11-6
Porch

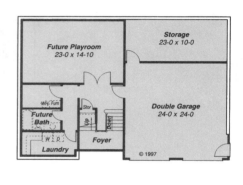

Future Playroom 23-0 x 14-10
Storage 23-0 x 10-0
WH Fun
Future Bath
Stor
Double Garage 24-0 x 24-0
W D
Laundry
Foyer
© 1997

DESIGN A104

Square Footage: 1,950
Bonus Room: 255 square feet

A cost-effective footprint makes this both a very attractive and sought-after house plan. An open dining room and gathering room with fireplace create an inviting atmosphere for entertaining. A large bay window helps ensure bright mornings in the breakfast area. The kitchen offers a walk-in pantry for convenient storage. Features in the spacious master suite include a tray ceiling and twin walk-in closets. The plan also provides for an optional basement level as well as a bonus area above its courtyard garage.

DECK/TERRACE
BREAKFAST 15'-0" x 8'-6"
SUITE 3 12'-0" x 12'-0"
GATHERING 14'-6" x 15'-4"
KITCHEN 12'-6" x 11'-0"
MASTER SUITE 13'-0" x 15'-4"
BATH
FOYER
SUITE 2 12'-0" x 12'-0"
DINING ROOM 11'-4" x 11'-4"
POR.
MASTER BATH
W.I.C. 10'-0" x 7'-6"
LAUNDRY
LOGGIA
GARAGE 21'-0" x 21'-0"

Design by
© Living Concepts Home Planning

DN
OPTIONAL BONUS ROOM 12'-4" x 16'-8"

OPTIONAL

Width 59'-4"
Depth 61'-4"

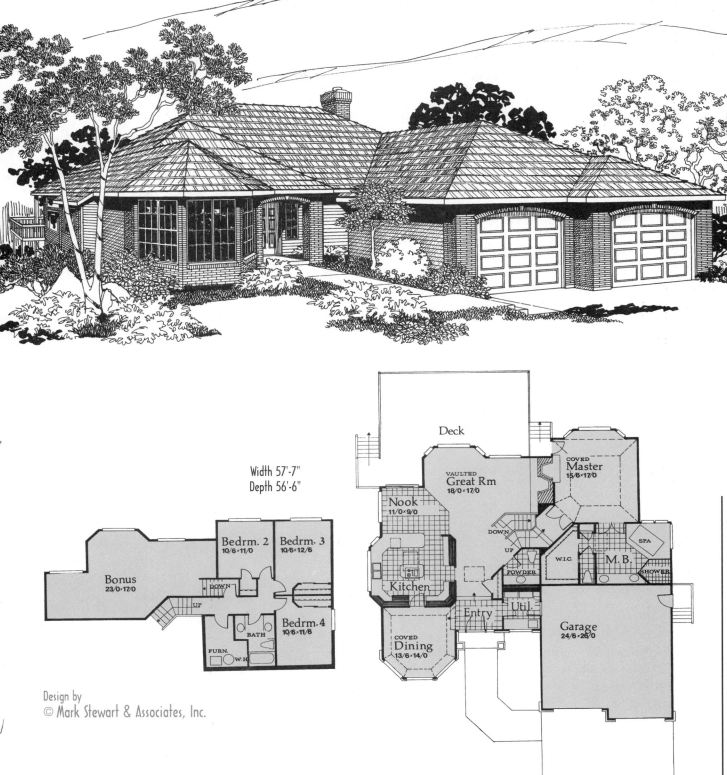

Width 57'-7"
Depth 56'-6"

Bonus 23/0×17/0

Bedrm. 2 10/6×11/0

Bedrm. 3 10/6×12/6

Bedrm. 4 10/6×11/6

DOWN

UP

BATH

FURN.

W.H.

Deck

Great Rm VAULTED 18/0×17/0

Master COVED 15/6×17/0

Nook 11/0×9/0

DOWN

UP

SPA

W.I.C.

M.B.

SHOWER

Kitchen

POWDER

Entry

Util.

Garage 24/6×26/0

Dining COVED 13/6×14/0

Design by
© Mark Stewart & Associates, Inc.

A ranch in appearance, a two-story in reality! This stucco home has plenty to offer in the way of amenities. From the bayed formal dining room at the front of the design to the answering bay in the great room at the rear, this design is perfect for families. The octagonal kitchen will delight the gourmet of the household with its island worktop and snack bar into the sunny nook. Located on the main level for privacy, the master bedroom pampers with a bay window, tray ceiling, walk-in closet and lavish bath. Downstairs, three secondary bedrooms share a full hall bath and access to a spacious bonus room.

DESIGN J166
Main Level: 1,758 square feet
Lower Level: 549 square feet
Total: 2,307 square feet

MULTI-LEVEL & HILLSIDE HOMES

DESIGN
P302
Square Footage: 1,258

Design by
© Frank Betz Associates, Inc.

An impressive front entrance adds interest to the gable roofline of this livable three-bedroom design. Inside, high ceilings add a sense of spaciousness. Ascend from the front foyer to a vaulted dining room, family room and kitchen. The sleeping wing is tucked away on the left side of the home, which includes two family bedrooms that share a hall bath. A luxurious master suite offers a tray ceiling and vaulted master bath. The foyer adds 60 square feet to the living space, and an unfinished basement offers room for future expansion.

Width 46'-4"
Depth 32'-0"

DESIGN
7229
Square Footage: 1,696

This convenient split-entry ranch design features a great room with a volume ceiling, a fireplace flanked by bookcases and a floor-to-ceiling view of the backyard. The efficient double-L kitchen includes a sunny bay-windowed breakfast area. Box ceilings grace both the breakfast nook and the formal dining room. The laundry room is strategically located near the sleeping wing. Two secondary bedrooms offer abundant closet space and a shared full bath. The deluxe master bedroom includes a vaulted ceiling, large walk-in closet and a bath with whirlpool tub and skylit dual vanity.

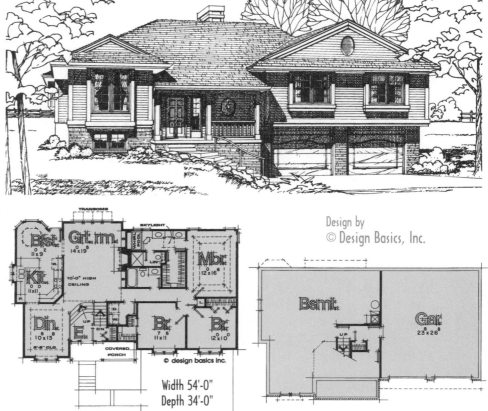

Design by
© Design Basics, Inc.

Width 54'-0"
Depth 34'-0"

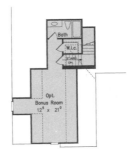

Design by
© Frank Betz Associates, Inc.

Width 61'-0"
Depth 64'-4"

DESIGN P201

Square Footage: 2,311
Bonus Room: 425 square feet

Brick-and-stucco detailing, hipped and gabled rooflines and elegant windows all combine to present European style with grace. The kitchen and the vaulted, bayed breakfast room combine to create a haven for both the gourmet of the family and for casual meal time. For larger gatherings there is the spacious, vaulted family room, where a fireplace waits to warm cool evenings, a serving bar from the kitchen adds convenience and a French door offers access to the rear yard. Please specify basement or crawlspace foundation when ordering.

DESIGN T078

Square Footage: 1,770

The country-cottage styling of this stately brick home includes brick detailing, gables and a multi-level roof. The foyer provides views into both the great room with hearth and the dining room with vaulted ceiling. From the great room, one enters the kitchen, with a spacious work area and adjacent breakfast room. The second level offers two bedrooms that share a bath. The master bedroom features a tray ceiling and French doors leading to a private deck. The master bath is complete with His and Hers vanities, garden tub and walk-in closet. This home is designed with a basement foundation.

Width 48'-0"
Depth 47'-0"

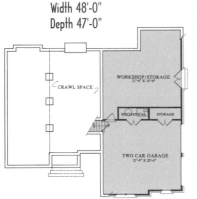

Design by
© Stephen Fuller,
American Home Gallery

Quote One®

Cost to build? See page 684 to order complete cost estimate to build this house in your area!

MULTI-LEVEL & HILLSIDE HOMES

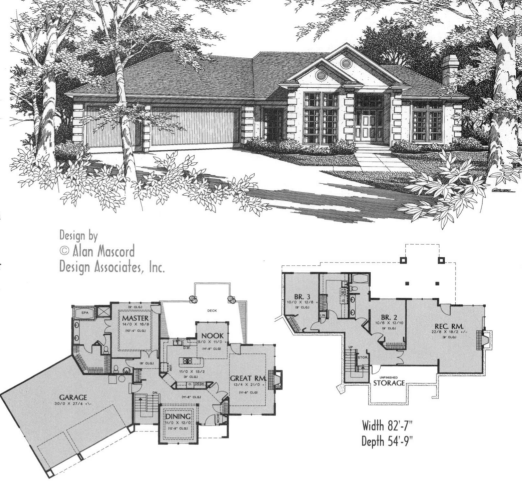

DESIGN 9537

Main Level: 1,687 square feet
Lower Level: 1,251 square feet
Total: 2,938 square feet

L

This striking home is perfect for daylight basement lots. An elegant dining room is near an expansive kitchen that features plenty of cabinet and counter space. A nook surrounded by a deck adds character. The comfortable great room includes a raised ceiling and a fireplace. The master suite includes private deck access and a superb bath with a spa tub and dual lavatories. Downstairs, two bedrooms, a laundry room with lots of counter space and a rec room with a fireplace cap off the plan.

Design by
© Alan Mascord
Design Associates, Inc.

Width 82'-7"
Depth 54'-9"

DESIGN 7436

Main Level: 1,537 square feet
Lower Level: 1,238 square feet
Total: 2,775 square feet

This stucco-and-siding exterior offers a plan with a daylight basement. On the main level, the U-shaped kitchen adjoins the formal dining room and the sunny nook. A tray ceiling, fireplace and built-in media center dress-up the living room. Down a short hall, the double-door den is convenient to the master suite, which has a walk-in closet, lavish bath and private balcony. The lower floor consists of a spacious family room with outdoor access, and two family bedrooms—each with a walk-in closet and direct access to a full bath.

Design by
© Alan Mascord
Design Associates, Inc.

Width 41'-0"
Depth 56'-0"

www.homeplanners.com

Design by
© Alan Mascord
Design Associates, Inc.

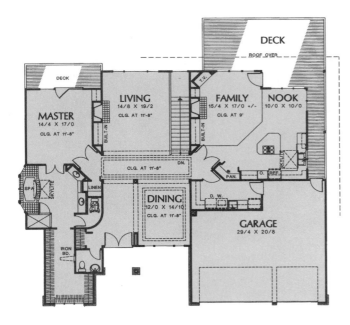

DECK

ROOF OVER

MASTER
14/4 X 17/0
CLG. AT 11'-8"

LIVING
14/8 X 19/2
CLG. AT 11'-8"

FAMILY
15/4 X 17/0 +/-
CLG. AT 9'

NOOK
10/0 X 10/0

DECK

BUILT-IN

BUILT-IN

T.V.

T.V.

CLG. AT 11'-8"

DN.

SKYLITE

SPA

SKYLITE

LINEN

DINING
12/0 X 14/10
CLG. AT 11'-8"

PAN.

O.

REF.

D. W.

IRON
BD.

GARAGE
29/4 X 20/8

DECK

BR. 2
14/0 X 12/0
CLG. AT 9'

BUILT-IN

GAMES RM.
14/8 X 19/2 +
CLG. AT 9'

DN. DN.
UP

DEN
15/4 X 16/6 +/-
CLG. AT 9'

OFFICE
15/4 X 20/8 +/-
CLG. AT 9'

WET
BAR

LIN.

STOR.

LINEN

BR. 3
14/0 X 14/0
CLG. AT 9'

CRAWLSPACE

Width 67'-6"
Depth 53'-0"

MULTI-LEVEL & HILLSIDE HOMES

It looks like a ranch home, but on the inside it's a two-story house. The formal dining room with detailed ceiling is to the right of the foyer, while directly ahead, the living room offers a warming fireplace. The kitchen features a cooktop island and a skylight. A fireplace, built-in entertainment shelves and a door to the rear deck enhance the family room. The master suite, on the main level, is full of amenities. Downstairs, you'll find two family bedrooms, a full bath, a spacious games room, a den and a home office with an outside door for clients. Note the wet bar and outside deck also on this level.

DESIGN
7440
Main Level: 2,177 square feet
Lower Level: 1,752 square feet
Total: 3,929 square feet

DESIGN 1974

Main Level: 1,680 square feet
Lower Level: 1,344 square feet
Total: 3,024 square feet

From the front, it looks as though all the livability is on one floor. If you choose, you can build the home without finishing the lower level immediately then adding it as your need for space increases. The main level includes grand livability on its own: a living and dining room, kitchen with breakfast room and three bedrooms with two full baths. The finished lower level would add a family room, game room, laundry and hobby room, bedroom or study and another full bath.

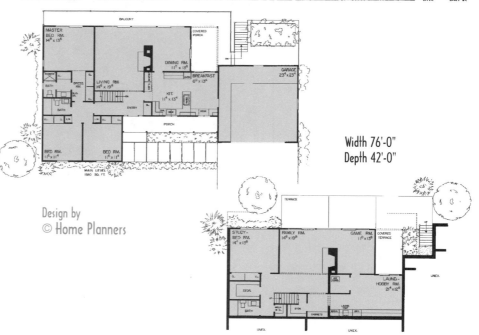

Design by
© Home Planners

Width 76'-0"
Depth 42'-0"

DESIGN X013

Main Level: 1,128 square feet
Lower Level: 604 square feet
Total: 1,732 square feet

A beautiful half-circle window tops a covered front porch on this fine three-bedroom home. Inside, the features start with the large, open great room and its warming fireplace. A uniquely shaped dining room is adjacent to the efficient kitchen that offers a small bay window over the sink. The master suite is complete with a cathedral ceiling, bay area for relaxing and a private bath with laundry facilities. On the lower level, a two-car garage shelters the family fleet, while two bedrooms—or make one a study— share a full hall bath.

Design by
© Jannis Vann & Associates, Inc.

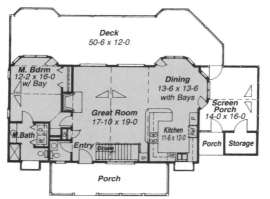

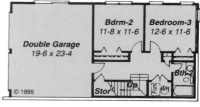

Width 59'-0"
Depth 46'-0"

MULTI-LEVEL & HILLSIDE HOMES

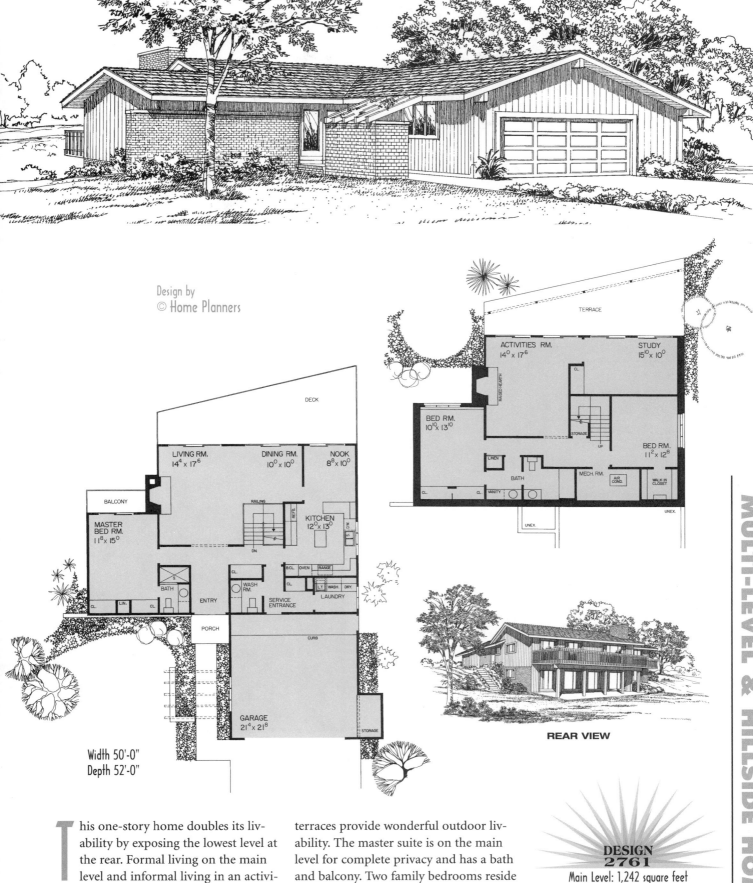

Design by
© Home Planners

LIVING RM.
14⁴ x 17⁶

DINING RM.
10⁰ x 10⁰

NOOK
8⁸ x 10⁰

DECK

BALCONY

MASTER BED RM.
11⁸ x 15⁰

KITCHEN
12⁰ x 13⁰

RAILING

BATH

WASH RM.

ENTRY

SERVICE ENTRANCE

LAUNDRY

PORCH

CURB

GARAGE
21⁴ x 21⁸

STORAGE

Width 50'-0"
Depth 52'-0"

TERRACE

ACTIVITIES RM.
14⁰ x 17⁶

STUDY
15¹⁰ x 10⁰

BED RM.
10¹⁰ x 13¹⁰

RAISED HEARTH

STORAGE

UP

BED RM.
11² x 12⁸

LINEN

BATH

VANITY

MECH. RM.

AIR COND.

WALK IN CLOSET

UNEX.

UNEX.

REAR VIEW

This one-story home doubles its livability by exposing the lowest level at the rear. Formal living on the main level and informal living in an activity room and study on the lower level create the best of floor plans. Decks and terraces provide wonderful outdoor livability. The master suite is on the main level for complete privacy and has a bath and balcony. Two family bedrooms reside on the lower level and share a bath that includes dual sinks.

DESIGN
2761
Main Level: 1,242 square feet
Lower Level: 1,242 square feet
Total: 2,484 square feet

L

MULTI-LEVEL & HILLSIDE HOMES

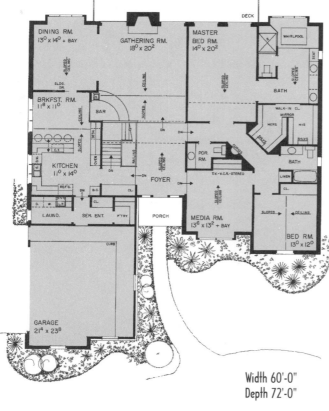

QUOTE ONE®
Cost to build? See page 684
to order complete cost estimate
to build this house in your area!

Width 60'-0"
Depth 72'-0"

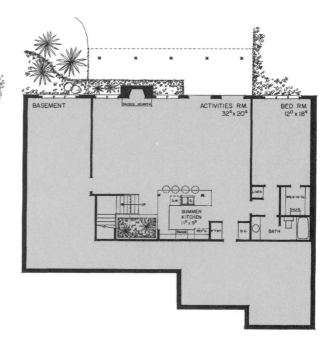

Design by
© Home Planners

DESIGN 3360
Main Level: 2,673 square feet
Lower Level: 1,389 square feet
Total: 4,062 square feet

L

This plan has the best of both worlds—a traditional exterior and a modern, multi-level floor plan. The central foyer routes traffic effectively to all areas: the kitchen, gathering room, sleeping area and media room. The lower level can be developed later. Plans include space for a summer kitchen, activities room and bedroom with full bath. The master suite features a luxurious bath with whirlpool tub, dual sinks and His and Hers walk-in closets.

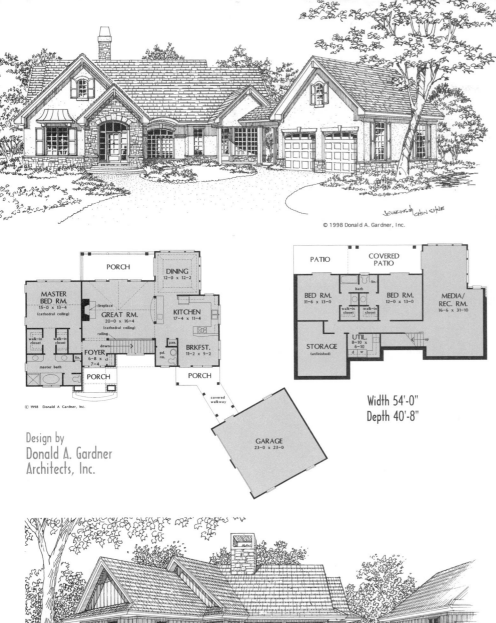

© 1998 Donald A. Gardner, Inc.

A stone-and-stucco exterior and exquisite window detailing give this home its Mediterranean appeal. A covered porch connects the garage to the main house via the breakfast room. The master suite includes two walk-in closets and a bath with separate vanities. Two family bedrooms in the basement feature walk-in closets and share a compartmented bath and a media or recreation room. Both bedrooms have private access to the patio. A utility room and storage room complete the basement level.

PORCH

DINING
12-0 x 12-2

MASTER BED RM.
15-0 x 13-4
(cathedral ceiling)

GREAT RM.
20-0 x 16-4
(cathedral ceiling)

KITCHEN
17-4 x 11-4

fireplace

walk-in closet   walk-in closet

FOYER
6-8 x
7-4

down
railing

BRKFST.
11-2 x 9-2

pan.
pd.
rm.

master bath

PORCH

PORCH

© 1998 Donald A Gardner, Inc.

covered walkway

GARAGE
23-0 x 23-0

Design by
Donald A. Gardner
Architects, Inc.

PATIO

COVERED PATIO

BED RM.
11-6 x 13-0

bath

lin.

BED RM.
12-0 x 13-0

MEDIA/ REC. RM.
16-6 x 31-10

walk-in closet   walk-in closet

STORAGE
(unfinished)

UTIL.
8-10 x
6-10
d w

up

Width 54'-0"
Depth 40'-8"

©1997 Donald A. Gardner Architects, Inc.

This rustic retreat is updated with contemporary angles and packs a lot of living into a small space. The covered front porch leads to a welcoming foyer. The beamed-ceilinged great room opens directly ahead and features a fireplace, a wall of windows, access to the screened porch. A highly efficient island kitchen provides a cathedral ceiling, access to the rear deck and tons of counter and cabinet space. Two family bedrooms, sharing a full bath, are located on one end of the plan while the secluded master suite is at the other end.

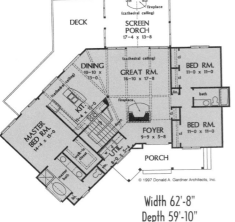

DECK

fireplace

SCREEN PORCH
17-4 x 13-8
(cathedral ceiling)

DINING
10-10 x
13-0
(cathedral ceiling)

GREAT RM.
16-10 x 17-8
(cathedral ceiling)

KIT.

fireplace

BED RM.
11-0 x 11-0

bath

MASTER BED RM.
14-4 x 15-0

UTIL

FOYER
9-9 x 5-8

BED RM.
11-0 x 11-0

PORCH

© 1997 Donald A. Gardner Architects, Inc.

REAR VIEW

GARAGE
22-0 x 22-0

Design by
Donald A. Gardner
Architects, Inc.

Width 62'-8"
Depth 59'-10"

DESIGN 4115

Main Level: 1,494 square feet
Upper Level: 597 square feet
Total: 2,091 square feet

Interior spaces in this home are dramatically proportioned because of the long and varied rooflines on the exterior. The two-story living area has a sloped ceiling, as does the master bedroom and two upper-level bedrooms. Two fireplaces, a huge wooden deck, a small upstairs sitting room and a liberal number of windows make this a most comfortable residence.

Design by
© Home Planners

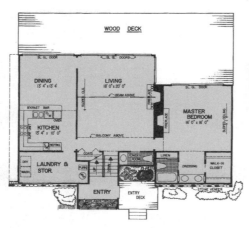

Width 50'-8"
Depth 47'-8"

DESIGN 4308

Main Level: 1,494 square feet
Upper Level: 597 square feet
Lower Level: 1,035 square feet
Total: 3,126 square feet

You can't help but feel spoiled by this design. Downstairs from the entry is a large living room with sloped ceiling and fireplace. Nearby is the U-shaped kitchen with a pass-through to the dining room. Also on this level, the master suite boasts a fireplace and a sliding glass door to the deck. Upstairs two bedrooms share a bath. A balcony sitting area overlooks the living room. The lower level includes a play room with a fireplace, half bath, large bar and sliding glass doors to the patio.

Design by
© Home Planners

Width 59'-0"
Depth 69'-8"

MULTI-LEVEL & HILLSIDE HOMES

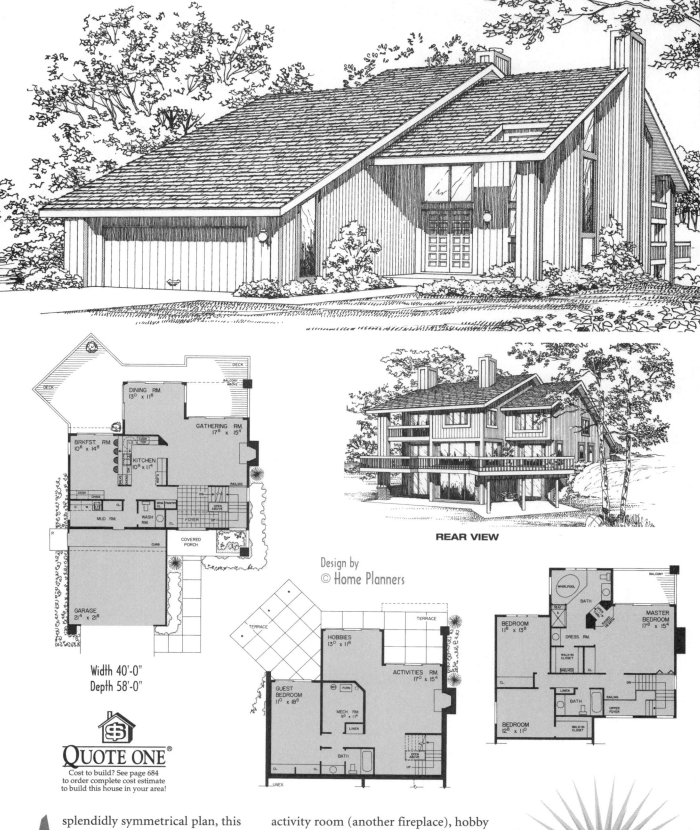

REAR VIEW

Design by
© Home Planners

Width 40'-0"
Depth 58'-0"

Quote One®
Cost to build? See page 684
to order complete cost estimate
to build this house in your area!

A splendidly symmetrical plan, this clean-lined, open-planned contemporary home is a great place for the outdoor minded. A gathering room (with fireplace), dining room and breakfast room all lead out to a deck off the main level. Similarly, the lower-level activity room (another fireplace), hobby room and guest bedroom contain separate doors to the backyard terrace. Upstairs are three bedrooms, including a suite with a through-fireplace, private balcony, walk-in closet, dressing room and whirlpool tub.

DESIGN 2937
Main Level: 1,096 square feet
Upper Level: 1,115 square feet
Lower Level: 1,104 square feet
Total: 3,315 square feet

L

COVERED PORCH

TERRACE

GATHERING RM.
21⁰x21⁶

DINING RM.
14²x11¹⁰

STUDY
11⁸x13⁴

MASTER
BED RM.
13⁰x18⁸

WALK-IN CLOSET

THRU
FIREPLACE

DRESSING/BATH

BREAKFAST
14⁰x11⁰

BAR

POWDER
RM.

TUB

BATH

PANTRY

FOYER

LINEN

WALK-IN
CLOSET

KITCHEN
13⁰x10⁰

COVERED
PORCH

BED RM.
11⁰x12⁰

BATH

BED RM.
11⁸x12⁰

STEP-UP

PATIO

TUB

GARAGE
31⁴x21⁸

CURB

Design by
© Home Planners

Width 85'-10"
Depth 72'-4"

DESIGN 2789
Square Footage: 2,732
L D

This elegant one-story contemporary home is designed for sites that slope slightly to the front. As a consequence, the major rooms of the home are sunken just a few steps from the grand entry foyer. The large gathering room is in line with the entry doors and has sliding glass doors to the terrace and a through-fireplace to the study. The dining room is nearby, with sliding glass doors to a covered porch.

The L-shaped kitchen and breakfast nook share the use of a patio just outside the nook. For real convenience, the study has built-ins and a powder room close at hand. Amenities in the master suite include a walk-in closet, spa tub and double sinks. Family bedrooms share a full bath that includes a garden tub and double sinks. A three-car garage connects to the home at the laundry room.

DECK

BREAKFAST
10'-0" x 10'-6"

KEEPING ROOM
14'-0" x 19'-3"

GREAT ROOM
17'-6" x 21'-3"

M. BATH
17'-4" x 12'-0"

KITCHEN
13'-6" x 14'-0"

HIS   HERS

LAUNDRY
9'-4" x 7'-6"

POWDER

MASTER SUITE
18'-0" x 13'-9"

TWO-CAR GARAGE
21'-6" x 21'-6"

DINING ROOM
13'-0" x 13'-0"

FOYER
7'-8" x 18'-8"

STUDY/
LIVING ROOM
13'-3" x 14'-0"

COVERED PORCH

Design by
© Stephen Fuller,
American Home Gallery

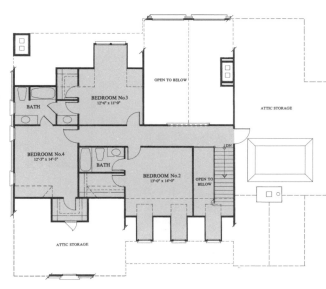

OPEN TO BELOW

ATTIC STORAGE

BATH

BEDROOM No.3
12'-6" x 11'-0"

BEDROOM No.4
12'-3" x 14'-3"

BATH

BEDROOM No.2
13'-6" x 14'-0"

OPEN TO
BELOW

ATTIC STORAGE

Width 61'-6"
Depth 52'-6"

T he front of this traditional home is characterized by the arch pattern evident in the windows, doorway and above the columned front porch. Left of the foyer is the dining room and the great room with a fireplace and vaulted ceiling. The large kitchen, with a cooking island, adjoins the breakfast room and keeping room, which has a corner fireplace. The master suite includes a study—with a vaulted ceiling—that also opens from the foyer. The study's dual-opening fireplace also warms the bedroom. Through the master suite and beyond the two walk-in closets is a bath with dual vanities. Upstairs are three more bedrooms and two baths. This home is designed with a basement foundation.

**DESIGN
T006**
First Floor: 2,355 square feet
Second Floor: 987 square feet
Total: 3,342 square feet

LUXURY HOMES

DESIGN 2991

First Floor: 2,658 square feet
Second Floor: 1,429 square feet
Total: 4,087 square feet

L D

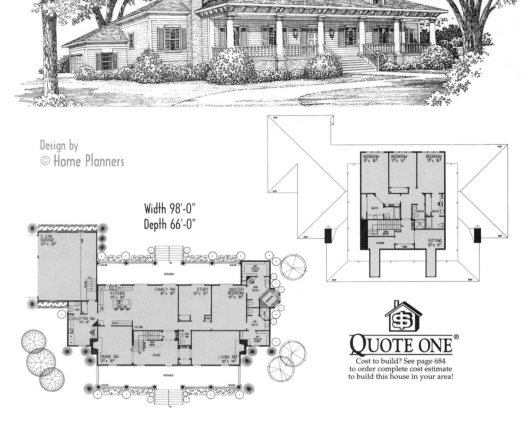

Design by
© Home Planners

Width 98'-0"
Depth 66'-0"

This antebellum Greek Revival manor represents the grace of Southern plantation style. Flanking a wide entry foyer are the formal living and dining rooms. Each has its own fireplace. Less formal activities take place in the family room, which is conveniently open to the island kitchen. A cooktop with snack-bar island serves both areas. Separating living areas from the master suite is a study. Three bedrooms and three baths reside on the second floor.

Cost to build? See page 684 to order complete cost estimate to build this house in your area!

DESIGN 3515

First Floor: 1,669 square feet
Second Floor: 1,627 square feet
Total: 3,296 square feet

L D

Design by
© Home Planners

Width 64'-0"
Depth 46'-0"

Two sets of twin dormers set off a signature hip roof and classic columns on this Southern home. An elegant tiled foyer opens to formal areas on each side, and leads to a rustic family area designed to allow generous views. Lovely French doors create a striking ambience in the formal areas—and each of these rooms offers a warming fireplace. A wraparound porch invites good indoor/outdoor flow. The second-floor sleeping zone offers three family bedrooms, a hall bath and a master suite with two walk-in closets, dual lavatories and a whirlpool tub.

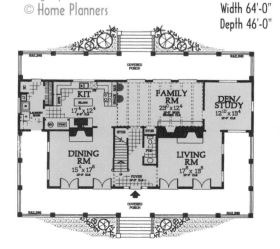

Cost to build? See page 684 to order complete cost estimate to build this house in your area!

LUXURY HOMES

www.homeplanners.com

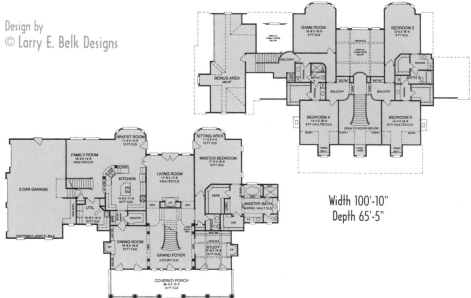

Design by
© Larry E. Belk Designs

Width 100'-10"
Depth 65'-5"

DESIGN 8269

First Floor: 3,170 square feet
Second Floor: 1,914 square feet
Total: 5,084 square feet
Bonus Room: 445 square feet

Reminiscent of the grand homes of the Old South, this elegantly appointed home is a beauty inside and out. A centerpiece stair rises gracefully from the two-story foyer and features balcony overlooks. The kitchen, breakfast room and family room provide open space for gatherings. The beam-ceilinged study and the dining room flank the grand foyer and each includes a fireplace. The master suite features a cozy sitting area and a luxury master bath with His and Hers vanities and walk-in closets. Three large bedrooms and a game room complete the second floor.

DESIGN 2686

First Floor: 1,683 square feet
Second Floor: 1,541 square feet
Total: 3,224 square feet

L D

This design has its roots in the South and is referred to as a raised cottage. This adaptation has front and rear covered porches whose columns reflect a modified Greek Revival style. Flanking the center foyer are the formal living areas of the living room and library and the informal country kitchen. Upstairs, two large family bedrooms share a full hall bath while the master bedroom offers a pampering bath complete with a whirlpool tub, separate shower, twin vanities and walk-in closet.

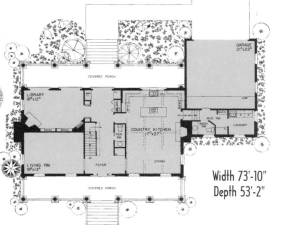

Design by
© Home Planners

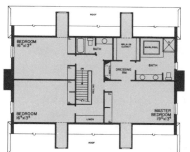

Width 73'-10"
Depth 53'-2"

LUXURY HOMES

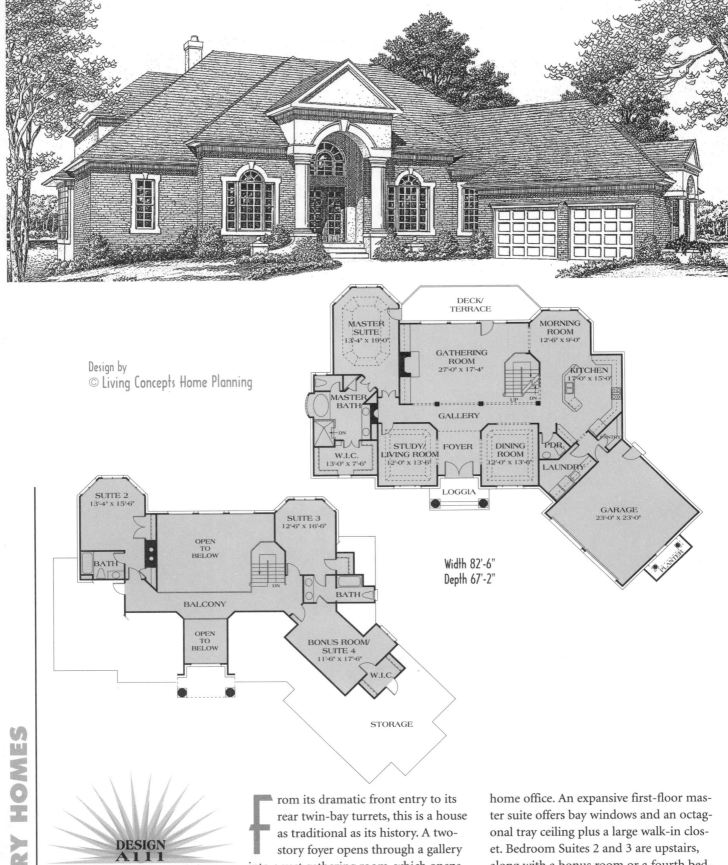

Design by
© Living Concepts Home Planning

MASTER SUITE 13'-4" x 19'-0"

DECK/TERRACE

MORNING ROOM 12'-6" x 9'-0"

GATHERING ROOM 27'-0" x 17'-4"

KITCHEN 17'-0" x 15'-0"

MASTER BATH

GALLERY

W.I.C. 13'-0" x 7'-6"

STUDY/LIVING ROOM 12'-0" x 13'-6"

FOYER

DINING ROOM 12'-0" x 13'-6"

PDR.

PANTRY

LAUNDRY

LOGGIA

GARAGE 23'-0" x 23'-0"

PLANTER

Width 82'-6"
Depth 67'-2"

SUITE 2 13'-4" x 15'-6"

SUITE 3 12'-6" x 16'-6"

OPEN TO BELOW

BATH

BATH

BALCONY

OPEN TO BELOW

BONUS ROOM/SUITE 4 11'-6" x 17'-6"

W.I.C.

STORAGE

DESIGN A111
First Floor: 2,293 square feet
Second Floor: 901 square feet
Total: 3,194 square feet
Bonus Room: 265 square feet

From its dramatic front entry to its rear twin-bay turrets, this is a house as traditional as its history. A two-story foyer opens through a gallery into a vast gathering room, which opens to the bay-windowed morning room and the counter-filled kitchen. A study/living room provides the perfect location for a home office. An expansive first-floor master suite offers bay windows and an octagonal tray ceiling plus a large walk-in closet. Bedroom Suites 2 and 3 are upstairs, along with a bonus room or a fourth bedroom suite that shares the Suite 3 bath. A screened porch provides for additional outdoor enjoyment on the basement level.

LUXURY HOMES

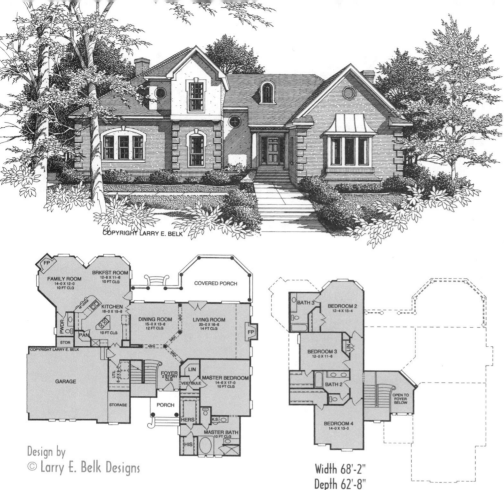

COPYRIGHT LARRY E. BELK

Design by
© Larry E. Belk Designs

Width 68'-2"
Depth 62'-8"

DESIGN 8121

First Floor: 2,144 square feet
Second Floor: 965 square feet
Total: 3,109 square feet

A covered porch opens to a foyer that leads to the living room with a fireplace and the nearby dining room. A breakfast room next to the family room with a fireplace is served by an angled kitchen with a cooktop island and snack bar. Three bedrooms share two full baths on the upper level. Please specify crawlspace or slab foundation when ordering.

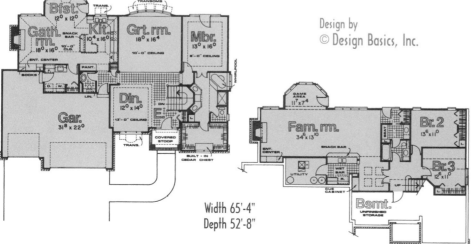

Design by
© Design Basics, Inc.

Width 65'-4"
Depth 52'-8"

DESIGN 7222

Main Level: 1,887 square feet
Lower Level: 1,338 square feet
Total: 3,225 square feet

A majestic window and brick exterior provides an extra measure of style to this handsome traditional home. Straight ahead, upon entering the foyer, is the spacious great room. The kitchen and breakfast area are integrated with the gathering room. Entertaining is easy in the adjacent dining room. The large, private master suite is highlighted by double doors opening into the master dressing area. The basement features a fabulous family room, two family bedrooms and offers a second fireplace.

LUXURY HOMES

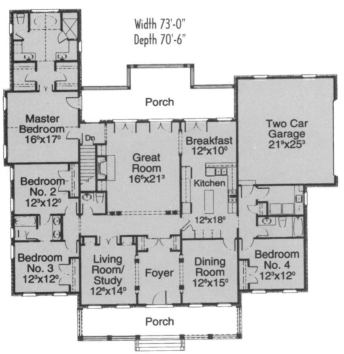

Width 73'-0"
Depth 70'-6"

Porch

Master Bedroom
16⁰x17⁰

Two Car Garage
21⁹x25³

Breakfast
12⁶x10⁰

Great Room
16⁶x21³

Kitchen

Bedroom No. 2
12³x12⁰

12⁶x18⁰

Bedroom No. 3
12³x12⁰

Living Room/ Study
12⁶x14⁰

Foyer

Dining Room
12⁶x15⁰

Bedroom No. 4
12³x12⁰

Porch

Design by
© Stephen Fuller,
American Home Gallery

DESIGN
T165
Square Footage: 3,066

Descended from the architecture that developed in America's Tidewater country, this updated adaptation retains the charm of a coastal cottage. At the same time, it offers an elegance that is appropriate for any setting in any climate today. Inside, the family living area is concentrated in the center of the house. Central to the social flow in the house, the great room opens to the kitchen, the breakfast room and the rear porch that runs across the back. The left wing contains a private master suite that includes twin walk-in closets leading into a lavish master bath. Two additional bedrooms share a bath, while Bedroom 4 (located on the right side of the house) enjoys a high level of privacy that makes it an ideal guest room. This home is designed with a basement foundation.

LUXURY HOMES

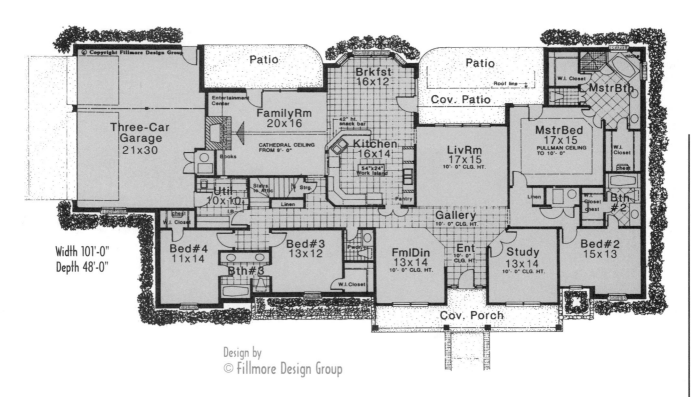

Width 101'-0"
Depth 48'-0"

Design by
© Fillmore Design Group

A distinctive exterior, complete with siding, stone and brick, presents a welcoming facade on this four-bedroom home. A cathedral ceiling in the large family room, which includes a fireplace and built-ins, makes this country-style home a great choice. The island kitchen has plenty of workspace and direct access to a sunny, bay-windowed breakfast room. A study and formal dining room flank the tiled entryway, which leads straight into a formal living room. Three family bedrooms are arranged across the front of the house. The master suite offers plenty of seclusion as well as two walk-in closets, a lavish bath and direct access to the rear patio. A stairway leads to a future upstairs area.

DESIGN
M139
Square Footage: 3,270

DESIGN T105

First Floor: 2,565 square feet
Second Floor: 1,375 square feet
Total: 3,940 square feet

A symmetrical facade with twin chimneys makes a grand statement. A covered porch opens to the entry foyer which is flanked by the formal living areas. An L-shaped kitchen provides a work island and a walk-in pantry and easily serves the nearby breakfast and sun rooms. The deck is accessible through the great room, the sun room or the master bedroom. The first-floor master bedroom suite is lavish in its luxuries. The second floor offers three bedrooms, two full baths and plenty of storage space. This home is designed with a basement foundation.

Width 88'-6"
Depth 50'-6"

Design by
© Stephen Fuller,
American Home Gallery

DESIGN T107

First Floor: 2,315 square feet
Second Floor: 1,200 square feet
Total: 3,515 square feet

D ormer windows and a traditional brick and siding exterior create a welcoming facade on this farmhouse. Inside, the entry foyer opens to a formal zone. The kitchen enjoys a pass-through to the breakfast area—the great room is just a step away. Double doors grant passage to the backyard. The master bedroom boasts a tray ceiling, window bay and lavish bath. Upstairs, each family bedroom has a walk-in closet and direct access to a full bath. This home is designed with a basement foundation.

Width 77'-4"
Depth 46'-8"

Design by
© Stephen Fuller,
American Home Gallery

LUXURY HOMES

www.homeplanners.com

Design by
© Ahmann Design, Inc.

PORCH

KIT.
10'4" x 13'0"

NK.
8'0" x 16'8"

GRT.RM.
CATHEDRAL CEILING
19'8" x 26'0"

DIN.
12'0" x 15'0"

MBR.
CATHEDRAL CEILING
14'0" x 18'8"

3 CAR GAR.
22'4" x 32'0"

PORCH

Width 66'-0"
Depth 62'-0"

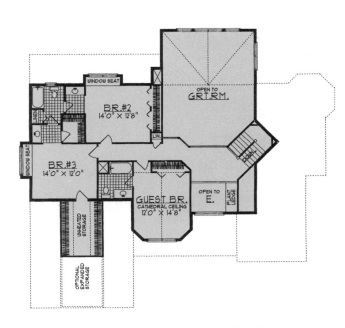

WINDOW SEAT

BR. #2
14'0" x 12'8"

OPEN TO
GRT.RM.

WINDOW SEAT

BR. #3
14'0" x 12'0"

GUEST BR.
CATHEDRAL CEILING
12'0" x 14'8"

OPEN TO
E.

PLANT
LEDGE

UNHEATED
STORAGE

OPTIONAL
EXPANDED
STORAGE

Victorian detailing accents the charm of this fine four-bedroom home. A covered front porch ushers you into the two-story foyer that leads to the formal dining room on the left and a spacious great room directly ahead. Located on the first floor for privacy, the master suite is lavish with its luxuries. Included in the list of pleasures are two walk-in closets and a whirlpool tub set in a bay. A guest suite is found on the second floor and has its own amenities to offer. A three-car garage is available for the family fleet.

DESIGN
U171
First Floor: 2,127 square feet
Second Floor: 1,069 square feet
Total: 3,196 square feet

LUXURY HOMES

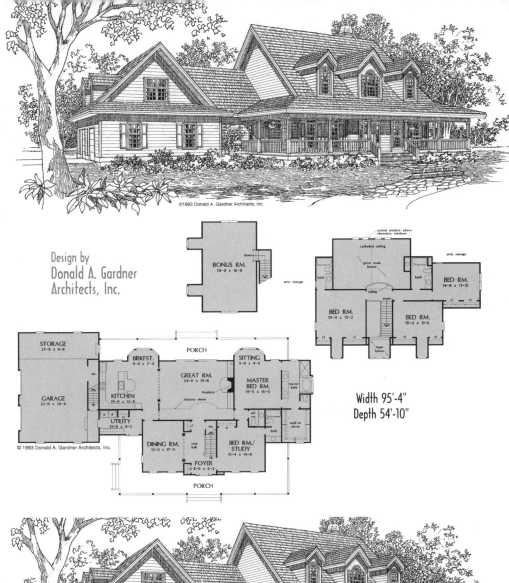

DESIGN 7651

First Floor: 2,357 square feet
Second Floor: 995 square feet
Total: 3,352 square feet
Bonus Room: 545 square feet

This home is a classic sprawling farmhouse, but elegantly refined. The two-level foyer, with its Palladian clerestory window, and the large great room, with a cathedral ceiling and a balcony, make dramatic statements. A bedroom or study with a private full bath is available on the first floor. The master bedroom, the open island kitchen and the great room all access the covered porch. Three family bedrooms and two full baths occupy the second floor.

Design by
Donald A. Gardner
Architects, Inc.

© 1993 Donald A. Gardner Architects, Inc.

Width 95'-4"
Depth 54'-10"

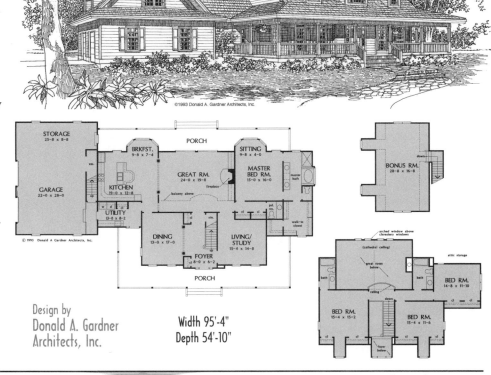

DESIGN 7648

First Floor: 2,357 square feet
Second Floor: 995 square feet
Total: 3,352 square feet
Bonus Room: 545 square feet

From the two-story foyer with a Palladian clerestory window and graceful stairway to the large great room with cathedral ceiling and curved balcony, impressive spaces prevail in this open plan. A columned opening from the great room introduces a spacious family kitchen with a center island counter and breakfast bay. The secluded master suite features a sitting bay, walk-in closet and bath with every possible luxury. Three bedrooms and two full baths make up the second floor, perfect for friends and family.

Design by
Donald A. Gardner
Architects, Inc.

Width 95'-4"
Depth 54'-10"

www.homeplanners.com

© 1993 Donald A. Gardner Architects, Inc.

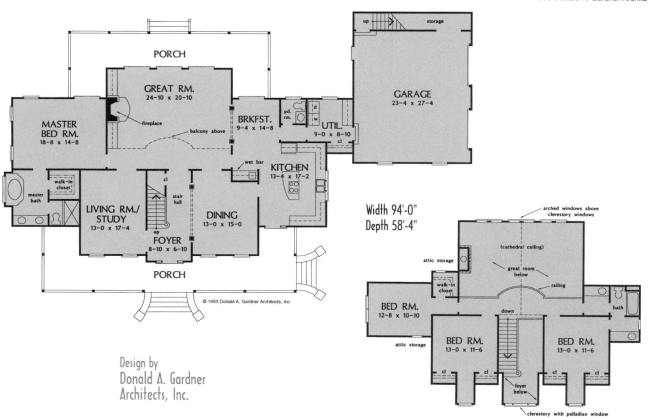

PORCH

GREAT RM.
24-10 x 20-10

fireplace

balcony above

BRKFST.
9-4 x 14-8

pd. rm.

d w

UTIL.
9-0 x 8-10

cl

up storage

GARAGE
23-4 x 27-4

MASTER
BED RM.
18-8 x 14-8

walk-in closet

master bath

wet bar

KITCHEN
13-4 x 17-2

cl

LIVING RM./
STUDY
13-0 x 17-4

stair hall

cl

up

FOYER
8-10 x 6-10

DINING
13-0 x 15-0

PORCH

© 1993 Donald A. Gardner Architects, Inc.

Width 94'-0"
Depth 58'-4"

arched windows above clerestory windows

(cathedral ceiling)

attic storage

walk-in closet

great room below

railing

BED RM.
12-8 x 10-10

down

bath

attic storage

BED RM.
13-0 x 11-6

BED RM.
13-0 x 11-6

cl cl

cl cl

foyer below

clerestory with palladian window

Design by
Donald A. Gardner
Architects, Inc.

Country living is at its best in this spacious four-bedroom farmhouse with a wraparound porch. A front Palladian window dormer and rear clerestory windows in the great room add exciting visual elements to the exterior, while providing natural light to the interior. In the great room, a fireplace, bookshelves, cathedral ceiling and balcony overlook create a comfortable atmosphere. The formal dining room is open to the foyer, while the living room could be used as a study instead. Special features, such as a large cooktop island in the kitchen, a wet bar, a generous bonus room over the garage and ample storage space, set this plan apart from others. You'll also love that the master bedroom suite, the great room and the breakfast room all directly access the rear porch.

LUXURY HOMES

DESIGN 9743
First Floor: 2,176 square feet
Second Floor: 861 square feet
Total: 3,037 square feet
Bonus Room: 483 square feet

DESIGN 7392

First Floor: 1,883 square feet
Second Floor: 1,801 square feet
Total: 3,684 square feet

Shuttered multi-pane windows and a wraparound porch offer countryside comfort with this charming farmhouse design. A tiled entry opens to a traditional living room and the formal dining room. An expansive kitchen has an island cooktop counter, double oven/microwave stack and a peninsula snack bar. The spacious breakfast area provides a bay window. A cozy fireplace warms the family room, which has a door to the porch. Upstairs, a grand master suite enjoys a luxurious bath. Two family bedrooms share a full bath, while an additional bedroom has its own bath.

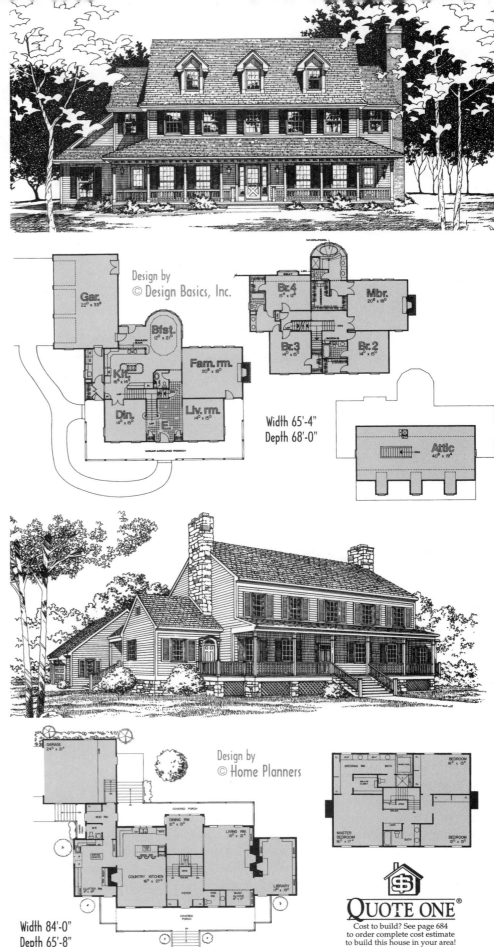

Design by
© Design Basics, Inc.

Width 65'-4"
Depth 68'-0"

DESIGN 2694

First Floor: 2,026 square feet
Second Floor: 1,386 square feet
Total: 3,412 square feet
L

This two-story design faithfully recalls the 18th-Century homestead of Secretary of Foreign Affairs John Jay. First-floor livability includes a grand living room with a fireplace and music alcove, a library with another fireplace and built-in bookshelves, a light-filled dining room, a large country kitchen with still another fireplace and snack bar, and a handy clutter room adjacent to the mudroom. Three upstairs bedrooms include a large master suite.

Design by
© Home Planners

Width 84'-0"
Depth 65'-8"

QUOTE ONE®
Cost to build? See page 684 to order complete cost estimate to build this house in your area!

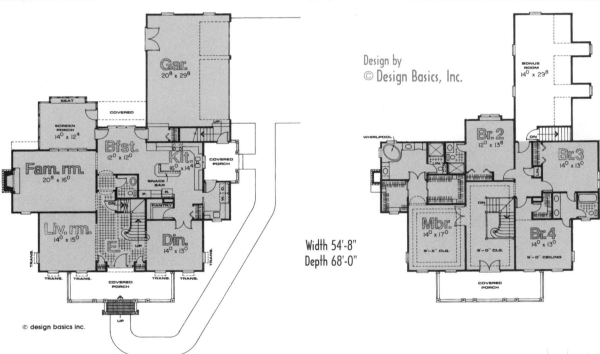

Design by
© Design Basics, Inc.

Width 54'-8"
Depth 68'-0"

© design basics inc.

Main- and second-level covered porches, accompanied by intricate detailing, and many multi-pane windows create a splendid Southern mansion. The prominent entry opens to formal dining and living rooms. The grand family room is warmed by a fireplace and views a screened porch with a cozy window seat. The roomy breakfast area provides access to the porch and the three-car garage. French doors open to the second-floor master suite, which features decorative ceiling details, His and Hers walk-in closets, a large dressing area, dual lavs, a whirlpool bath and separate shower area.

**DESIGN
7267**
First Floor: 1,598 square feet
Second Floor: 1,675 square feet
Total: 3,273 square feet
Bonus Room: 534 square feet

LUXURY HOMES

© 1996 Donald A. Gardner Architects, Inc.

PORCH

MASTER BD. RM.
15-6 x 14-0

FAMILY RM.
18-8 x 23-2
(two story ceiling)

fireplace
balcony above

BRKFST.
13-4 x 13-8

pd. rm.

cl

storage

walk-in closet

lin.

cl

KIT.
13-4 x 12-0

UTIL.
6-10 x 10-0

GARAGE
21-8 x 28-4

master bath

walk-in closet

pan.

w
d

LIVING RM.
13-4 x 13-6

FOYER
8-8 x 10-2
up

DINING
13-4 x 13-6

up

PORCH

© 1996 Donald A. Gardner Architects, Inc.

Width 81'-10"
Depth 51'-8"

Design by
Donald A. Gardner
Architects, Inc.

family room below

LOFT/STUDY
8-8 x 10-2

BED RM.
13-4 x 11-10

attic storage

railing

cl cl

lin.

skylights

walk-in closet

bath

shelves

down

walk-in closet

bath

down

down

BONUS RM.
21-8 x 16-5

BED RM.
13-4 x 12-2

railing

balcony

BED RM.
13-4 x 13-6

LUXURY HOMES

DESIGN 7650
First Floor: 2,086 square feet
Second Floor: 1,077 square feet
Total: 3,163 square feet
Bonus Room: 403 square feet

This beautiful farmhouse with prominent twin gables and bays adds just the right amount of country style to modern family life. The master suite is quietly tucked away downstairs with no rooms directly above, and the cook of the family will love the spacious U-shaped kitchen. The bonus room is easily accessible from the back stairs or second floor, where three bedrooms share two full baths. A curved balcony borders a versatile loft/study, which overlooks the stunning two-story great room. A two-car garage loads from the side.

www.homeplanners.com

DESIGN T057

First Floor: 1,570 square feet
Second Floor: 1,630 square feet
Total: 3,200 square feet

This classic design employs wood siding, a variety of window styles and a detailed front porch. Inside, the large two-story foyer flows into the formal dining room and the living room highlighted by a bay window. A short passage with a wet bar accesses the family room with its wall of windows, French doors and fireplace. The large breakfast area and open island kitchen are spacious as well as efficient. Upstairs, the master suite's sleeping and sitting rooms feature columns, tray ceilings and a fireplace. This home is designed with a basement foundation.

QUOTE ONE®
Cost to build? See page 684 to order complete cost estimate to build this house in your area!

Design by
© Stephen Fuller,
American Home Gallery

Width 60'-0"
Depth 47'-6"

DESIGN T104

First Floor: 1,700 square feet
Second Floor: 1,585 square feet
Total: 3,285 square feet
Bonus Room: 176 square feet

The covered front stoop of this two-story traditionally styled home gives way to the foyer and formal areas inside. A cozy living room with a fireplace sits on the right and an elongated dining room is on the left. A great room with a fireplace and a kitchen/breakfast area account for the rear of the first-floor plan. Upstairs, four bedrooms include a master suite with a bayed sitting area and a private bath. This home is designed with a basement foundation.

LUXURY HOMES

DESIGN P283

First Floor: 2,098 square feet
Second Floor: 2,037 square feet
Total: 4,135 square feet

This two-story farmhouse has much to offer such as the opulent master suite: French doors access the main bedroom, steps lead to a separate sitting room with a fireplace and bay window and His and Hers walk-in closets lead to a vaulted master bath with a whirlpool tub. Three family bedrooms, all with walk-in closets, and two full baths complete the second floor. On the first floor, an island kitchen and a bayed breakfast room flow into a two-story family room with a raised-hearth fireplace. Please specify basement or crawlspace foundation when ordering.

Design by
© Frank Betz Associates, Inc.

Width 68'-6"
Depth 53'-0"

DESIGN 2953

First Floor: 2,995 square feet
Second Floor: 1,831 square feet
Total: 4,826 square feet
L D

A magnificent, finely wrought covered porch wraps around this impressive Victorian home. The two-story foyer provides a direct view into the great room with a large central fireplace. To the left of the foyer is a bookshelf-lined library and to the right is a octagonal-shaped dining room. The island cooktop completes a convenient work triangle in the kitchen. The first-floor master suite opens to the rear covered porch. Four bedrooms, three full baths and a restful lounge with fireplace are located on the second floor.

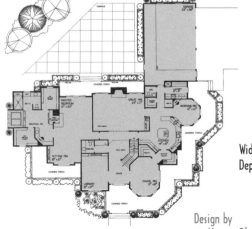

Width 95'-0"
Depth 99'-3"

Design by
© Home Planners

Quote One®
Cost to build? See page 684
to order complete cost estimate
to build this house in your area!

LUXURY HOMES

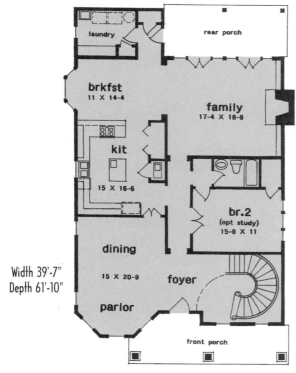

laundry

rear porch

brkfst
11 X 14-4

family
17-4 X 18-8

kit
15 X 16-6

br.2
(opt study)
15-8 X 11

dining
15 X 20-9

foyer

parlor

front porch

Width 39'-7"
Depth 61'-10"

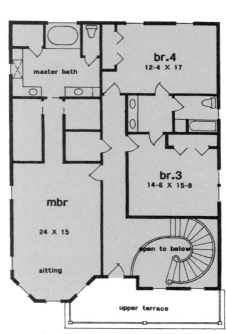

master bath

br.4
12-4 X 17

br.3
14-6 X 15-8

mbr
24 X 15

sitting

open to below

upper terrace

Design by
© Andy McDonald Design Group

LUXURY HOMES

Two porches and an upper terrace provide a variety of outside areas. The two-story cupola-style tower forms bay windows in the parlor near the formal dining room downstairs and in the sitting area in the master bedroom above. An open circular staircase, a fireplace in the family room and a bay window in the breakfast room are some of the charming features in this classic Queen Anne. Four bedrooms, three bathrooms and a well-designed kitchen complete this charming home. A rear porch can be reached from the family room.

DESIGN M525
First Floor: 1,844 square feet
Second Floor: 1,546 square feet
Total: 3,390 square feet

Design by
© Living Concepts Home Planning

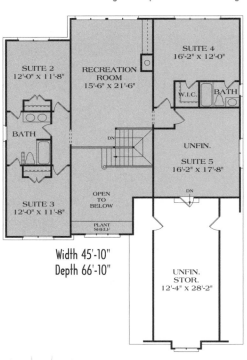

Width 45'-10"
Depth 66'-10"

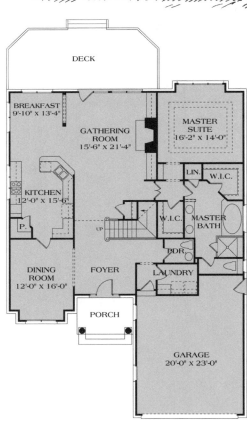

DESIGN A298
First Floor: 1,882 square feet
Second Floor: 1,269 square feet
Total: 3,151 square feet
Bonus Room: 284 square feet

Craftsman architecture in this four-bedroom home is so distinct that one could hardly miss the rafter tails, shingles, double-hung windows and pillars at the front porch. In the gathering room, built-ins flank the warming fireplace, while access to the rear deck is nearby. Located on the first floor for pri-vacy, the master suite is full of amenities: His and Hers walk-in closets, a double-bowl vanity and a separate tub and shower in the compartmented bath and a tray ceiling in the bedroom. The second floor is complete with three bedrooms, two full baths and an unfinished bonus room with access to unfinished storage.

The home, as shown in the photograph, may differ from the actual blueprints. For more detailed information, please check the floor plans carefully.

Photo by Northlight Photography

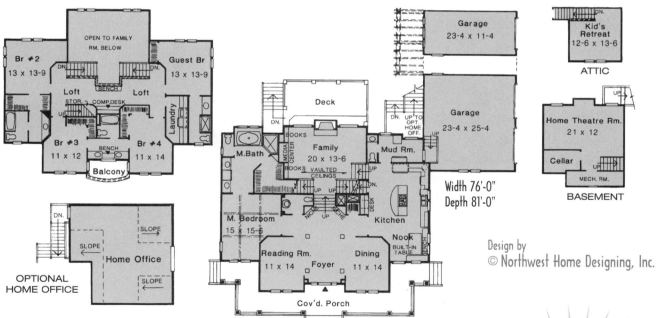

Br #2 13 x 13-9

OPEN TO FAMILY RM. BELOW

Guest Br 13 x 13-9

Loft STOR. COMP.DESK

Loft

DN. DN.

BENCH

Br #3 11 x 12

Laundry

Br #4 11 x 14

BENCH

Balcony

DN.

SLOPE

SLOPE

Home Office

SLOPE

OPTIONAL HOME OFFICE

Deck

DN.

BOOKS

M.Bath

MEDIA CENTER

Family 20 x 13-6 VAULTED CEILINGS

Mud Rm.

DN. UP TO OPT. HOME OFF.

Garage 23-4 x 11-4

Garage 23-4 x 25-4

M. Bedroom 15 x 15-6

NICHE NICHE

DESK

UP

Kitchen

Reading Rm. 11 x 14

Foyer

Dining 11 x 14

Nook BUILT-IN TABLE

BENCH

Cov'd. Porch

Width 76'-0" Depth 81'-0"

Kid's Retreat 12-6 x 13-6

DN.

ATTIC

UP

Home Theatre Rm. 21 x 12

Cellar

UP

MECH. RM.

BASEMENT

Design by
© Northwest Home Designing, Inc.

This Craftsman-style home has a great layout and offers many options for your changing family needs. Inside, the formal dining room and a cozy reading room flank the foyer. To the left is the large efficient kitchen with work island, snack bar and built-in breakfast table. The family room at the back of the house has vaulted ceilings, a fireplace and a built-in media center. The master bedroom features a beamed ceiling, walk-in closet and sumptuous bath. On the second floor, two family bedrooms share a full bath and a balcony, while a third bedroom offers a private bath. The spacious guest bedroom also has a private bath. The attic on the third level can be used for a kid's retreat or storage.

DESIGN W311
First Floor: 2,120 square feet
Second Floor: 1,520 square feet
Total: 3,640 square feet
Optional Finished Basement: 377 square feet
Optional Home Office: 526 square feet
Attic: 183 square feet

LUXURY HOMES

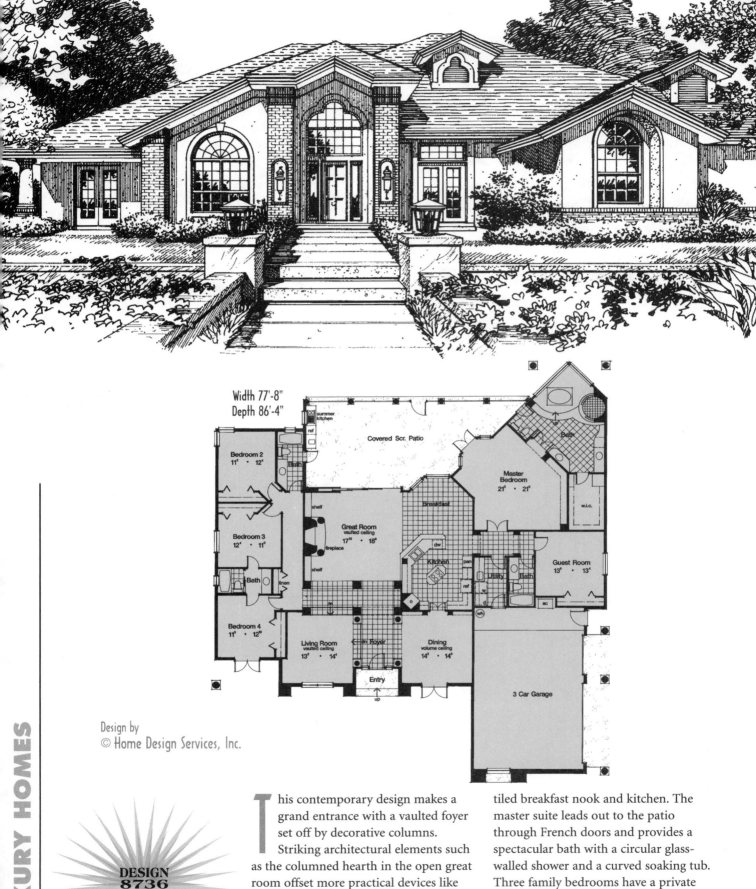

Width 77'-8"
Depth 86'-4"

Design by
© Home Design Services, Inc.

DESIGN 8736
Square Footage: 3,448

This contemporary design makes a grand entrance with a vaulted foyer set off by decorative columns. Striking architectural elements such as the columned hearth in the open great room offset more practical devices like the twelve-foot sliding glass door to the back patio. A bay window brightens the tiled breakfast nook and kitchen. The master suite leads out to the patio through French doors and provides a spectacular bath with a circular glass-walled shower and a curved soaking tub. Three family bedrooms have a private wing with two full baths. A three-car garage sits to the front.

The home, as shown in the photograph, may differ from the actual blueprints.
For more detailed information, please check the floor plans carefully.

Photo by Allen Maertz

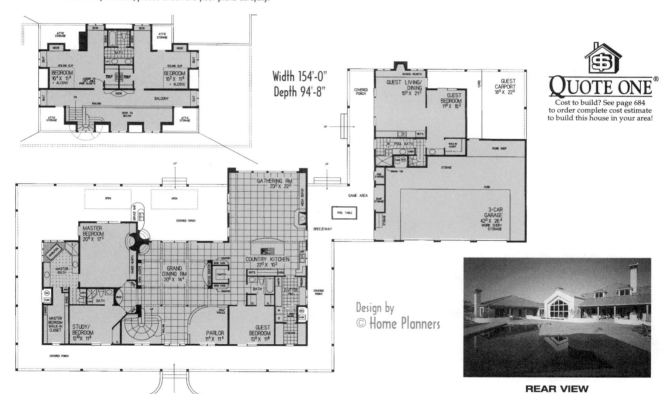

Width 154'-0"
Depth 94'-8"

Design by
© Home Planners

REAR VIEW

LUXURY HOMES

Western farmhouse-style living is captured in this handsome design. The central entrance leads into a cozy parlor—half walls provide a view of the grand dining room. Entertaining's a cinch with the dining room's built-in china alcove, service counter and fireplace. The country kitchen, with a large island cooktop, overlooks the gathering room with its full wall of glass. The master bedroom will satisfy even the most discerning tastes. It boasts a raised hearth, porch access and a bath with a walk-in closet, separate vanities and a whirlpool tub. You may want to use one of the additional first-floor bedrooms as a study, the other as a guest room. To round out the first floor, you'll also find a clutter room with a pantry, freezer space and access to storage space. Two family bedrooms and attic storage make up the second floor. Note, too, the separate garage and guest house, which make this such a winning design.

DESIGN 3471

First Floor: 3,166 square feet
Second Floor: 950 square feet
Guest Living Area: 680 square feet
Total: 4,796 square feet

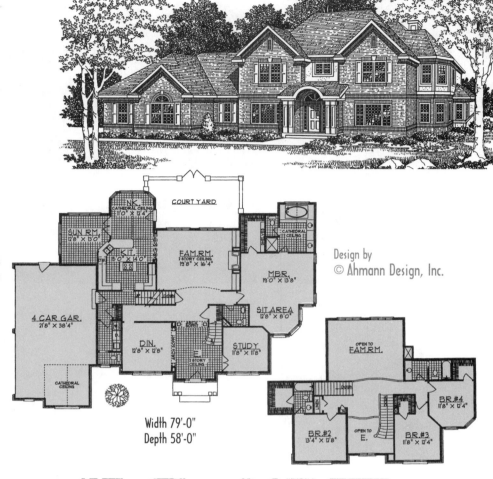

DESIGN U114

First Floor: 2,470 square feet
Second Floor: 1,000 square feet
Total: 3,470 square feet

Double columns flank the elegant entry, while inside, the two-story foyer leads to a cozy study on the right and a formal dining room on the left. The kitchen features a cooktop island, snack bar into the nook and access to the nearby sun room. The first-floor master bedroom is full of amenities. Upstairs, a balcony overlooks the family room and the foyer and leads to three secondary bedrooms—each with walk-in closets. Bedrooms 3 and 4 share a full bath, while Bedroom 2 offers a private bath. The four-car garage features plenty of storage space.

Design by
© Ahmann Design, Inc.

Width 79'-0"
Depth 58'-0"

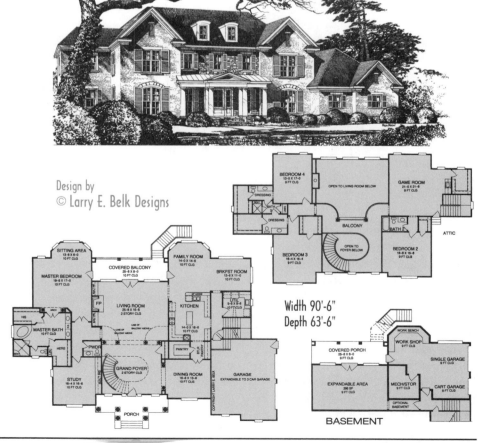

DESIGN 8273

First Floor: 3,413 square feet
Second Floor: 2,076 square feet
Total: 5,489 square feet
Bonus Room: 430 square feet

Classic design combined with dynamite interiors make this home a real gem. Inside, a free-floating curved staircase rises majestically to the second floor. The enormous living room features a dramatic two-story window wall. Family room, breakfast room and kitchen are conveniently grouped. The master secluded suite includes a sitting area and sumptuous master bath. The second floor includes a second bedroom with a private bath. Bedrooms 3 and 4 share a bath that includes two private dressing areas.

Design by
© Larry E. Belk Designs

Width 90'-6"
Depth 63'-6"

LUXURY HOMES

The home, as shown in the photograph, may differ from the actual blueprints. For more detailed information, please check the floor plans carefully.

Photo by Terrebonne Photography; Builder: Barrington Homes

Width 76'-0"
Depth 73'-10"

Design by
© Frank Betz Associates, Inc.

his design features a breathtaking rear exterior with an upper balcony, four covered porches and an inconspicuous side garage. The foyer is flanked by the dining room and the two-story library, which includes a fireplace and an upper balcony with built-in bookcases. The master bath is elegant, with dual vanities, a bright radius window and a 7x7-foot shower with leaded glass. A unique double-decker walk-in closet provides plenty of storage for the most avid shopper. Just a few steps away, a home office offers a quiet place to work amid stunning views of the backyard. Upstairs, two family bedrooms share a compartmented bath and a covered porch, while a third bedroom has a private bath. A bonus room is included for future expansion.

DESIGN
P285
First Floor: 3,218 square feet
Second Floor: 1,240 square feet
Total: 4,458 square feet
Bonus Room: 656 square feet

LUXURY HOMES

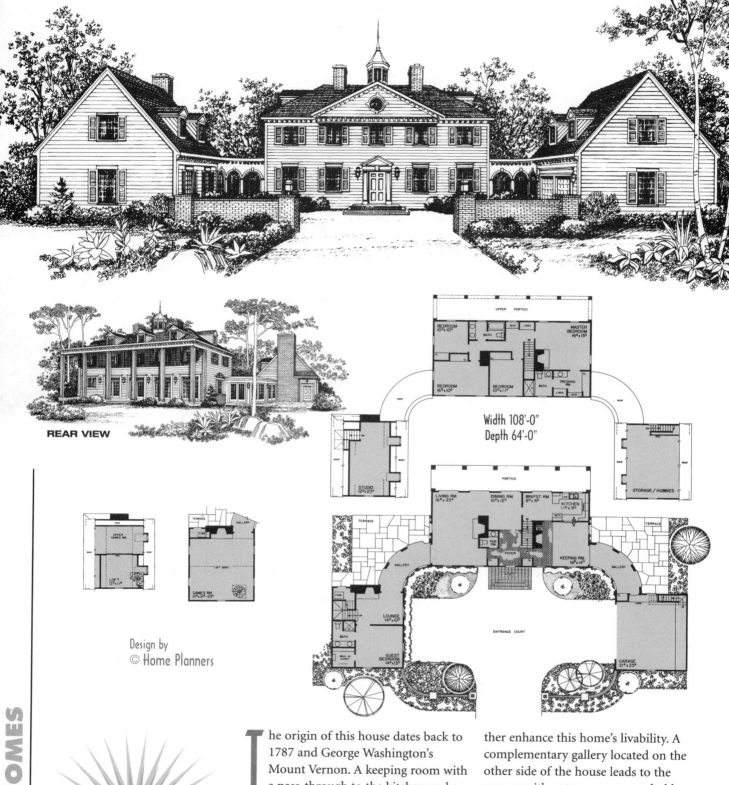

REAR VIEW

Width 108'-0"
Depth 64'-0"

Design by
© Home Planners

DESIGN 2665

First Floor: 1,992 square feet
Second Floor: 1,458 square feet
Total: 3,450 square feet
Bonus Room: 380 square feet

The origin of this house dates back to 1787 and George Washington's Mount Vernon. A keeping room with a pass-through to the kitchen and a fireplace with built-in wood box, a formal dining room, a breakfast room and a formal living room with a fireplace allow plenty of social possibilities. Separate guest quarters with a full bath, a lounge area and an upstairs studio which is connected to the main house by a gallery further enhance this home's livability. A complementary gallery located on the other side of the house leads to the garage, with a storage room or hobby room situated above. Four bedrooms with two full baths are found on the second floor, including the master suite with a fireplace. In the left wing, the guest bedroom/lounge with its upstairs study can be designed as a game room with a spiral staircase and a loft area.

DESIGN 2660

First Floor: 1,479 square feet
Second Floor: 1,501 square feet
Third Floor: 912 square feet
Activities Room: 556 square feet
Total: 4,448 square feet

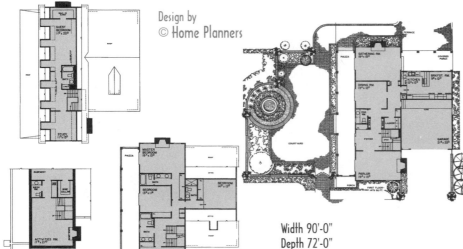

Width 90'-0"
Depth 72'-0"

The "single house" style represented here is true to its nature: one-room wide with a two-story piazza down the side. The one-room width allows for extra ventilation. The foyer opens to a parlor and, down the hall, a dining room and gathering room. The kitchen is located at the back of the wing created by the garage. The second floor is comprised of four bedrooms. A third floor holds a guest bedroom and a study. The basement holds a hearth-warmed activities room, a powder room and wine cellar.

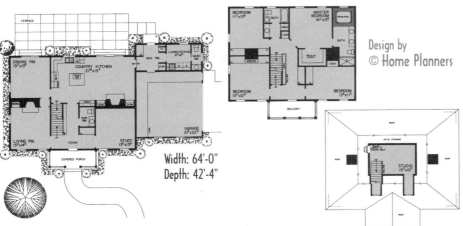

DESIGN 2690

First Floor: 1,559 square feet
Second Floor: 1,344 square feet
Third Floor: 176 square feet
Total: 3,079 square feet

Width: 64'-0"
Depth: 42'-4"

This Cape Cod Georgian home recalls the Julia Wood House, built around 1790 in Falmouth, Mass. Such homes generally featured a balustraded roof deck or "widow's walk" where wives of captains looked to the sea for signs of returning ships. Our updated floor plan features four bedrooms, including a master suite, on the second floor, and a country kitchen, study, dining room and living room on the first floor. The third floor makes a fine studio, with a ladder leading to the widow's walk.

LUXURY HOMES

DESIGN 3349

First Floor: 2,807 square feet
Second Floor: 1,363 square feet
Total: 4,170 square feet

L D

Grand traditional design comes to the forefront in this elegant two-story home. From the dramatic front entry with curving double stairs, to the less-formal gathering room with a fireplace and terrace access, this plan accommodates family lifestyles. Notice the split bedroom plan with the master suite, complete with a separate study, His and Hers walk-in closets and a lavish bath, on the first floor and four family bedrooms, sharing two full baths, upstairs. A four-car garage handles the largest of family fleets.

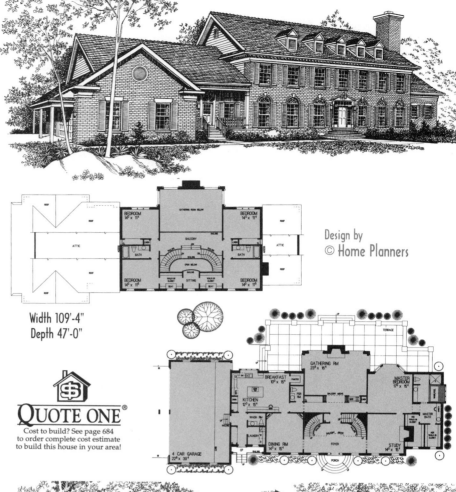

Width 109'-4"
Depth 47'-0"

Design by
© Home Planners

QUOTE ONE®

Cost to build? See page 684
to order complete cost estimate
to build this house in your area!

DESIGN F129

First Floor: 2,938 square feet
Second Floor: 1,273 square feet
Total: 4,211 square feet

The secluded master bedroom suite of this staunch New England four-bedroom design provides all the extras. The oversized master bedroom opens into a bay window with petit dejeuner with access to a private terrace. A study, family room with fireplace and sunken living room provide a variety of activity options. Family bedrooms are on the second floor and include one bedroom with a private bath.

Width 101'-10"
Depth 74'-2"

Design by
© R.L. Pfotenhauer

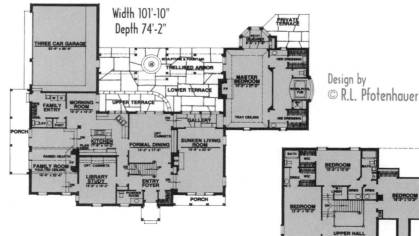

DESIGN F107

First Floor: 1,830 square feet
Second Floor: 1,723 square feet
Total: 3,553 square feet
Bonus Room: 534 square feet

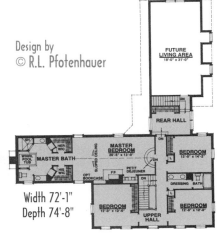

Design by
© R.L. Pfotenhauer

Width 72'-1"
Depth 74'-8"

Twin chimneys top the ridge of this grand home. Inside, the foyer extends a cordial welcome. The living room shares the warmth of a double-facing fireplace with the formal dining room. Across the hall is a study that easily serves as a library. Located to the side of the kitchen with its adjacent morning room is a huge family room with a warming fireplace, wraparound porch and nine-foot ceiling. Convenient back stairs lead to the second-floor master suite. Three additional bedrooms and a full bath complete the second floor.

Width 76'-10"
Depth 38'-10"

Design by
© Home Planners

DESIGN 1858

First Floor: 1,794 square feet
Second Floor: 1,474 square feet
Studio: 424 square feet
Total: 3,692 square feet

D

The stately facade of this Georgian design seems to foretell all of the exceptional features to be found inside. Both the family and formal living rooms feature a fireplace, while the quiet library is warmed by a raised corner hearth. The kitchen's adjoining breakfast room offers stairs that rise to the studio apartment over the garage. The grand stairway from the entry foyer leads to three family bedrooms that share a dual-vanity hall bath. The master suite features a bookshelf hearth.

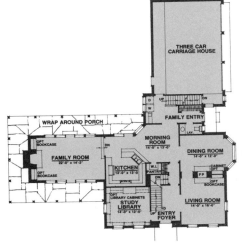

LUXURY HOMES

DESIGN M137

First Floor: 2,432 square feet
Second Floor: 903 square feet
Total: 3,335 square feet

The elegant symmetry of this Southern traditional four-bedroom plan makes it a joy to own. Six columns frame the covered porch, and two chimneys add interest to the exterior roofline. The two-story foyer opens to a formal living room with built-in wet bar and fireplace. A massive family room with cathedral ceiling leads outside to a large covered patio or to the breakfast room and kitchen. The first-floor master bedroom suite features vaulted ceilings, a secluded covered patio and plant ledge in the master bath. The three upstairs bedrooms share 2½ baths.

Design by
© Fillmore Design Group

Width 90'-0"
Depth 53'-10"

DESIGN 2889

First Floor: 2,348 square feet
Second Floor: 1,872 square feet
Total: 4,220 square feet

L D

This classic Georgian design contains a variety of features that make it outstanding: a pediment gable with cornice work and dentils, beautifully proportioned columns and distinct window treatment. The first floor contains some special appointments: a fireplace in the living room, a wet bar in the gathering room and sliding glass doors from the study to the rear terrace. Upstairs, an extension over the garage allows for a huge walk-in closet in the deluxe master suite and a full bath with tub in the left front bedroom.

The home, as shown in the photograph, may differ from the actual blueprints. For more detailed information, please check the floor plans carefully.

Photo by Andrew D. Lautman

Width 90'-4"
Depth 44'-8"

Design by
© Home Planners

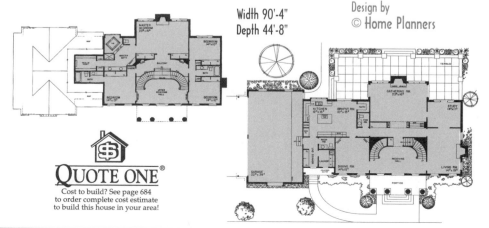

QUOTE ONE®

Cost to build? See page 684 to order complete cost estimate to build this house in your area!

LUXURY HOMES

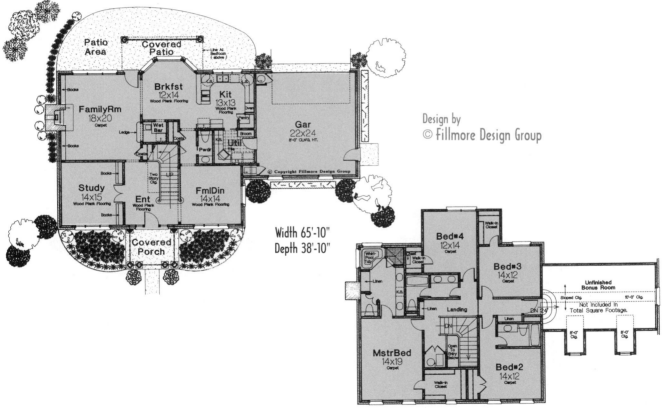

Design by
© Fillmore Design Group

Width 65'-10"
Depth 38'-10"

A lovely facade graces this striking four-bedroom traditional home with double columns supporting the impressive gabled entry. The hardwood floor in the foyer continues through double doors into a large study with built-in bookshelves and extends to the right into the formal dining room. The bright open area across the back holds the family room with fireplace, breakfast room with bay window and U-shaped kitchen with pantry. The master suite on the second level features a corner whirlpool tub. Three family or guest bedrooms access two additional full baths. A large well-lighted bonus room over the garage awaits future development as an additional bedroom or as office space.

DESIGN M143
First Floor: 1,573 square feet
Second Floor: 1,449 square feet
Total: 3,022 square feet

LUXURY HOMES

DESIGN 3337

First Floor: 2,167 square feet
Second Floor: 1,992 square feet
Total: 4,159 square feet

L

The elegant facade of this design, with its columned portico, fanlights and dormers, houses an amenity-filled interior. The gathering room, study and dining room, each with a fireplace, provide plenty of room for relaxing and entertaining. A large work area contains a kitchen with a breakfast room, snack bar, laundry room and pantry. The four-bedroom second floor includes a master suite with a sumptuous bath and an exercise room.

Design by
© Home Planners

Width 94'-4"
Depth 42'-9"

QUOTE ONE®
Cost to build? See page 684
to order complete cost estimate
to build this house in your area!

DESIGN 9364

First Floor: 1,717 square feet
Second Floor: 1,518 square feet
Total: 3,235 square feet

Stately columns highlight the facade of this home. The open entry allows for views into formal areas and up the tapering staircase. The dining room with hutch space accesses the kitchen through double doors. The living room accesses the sunken family room through pocket doors. The sunken family room offers large windows, a fireplace, a built-in entertainment center and bookcases. The kitchen adjoins the sunny, semi-gazebo breakfast area. The private master suite features a tiered ceiling, two walk-in closets and a roomy, bayed sitting area.

QUOTE ONE®
Cost to build? See page 684
to order complete cost estimate
to build this house in your area!

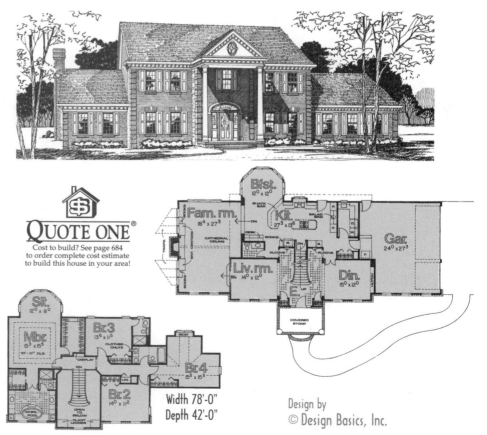

Width 78'-0"
Depth 42'-0"

Design by
© Design Basics, Inc.

LUXURY HOMES

DESIGN
2984

First Floor: 3,116 square feet
Second Floor: 1,997 square feet
Total: 5,113 square feet

L

An echo of Whitehall, built in 1765 in Anne Arundel County, Maryland, resounds in this home. Its classic symmetry and columned facade herald a grand interior. Inside, all are kept cozy with fireplaces in the gathering room, study and family room. An island kitchen with attached breakfast room handily serves the nearby dining room. Four second-floor bedrooms include a large master suite with another fireplace, a whirlpool tub and His and Hers closets in the bath. Three more full baths are found on this floor.

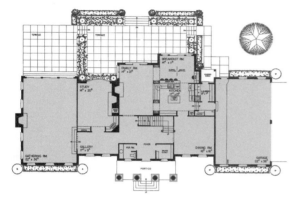

Width 104'-0"
Depth 54'-8"

Design by
© Home Planners

QUOTE ONE®
Cost to build? See page 684
to order complete cost estimate
to build this house in your area!

DESIGN
2693

Square Footage: 3,462

This imposing design recalls Rose Hill, built near Lexington, Kentucky, around 1820. The living room, dining room and library each have a fireplace flanked by built-in cabinets. The large country kitchen, with a fourth fireplace, provides an efficient work station that includes an island cooktop. A clutter room with a workbench and a potting counter is a welcome amenity. Terrace access and a large bow window are highlights in the master bedroom. Three additional bedrooms complete the plan.

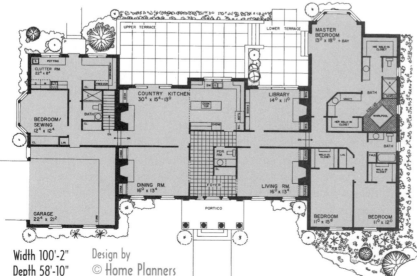

Width 100'-2"
Depth 58'-10"

Design by
© Home Planners

LUXURY HOMES

COVERED PORCH

BREAKFAST
13'-5" x 10'-0"

TWO-CAR GARAGE
22'-0" x 21'-6"

FAMILY ROOM
15'-6" x 16'-0"

KITCHEN
13'-5" x 12'-0"

LAUNDRY
7'-10" x 7'-0"

LIVING ROOM
13'-6" x 12'-0"

TWO-STORY
FOYER
15'-6" x 9'-2"

DINING ROOM
13'-4" x 15'-0"

Width 53'-0"
Depth 46'-0"

COVERED PORCH

SITTING
5'-0" x 4'-8"

MASTER BATH
13'-4" x 15'-10"

BEDROOM No.4
16'-10" x 11'-10"

MASTER BEDROOM
15'-6" x 16'-0"

MASTER CLOSET

BATH

BATH

BEDROOM No.2
17'-4" x 12'-0"

OPEN TO FOYER BELOW

BEDROOM No.3
17'-4" x 12'-0"

Quote One®

Cost to build? See page 684
to order complete cost estimate
to build this house in your area!

Design by
© Stephen Fuller,
American Home Gallery

**DESIGN
T027**
First Floor: 1,455 square feet
Second Floor: 1,649 square feet
Total: 3,104 square feet

LUXURY HOMES

The double wings, twin chimneys and the center portico of this home work in concert to create a classic architectural statement. The two-story foyer is flanked by the spacious dining room and formal living room, each containing its own fireplace. A large family room with a full wall of glass beckons the outside in while it opens conveniently to the sunlit kitchen and breakfast room. The master suite features a tray ceiling and French doors that open to a covered porch. A grand master bath with all the amenities, including a garden tub and huge closet, completes the master suite. Two other bedrooms share a bath while another has its own private bath. The fourth bedroom also features a sunny nook for sitting or reading. This home is designed with a basement foundation.

Width 85'-3"
Depth 74'-0"

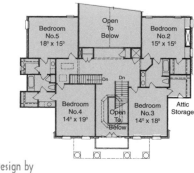

Design by
© Stephen Fuller,
American Home Gallery

DESIGN T126

First Floor: 3,902 square feet
Second Floor: 2,159 square feet
Total: 6,061 square feet

The entry to this classic home is framed with a sweeping double staircase and four large columns topped with a pediment. Beyond the foyer, the home is designed with rooms that offer maximum livability. The two-story family room, which has a central fireplace, opens to the study and a solarium. A spacious U-shaped kitchen features a central island cooktop. The impressive master suite features backyard access and a bath fit for royalty. Four second-floor bedrooms enjoy large proportions. This home is designed with a basement foundation.

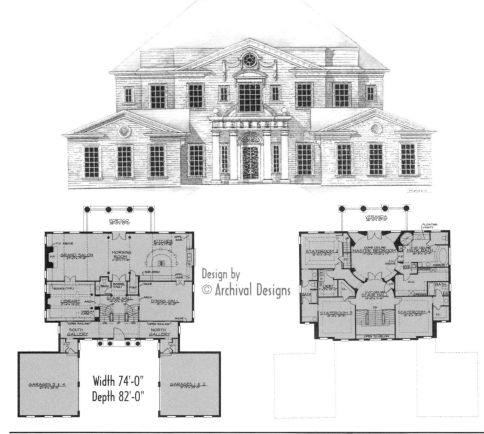

Design by
© Archival Designs

Width 74'-0"
Depth 82'-0"

DESIGN S122

First Floor: 2,175 square feet
Second Floor: 1,927 square feet
Total: 4,102 square feet

Simply elegant, with dignified details, this beautiful home is reminiscent of English estate homes. Two double garages flank a columned front door and are attached to the main floor by galleries leading to the entry foyer. Here a double staircase leads to the upstairs, and encourages a view of the morning room, grand salon and rear portico. The gourmet kitchen has a uniquely styled island counter with cooktop. A formal library with beam ceiling and fireplace rests just beyond the foyer. Impressive bedroom suites are upstairs.

LUXURY HOMES

DESIGN 3500

First Floor: 1,968 square feet
Second Floor: 1,901 square feet
Total: 3,869 square feet

Here is a stately antebellum manor in the Greek Revival tradition. Stepping into the foyer, the dramatic impact of the open, curving staircase to the second floor and its spacious hall is a delight to behold. Notice the fireplaces and built-ins in the living, dining and family rooms. The L-shaped kitchen has an island cooking surface and opens to the breakfast area. Two of the second-floor bedrooms share a common bath with twin lavatories, while a third includes a private bath. Down the hall and past the doors to the balcony is the master bedroom.

Width 52'-0"
Depth 38'-0"

Design by
© Home Planners

Quote One®
Cost to build? See page 684
to order complete cost estimate
to build this house in your area!

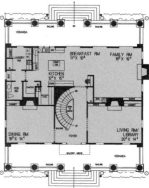

DESIGN 3527

First Floor: 2,000 square feet
Second Floor: 2,000 square feet
Total: 4,000 square feet
Bonus Room: 264 square feet

From the temple-style front to the angled balustrade on the roof, this home is a standout. Tall columns support porches on two levels on the front and back of the house. A tiled foyer leads back to the family area, which includes a U-shaped kitchen with a snack bar, a fireplace flanked by window seats and three sets of sliding glass doors to the rear porch. Fireplaces in the formal living and dining rooms add their welcoming glow for guests, while the master-bedroom fireplace warms the homeowner's quiet time.

Quote One®
Cost to build? See page 684
to order complete cost estimate
to build this house in your area!

Design by
© Home Planners

Width 50'-8"
Depth 56'-8"

LUXURY HOMES

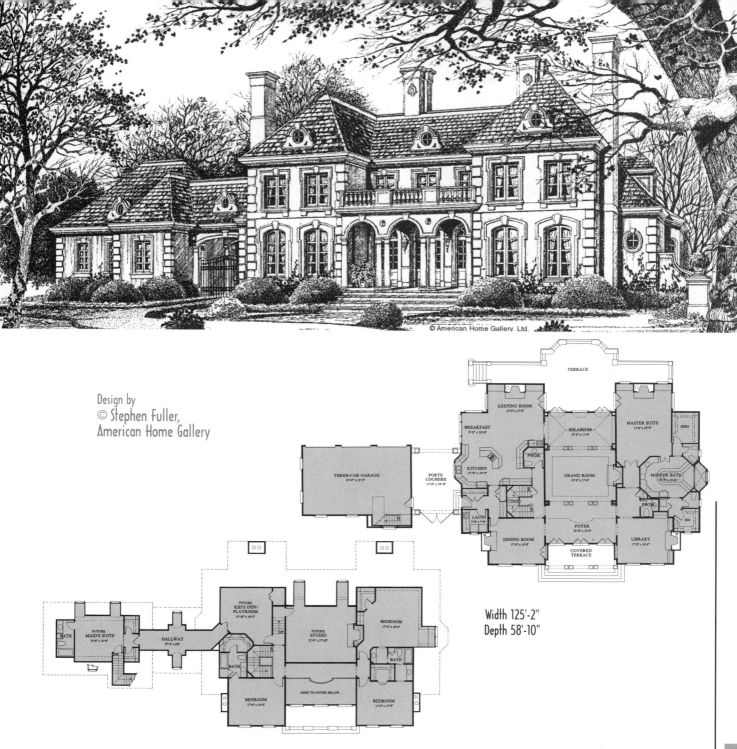

Design by
© Stephen Fuller,
American Home Gallery

Width 125'-2"
Depth 58'-10"

This magnificent estate is detailed with exterior charm: a porte cochere connecting the detached garage to the house, a covered terrace and oval windows. The first floor consists of a lavish master suite, a cozy library with a fireplace, a stupendous grand room/solarium combination, an elegantly formal dining room with another fireplace and a kitchen/breakfast room/keeping room that will delight everyone in the family.

Three large bedrooms dominate the second floor, each with a walk-in closet. For the kids there is a play room/kid's den and up another flight of stairs is a room for future expansion into a deluxe studio with a fireplace. Over the three-car garage and attached to the second floor via the roof of the porte cochere, there is a room for a future mother-in-law suite or maid's suite. This home is designed with a basement foundation.

DESIGN T127

First Floor: 3,703 square feet
Second Floor: 1,427 square feet
Total: 5,130 square feet
Bonus Space: 1,399 square feet

LUXURY HOMES

DESIGN T066

First Floor: 1,554 square feet
Second Floor: 1,648 square feet
Total: 3,202 square feet

The classic styling of this brick American traditional home is defined by a double-door entrance with transom and Palladian window above. A large family room with a full wall of glass opens conveniently to the kitchen and breakfast room. The second-floor master suite features a sitting room with fireplace separated from the sleeping area by a majestic colonnade. Two additional bedrooms share a bath while a fourth bedroom has its own private bath. This home is designed with a basement foundation.

Design by
© Stephen Fuller,
American Home Gallery

QUOTE ONE®
Cost to build? See page 684 to order complete cost estimate to build this house in your area!

Width 60'-0"
Depth 43'-0"

DESIGN 9367

First Floor: 2,500 square feet
Second Floor: 973 square feet
Total: 3,473 square feet

Step between the columns and into the entry of this grand design. Large living and dining rooms flank a formal staircase. The dramatic great room offers a fourteen-foot-high beamed ceiling, a fireplace and wonderful views. Fancy the octagon-shaped breakfast nook or the kitchen with abundant counter space. A tiered ceiling, two walk-in closets and a luxurious bath with His and Hers vanities, shower and a spa tub all characterize the master suite. On the second floor you'll find three bedrooms and two full baths.

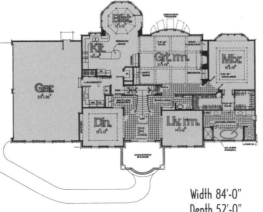

Design by
© Design Basics, Inc.

Width 84'-0"
Depth 52'-0"

LUXURY HOMES

DESIGN
2543

First Floor: 2,345 square feet
Second Floor: 1,687 square feet
Total: 4,032 square feet

L D

This best-selling French adaptation is highlighted by many exterior details and excellent proportion. Inside, a large, two-story foyer leads under the arch of a dual staircase to a gathering room graced by a central fireplace and access to the rear terrace. The formal living and dining rooms flank the foyer. The gourmet kitchen offers a work island and has an attached breakfast room with access to the terrace. Upstairs a deluxe master suite is lavish in its efforts to pamper you. Three secondary bedrooms also share this level.

Design by
© Home Planners

Width 90'-4"
Depth 44'-0"

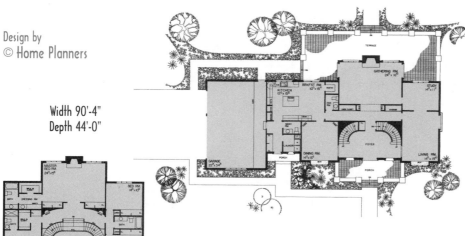

DESIGN
3380

First Floor: 3,350 square feet
Second Floor: 1,298 square feet
Total: 4,648 square feet

Reminiscent of a Mediterranean villa, this grand manor is a comfortable residence on the inside. An elegant receiving hall boasts a double staircase and is flanked by the formal dining room and the library. A huge gathering room to the back is graced by a fireplace and a wall of sliding glass doors to the rear terrace. With a lavish bath and His and Hers walk-in closets, the master suite will be a delight. Upstairs are four additional bedrooms with ample storage space, a large balcony overlooking the gathering room and two full baths.

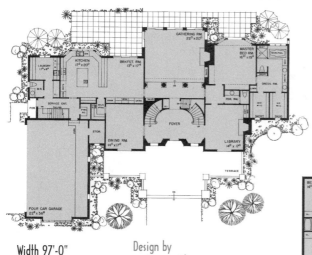

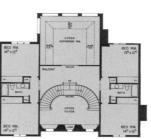

$ QUOTE ONE®

Cost to build? See page 684
to order complete cost estimate
to build this house in your area!

Width 97'-0"
Depth 74'-4"

Design by
© Home Planners

LUXURY HOMES

DESIGN 3305

First Floor: 3,644 square feet
Second Floor: 2,005 square feet
Total: 5,649 square feet

A steeply pitched roof, a generous supply of multi-pane windows, and fanlights and glass side panels that accent the front entry enhance the grand design of this beautiful home. Highlights include a magnificent first-floor master suite, a sun-filled living room overlooking the rear grounds and bay windows in the family room, dining room and study. Note the three fireplaces, plenty of outdoor access and the three-car garage.

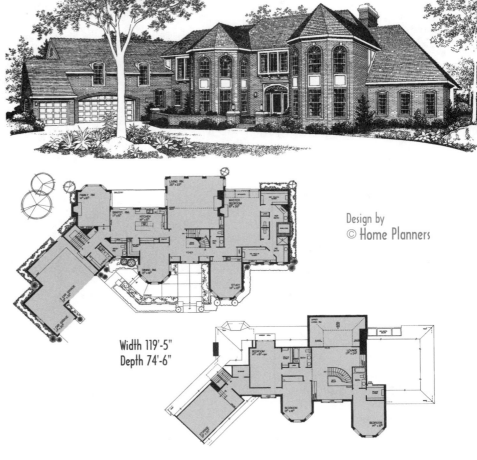

Design by
© Home Planners

Width 119'-5"
Depth 74'-6"

DESIGN 2968

First Floor: 3,736 square feet
Second Floor: 2,264 square feet
Total: 6,000 square feet

L

Twin turrets flank the distinctive covered entry to this stunning manor. The plan opens from the foyer to a formal dining room, a master study and a step-down gathering room. The spacious kitchen includes an island work station and a built-in desk. The adjacent morning room and the gathering room, with a wet bar and a raised-hearth fireplace, open to the terrace. The luxurious and secluded master suite provides two walk-in closets, a dressing area and an exercise area with a spa. The second floor features four bedrooms and an activities room.

QUOTE ONE®
Cost to build? See page 684
to order complete cost estimate
to build this house in your area!

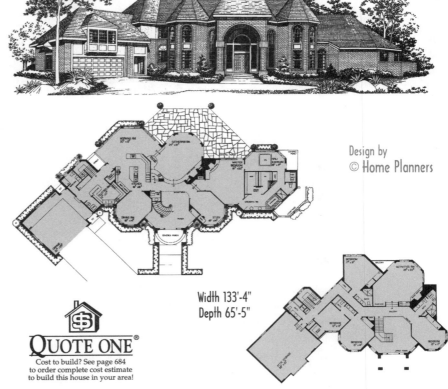

Design by
© Home Planners

Width 133'-4"
Depth 65'-5"

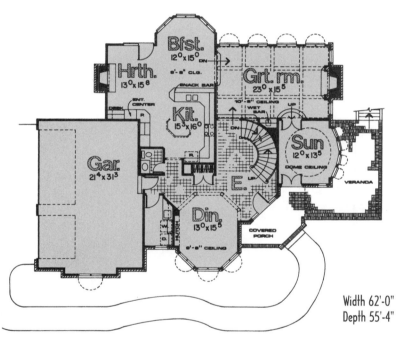

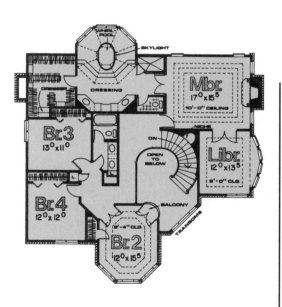

Width 62'-0"
Depth 55'-4"

Two-story bays, luminous windows and brick details embellish this stately, traditional castle. Wouldn't you love to call it home? Inside, the soaring foyer is angled to provide impressive views of the spectacular curving staircase and columns that define the octagonal dining room. Although hard to choose, this home's most outstanding feature may be the sun room, which is crowned with a dome ceiling and lit with a display of bowed windows. This room gives access to the multi-windowed great room and an expansive veranda. A cozy hearth room, a breakfast room and an oversized kitchen complete the casual living area. The sumptuous master suite features a fireplace, a library and an opulent master bath with a gazebo ceiling and a skylight above the magnificent whirlpool tub. Three secondary bedrooms, one with a dramatic French-door balcony overlooking the foyer, and a full hall bath complete the second floor.

DESIGN 7273
First Floor: 1,719 square feet
Second Floor: 1,688 square feet
Total: 3,407 square feet

LUXURY HOMES

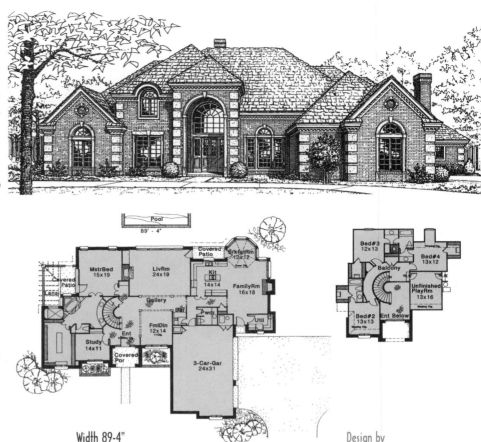

DESIGN M153

First Floor: 2,997 square feet
Second Floor: 983 square feet
Total: 3,980 square feet

The distinctive covered entry to this stunning manor leads to a gracious entry with impressive two-story semi-circular fanlights. The entry leads to a study, formal dining and living rooms and the master suite. The kitchen includes an island workstation and built-in pantry. The breakfast room features a cone ceiling. The luxurious master bath, secluded in its own wing, is complete with a covered patio. The master bedroom has a huge walk-in closet. Upstairs are three bedrooms, two baths and a future playroom area.

Width 89-4"
Depth 71'-0"

Design by
© Fillmore Design Group

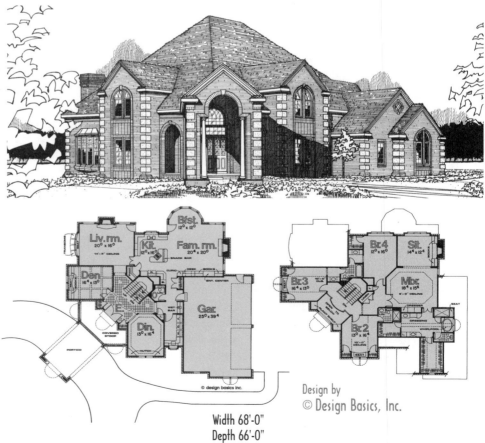

DESIGN 7268

First Floor: 2,040 square feet
Second Floor: 1,952 square feet
Total: 3,992 square feet

This stately brick home offers a magnificent elevation from every angle. The entry hall is highlighted by a majestic staircase. Between the formal rooms is a den with floor-to-ceiling cabinetry, a window seat and spider-beam ceiling. A gourmet kitchen with walk-in pantry and island cooktop/snack bar opens to a family room featuring a built-in rolltop desk, entertainment center and raised-hearth fireplace. The nearby breakfast nook offers views to the outside. Upstairs, a lavish master suite and three family bedrooms complete the plan.

Width 68'-0"
Depth 66'-0"

Design by
© Design Basics, Inc.

LUXURY HOMES

Design by
© Fillmore Design Group

Width 108'-10"
Depth 53'-10"

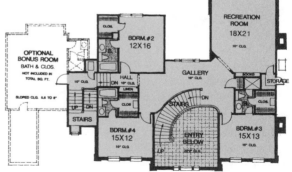

A grand facade detailed with brick corner quoins, stucco flourishes, arched windows and an elegant entrance presents this home and preludes the amenities inside. A spacious foyer is accented by a curving stair and flanked by a formal living room and a formal dining room. For cozy times, a through-fireplace is located between a large family room and a quiet study. The master suite is designed to pamper, with two walk-in closets (one is absolutely huge), a two-sided fireplace sharing its heat with a bayed sitting area and the bedroom and a lavish master bath filled with attractive amenities. Upstairs, three secondary bedrooms each have a private bath and walk-in closet. Also on this level is a spacious recreation room, perfect for a game room or children's playroom.

DESIGN M155
First Floor: 3,599 square feet
Second Floor: 1,621 square feet
Total: 5,220 square feet

LUXURY HOMES

DESIGN 2951

First Floor: 4,195 square feet
Second Floor: 2,094 square feet
Total: 6,289 square feet

A turret with two-story divided windows is the focal point on the exterior of this stately Tudor home. The large gathering room features a wet bar and a fireplace with a raised hearth that runs the entire length of the wall. An octagon-shaped sitting room is tucked into the corner of the impressive first-floor master suite. Three bedrooms—one a guest suite with sitting room—three baths and a study are located on the second floor.

Design by
© Home Planners

Width 111'-4"
Depth 87'-6"

DESIGN 2966

Square Footage: 3,403
Bonus Room: 284 square feet

This Tudor adaptation is as dramatic inside as it is outside. From the front entrance courtyard to the rear terrace, there is much that catches the eye. The spacious foyer with its sloping ceiling looks up into the balcony lounge and down the open stairwell to the lower level. The focal point of the living zone is the delightful atrium. Both the formal living room and the informal family room feature a fireplace. Both of the full baths include a tub, separate shower, vanity and twin lavatories.

Width 106'-0"
Depth 58'-0"

Design by
© Home Planners

LUXURY HOMES

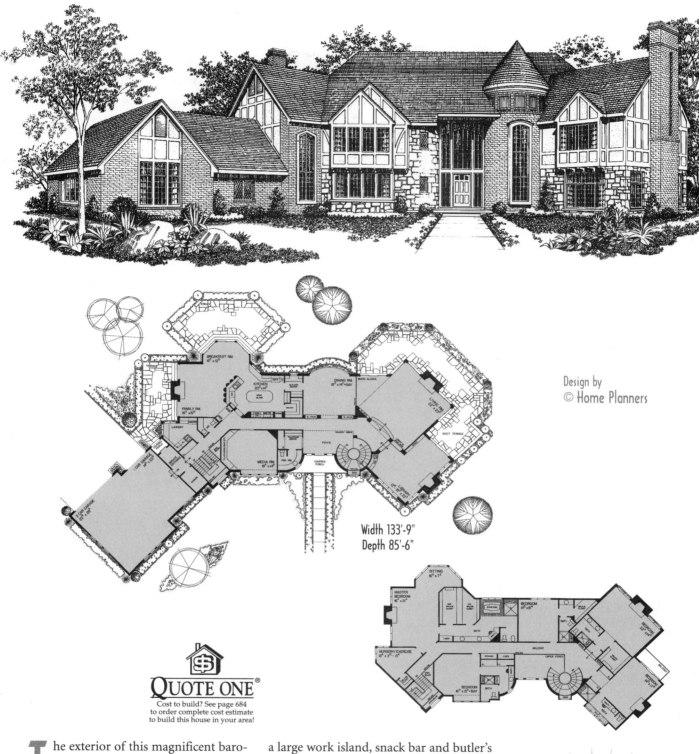

Width 133'-9"
Depth 85'-6"

Design by
© Home Planners

QUOTE ONE®

Cost to build? See page 684
to order complete cost estimate
to build this house in your area!

The exterior of this magnificent baronial Tudor conceals an interior fit for royalty. The two-story foyer reveals a circular staircase housed in a turret plus a powder room and a telephone center located for easy use by guests. Two steps lead down to the elegant living room with its music alcove or to the sumptuous library with a wet bar. Both rooms offer fireplaces, as does the family room. The kitchen is a chef's delight, with a large work island, snack bar and butler's pantry leading into the formal dining room. The second floor features four family bedrooms, two with fireplaces, and each with a private bath. The master suite pampers with a fireplace, His and Hers walk-in closets, a whirlpool bath and a sunny sitting area. Adjacent to the master suite is a nursery that would also make an ideal exercise room. A three-car garage nicely finishes the plan.

DESIGN 2955
First Floor: 3,840 square feet
Second Floor: 3,435 square feet
Total: 7,275 square feet

LUXURY HOMES

DESIGN U279

First Floor: 3,536 square feet
Second Floor: 1,690 square feet
Total: 5,226 square feet
Bonus Room: 546 square feet

Lavish, grand, luxurious—all of these words apply to this beautiful brick mansion with its expansive entrance. Inside, the two-story foyer leads to the formal rooms. A curving staircase points the way to the upper level with a balcony. The kitchen includes a cooktop island with snack bar, a walk-in pantry, plenty of counter and cabinet space, an adjacent nook and access to the porch. The master suite offers—among its many other amenities—a separate sitting area with a fireplace. Upstairs, each bedroom has a walk-in closet and private bath.

Design by
© Ahmann Design, Inc.

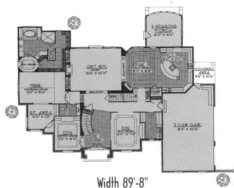

Width 89'-8"
Depth 76'-0"

REAR VIEW

DESIGN A212

First Floor: 2,588 square feet
Second Floor: 1,375 square feet
Total: 3,963 square feet
Bonus Room: 460 square feet

Though it looks like there are two entrances to this fine home, the one on the left is the main entry. Inside here, formal rooms flank the foyer. Directly ahead, the spacious lake gathering room offers a welcoming fireplace and access to the rear veranda. A huge kitchen features a worktop island, wet bar and adjacent morning room. The main-level master suite is complete with a huge dressing closet, access to the veranda and a lavish bath. Three suites inhabit the second-floor and share two full baths.

Design by
© Living Concepts Home Planning

Width 91'-4"
Depth 51'-10

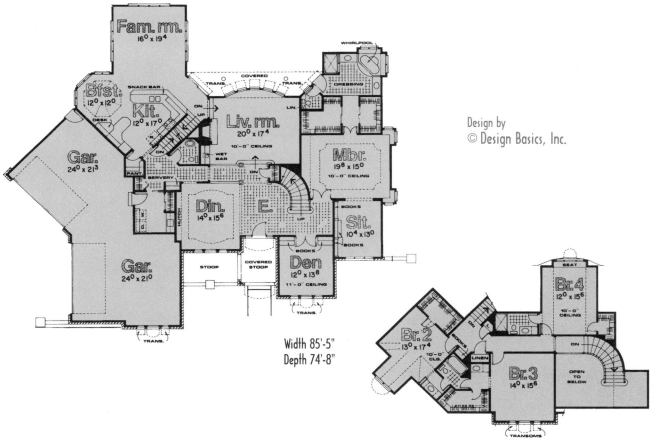

Design by
© Design Basics, Inc.

Width 85'-5"
Depth 74'-8"

The stone facade of this elegant traditional home evokes images of a quieter life, a life of harmony and comfortable luxury. An elegant floor plan allows you to carry that feeling inside. The tiled foyer offers entry to any room you choose, whether it be the secluded den with its built-in bookshelves, the formal dining room, the formal living room with its fireplace, wet bar and wall of windows, or the spacious rear family area and kitchen with its sunny breakfast nook. The master bedroom offers privacy on the first floor and features a sitting room with bookshelves, two walk-in closets and a master bath with a corner whirlpool tub. Three family bedrooms, each with a walk-in closet, and two baths make up the second floor. Bedroom 4 has a window seat and private bath.

DESIGN 7246
First Floor: 2,813 square feet
Second Floor: 1,091 square feet
Total: 3,904 square feet

LUXURY HOMES

DESIGN 7204

First Floor: 2,789 square feet
Second Floor: 1,038 square feet
Total: 3,827 square feet

The sophisticated lines and brick details of this house are stunning enhancements. The entry surveys a dramatic, curved staircase. French doors open to the den. The living room enjoys an eleven-foot ceiling and a fireplace flanked by transom windows. The casual family room includes a raised-hearth fireplace and a built-in desk. The gourmet kitchen provides two pantries, an island cooktop, wrapping counter, snack bar and private stairs to the second level. Four bedrooms include a pampering master suite.

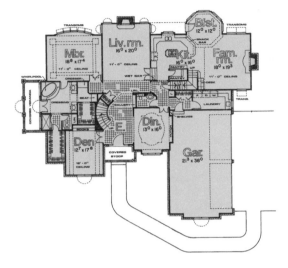

Design by
© Design Basics, Inc.

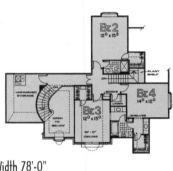

Width 78'-0"
Depth 73'-8"

DESIGN 7036

First Floor: 2,461 square feet
Second Floor: 1,019 square feet
Total: 3,480 square feet

Asymmetrical gables and arch-top windows define this traditional facade. Inside, the formal dining room features a stunning bay window. A secluded master suite enjoys a sitting area, lavish bath and walk-in closet designed for two. The family room contains a fireplace and its own bay window, which also brings light into the gourmet kitchen. Upstairs, three secondary bedrooms and a loft complete the plan.

Design by
© Design Basics, Inc.

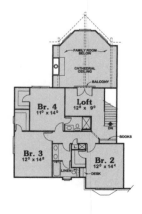

Width 74'-0"
Depth 79'-6"

Design by
© Design Basics, Inc.

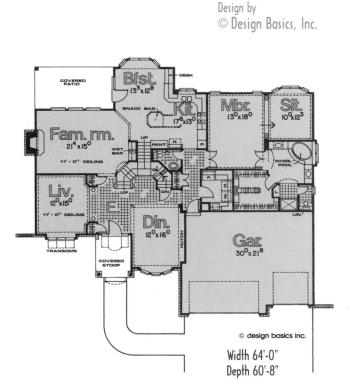

Width 64'-0"
Depth 60'-8"

© design basics inc.

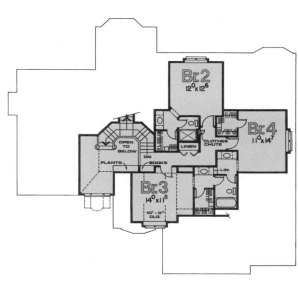

REAR VIEW

This elevation features wing walls and an elegant window-framed doorway. The tiled entry displays a curved staircase and opens to the formal living and dining rooms. The family room offers a window wall, wet bar and fireplace. A nearby breakfast bay provides a planning desk and access to the covered patio. The powder room has its own linen closet, while the laundry room offers space for a freezer. The master suite includes a raised sitting room with bay window and a pampering bath. Upstairs, one family bedroom enjoys a private bath, while two bedrooms share a compartmented bath. A clothes chute to the laundry room, a plant shelf and a built-in bookcase are appreciated extras on this level. A three-car garage sits to the front of the plan.

DESIGN 7242
First Floor: 2,169 square feet
Second Floor: 898 square feet
Total: 3,067 square feet

LUXURY HOMES

First Floor: 2,252 square feet
Second Floor: 920 square feet
Total: 3,172 square feet

A curving staircase graces the entry to this beautiful home and hints at the wealth of amenities found in the floor plan. Besides an oversized great room with fireplace and arched windows, there's a cozy hearth room with its own fireplace. The gourmet kitchen has a work island and breakfast area. A secluded den contains bookcases and an arched transom above double doors. The first-floor master bedroom is separated from three family bedrooms upstairs. Bedrooms 2 and 4 share a full bath while Bedroom 3 has its own private bath.

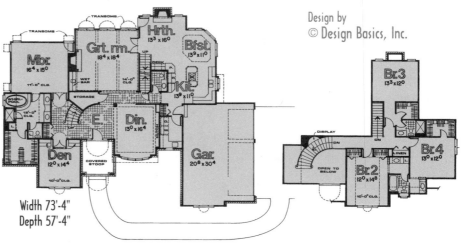

Design by
© Design Basics, Inc.

Width 73'-4"
Depth 57'-4"

First Floor: 1,631 square feet
Second Floor: 1,426 square feet
Total: 3,057 square feet

S tucco accents and graceful window treatments enhance the facade of this elegant home. Inside, the two-story foyer is flanked by a formal living room on the left and a bay-windowed den on the right. The efficient kitchen easily serves a beautiful breakfast room and a comfortable family room. Note the cathedral ceiling, transom windows, built-in bookcases and warming fireplace in the family room. The deluxe master suite is sure to please with its detailed ceiling, bayed sitting area, two walk-in closets and luxurious bath.

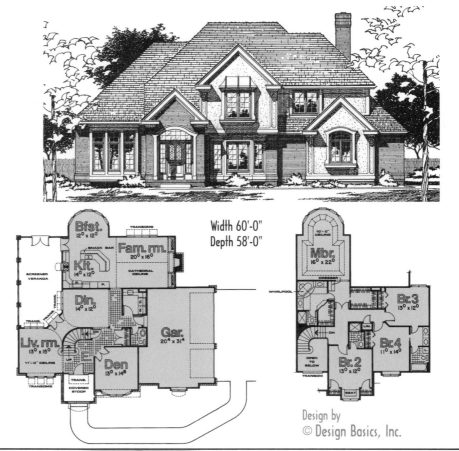

Width 60'-0"
Depth 58'-0"

Design by
© Design Basics, Inc.

LUXURY HOMES

www.homeplanners.com

Design by
© Design Basics, Inc.

Width 83'-5"
Depth 73'-4"

spectacular volume entry with a curving staircase opens through columns to the formal areas of this home. The sunken living room contains a fireplace, wet bar and bowed window overlooking the back property, while the front-facing dining room offers a built-in hutch and a handy servery. The family room, with bookcases surrounding a fireplace, is open to a bayed breakfast nook, and both are easily served from the nearby kitchen. Placed away from the living area of the home, the den provides a quiet retreat with a stunning window. The master suite is located on the first floor and has a most elegant bath and a huge walk-in closet. Second-floor bedrooms also include walk-in closets and private baths. A garage with angled bays holds four cars.

DESIGN 9346
First Floor: 2,617 square feet
Second Floor: 1,072 square feet
Total: 3,689 square feet

LUXURY HOMES

DESIGN 9366

First Floor: 2,603 square feet
Second Floor: 1,020 square feet
Total: 3,623 square feet

Perhaps the most notable characteristic of this traditional house is its masterful use of space. The glorious great room, open dining room and handsome den serve as the heart of the house. A cozy hearth room with a fireplace rounds out the kitchen and breakfast areas. The master bedroom, thoughtfully secluded on the first floor, opens to a private sitting room with fireplace. The second floor holds the three family bedrooms, each with its own private bath and walk-in closet.

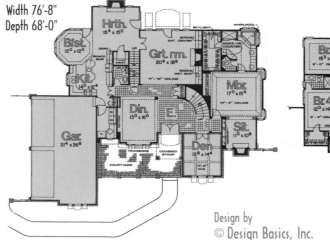

Width 76'-8"
Depth 68'-0"

Design by
© Design Basics, Inc.

Quote One®
Cost to build? See page 684
to order complete cost estimate
to build this house in your area!

DESIGN 9337

First Floor: 1,923 square feet
Second Floor: 1,852 square feet
Total: 3,775 square feet

Breathtaking details and bright windows highlight this luxurious two-story home. Just off the spectacular entry is an impressive private den. In the family room, three arched windows, a built-in entertainment center and a fireplace flanked by bookcases enhance comfort. Three secondary bedrooms provide private access to a bath. A sumptuous master suite awaits the homeowners with its built-in entertainment center, His and Hers walk-in closets, a whirlpool bath, through-fireplace and bayed gazebo sitting area.

Width 70'-0"
Depth 60'-0"

Design by
© Design Basics, Inc.

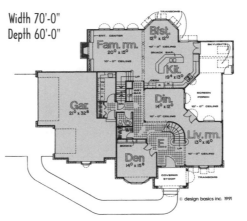

© design basics inc. 1991

LUXURY HOMES

Design by
© Design Basics, Inc.

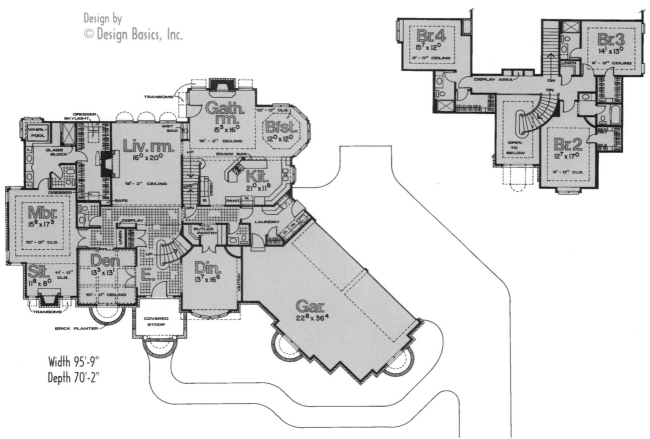

Width 95'-9"
Depth 70'-2"

A two-story foyer introduces the formal living zones of this plan—a den with a ten-foot ceiling, a dining room with an adjoining butler's pantry and a living room with a fireplace and a twelve-foot ceiling. For more casual living, the gathering room shares space with the octagonal breakfast area and the amenity-filled kitchen. Sleeping arrangements include a first-floor master bedroom. It offers a sitting area with a fireplace, a bath with a corner whirlpool tub and compartmented toilet, and an extensive closet. The second floor holds three bedrooms, each with a walk-in closet and a private bath.

DESIGN
9351
First Floor: 2,839 square feet
Second Floor: 1,111 square feet
Total: 3,950 square feet

LUXURY HOMES

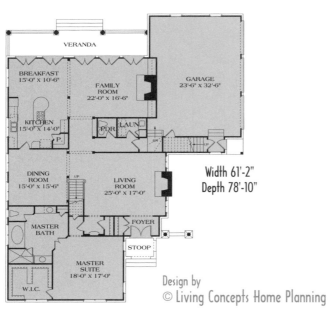

VERANDA

BREAKFAST
15'-0" x 10'-6"

FAMILY
ROOM
22'-0" x 16'-6"

GARAGE
23'-6" x 32'-6"

KITCHEN
15'-0" x 14'-0"

PDR.   LAUN.

DINING
ROOM
15'-0" x 15'-6"

LIVING
ROOM
25'-0" x 17'-0"

Width 61'-2"
Depth 78'-10"

MASTER
BATH

FOYER

STOOP

MASTER
SUITE
18'-0" x 17'-0"

W.I.C.

Design by
© Living Concepts Home Planning

REC.
ROOM
20'-0" x 15'-8"

MOTHER
IN-LAW
SUITE
12'-8" x 25'-6"

BATH

SUITE 5
15'-0" x 13'-0"

SUITE 4
15'-4" x 12'-6"

W.I.C.

W.I.C.

BATH

W.I.C.

BATH

SUITE 2
14'-4" x 17'-0"

SUITE 3
14'-6" x 17'-0"

**DESIGN
A295**

First Floor: 2,446 square feet
Second Floor: 1,988 square feet
Total: 4,434 square feet
Bonus Room: 651 square feet

Here is a home with Old World charm and the perfect footprint for a narrow lot. Decorative balustrades, vertical shutters and arches add nice finishing touches to the brick exterior. Inside, eleven-foot ceilings give added spaciousness throughout the first floor. The front stoop leads to a small foyer, then to the formal living room. A second fireplace is found in the family room, which is separated by columned arches from the breakfast area and the island kitchen. A wall of French doors brightens this area and opens to a veranda stretching across the back of the house. The master suite at the front pampers the homeowners with a large walk-in closet, dual vanities and a garden tub. Family members and guests will appreciate the second-floor sleeping quarters and recreation room. The mother-in-law-suite can be accessed at two points.

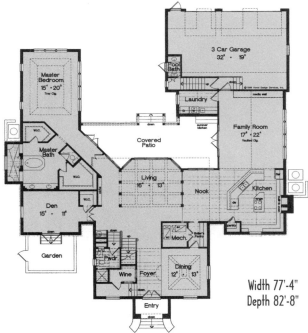

Width 77'-4"
Depth 82'-8"

Imagine yourself in the south of France with this French Provincial home. Inside, head straight for the beam-ceilinged living room, which looks out to the covered porch. The breakfast room, kitchen, and family room are all connected by the kitchen's island/ snack bar. The formal dining room at the front of the house contains a tray ceiling. The master suite at the back of the house features a wall of windows, two walk-in closets and a luxurious master bath. On the second level are three bedrooms, two of which share a bathroom and one that has its own. Other amenities include a den, which has a walk-in closet and French doors leading to a private garden, a wine cellar, and a powder room off of the garage for swimming parties. The garage holds three vehicles.

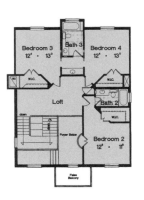

DESIGN 8701
First Floor: 3,079 square feet
Second Floor: 1,015 square feet
Total: 4,094 square feet
Bonus Room: 425 square feet

LUXURY HOMES

DESIGN A140

First Floor: 1,846 square feet
Second Floor: 1,249 square feet
Total: 3,095 square feet
Bonus Room: 394 square feet

A striking cove entrance sets the tone for this well-planned, two-story traditional design. Inside, the foyer leads directly into the imposing gathering room, with double-door access to the large rear deck. To the right, the efficient kitchen is nestled between a dining room and breakfast nook. The master suite has a garden bath and large walk-in closet, plus direct access to the deck. Three additional bedrooms are arranged upstairs off the long balcony overlooking the gathering room.

Width 52'-2"
Depth 66'-2"

Design by
© Living Concepts Home Planning

DESIGN A204

First Floor: 1,741 square feet
Second Floor: 1,884 square feet
Total: 3,625 square feet

Corner quoins, gabled rooflines and attractive shutters give this four-bedroom home plenty of curb appeal. Inside, the floor plan is designed for entertaining. For formal occasions, there is the living/dining room combination. Casual gatherings will be welcomed in the spacious family room, which features a fireplace and access to the rear deck. Upstairs, three bedrooms share two baths and access to a large playroom/loft. The master suite features a tray ceiling, two walk-in closets and a luxurious bath.

Width 61'-9"
Depth 48'-10"

Design by
© Living Concepts Home Planning

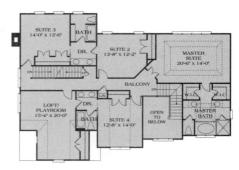

LUXURY HOMES

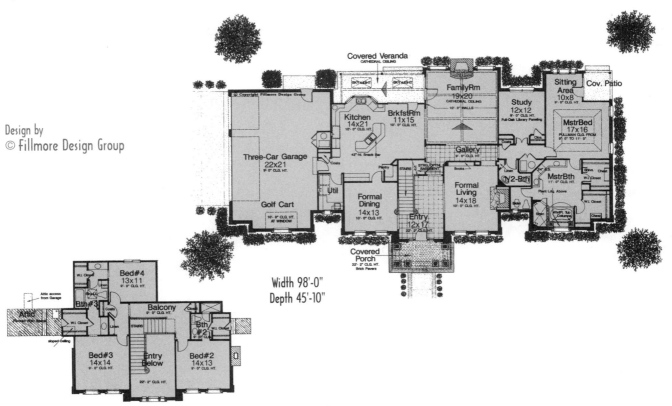

Design by
© Fillmore Design Group

Width 98'-0"
Depth 45'-10"

A covered, columned porch and symmetrically placed windows welcome you to this elegant brick home. The formal living room offers built-in bookshelves and one of two fireplaces, the other being found in the spacious family room. A gallery running between these rooms leads to the sumptuous master suite, which includes a sitting area, private covered patio and bath with two walk-in closets, dual vanities, large shower and garden tub. The step-saving kitchen features a work island and snack bar. The breakfast and family rooms have doors to the large covered veranda. Upstairs, you'll find three bedrooms and attic storage space. The three-car garage even has room for a golf cart.

DESIGN M149
First Floor: 2,814 square feet
Second Floor: 979 square feet
Total: 3,793 square feet

DESIGN S150

First Floor: 1,950 square feet
Second Floor: 1,680 square feet
Total: 3,630 square feet

Interesting windows and rooflines give a unique character to this stucco facade. To the right of the foyer, the study is highlighted by a beam ceiling, built-ins and floor-to-ceiling windows. The grand room includes a bayed sitting area and a fireplace. Another bay window brightens the breakfast room, which is found between the island kitchen and a den. The living room and a grand stair hall complete the first floor. The elegant stairway leads up to three family bedrooms and a sumptuous master suite.

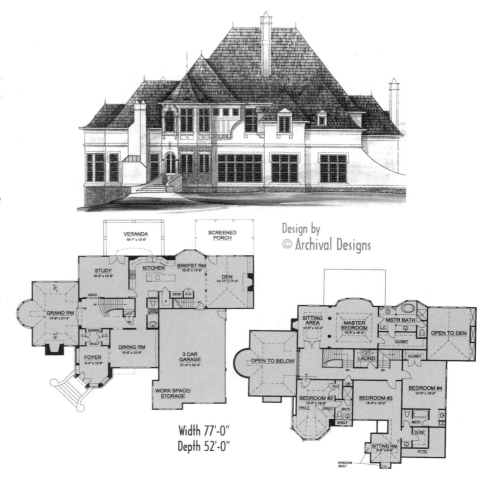

Design by
© Archival Designs

Width 77'-0"
Depth 52'-0"

DESIGN S101

First Floor: 2,032 square feet
Second Floor: 1,028 square feet
Total: 3,060 square feet

This narrow-lot design would be ideal for a golf course or lake lot. Inside the arched entry, the formal dining room is separated from the foyer and the massive grand room by decorative pillars. The family will enjoy gathering in the cozy keeping room with its fireplace and easy access to the large island kitchen and the sunny gazebo-style breakfast room. The secluded master suite features a uniquely designed bedroom and a luxurious bath with His and Hers walk-in closets.

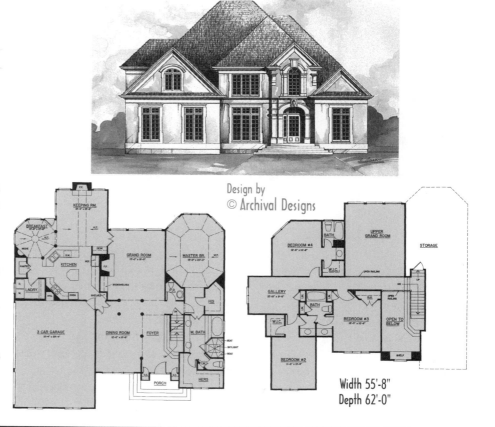

Design by
© Archival Designs

Width 55'-8"
Depth 62'-0"

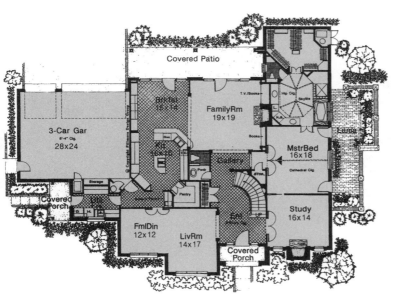

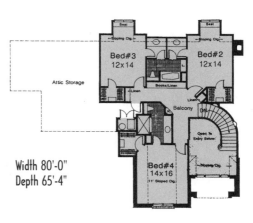

Covered Patio

Brkfst
15x14

FamilyRm
19x19

T.V./Books

Hip Clg.

Skylite

3-Car Gar
28x24
8'-4" Clg.

KIT.
15x16

Gallery

MstrBed
16x18

Cathedral Clg.

Lanai

storage

pantry

Covered
Porch

FmlDin
12x12

LivRm
14x17

Ent.

UP

Study
16x14

Covered
Porch

Bed#3
12x14

Bed#2
12x14

Attic Storage

Books/Linen

Linen

Linen

Balcony

Open To
Entry Below

Bed#4
14x16
11' Sloped Clg.

Width 80'-0"
Depth 65'-4"

Design by
© Fillmore Design Group

E uropean exterior styling with exquisite door and window detailing give this home plenty of curb appeal. Inside, a curving stairway in the large foyer leads to the upper level. Formal rooms reside to the left—a living room and dining room open to one another, perfect for entertaining. The kitchen features a walk-in pantry, work-top island and snack bar into the breakfast room. A volume ceiling in the master bath is just the beginning of the amenities found here, and is echoed by a cathedral ceiling in the master bedroom. Three secondary bedrooms—each with walk-in closets—share two full baths on the upper level. The three-car garage easily shelters the family fleet.

DESIGN M159
First Floor: 2,807 square feet
Second Floor: 1,063 square feet
Total: 3,870 square feet

LUXURY HOMES

DESIGN P394

First Floor: 1,488 square feet
Second Floor: 1,551 square feet
Total: 3,039 square feet

Dozens of windows bring light into this home. Windows frame the fireplace in the family room. Both the dining room and living room feature tall windows, and the guest suite has a pair of corner windows. In addition to a corner pantry and a cooktop island with a serving bar, the kitchen offers French doors to the outside. On the second floor, the master suite includes a vaulted bath with a radius window over the tub. Three secondary bedrooms offer pairs of windows and walk-in closets. Please specify basement or crawlspace foundation when ordering.

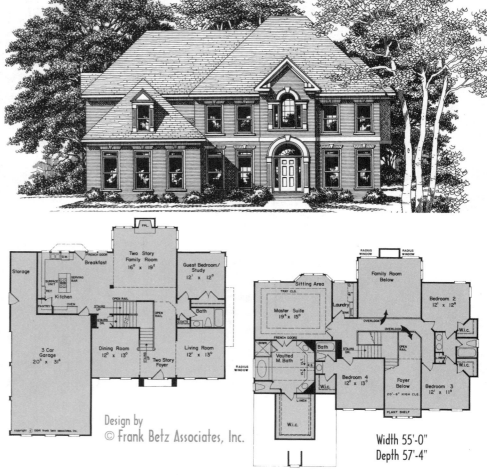

Design by
© Frank Betz Associates, Inc.

Width 55'-0"
Depth 57'-4"

DESIGN P138

First Floor: 1,415 square feet
Second Floor: 1,632 square feet
Total: 3,047 square feet

This impressive traditional design offers unique room placement to set it apart from the rest. The foyer leads to an angled two-story family room with a corner fireplace, a balcony overlook and a pass-through to the island kitchen. The bayed breakfast nook offers French-door access to the rear yard. Upstairs, two bedrooms share a full bath while Bedroom 4 features its own bath and a walk-in closet. The master suite offers a bayed sitting room. Please specify basement or crawlspace foundation when ordering.

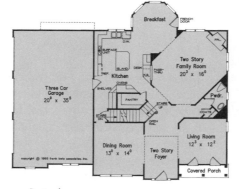

Design by
© Frank Betz Associates, Inc.

Width 56'-0"
Depth 47'-6"

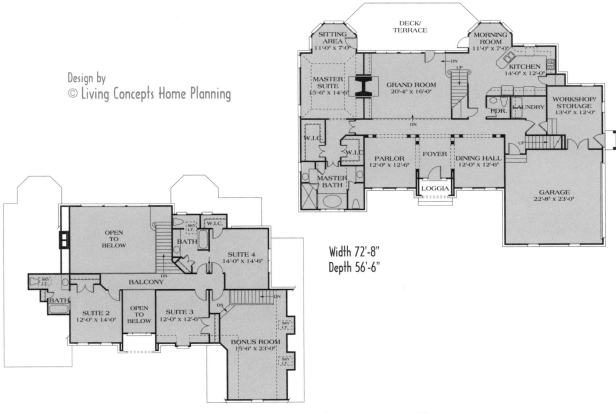

Design by
© Living Concepts Home Planning

Width 72'-8"
Depth 56'-6"

Designed for active lifestyles, this home caters to homeowners who enjoy dinner guests, privacy, luxurious surroundings and open spaces. Sets of columns define the foyer, parlor and dining hall, which all share a gallery hall that runs through the center of the plan. The grand room, on the other side of the gallery hall, opens to the wide deck/terrace, which is also accessed from the sitting area and morning room. The right wing contains a well-appointed kitchen, powder room, laundry room, workshop or storage area and garage. The left wing is dominated by the master suite with its sitting bay, fireplace, two walk-in closets and compartmented bath. The second floor features three bedrooms, one with a private bath. A large bonus room can be developed later.

LUXURY HOMES

**DESIGN
A188**
First Floor: 2,198 square feet
Second Floor: 1,028 square feet
Total: 3,226 square feet
Bonus Room: 466 square feet

DESIGN P222

First Floor: 2,294 square feet
Second Floor: 869 square feet
Total: 3,163 square feet
Bonus Room: 309 square feet

I t will be a pleasure to come home to this traditional French design. From the pleasing covered porch, the two-story foyer leads through an arched opening to the formal dining room and also to the charming bayed living room. The first-floor master suite provides its own vaulted sitting room, walk-in closet and spacious bath. The two-story family room features a fireplace and rear views. Three more bedrooms and two baths complete the upper level. Please specify basement or crawlspace foundation when ordering.

Design by
© Frank Betz Associates, Inc.

Width 63'-6"
Depth 63'-0"

DESIGN P224

First Floor: 2,429 square feet
Second Floor: 654 square feet
Total: 3,083 square feet
Bonus Room: 420 square feet

K eystones that cap each window, a terrace that dresses up the entrance, and a bay-windowed turret add up to a totally refined exterior. Inside, open planning employs columns to define the foyer, dining room and two-story family room. A first-floor master suite is designed with every amenity. The second floor contains two bedrooms, two baths and an optional bonus room. Please specify basement or crawlspace foundation when ordering.

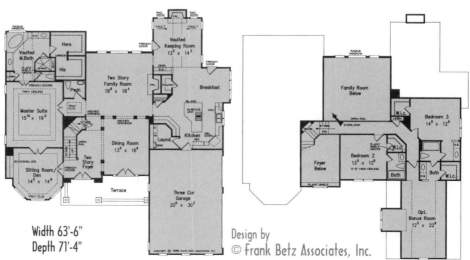

Width 63'-6"
Depth 71'-4"

Design by
© Frank Betz Associates, Inc.

LUXURY HOMES

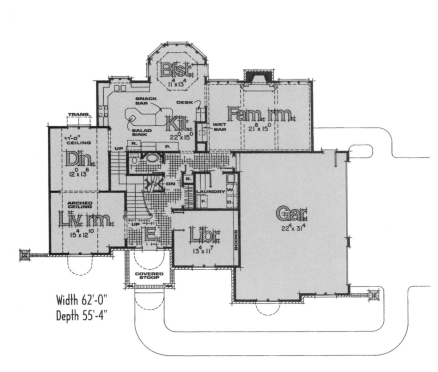

Width 62'-0"
Depth 55'-4"

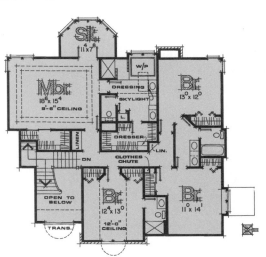

Design by
© Design Basics, Inc.

An attractive facade and an amenity-filled interior make this home a showplace both outside and in. Immediately off the two-story foyer are the living room and connecting formal dining room, both with arched ceilings, and the quiet library with built-in bookcases. The enormous gourmet kitchen features a large island work counter/snack bar, a pantry, desk and gazebo breakfast nook. Just steps away is the spacious family room with a grand fireplace and windows overlooking the backyard. Upstairs two baths serve three family bedrooms and a luxurious master suite contains a bay-windowed sitting room, detailed ceiling and skylit bath with whirlpool tub.

DESIGN 9229
First Floor: 1,709 square feet
Second Floor: 1,597 square feet
Total: 3,306 square feet

LUXURY HOMES

Design by
© Fillmore Design Group

Width 84'-0"
Depth 55'-7"

DESIGN M169
First Floor: 2,612 square feet
Second Floor: 1,242 square feet
Total: 3,854 square feet

Stones with brick accents create an exterior with rear country charm. The feeling continues inside, where brick pavers are used as flooring for the entry, gallery, kitchen and breakfast room. To the left of the entry, the formal living and dining rooms range across the front of the house, while a study with wood flooring, bookshelves and a fireplace is to the right. The great room also boasts a fireplace, as well as access to a covered patio. The master suite includes a bayed sitting area and an elegant bath with dual vanities and walk-in closets and an angled garden tub. Upstairs, two bedrooms share a bath that has twin vanities, while a third bedroom includes a private bath. A sitting area in the balcony overlooks the entry. A three-car garage faces to the back of the plan.

www.homeplanners.com

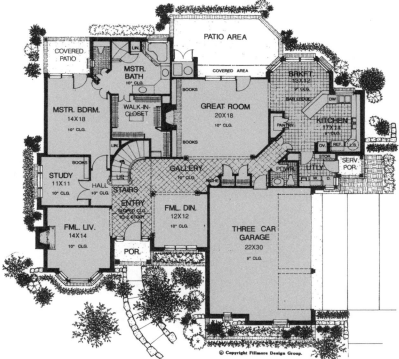

PATIO AREA

COVERED AREA

COVERED PATIO

MSTR. BATH
10" CLG.

BOOKS

BRKFST
12X12
9" CLG.
BAR-BEQUE

WALK-IN CLOSET

MSTR. BDRM.
14X18
10" CLG.

GREAT ROOM
20X18
10" CLG.

KITCHEN
17X18
9" CLG.

BOOKS

PANTRY

OV. REF.

DW

STOR.

SERV. POR.

GALLERY
10" CLG.

POWD.

UTLY

W D

BOOKS

STUDY
11X11
10" CLG.

HALL
10" CLG.

STAIRS UP

ENTRY
SLOPED CLG. TO 2 STORY

FML. DIN.
12X12
10" CLG.

THREE CAR GARAGE
22X30
9" CLG.

FML. LIV.
14X14
10" CLG.

POR.

© Copyright Fillmore Design Group.

BDRM.#3
12X14
SLOPED CLG. TO 8'

HALL

BDRM.#2
12X12
8" CLG.

STAIRS DN.

OPEN ABOVE ENTRY
SLOPED CLG. TO 2 STORY

BDRM.#4
12X12
8" CLG.

FUTURE BONUS ROOM

Width 70'-0"
Depth 63'-2"

H ere's a cottage that would have provided plenty of room for Goldilocks AND the three bears! Wonderful rooflines top a brick exterior with cedar and stone accents— and lots of English country charm. Stone wing walls extend the front profile and a cedar hood tops the large bay window. The two-story entry reveals a graceful curving staircase and opens to the formal living and dining rooms. Fireplaces are found in the living room as well as the great room, which also boasts built-in bookcases and access to the rear patio. The kitchen and breakfast nook add to the informal area and include a snack bar. A private patio is part of the master suite, which also offers an intriguing corner tub, twin vanities, a large walk-in closet and nearby study. Three family bedrooms and a bonus room comprise the second floor.

DESIGN M176
First Floor: 2,438 square feet
Second Floor: 882 square feet
Total: 3,320 square feet

LUXURY HOMES

DESIGN C118

First Floor: 2,190 square feet
Second Floor: 854 square feet
Total: 3,044 square feet
Bonus Room: 282 square feet

Design by
© James Fahy Design

Repeating elliptical transom glass highlights this brick and clapboard-sided transitional front elevation. The adjoining living and dining rooms with pillared entries provide a luxurious formal area off the front foyer. The first-floor master suite features a walk-through dressing area with generous closets opening to a luxurious master bath. The spacious kitchen opens to an octagon-shaped dinette and tray ceiling. The second floor features a large balcony/loft with three bedrooms and a bonus room.

Width 77'-8"
Depth 48'-0"

DESIGN P178

First Floor: 1,849 square feet
Second Floor: 1,773 square feet
Total: 3,622 square feet

Asymmetrical gables set off a fresh blend of shingles and siding on this Victorian adaptation. Interior amenities draw on the future, starting with a balcony bridge that overlooks both the foyer and the family room. Upstairs, a luxuriant master bedroom opens to a vaulted sitting area with its own fireplace. A nearby family bedroom offers its own bath, while two additional bedrooms share a full bath. Please specify basement or crawlspace foundation when ordering.

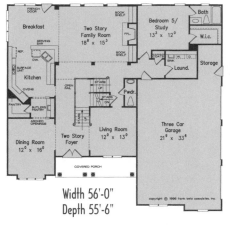

Width 56'-0"
Depth 55'-6"

Design by
© Frank Betz Associates, Inc.

LUXURY HOMES

DOHERTY

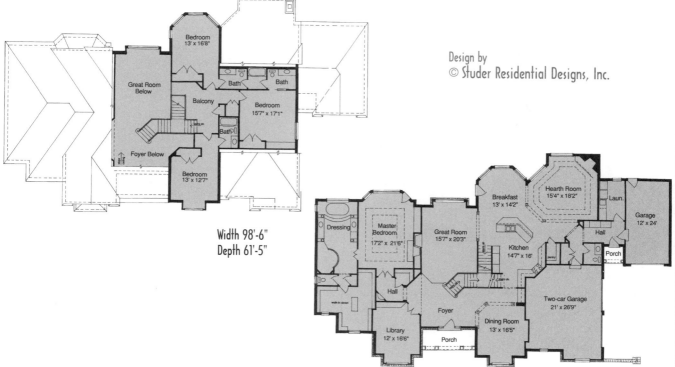

Bedroom
13' x 16'8"

Great Room
Below

Balcony

Bath

Bath

Bedroom
15'7" x 17'1"

Bath

Foyer Below

Bedroom
13' x 12'7"

Width 98'-6"
Depth 61'-5"

Design by
© Studer Residential Designs, Inc.

Breakfast
13' x 14'2"

Hearth Room
15'4" x 18'2"

Laun.

Garage
12' x 24'

Dressing

Master
Bedroom
17'2" x 21'6"

Great Room
15'7" x 20'3"

Kitchen
14'7" x 16'

Hall

Porch

Hall

walk-in closet

Hall

Foyer

Two-car Garage
21' x 26'9"

Library
12' x 16'6"

Porch

Dining Room
13' x 16'5"

The richness of natural stone and brick set the tone for the warmth and charm of this transitional home. The expansive entry is adorned with an angled stairway, a grand opening to the formal dining room and a view of the spectacular great room. A deluxe bath and a dressing area with a walk-in closet complement the master bedroom. The spacious island kitchen opens to the breakfast room and

the cozy hearth room. The library retreat boasts built-in bookshelves and a fourteen-foot ceiling. Access to the second floor is provided from the foyer or the kitchen. A dramatic view greets you at the second-floor balcony. Two family bedrooms share a tandem bath that has separate vanities while a third bedroom includes a private bath. The plan includes one– and two-car garages.

DESIGN
B568
First Floor: 3,364 square feet
Second Floor: 1,198 square feet
Total: 4,562 square feet

LUXURY HOMES

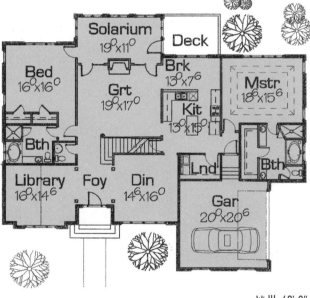

Solarium
19⁰x11⁰

Deck

Brk
13⁰x7⁶

Mstr
18⁰x15⁶

Bed
16⁰x16⁰

Grt
19⁰x17⁰

Kit
13⁰x15⁰

Bth

Bth

Library
16⁰x14⁶

Foy

Din
14⁶x16⁰

Lnd

Gar
20⁰x20⁶

Design by
© United Design Association, Inc.

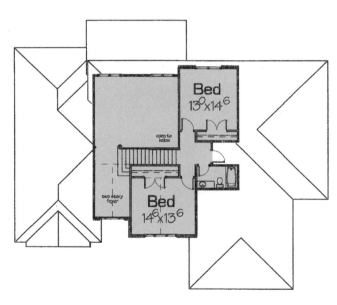

Bed
13⁰x14⁶

open to below

two-story foyer

Bed
14⁶x13⁶

Width 68'-0"
Depth 59'-8"

DESIGN V012

First Floor: 2,586 square feet
Second Floor: 583 square feet
Total: 3,169 square feet
Bonus Room: 805 square feet

This traditional estate home embodies the majestic grace of centuries-old architecture. The two-story foyer and great room showcase a beautiful open staircase and second-floor balcony. The great room offers access to a beautiful solarium. The spacious kitchen includes an island and breakfast area overlooking the rear deck. The first-floor master suite features a tray ceiling, large walk-in closet and master bath with whirlpool tub. A second bedroom on this level is complete with a private bath and access to the solarium. For reading pleasure, a library with a bumped-out window is located toward the front. The second floor includes two bedrooms and a bath, with direct attic access.

Design by
© Fillmore Design Group

Width 99'-10"
Depth 74'-10"

Multiple rooflines, a stone, brick and siding facade and an absolutely grand entrance combine to give this home the look of luxury. Things to note inside: a guest suite on the first floor, a large study next to the first-floor master suite, fireplaces in both the family room and the formal living room, private baths for each of the second-floor bedrooms and a spacious playroom. The kitchen offers a large walk-in pantry and an angled snack bar to the breakfast room. Note the nearby utility room, rear entry and powder room. The three-car garage provides space for a covered drive and a parking court.

DESIGN M154
First Floor: 3,248 square feet
Second Floor: 1,426 square feet
Total: 4,674 square feet

LUXURY HOMES

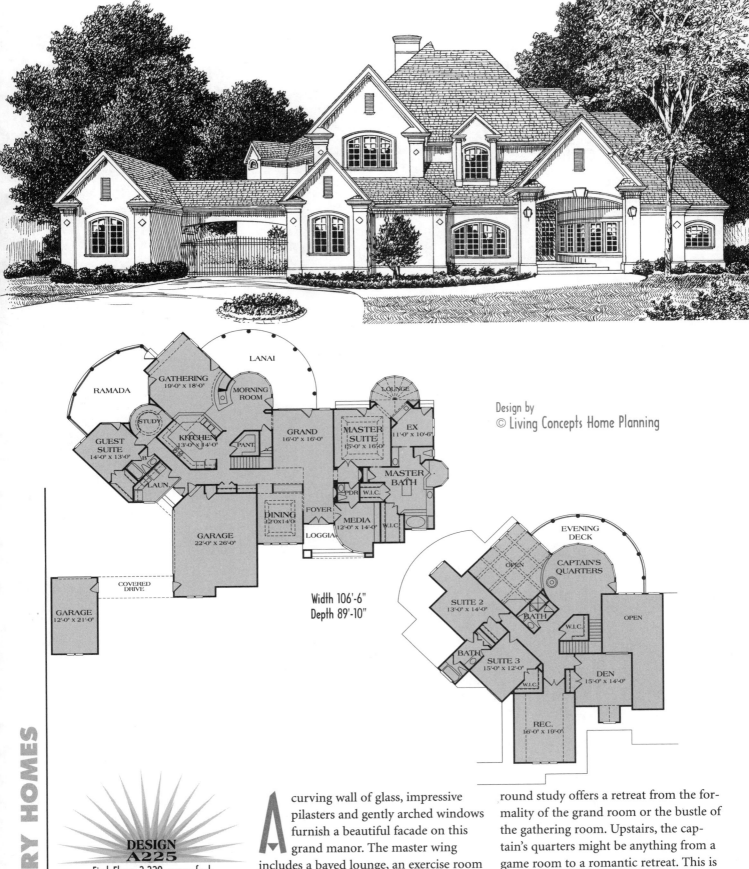

RAMADA

GATHERING
19'-0" x 18'-0"

LANAI

MORNING
ROOM

STUDY

GUEST
SUITE
14'-0" x 13'-0"

KITCHEN
13'-0" x 14'-0"

PANT.

GRAND
16'-0" x 16'-0"

MASTER
SUITE
15'-0" x 16'-0"

LOUNGE

EX
11'-0" x 10'-6"

Design by
© Living Concepts Home Planning

B.

LAUN.

MASTER
BATH

PDR

W.I.C.

GARAGE
22'-0" x 26'-0"

DINING
12'0x14'0

FOYER

MEDIA
12'-0" x 14'-0"

W.I.C.

LOGGIA

COVERED
DRIVE

GARAGE
12'-0" x 21'-0"

Width 106'-6"
Depth 89'-10"

EVENING
DECK

OPEN

CAPTAIN'S
QUARTERS

SUITE 2
13'-0" x 14'-0"

BATH

W.I.C.

OPEN

BATH

SUITE 3
15'-0" x 12'-0"

DEN
15'-0" x 14'-0"

W.I.C.

REC.
16'-0" x 19'-0"

LUXURY HOMES

DESIGN
A225
First Floor: 3,329 square feet
Second Floor: 1,485 square feet
Total: 4,814 square feet
Bonus Room: 300 square feet

A curving wall of glass, impressive pilasters and gently arched windows furnish a beautiful facade on this grand manor. The master wing includes a bayed lounge, an exercise room and a media room, as well as a sumptuous bath. A glass-enclosed morning room completes the gourmet kitchen, while a round study offers a retreat from the formality of the grand room or the bustle of the gathering room. Upstairs, the captain's quarters might be anything from a game room to a romantic retreat. This is truly a home to challenge your imagination! Note the double garages connected by a covered drive.

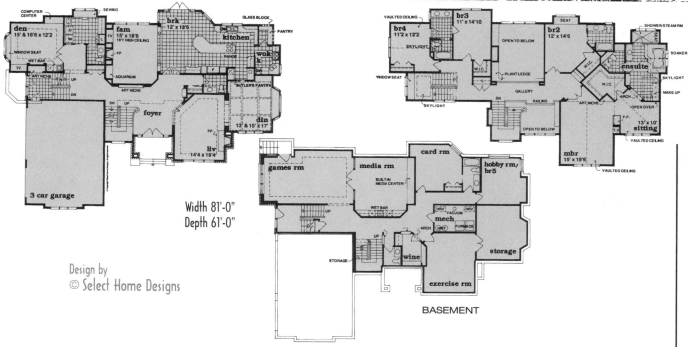

Width 81'-0"
Depth 61'-0"

Design by
© Select Home Designs

BASEMENT

This grand, two-story European home is adorned with a facade of stucco and brick, meticulously appointed with details for gracious living. Guests enter through a portico to find a stately, two-story foyer. The formal living room features a tray ceiling and fireplace and is joined by a charming dining room with large bay window. A butler's pantry joins the dining room to the gourmet kitchen that holds a separate wok kitchen, an island work center and a breakfast room with double doors leading to a rear patio. The nearby family room holds a built-in aquarium, a media center and fireplace. A den with tray ceiling, window seat and built-in computer center is tucked in a corner for privacy. The laundry is large enough to accommodate a sewing center. Served by two separate staircases, the second floor features a spectacular master suite with a separate sitting room, oversized closet and bath with shower/steam room and spa tub. If you choose, you may develop the lower level to include an exercise room, hobby room, card room, game room, media room, wine cellar and large storage space.

DESIGN Q457
First Floor: 2,596 square feet
Second Floor: 2,233 square feet
Total: 4,829 square feet
Bonus Space: 2,012 square feet

LUXURY HOMES

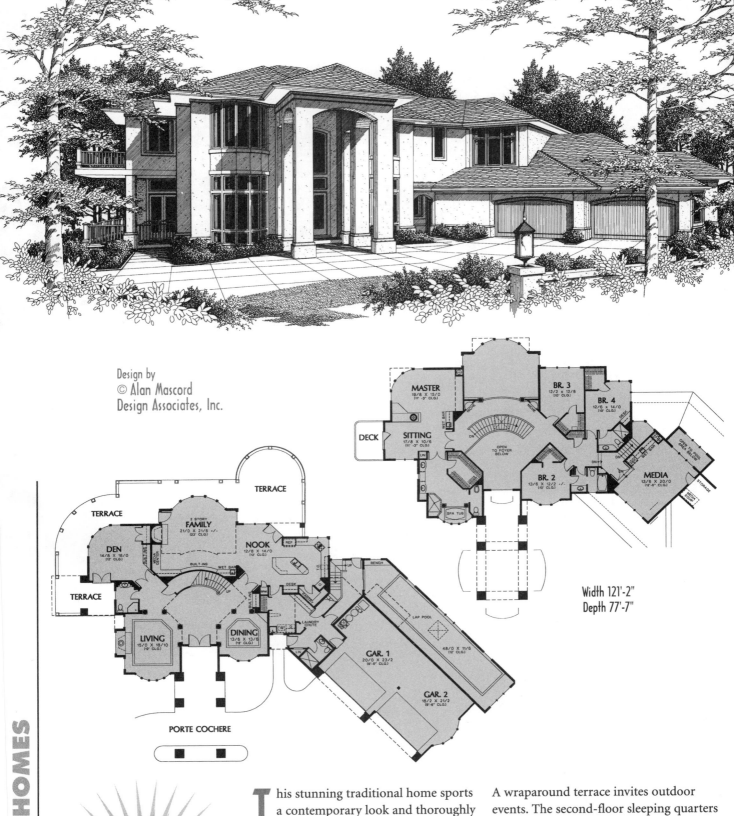

Design by
© Alan Mascord
Design Associates, Inc.

MASTER
19/8 X 15/0
(11' -3" CLG.)

BR. 3
12/2 X 12/6
(10' CLG.)

BR. 4
12/6 X 14/0
(10' CLG.)

DECK

SITTING
17/8 X 10/6
(11' -3" CLG.)

WET BAR

OPEN TO FOYER BELOW

BR. 2
13/6 X 12/2
(10' CLG.)

MEDIA
13/6 X 20/0
(12' -6" CLG.)

OPEN TO POOL AREA BELOW

SPA TUB

Width 121'-2"
Depth 77'-7"

TERRACE

TERRACE

TERRACE

2 STORY
FAMILY
21/0 X 21/6 +/-
(23' CLG.)

NOOK
12/8 X 14/0
(12' CLG.)

DEN
14/8 X 16/0
(12' CLG.)

REF.

WET BAR

BUILT-INS

BENCH

DESK

LIVING
15/0 X 18/10
(12' CLG.)

DINING
13/6 X 13/6
(12' CLG.)

LAUNDRY CHUTE

GAR. 1
20/0 X 23/2
(9'-6" CLG.)

LAP POOL
48/0 X 11/6
(12' CLG.)

GAR. 2
18/2 X 21/2
(9'-6" CLG.)

PORTE COCHERE

DESIGN 7530
First Floor: 2,709 square feet
Second Floor: 2,321 square feet
Total: 5,030 square feet

This stunning traditional home sports a contemporary look and thoroughly up-to-date amenities inside. A dazzling, spacious foyer opens to the formal living and dining rooms through arched columns. The heart of the home is a grand family room, which features a curved wall of glass offering great views.

A wraparound terrace invites outdoor events. The second-floor sleeping quarters include a grand master suite, which provides a sitting area that opens to a private deck. Three secondary bedrooms cluster around a hall leading to a sizable media room. Notice the large double garages on the right side of the plan.

Main Level: 2,773 square feet
Lower Level: 1,214 square feet
Total: 3,987 square feet

An understated stucco facade creates an elegant picture of this sloping-lot home. The foyer features a barrel-vaulted ceiling, which ties into the arched opening leading to the great room and its fourteen-foot ceiling. The master suite, the great room, the kitchen and breakfast room all provide access to the large deck. Downstairs, the basement includes two bedrooms with private baths. Nine-foot ceilings in the basement give the rooms an open, spacious feeling. This home may also be built with a slab foundation.

Width 70'-8"
Depth 91'-2"

Design by
© Larry E. Belk Designs

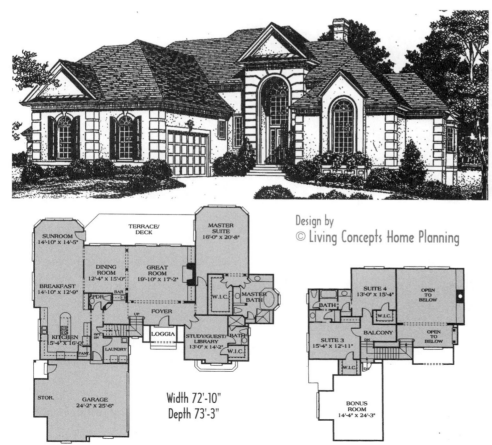

First Floor: 2,520 square feet
Second Floor: 723 square feet
Total: 3,243 square feet
Bonus Room: 321 square feet

Corner quoins, high arched windows and a dramatic entry all spell classic estate details. Note the multi-purpose room just off the foyer that can be used as a study or a guest room. The great room is separated from the dining room by only columns. The U-shaped island kitchen is open to the breakfast room and its adjoining sun room. The master bath holds a spa tub in a bay window, separate shower and double sinks. Two family bedrooms with walk-in closets share a full bath.

Design by
© Living Concepts Home Planning

Width 72'-10"
Depth 73'-3"

LUXURY HOMES

Design by
© Larry E. Belk Designs

Width 73'-8"
Depth 58'-6"

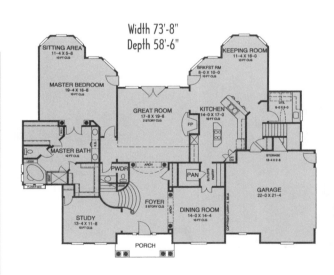

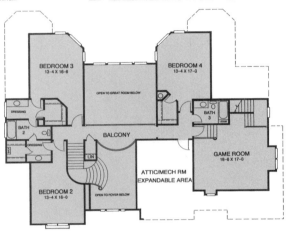

REAR VIEW

DESIGN 8034

First Floor: 2,639 square feet
Second Floor: 1,625 square feet
Total: 4,264 square feet

European traditional style is the hallmark of this bestselling plan. The two-story foyer is graced by a lovely staircase and a balcony overlook from upstairs. Two columns flank the entry to the great room notable for its beautiful window wall facing the rear grounds. Two-story double bays on the rear of the home form the keeping room and the breakfast room on one side and the master bedroom and its sitting area on the other. A huge walk-in pantry and an adjacent butler's pantry connect the dining room to the kitchen. Rear stairs from the kitchen join the family gathering area with the three bedrooms and game room upstairs. With a large study downstairs and walk-in attic storage available for expansion upstairs, this home provides all the amenities needed for today's busy family. Please specify basement or slab foundation when ordering.

HIS

MASTER BATH
10 FT CLG

HERS

MASTER BEDROOM
16-0 X 15-4
10 FT CLG

COVERED PORCH

BRKFST
12-6 X 10-6
10 FT CLG

LIVING ROOM
19-0 X 15-4
VAULTED TO 2 STORY

KIT
12-6 X 15-4
10 FT CLG

FAMILY ROOM
15-0 X 19-0
10 FT CLG

FP

BATH 2

UTIL

PWDR

BEDRM 2/STUDY
13-8 X 12-4
10 FT CLG

FOYER
2 STORY CEILING

DINING ROOM
10-8 X 12-8
10 FT CLG

PORCH

3 CAR GARAGE

COPYRIGHT LARRY E. BELK

Quote One®
Cost to build? See page 684
to order complete cost estimate
to build this house in your area!

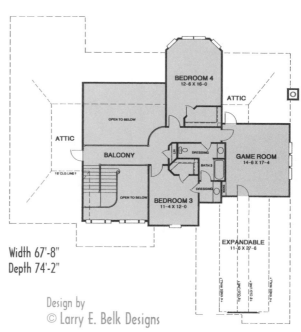

ATTIC

BEDROOM 4
12-6 X 16-0

ATTIC

OPEN TO BELOW

BALCONY

DRESSING

BATH 3

GAME ROOM
14-6 X 17-4

18' CLG LINE

DRESSING

BEDROOM 3
11-4 X 12-0

OPEN TO BELOW

EXPANDABLE
11-6 X 27-6

4' KNEE WALLS

18' CLG LINE

Width 67'-8"
Depth 74'-2"

Design by
© Larry E. Belk Designs

An arresting double arch gives this European-style home a commanding presence. Once inside, a two-story foyer provides an open view directly through the formal living room to the rear grounds beyond. The use of square columns defining the formal dining room adds an air of elegance to the home. A spacious kitchen with a prep island and bayed breakfast area share space with the family room. A welcoming fireplace is visible to all areas and creates an area for gatherings. The private master suite features dual lavs, His and Hers walk-in closets, a corner garden tub and separate shower. A second bedroom, which doubles as a nursery or a study, and a full bath are located nearby. Two bedrooms and a bath with two dressing areas are located on the second floor. A large game room completes this wonderful family home. Expandable space for an additional bedroom is available over the three-car garage. Please specify basement, crawlspace or slab foundation when ordering.

DESIGN 8048
First Floor: 2,469 square feet
Second Floor: 1,025 square feet
Total: 3,494 square feet

L

LUXURY HOMES

Photo by Mark Englund

The home, as shown in the photograph, may differ from the actual blueprints. For more detailed information, please check the floor plans carefully.

Width 79'-0"
Depth 60'-4"

Design by
© Frank Betz Associates, Inc.

DESIGN P336
First Floor: 2,190 square feet
Second Floor: 1,865 square feet
Total: 4,055 square feet

This European-style home offers an array of stunning windows that serve both aesthetic and practical purposes. Inside, the two-story foyer leads to the grand staircase and balcony overlook above. A gallery hall leads to the generous family room, dressed with a plant shelf, fireplace and columns. The space between the breakfast area and kitchen is defined by a food-prep island. The kitchen also contains dual ovens, extra counter space and a sizable pantry. The right wing of the second floor is dedicated to a rambling master suite, with its own sitting room, fireplace, master bath and two very large walk-in closets. The other three bedrooms have access to a bathroom. Also notice the three-car garage, second staircase and fifth bedroom/study on the first floor. Please specify basement or slab foundation when ordering.

Photo by Exposures Unlimited, Ron & Donna Kolb

The home, as shown in the photograph, may differ from the actual blueprints. For more detailed information, please check the floor plans carefully.

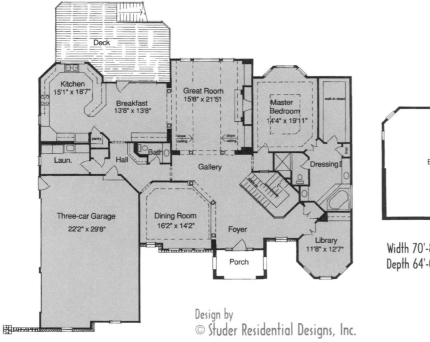

Deck

Kitchen
15'1" x 18'7"

Breakfast
13'8" x 13'8"

Great Room
15'8" x 21'5"

Master Bedroom
14'4" x 19'11"

walk-in closet

pantry

Laun.

Hall

Bath

Gallery

slope ceiling

slope ceiling

Dressing

Three-car Garage
22'2" x 29'8"

Dining Room
16'2" x 14'2"

Foyer

Library
11'8" x 12'7"

Porch

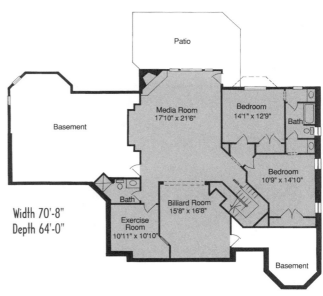

Patio

Basement

Media Room
17'10" x 21'6"

Bedroom
14'1" x 12'9"

Bath

Bedroom
10'9" x 14'10"

Bath

Billiard Room
15'8" x 16'8"

Exercise Room
10'11" x 10'10"

Basement

Width 70'-8"
Depth 64'-0"

Design by
© Studer Residential Designs, Inc.

Stone accents provide warmth and character to the exterior of this home. An arched entry leads to the interior, where elegant window styles and dramatic ceiling treatments create an impressive showplace. The gourmet kitchen and breakfast room offer a spacious area for chores and family gatherings, while providing a striking view through the great room to the fireplace wall. For convenience, the butler's pantry is located in the hall leading to the dining room. An extravagant master suite and a library with built-in shelves round out the main floor. Accented by a wood rail, an extra-wide stairway leads to the lower level, where two additional bedrooms, a media room, a billiards room and an exercise room complete the home. Note the three-car garage at left.

DESIGN B502
Main Level: 2,582 square feet
Lower Level: 1,746 square feet
Total: 4,328 square feet

LUXURY HOMES

DESIGN A145

First Floor: 2,452 square feet
Second Floor: 1,079 square feet
Total: 3,531 square feet
Bonus Room: 273 square feet

A central peaked gable above a copper-hooded bay window lends a touch of class to the exterior facade of this four-bedroom plan. Inside, two fireplaces warm the parlor/study. The spacious grand room provides doors leading to the rear deck. A secluded master retreat features a sloped ceiling in the bedroom with a dual-entry walk-in closet and master bath with all the amenities. The open island kitchen and morning room look out onto the rear deck. Please specify basement or crawlspace foundation when ordering.

Design by
© Living Concepts Home Planning

Width 68'-0"
Depth 77'-8"

DESIGN A222

First Floor: 2,886 square feet
Second Floor: 1,561 square feet
Total: 4,447 square feet
Bonus Room: 338 square feet

A stucco exterior with stone accents and a three-car garage provide an impressive introduction to this well-planned home. The two-story foyer opens to the great room. On the left, the kitchen serves the morning room, family room and dining room. The den/office stands adjacent to a hall bath. On the opposite side of the plan, the master suite opens to the terrace and features two walk-in closets and a luxurious bath. The second floor contains four family bedrooms, three baths and a bonus room.

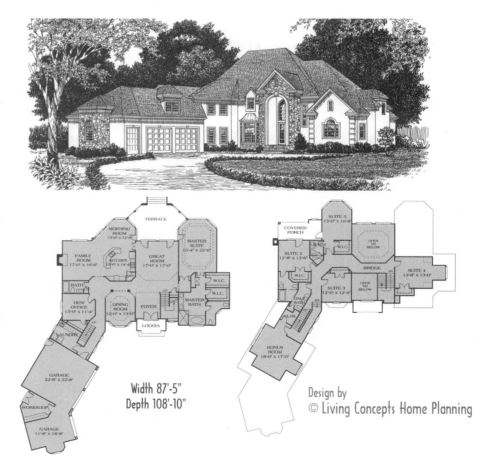

Width 87'-5"
Depth 108'-10"

Design by
© Living Concepts Home Planning

LUXURY HOMES

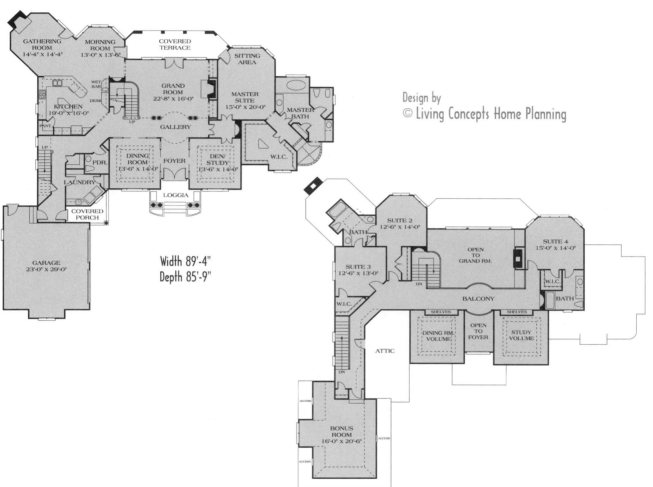

Design by
© Living Concepts Home Planning

Width 89'-4"
Depth 85'-9"

Double columns flank a raised loggia that leads to a beautiful two-story foyer. Flanking this elegance, a formal dining room lies to the left while a den or study opens to the right. Straight ahead, under a balcony and defined by yet more pillars, is the spacious grand room. Here, a warming fireplace and direct access to the rear covered terrace are offered. For casual get-togethers, the gathering room presents another

fireplace, as well as an adjacent morning room full of natural light from a bay window. The master suite is lavish with its amenities, which include a bayed sitting area, direct access to the rear terrace, a huge walk-in closet and a sumptuous bath. The rest of the sleeping zone is located upstairs. Here, Suites 2 and 3 share a skylit bath, while Suite 4 has a private bath—perfect for a guest suite. A bonus room sits over the garage.

DESIGN A223
First Floor: 3,143 square feet
Second Floor: 1,348 square feet
Total: 4,491 square feet
Bonus Room: 368 square feet

LUXURY HOMES

DESIGN P248

First Floor: 1,786 square feet
Second Floor: 1,739 square feet
Total: 3,525 square feet

European details bring charm and *joie de vivre* to this traditional home. Casual living space includes a two-story family room with a centered fireplace. A sizable kitchen, with an island serving bar and a French door to the rear property, leads to the formal dining room through a butler's pantry. The second floor includes a generous master suite and three family bedrooms—one with a private bath. Please specify basement or crawlspace foundation when ordering.

Design by
© Frank Betz Associates, Inc.

Width 59'-0"
Depth 53'-0"

DESIGN P247

First Floor: 1,583 square feet
Second Floor: 1,632 square feet
Total: 3,215 square feet

An arch-top entry and a clerestory window add European spirit to this stunning country home. Inside, arched openings help define the formal rooms, while a two-story family room enjoys wide views of the outdoors complemented by the coziness of an extended-hearth fireplace. Upstairs, a lavish master suite offers a vaulted sitting room with its own hearth, and a rambling bath with two walk-in closets with a skylit spa tub. Please specify basement or crawlspace foundation when ordering.

Width 58'-4"
Depth 50'-0"

Design by
© Frank Betz Associates, Inc.

LUXURY HOMES

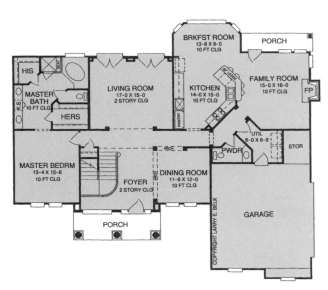

Design by
© Larry E. Belk Designs

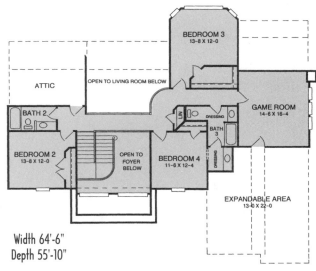

Width 64'-6"
Depth 55'-10"

A uniquely beautiful entrance is framed by huge columns topped by elegant arches to welcome you into this classic European home. Inside, the formal dining room to the right of the foyer is defined by yet another set of columns and arches. The appealing living room offers access to the rear yard via two sets of double French doors. A gourmet kitchen is conveniently located between the dining room and the sunny breakfast room. An inviting family room with a fireplace and access to the rear porch is also nearby. The deluxe master suite, with its lavish bath and His and Hers walk-in closets, completes the main level. Upstairs, one large bedroom includes its own full bath and may be used as a guest suite. Two other bedrooms share a full bath and access to a huge game room. Please specify basement, crawlspace or slab foundation when ordering.

DESIGN 8186
First Floor: 1,919 square feet
Second Floor: 1,190 square feet
Total: 3,109 square feet

LUXURY HOMES

DESIGN P180

First Floor: 1,468 square feet
Second Floor: 1,559 square feet
Total: 3,027 square feet

Stone accents and a variety of gables decorate the front of this stucco home. The impressive entry opens to a two-story foyer with the formal living area to the right. The sunken living room features a fireplace and a vaulted ceiling. Serving bars separate the kitchen from the two-story family room—which boasts a second fireplace and a nice view of the backyard—and the bumped-out breakfast nook. The elegant master suite and three family bedrooms make up the second floor. Please specify basement or crawlspace foundation when ordering.

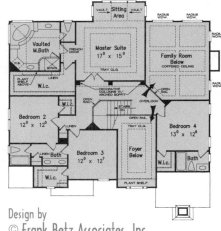

Width 52'-4"
Depth 55'-4"

Design by
© Frank Betz Associates, Inc.

DESIGN P152

First Floor: 2,467 square feet
Second Floor: 928 square feet
Total: 3,395 square feet
Bonus Room: 296 square feet

A chic combination of European style and farmhouse charm gives this two-story home an eclectic appeal. Living areas are open and divided by decorative columns. The spacious kitchen provides wraparound counters, a serving bar and a sunny breakfast room. The master suite enjoys a lovely, vaulted sitting room with a three-sided fireplace and a spa-style bath. Upstairs, two bedrooms share a bath, with another having a private bath. Please specify basement, crawlspace or slab foundation.

Width 64'-6"
Depth 62'-10"

Design by
© Frank Betz Associates, Inc.

www.homeplanners.com

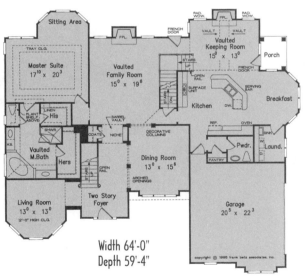

Width 64'-0"
Depth 59'-4"

copyright © 1995 frank betz associates, inc.

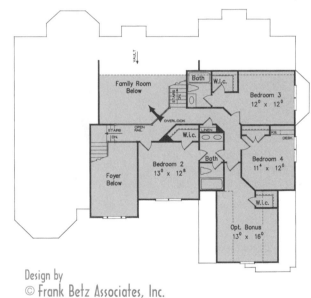

Design by
© Frank Betz Associates, Inc.

The arched front doorway bids a warm welcome to this spacious home. The formal dining room opens to the right—its outline punctuated by decorative columns. The family and keeping rooms each have a fireplace and a vaulted ceiling, while the large kitchen offers a work island and a serving bar to make mealtimes in the breakfast nook a cinch. On the left side of the plan are a gazebo-shaped formal living room and the elegant master suite with a bayed sitting area. Two staircases lead to three family bedrooms and the optional bonus room on the second floor. Bedroom 3 has a private bath, making it a fine guest suite. Please specify basement or crawlspace foundation when ordering.

DESIGN
P169

First Floor: 2,302 square feet
Second Floor: 845 square feet
Total: 3,147 square feet
Bonus Room: 247 square feet

DESIGN
P225

First Floor: 1,665 square feet
Second Floor: 1,445 square feet
Total: 3,110 square feet

There are plenty of extras in this well-designed house, including a large work island and serving bar in the kitchen, and a handy laundry area. The vaulted family room is warmed by its own fireplace and conveniently opens to the breakfast area and kitchen. Upstairs, the master suite includes a large walk-in closet and a compartmented bath. Three more bedrooms include one with a private bath. Please specify basement, crawlspace or slab foundation when ordering.

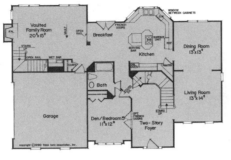

Design by
© Frank Betz Associates, Inc.

Width 60'-4"
Depth 41'-0"

DESIGN
P230

First Floor: 2,764 square feet
Second Floor: 1,598 square feet
Total: 4,362 square feet

The heart of this magnificent design is the two-story living room with its coffered ceiling, fireplace flanked by built-ins, and wall of windows. The family living area consists of a formal dining room, island kitchen, sunny breakfast nook with French-door access to the rear patio and a vaulted family room with fireplace. The private owner's wing features a secluded sitting room and a large master suite. Located upstairs are three family bedrooms, all with walk-in closets, and a large loft. Please specify basement or crawlspace foundation when ordering.

Design by
© Frank Betz Associates, Inc.

Width 74'-6"
Depth 65'-10"

www.homeplanners.com

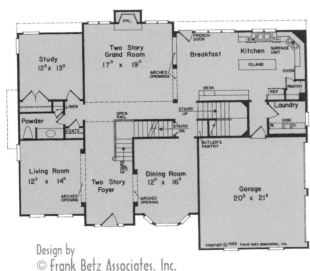

Design by
© Frank Betz Associates, Inc.

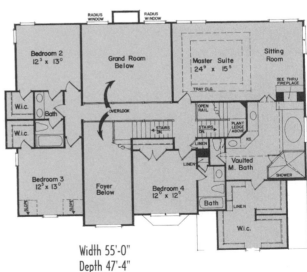

Width 55'-0"
Depth 47'-4"

Here's a lovely European-style home with just the right amount of space for a family. Second-floor sleeping quarters include three secondary bedrooms as well as a master suite, which contains a vaulted bath and a walk-in closet designed for two. On the first floor, the two-story grand room includes a fireplace. The formal living and dining rooms flank the foyer, while the study is secluded to the rear of the plan. The L-shaped kitchen features a work island and a desk in the breakfast area, which offers French-door access outside. Please specify basement or crawlspace foundation when ordering.

DESIGN P406
First Floor: 1,738 square feet
Second Floor: 1,665 square feet
Total: 3,403 square feet

Design by
© Home Design Services, Inc.

Width 87'-0"
Depth 97'-6"

LUXURY HOMES

**DESIGN
8628**
First Floor: 3,770 square feet
Second Floor: 634 square feet
Total: 4,404 square feet

This fresh and innovative design creates unbeatable ambience. Octagon-shaped rooms, columns and flowing spaces will delight all. The breakfast nook and family room both open to a patio—a perfect arrangement for informal entertaining. The dining room is sure to please with elegant pillars separating it from the sunken living room. A media room delights with its shape and by being convenient to the nearby kitchen—perfect for snack runs. A private garden surrounds the master bath and its spa tub and enormous walk-in closet. The master bedroom is enchanting with a fireplace and access to the outdoors. Additional family bedrooms come in a variety of different shapes and sizes; Bedroom 4 reigns over the second floor and features its own full bath.

www.homeplanners.com

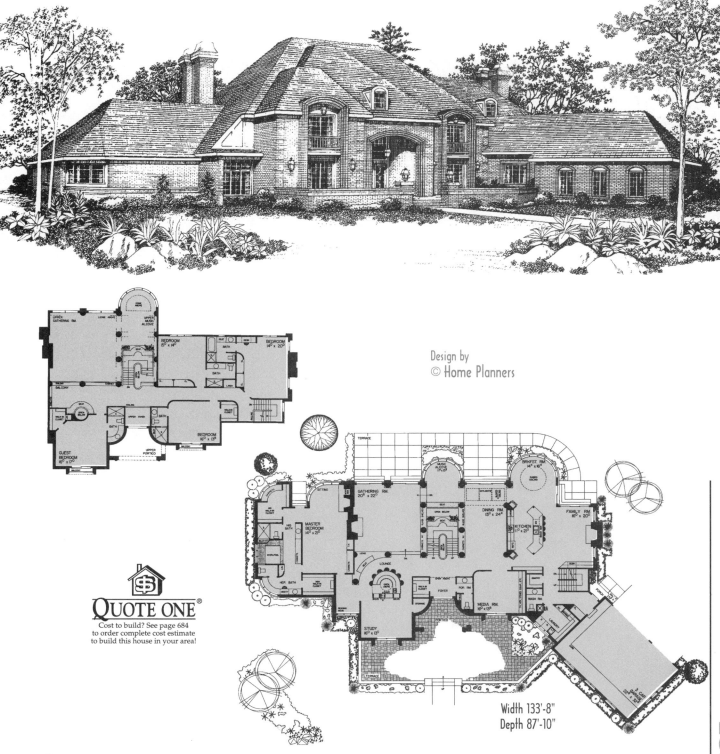

Design by
© Home Planners

QUOTE ONE®
Cost to build? See page 684
to order complete cost estimate
to build this house in your area!

Width 133'-8"
Depth 87'-10"

Graceful window arches soften the massive chimneys and steeply gabled roof of this grand Norman manor. A two-story gathering room is two steps down from the adjacent lounge with an impressive wet bar and semi-circular music alcove. The highly efficient galley-style kitchen overlooks the family-room fireplace and spectacular windowed breakfast room. The master suite is a private retreat with a fireplace and a wood box tucked into the corner of its sitting room. Separate His and Hers baths and dressing rooms guarantee plenty of space and privacy. A large, built-in whirlpool tub adds the final touch. Upstairs, a second-floor balcony overlooks the gathering room below. Four additional bedrooms each include a private bath.

DESIGN 2940
First Floor: 4,786 square feet
Second Floor: 1,842 square feet
Total: 6,628 square feet
L D

LUXURY HOMES

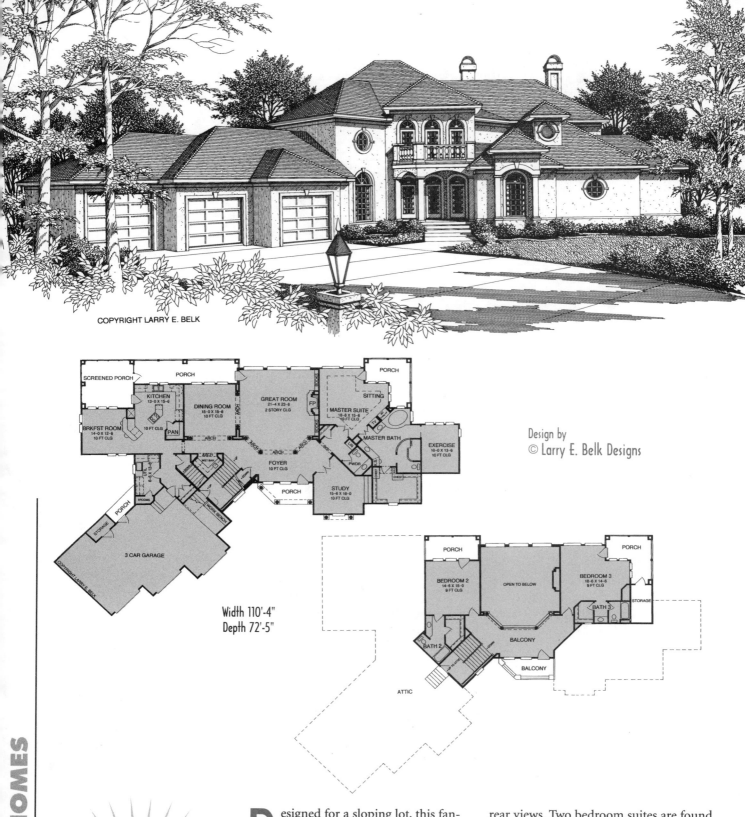

COPYRIGHT LARRY E. BELK

Design by
© Larry E. Belk Designs

Width 110'-4"
Depth 72'-5"

DESIGN 8145
First Floor: 2,959 square feet
Second Floor: 1,055 square feet
Total: 4,014 square feet

Designed for a sloping lot, this fantastic Mediterranean features all the views to the rear, making it the perfect home for an ocean, lake or golf-course view. Inside, the two-story great room features a full window wall to the rear. The breakfast room, kitchen, dining room and master suite also have rear views. Two bedroom suites are found upstairs, each with a private bath and a porch. An optional basement can add up to 1,270 square feet of space for another bedroom suite and a large game room. This home may also be built with a slab foundation. Please specify your preference when ordering.

DESIGN
S149
First Floor: 3,102 square feet
Second Floor: 1,487 square feet
Total: 4,589 square feet
Bonus Room: 786 square feet

Width 106'-0"
Depth 56'-6"

Design by
© Archival Designs

A s you approach this magnificent estate, you will be transformed back in time to the land of gentry. Inside, the circular stairway floats in front of the grand salon and floor-to-ceiling windows. The dining hall utilizes a butler's pantry on the way to the oversized octogonal-shaped kitchen. To the left of the foyer is a master suite with all the finest appointments. The second floor holds a large stateroom with a sitting room and bath and two additional bedrooms, each with its own bathroom.

DESIGN
A283
First Floor: 3,767 square feet
Second Floor: 2,602 square feet
Total: 6,369 square feet
Bonus Room: 677 square feet

S hake-covered dormers and stone accents highlight this brick country home. Tall chimneys support three fireplaces—in the gathering room, the grand room and the study. Distinctive features include built-ins flanking the fireplaces and a walk-in pantry in the kitchen. The master suite offers private access to the terrace, two huge walk-in closets and His and Hers baths sharing only the tub and shower area. Three flights of stairs lead upstairs to four family bedrooms with private baths and a home theater.

Width 131'-0"
Depth 99'-11"

Design by
© Living Concepts Home Planning

LUXURY HOMES

DESIGN 6656

First Floor: 3,027 square feet
Second Floor: 1,079 square feet
Total: 4,106 square feet

The inside of this design is just as majestic as the outside. Pillars highlight the grand foyer, which opens to a two-story living room with a fireplace and access to both rear verandas. The casual family area includes a well-designed kitchen, a sunny nook and a leisure room with fireplace and outdoor access. The master wing includes a separate study and an elegant master bath. The second level features a guest suite, two family bedrooms and a gallery loft. Please specify basement or slab foundation when ordering.

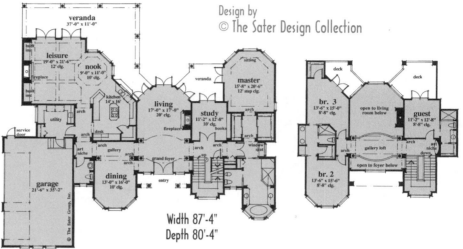

Design by
© The Sater Design Collection

Width 87'-4"
Depth 80'-4"

DESIGN 6651

First Floor: 3,546 square feet
Second Floor: 1,213 square feet
Total: 4,759 square feet

A marvelously arched entry welcomes you to this beautiful home. Special details abound inside: a through-fireplace between the living room and study, multiple sets of French doors to the rear terrace, a built-in entertainment center in the leisure room, and a cooktop island in the kitchen. The master suite is loaded with amenities. Upstairs, two family bedrooms share a full bath that has twin vanities while the third has a private bath. Please specify basement or slab foundation when ordering.

Design by
© The Sater Design Collection

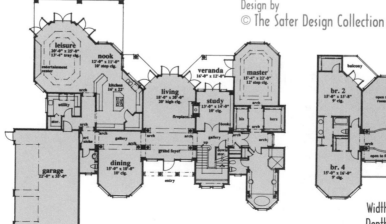

Width 95'-4"
Depth 83'-0"

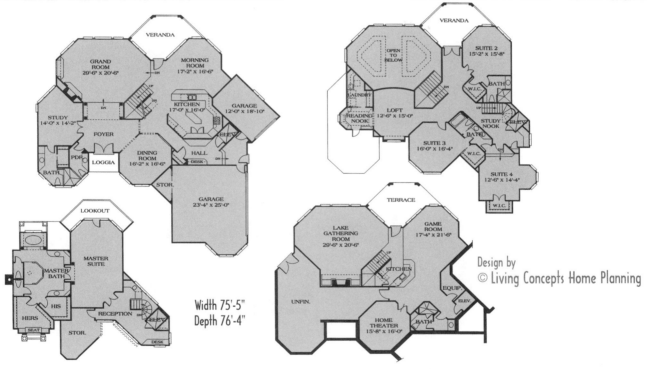

Width 75'-5"
Depth 76'-4"

Design by
© Living Concepts Home Planning

f an opulent manor is cast for your future, this four-level plan has everything. Wake up in the master suite, step out on the lookout balcony to watch the sunrise, then take the elevator to the basement for a workout with your own equipment. A quick cup of coffee in the basement kitchen is followed by a shower in the nearby bath. Breakfast waits in the first-floor morning room, then a morning in the study takes care of the day's work, or go up to the second-floor reading nook, just off the loft that over-looks the grand room. Three bedrooms on this floor share two baths and a veranda. Later in the day, enjoy a relaxing hour in the master bath's garden tub, and select evening wear from a walk-in closet that doubles as a dressing room. After an elegant dinner in the formal dining room, a viewing of a new movie release is offered in the home theater. The evening is complete with midnight supper in front of the fireplace in the gathering room—the end of a perfect day. Two separate garages hold up to three vehicles.

DESIGN A235

First Floor: 2,347 square feet
Second Floor: 1,800 square feet
Third Floor: 1,182 square feet
Basement: 1,688 square feet
Total: 7,017 square feet

LUXURY HOMES

DESIGN 6635

First Floor: 4,760 square feet
Second Floor: 1,552 square feet
Total: 6,312 square feet

L

This home features a spectacular blend of arch-top windows, French doors and balusters. Dramatic two-story ceilings and tray details add custom spaciousness. An informal leisure room features a sixteen-foot-high tray ceiling and an entertainment center. The gourmet kitchen easily serves the nook and formal dining room. The master suite holds a bayed sitting area. His and Hers vanities and walk-in closets and a curved, glass-block shower are highlights in the bath. The staircase leads to the deluxe guest suites, two of which have observation decks.

Design by
© The Sater Design Collection

Width 98'-0"
Depth 103'-8"

Quote One®
Cost to build? See page 684 to order complete cost estimate to build this house in your area!

DESIGN 6660

First Floor: 2,853 square feet
Second Floor: 627 square feet
Guest House: 312 square feet
Total: 3,792 square feet

L

A unique courtyard provides a happy marriage of indoor-outdoor relationships. Inside, the foyer opens to a grand salon with a wall of glass, providing unobstructed views of the backyard. Informal areas include a leisure room with an entertainment center and glass doors that open to a covered poolside lanai. An outdoor fireplace enhances casual gatherings. The master wing is filled with amenities. Upstairs, two bedrooms—both with private decks—share a full bath.

Design by
© The Sater Design Collection

Width 80'-0"
Depth 96'-0"

LUXURY HOMES

Photo by Home Design Services

The home, as shown in the photograph, may differ from the actual blueprints. For more detailed information, please check the floor plans carefully.

Width 78'-0"
Depth 84'-6"

DESIGN 8625

First Floor: 2,669 square feet
Second Floor: 621 square feet
Total: 3,290 square feet

Rooflines, arches and corner quoins adorn the facade of this magnificent home. Inside, a wet bar serves the sunken living room and overlooks the pool area. The dining room has a tray ceiling and is located near the gourmet kitchen with prep island and angled counter. The generous family room, warmed by a fireplace, opens to the screened patio. The master bedroom has a sitting room and a fireplace that's set into an angled wall. Upstairs, two bedrooms share the oversized balcony and nearby observation room.

Width 66'-0"
Depth 83'-0"

DESIGN 8655

First Floor: 2,624 square feet
Second Floor: 540 square feet
Total: 3,164 square feet

This award-winning design has been recognized for its innovative use of space. The formal spaces separate the master suite and den/study from family spaces. A convenient bath with outside access turns the den/study into a guest bedroom when needed. The master retreat contains a master bath with His and Hers vanities, private toilet room and walk-in closet. The perfect touch in this two-story design is the placement of two bedrooms downstairs with two extra bedrooms on the second floor. Study space overlooks the rooms below.

LUXURY HOMES

Design by
© Home Design Services, Inc.

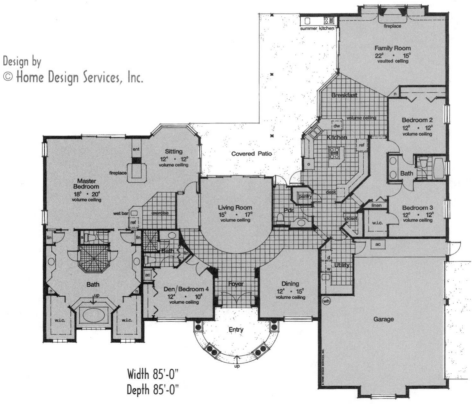

Width 85'-0"
Depth 85'-0"

DESIGN 8690
Square Footage: 3,556

A beautiful curved portico provides a majestic entrance to this one-story home. Curved ceilings in the formal living and dining rooms continue the extraordinary style. To the left of the foyer is a den/bedroom with a private bath, ideal for use as a guest suite. The exquisite master suite features a see-through fireplace and an exercise area with a wet bar. A sumptuous soaking tub and island shower in the master bath invite relaxation. The family wing is geared for casual living with a powder room/patio bath, a huge island kitchen with a walk-in pantry, a glass-walled breakfast nook and a grand family room with a fireplace and media wall. Two family bedrooms share a private bath.

© The Sater Group, Inc.

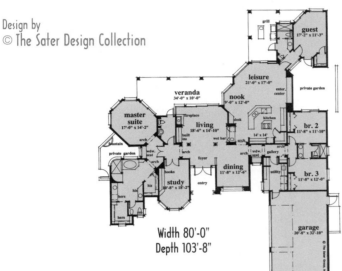

Width 80'-0"
Depth 103'-8"

DESIGN 6661
Square Footage: 3,265

A turret study and a raised entry with half-round columns add elegance to this marvelous stucco home. Inside, columns frame the living room, which features glass doors that open to the veranda and provide spectacular views of the rear grounds. A guest suite—adjacent to the leisure room—includes a full bath, porch access and a private garden entry, making it perfect for use as an in-law suite. Secondary bedrooms share a full bath. The master suite has a foyer with a window seat overlooking a private garden and fountain area.

Width 62'-0"
Depth 83'-8"

DESIGN 8678
Square Footage: 3,091

With elegantly formal columns standing at attention around the entryway, this design only gets better. Inside, ceiling detail in the foyer and the formal dining room immediately reinforces the graceful qualities of this beautiful home. A large and airy living room awaits to entertain, while the spacious family room includes a fireplace and access to the covered patio. An angled kitchen offers a sunny breakfast room. Three secondary bedrooms accommodate both family and friends, while a lavish master suite promises pampering for the homeowner.

LUXURY HOMES

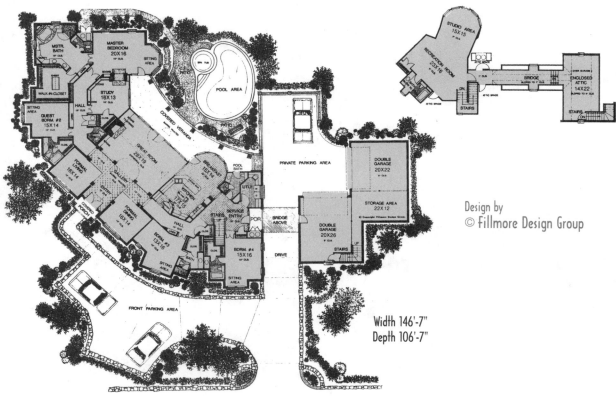

Design by
© Fillmore Design Group

Width 146'-7"
Depth 106'-7"

DESIGN M152

First Floor: 5,152 square feet
Second Floor: 726 square feet
Total: 5,878 square feet

From the master bedroom suite to the detached four-car garage, this design will delight even the most discerning palates. While the formal living and dining rooms bid greeting as you enter, the impressive great room, with its cathedral ceiling, raised-hearth fireplace and veranda access, will take your breath away. A gallery hall leads to the kitchen and the family sleeping wing on the right and to the study, guest suite and master suite on the left. The large island kitchen, with its sunny breakfast nook, will be a gourmet's delight. The master suite includes a bayed sitting area, a dual fireplace shared with the study and a luxurious bath. Each additional bedroom features its own bath and sitting area. The second floor offers a massive recreation room with a sunlit studio area and a bridge leading to an attic over the garage and storage area.

DESIGN F120

First Floor: 3,182 square feet
Second Floor: 1,190 square feet
Total: 4,372 square feet
Bonus Room: 486 square feet

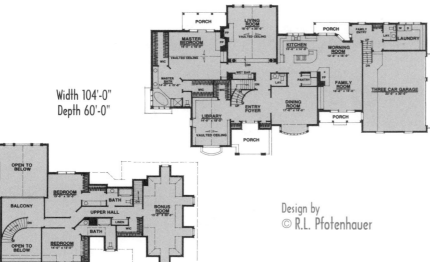

Width 104'-0"
Depth 60'-0"

Design by
© R.L. Pfotenhauer

I n the Pays Basque region of rural France are found finished farmhouses such as this beauty. The two-story entry is graced with a beautiful curved stair, opening to a two-story living room with vaulted ceiling. To the right is a formal dining room and to the left, a finely detailed library with a vaulted ceiling and an impressive arched window. The private master bedroom, with its vaulted ceiling, king-size bath and huge walk-in closets, will never go out of style. The second floor has two bedrooms with their own bathrooms.

DESIGN A265

First Floor: 2,351 square feet
Second Floor: 866 square feet
Apartment: 596 square feet
Total: 3,813 square feet

I f you've ever dreamed of living in a castle, this could be the home for you. The interior is also fit for royalty, from the formal dining room to the multi-purpose grand room to the comfortable sitting area off the kitchen. The master suite has a fireplace, two walk-in closets and a compartmented bath. One stairway, housed in the turret, leads to a sitting area and a balcony overlooking the grand room. The balcony leads to two more bedrooms and a rec room (or apartment) with a deck.

Width 113'-7"
Depth 57'-5"

Design by
© Living Concepts Home Planning

LUXURY HOMES

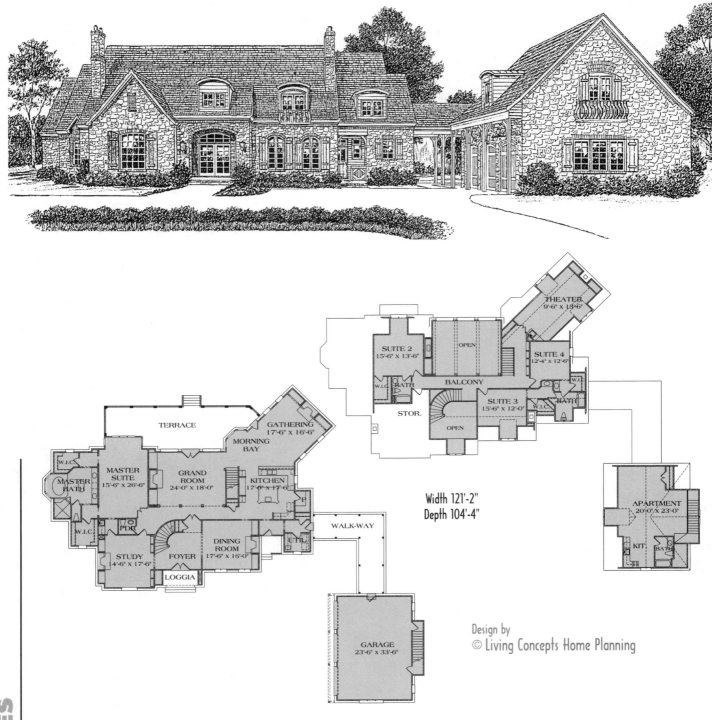

Width 121'-2"
Depth 104'-4"

Design by
© Living Concepts Home Planning

DESIGN A128

First Floor: 3,560 square feet
Second Floor: 1,783 square feet
Total: 5,343 square feet
Apartment: 641 square feet

Multi-pane windows complement the porte cochere and dress up the natural stone facade on this French country estate. A two-story foyer leads to a central grand room with French doors to the terrace. A formal dining room to the front offers a fireplace. To the left, a cozy study with a second fireplace features built-in cabinetry. The sleeping quarters offer luxurious amenities. The master bath includes a whirlpool tub in a bumped-out bay, twin lavatories and two walk-in closets. Upstairs, three suites, each with a walk-in closet and one with its own bath, share a balcony hall that leads to a home theater. A guest apartment over the garage will house visiting or live-in relatives, or may be used as a maid's quarters or as a convenient home office.

Photo by Living Concepts Home Planning

The home, as shown in the photograph, may differ from the actual blueprints. For more detailed information, please check the floor plans carefully.

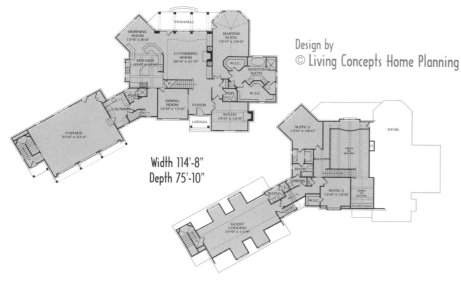

Design by
© Living Concepts Home Planning

Width 114'-8"
Depth 75'-10"

Gently curved arches and dormers contrast with the straight lines of gables and wooden columns on this French-style stone exterior. Inside, a spacious gathering room with an impressive fireplace opens to a cheery morning room. The kitchen is a delight, with a beam ceiling, triangular work island, walk-in pantry and snack bar. The first-floor master suite boasts a bay-windowed sitting nook, deluxe bath and handy study. The second floor includes a balcony overlooking the gathering room, two suites and a large guest area over the garage.

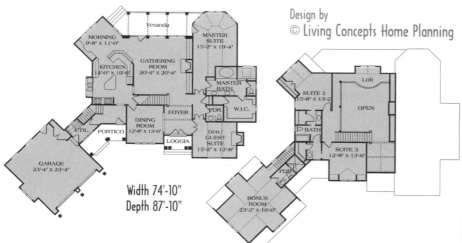

Design by
© Living Concepts Home Planning

Width 74'-10"
Depth 87'-10"

The grand exterior of this Normandy country design features a steep-pitched gable roofline. Arched dormers repeat the window accents. Inside, a large gathering room fills the center of the house and opens to a long trellised veranda. A den or guest suite with fireplace, an adjacent powder room and a master suite with vaulted ceiling and access to the veranda are in the right wing. Two additional bedrooms with two baths and a loft overlooking the gathering room are upstairs.

LUXURY HOMES

DESIGN
M150
Square Footage: 4,615

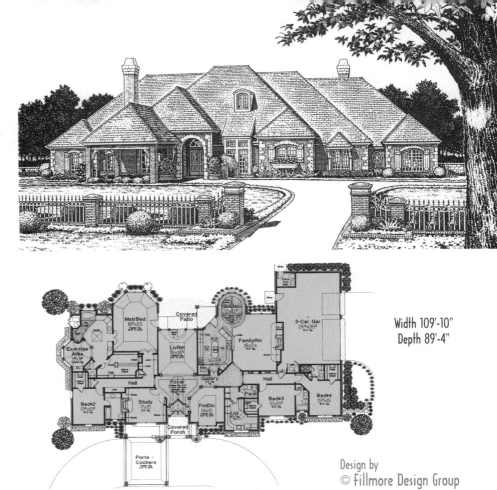

The hip-roof French country exterior and porte cochere entrance are just the beginning of this unique, and impressive, design. An unusual pullman ceiling graces the foyer as it leads to the formal dining room on the right, to the study with a fireplace on the left and straight ahead to the formal living room with its covered patio access. A gallery directs you to the island kitchen with its abundant counter space and adjacent sun-filled breakfast bay. All of the family bedrooms offer private baths and walk-in closets.

Width 109'-10"
Depth 89'-4"

Design by
© Fillmore Design Group

DESIGN
M180
Square Footage: 4,825

In this English country design, a series of hip roofs covers an impressive brick facade accented by fine wood detailing. Formal living and dining rooms flank the foyer. The nearby media room is designed for home theater and surround sound. Fireplaces warm the living room and the family room, which also boasts a cathedral ceiling. The kitchen offers plenty of work space, a bright breakfast nook and access to two covered patios. All four bedrooms include private baths and walk-in closets. The master suite provides the added luxury of a glass-enclosed sitting area.

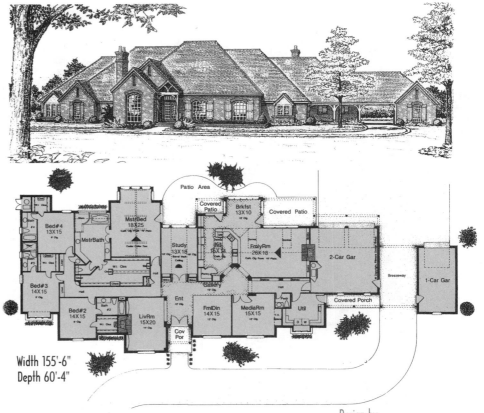

Width 155'-6"
Depth 60'-4"

Design by
© Fillmore Design Group

LUXURY HOMES

Width 91'-0"
Depth 71'-9"

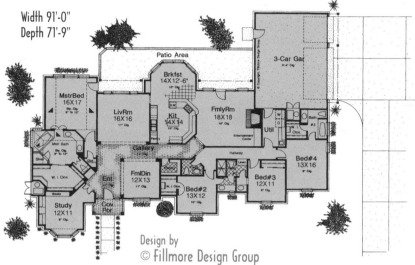

Design by
© Fillmore Design Group

This home combines the rustic charm of shutters and a stonework wall with the elegance of molded cornices and arched multi-pane windows. Enter the formal dining room to the right and living room to the rear. The arched gallery leads past the kitchen to the family room with fireplace and built-in entertainment center. The bay-windowed breakfast nook looks out to the rear patio. Bedroom 4 offers a private full bath, while Bedrooms 2 and 3 each have their own private vanity in the shared full bath. The left wing holds the master suite and the double-doored, bay-windowed study with built-ins.

Design by
© Fillmore Design Group

Width 80'-0"
Depth 79'-0"

This home depends on European and French influences for its exterior beauty. A volume roofline allows for vaulted ceilings in many of the interior spaces. There are more than enough living areas in this plan: formal living and dining rooms, a huge family room with fireplace and a study with bay window. The kitchen opens to an attached, light-filled breakfast area and the family room. Four bedrooms include three family bedrooms; two on the right and one on the left. The master suite has a private covered patio, a vaulted ceiling, two walk-in closets and a bath fit for a king.

LUXURY HOMES

DESIGN 7660
Square Footage: 4,523

Large and rambling, this four-bedroom home is sure to please every member of the family. The homeowner will especially appreciate the master bedroom suite. Here, luxuries such as His and Hers bathrooms, two walk-in closets and a tray ceiling wait to pamper. For gatherings, the spacious great room lives up to its name, with a fireplace, built-ins, a tray ceiling and access to the rear porch. The kitchen features an island cooktop/snack bar, a walk-in pantry and an adjacent bayed breakfast room. A sun room is also nearby.

©1997 Donald A. Gardner Architects, Inc.

Design by
Donald A. Gardner
Architects, Inc.

© 1997 Donald A. Gardner Architects, Inc.

Width 114'-4"
Depth 82'-3"

DESIGN 2977
First Floor: 4,104 square feet
Second Floor: 979 square feet
Total: 5,083 square feet
L

Both front and rear facades of this elegant brick manor depict classic Georgian symmetry. A columned Greek entry opens to an impressive two-story foyer. Fireplaces, built-in shelves and cabinets highlight the living room, dining room, family room and library. The kitchen features a work island, a pass-through to the dining room and a snack bar. The master suite in its own wing includes a private atrium entrance, lounge/exercise room and fifth fireplace. Two bedrooms, each with a private bath, are located on the second floor.

Design by
© Home Planners

Width 132'-0"
Depth 53'-6"

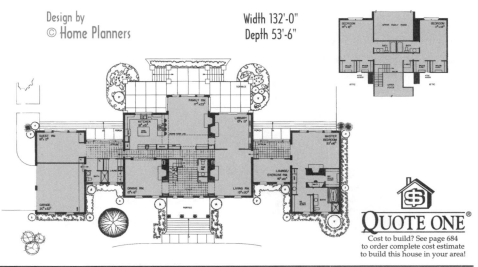

Quote One®
Cost to build? See page 684
to order complete cost estimate
to build this house in your area!

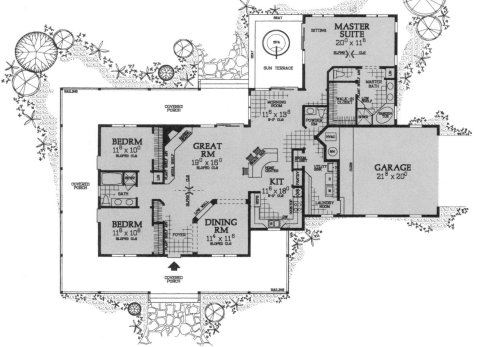

Design by
© Home Planners

Width 84'-6"
Depth 64'-0"

DESIGN
3672
Square Footage: 2,090

This classic farmhouse enjoys a wrap-around porch that's perfect for enjoyment of the outdoors. To the rear of the plan, a sun terrace with a spa opens from the master suite and the morning room. A grand great room offers a sloped ceiling and a corner fireplace with a raised hearth. The formal dining room is defined by a low wall and by graceful archways set off by decorative columns. The tiled kitchen provides a centered island counter with a snack bar and adjoins the laundry area. Two family bedrooms reside to the side of the plan, and each enjoys private access to the covered porch. A secluded master suite nestles in its own wing and features a sitting area with access to the rear terrace and spa. A two-car garage opens to the side and accesses the main house at the laundry.

ONE-STORY FARMHOUSES

© 1995 Donald A. Gardner Architects, Inc.

DESIGN 9792

First Floor: 1,480 square feet
Second Floor: 511 square feet
Total: 1,991 square feet
Bonus Room: 363 square feet

A quaint covered porch, dormers and arch-top windows stir memories of gentler times with this country home, but the interior is designed for active lifestyles. The foyer opens to a formal dining room with a bay window, and leads to a two-story great room with a fireplace and outdoor views. The first-floor master suite opens to a rear deck and spa and offers a whirlpool bath with a windowed walk-in closet. Two family bedrooms share a full bath and a balcony hall upstairs.

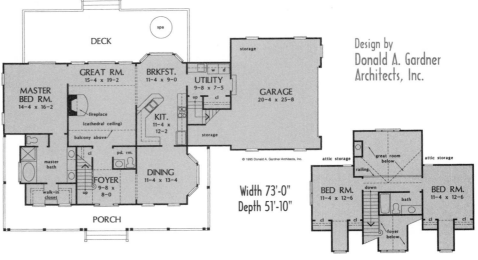

Design by
**Donald A. Gardner
Architects, Inc.**

Width 73'-0"
Depth 51'-10"

© 1995 Donald A. Gardner Architects, Inc.

ONE-STORY FARMHOUSES

DESIGN 9738

Square Footage: 2,136
Bonus Room: 405 square feet

Details such as columns, cathedral ceilings and open living areas combine to create the ideal floor plan. The spacious great room features built-in cabinets, a fireplace and cathedral ceiling. An efficient island kitchen is convenient to the great room, dining room and skylit breakfast area. A private master bedroom features a cathedral ceiling, walk-in closet and relaxing master bath. Two family bedrooms share a full bath at the opposite end of the home.

© 1994 Donald A. Gardner Architects, Inc.

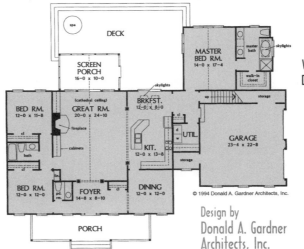

© 1994 Donald A. Gardner Architects, Inc.

Width 76'-4"
Depth 64'-4"

Design by
**Donald A. Gardner
Architects, Inc.**

QUOTE ONE®
Cost to build? See page 684
to order complete cost estimate
to build this house in your area!

© 1995 Donald A. Gardner Architects, Inc.

R. NATHAN

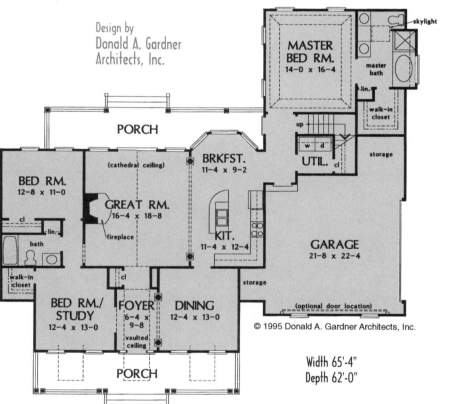

Design by
**Donald A. Gardner
Architects, Inc.**

PORCH

**MASTER
BED RM.**
14-0 x 16-4

skylight

master
bath

lin.

walk-in
closet

up

UTIL.

w d

cl

storage

BRKFST.
11-4 x 9-2

(cathedral ceiling)

BED RM.
12-8 x 11-0

cl

lin.

GREAT RM.
16-4 x 18-8

fireplace

bath

walk-in
closet

KIT.
11-4 x 12-4

GARAGE
21-8 x 22-4

storage

BED RM./
STUDY
12-4 x 13-0

FOYER
6-4 x
9-8

vaulted
ceiling

cl

DINING
12-4 x 13-0

storage

(optional door location)

© 1995 Donald A. Gardner Architects, Inc.

PORCH

Width 65'-4"
Depth 62'-0"

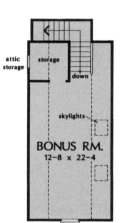

attic
storage

storage

down

skylights

BONUS RM.
12-8 x 22-4

Cost to build? See page 684
to order complete cost estimate
to build this house in your area!

The charm of this home is evident at first glance, but you'll especially appreciate its qualities the moment you step inside. The vaulted foyer ushers guests to the formal dining room and leads back to casual living space. A magnificent great room beckons with a cathedral ceiling and an extended-hearth fireplace, while sliding glass doors, framed by tall windows, provide access to the rear covered porch. The gourmet kitchen with island counter enjoys sunlight from the nearby breakfast bay, and leads to a hall with rear-porch access. A first-floor master suite features a tray ceiling and a skylit bath with a garden tub and U-shaped walk-in closet. A bonus room over the garage has skylights and a storage area.

**DESIGN
9783**

Square Footage: 1,832
Bonus Room: 425 square feet

DESIGN 9742
Square Footage: 1,954
Bonus Room: 436 square feet

This beautiful brick country home offers style and comfort for an active family. Join the outdoors with two covered porches and a spa on the rear deck. A well-defined interior enjoys a cathedral ceiling that soars above the central great room, with an raised-hearth fireplace and sunlit arch-top clerestory window. A splendid master suite enjoys its own secluded wing. Two family bedrooms share a full bath.

Design by
Donald A. Gardner Architects, Inc.

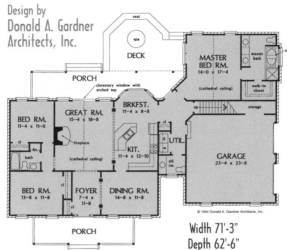

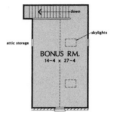

Width 71'-3"
Depth 62'-6"

QUOTE ONE®
Cost to build? See page 684 to order complete cost estimate to build this house in your area!

DESIGN 9780
Square Footage: 1,561

Fine country details such as a front porch encourage the joy of summer breezes. The entry foyer leads to a formal dining room defined by columns. Beyond it is the large great room with a cathedral ceiling and a fireplace. The kitchen and the breakfast room are open to the living area and include porch access. The master suite is tucked away in its own private space. The two-car garage contains extra storage space.

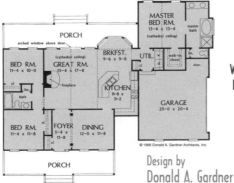

Width 60'-10"
Depth 51'-6"

QUOTE ONE®
Cost to build? See page 684 to order complete cost estimate to build this house in your area!

REAR VIEW

Design by
Donald A. Gardner Architects, Inc.

©1997 Donald A. Gardner Architects, Inc.

B.NATHAN.

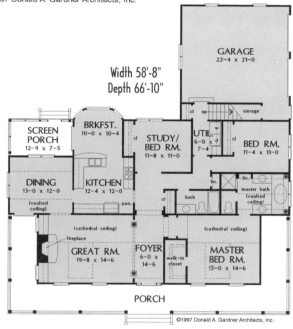

Width 58'-8"
Depth 66'-10"

GARAGE
22-4 x 21-0

SCREEN PORCH
12-9 x 7-5

BRKFST.
10-0 x 10-4

STUDY/ BED RM.
11-8 x 11-0

UTIL.
6-0 x 7-4

BED RM.
11-4 x 11-0

DINING
13-0 x 12-0
(vaulted ceiling)

KITCHEN
12-4 x 12-0

bath

lin.

master bath
(vaulted ceiling)

(cathedral ceiling)

fireplace

GREAT RM.
19-8 x 14-6

FOYER
6-0 x 14-6

walk-in closet

(cathedral ceiling)

MASTER BED RM.
15-0 x 14-6

PORCH

©1997 Donald A. Gardner Architects, Inc.

Design by
Donald A. Gardner
Architects, Inc.

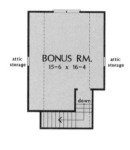

attic storage

BONUS RM.
15-6 x 16-4

attic storage

down

C ountry charm in a one-story home—but it looks like a two-story. The upper-level dormers provide light to the floor plan and add detailing to the exterior. A covered porch wraps around three sides of the plan and is accessed at two separate points. Both the great room and the master bedroom have cathedral ceilings, while the formal dining room has a vaulted ceiling. A screened porch to the rear can be reached from the breakfast room (note the bay window here). The plan calls for three bedrooms, but one may be used as a study or home office if you choose. The two-car garage sits to the rear of the plan, taking nothing away from the beauty of the facade. Appointments in the master suite include a bath with vaulted ceiling, garden whirlpool tub and compartmented toilet. A bonus room over the garage allows space to expand.

DESIGN 7658
Square Footage: 1,899
Bonus Room: 315 square feet

ONE-STORY FARMHOUSES

© 1995 Donald A. Gardner Architects, Inc.

DESIGN 9779
Square Footage: 1,632

This country home has more than just elegance, style and a host of amenities—it has heart. A cathedral ceiling highlights the great room, while a clerestory window and sliding glass doors really let in the light. The private master suite, with a tray ceiling and walk-in closet, boasts luxurious amenities: a skylit bath, whirlpool tub, separate shower and dual vanity. Two additional bedrooms share a full bath. The front bedroom features a walk-in closet and could double as a study.

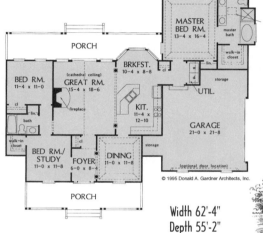

© 1995 Donald A. Gardner Architects, Inc.

Width 62'-4"
Depth 55'-2"

QUOTE ONE®
Cost to build? See page 684 to order complete cost estimate to build this house in your area!

Design by
Donald A. Gardner
Architects, Inc.

REAR VIEW

DESIGN 9782
Square Footage: 2,192
Bonus Room: 390 square feet

This comfortable, open plan features secluded bedrooms that are pleasant retreats. Sunlight fills the airy foyer from a vaulted dormer and streams into the great room. A formal dining room, delineated from the foyer by columns, features a tray ceiling. The kitchen enjoys entertaining with only columns separating it from the great room. The master suite is highlighted by a tray ceiling and a spacious master bath with a walk-in closet.

©1995 Donald A. Gardner Architects, Inc.

Width 74'-10"
Depth 55'-8"

REAR VIEW

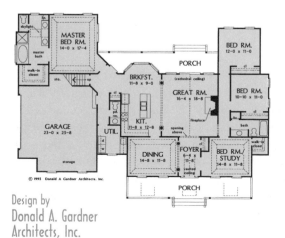

© 1995 Donald A Gardner Architects, Inc.

Design by
Donald A. Gardner
Architects, Inc.

© 1997 Donald A. Gardner Architects, Inc.

B. NATHAN

Design by
Donald A. Gardner
Architects, Inc.

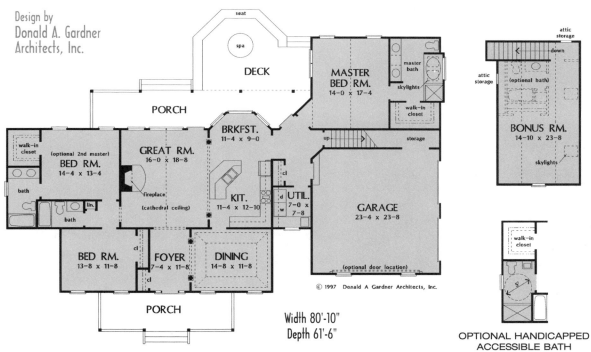

© 1997 Donald A. Gardner Architects, Inc.

Width 80'-10"
Depth 61'-6"

OPTIONAL HANDICAPPED
ACCESSIBLE BATH

With its clean lines and symmetry, this home radiates grace and style. Inside, cathedral and tray ceilings add volume and elegance. The L-shaped kitchen includes an angled snack bar to the breakfast bay and great room. Secluded at the back of the house is the vaulted master suite with a skylit bath. Of the two secondary bedrooms, one acts as a "second" master suite with its own private bath, and an alternate bath design creates a wheelchair accessible option for the disabled. The bonus room makes a great craft room, playroom, office or optional fourth bedroom with a bath. The garage loads to the side.

DESIGN
7725
Square Footage: 2,057
Bonus Room: 444 square feet

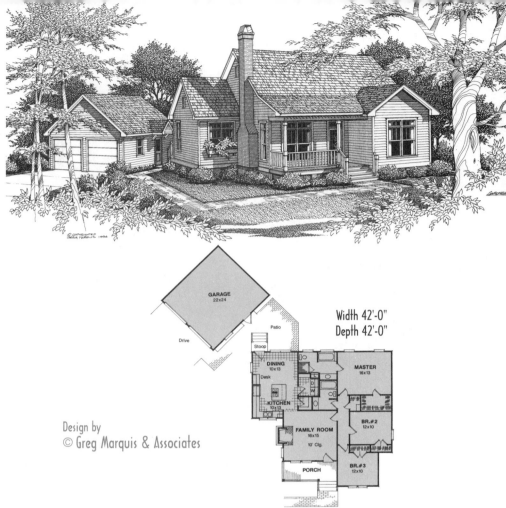

DESIGN B103
Square Footage: 1,393

A welcoming front porch ushers you into a large family room complete with a warming fireplace. The well-designed kitchen features a cooktop island with an adjoining eating bar, a large pantry, plus a convenient built-in desk area. The dining area looks out to the angled patio, providing an inviting outdoor dining area. Three bedrooms with ample closets and two baths provide plenty of room for quiet retreats.

Width 42'-0"
Depth 42'-0"

Design by
© Greg Marquis & Associates

GARAGE 22x24

Drive

Patio

Stoop

DINING 10x13

Desk

KITCHEN 10x13

MASTER 16x13

BR.#2 12x10

FAMILY ROOM 16x15
10' Clg.

BR.#3 12x10

PORCH

DESIGN Z050
Square Footage: 920

Compact yet comfortable, this country cottage has many appealing amenities. From the covered front porch that invites relaxed living, the entrance opens to the living room with access to the dining room and snack bar at the rear. Two bedrooms are secluded to the right of the plan, and the kitchen, bathroom/laundry facilities are located on the left side. A second porch off the kitchen provides room for dining and quiet moments. This home is designed with a basement foundation.

Width 38'-0"
Depth 28'-0"

5,70 X 3,50
19'-0" X 11'-8"

3,65 X 3,50
12'-2" X 11'-8"

4,60 X 3,60
15'-4" X 12'-0"

2,70 X 3,00
9'-0" X 10'-0"

Design by
© Drummond Designs, Inc.

ONE-STORY FARMHOUSES

This country cottage is sure to please with its many amenities! Included in the long list are a fireplace in the family room, a work island in the U-shaped kitchen and a convenient—yet hidden—laundry room. Two family bedrooms share a full bath while the master suite offers a private bath and a large walk-in closet. Note the huge storage area beyond the carport.

Design by
© Greg Marquis & Associates

Width 55'-6"
Depth 64'-3"

© 1994 Donald A. Gardner Architects, Inc.

A country farmhouse exterior combined with an open floor plan creates a comfortable home or vacation getaway. The great room, warmed by a fireplace and opened by a cathedral ceiling, combines well with the dining room and the kitchen. A front bedroom and full bath easily double as a home office. The second floor contains the master bedroom with a walk-in closet and a private bath. Front and rear porches provide plenty of room for outdoor enjoyment.

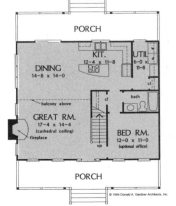

Width 35'-9"
Depth 43'-0"

QUOTE ONE
Cost to build? See page 684
to order complete cost estimate
to build this house in your area!

© 1994 Donald A. Gardner Architects, Inc.

Design by
Donald A. Gardner
Architects, Inc.

ONE-STORY FARMHOUSES

© 1994 Donald A. Gardner Architects, Inc.

DESIGN 9748
Square Footage: 1,737

Inviting porches are just the beginning of amenities found in this lovely country home. Casual lifestyles will love the massive great room with a cathedral ceiling, built-in bookshelves and a fireplace. An octagonal dining room with a tray ceiling makes every meal a special occasion. The breakfast area is a perfect extension to the efficient kitchen that includes an island cooktop and built-in pantry. The master bedroom, set to the rear of the plan, offers privacy and comfort.

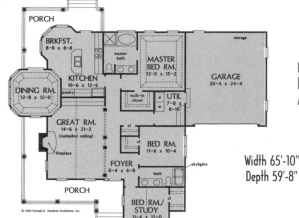

© 1994 Donald A. Gardner Architects, Inc.

Design by
Donald A. Gardner
Architects, Inc.

Width 65'-10"
Depth 59'-8"

DESIGN 3689
Square Footage: 1,295

L D

Equally gracious outside and inside, this one- or two-bedroom cottage presents a post-and-rail covered porch hugging one wing, with convenient access through double doors or pass-through windows in the dining room and kitchen. The columned entry foyer features a sloped ceiling and leads past a second bedroom or media room into a great room with sloped ceiling and fireplace. The master suite fills the right wing and features a plant shelf in the bedroom and garden tub in the master bath, plus a large walk-in closet and laundry facilities.

Design by
© Home Planners

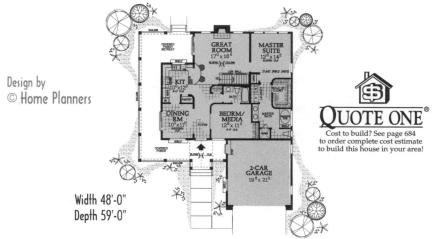

QUOTE ONE®
Cost to build? See page 684 to order complete cost estimate to build this house in your area!

Width 48'-0"
Depth 59'-0"

BASIC PLAN

Design by
© Home Planners

ENHANCED PLAN

Width 35'-0"
Depth 78'-0"

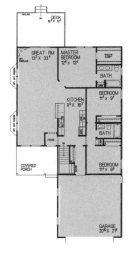

This eye-catching three-bedroom ranch home is designed specifically for narrow lots. All the many features you've been looking for in a family home can be found here. The master bedroom includes a bath and a walk-in closet. A second bath is located between the two family bedrooms. The huge great room offers plenty of space for all your gatherings. The blueprints for this house show how to build both a basic, low-cost version and an enhanced, upgraded version.

BASIC PLAN

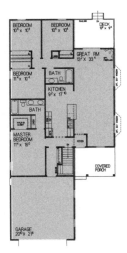

Width 35'-0"
Depth 76'-0"

Design by
© Home Planners

ENHANCED PLAN

If you have a narrow lot to build your home on, then this elegant ranch design is for you! The master bedroom includes a full bath and a walk-in closet, while a second full bath serves the remaining three bedrooms. A galley kitchen with an eat-in nook opens up to a huge great room that easily accommodates friends and family. The house may be built with or without the two-car garage, rear deck, bay windows and fireplace. Blueprints include details for both the basic and the enhanced versions.

ONE-STORY FARMHOUSES

© 1995 Donald A. Gardner Architects, Inc.

DESIGN 9795
Square Footage: 1,298

This design provides plenty of curb appeal. From its gable roof and covered front porch to its large rear deck, this home will brighten any neighborhood. Inside, open planning is the theme in the dining room/great room, with a cathedral ceiling combining the two areas into a comfortable unit. The kitchen contributes to the openness with its snack bar/work island. Three bedrooms—or two and a study—complete this attractive home.

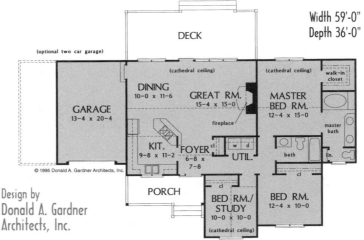

Width 59'-0"
Depth 36'-0"

DECK

(optional two car garage)

(cathedral ceiling)

DINING 10-0 x 11-6

GREAT RM. 15-4 x 15-0

fireplace

(cathedral ceiling)

MASTER BED RM. 12-4 x 15-0

walk-in closet

master bath

GARAGE 13-4 x 20-4

KIT. 9-8 x 11-2

FOYER 6-8 x 7-8

UTIL.

bath

PORCH

BED RM./ STUDY 10-0 x 10-0

(cathedral ceiling)

BED RM. 12-4 x 10-0

© 1995 Donald A. Gardner Architects, Inc.

Design by
Donald A. Gardner
Architects, Inc.

DESIGN 9693
Square Footage: 1,677

Cathedral ceilings grace both the great room and the bedroom/study, while tray ceilings appear in the dining room and master bedroom in this elegant, three-bedroom home. The open kitchen allows for a serving island convenient to the breakfast area, dining room and rear porch. The master suite directly accesses the deck and also features a walk-in closet and master bath with double-bowl vanity, shower and whirlpool tub. A covered breezeway connects the garage to the house.

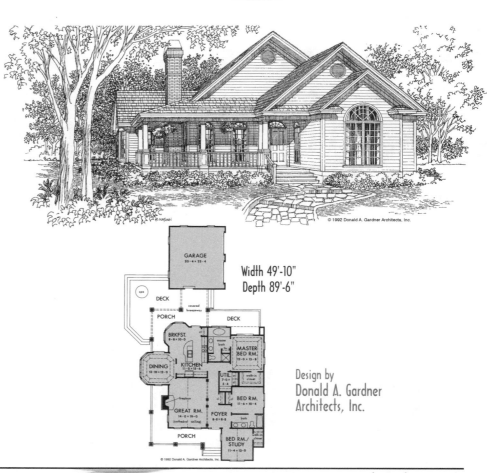

© 1992 Donald A. Gardner Architects, Inc.

GARAGE 20-4 x 23-4

Width 49'-10"
Depth 89'-6"

DECK

PORCH

covered breezeway

DECK

BRKFST. 8-8 x 10-0

KITCHEN 11-0 x 15-6

MASTER BED RM. 12-0 x 13-6

DINING 12-10 x 12-0

UTIL. 7-0 x 5-4

walk-in closet

BED RM. 11-6 x 10-4

GREAT RM. 14-0 x 19-0 (cathedral ceiling)

FOYER 8-0 x 8-8

bath

PORCH

BED RM./ STUDY 11-4 x 12-0

© 1992 Donald A. Gardner Architects, Inc.

Design by
Donald A. Gardner
Architects, Inc.

© 1995 Donald A. Gardner Architects, Inc.

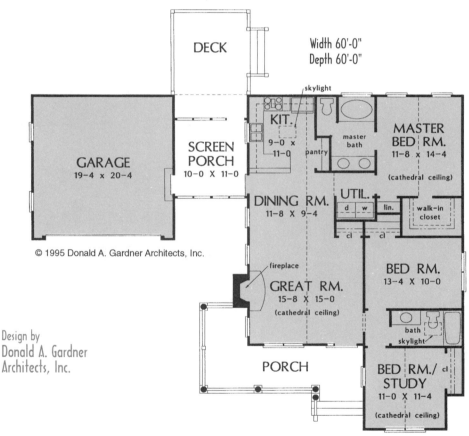

DECK

Width 60'-0"
Depth 60'-0"

skylight

KIT.
9-0 x
11-0

master bath

pantry

MASTER BED RM.
11-8 x 14-4

(cathedral ceiling)

GARAGE
19-4 x 20-4

SCREEN PORCH
10-0 X 11-0

DINING RM.
11-8 X 9-4

UTIL.
d w   lin.

cl   cl

walk-in closet

© 1995 Donald A. Gardner Architects, Inc.

fireplace

GREAT RM.
15-8 X 15-0

(cathedral ceiling)

BED RM.
13-4 x 10-0

bath
skylight

Design by
Donald A. Gardner
Architects, Inc.

PORCH

BED RM./ STUDY
11-0 X 11-4

(cathedral ceiling)

This one-story home offers tremendous curb appeal and many extras found only in much larger homes. A continuous cathedral ceiling in the great room, dining room and kitchen gives a spacious feel to an efficient plan. The kitchen, brightened by a skylight, features a pantry and a peninsula counter for easy preparation and service to the dining room and screened porch. The deck joins the screened porch for extra entertaining space. The master suite opens up with a cathedral ceiling, walk-in and linen closets and a private bath including a garden tub and double-bowl vanity. A cathedral ceiling highlights the front bedroom/study, separated from the other bedroom by a skylit bath.

DESIGN 9781
Square Footage: 1,246

DESIGN 9797
Square Footage: 1,417

B. NATHAN © 1995 Donald A. Gardner Architects, Inc.

A wide-open floor plan emphasizes family living in this modest, single-story home. A cathedral ceiling stretches the length of the plan, stylishly topping the dining room, great room and master bedroom. The kitchen is open to the dining room and great room. The master suite has a walk-in closet and a compartmented bath with a garden tub and twin vanities. One of the two family bedrooms has a cathedral ceiling as well, making it an optional study.

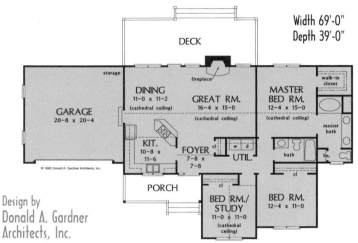

Width 69'-0"
Depth 39'-0"

Design by
Donald A. Gardner
Architects, Inc.

DESIGN 9696
Square Footage: 1,625

This family-pleasing design is thoughtful, indeed. Living areas include a kitchen with efficient work triangle, an adjoining breakfast room, a dining room with bay window, and of course, the great room with fireplace and access to a rear porch. The master bedroom also has porch access, along with a walk-in closet and a lavish bath. One of the two family bedrooms includes a half-round transom window, adding appeal to the exterior and interior.

© 1992 Donald A. Gardner Architects, Inc.

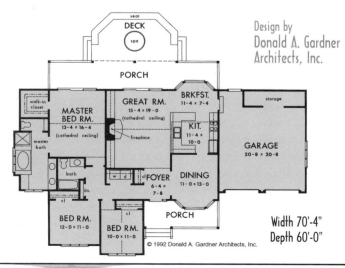

Design by
Donald A. Gardner
Architects, Inc.

Width 70'-4"
Depth 60'-0"

© 1992 Donald A. Gardner Architects, Inc.

www.homeplanners.com

© 1992 Donald A. Gardner Architects, Inc.

B. NATHAN

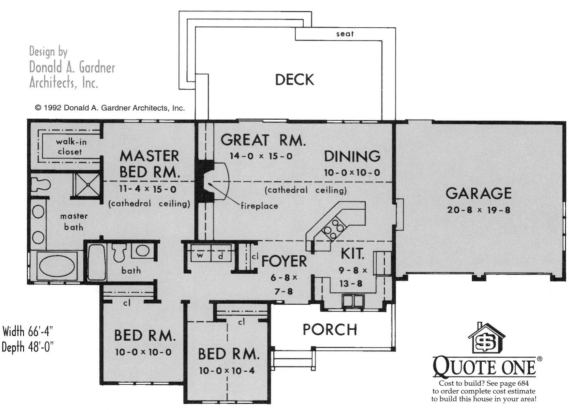

Design by
Donald A. Gardner
Architects, Inc.

© 1992 Donald A. Gardner Architects, Inc.

DECK

seat

walk-in closet

MASTER BED RM.
11-4 × 15-0
(cathedral ceiling)

GREAT RM.
14-0 × 15-0

DINING
10-0 × 10-0

GARAGE
20-8 × 19-8

master bath

(cathedral ceiling)

fireplace

w | d | cl

FOYER
6-8 × 7-8

KIT.
9-8 × 13-8

bath

cl

Width 66'-4"
Depth 48'-0"

BED RM.
10-0 × 10-0

cl

BED RM.
10-0 × 10-4

PORCH

Quote One®
Cost to build? See page 684
to order complete cost estimate
to build this house in your area!

This economical plan offers an impressive visual statement with its comfortable and well-appointed appearance. The entrance foyer leads to all areas of the home. The great room, dining area and kitchen are all open to one another, allowing visual interaction. The great room and dining area are joined under a dramatic cathedral ceiling. Bookshelves and cabinets flank the fire-place. The master suite contains a cathedral ceiling, walk-in closet and master bath with double-bowl vanity, whirlpool tub and shower. Two family bedrooms and a full hall bath complete this cozy house. A basement or crawlspace foundation is available. A two-car garage opens to the front. A wide deck with built-in seat opens off the great room.

DESIGN 9664
Square Footage: 1,287

ONE-STORY FARMHOUSES

DESIGN
7704
Square Footage: 1,246

D. NATAN
© 1997 Donald A. Gardner Architects, Inc.

Open living spaces allow an easy flow while vaulted ceilings add volume in this gracious country cottage. The front porch wraps slightly, giving the illusion of a larger home, while a cathedral ceiling maximizes space in the open great room and dining room. The kitchen features a center skylight, breakfast bar and screened-porch access. Two bedrooms share a bath up front, while the master suite enjoys a private location to the back of the plan.

Width 60'-0"
Depth 48'-0"

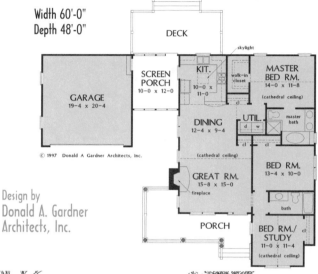

© 1997 Donald A Gardner Architects, Inc.

Design by
Donald A. Gardner
Architects, Inc.

DESIGN
9764
Square Footage: 1,815
Bonus Room: 336 square feet

Dormers, arched windows and covered porches lend this home its country appeal. Inside, the foyer opens to the dining room on the right and leads through a columned entrance to the great room warmed by a fireplace. The open kitchen easily serves the great room, the bayed breakfast area and the dining room. A cathedral ceiling graces the master bedroom, which also features a walk-in closet and private bath with a dual vanity and a whirlpool tub. Two additional bedrooms share a full bath.

© 1994 Donald A. Gardner Architects, Inc.

Design by
Donald A. Gardner
Architects, Inc.

Width 70'-8"
Depth 70'-2"

Quote One®
Cost to build? See page 684
to order complete cost estimate
to build this house in your area!

ONE-STORY FARMHOUSES

© 1994 Donald A. Gardner Architects, Inc.

Width 65'-0"
Depth 44'-2"

MASTER BED RM.
14-8 x 13-0

DECK

master bath
walk-in closet
UTIL.
w d
lin. sto.

GREAT RM.
15-8 x 15-0
(cathedral ceiling)
fireplace

DINING
11-4 x 11-0

GARAGE
21-0 x 21-0

FOYER
6-8 x 5-8

KIT.
11-4 x 12-4

bath
cl

BED RM.
10-0 x 10-4

BED RM.
10-0 x 10-4

PORCH

© 1994 Donald A. Gardner Architects, Inc.

Design by
Donald A. Gardner
Architects, Inc.

REAR VIEW

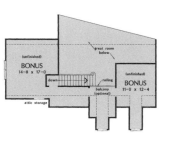

QUOTE ONE®
Cost to build? See page 684
to order complete cost estimate
to build this house in your area!

DESIGN
9753
Square Footage: 1,346

A great room that stretches into the dining room makes this design perfect for entertaining. A fireplace and built-ins, as well as a cathedral ceiling, further the possibilities. A rear deck allows for great outdoor livability. It can be reached from the master bedroom and the great room. The ample kitchen features lots of counter and cabinet space as well as an angled cooktop. Three bedrooms include a master suite with sloped ceiling, private bath and walk-in closet.

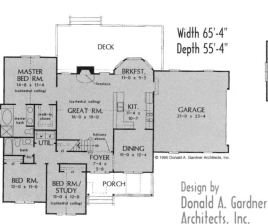

© 1995 Donald A. Gardner Architects, Inc.

Width 65'-4"
Depth 55'-4"

MASTER BED RM.
14-8 x 13-4
(cathedral ceiling)

DECK

master bath
walk-in closet
UTIL.
w d
bath
cl

fireplace

GREAT RM.
16-0 x 19-0
(cathedral ceiling)

BRKFST.
11-0 x 9-5

KIT.
11-4 x 10-7

GARAGE
21-0 x 23-4

balcony above

DINING
11-0 x 12-4

FOYER
7-4 x 5-8

BED RM.
12-0 x 11-0

BED RM./
STUDY
11-0 x 12-0
(cathedral ceiling)

PORCH

Design by
Donald A. Gardner
Architects, Inc.

(unfinished)
BONUS
14-8 x 17-0

great room below

down

(unfinished)
BONUS
11-0 x 12-4

railing
balcony (optional)

attic storage

DESIGN
9794
Square Footage: 1,633
Bonus Room: 595 square feet

Stylish rooms and comfortable arrangements make this country home unique and inviting. The foyer opens from a quaint covered porch and leads to the expansive great room, which boasts a cathedral ceiling, an extended-hearth fireplace and access to the rear deck. The kitchen serves the formal dining room as well as the bayed breakfast nook. A secluded master suite nestles to the rear of the plan and features a U-shaped walk-in closet, a garden tub and twin vanities. Two nearby bedrooms—or make one a study—share a full bath.

ONE-STORY FARMHOUSES

DESIGN 9771
Square Footage: 1,927

With so many windows, sunlight takes center stage in this delightful country home. Two bedrooms and a full bath are to the left of the foyer. To the right is the dining room, which leads into the L-shaped kitchen that has a peninsular cooktop and connecting breakfast area with a bay window. The central great room offers a cathedral ceiling, a fireplace and access to the rear porch. The secluded master suite features a lovely display of windows, large walk-in closet and luxurious whirlpool bath with skylights.

© 1994 Donald A. Gardner Architects, Inc.

Design by
Donald A. Gardner
Architects, Inc.

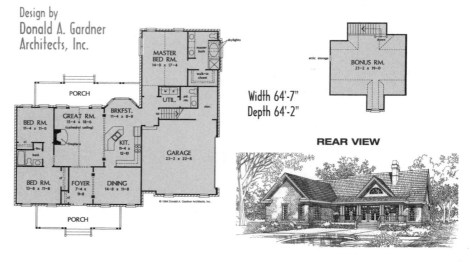

Width 64'-7"
Depth 64'-2"

REAR VIEW

DESIGN 7679
Square Footage: 1,517
Bonus Room: 287 square feet

The foyer opens to a spacious great room with a fireplace and a cathedral ceiling in this lovely traditional home. Sliding doors open to a rear deck from the great room, posing a warm welcome to the outdoors. The U-shaped kitchen features an angled peninsula counter with a cooktop. A private hall leads to the family sleeping quarters, which include two bedrooms and a full bath with a double-bowl lavatory. Sizable bonus space above the garage provides a skylight.

© 1997 Donald A. Gardner Architects, Inc.

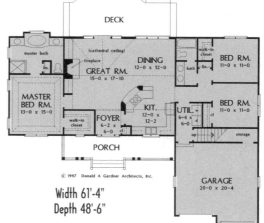

Design by
Donald A. Gardner
Architects, Inc.

Width 61'-4"
Depth 48'-6"

ONE-STORY FARMHOUSES

496

www.homeplanners.com

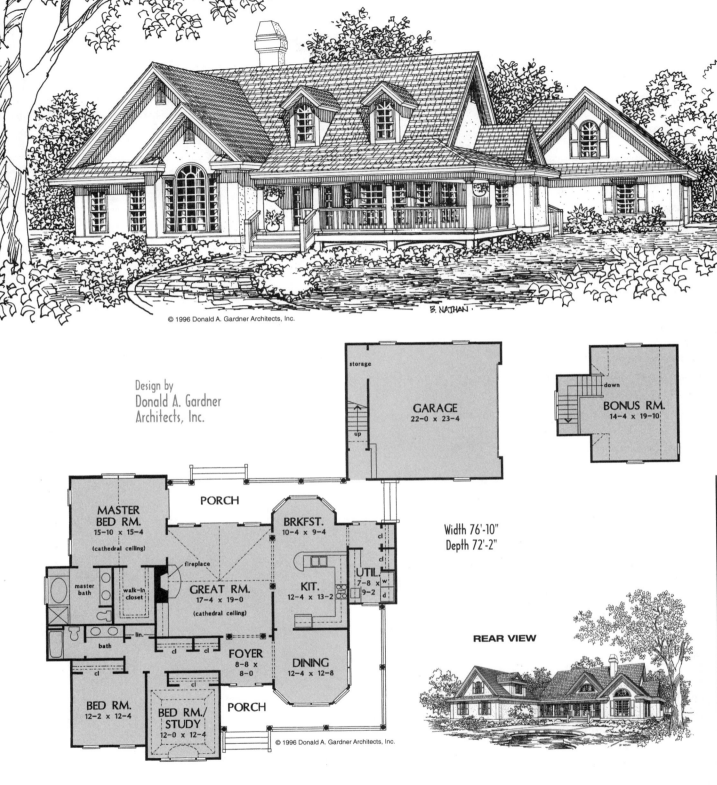

© 1996 Donald A. Gardner Architects, Inc.

B. NATHAN

Design by
Donald A. Gardner
Architects, Inc.

storage

GARAGE
22-0 x 23-4

up

BONUS RM.
14-4 x 19-10

down

PORCH

MASTER
BED RM.
15-10 x 15-4
(cathedral ceiling)

BRKFST.
10-4 x 9-4

master bath

walk-in closet

fireplace

GREAT RM.
17-4 x 19-0
(cathedral ceiling)

KIT.
12-4 x 13-2

UTIL.
7-8 x
9-2

w
d

cl

Width 76'-10"
Depth 72'-2"

bath

lin.

cl   cl

FOYER
8-8 x
8-0

DINING
12-4 x 12-8

BED RM.
12-2 x 12-4

cl

BED RM./
STUDY
12-0 x 12-4

PORCH

© 1996 Donald A. Gardner Architects, Inc.

REAR VIEW

ONE-STORY FARMHOUSES

Quaint and cozy on the outside, this country charmer offers an open floor plan with soaring, sparkling space as well as plenty of niches to nestle in. A cathedral ceiling and an extended-hearth fireplace highlight the great room, which opens to the breakfast room and leads out to the rear porch. The formal dining room enjoys a bay of windows and is easily served by a spacious, U-shaped kitchen. A cathedral ceiling and relaxing bath amenities, such as a spa-style tub, enhance the secluded master suite. Two additional bedrooms—or make one a study—share a gallery hall that leads to a full bath and extra linen storage.

DESIGN 7625
Square Footage: 2,006
Bonus Room: 329 square feet

© 1997 Donald A. Gardner Architects, Inc.

B. NATHAN

DESIGN 7714
Square Footage: 2,203
Bonus Room: 395 square feet

Bay windows, transoms and gables charm the exterior of this friendly plan, while inside, decorative columns and dramatic ceiling treatments highlight the open layout. Sharing a cathedral ceiling, the great room and kitchen are open to the breakfast bay. The private master suite features a tray ceiling and skylit garden tub. Three additional bedrooms, one with an optional arrangement for wheelchair accessibility, are to the opposite side of the plan.

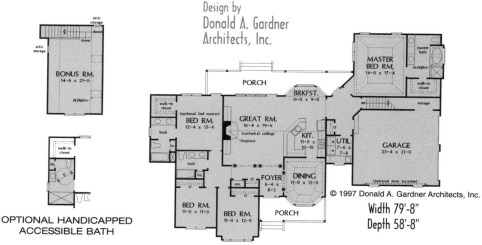

Design by
Donald A. Gardner
Architects, Inc.

© 1997 Donald A. Gardner Architects, Inc.

Width 79'-8"
Depth 58'-8"

OPTIONAL HANDICAPPED
ACCESSIBLE BATH

BONUS RM.
14-6 x 21-0

R. NATHAN

© 1998 Donald A. Gardner, Inc.

DESIGN 7682
Square Footage: 1,762
Bonus Room: 316 square feet

Horizontal siding and charming multi-pane windows set off the exterior of this lovely country home. Inside, the foyer leads to the great room, which has a cathedral ceiling and a fireplace. Open planning allows the formal dining room to enjoy the glow of the hearth as well as views of the back property. The secluded master wing holds two walk-in closets, a tray ceiling and a lavish bath with a garden tub.

© 1998 Donald A. Gardner Architects, Inc.

Design by
Donald A. Gardner
Architects, Inc.

Width 56'-8"
Depth 59'-0"

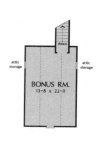

BONUS RM.
13-8 x 22-0

©1997 Donald A. Gardner Architects, Inc.

B. NATHAN

Design by
Donald A. Gardner
Architects, Inc.

Width 62'-10"
Depth 65'-10"

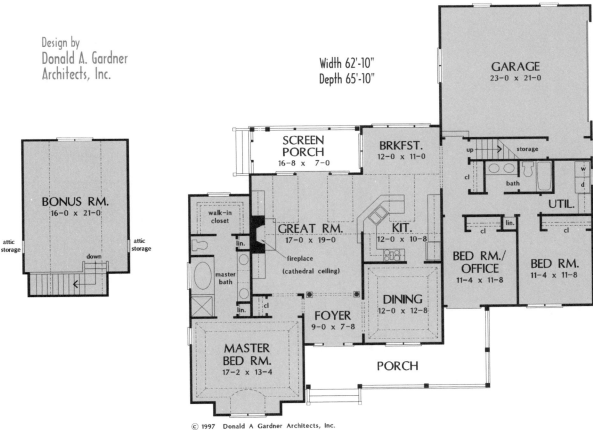

© 1997 Donald A Gardner Architects, Inc.

The perfect picture of country comfort, this lovely home offers ample space and flexibility for its moderate size. Columns mark the entrance to an exceptional great room that boasts rear clerestory dormer windows, access to the screened porch, a shared cathedral ceiling with the adjacent kitchen, and functional built-ins on either side of its soothing fireplace. The master suite features a bay window, tray ceiling, whirlpool bath, separate shower and dual-sink vanity. Two more bedrooms at the other side of the home share a full bath. Above the garage, a bonus room can be developed in the future.

DESIGN
7716
Square Footage: 1,911
Bonus Room: 406 square feet

©1997 Donald A. Gardner Architects, Inc.

B. NATHAN

Design by
Donald A. Gardner
Architects, Inc.

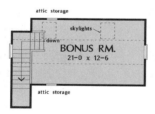

attic storage

skylights

down

BONUS RM.
21-0 x 12-6

attic storage

storage

GARAGE
21-0 x 21-4

up

covered breezeway

Width 74'-8"
Depth 75'-10"

MASTER
BED RM.
16-0 x 15-0

PORCH

BRKFST.
11-8 x 9-0

cl

master bath

walk-in closet

fireplace

KIT.
14-8 x 12-8

pd. rm.

UTIL.
8-8 x 6-4

linen

GREAT RM.
17-4 x 20-4

d w

lin.

(cathedral ceiling)

bath

BED RM.
11-0 x 12-6

lin.

cl

FOYER
8-8 x
7-10

DINING
13-0 x 15-10

cl

cl cl

BED RM./
STUDY
12-0 x 12-4

PORCH

BED RM.
12-4 x 12-0

© 1997 Donald A Gardner Architects, Inc.

DESIGN
7715
Square Footage: 2,273
Bonus Room: 342 square feet

An exciting blend of styles, this home features the wrapping porch of a country farmhouse with a brick-and-siding exterior, for a uniquely pleasing effect. The great room shares its cathedral ceiling with an open kitchen while the octagonal shaped dining room is complemented by a tray ceiling. Built-ins flank the great room's fireplace for added convenience. The master suite at the back of the home includes access to the porch, walk-in closet, whirlpool tub, separate shower and dual-sink vanity. The other three bedrooms share a full bath, also with dual-sink vanity. The two-car garage is reached via a breezeway.

©1993 Donald A. Gardner Architects, Inc.

Design by
**Donald A. Gardner
Architects, Inc.**

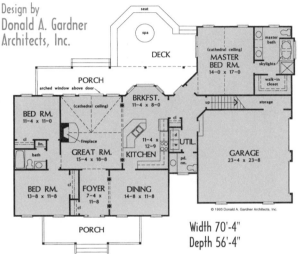

seat

spa

DECK

PORCH
arched window above door

(cathedral ceiling)

(cathedral ceiling)
MASTER
BED RM.
14-0 x 17-0

master
bath

skylights

walk-in
closet

BRKFST.
11-4 x 8-0

BED RM.
11-4 x 11-0

storage

GREAT RM.
15-4 x 18-8

fireplace

KITCHEN

11-4 x
12-9

up

UTIL.

d
w

GARAGE
23-4 x 23-8

pd.
rm.

BED RM.
13-8 x 11-8

FOYER
7-4 x
11-8

DINING
14-8 x 11-8

PORCH

© 1993 Donald A. Gardner Architects, Inc.

Width 70'-4"
Depth 56'-4"

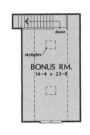

down

skylights

BONUS RM.
14-4 x 23-8

QUOTE ONE®
Cost to build? See page 684
to order complete cost estimate
to build this house in your area!

Quaint and cozy on the outside with porches front and back, this three-bedroom country home surprises with an open floor plan that features a large great room with a cathedral ceiling. A central kitchen with an angled counter opens to the breakfast and great rooms for easy entertaining. The secluded master bedroom includes a cathedral ceiling and access to the deck. Operable skylights over the tub accent the luxurious master bath.

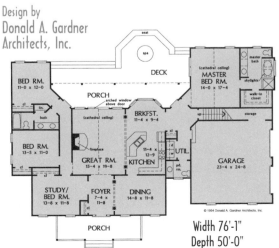

© 1994 Donald A. Gardner Architects, Inc.

Design by
**Donald A. Gardner
Architects, Inc.**

seat

spa

DECK

PORCH
arched window above door

(cathedral ceiling)

(cathedral ceiling)
MASTER
BED RM.
14-0 x 17-4

master
bath

skylights

walk-in
closet

BRKFST.
11-4 x 9-4

BED RM.
11-0 x 12-0

storage

GREAT RM.
15-4 x 19-8

fireplace

KITCHEN

11-4 x
12-9

up

UTIL.

d
w

GARAGE
23-4 x 24-8

pd.
rm.

BED RM.
13-5 x 11-0

STUDY/
BED RM.
13-8 x 11-8

FOYER
7-4 x
11-8

DINING
14-8 x 11-8

PORCH

© 1994 Donald A. Gardner Architects, Inc.

Width 76'-1"
Depth 50'-0"

down

BONUS RM.
14-4 x 24-8

QUOTE ONE®
Cost to build? See page 684
to order complete cost estimate
to build this house in your area!

This quaint four-bedroom home with front and rear porches reinforces its beauty with arched windows and dormers. The pillared dining room opens on the right while a study lies to the left. The massive great room features a cathedral ceiling, enchanting fireplace and access to the rear porch. The master suite enjoys a cathedral ceiling, rear-deck access and an amenity-filled master bath. Two additional bedrooms at the opposite end of the house share a full bath that contains dual vanities.

ONE-STORY FARMHOUSES

DESIGN
9763
Square Footage: 1,807
Bonus Room: 419 square feet

Dormers and arched windows provide this country home with lots of charm. An open kitchen easily serves the great room, the bayed breakfast area and the dining room. Outdoor living is enhanced with a rear skylit porch. The master bedroom contains a huge walk-in closet and a private bath featuring a whirlpool tub, separate shower and double-bowl vanity. Two family bedrooms share a full bath. A bonus room over the garage can be developed as additional space is needed.

© 1994 Donald A. Gardner Architects, Inc.

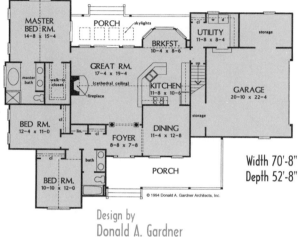

MASTER BED RM.
14-8 x 15-4

PORCH
skylights

UTILITY
11-8 x 8-4

storage

master bath

walk-in closet

BRKFST.
10-4 x 8-6

GREAT RM.
17-4 x 19-4
(cathedral ceiling)
fireplace

KITCHEN
11-8 x 10-6

up

GARAGE
20-10 x 22-4

BED RM.
12-4 x 11-0

storage

lin.

FOYER
8-8 x 7-8

DINING
11-4 x 12-8

BED RM.
10-10 x 12-0

bath

PORCH

© 1994 Donald A. Gardner Architects, Inc.

Width 70'-8"
Depth 52'-8"

Design by
Donald A. Gardner
Architects, Inc.

QUOTE ONE®
Cost to build? See page 684 to order complete cost estimate to build this house in your area!

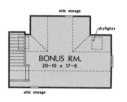

attic storage

skylights

BONUS RM.
20-10 x 17-8

attic storage

DESIGN
9750
Square Footage: 1,575
Bonus Room: 276 square feet

A covered porch and dormers combine to create the inviting exterior on this three-bedroom country home. The foyer leads through columns to an expansive great room with a cozy fireplace, bookshelves and access to the rear covered porch. To the right, an open kitchen easily serves the bay-windowed breakfast area and the formal dining room. The master suite enjoys access to the covered porch, a walk-in closet and a relaxing master bath complete with double-bowl vanities, whirlpool tub and separate shower.

© 1994 Donald A. Gardner Architects, Inc.

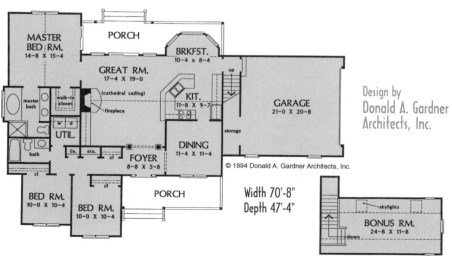

MASTER BED RM.
14-8 X 15-4

PORCH

BRKFST.
10-4 x 8-4

GREAT RM.
17-4 x 19-0
(cathedral ceiling)
fireplace

KIT.
11-8 x 9-7

up

GARAGE
21-0 X 20-8

master bath

walk-in closet

w   d

UTIL.

storage

lin.   sto.

FOYER
8-8 X 5-8

DINING
11-4 x 11-4

BED RM.
10-0 X 10-4

BED RM.
10-0 X 10-4

PORCH

© 1994 Donald A. Gardner Architects, Inc.

Width 70'-8"
Depth 47'-4"

Design by
Donald A. Gardner
Architects, Inc.

skylights

BONUS RM.
24-8 X 11-8

down

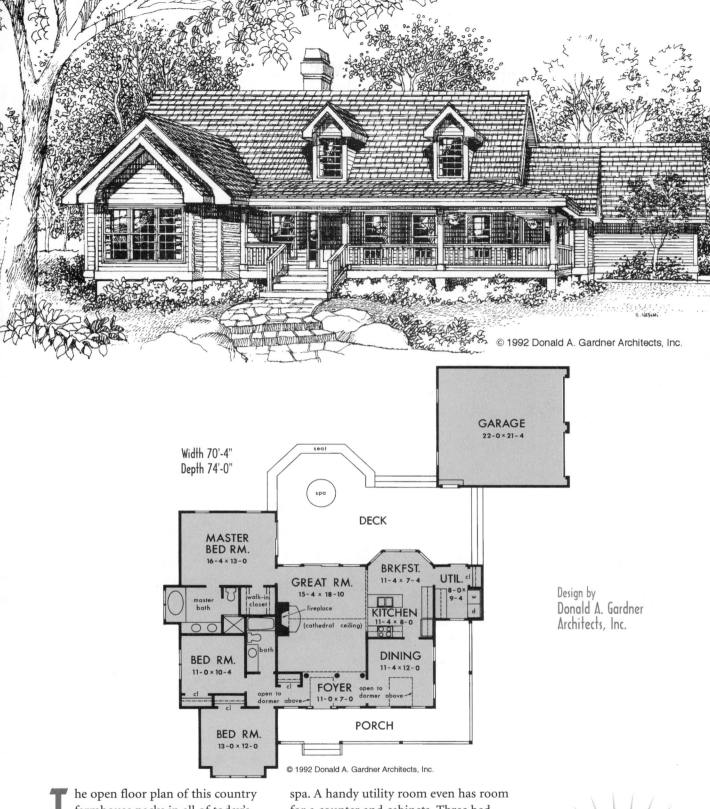

© 1992 Donald A. Gardner Architects, Inc.

Width 70'-4"
Depth 74'-0"

GARAGE
22-0 × 21-4

seat

spa

DECK

MASTER
BED RM.
16-4 × 13-0

master bath

walk-in closet

GREAT RM.
15-4 × 18-10

fireplace

(cathedral ceiling)

BRKFST.
11-4 × 7-4

UTIL.
8-0 × 9-4

cl

w

d

KITCHEN
11-4 × 8-0

Design by
Donald A. Gardner
Architects, Inc.

BED RM.
11-0 × 10-4

bath

DINING
11-4 × 12-0

cl

cl

open to dormer above

FOYER
11-0 × 7-0

open to dormer above

cl

BED RM.
13-0 × 12-0

PORCH

© 1992 Donald A. Gardner Architects, Inc.

The open floor plan of this country farmhouse packs in all of today's amenities in only 1,590 square feet. Columns separate the foyer from the great room, with its cathedral ceiling and fireplace. Serving meals has never been easier—the kitchen makes use of direct access to the dining room as well as a breakfast nook overlooking the deck and spa. A handy utility room even has room for a counter and cabinets. Three bedrooms make this an especially desirable design. The master bedroom, off of the great room, provides private access to the deck. A two-car garage sits to the back, beyond the deck. This design is flexible enough to be accommodated by a narrow lot if the garage is relocated.

DESIGN
9713
Square Footage: 1,590

ONE-STORY FARMHOUSES

DESIGN 9639
Square Footage: 1,541

© 1991 Donald A. Gardner Architects, Inc.

This traditional three-bedroom home, with front and side porches, arched windows and dormers, projects the appearance of a much larger home. The great room features a cathedral ceiling, fireplace and arched window above the sliding glass door to the expansive rear deck. Elegant round columns define the dining room. The master suite contains a pampering master bath with a whirlpool tub, separate shower, double-bowl vanity and walk-in closet. Two other bedrooms share a full bath that includes a double-bowl vanity.

Design by
Donald A. Gardner
Architects, Inc.

Width 71'-0"
Depth 59'-0"

© 1991 Donald A. Gardner Architects, Inc.

DESIGN 9620
Square Footage: 1,310

A multi-pane bay window, decorative dormers and a covered porch dress up this one-story cottage. The entrance foyer leads to an impressive great room with a cathedral ceiling and fireplace. The U-shaped kitchen, adjacent to the dining room, provides an ideal layout for food preparation. The luxurious master bedroom, located to the rear of the house, takes advantage of the deck area and is assured privacy from two other bedrooms at the front of the house. These family bedrooms share a full bath.

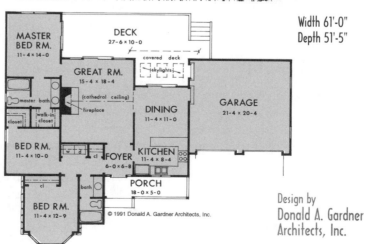

© 1991 Donald A. Gardner Architects, Inc.

Width 61'-0"
Depth 51'-5"

Design by
Donald A. Gardner
Architects, Inc.

ONE-STORY FARMHOUSES

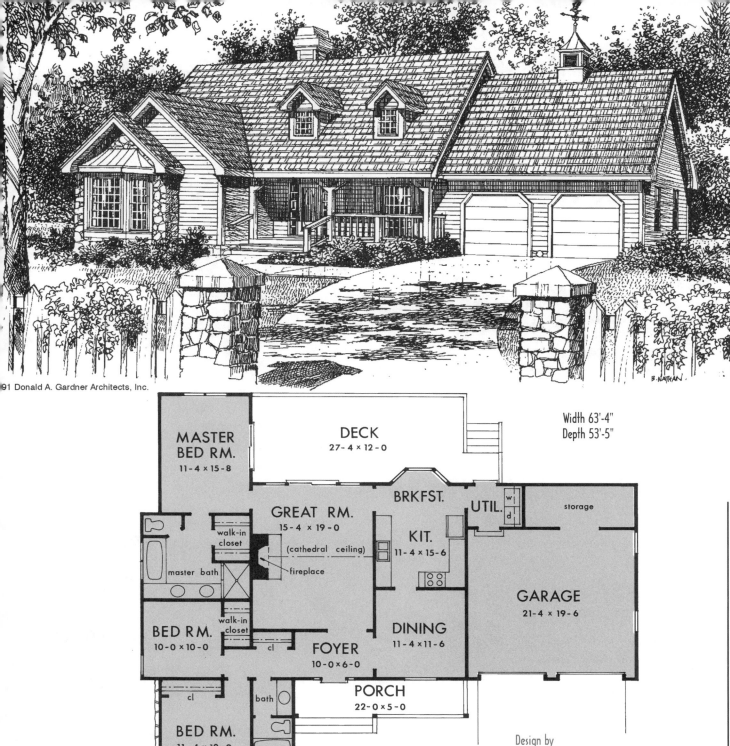

Width 63'-4"
Depth 53'-5"

MASTER BED RM.
11- 4 × 15- 8

DECK
27- 4 × 12- 0

BRKFST.

UTIL.

storage

walk-in closet

GREAT RM.
15- 4 × 19- 0

(cathedral ceiling)

KIT.
11- 4 × 15- 6

master bath

fireplace

GARAGE
21- 4 × 19- 6

BED RM.
10- 0 × 10- 0

walk-in closet

cl

DINING
11- 4 × 11- 6

FOYER
10- 0 × 6- 0

cl

bath

PORCH
22- 0 × 5- 0

BED RM.
11- 4 × 12- 9

© 1991 Donald A. Gardner Architects, Inc.

Design by
Donald A. Gardner
Architects, Inc.

ONE-STORY FARMHOUSES

A multi-pane bay window, dormers, a cupola, a covered porch and a variety of building materials all combine to dress up this intriguing country cottage. The generous entry foyer leads to a formal dining room and an impressive great room with a cathedral ceiling and fireplace. The kitchen includes a breakfast area with a bay window overlooking the deck. The great room and master bedroom also access the deck. An amenity-filled master suite is highlighted by a master bath that includes a double-bowl vanity, shower and garden tub. Two additional bedrooms at the front of the house share a full bath.

DESIGN 9679
Square Footage: 1,512

© 1993 Donald A. Gardner Architects, Inc.

DESIGN 9727
Square Footage: 1,322

Small doesn't necessarily mean boring in this well-proportioned, three-bedroom country home. A gracious foyer leads to the great room through a set of elegant columns. In this living area, a cathedral ceiling works well with a fireplace and skylights to bring the utmost livability to the homeowner. Outside, an expansive deck includes room for a spa. A handsome master suite contains a tray ceiling and a private bath. Two additional bedrooms to the left of the plan both enjoy ample closet space and share a hall bath.

Design by
Donald A. Gardner
Architects, Inc.

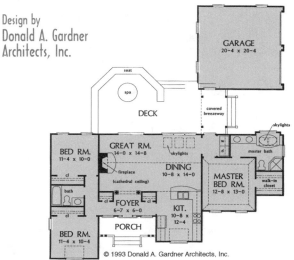

Width 56'-8"
Depth 63'-4"

© 1993 Donald A. Gardner Architects, Inc.

DESIGN 9726
Square Footage: 1,498

This charming country home utilizes multi-pane windows, columns, dormers and a covered porch to provide a welcoming front exterior. Inside, the great room with a dramatic cathedral ceiling commands attention; the kitchen and breakfast room are just beyond a set of columns. A tray ceiling in the master bedroom contributes to its pleasant atmosphere, as do the large walk-in closet and the gracious master bath with a garden tub and separate shower.

Design by
Donald A. Gardner
Architects, Inc.

Width 59'-8"
Depth 50'-8"

© 1993 Donald A. Gardner Architects, Inc.

© 1996 Donald A. Gardner Architects, Inc.

DECK

spa

BED RM.
11-4 x 12-4

GREAT RM.
15-4 x 19-8
(cathedral ceiling)

fireplace

BRKFST.
11-4 x 8-0

MASTER
BED RM.
13-4 x 14-8

master
bath

lin.

skylights

walk-in
closet

storage

KIT.
11-4 x 10-4

w
d

down

FOYER
8-2 x 6-2

cl

cl

BED RM./
STUDY
11-4 x 11-4

PORCH

DINING
11-4 x 12-4

storage

GARAGE
20-0 x 19-8

storage

(optional door location)

bath

lin.

cl

Width 61'-0"
Depth 53'-8"

© 1996   Donald A Gardner Architects, Inc.

Design by
Donald A. Gardner
Architects, Inc.

Quote One®
Cost to build? See page 684
to order complete cost estimate
to build this house in your area!

REAR VIEW

DESIGN
9778
Square Footage: 1,655

B. NATHAN

Covered front-porch dormers and arched windows welcome you to this modified version of one of our most popular country home plans. Interior columns dramatically open the foyer and the kitchen to the spacious great room. The drama is heightened by the great room's cathedral ceiling and fireplace. The kitchen, with its food-preparation island, easily serves the breakfast room and the formal dining room. The master suite features a tray ceiling and access to the rear deck. Added luxuries include a walk-in closet and a skylit master bath with a double vanity, garden tub and separate shower. Two generous bedrooms share the second bath. The two-car garage loads from the side of the plan and includes a large storage area. Relocate the garage doors to the front, if desired.

ONE-STORY FARMHOUSES

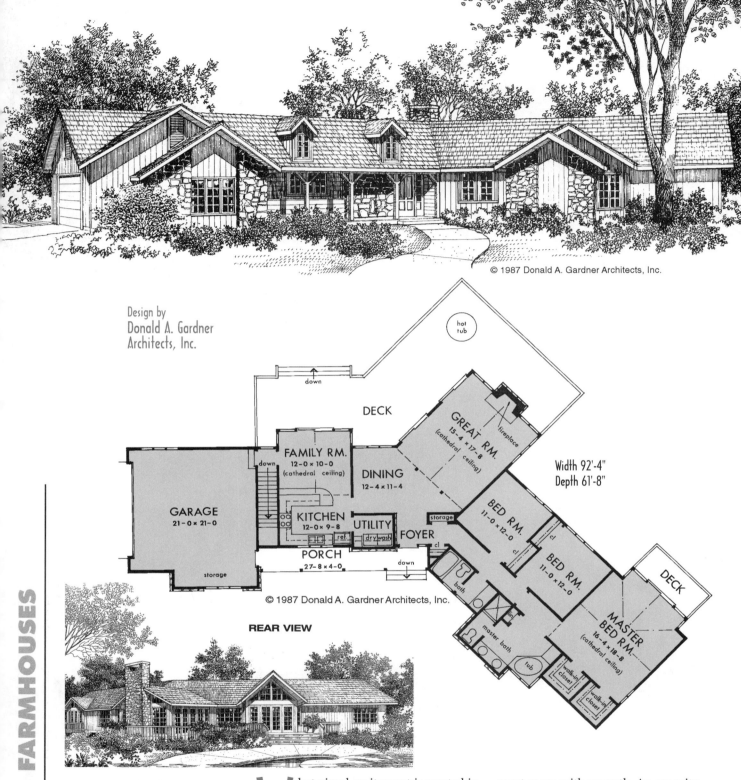

© 1987 Donald A. Gardner Architects, Inc.

Design by
Donald A. Gardner
Architects, Inc.

hot tub

down

DECK

FAMILY RM.
12-0 × 10-0
(cathedral ceiling)

DINING
12-4 × 11-4

GREAT RM.
15-4 × 17-8
(cathedral ceiling)

fireplace

Width 92'-4"
Depth 61'-8"

down

GARAGE
21-0 × 21-0

KITCHEN
12-0 × 9-8

UTILITY

dry wash

ref.

storage

BED RM.
11-0 × 12-0

cl

cl

BED RM.
11-0 × 12-0

DECK

FOYER

cl

PORCH
27-8 × 4-0

storage

down

bath

master bath

tub

MASTER
BED RM.
16-4 × 18-8
(cathedral ceiling)

walk-in closet

walk-in closet

© 1987 Donald A. Gardner Architects, Inc.

REAR VIEW

ONE-STORY FARMHOUSES

DESIGN 9622
Square Footage: 1,842

What visual excitement is created in this country ranch with the use of a combination of exterior building materials and shapes! The angular nature of the plan allows for flexibility in design—lengthen the great room or family room, or both, to suit individual space needs. Cathedral ceilings grace both rooms and a fireplace embellishes the great room with warmth. An amenity-filled master bedroom features a cathedral ceiling, private deck and master bath with whirlpool tub. Two family bedrooms share a full bath. An expansive deck area with a hot tub wraps around interior family gathering areas for enhanced outdoor living. The two-car garage offers a large storage area.

www.homeplanners.com

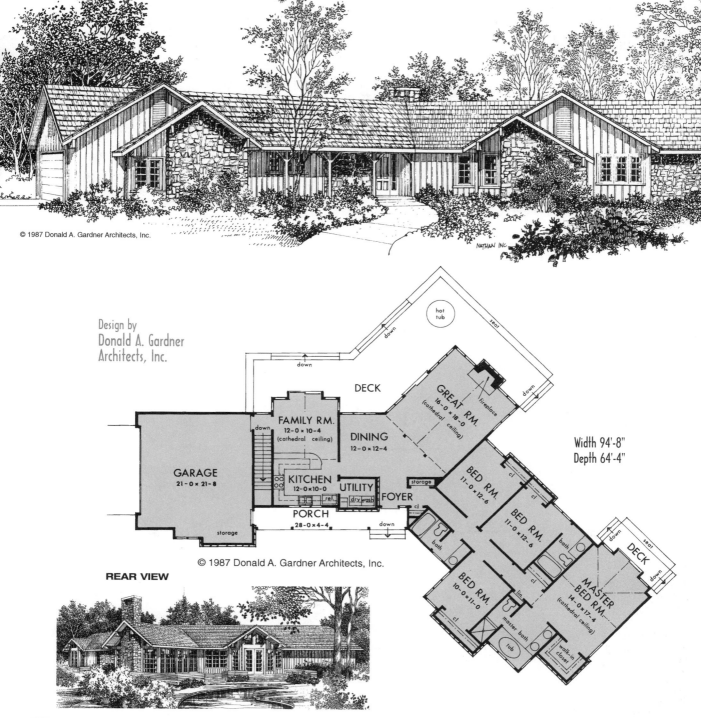

© 1987 Donald A. Gardner Architects, Inc.

Design by
Donald A. Gardner
Architects, Inc.

© 1987 Donald A. Gardner Architects, Inc.

hot tub

DECK

GREAT RM.
16-0 × 18-0
(cathedral ceiling)

fireplace

FAMILY RM.
12-0 × 10-4
(cathedral ceiling)

DINING
12-0 × 12-4

GARAGE
21-0 × 21-8

KITCHEN
12-0 × 10-0

UTILITY

FOYER

storage

BED RM.
11-0 × 12-6

BED RM.
11-0 × 12-6

PORCH
28-0 × 4-4

BED RM.
10-0 × 11-0

DECK

MASTER BED RM.
14-0 × 17-4
(cathedral ceiling)

bath

master bath

tub

walk-in closet

Width 94'-8"
Depth 64'-4"

REAR VIEW

This country-style ranch home is the essence of excitement with its combination of exterior building materials and interesting shapes. Because it is angled, it allows for flexibility in design—the great room and/or the family room can be lengthened to meet family space requirements. Both the family room and great room feature cathedral ceilings. The great room is framed with a dramatic wall of windows and has a cozy fireplace. The master bedroom includes a cathedral ceiling, walk-in closet, private deck and a spacious master bath with whirlpool tub. There are three family bedrooms—two that share a full bath and one that has a private bath. The expansive deck area with space for a hot tub wraps around interior family gathering areas. Note the storage space in the garage.

**DESIGN
9601**
Square Footage: 1,988

ONE-STORY FARMHOUSES

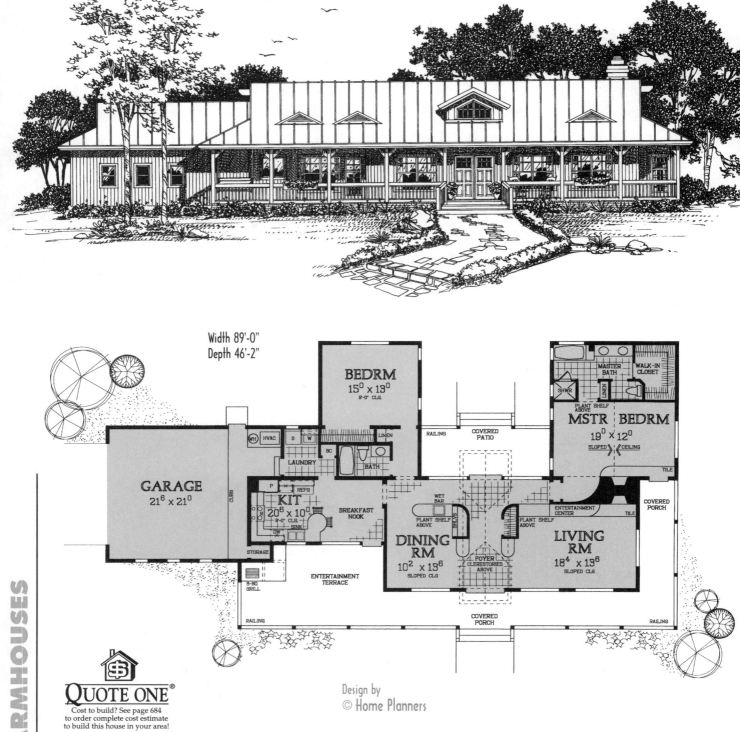

Width 89'-0"
Depth 46'-2"

BEDRM
15⁰ x 13⁰
9'-0" CLG.

COVERED PATIO

RAILING

MASTER BATH

WALK-IN CLOSET

SHWR LINEN

PLANT SHELF ABOVE

MSTR BEDRM
19⁰ x 12⁰

SLOPED CEILING

TILE

GARAGE
21⁶ x 21⁰

WH HVAC D W

BC

LAUNDRY

LINEN

BATH

P

REFG

KIT
20⁶ x 10⁰
9'-0" CLG.

BREAKFAST NOOK

SINK

R

DW

STORAGE

CURB

WET BAR

PLANT SHELF ABOVE

SHLVS

ENTERTAINMENT CENTER

PLANT SHELF ABOVE

COVERED PORCH

TILE

B-B-Q GRILL

ENTERTAINMENT TERRACE

DINING RM
10² x 13⁶
SLOPED CLG

FOYER CLERESTORIES ABOVE

LIVING RM
18⁴ x 13⁶
SLOPED CLG

RAILING

COVERED PORCH

RAILING

QUOTE ONE®
Cost to build? See page 684
to order complete cost estimate
to build this house in your area!

Design by
© Home Planners

ONE-STORY FARMHOUSES

DESIGN
3466
Square Footage: 1,800
L D

mall but inviting, this ranch-style farmhouse is the perfect choice for a small family or empty-nesters. It's loaded with amenities even the most particular homeowner will appreciate. For example, the living room and dining room include plant shelves, sloped ceilings and built-in cabinetry to enhance livability. The living room also sports a

warming fireplace. The master bedroom contains a well-appointed bath with a dual vanity and walk-in closet. The additional bedroom has its own bath with linen storage. The kitchen is separated from the breakfast nook by a clever bar area. Access to the two-car garage is through a laundry area with washer/dryer hook-up space.

www.homeplanners.com

© 1994 Donald A. Gardner Architects, Inc.

B. NATHAN

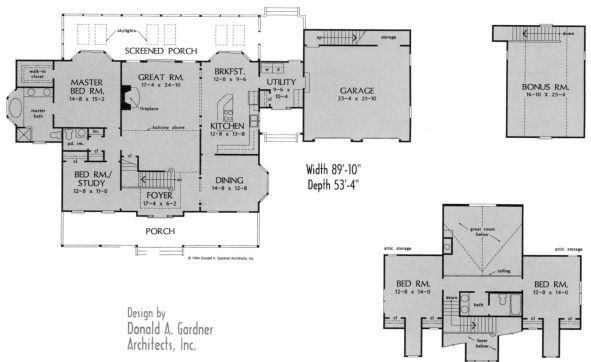

skylights

SCREENED PORCH

walk-in closet

MASTER BED RM.
14-8 x 15-2

master bath

pd. rm.

BED RM./ STUDY
12-8 x 11-0

FOYER
17-4 x 6-2

PORCH

GREAT RM.
17-4 x 24-10

fireplace

balcony above

BRKFST.
12-8 x 9-6

KITCHEN
12-8 x 13-8

UTILITY
9-6 x 10-4

DINING
14-8 x 12-8

up   storage

GARAGE
23-4 x 21-10

© 1994 Donald A. Gardner Architects, Inc.

Width 89'-10"
Depth 53'-4"

BONUS RM.
16-10 x 25-4

down

Design by
Donald A. Gardner
Architects, Inc.

great room below

attic storage   attic storage

BED RM.
12-8 x 14-0

railing

bath

down

BED RM.
12-8 x 14-0

foyer below

S unny bay windows splash this favorite farmhouse with style, and create a charming facade that's set off by an old-fashioned country porch. Inside, the two-story foyer opens to a formal dining room and to a study—this room could be used as a guest suite. The casual living area enjoys a fireplace with an extended hearth and access to an expansive screened porch. The sensational master suite offers a walk-in closet and a bath with a bumped-out bay tub, twin vanities and a separate shower. The two family bedrooms share a full bath upstairs. A bonus room over the garage may be developed later, as space is needed.

DESIGN 9761
First Floor: 1,907 square feet
Second Floor: 656 square feet
Total: 2,563 square feet
Bonus Room: 467 square feet

TWO-STORY FARMHOUSES

DESIGN 9751

First Floor: 1,975 square feet
Second Floor: 631 square feet
Total: 2,606 square feet

© 1994 Donald A. Gardner Architects, Inc.

The two-story great room will become the focal point of this exquisite farmhouse. It features a cathedral ceiling, interior columns and an inviting fireplace. The kitchen includes an island cooktop, large pantry and nearby utility room. The master bedroom directly accesses the covered porch and offers a master bath with a double-bowl vanity, whirlpool tub, separate shower and large walk-in closet. The front bedroom, with its separate full bath, can also convert to a study. Two additional bedrooms on the second floor share a full bath.

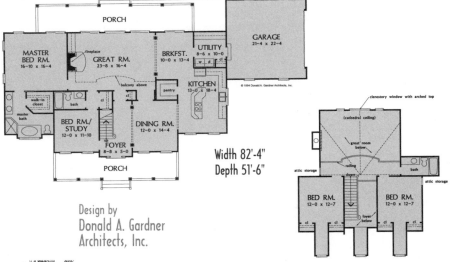

Width 82'-4"
Depth 51'-6"

Design by
Donald A. Gardner
Architects, Inc.

TWO-STORY FARMHOUSES

DESIGN 9703

First Floor: 1,783 square feet
Second Floor: 611 square feet
Total: 2,394 square feet

Onlookers will delight in the symmetry of this facade's arched windows and dormers. The interior offers a great room with a cathedral ceiling. This open plan also includes a kitchen with large island and wet bar, a bedroom/study combo on the first floor and a gorgeous master suite with a spa-style bath. Upstairs, two family bedrooms share a compartmented hall bath. An expansive rear deck and generous covered front porch offer maximum outdoor livability.

© 1993 Donald A. Gardner Architects, Inc.

Design by
Donald A. Gardner
Architects, Inc.

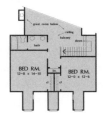

Width 70'-0"
Depth 79'-2"

© 1993 Donald A. Gardner Architects, Inc.

www.homeplanners.com

© 1992 Donald A. Gardner Architects, Inc.

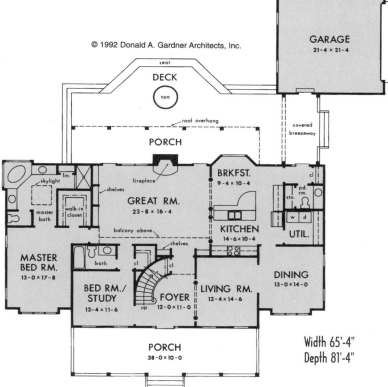

© 1992 Donald A. Gardner Architects, Inc.

GARAGE
21-4 x 21-4

seat

DECK
spa

roof overhang

covered breezeway

PORCH

skylight   lin.
master
bath   walk-in
closet   shelves
fireplace   BRKFST.
9-4 x 10-4

GREAT RM.
23-8 x 16-4   pd.
rm.
sto.
cl

KITCHEN
14-6 x 10-4   w   d

balcony above   shelves   UTIL.

MASTER
BED RM.
13-0 x 17-8   bath

cl   cl
BED RM./
STUDY
12-4 x 11-6   FOYER
12-0 x 11-0

up

LIVING RM.
12-4 x 14-6   DINING
13-0 x 14-0

PORCH
38-0 x 10-0

Width 65'-4"
Depth 81'-4"

Design by
Donald A. Gardner
Architects, Inc.

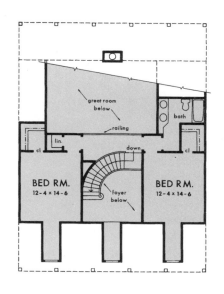

great room
below

railing   bath

cl   lin.

down

BED RM.
12-4 x 14-6   foyer
below   BED RM.
12-4 x 14-6

DESIGN
9671
First Floor: 2,156 square feet
Second Floor: 707 square feet
Total: 2,863 square feet

This striking country home is enhanced by large front and rear porches and an expansive rear deck for great outdoor living. The foyer with a curved stair adds a touch of elegance along with the round columns between the foyer and living room and between the great room and kitchen/breakfast area. The great room boasts a cathedral ceiling, allowing a second-level balcony overlook. The master bedroom is located on the first level for convenience. The luxurious master bath provides a dual vanity, whirlpool tub and separate shower. A second bedroom with full bath on the first floor can double as a study. Two large bedrooms with walk-in closets on the second level share a full bath that includes a double-bowl vanity. Note the two-car garage at the back.

TWO-STORY FARMHOUSES

DESIGN 7640

First Floor: 1,939 square feet
Second Floor: 657 square feet
Total: 2,596 square feet
Bonus Room: 386 square feet

© 1997 Donald A. Gardner Architects, Inc.

This country farmhouse offers an inviting wraparound porch for comfort and three gabled dormers for style. The foyer leads to a generous great room with an extended-hearth fireplace, a cathedral ceiling and access to the back covered porch. The first-floor master suite enjoys a sunny bay window and features a private bath with a cathedral ceiling, twin vanities and a windowed whirlpool tub. Upstairs, two family bedrooms share an elegant bath.

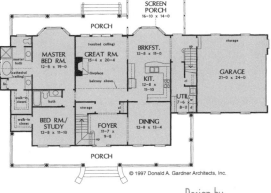

© 1997 Donald A. Gardner Architects, Inc.

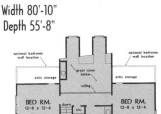

Width 80'-10"
Depth 55'-8"

Design by
Donald A. Gardner
Architects, Inc.

DESIGN 7653

First Floor: 1,471 square feet
Second Floor: 577 square feet
Total: 2,048 square feet
Bonus Room: 368 square feet

© 1997 Donald A. Gardner Architects, Inc.

For the family that enjoys outdoor living, this wraparound porch that becomes a screened porch and then turns into a deck is the best of all worlds! The dining-room bay window at the front of the plan mirrors the breakfast bay at the back, with the kitchen in between. On the opposite side of the plan, the master suite, with two walk-in closets and a deluxe bath, accesses the rear porch. Two family bedrooms upstairs are off a balcony that overlooks the great room.

Width 75'-5"
Depth 52'-0"

Design by
Donald A. Gardner
Architects, Inc.

© 1997 Donald A Gardner Architects, Inc.

TWO-STORY FARMHOUSES

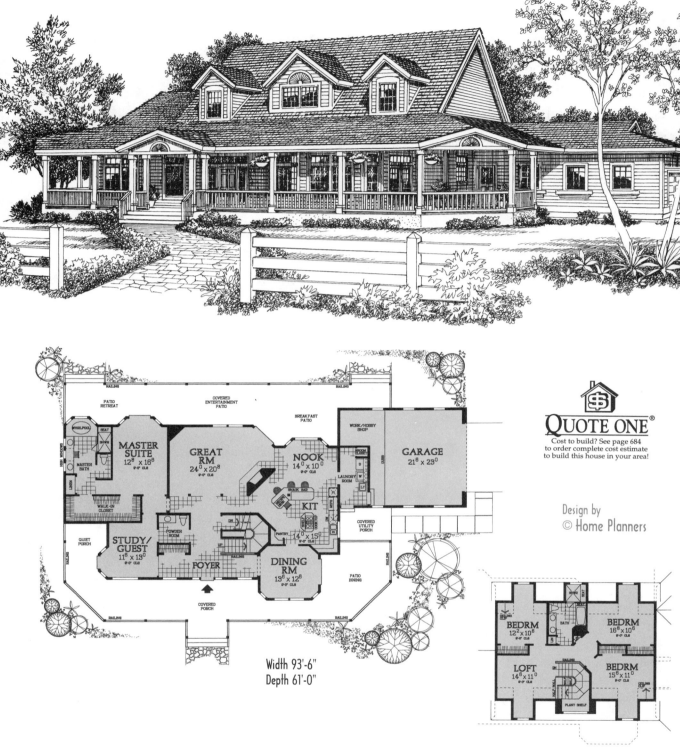

PATIO RETREAT

COVERED ENTERTAINMENT PATIO

BREAKFAST PATIO

WORK/HOBBY SHOP

GARAGE
21⁸ x 23⁰

WHIRLPOOL SEAT

MASTER SUITE
12⁸ x 16⁸
9'-0" CLG

GREAT RM
24⁰ x 20⁸
9'-0" CLG

NOOK
14⁰ x 10⁰
9'-0" CLG

LAUNDRY ROOM

MASTER BATH

SNACK BAR

WALK-IN CLOSET

KIT

QUIET PORCH

STUDY/ GUEST
11⁸ x 13⁰
9'-0" CLG

POWDER ROOM

PANTRY

14⁰ x 15⁰
9'-0" CLG

COVERED UTILITY PORCH

FOYER

DINING RM
13⁸ x 12⁸
9'-0" CLG

PATIO DINING

COVERED PORCH

Width 93'-6"
Depth 61'-0"

BEDRM
12² x 10⁸
9'-0" CLG

BEDRM
16⁸ x 10⁸
9'-0" CLG

BATH

LOFT
14⁸ x 11⁰
9'-0" CLG

BEDRM
15⁸ x 11⁰
9'-0" CLG

PLANT SHELF

$ **QUOTE ONE**®
Cost to build? See page 684
to order complete cost estimate
to build this house in your area!

Design by
© Home Planners

DESIGN 3608
First Floor: 2,347 square feet
Second Floor: 1,087 square feet
Total: 3,434 square feet

L

Dutch gable rooflines and a gabled wraparound porch with star-burst trim provide an extra measure of farmhouse style. The clerestory window sheds light on the stairway leading from the foyer to the upstairs bedrooms and loft. On the main level, the foyer leads to the study or guest bedroom that connects to the master suite on the left, to the formal dining room on the right and to the massive great room in the center of the home where a warming fireplace creates a cozy centerpiece. The kitchen conveniently combines with the great room, the breakfast nook and the dining room. The master suite includes access to the covered patio, a spacious walk-in closet and a master bath with a whirlpool tub. The two-car garage includes a work or hobby shop.

TWO-STORY FARMHOUSES

© 1991 Donald A. Gardner Architects, Inc.

DESIGN 9645

First Floor: 1,356 square feet
Second Floor: 542 square feet
Total: 1,898 square feet
Bonus Room: 393 square feet

The welcoming charm of this country farmhouse is expressed by its many windows and its covered, wraparound porch. A two-story entrance foyer is enhanced by a Palladian window in a clerestory dormer above to allow natural lighting. A first-floor master suite allows privacy and accessibility. The second floor provides two additional bedrooms, a full bath and plenty of storage space.

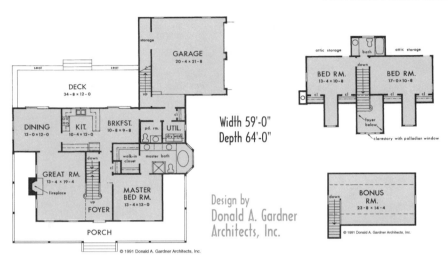

Width 59'-0"
Depth 64'-0"

Design by
Donald A. Gardner
Architects, Inc.

© 1991 Donald A. Gardner Architects, Inc.

DESIGN 9623

First Floor: 1,651 square feet
Second Floor: 567 square feet
Total: 2,218 square feet

A wonderful wraparound covered porch at the front and sides of this house and the open deck with spa at the back provide plenty of outside living area. Inside, the spacious great room is appointed with a fireplace, cathedral ceiling and clerestory with arched window. The centrally located kitchen features a food preparation island. Aside from the master bedroom with access to the sun room, there are two second-floor bedrooms that share a full bath.

© 1990 Donald A. Gardner Architects, Inc.

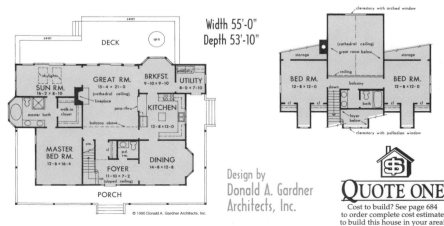

Width 55'-0"
Depth 53'-10"

Design by
Donald A. Gardner
Architects, Inc.

© 1990 Donald A. Gardner Architects, Inc.

Quote One®
Cost to build? See page 684
to order complete cost estimate
to build this house in your area!

TWO-STORY FARMHOUSES

© 1994 Donald A. Gardner Architects, Inc.

P. NATHAN

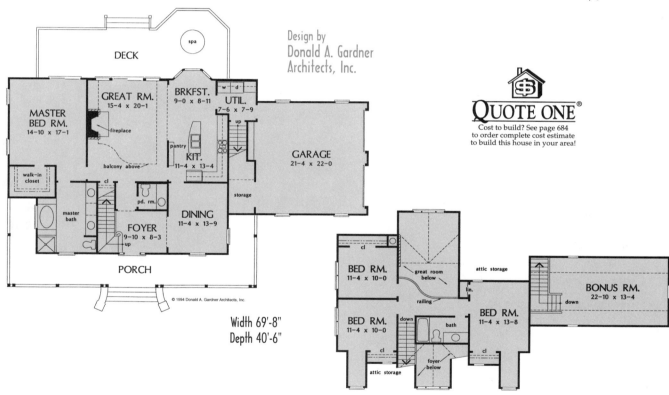

Design by
Donald A. Gardner
Architects, Inc.

DECK

spa

GREAT RM.
15-4 x 20-1

BRKFST.
9-0 x 8-11

UTIL.
7-6 x 7-9

w d

MASTER
BED RM.
14-10 x 17-1

fireplace

GARAGE
21-4 x 22-0

walk-in
closet

balcony above

pantry

KIT.
11-4 x 13-4

up

storage

master
bath

cl

pd. rm.

DINING
11-4 x 13-9

FOYER
9-10 x 8-3
up

PORCH

© 1994 Donald A. Gardner Architects, Inc.

Width 69'-8"
Depth 40'-6"

cl

BED RM.
11-4 x 10-0

great room
below

attic storage

BONUS RM.
22-10 x 13-4

down

lin.

railing

BED RM.
11-4 x 10-0

down

BED RM.
11-4 x 13-8

bath

attic storage

cl

foyer
below

cl

attic storage

Quote One®
Cost to build? See page 684
to order complete cost estimate
to build this house in your area!

The warm, down-home appeal of this
country house is as apparent inside
as it is out. A wraparound front
porch and a rear deck with a spa
provide plenty of space to enjoy the surrounding scenery. Inside, a two-story
foyer and a great room give the home an
open feel. The great room leads to a
breakfast area and an efficient kitchen
with an island work area and a large
pantry. The master bedroom is situated
on the left side of the house for privacy. It
features deck access, a large walk-in closet
and a bath that includes dual vanities, a
whirlpool tub and separate shower. Three
bedrooms, a full bath and bonus space are
located upstairs. The two-car garage connects via the utility room.

**DESIGN
9773**
First Floor: 1,499 square feet
Second Floor: 665 square feet
Total: 2,164 square feet
Bonus Room: 380 square feet

TWO-STORY FARMHOUSES

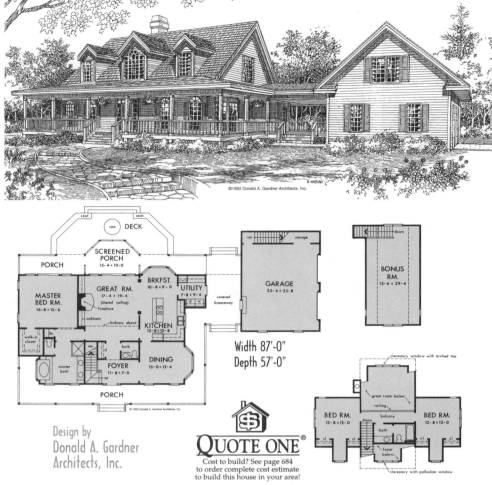

DESIGN 9702

First Floor: 1,618 square feet
Second Floor: 570 square feet
Total: 2,188 square feet
Bonus Room: 495 square feet

A wraparound covered porch, an open deck, arched windows and dormers enhance the already impressive character of this three-bedroom farmhouse. The entrance foyer and great room with sloped ceilings have Palladian window clerestories. The spacious great room boasts a fireplace and built-ins. The kitchen, with a cooking island, serves both the dining room and breakfast room. A generous master bedroom has plenty of closet space and an expansive master bath.

Width 87'-0"
Depth 57'-0"

Design by
Donald A. Gardner
Architects, Inc.

©1993 Donald A. Gardner Architects, Inc.

QUOTE ONE®
Cost to build? See page 684
to order complete cost estimate
to build this house in your area!

DESIGN 9706

First Floor: 1,585 square feet
Second Floor: 731 square feet
Total: 2,316 square feet
Bonus Room: 401 square feet

This complete farmhouse projects an exciting and comfortable feeling with its wraparound porch, arched windows and dormers. The large kitchen, with carefully planned layout incorporating a cooking island, easily services the breakfast area and dining room. The generous great room with fireplace is accessible to the spacious screened porch. The first-floor master suite contains a luxurious master bath. The second level allows for three bedrooms and a full bath.

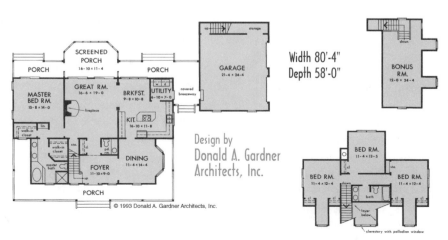

© 1993 Donald A. Gardner Architects, Inc.

Width 80'-4"
Depth 58'-0"

Design by
Donald A. Gardner
Architects, Inc.

© 1993 Donald A. Gardner Architects, Inc.

TWO-STORY FARMHOUSES

© 1992 Donald A. Gardner Architects, Inc.

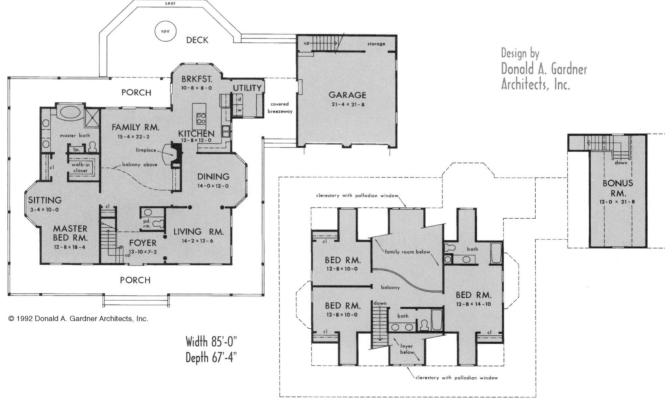

© 1992 Donald A. Gardner Architects, Inc.

Width 85'-0"
Depth 67'-4"

Design by
Donald A. Gardner
Architects, Inc.

This complete four-bedroom country farmhouse encourages both indoor and outdoor living with the well-organized open layout and the continuous flowing porch and deck encircling the house. Front and rear Palladian window dormers allow natural light to penetrate the foyer and family room below as well as adding exciting visual elements to the exterior. The dramatic family room with sloped ceiling envelopes a curved balcony. The master suite includes a large walk-in closet, special sitting area and master bath with whirlpool tub, shower and double-bowl vanity. Two secondary bedrooms share a full hall bath while a third has its own private bath. A bonus room over the garage adds to the versatility of this house. Make it a home office or hobby room.

DESIGN 9669
First Floor: 1,759 square feet
Second Floor: 888 square feet
Total: 2,647 square feet
Bonus Room: 324 square feet

TWO-STORY FARMHOUSES

DESIGN 9733

First Floor: 1,871 square feet
Second Floor: 731 square feet
Total: 2,602 square feet
Bonus Room: 402 square feet

This fetching four-bedroom country home, with porches and dormers at both front and rear, offers a welcoming touch to an open floor plan. The spacious great room enjoys a large fireplace, cathedral ceiling and clerestory with an arched window. The expansive first-floor master suite features a generous walk-in closet and a luxurious master bath, which boasts a bumped-out whirlpool tub, twin vanities and a separate shower.

© 1993 Donald A. Gardner Architects, Inc.

Width 77'-6"
Depth 70'-0"

Design by
Donald A. Gardner
Architects, Inc.

© 1993 Donald A. Gardner Architects, Inc.

DESIGN 9694

First Floor: 1,537 square feet
Second Floor: 641 square feet
Total: 2,178 square feet
Bonus Room: 418 square feet

The welcoming charm of this country farmhouse is expressed by its many windows and its covered wrap-around porch. The two-story entrance foyer has a Palladian window in a clerestory dormer. The master suite, with its large walk-in closet, is on the first level for privacy. The master bath includes a whirlpool tub, shower and double-bowl vanity. The second level contains two bedrooms, a full bath and plenty of storage.

© 1992 Donald A. Gardner Architects, Inc.

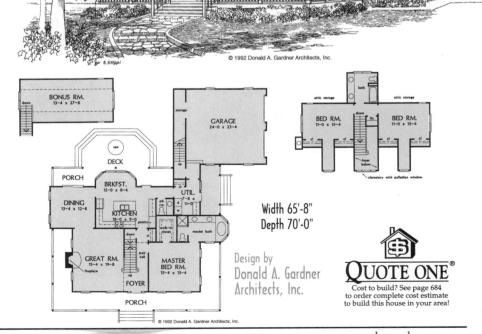

Width 65'-8"
Depth 70'-0"

Design by
Donald A. Gardner
Architects, Inc.

QUOTE ONE®
Cost to build? See page 684
to order complete cost estimate
to build this house in your area!

© 1992 Donald A. Gardner Architects, Inc.

© 1994 Donald A. Gardner Architects, Inc.   B. NATHAN

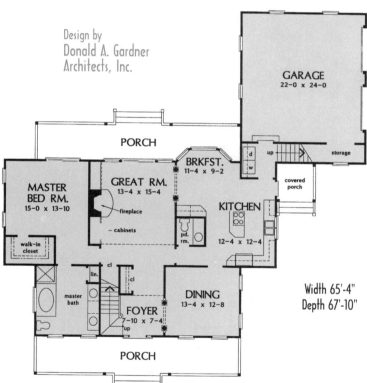

Design by
Donald A. Gardner
Architects, Inc.

GARAGE
22-0 x 24-0

PORCH

storage

up

covered porch

BRKFST.
11-4 x 9-2

GREAT RM.
13-4 x 15-4

d
w

fireplace

KITCHEN
12-4 x 12-4

MASTER BED RM.
15-0 x 13-10

cabinets

pd. rm.

walk-in closet

cl

cl

lin.

master bath

DINING
13-4 x 12-8

FOYER
7-10 x 7-4

up

PORCH

Width 65'-4"
Depth 67'-10"

© 1994 Donald A. Gardner Architects, Inc.

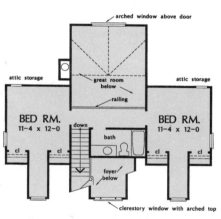

arched window above door

great room below

attic storage

attic storage

BED RM.
11-4 x 12-0

BED RM.
11-4 x 12-0

railing

down

bath

cl

cl

cl

cl

foyer below

clerestory window with arched top

skylights

BONUS RM.
13-4 x 24-0

down

This three-bedroom, country home with front and rear porches offers an open plan with minimal "empty" space. A front Palladian window dormer and a rear arched window add to its exterior visual intrigue. The entrance foyer rises with a sloped ceiling and enjoys an abundance of light from a Palladian window clerestory. In the spa-cious great room, a fireplace, cathedral ceiling and a clerestory with an arched window all add to the appeal. A second-level balcony overlooks the great room. The master suite features all of the ameni-ties, while two secondary bedrooms reside on the second level. A bonus room offers room to grow. It sits above the two-car garage and has skylights.

DESIGN 9732

First Floor: 1,506 square feet
Second Floor: 513 square feet
Total: 2,019 square feet
Bonus Room: 397 square feet

TWO-STORY FARMHOUSES

DESIGN 9746

First Floor: 1,966 square feet
Second Floor: 634 square feet
Total: 2,600 square feet
Bonus Room: 396 square feet

Three bay windows enhance the romance of this country home. Enter from the front porch to the great room with a cathedral ceiling and a fireplace. Enjoy a scenic dinner in the dining room. The kitchen includes an island cooktop, built-in pantry and sunny breakfast area with a view of the massive deck. The master bedroom completes the picture with a bay window, deck access and a luxurious bath with a whirlpool tub. Two family bedrooms and a full hall bath are located upstairs.

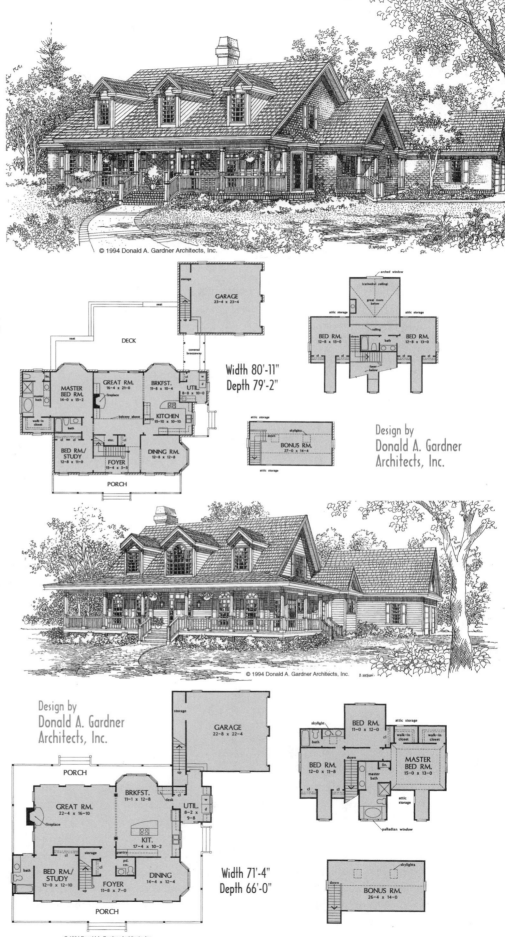

© 1994 Donald A. Gardner Architects, Inc.

Width 80'-11"
Depth 79'-2"

Design by
Donald A. Gardner
Architects, Inc.

DESIGN 9745

First Floor: 1,576 square feet
Second Floor: 947 square feet
Total: 2,523 square feet
Bonus Room: 405 square feet

Enjoy balmy breezes as you relax on the wraparound porch of this delightful country farmhouse. The foyer introduces a dining room to the right and a bedroom or study to the left. The expansive great room—with its cozy fireplace—has direct access to the rear porch. Columns define the kitchen and breakfast area. The house gourmet will enjoy preparing meals at the island cooktop. The master bedroom features a tray ceiling along with a luxurious bath. Two additional bedrooms share a skylit bath.

© 1994 Donald A. Gardner Architects, Inc.

Design by
Donald A. Gardner
Architects, Inc.

Width 71'-4"
Depth 66'-0"

www.homeplanners.com

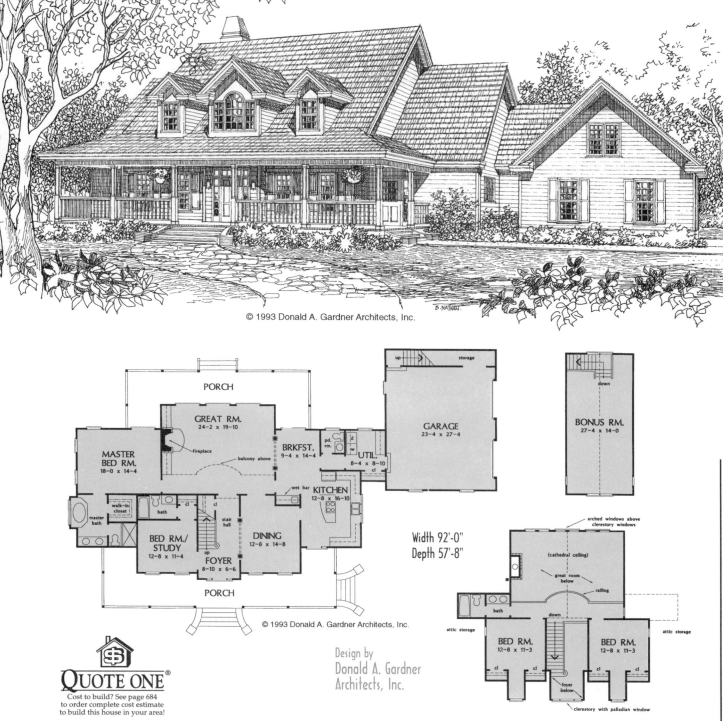

© 1993 Donald A. Gardner Architects, Inc.

B·NATHAN·

Floor plan labels:

PORCH

GREAT RM.
24-2 x 19-10

fireplace

balcony above

MASTER BED RM.
18-0 x 14-4

BRKFST.
9-4 x 14-4

pd. rm.
fireplace

UTIL.
8-4 x 8-10

GARAGE
23-4 x 27-4

up · storage

BONUS RM.
27-4 x 14-0

down

wet bar

KITCHEN
12-8 x 16-10

walk-in closet

master bath

bath

cl

BED RM./ STUDY
12-8 x 11-4

stair hall

DINING
12-8 x 14-8

up

FOYER
8-10 x 6-6

PORCH

Width 92'-0"
Depth 57'-8"

© 1993 Donald A. Gardner Architects, Inc.

arched windows above clerestory windows

(cathedral ceiling)

great room below

railing

bath

attic storage

BED RM.
12-8 x 11-3

BED RM.
12-8 x 11-3

attic storage

cl

foyer below

down

clerestory with palladian window

Design by
Donald A. Gardner
Architects, Inc.

You'll find country living at its best when meandering through this spacious four-bedroom farmhouse with wraparound porch. A front Palladian window dormer and rear clerestory windows at the great room add exciting visual elements to the exterior while providing natural light to the interior. The large great room boasts a fireplace, bookshelves and a raised cathedral ceiling, allowing a curved balcony overlook above. The great room, master bedroom and breakfast room are accessible to the rear porch for greater circulation and flexibility. Special features such as the large cooktop island in the kitchen, the wet bar, the bedroom/study, the generous bonus room over the garage and ample storage set this plan apart. Finish the bonus room later as an office or guest suite.

DESIGN 9723

First Floor: 2,064 square feet
Second Floor: 594 square feet
Total: 2,658 square feet
Bonus Room: 483 square feet

TWO-STORY FARMHOUSES

DESIGN 3682

First Floor: 1,093 square feet
Second Floor: 603 square feet
Total: 1,696 square feet

L D

A wraparound porch, stone chimney and arched windows set in dormers enhance this home's rustic country appeal. A great room with a sloped ceiling enjoys a raised-hearth fireplace whose warmth radiates into the kitchen/nook. The first-floor master bedroom includes plenty of closet space and a master bath filled with amenities. The second floor contains two secondary bedrooms, a full bath and a loft/study with a window seat.

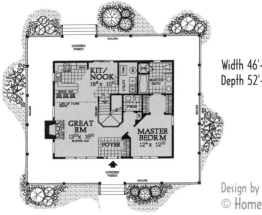

Width 46'-0"
Depth 52'-0"

Design by
© Home Planners

QUOTE ONE®
Cost to build? See page 684 to order complete cost estimate to build this house in your area!

DESIGN 3697

First Floor: 586 square feet
Second Floor: 486 square feet
Total: 1,072 square feet

The wraparound porch of this plan provides entry to the three primary areas of the main level—greatroom, kitchen, and dining nook. Amenities include a fireplace in the greatroom and a laundry room convenient to the U-shaped kitchen. The upper level is divided into two suites, each with ample closet space, an arched window and a private bath.

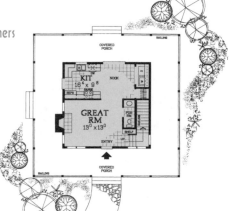

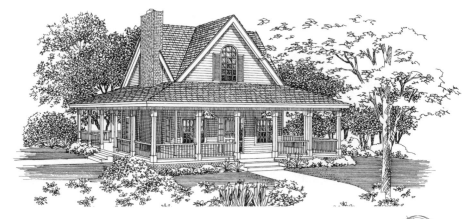

Design by
© Home Planners

Width 40'-0"
Depth 40'-0"

QUOTE ONE®
Cost to build? See page 684 to order complete cost estimate to build this house in your area!

TWO-STORY FARMHOUSES

DESIGN 3681

First Floor: 1,093 square feet
Second Floor: 576 square feet
Total: 1,669 square feet

L D

A two-story great room, warmed by a fireplace, sets a spirited mood in this country home. Nearby, a snack bar joins the living area with the U-shaped kitchen and attached nook. Two family bedrooms, a full bath and a utility room complete the first floor. The second-floor master suite is filled with amenities. Curl up in the window seat with a good book or enjoy fresh air from your own private balcony. A walk-in closet, master bath and a loft/study complete this special retreat.

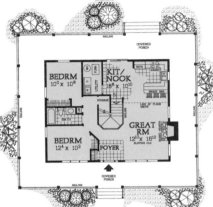

Width 52'-0"
Depth 46'-0"

Design by
© Home Planners

QUOTE ONE®
Cost to build? See page 684
to order complete cost estimate
to build this house in your area!

DESIGN 3683

First Floor: 1,139 square feet
Second Floor: 576 square feet
Total: 1,715 square feet

L D

A rustically royal welcome extends from the wraparound porch, inviting one and all into a comfortable interior. To the right of the foyer, a two-story great room enhanced by a raised-hearth fireplace sets a spirited country mood. Nearby, a snack bar joins the living area with an efficient, U-shaped kitchen and an attached nook. The second-floor master suite features amenities that create a private, restful getaway. Note the window seat and the private balcony.

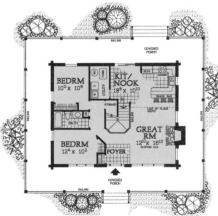

Width 52'-0"
Depth 46'-0"

Design by
© Home Planners

QUOTE ONE®
Cost to build? See page 684
to order complete cost estimate
to build this house in your area!

TWO-STORY FARMHOUSES

© 1993 Donald A. Gardner Architects, Inc.

Design by
**Donald A. Gardner
Architects, Inc.**

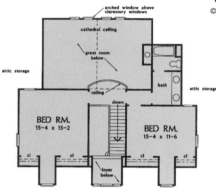

arched window above
clerestory windows

cathedral ceiling

attic storage

great room
below

railing

bath

attic storage

BED RM.
15-4 x 15-2

BED RM.
15-4 x 11-6

down

cl

cl

cl

cl

foyer
below

STORAGE
25-8 x 8-8

GARAGE
22-0 x 28-0

sto.

up

BRKFST.
9-8 x 7-4

KITCHEN
19-0 x 12-8

UTILITY
13-8 x 8-2

PORCH

GREAT RM.
24-0 x 19-8

fireplace

balcony above

DINING RM.
13-0 x 17-0

stair
hall

up

cl

sto.

FOYER
8-0 x 6-2

cl

SITTING
9-8 x 4-0

MASTER
BED RM.
15-0 x 16-0

master
bath

walk-in
closet

pd.
rm.

lin.

bath

walk-in
closet

BED RM./
STUDY
15-4 x 12-2

PORCH

© 1993 Donald A. Gardner Architects, Inc.

Width 95'-4"
Depth 54'-10"

QUOTE ONE®
Cost to build? See page 684
to order complete cost estimate
to build this house in your area!

TWO-STORY FARMHOUSES

**DESIGN
9721**
First Floor: 2,316 square feet
Second Floor: 721 square feet
Total: 3,037 square feet
Bonus Room: 545 square feet

This gracious farmhouse with its wraparound porch offers a touch of symmetry in a well-defined, open plan. The entrance foyer has a Palladian clerestory window that gives an abundance of natural light to the interior. The vaulted great room furthers this feeling of airiness with a second-floor balcony above and two sets of sliding glass doors leading to the rear porch. The country kitchen with an island counter-top, the bayed breakfast nook and the dining room all enjoy nine-foot ceilings. Upstairs, each family bedroom has two closets. A full bath with a double-bowl vanity rests to one side of the hall. For privacy, the master suite occupies the right side of the first floor. With a sitting room and all the amenities of a spa-style bath, this suite won't fail to please. Note the large storage area in the two-car garage and the large utility room.

© 1992 Donald A. Gardner Architects, Inc.

Width 76'-4"
Depth 74'-2"

DECK
spa
seat
storage

GARAGE
23-4 x 21-4

covered breezeway

up

BONUS RM.
27-0 x 12-0

downs

SCREENED PORCH
16-0 x 10-6
skylights

master bath

GREAT RM.
16-0 x 19-2
fireplace

walk-in closet

loft above

BRKFST.
12-4 x 10-2

KITCHEN
12-4 x 11-0

UTIL.

cl

MASTER BED RM.
12-4 x 16-0

FOYER
12-6 x 8-0

DINING
14-4 x 12-4

PORCH

clerestory window with arched top

great room below
railing

BED RM.
12-4 x 10-4

shelves

BED RM.
12-4 x 11-8

LOFT/STUDY
9-0 x 10-8

down

bath

railing

foyer below

clerestory window with arched top

Design by
Donald A. Gardner Architects, Inc.

© 1992 Donald A. Gardner Architects, Inc.

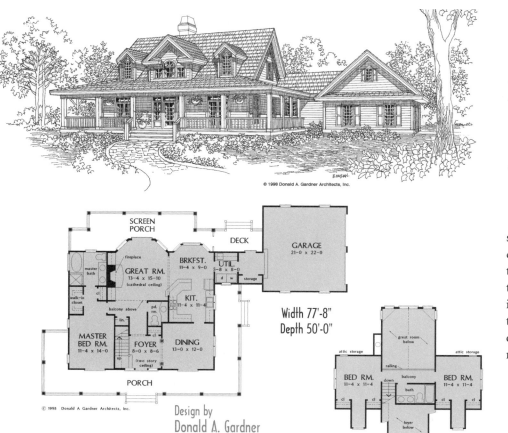

© 1998 Donald A. Gardner Architects, Inc.

SCREEN PORCH

DECK

GARAGE
21-0 x 22-0

master bath

GREAT RM.
13-4 x 15-10
(cathedral ceiling)

fireplace

BRKFST.
11-4 x 9-0

UTIL.
5-8 x 8-0

d w storage

walk-in closet

cl

KIT.
11-4 x 11-4

balcony above

lin.

pd. rm.

MASTER BED RM.
11-4 x 14-0

FOYER
8-0 x 8-6
(two story ceiling)

up

DINING
13-0 x 12-0

PORCH

Width 77'-8"
Depth 50'-0"

great room below

attic storage

railing

attic storage

balcony

BED RM.
11-4 x 11-4

BED RM.
11-4 x 11-4

down

bath

cl

cl

foyer below

© 1998 Donald A. Gardner Architects, Inc.

Design by
Donald A. Gardner Architects, Inc.

DESIGN 9673

First Floor: 1,526 square feet
Second Floor: 635 square feet
Total: 2,161 square feet

This beautiful farmhouse boasts all the extras a three-bedroom design could offer. A kitchen with an island counter and a breakfast area is open to the spacious great room through a cased opening with a colonnade. The exquisite master suite has a walk-in closet and a dramatic master bath, providing emphasis on the whirlpool tub flanked by double columns. The second level holds two bedrooms sharing a full bath and a loft/study area overlooking the great room.

DESIGN 7717

First Floor: 1,271 square feet
Second Floor: 490 square feet
Total: 1,761 square feet

This country farmhouse looks and lives larger than its square footage due to its wrapping front porch and generous, screened back porch. The large center dormer directs light through clerestory windows into the dramatic two-story foyer where interior columns mark entrance to the formal dining room. The heart of the home is the central great room with a fireplace.

TWO-STORY FARMHOUSES

© 1990 Donald A. Gardner Architects, Inc.

Design by
Donald A. Gardner
Architects, Inc.

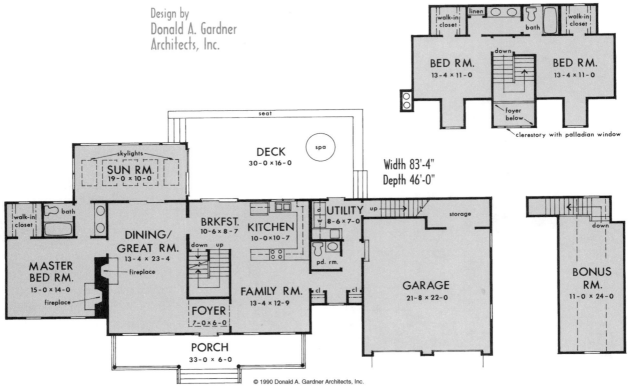

Width 83'-4"
Depth 46'-0"

© 1990 Donald A. Gardner Architects, Inc.

Second Floor:

walk-in closet | linen | bath | walk-in closet

BED RM.
13-4 × 11-0

down

BED RM.
13-4 × 11-0

foyer below

clerestory with palladian window

First Floor:

seat

DECK
30-0 × 16-0

spa

SUN RM.
19-0 × 10-0
skylights

walk-in closet | bath

DINING/
GREAT RM.
13-4 × 23-4

fireplace

BRKFST.
10-6 × 8-7

KITCHEN
10-0 × 10-7

UTILITY
8-6 × 7-0

up

storage

MASTER
BED RM.
15-0 × 14-0

fireplace

down | up

pd. rm.

FAMILY RM.
13-4 × 12-9

cl | cl

GARAGE
21-8 × 22-0

FOYER
7-0 × 6-0

PORCH
33-0 × 6-0

Bonus:

BONUS
RM.
11-0 × 24-0

down

TWO-STORY FARMHOUSES

DESIGN 9654

First Floor: 1,578 square feet
Second Floor: 554 square feet
Total: 2,132 square feet

Enjoy outdoor living with a covered porch at the front of this home and an expansive deck to the rear. The floor plan allows for great livability and features split-bedroom styling with the master suite on the first floor. The U-shaped kitchen opens to the breakfast room and easily accesses the dining/great-room and the family room. Second-floor bedrooms share a full bath that includes a double-bowl vanity. There is also bonus space above the garage for a studio, study or play room. A large storage area in the two-car garage extends its usefulness.

www.homeplanners.com

© 1990 Donald A. Gardner Architects, Inc.

DESIGN 9626

First Floor: 1,057 square feet
Second Floor: 500 square feet
Total: 1,557 square feet
Bonus Room: 342 square feet

This compact, two-story, cozy country cottage is perfect for the economically conscious family. Its entrance foyer is highlighted by a clerestory dormer above for natural light. The master bath boasts a whirlpool tub with skylight, a separate shower and double-bowl vanity. Second-level bedrooms share a full bath and there's a wealth of storage on this level. A bonus room over the garage can be finished later.

Width 59'-4"
Depth 50'-0"

© 1990 Donald A. Gardner Architects, Inc.

BASEMENT PLAN

Design by
Donald A. Gardner
Architects, Inc.

Quote One®
Cost to build? See page 684
to order complete cost estimate
to build this house in your area!

DESIGN 9606

First Floor: 1,289 square feet
Second Floor: 542 square feet
Total: 1,831 square feet
Bonus Room: 393 square feet

This cozy country cottage is perfect for the growing family—offering both an unfinished basement option and a bonus room. Enter through the two-story foyer with a Palladian window in a clerestory dormer above. The first-floor master suite's bath boasts a whirlpool tub with skylight above and a double-bowl vanity. The second floor contains two bedrooms, a full bath and plenty of storage. All first-floor rooms except the kitchen and utility room boast nine-foot ceilings.

Design by
Donald A. Gardner
Architects, Inc.

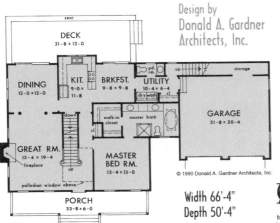

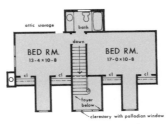

© 1990 Donald A. Gardner Architects, Inc.

Width 66'-4"
Depth 50'-4"

Quote One®
Cost to build? See page 684
to order complete cost estimate
to build this house in your area!

TWO-STORY FARMHOUSES

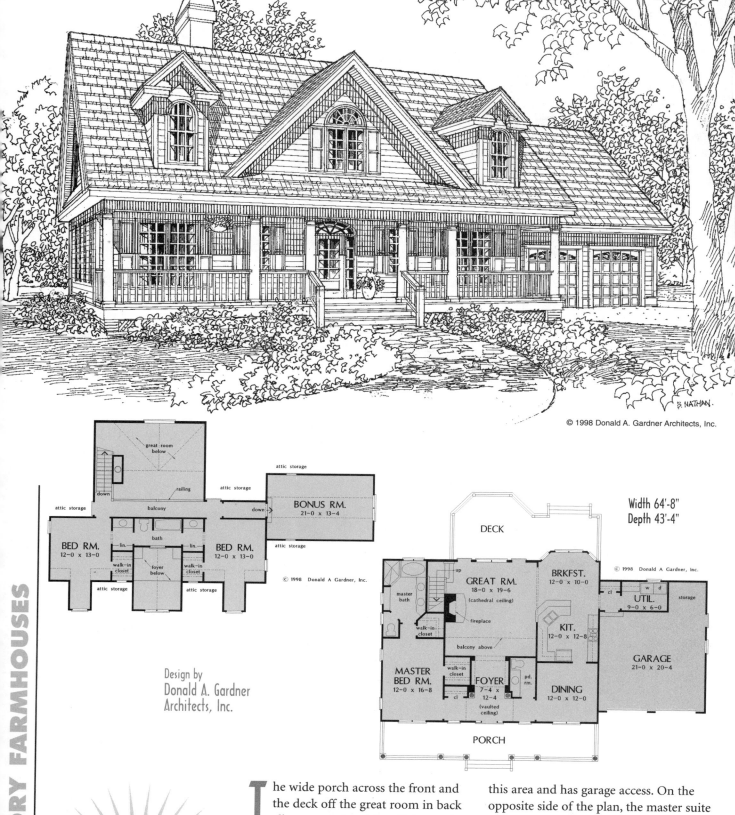

© 1998 Donald A. Gardner Architects, Inc.

great room below

down

attic storage

railing

attic storage

attic storage

balcony

down →

BONUS RM.
21-0 x 13-4

attic storage

BED RM.
12-0 x 13-0

lin.

bath

lin.

BED RM.
12-0 x 13-0

walk-in closet

foyer below

walk-in closet

attic storage

attic storage

attic storage

© 1998 Donald A Gardner, Inc.

Design by
Donald A. Gardner
Architects, Inc.

Width 64'-8"
Depth 43'-4"

DECK

master bath

GREAT RM.
18-0 x 19-6
(cathedral ceiling)

BRKFST.
12-0 x 10-0

© 1998 Donald A Gardner, Inc.

UTIL.
9-0 x 6-0

w d

storage

walk-in closet

fireplace

KIT.
12-0 x 12-8

cl

balcony above

GARAGE
21-0 x 20-4

MASTER
BED RM.
12-0 x 16-8

walk-in closet

FOYER
7-4 x
12-4
(vaulted ceiling)

pd. rm.

DINING
12-0 x 12-0

cl

PORCH

www.homeplanners.com

TWO-STORY FARMHOUSES

DESIGN 7677
First Floor: 1,569 square feet
Second Floor: 682 square feet
Total: 2,251 square feet

The wide porch across the front and the deck off the great room in back allow as much outdoor living as the weather permits. The foyer opens through columns off the front porch to the dining room, with a nearby powder room, and the great room. The breakfast room is open to the great room and the adjacent kichen. The utility room adjoins this area and has garage access. On the opposite side of the plan, the master suite offers a compartmented bath and two walk-in closets. A staircase leads upstairs to two family bedrooms—one at each end of a balcony that overlooks the great room. Each bedroom has a walk-in closet, a dormer window and private access to the bath through a private vanity area.

B. NATHAN.

© 1991 Donald A. Gardner Architects, Inc.

Quote One®
Cost to build? See page 684
to order complete cost estimate
to build this house in your area!

Design by
Donald A. Gardner
Architects, Inc.

Width 48'-4"
Depth 51'-10"

© 1991 Donald A. Gardner Architects, Inc.

DESIGN 9621

First Floor: 1,325 square feet
Second Floor: 453 square feet
Total: 1,778 square feet

This compact design has all the amenities available in larger plans with little wasted space. In addition, a wraparound covered porch, a front Palladian window, dormers and rear arched windows provide exciting visual elements to the exterior. The spacious great room has a fireplace, a cathedral ceiling and clerestory windows. The centrally located kitchen features a pass-through to the great room. Aside from the generous master suite, there are two second-floor family bedrooms sharing a full bath that has a double vanity.

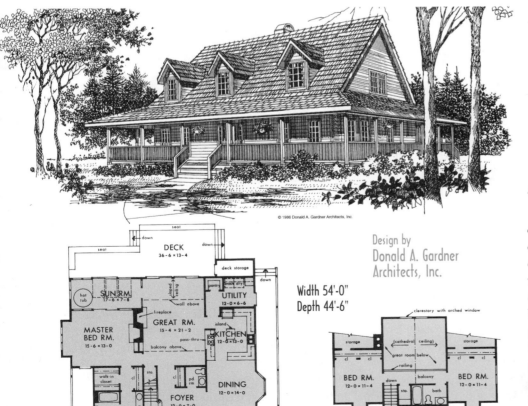

© 1986 Donald A. Gardner Architects, Inc.

Design by
Donald A. Gardner
Architects, Inc.

Width 54'-0"
Depth 44'-6"

© 1986 Donald A. Gardner Architects, Inc.

DESIGN 9605

First Floor: 1,562 square feet
Second Floor: 537 square feet
Total: 2,099 square feet

Enjoy outdoor living with the wraparound covered porch at the front and sides of this house, as well as on the open deck. Inside, you'll find the spacious great room with fireplace, cathedral ceiling and clerestory with arched windows. The kitchen occupies a central location between the dining room and the great room for equally convenient formal and informal occasions. A generous master suite has a fireplace and access to the sun room and covered porch. On the second level are two more bedrooms, a full bath and storage space.

TWO-STORY FARMHOUSES

Design by
© Home Planners

MASTER SUITE 20⁰ x 11⁶

SITTING

SUN TERRACE

SPA

SEAT

MASTER BATH

WALK-IN CLOSET

POWDER RM

MORNING ROOM 11⁶ x 13⁶

COVERED PATIO

RAILING

BEDRM 11⁶ x 10⁰ SLOPED CLG

GREAT RM 19⁰ x 13⁰ SLOPED CLG

HOME CENTER

KIT 11⁶ x 18⁰

HVAC

WH

GARAGE 21⁸ x 20⁰

UTILITY SINK

LAUNDRY ROOM

BATH

BEDRM 11⁶ x 10⁶ SLOPED CLG

FOYER

DINING RM 11⁴ x 11⁶ SLOPED CLG

COVERED PORCH

RAILING

Width 76'-0"
Depth 64'-0"

QUOTE ONE®
Cost to build? See page 684
to order complete cost estimate
to build this house in your area!

DESIGN 3677
Square Footage: 2,090
L D

This charming country home offers split-bedroom planning further enhanced by the covered front porch that provides a perfect spot for enjoying cool evening breezes. To the right of the foyer is the formal dining room. The nearby great room offers a raised-hearth fireplace with an extended media shelf. Easily accessible from any room, the U-shaped kitchen opens to a morning room filled with natural light. A conveniently located laundry room completes the design. The secluded master suite includes a walk-in closet, a compartmented bath and private access to the sun terrace.

DESIGN 3675

First Floor: 1,093 square feet
Second Floor: 580 square feet
Total: 1,673 square feet

L D

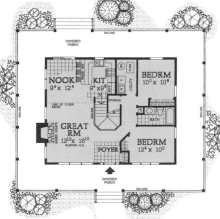

Width 46'-0"
Depth 52'-0"

QUOTE ONE®

Cost to build? See page 684
to order complete cost estimate
to build this house in your area!

Design by
© Home Planners

Comfortable covered porches lead you into a home tailor-made for casual living. The foyer offers access to the great room with a raised-hearth fireplace. The great room then flows into the breakfast nook, with outdoor access, and on to the efficient kitchen. Two family bedrooms, a shared bath and a utility room complete the first floor. Curved stairs lead you up to the master bedroom with its private balcony, large walk-in closet and amenity-filled bath. A loft/study with attic access finishes the second floor.

DESIGN 3679

First Floor: 1,093 square feet
Second Floor: 580 square feet
Total: 1,673 square feet

L D

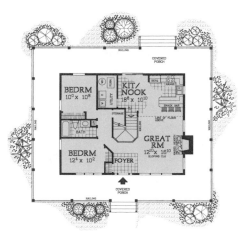

Width 52'-0"
Depth 46'-0"

QUOTE ONE®

Cost to build? See page 684
to order complete cost estimate
to build this house in your area!

Design by
© Home Planners

A cozy little plan, this 1½-story home allows all the comforts of home in a smaller square footage. The first floor holds a great room open to the kitchen and breakfast nook. A warm fireplace lends its glow to both areas. Family bedrooms on this floor share a full bath and are separated from the master suite on the second floor. With its own private balcony, the master bedroom offers a fine bath with a separate shower and tub and compartmented toilet. A loft or study area overlooks the great room.

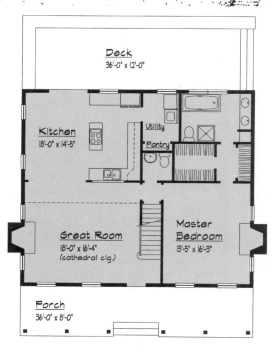

Deck
36'-0" x 12'-0"

Kitchen
18'-0" x 14'-5"

Utility

Pantry

Great Room
18'-0" x 16'-4"
(cathedral clg.)

Master Bedroom
13'-5" x 16'-3"

Porch
36'-0" x 8'-0"

Design by
© TAG Archetiects

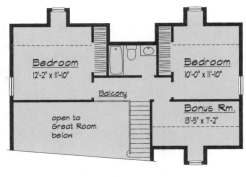

Bedroom
12'-2" x 11'-10"

Bedroom
10'-0" x 11'-10"

Balcony

open to
Great Room
below

Bonus Rm.
13'-5" x 7'-2"

Width 36'-0"
Depth 40'-0"

DESIGN W006
First Floor: 1,152 square feet
Second Floor: 452 square feet
Total: 1,604 square feet
Bonus Room: 115 square feet

Three dormers, two chimneys and a covered front porch combine to make this home attractive in any neighborhood. Inside, a great room greets both family and friends with a cathedral ceiling and a warming fireplace. Toward the rear, an L-shaped kitchen features a work-top island with a stove surface. The nearby dining area offers rear-porch access. The master suite contains a second fireplace, as well as two closets and a private bath with separate tub and shower. Upstairs, two secondary bedrooms share a hall bath and have access to a bonus room—perfect for a study or computer room. Note the dormer windows in the family bedrooms upstairs. Please specify basement or crawlspace foundation when ordering.

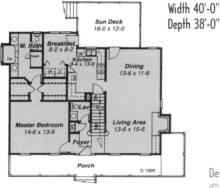

Width 40'-0"
Depth 38'-0"

Sun Deck
16-0 x 12-0

M. Bath
Breakfast
8-2 x 8-2

Kitchen
9-4 x 13-6

Dining
13-6 x 11-6

W.D.

Master Bedroom
14-6 x 13-6

Living Area
13-6 x 15-6

Lav.

Foyer

Porch

© 1995

Bedroom-3
14-10 x 11-6

Bath 3

Bath 2

Bedroom-4
14-0 x 10-6

Bedroom-2
13-6 x 14-0

Design by
© Jannis Vann & Associates, Inc.

DESIGN
X016

First Floor: 1,143 square feet
Second Floor: 876 square feet
Total: 2,019 square feet

A metal-roofed porch adds character to a simple Cape Cod design. Inside, the home provides a spacious living and dining area with a fireplace and sun-deck access. A cozy breakfast nook also accesses the sun deck. The first-floor master suite offers two walk-in closets and His and Hers vanities flanking a garden tub. Upstairs a guest bedroom includes a private bath and walk-in closet, while the other bedrooms share a compartmented hall bath.

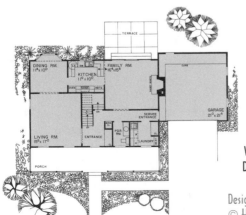

TERRACE

DINING RM.
11⁸ x 10⁰

KITCHEN
13⁰ x 10⁰

FAMILY RM.
16⁵ x 15⁶

GARAGE
21⁰ x 21⁸

SERVICE ENTRANCE

LIVING RM.
15⁸ x 17⁰

PDR. RM.

ENTRANCE

LAUNDRY

PORCH

WALK-IN CLOSET

BATH

BATH

MASTER BED RM.
15⁶ x 13⁴

BED RM.
11⁸ x 10⁰

BED RM.
14⁸ x 10⁰

ROOF

Width 61'-4"
Depth 38'-0"

Design by
© Home Planners

QUOTE ONE®

Cost to build? See page 684
to order complete cost estimate
to build this house in your area!

DESIGN
2776

First Floor: 1,134 square feet
Second Floor: 874 square feet
Total: 2,008 square feet

L D

W arm weather will invite friends and family out to the large, front covered porch. Just off the front entrance is a spacious living room that opens to the formal dining room, which enjoys a bay window and easy service from the U-shaped kitchen. The family room offers casual living space warmed by a raised-hearth fireplace and extended by double-door access to the rear terrace. The second floor houses two family bedrooms, which share a full bath, and a generous master suite with a walk-in closet and a private bath.

TWO-STORY FARMHOUSES

DESIGN 3328

First Floor: 2,300 square feet
Second Floor: 812 square feet
Total: 3,112 square feet

Dormered windows, a covered porch and symmetrical balustrades provide a warm country welcome. Formal living and dining rooms flank the foyer. The spacious family room contains a raised-hearth fireplace. It is conveniently located near the breakfast/kitchen area, which features an island cooktop, pantry and planning desk. A three-sided fireplace warms both the sitting room and the master bedroom. A lavish master bath is complete with a whirlpool tub and separate His and Her dressing areas. The second floor contains two family bedrooms and a full bath.

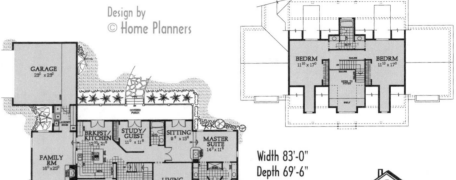

Width 83'-0"
Depth 69'-6"

QUOTE ONE®
Cost to build? See page 684
to order complete cost estimate
to build this house in your area!

DESIGN 3397

First Floor: 1,855 square feet
Second Floor: 1,241 square feet
Total: 3,096 square feet

L D

Five second-story dormers and a wide covered front porch add to the charm of this farmhouse design. Inside, the entry foyer opens to the left to a formal living room with fireplace and attached dining room. To the right is a private study. The back of the plan is dominated by a huge country kitchen featuring an island cooktop. On this floor is the master suite with a large walk-in closet. The second floor holds three bedrooms (or two and a sitting room) with two full baths.

QUOTE ONE®
Cost to build? See page 684
to order complete cost estimate
to build this house in your area!

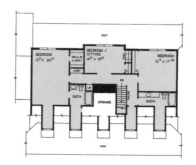

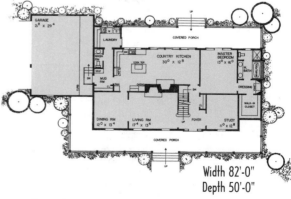

Width 82'-0"
Depth 50'-0"

TWO-STORY FARMHOUSES

www.homeplanners.com

Width 72'-0"
Depth 45'-4"

Design by
© Design Basics, Inc.

QUOTE ONE®
Cost to build? See page 684
to order complete cost estimate
to build this house in your area!

Oval windows and an appealing covered porch lend character to this 1½-story home. Inside, a volume entry views the formal living and dining rooms. Three large windows and a raised-hearth fireplace flanked by bookcases highlight a volume great room. An island kitchen with a huge pantry and two lazy Susans serves a captivating gazebo dinette. In the master suite, a cathedral ceiling, corner whirlpool tub and roomy dressing area deserve careful study. A gallery wall for displaying family mementos and prized heirlooms graces the upstairs corridor. Each secondary bedroom has convenient access to the bathrooms. This home's charm and blend of popular amenities will fit your lifestyle!

DESIGN 9298
First Floor: 1,881 square feet
Second Floor: 814 square feet
Total: 2,695 square feet

© 1993 Donald A. Gardner Architects, Inc.

DESIGN 9707

First Floor: 1,632 square feet
Second Floor: 669 square feet
Total: 2,301 square feet
Bonus Room: 528 square feet

This open country plan boasts front and rear covered porches. The entrance foyer with a sloped ceiling has a Palladian window clerestory to allow in natural light. The spacious great room provides a fireplace, cathedral ceiling and a clerestory with arched windows. The second-floor balcony overlooks the great room. A U-shaped kitchen provides the ideal layout for food preparation. Access to the bonus room is provided from both the first and second floors.

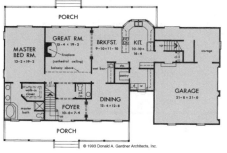
© 1993 Donald A. Gardner Architects, Inc.

Design by
Donald A. Gardner
Architects, Inc.

Width 72'-6"
Depth 46'-10"

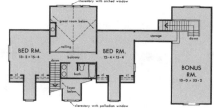

QUOTE ONE®
Cost to build? See page 684
to order complete cost estimate
to build this house in your area!

DESIGN 9752

First Floor: 1,484 square feet
Second Floor: 660 square feet
Total: 2,144 square feet

Overlooking a covered porch and a deck with a spa, this home's kitchen will be a gourmet's delight. A wraparound counter gives plenty of space while a snack bar opens to the breakfast nook. In the great room—which delights with a fireplace—quiet gatherings and entertaining will be a pleasure. The master bedroom, complete with a spa-style bath, rests to the right side of the first floor. Upstairs, two bedrooms and a full hall bath comfortably house family and guests.

© 1993 Donald A. Gardner Architects, Inc.

Design by
Donald A. Gardner
Architects, Inc.

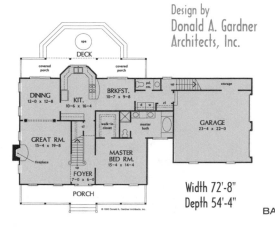
© 1993 Donald A. Gardner Architects, Inc.

Width 72'-8"
Depth 54'-4"

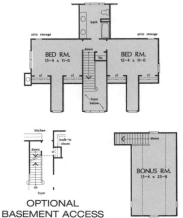

OPTIONAL
BASEMENT ACCESS

© 1992 Donald A. Gardner Architects, Inc.

DESIGN 9690

First Floor: 1,145 square feet
Second Floor: 518 square feet
Total: 1,663 square feet
Bonus Room: 380 square feet

A wraparound porch welcomes visitors to the home. Inside lies an enormous great room with a fireplace. To the rear of the home, the breakfast and dining rooms have sliding glass doors to a large deck with room for a spa. The master bedroom contains a walk-in closet and an airy bath with a whirlpool tub. Two bedrooms are found on the second floor, as well as a bonus room over the garage.

BONUS RM. 24-8 × 14-4

Width 59'-4"
Depth 56'-6"

Design by Donald A. Gardner Architects, Inc.

BED RM. 13-4 × 10-2
BED RM. 13-4 × 10-2

DECK
BRKFST. 10-10 × 7-6
DINING 12-4 × 11-6
KITCHEN 13-2 × 8-2
GARAGE 21-0 × 21-8
GREAT RM. 13-4 × 19-4
MASTER BED RM. 13-4 × 13-0
PORCH

© 1992 Donald A. Gardner Architects, Inc.

QUOTE ONE®
Cost to build? See page 684 to order complete cost estimate to build this house in your area!

©1993 Donald A. Gardner Architects, Inc.

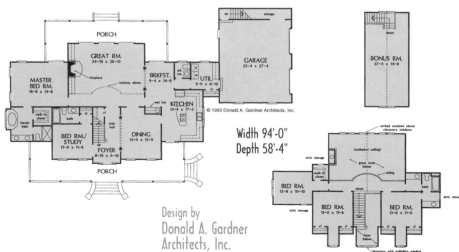

DESIGN 9729

First Floor: 2,176 square feet
Second Floor: 861 square feet
Total: 3,037 square feet

Country living is at its best in this spacious, five-bedroom farmhouse with a wrap-around porch. A front Palladian window dormer and rear clerestory windows add exciting visual elements to the exterior and provide natural light to the interior. The large great room boasts a fireplace, bookshelves and a raised cathedral ceiling allowing the curved-balcony overlook. Special features such as a large cooktop island in the kitchen, a wet bar, a bedroom/study combo and generous bonus room over the garage set this plan apart.

PORCH
GREAT RM. 24-10 × 20-10
MASTER BED RM. 18-8 × 14-8
BRKFST. 9-4 × 14-8
UTIL. 9-0 × 8-10
GARAGE 23-4 × 27-4
BONUS RM. 27-4 × 14-0
KITCHEN 13-4 × 17-2
BED RM./STUDY 13-0 × 11-8
FOYER 8-10 × 6-10
DINING 13-0 × 15-0
PORCH

© 1993 Donald A. Gardner Architects, Inc.

Width 94'-0"
Depth 58'-4"

BED RM. 12-8 × 10-10
BED RM. 13-0 × 11-6
BED RM. 13-0 × 11-6

Design by Donald A. Gardner Architects, Inc.

TWO-STORY FARMHOUSES

DESIGN 9711

First Floor: 1,271 square feet
Second Floor: 665 square feet
Total: 1,936 square feet

This gabled and dormered country home with an L-shaped wrapping porch fits unexpected luxury into this compact plan. A balcony adds drama to the vaulted great room and the large, center island kitchen opens to rear porches and a deck with spa area for great entertaining. The second-floor master bedroom features a bath with all of the extras.

© 1993 Donald A. Gardner Architects, Inc.

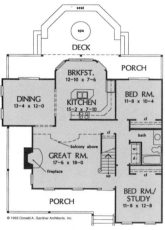

© 1993 Donald A. Gardner Architects, Inc.

Width 41'-6"
Depth 44'-8"

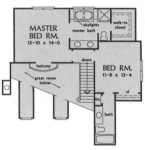

Design by
Donald A. Gardner
Architects, Inc.

DESIGN 3461

First Floor: 1,391 square feet
Second Floor: 611 square feet
Total: 2,002 square feet

Muntin windows, shutters and flower boxes add exterior appeal to this well-designed family farmhouse. Informal living takes off in the open kitchen and family room. An island cooktop will be a favorite feature, as will be the fireplace. Sleeping accommodations are defined by the master bedroom where a bay window provides a perfect sitting nook. The master bath has a large walk-in closet, twin lavatories, a separate shower and whirlpool tub. Three bedrooms reside upstairs.

Width 64'-0"
Depth 44'-0"

Design by
© Home Planners

QUOTE ONE®
Cost to build? See page 684
to order complete cost estimate
to build this house in your area!

© 1992 Donald A. Gardner Architects, Inc.

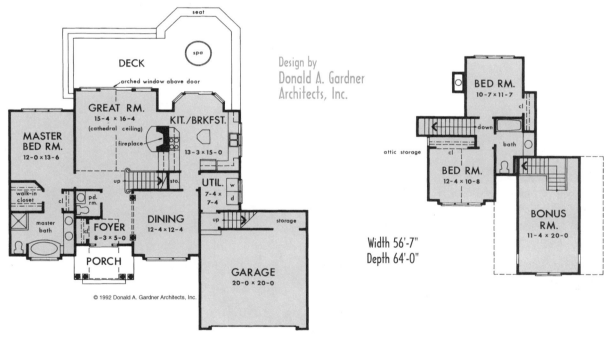

Design by
Donald A. Gardner
Architects, Inc.

DECK

seat

spa

arched window above door

GREAT RM.
15-4 × 16-4
(cathedral ceiling)

fireplace

KIT./BRKFST.

13-3 × 15-0

MASTER
BED RM.
12-0 × 13-6

walk-in
closet

cl

up

sto.

UTIL.
7-4 ×
7-4

w

d

master
bath

pd.
rm.

FOYER
8-3 × 5-0

DINING
12-4 × 12-4

up

storage

PORCH

GARAGE
20-0 × 20-0

© 1992 Donald A. Gardner Architects, Inc.

BED RM.
10-7 × 11-7

cl

down

attic storage

cl

bath

BED RM.
12-4 × 10-8

BONUS
RM.
11-4 × 20-0

Width 56'-7"
Depth 64'-0"

A n arched entrance and multi-pane windows combine with the round columns to create a touch of class on the exterior of this three-bedroom plan. There is little, if any, wasted space in the layout of this plan. The foyer leads to all areas of the house, minimizing corridor space. The dining room features round columns at the entrance, while the great room boasts a cathedral ceiling, fire-place and arched windows over exterior doors to the deck. A large open kitchen includes an island and separate entrance to the deck. A master bedroom with plenty of walk-in closet space contains a bath with a double-bowl vanity, shower and whirlpool tub. The expansive rear deck allows space for a spa and outdoor living. The second level houses two bedrooms that share a full bath.

DESIGN 9692

First Floor: 1,288 square feet
Second Floor: 410 square feet
Total: 1,698 square feet
Bonus Room: 289 square feet

TWO-STORY FARMHOUSES

© 1996 Donald A. Gardner Architects, Inc.

DESIGN 7605

First Floor: 1,099 square feet
Second Floor: 647 square feet
Total: 1,746 square feet
Bonus Room: 377 square feet

The front gable of this farmhouse design features a clerestory window that illuminates the oversized great room. The efficient kitchen opens to the dining room, which accesses the deck and provides a service entrance from the garage. Family bedrooms on the first floor feature triple windows and a shared full bath. The master retreat, located upstairs, includes a bath with a garden tub and separate vanities, as well as a loft/study that can be converted into an additional bedroom or nursery.

Width 61'-6"
Depth 36'-4"

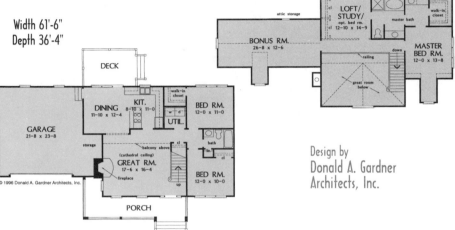

Design by
Donald A. Gardner
Architects, Inc.

DESIGN 7700

First Floor: 1,219 square feet
Second Floor: 450 square feet
Total: 1,669 square feet
Bonus Room: 406 square feet

This narrow-lot home offers some of the extras usually reserved for wider lots, such as a wraparound porch and a two-car garage. A vaulted ceiling adds volume to the great room, while columns and a bay window add distinction to the dining room. The kitchen is designed for efficiency and offers access to the side porch and rear deck for outdoor dining options.

© 1997 Donald A. Gardner Architects, Inc.

Width 50'-4"
Depth 49'-2"

Design by
Donald A. Gardner
Architects, Inc.

TWO-STORY FARMHOUSES

DESIGN 9238

First Floor: 1,421 square feet
Second Floor: 448 square feet
Total: 1,869 square feet

Always a welcome sight, the covered front porch of this home invites entry to its delightful floor plan. Living areas to the back of the house include the great room with a see-through fireplace to the hearth kitchen with bayed dinette, planning desk and large corner walk-in pantry. The front formal dining room features built-in hutch space. A split-bedroom sleeping plan puts the master suite with whirlpool tub, walk-in closet and double vanity on the first floor, away from two second-floor bedrooms and shared full bath.

Design by
© Design Basics, Inc.

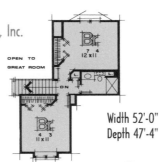

Width 52'-0"
Depth 47'-4"

QUOTE ONE®
Cost to build? See page 684
to order complete cost estimate
to build this house in your area!

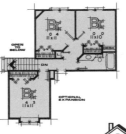

DESIGN 9206

First Floor: 1,421 square feet
Second Floor: 578 square feet
Total: 1,999 square feet

Growing families will love this unique plan that combines all the essentials with an abundance of stylish touches. A spacious great room includes high ceilings, windows, a through-fireplace to the kitchen and access to the rear yard. A dining room with hutch space accommodates formal occasions. The master suite with whirlpool tub and a walk-in closet is found downstairs while three family bedrooms are upstairs. Please specify basement or slab foundation when ordering.

Width 52'-0"
Depth 47'-4"

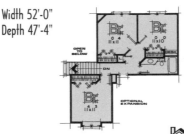

Design by
© Design Basics, Inc.

QUOTE ONE®
Cost to build? See page 684
to order complete cost estimate
to build this house in your area!

TWO-STORY FARMHOUSES

© 1990 Donald A. Gardner Architects, Inc.

Design by
Donald A. Gardner
Architects, Inc.

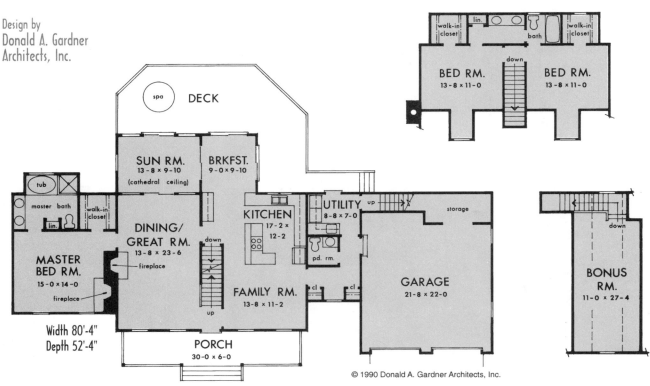

© 1990 Donald A. Gardner Architects, Inc.

TWO-STORY FARMHOUSES

**DESIGN
9625**
First Floor: 1,581 square feet
Second Floor: 549 square feet
Total: 2,130 square feet
Bonus Room: 334 square feet

Great flexibility is available in this plan—the great room/dining room can be reworked into one large great room with the dining room relocated to the family room. A sun room with cathedral ceiling and sliding glass door to the deck is accessible from both the breakfast and dining rooms. A large kitchen boasts a convenient cook- ing island. The master bedroom adds a fireplace, walk-in closet and spacious master bath. Two second-level bedrooms are equal in size and share a full bath, that has double-bowl vanity. Both bed- rooms have a dormer window and a walk-in closet. A large bonus room over the garage is accessible from the utility room below.

© 1994 Donald A. Gardner Architects, Inc.

This farmhouse exudes welcoming charm. Inside, the large great room with cathedral ceiling, fireplace and rear-deck access is convenient to the efficient kitchen. The breakfast room has sliding glass doors to a screened-in porch for carefree outdoor dining. The location of the master bedroom downstairs and two other bedrooms upstairs maintains privacy.

Design by
Donald A. Gardner Architects, Inc.

DECK

SCREEN PORCH
12-0 x 12-0

(vaulted ceiling)

BRKFST.
7-10 x 8-0

UTIL.
7-2 x 6-0

GREAT RM.
23-6 x 17-0

plant shelf above

fireplace

balcony above

KIT.
11-4 x 10-0

storage

GARAGE
19-8 x 20-0

master bath

walk-in closet

pd. rm.

cl

DINING
11-4 x 13-0

plant shelf above

FOYER
9-10 x 5-4

MASTER BED RM.
13-4 x 15-0

PORCH

(cathedral ceiling)

© 1994 Donald A. Gardner Architects, Inc.

Width 61'-6"
Depth 54'-0"

great room below

skylight

attic storage

BED RM.
12-2 x 12-0

railing

bath

down

BED RM.
11-4 x 12-0

cl

cl

cl

foyer below

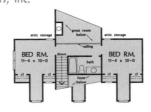

Quote One®
Cost to build? See page 684
to order complete cost estimate
to build this house in your area!

© 1994 Donald A. Gardner Architects, Inc.

Open floor planning gives this efficient three-bedroom home a much larger feeling. The two-story foyer leads to the great room and dining area, which sports a vaulted ceiling accented with skylights. The eat-in kitchen features a stylish angled snack bar that opens to the great room. Privacy is assured in the first-floor master suite, which contains a walk-in closet and a pampering bath. Upstairs, a balcony hall overlooks the great room and leads to two family bedrooms with a shared full bath.

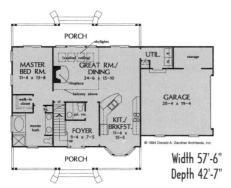

PORCH

skylights

(vaulted ceiling)

MASTER BED RM.
11-4 x 13-8

GREAT RM./ DINING
24-6 x 15-10

UTIL.

storage

fireplace

balcony above

walk-in closet

GARAGE
20-4 x 19-4

master bath

pd. rm.

cl

FOYER
9-4 x 7-5

KIT./ BRKFST.
11-4 x 15-5

PORCH

© 1994 Donald A. Gardner Architects, Inc.

Design by
Donald A. Gardner Architects, Inc.

attic storage

great room below

attic storage

BED RM.
11-4 x 10-0

down

railing

bath

BED RM.
11-4 x 10-0

foyer below

Width 57'-6"
Depth 42'-7"

Two-Story Farmhouses

B. NATHAN. © 1994 Donald A. Gardner Architects, Inc.

Width 58'-0"
Depth 44'-0"

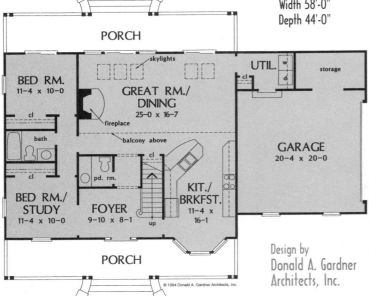

PORCH

BED RM.
11-4 x 10-0

cl

bath

cl

BED RM./
STUDY
11-4 x 10-0

pd. rm.

FOYER
9-10 x 8-1

up

GREAT RM./
DINING
25-0 x 16-7

skylights

fireplace

balcony above

cl

KIT./
BRKFST.
11-4 x
16-1

UTIL.

w
d

cl

storage

GARAGE
20-4 x 20-0

PORCH

© 1994 Donald A. Gardner Architects, Inc.

Design by
Donald A. Gardner
Architects, Inc.

Quote One®
Cost to build? See page 684
to order complete cost estimate
to build this house in your area!

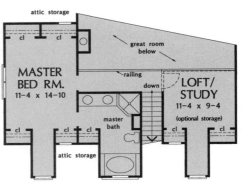

attic storage

cl   cl

MASTER
BED RM.
11-4 x 14-10

cl   cl

attic storage

master
bath

great room
below

railing

down

LOFT/
STUDY
11-4 x 9-4
(optional storage)

cl   cl

**DESIGN
9775**
First Floor: 1,234 square feet
Second Floor: 609 square feet
Total: 1,843 square feet

Interesting room arrangements make this home unique and inviting. From the wide front porch, enter the foyer to find the family bedrooms and a shared full bath on the left and a small hallway on the right that leads to the sunny kitchen. Ahead of the foyer and the kitchen is a combination great room and dining area that features a fireplace, access to the large back porch and plenty of windows and skylights. A large utility area with access to the garage and an abundance of storage space completes the first floor. The second floor is reserved for a grand master suite that features plenty of closet space, a separate loft or study area and a wonderful master bath with a bumped-out whirlpool tub.

www.homeplanners.com

© 1994 Donald A. Gardner Architects, Inc.

BED RM. 12-8 x 12-0
attic storage
great room below
attic storage
BED RM. 12-8 x 12-0
attic storage
BONUS RM. 21-6 x 14-0
attic storage
bath
down
railing
foyer below

Design by
Donald A. Gardner
Architects, Inc.

MASTER BED RM. 13-0 x 17-6
walk-in closet
master bath
GREAT RM. 15-4 x 21-0
fireplace
skylights
(cathedral ceiling)
balcony above
BRKFST. 10-8 x 10-2
UTIL. 9-0 x 7-10
pantry
GARAGE 21-6 x 23-0
storage
KIT. 13-0 x 13-0
BED RM./ STUDY 13-0 x 11-0
walk-in closet
FOYER 15-4 x 5-4
DINING 13-0 x 12-8
PORCH

Width 82'-2"
Depth 48'-10"

© 1994 Donald A. Gardner Architects, Inc.

DESIGN 9767

First Floor: 1,841 square feet
Second Floor: 594 square feet
Total: 2,435 square feet
Bonus Room: 391 square feet

Spaciousness and lots of amenities earmark this design as a family favorite. The front wraparound porch leads to the foyer where a bedroom/study and dining room open. The central great room presents a warming fireplace, a cathedral ceiling and access to the rear porch. In the master bedroom suite, a private bath with a bumped-out tub and a walk-in closet are extra enhancements. Upstairs, two bedrooms flank a full bath. A bonus room over the garage allows for future expansion.

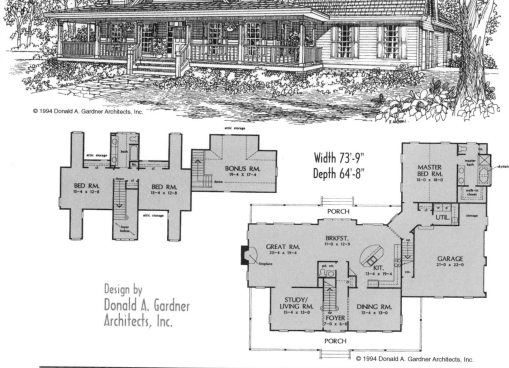

© 1994 Donald A. Gardner Architects, Inc.

BED RM. 15-4 x 12-8
attic storage
bath
BED RM. 15-4 x 12-8
attic storage
BONUS RM. 19-4 x 17-4
down
down
foyer below

Width 73'-9"
Depth 64'-8"

Design by
Donald A. Gardner
Architects, Inc.

GREAT RM. 20-4 x 19-4
fireplace
PORCH
BRKFST. 11-0 x 12-9
pd. rm.
KIT. 13-4 x 19-4
MASTER BED RM. 16-0 x 18-0
master bath
skylight
walk-in closet
UTIL.
storage
GARAGE 21-0 x 22-0
up
stn.
STUDY/ LIVING RM. 15-4 x 13-0
FOYER 7-0 x 6-0
DINING RM. 15-4 x 13-0
PORCH

© 1994 Donald A. Gardner Architects, Inc.

DESIGN 9766

First Floor: 2,087 square feet
Second Floor: 758 square feet
Total: 2,845 square feet

This handsome country exterior will be a pleasure to come home to and it offers both a front covered porch and a rear porch for added outdoor livability. The great room presents lots of windows and a fireplace for added warmth. The breakfast area takes advantage of rear views while the kitchen serves this area with a large island cooktop. A formal dining room is available for extra-special occasions. The private master suite enjoys a luxury bath. Two secondary bedrooms upstairs and a bonus room over the garage finish the plan.

TWO-STORY FARMHOUSES

DESIGN 7663

First Floor: 1,336 square feet
Second Floor: 523 square feet
Total: 1,859 square feet
Bonus Room: 225 square feet

A centered fireplace warms the great room, which opens to the rear covered porch through lovely French doors. The U-shaped kitchen serves a snack counter as well as the formal dining room, with its own porch access. A tray ceiling, garden tub, double-bowl vanity and walk-in closet highlight the master suite. Two upper-level bedrooms are connected by a gallery hall with an overlook to the greatroom.

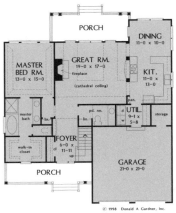

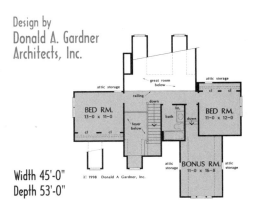

Design by
Donald A. Gardner
Architects, Inc.

Width 45'-0"
Depth 53'-0"

© 1998 Donald A Gardner, Inc.

DESIGN 7654

First Floor: 1,055 square feet
Second Floor: 572 square feet
Total: 1,627 square feet

What could be more charming than this country cottage? The covered front porch with special wood detailing invites you to put your feet up and take it easy. The interior is equally charming. The great room boasts a cathedral ceiling and fireplace while the adjacent kitchen and dining area access a rear covered porch to extend indoor/outdoor living. Two family bedrooms share a hall bath and complete the main level. Upstairs is located the master bedroom suite with attic storage and a roomy loft/study.

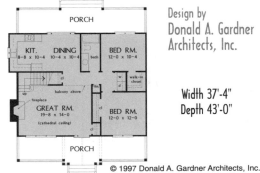

Design by
Donald A. Gardner
Architects, Inc.

Width 37'-4"
Depth 43'-0"

© 1997 Donald A. Gardner Architects, Inc.

TWO-STORY FARMHOUSES

www.homeplanners.com

© 1994 Donald A. Gardner Architects, Inc.

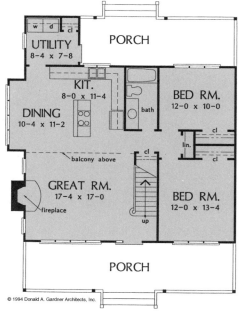

UTILITY
8-4 x 7-8

PORCH

KIT.
8-0 x 11-4

bath

BED RM.
12-0 x 10-0

DINING
10-4 x 11-2

cl

balcony above

lin.

cl

cl

GREAT RM.
17-4 x 17-0

up

fireplace

BED RM.
12-0 x 13-4

PORCH

© 1994 Donald A. Gardner Architects, Inc.

Design by
**Donald A. Gardner
Architects, Inc.**

QUOTE ONE®
Cost to build? See page 684
to order complete cost estimate
to build this house in your area!

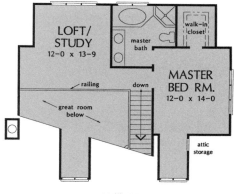

LOFT/
STUDY
12-0 x 13-9

master
bath

walk-in
closet

railing

MASTER
BED RM.
12-0 x 14-0

down

great room
below

attic
storage

Width 36'-8"
Depth 45'-0"

A relaxing country image projects from the front and rear covered porches of this rustic three-bedroom home. Open planning extends to the great room, the dining room and the efficient kitchen. A shared cathedral ceiling creates an impressive space. Completing the first floor are two family bedrooms, a full bath and a handy utility area with washer/dryer space, a closet and access to the rear porch. The second floor contains the master suite which features a spacious walk-in closet and a master bath with a whirlpool tub and a separate corner shower. A generous loft/study overlooks the great room below.

**DESIGN
9759**
First Floor: 1,100 square feet
Second Floor: 584 square feet
Total: 1,684 square feet

TWO-STORY FARMHOUSES

DESIGN
Q219

First Floor: 1,026 square feet
Second Floor: 994 square feet
Total: 2,020 square feet
Bonus Room: 377 square feet

This inviting country home is enhanced by a full-width covered front porch, a fieldstone exterior and a trio of dormers. Double doors open to a foyer flanked by the formal rooms. The living room extends the full depth of the house and has a fireplace and sliding glass doors to the rear patio. A U-shaped kitchen adjoins a breakfast room with sliding glass doors to the patio. Second-floor space includes two family bedrooms with a shared bath and a master suite that features a full bath and walk-in closet.

Design by
© Select Home Designs

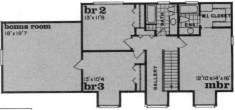

Width 58'-0"
Depth 32'-0"

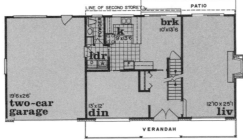

DESIGN
Q386

First Floor: 1,404 square feet
Second Floor: 640 square feet
Total: 2,044 square feet
Bonus Room: 695 square feet

This home is made for country living. The living room shares a three-sided fireplace with the dining room and features columns and a half wall at its entry. The master suite opens through double doors and offers a walk-in closet and full bath with a whirlpool tub. Across the back of the plan is the country kitchen with an island cooktop, an L-shaped work center and a bayed eating area. The second floor has two family bedrooms and a full bath. Plans include basement and crawlspace options.

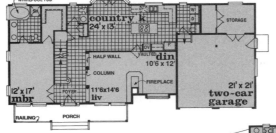

Design by
© Select Home Designs

Width 68'-6"
Depth 36'-0"

TWO-STORY FARMHOUSES

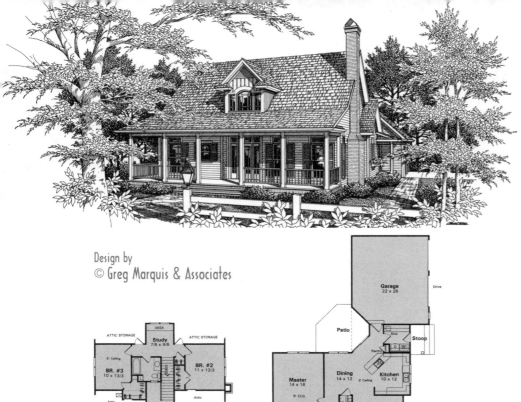

DESIGN B126

First Floor: 1,271 square feet
Second Floor: 537 square feet
Total: 1,808 square feet

The foyer of this traditional country design is open to the second-floor dormer above to fill the house with natural light. The family room with high ceilings and fireplace is to the right of the foyer. The open dining room and kitchen have an angled cooking area, full pantry and access to the rear patio. The master suite features a walk-in closet, double vanities and a linen closet in the bath. Two bedrooms share a hall bath on the second floor, plus a built-in desk in the study area.

Design by
© Greg Marquis & Associates

Width 44'-4"
Depth 73'-2"

BASIC PLAN

Design by
© Home Planners

Width 68'-0"
Depth 30'-0"

ENHANCED PLAN

DESIGN 3715

First Floor: 1,312 square feet
Second Floor: 795 square feet
Total: 2,107 square feet

The design of this 1½-story Cape Cod provides plenty of room for all your family's needs. The kitchen extends as one large room over the snack bar into an expansive family room. Both the family and living rooms open directly to the center hall, which also leads into the dining room at the back of the house. A study downstairs could be converted into another bedroom with an adjacent full bath. The house may be enhanced by the addition of a fireplace, bay window, two-car garage, laundry room and rear deck.

TWO-STORY FARMHOUSES

DESIGN 3635

First Floor: 2,026 square feet
Second Floor: 849 square feet
Total: 2,875 square feet

L

Sunny bay windows splash this favoite farmhouse with uptown, down-home style, set off by an old-fashioned country porch. Inside, the tiled foyer opens to a study, or guest suite, with a powder room. The casual living area enjoys a raised-hearth fireplace and a media niche. The gourmet kitchen enjoys natural light from a breakfast bay and a skylight. Two family bedrooms share a full bath on the second floor, while a fourth bedroom, or guest suite, enjoys a private bath.

Design by
© Home Planners

QUOTE ONE®
Cost to build? See page 684
to order complete cost estimate
to build this house in your area!

Width 70'-8"
Depth 61'-4"

DESIGN 3687

First Floor: 1,374 square feet
Second Floor: 600 square feet
Total: 1,974 square feet

L D

Balustrades and brackets, dual balconies and a wraparound porch create a country-style exterior meant for soft summer evenings. An aura of hospitality pervades the well-planned interior, starting with a tiled foyer that opens to a two-story great room. The sunny, bayed nook invites casual dining and shares its natural light with a snack counter and a well-appointed U-shaped kitchen. A spacious master suite offers a corner whirlpool tub and a walk-in closet.

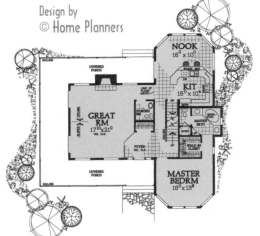

Design by
© Home Planners

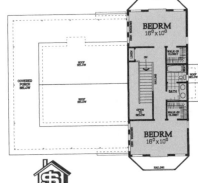

QUOTE ONE®
Cost to build? See page 684
to order complete cost estimate
to build this house in your area!

Width 51'-8"
Depth 50'-8"

TWO-STORY FARMHOUSES

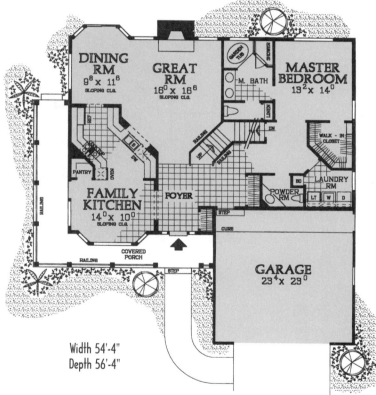

Width 54'-4"
Depth 56'-4"

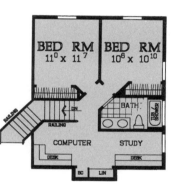

QUOTE ONE®
Cost to build? See page 684
to order complete cost estimate
to build this house in your area!

Design by
© Home Planners

This home's front-projecting garage allows utilization of a narrow, less-expensive building site. The wrap-around porch provides sheltered entrances and outdoor living access from the family kitchen. Open planning, sloping ceilings and an abundance of windows highlight the formal dining room/great room. Notice the second bay window in the dining room. The great room has a centered fireplace as its focal point. The master bedroom contains a large walk-in closet and the master bath includes twin lavatories, a garden tub, stall shower and compartmented toilet with linen closet. Upstairs are two bedrooms, a bath with twin lavatories and an outstanding computer/study area.

DESIGN 3609
First Floor: 1,624 square feet
Second Floor: 596 square feet
Total: 2,220 square feet

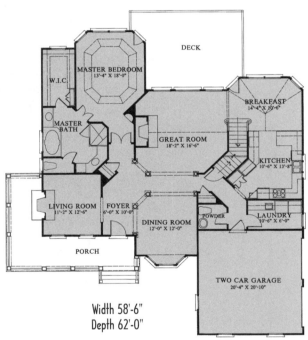

DECK

MASTER BEDROOM
13'-4" X 18'-0"

W.I.C.

MASTER BATH

BREAKFAST
14'-4" X 10'-6"

GREAT ROOM
18'-2" X 16'-6"

KITCHEN
10'-6" X 13'-8"

LIVING ROOM
11'-2" X 12'-6"

FOYER
6'-0" X 10'-0"

DINING ROOM
12'-0" X 12'-0"

POWDER

LAUNDRY
10'-6" X 6'-0"

PORCH

TWO CAR GARAGE
20'-4" X 20'-10"

Width 58'-6"
Depth 62'-0"

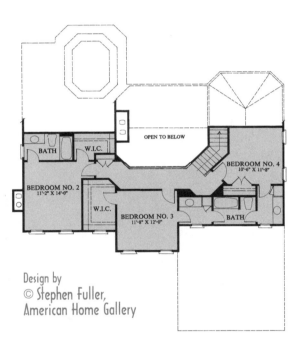

BATH

W.I.C.

OPEN TO BELOW

BEDROOM NO. 2
11'-2" X 14'-0"

W.I.C.

BEDROOM NO. 3
11'-8" X 12'-0"

BEDROOM NO. 4
10'-6" X 11'-8"

BATH

Design by
© Stephen Fuller,
American Home Gallery

TWO-STORY FARMHOUSES

DESIGN
TO51
First Floor: 1,840 square feet
Second Floor: 950 square feet
Total: 2,790 square feet

The appearance of this Early American home brings the past to mind with its wraparound porch, wood siding and flower-box detailing. The uniquely shaped foyer leads to the dining room accented by columns. Nearby, columns frame the great room as well, while a ribbon of windows creates a wall of glass at the back of the house from the great room to the breakfast area. The asymmetrical theme continues through the kitchen as it leads back to the hallway, accessing the laundry and two-car garage.

Left of the foyer lies the living room with a warming fireplace. The master suite begins with double doors that open to a large living space with an octagonal tray ceiling and a bay window. The spacious master bath and walk-in closet complete the suite. Stairs to the second level lead from the breakfast area to an open landing overlooking the great room. Three additional bedrooms with large walk-in closets and a variety of bath arrangements complete this level. This home is designed with a basement foundation.

www.homeplanners.com

DESIGN Z010

First Floor: 1,246 square feet
Second Floor: 1,046 square feet
Total: 2,292 square feet

Stone accents enhance the exterior of this two-story farmhouse. A country kitchen is conveniently located near the dining room and opens to the wraparound front porch and the back porch. A breakfast bar divides the kitchen from the living room. A few steps down, the family room can be used as a home office. Upstairs, the master bedroom features a luxurious bathroom, walk-in closet, fireplace and sitting area. Two additional bedrooms complete the sleeping zone. This home is designed with a basement foundation.

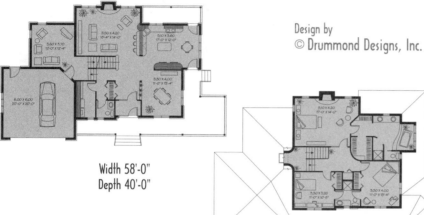

Design by
© Drummond Designs, Inc.

Width 58'-0"
Depth 40'-0"

Design by
© Home Planners

Width 50'-0"
Depth 44'-0"

Quote One®

Cost to build? See page 684
to order complete cost estimate
to build this house in your area!

DESIGN 3619

First Floor: 1,171 square feet
Second Floor: 600 square feet
Total: 1,771 square feet

L D

There's nothing that tops a gracious Southern-style farmhouse! The entry hall opens through an archway on the right to a formal dining room. Nearby, the efficient country kitchen shares space with an eating bay. The two-story family/great room includes a fireplace. The first-floor master suite offers a bay window and accesses the porch through French doors. The second floor holds two family bedrooms that share a full bath. Plans for an optional indoor swimming pool/spa and detached garage are included.

TWO-STORY FARMHOUSES

DESIGN 3653

First Floor: 1,216 square feet
Second Floor: 1,191 square feet
Total: 2,407 square feet

L D

Symmetrical gables and clap-board siding lend a Midwestern style to this prairies-and-plains farmhouse. A spacious foyer opens to formal rooms and leads to a casual living area with a tiled-hearth fireplace. The U-shaped kitchen enjoys an easy-care ceramic tile floor and a walk-in pantry. The second-floor sleeping quarters include a generous master suite with a window-seat dormer and a private bath with a whirlpool tub, walk-in closet and twin vanities. Three family bedrooms share a full bath and a central hall.

Design by
© Home Planners

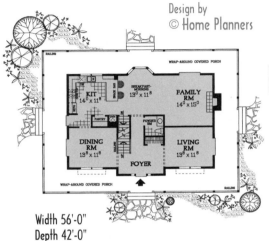

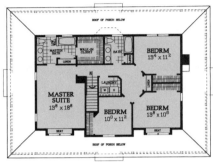

Width 56'-0"
Depth 42'-0"

QUOTE ONE®
Cost to build? See page 684 to order complete cost estimate to build this house in your area!

DESIGN 5548

First Floor: 1,239 square feet
Second Floor: 1,120 square feet
Total: 2,359 square feet
Bonus Room: 415 square feet

A long covered porch with room for rocking chairs offers a hearty welcome to this two-story home. To the left of the foyer is a spacious living room/dining room combination. The U-shaped kitchen offers plenty of counter space and a snack-bar pass-through to the breakfast nook. A media room or den, and a powder room complete the first floor. On the second floor, the master bedroom features a large walk-in closet and a luxurious master bath. Three additional bedrooms share a full hall bath.

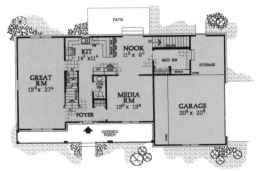

Design by
© Home Planners

Width 61'-8"
Depth 35'-4"

QUOTE ONE®
Cost to build? See page 684 to order complete cost estimate to build this house in your area!

© 1992 Donald A. Gardner Architects, Inc.

Design by
Donald A. Gardner
Architects, Inc.

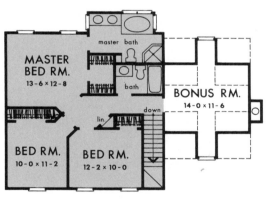

MASTER
BED RM.
13-6 × 12-8

master bath

bath

BONUS RM.
14-0 × 11-6

down

lin.

BED RM.
10-0 × 11-2

BED RM.
12-2 × 10-0

Width 45'-0"
Depth 69'-2"

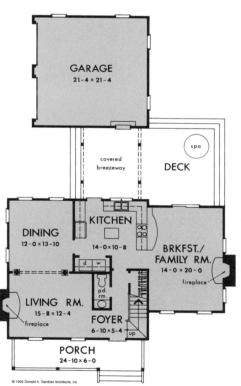

GARAGE
21-4 × 21-4

covered
breezeway

DECK

spa

KITCHEN
14-0 × 10-8

DINING
12-0 × 13-10

BRKFST./
FAMILY RM.
14-0 × 20-0
fireplace

d w

pd.
rm.

LIVING RM.
15-8 × 12-4
fireplace

FOYER
6-10 × 5-4

up

PORCH
24-10 × 6-0

© 1992 Donald A. Gardner Architects, Inc.

This two-level, three-bedroom country home is ideal for narrow lots. The spacious living room and the family room, both with fireplaces, add flexibility to entertaining. The U-shaped kitchen with island counter offers maximum efficiency for food preparation. A covered breezeway connects the garage to the main house and provides a partially sheltered deck area. The second level boasts a master bedroom that offers a master bath with a double-bowl vanity, whirlpool tub and separate shower. In addition, two family bedrooms with a full bath and a bonus room are located on the second floor.

DESIGN
9687
First Floor: 1,044 square feet
Second Floor: 719 square feet
Total: 1,763 square feet

DESIGN 9616

First Floor: 1,734 square feet
Second Floor: 958 square feet
Total: 2,692 square feet

A wraparound covered porch at the front and sides of this home and the open deck with spa and seating provide plenty of outside living area. A central great room features a vaulted ceiling, loft overlook, fireplace and clerestory windows above. Besides a formal dining room, kitchen, breakfast room and sun room on the first floor, there is also a generous master suite with a garden tub. Three second-floor bedrooms complete the sleeping accommodations.

© 1990 Donald A. Gardner Architects, Inc.

B·NATHAN·

Design by
Donald A. Gardner
Architects, Inc.

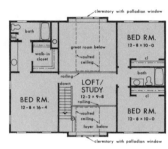

Width 55'-0"
Depth 59'-10"

TWO-STORY FARMHOUSES

DESIGN Q299

First Floor: 1,291 square feet
Second Floor: 1,291 square feet
Total: 2,582 square feet

Traditional with an essence of farmhouse flavor, this four-bedroom home begins with a wraparound covered porch. The floor plan revolves around a central hall with formal rooms on the left and the private den on the right. The family room sits to the rear and is open to the breakfast bay and the L-shaped island kitchen. Two rear porches are reached through doors in the dining and family rooms. The master suite on the second level enjoys a sitting bay and bath with whirlpool tub and separate shower.

Design by
© Select Home Designs

Width 64'-6"
Depth 47'-0"

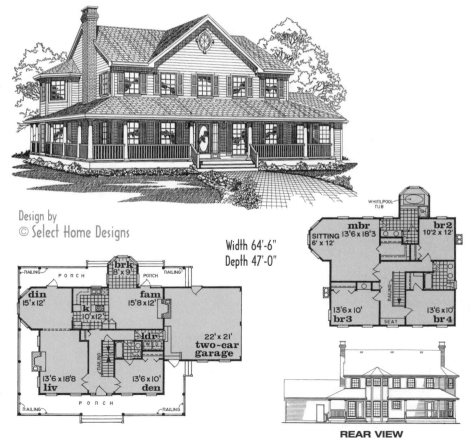

REAR VIEW

www.homeplanners.com

© 1993 Donald A. Gardner Architects, Inc.

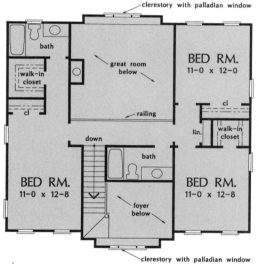

clerestory with palladian window

bath

walk-in closet

cl

great room below

railing

down

BED RM. 11-0 x 12-0

cl

walk-in closet

lin.

BED RM. 11-0 x 12-8

bath

foyer below

BED RM. 11-0 x 12-8

clerestory with palladian window

Design by
Donald A. Gardner
Architects, Inc.

Width 49'-5"
Depth 45'-4"

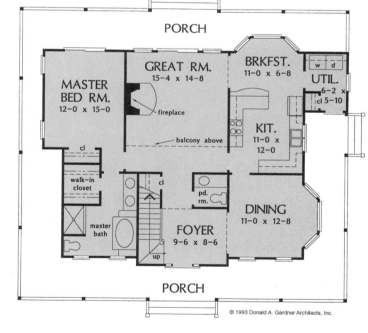

PORCH

MASTER BED RM. 12-0 x 15-0

GREAT RM. 15-4 x 14-8

fireplace

BRKFST. 11-0 x 6-8

UTIL. 6-2 x cl 5-10

w d

KIT. 11-0 x 12-0

balcony above

cl

walk-in closet

master bath

cl

pd. rm.

DINING 11-0 x 12-8

FOYER 9-6 x 8-6

up

PORCH

© 1993 Donald A. Gardner Architects, Inc.

TWO-STORY FARMHOUSES

This classy, two-story home with wraparound covered porch offers a dynamic open floor plan. The entrance foyer and the spacious great room both rise to two stories—a Palladian window at the second level floods these areas with natural light. The kitchen is centrally located for maximum flexibility in layout and, as an added feature, also has a breakfast bar. The large dining room will delight with a bay window. The generous master suite provides plenty of closet space as well as a bath with a whirlpool tub, shower and double-bowl vanity. On the second level, three bedrooms branch off the balcony that overlooks the great room. One large bedroom has a private bath and a walk-in closet while the other bedrooms share a full bath.

DESIGN 9725
First Floor: 1,346 square feet
Second Floor: 836 square feet
Total: 2,182 square feet

© 1992 Donald A. Gardner Architects, Inc.

DESIGN 9667

First Floor: 1,357 square feet
Second Floor: 1,204 square feet
Total: 2,561 square feet

This grand four-bedroom farmhouse with a wrap-around porch offers eye-catching features. The living room opens to the foyer and provides a formal entertaining area. The exceptionally large family room allows for more casual living. The lavish kitchen boasts a cooking island and serves the dining room, breakfast and deck areas. The master suite on the second level has a large walk-in closet and a master bath with a whirlpool tub, shower and double-bowl vanity. Three additional bedrooms share a full bath.

Design by
Donald A. Gardner
Architects, Inc.

Quote One®
Cost to build? See page 684
to order complete cost estimate
to build this house in your area!

Width 80'-0"
Depth 57'-0"

© 1992 Donald A. Gardner Architects, Inc.

DESIGN 9662

First Floor: 1,025 square feet
Second Floor: 911 square feet
Total: 1,936 square feet
Bonus Room: 410 square feet

The exterior of this three-bedroom country-style home is enhanced by its many gables, arched windows and the wraparound porch. A large great room with an impressive fireplace leads to both the dining room and screened porch. Sized for entertaining, the deck wraps to provide room for a spa and outdoor dining space. An open kitchen offers a country atmosphere. The second-floor master suite has two walk-in closets and an impressive bath enhanced by a spa tub in a bumped-out bay.

© 1991 Donald A. Gardner Architects, Inc.

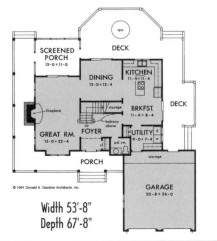

Width 53'-8"
Depth 67'-8"

© 1991 Donald A. Gardner Architects, Inc.

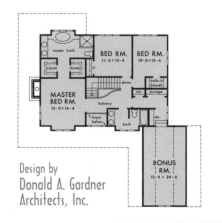

Design by
Donald A. Gardner
Architects, Inc.

TWO-STORY FARMHOUSES

www.homeplanners.com

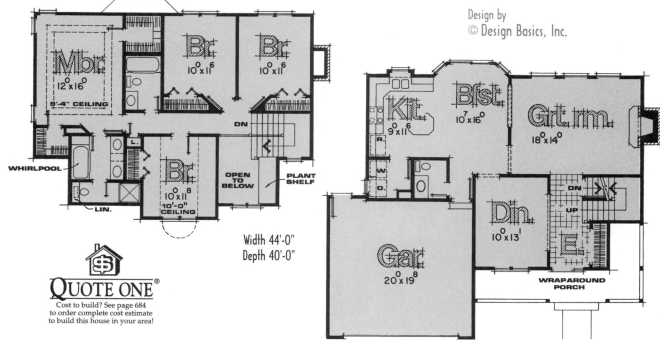

Mbr
12⁰x16⁰

9'-4" CEILING

Br
10⁰x11

Br
10⁰x11

WHIRLPOOL

L.

DN

Br
10⁰x11
10'-0" CEILING

OPEN TO BELOW

PLANT SHELF

LIN.

Width 44'-0"
Depth 40'-0"

Design by
© Design Basics, Inc.

Kit
9⁰x11

Bfst
10⁷x16⁰

Grt. rm.
18⁰x14⁰

R.

W.
D.

Gar
20⁰x19⁸

Din.
10⁰x13¹

DN

UP

WRAPAROUND PORCH

QUOTE ONE®
Cost to build? See page 684
to order complete cost estimate
to build this house in your area!

A wonderful design begins with the wraparound porch of this plan. Explore further and find a two-story entry with a coat closet and plant shelf above and a strategically placed staircase alongside. The island kitchen with a boxed window over the sink is adjacent to a large bay-windowed dinette. The great room includes many windows and a fireplace. A powder bath and laundry room are both conveniently placed on the first floor. Upstairs, the large master suite contains His and Hers walk-in closets, corner windows and a bath area featuring a double vanity and whirlpool tub. Two pleasant secondary bedrooms have interesting angles and a third bedroom in the front features a volume ceiling and arched window. The two-car garage connects to the main house at the powder room. Please specify basement or slab foundation when ordering.

**DESIGN
9235**
First Floor: 919 square feet
Second Floor: 927 square feet
Total: 1,846 square feet

TWO-STORY FARMHOUSES

DESIGN 9644

First Floor: 943 square feet
Second Floor: 840 square feet
Total: 1,783 square feet
Bonus Room: 323 square feet

Roundtop windows and an inviting covered porch offer an irresistible appeal for this three-bedroom plan. A two-story foyer provides a spacious feeling to this well-organized open layout. Round columns between the great room and kitchen add to the impressive quality of the plan. Enjoy casual meals from the bay-windowed breakfast nook that overlooks the expansive deck. The master suite with walk-in closet and complete master bath is on the second floor along with two additional bedrooms and a full bath.

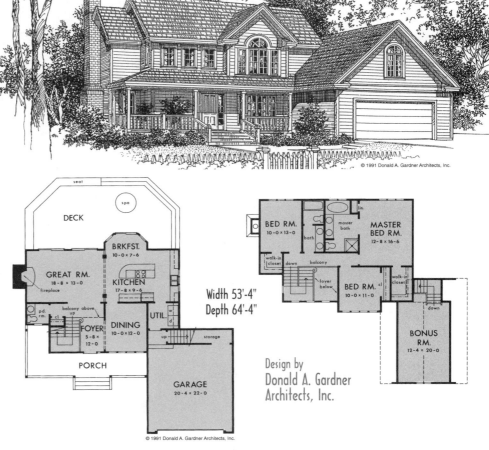

© 1991 Donald A. Gardner Architects, Inc.

Width 53'-4"
Depth 64'-4"

Design by
Donald A. Gardner
Architects, Inc.

© 1991 Donald A. Gardner Architects, Inc.

DESIGN 9798

First Floor: 1,483 square feet
Second Floor: 1,349 square feet
Total: 2,832 square feet
Bonus Room: 486 square feet

This country home displays a quaint rural character outside and a savvy sophistication within. The foyer opens on either side to elegant formal areas, beautifully lit with natural light from multi-pane windows. A casual living area opens to the U-shaped kitchen and bayed breakfast nook, and features a focal-point fireplace. The second-floor master suite offers a sumptuous bath. Three family bedrooms share a gallery hall that leads to a spacious bonus room.

© 1995 Donald A. Gardner Architects, Inc.

Width 66'-10"
Depth 47'-8"

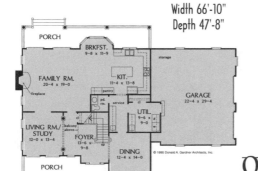

© 1995 Donald A. Gardner Architects, Inc.

Quote One®
Cost to build? See page 684
to order complete cost estimate
to build this house in your area!

Design by
Donald A. Gardner
Architects, Inc.

www.homeplanners.com

© 1993 Donald A. Gardner Architects, Inc.

B. NATHAN

Design by
Donald A. Gardner
Architects, Inc.

Width 58'-8"
Depth 66'-4"

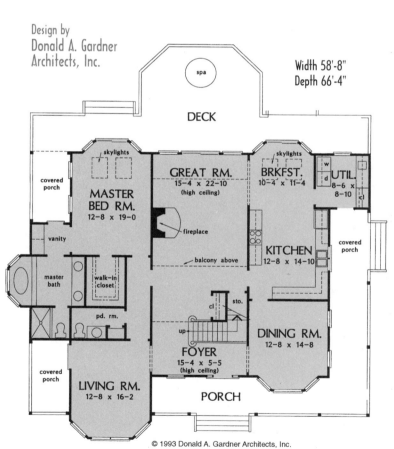

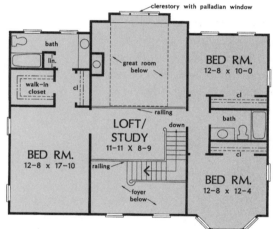

clerestory with palladian window

REAR VIEW

This stylish country farmhouse offers flexibility in the total number of bedrooms while maximizing the use of space. The master bedroom and the breakfast area admit natural light through bay windows and skylights.

Private covered porches are accessible from the master bedroom and the living room/study. Upstairs, three bedrooms share two full baths and a loft/study overlooking the foyer and the great room. Note the fine outdoor areas.

**DESIGN
9730**
First Floor: 1,976 square feet
Second Floor: 970 square feet
Total: 2,946 square feet

TWO-STORY FARMHOUSES

DESIGN 7671

First Floor: 1,943 square feet
Second Floor: 1,000 square feet
Total: 2,943 square feet
Bonus Room: 403 square feet

Two symmetrical bay windows accent the formal rooms of this design. The foyer leads straight back to the family room and rear porch. A fireplace, built-ins and an overhead balcony grace the family room. Between the dining room and kitchen, there's a handy pantry area. The utility room and a powder room are to the right of the breakfast room. The first-floor master suite includes a walk-in closet and a bath with a double-bowl vanity. Upstairs, three bedrooms share a hall bath and a loft/study.

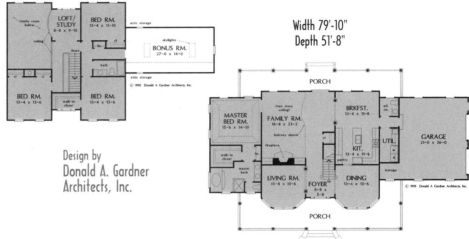

Width 79'-10"
Depth 51'-8"

Design by
Donald A. Gardner Architects, Inc.

DESIGN 7661

First Floor: 1,614 square feet
Second Floor: 892 square feet
Total: 2,506 square feet
Bonus Room: 341 square feet

At the front of this farmhouse design, the master suite includes a sitting bay, two walk-in closets, a door to the front porch and a compartmented bath with a double-bowl vanity. The formal dining room is in the second bay, also with a door to the front porch. Access to the rear porch is from the great room, which is open under a balcony to the breakfast room. On the second floor, three family bedrooms share a bath that has a double-bowl vanity.

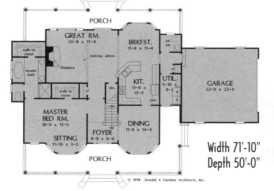

Design by
© **Design Basics, Inc.**

Width 71'-10"
Depth 50'-0"

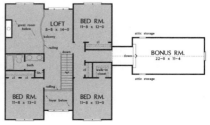

TWO-STORY FARMHOUSES

Design by
© Greg Marquis & Associates

Deck/Patio

Storage

Master
12x14

9' ceiling

up

Dining
11x10

Kitchen
10x10

Garage
22x26

9' ceiling

Walk

shelves

D   W

Family Room
14x16/10

Porch
28x7

down

Br.#3
10x11/8

Br.#4
12x10

Desk

Br.#2
10/8x11/8

roof

Width 71'-0"
Depth 42'-6"

A two-windowed gable tops a covered porch in this comfortable two-story design. The family room includes a fireplace and windows that look out to the front porch, and is open to the dining room at the back of the house. The

L-shaped kitchen offers a snack bar to the dining room and looks out to the rear deck. The master suite completes the main floor. Upstairs, three bedrooms share a full bath. Look for the large storage area in the two-car garage.

DESIGN
B142

First Floor: 982 square feet
Second Floor: 615 square feet
Total: 1,597 square feet

TWO-STORY FARMHOUSES

© 1992 Donald A. Gardner Architects, Inc.

DESIGN 9688

First Floor: 1,569 square feet
Second Floor: 929 square feet
Total: 2,498 square feet

This home's striking exterior is reinforced by its gables and arched glass window. The central foyer leads to all spaces in the home's open layout. Both the living room and great room boast fireplaces and round columns. The efficient U-shaped kitchen offers a cooking island for added luxury to serve both the dining room and breakfast area. All the bedrooms are on the second floor. A study on the first level can easily double as a bedroom.

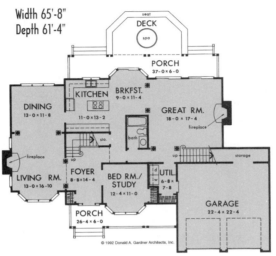

Width 65'-8"
Depth 61'-4"

Design by
Donald A. Gardner
Architects, Inc.

DESIGN 9791

First Floor: 1,484 square feet
Second Floor: 1,061 square feet
Total: 2,545 square feet
Bonus Room: 486 square feet

With two covered porches to encourage outdoor living and an open layout, this farmhouse has plenty to offer. Columns define the living room/study. The great room is graced by a fireplace and has access to the rear porch. A sunny, bayed breakfast room is convenient to the U-shaped island kitchen. A formal dining room with box-bay window is located to the front. Three bedrooms upstairs include a deluxe master suite. Two secondary bedrooms share a full hall bath.

© 1995 Donald A. Gardner Architects, Inc.

Design by
Donald A. Gardner
Architects, Inc.

Width 66'-10"
Depth 47'-8"

Quote One®
Cost to build? See page 684
to order complete cost estimate
to build this house in your area!

www.homeplanners.com

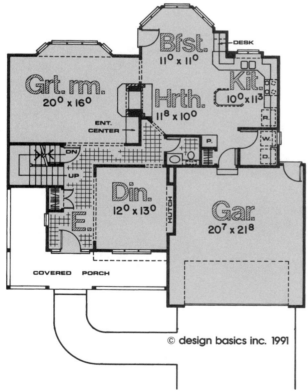

Grt. rm.
20⁰ x 16⁰

Bfst.
11⁰ x 11⁰

DESK

Hrth.
11⁸ x 10⁰

Kit.
10⁰ x 11³

ENT. CENTER

R.

P.

W.

D.

DN

UP

Din.
12⁰ x 13⁰

HUTCH

Gar.
20⁷ x 21⁸

COVERED PORCH

© design basics inc. 1991

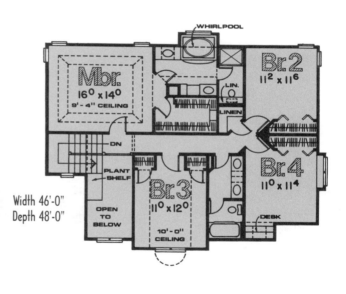

WHIRLPOOL

Mbr.
16⁰ x 14⁰
9'- 4" CEILING

Br. 2
11² x 11⁶

LIN.

LINEN

DN

PLANT SHELF

OPEN TO BELOW

Br. 3
11⁰ x 12⁰
10'- 0" CEILING

Br. 4
11⁰ x 11⁴

DESK

Width 46'-0"
Depth 48'-0"

Design by
© Design Basics, Inc.

A covered porch enhances the elevation of this popular farmhouse. The spacious two-story entry provides a fine introduction to the formal dining room. A fireplace and bayed windows add appeal to the great room. Families will love the spacious kitchen, breakfast area and hearth room. Enhancements to this casual living area include a through-fireplace, gazebo dinette, wrapping counters, an island kitchen and planning desk. Secondary bedrooms and a sumptuous master suite provide privacy. Bedroom 3 is highlighted by a half-circle window while Bedroom 4 features a built-in desk. The master bedroom has a private bath.

DESIGN 9312
First Floor: 1,150 square feet
Second Floor: 1,120 square feet
Total: 2,270 square feet

TWO-STORY FARMHOUSES

DESIGN 7611

First Floor: 1,395 square feet
Second Floor: 502 square feet
Total: 1,897 square feet
Bonus Room: 316 square feet

This traditional plan blends a country exterior with a stylish interior plan. The foyer opens to a U-shaped staircase on the right and a bay-windowed formal dining room on the left. Directly ahead is a stunning, two-story great room with a fireplace as well as access to a covered porch. The secluded master suite enjoys a raised ceiling and a luxury bath with a windowed garden tub. Two family bedrooms share a full bath on the second floor.

Design by
Donald A. Gardner
Architects, Inc.

Width 53'-4"
Depth 51'-4"

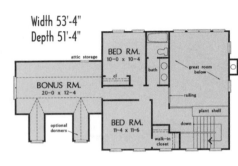

DESIGN 9717

First Floor: 1,377 square feet
Second Floor: 714 square feet
Total: 2,091 square feet

An inviting covered porch and roundtop windows offer an irresistible appeal to this four-bedroom plan. The great room with a fireplace and the breakfast bay both provide access to a rear deck. The master bedroom, located on the first level, has a walk-in closet and a bath consisting of a shower and a garden tub with a skylight overhead. The second level has three bedrooms, a bath and a large bonus room for future development.

Width 55'-8"
Depth 62'-4"

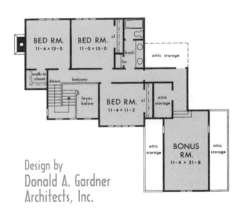

Design by
Donald A. Gardner
Architects, Inc.

TWO-STORY FARMHOUSES

© 1995 Donald A. Gardner Architects, Inc.

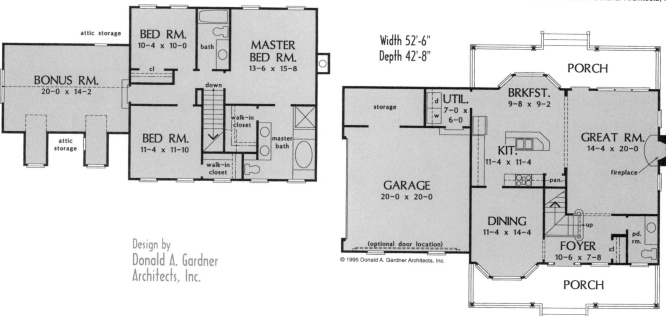

attic storage

BED RM.
10-4 x 10-0

bath

MASTER
BED RM.
13-6 x 15-8

BONUS RM.
20-0 x 14-2

cl

down

attic storage

walk-in closet

BED RM.
11-4 x 11-10

master bath

walk-in closet

Design by
Donald A. Gardner
Architects, Inc.

Width 52'-6"
Depth 42'-8"

storage

UTIL.
7-0 x
6-0

BRKFST.
9-8 x 9-2

PORCH

d w

KIT.
11-4 x 11-4

GREAT RM.
14-4 x 20-0

fireplace

pan.

GARAGE
20-0 x 20-0

DINING
11-4 x 14-4

up

FOYER
10-6 x 7-8

cl

pd. rm.

(optional door location)

© 1995 Donald A. Gardner Architects, Inc.

PORCH

TWO-STORY FARMHOUSES

Alarge, center front gable and a covered porch set the tone for a down-home country welcome. The formal dining room is filled with light from a bay window and has direct access to an efficient island kitchen. A matching bay is found in the breakfast room, furnishing the perfect location for a leisurely cup of morning tea. Active families will enjoy the large great room graced with a warming fireplace and an abundance of windows. For extra flexibility, living space extends out to the covered porch from the great room. An L-shaped staircase leads to the second floor, which contains two family bedrooms, a full bath and a master suite full of amenities. A bonus room extending over the garage can be developed into a game room, fourth bedroom, study or home office at a later date.

**DESIGN
7600**
First Floor: 959 square feet
Second Floor: 833 square feet
Total: 1,792 square feet
Bonus Room: 344 square feet

21'-0" X20'-8"

5,10 X 3,50
17'-0" X 11'-8"

2,90 X 2,60
9'-8" X 8'-8"

2,70 X 3,00
9'-0" X 10'-0"

3,00 X 3,60
10'-0" X 12'-0"

2,90 X 2,80
9'-8" X 9'-4"

3,60 X 6,20
12'-0" X 20'-8"

Design by
© Drummond Designs, Inc.

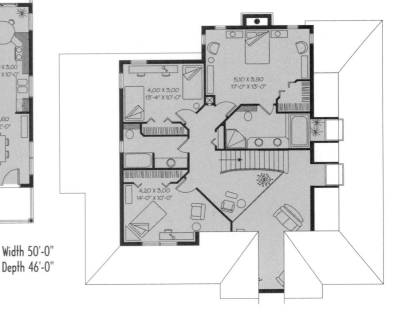

4,00 X 3,00
13'-4" X 10'-0"

5,10 X 3,90
17'-0" X 13'-0"

4,20 X 3,00
14'-0" X 10'-0"

Width 50'-0"
Depth 46'-0"

DESIGN Z018
First Floor: 1,274 square feet
Second Floor: 983 square feet
Total: 2,257 square feet

Special attention to exterior details and interior nuances give this relaxed farmhouse fine distinction on any street. From the large covered porch, enter to find a roomy, well-zoned plan. A striking, central staircase separates the first-floor living area, which boasts a home office, and cathedral ceiling in the living room. The second floor includes a master suite, two bedrooms that share a full bath and a flexible upstairs sitting area. The master suite contains a bath with double-bowl vanities and a walk-in closet. A two-car garage sits to the back of the plan and has two pedestrian doors. This home has a daylight basement.

Two covered porches will entice you outside, while a special sun room on the first floor brings the outdoors in. The foyer opens on the right to a comfortable family room that may be used as a home office. On the left, the living area is warmed by the sun room and a corner fireplace. The efficient kitchen includes a central island and breakfast nook. A spacious master suite with walk-in closet and luxurious master bath completes the second floor. This home has a daylight basement.

Design by
© Drummond Designs, Inc.

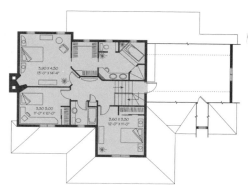

Width 56'-0"
Depth 38'-0"

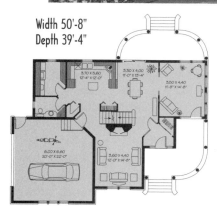

Width 50'-8"
Depth 39'-4"

Design by
© Drummond Designs, Inc.

This lovely country design features a stunning wrapping porch and plenty of windows to provide the interior with natural light. The living room boasts a centered fireplace, which helps to define this spacious open area. The casual living room leads outdoors to a rear porch. Upstairs, four bedrooms cluster around a central hall. The master suite features a walk-in closet and a deluxe bath with an oval tub and a separate shower. This home is designed with a basement foundation.

TWO-STORY FARMHOUSES

© 1997 Donald A. Gardner Architects, Inc.

Design by
Donald A. Gardner
Architects, Inc.

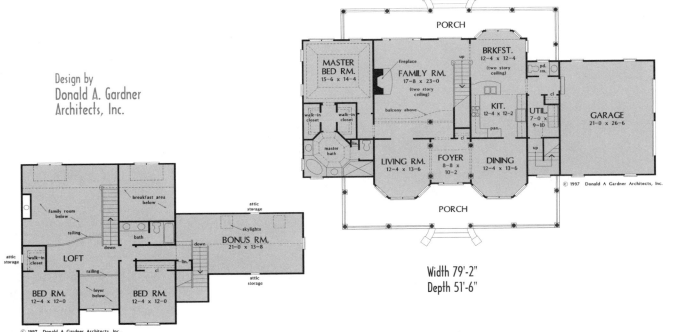

Width 79'-2"
Depth 51'-6"

PORCH

MASTER BED RM.
15-6 x 14-4

FAMILY RM.
17-8 x 23-0
(two-story ceiling)

fireplace

BRKFST.
12-4 x 12-4
(two story ceiling)

up

walk-in closet   walk-in closet

balcony above

KIT.
12-4 x 12-2

UTIL.
7-0 x 9-10

pd. rm.

cl

GARAGE
21-0 x 26-6

master bath

lin.

LIVING RM.
12-4 x 13-6

FOYER
8-8 x 10-2

DINING
12-4 x 13-6

up

PORCH

© 1997 Donald A Gardner Architects, Inc.

family room below

breakfast area below

attic storage

skylights

railing

bath

down

BONUS RM.
21-0 x 13-8

attic storage

attic storage

walk-in closet

LOFT

railing

cl

lin.

down

BED RM.
12-4 x 12-0

foyer below

BED RM.
12-4 x 12-0

© 1997 Donald A Gardner Architects, Inc.

TWO-STORY FARMHOUSES

DESIGN 7656
First Floor: 1,914 square feet
Second Floor: 597 square feet
Total: 2,511 square feet
Bonus Room: 487 square feet

Filled with the charm of farmhouse details, this design opens with a classic front porch. The entry leads to a foyer flanked by columns that separate it from the formal dining room on the right and formal living room on the left. Straight ahead, decorated by another column, is the family room a with two-story ceiling, fireplace and sliding glass doors to the rear covered porch. The U-shaped kitchen separates the dining room from the bayed breakfast room. The first-floor master suite features a bedroom with tray ceiling and a bath with whirlpool tub, dual sinks and separate shower. Two walk-in closets complete the suite. Two family bedrooms on the second floor are joined by a loft overlooking the family room. A skylit bonus room here could become a game room or additional bedroom. Note the two-car garage at the side of the plan.

www.homeplanners.com

*****
DESIGN
5511
First Floor: 1,160 square feet
Second Floor: 1,135 square feet
Total: 2,295 square feet

Width 54'-0"
Depth 42'-0"

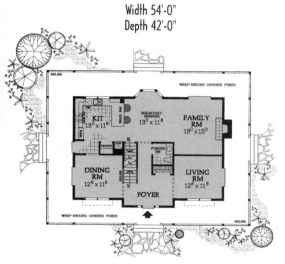

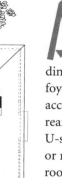

Design by
© Home Planners

QUOTE ONE®
Cost to build? See page 684
to order complete cost estimate
to build this house in your area!

Amenities fill this two-story country home, beginning with a full wraparound porch. Formal living and dining rooms border the central foyer, each with French-door access to the covered porch. At the rear is an open family area with a U-shaped kitchen, bayed breakfast or morning area and large family room with fireplace and access to the rear porch. Upstairs, three family bedrooms share a utility room and a full hall bath with dual sinks. The master bedroom features a box-bay window seat and an amenity-filled master bath.

*****
DESIGN
3654
First Floor: 1,378 square feet
Second Floor: 912 square feet
Total: 2,290 square feet
L

Countrified splendor is what you'll get with this plan— along with a most agreeable floor plan. The front porch leads through the two-story foyer to a formal living area and a formal dining room. A three-sided fireplace is shared by the dining and family rooms. A gourmet kitchen with a snack bar and a large pantry is open to the family room. The first-floor master suite provides a door to the front porch and a bath with all the amenities. Upstairs are three family bedrooms, a full bath, a multi-media room and huge laundry room.

Width 74'-0"
Depth 46'-0"

Design by
© Home Planners

QUOTE ONE®
Cost to build? See page 684
to order complete cost estimate
to build this house in your area!

TWO-STORY FARMHOUSES

Design by
© Home Planners

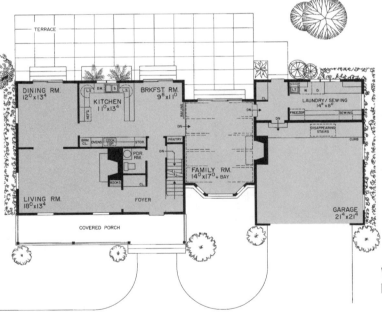

Width 70'-0"
Depth 34'-0"

Quote One®
Cost to build? See page 684
to order complete cost estimate
to build this house in your area!

TWO-STORY FARMHOUSES

**DESIGN
2908**
First Floor: 1,427 square feet
Second Floor: 1,153 square feet
Total: 2,580 square feet

LD

This Early American home offers plenty of modern comfort with its covered front porch with pillars and rails, double chimneys, spacious rooms and large country kitchen with breakfast room. A step-down family room features a fireplace, as does the formal living room. Upstairs, three family bed-rooms share a full hall bath. The master suite is complete with a dual vanity and a compartmented bath with dressing room. Special features of this home include a laundry/sewing room with freezer and washer/dryer space, a large rear terrace and an entry-hall powder room. The two-car garage connects at the laundry room.

www.homeplanners.com

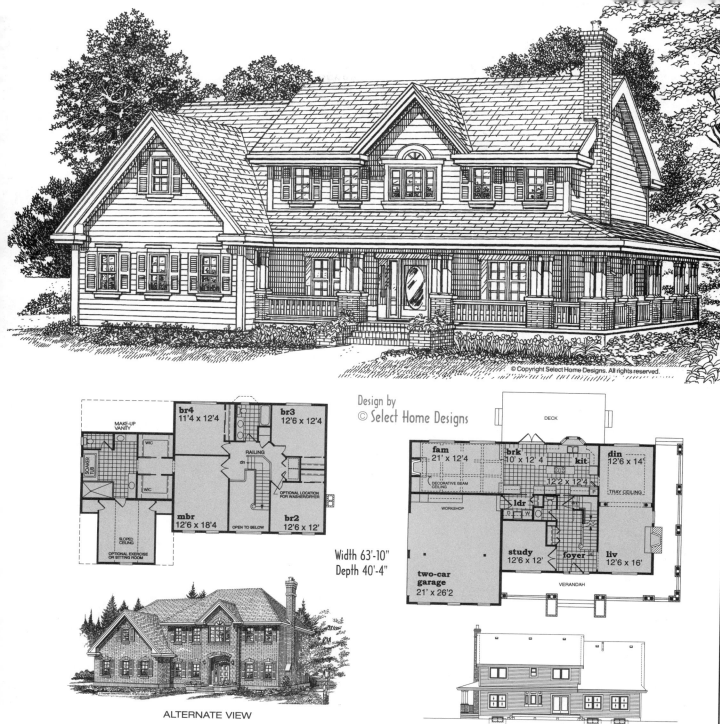

Design by
© Select Home Designs

Width 63'-10"
Depth 40'-4"

br4 11'4 x 12'4
br3 12'6 x 12'4
MAKE-UP VANITY
WIC
WIC
SOAKER TUB
RAILING
dn
OPTIONAL LOCATION FOR WASHER/DRYER
mbr 12'6 x 18'4
OPEN TO BELOW
br2 12'6 x 12'
SLOPED CEILING
OPTIONAL EXERCISE OR SITTING ROOM

DECK
fam 21' x 12'4
DECORATIVE BEAM CEILING
brk 10' x 12'4
kit 12'2 x 12'4
din 12'6 x 14'
TRAY CEILING
WORKSHOP
ldr
D W
P
study 12'6 x 12'
foyer
liv 12'6 x 16'
two-car garage 21' x 26'2
VERANDAH

ALTERNATE VIEW

REAR VIEW

Choose from one of two exteriors for this grand design—a lovely wood-sided farmhouse or a stately brick traditional. Plans include details for both facades. Special mouldings and trim add interest to the nine-foot ceilings on the first floor. The dining room features a tray ceiling and is separated from the hearth-warmed living room by decorative columns. A study is secluded behind double doors just off the entry. The centrally located kitchen features a large cooking island, pantry, telephone desk and ample cupboard and counter space. The family room has a decorative beam ceiling and fireplace. The private master bedroom has an exquisite bath with His and Hers walk-in closets, a soaking tub, separate shower and make-up vanity. An optional exercise/sitting room adds 241 square feet to the total. Family bedrooms share a full bath. If you choose, situate the washer and dryer in an alcove on the second floor.

DESIGN Q454
First Floor: 1,439 square feet
Second Floor: 1,419 square feet
Total: 2,858 square feet
Bonus Room: 241 square feet

TWO-STORY FARMHOUSES

DESIGN 2945

First Floor: 1,644 square feet
Second Floor: 971 square feet
Total: 2,615 square feet
Bonus Room: 971 square feet

This affordable farmhouse manages to include all the basics then adds a little more. Note the wraparound covered porch, large family room with raised-hearth fireplace, spacious kitchen with island cooktop, formal dining room and rear terrace. Upstairs, the plan is as flexible as they come: three or four bedrooms (the fourth could easily be a study or playroom) and plenty of unfinished attic waiting to be transformed into living space.

Design by
© Home Planners

Width 59'-8"
Depth 56'-0"

QUOTE ONE®

Cost to build? See page 684
to order complete cost estimate
to build this house in your area!

DESIGN 9214

First Floor: 1,188 square feet
Second Floor: 1,172 square feet
Total: 2,360 square feet

Beginning with the interest of a wraparound porch, there's a feeling of country charm in this two-story plan. Formal dining and living rooms offer ample space for gracious entertaining. The large family room is truly a place of warmth and welcome with its gorgeous bay window, fireplace and French doors to the living room. The kitchen, with island counter, pantry and desk, makes cooking a delight. Upstairs, the secondary bedrooms share an efficient compartmented bath. The expansive master suite has its own luxury bath.

Design by
© Design Basics, Inc.

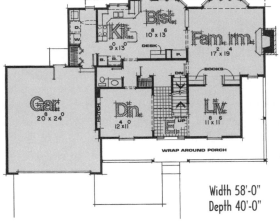

Width 58'-0"
Depth 40'-0"

www.homeplanners.com

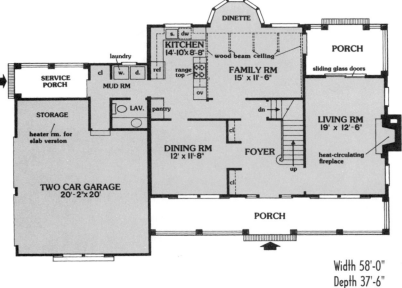

KITCHEN 14'-10"x 8'-8"

s. | dw

DINETTE

wood beam ceiling

FAMILY RM 15' x 11'-6"

PORCH

sliding glass doors

laundry

cl | w. | d. | ref

range top

ov

SERVICE PORCH

MUD RM

LAV. | pantry

dn

LIVING RM 19' x 12'-6"

STORAGE

heater rm. for slab version

cl

DINING RM 12' x 11'-8"

FOYER

up

heat-circulating fireplace

TWO CAR GARAGE 20'-2"x 20'

cl

PORCH

Width 58'-0"
Depth 37'-6"

Design by
© Perfect Home Plans, Inc.

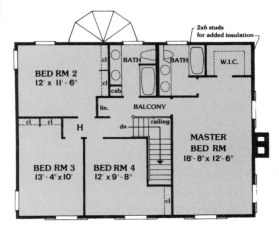

2x6 studs for added insulation

BED RM 2 12' x 11'-6"

BATH

BATH

W.I.C.

cl

cab

lin.

BALCONY

cl | cl

H

dn | railing

MASTER BED RM 18'-8" x 12'-6"

BED RM 3 13'-4"x10'

BED RM 4 12' x 9'-8"

cl

This economical, two-story Colonial farmhouse has a center hall enhanced by a decorative stairway leading to four bedrooms on the second floor. A formal living room with fireplace and a formal dining room flank the entry foyer. Beyond the foyer is an open kitchen and beamed family room with a large bay window in the charming dinette area. A front porch spans the front of the house and a corner rear porch can be accessed from either the family room or living room. The one-story left wing features a mudroom, laundry, lavatory, serving porch, two-car garage and large storage area. The four second-floor bedrooms provide lots of closet space and two bathrooms feature double-sink vanities. Please specify basement or crawlspace foundation when ordering.

DESIGN
N100
First Floor: 1,082 square feet
Second Floor: 1,013 square feet
Total: 2,095 square feet

DESIGN 9242

First Floor: 1,322 square feet
Second Floor: 1,272 square feet
Total: 2,594 square feet

Here's the luxury you've been looking for—from the wraparound covered front porch to the bright sun room at the rear off the breakfast room. A sunken family room with fireplace serves everyday casual gatherings, while the more formal living and dining rooms are reserved for special entertaining situations. The kitchen has a central island with snack bar. Upstairs are four bedrooms, one a lovely master suite with French doors into the master bath and a whirlpool tub in a dramatic bay window.

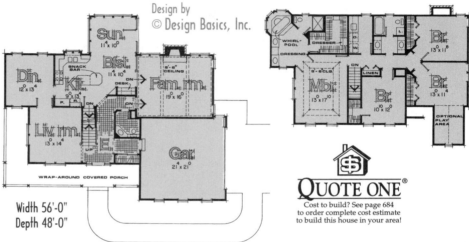

Design by
© Design Basics, Inc.

Width 56'-0"
Depth 48'-0"

Cost to build? See page 684
to order complete cost estimate
to build this house in your area!

DESIGN 3325

First Floor: 1,595 square feet
Second Floor: 1,112 square feet
Total: 2,707 square feet

L D

Horizontal clapboard siding, varying roof planes and finely detailed window treatments set a delightful tone for this farmhouse favorite. A tiled foyer leads past a convenient powder room to a spacious central morning room with an exposed beam ceiling and a wide door to the entertainment terrace. The U-shaped island kitchen serves the formal dining room, which enjoys a bay window and leads to an expansive living room. Upstairs, a gallery hall connects the master suite, three family bedrooms and a hall bath.

Width 63'-6"
Depth 48'-0"

Design by
© Home Planners

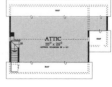

Cost to build? See page 684
to order complete cost estimate
to build this house in your area!

www.homeplanners.com

Photo by Andrew D. Lautman

The home, as shown in the photograph, may differ from the actual blueprints. For more detailed information, please check the floor plans carefully.

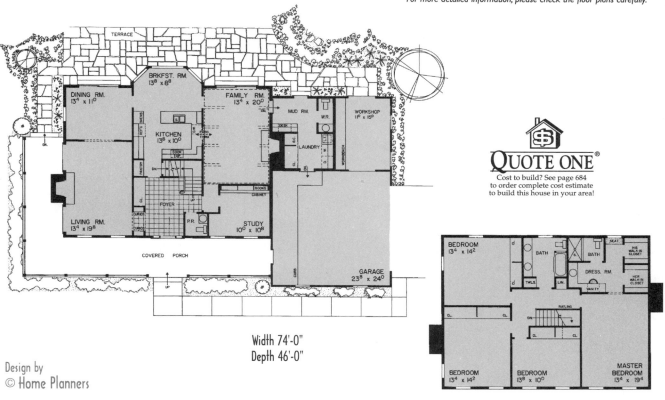

Width 74'-0"
Depth 46'-0"

Design by
© Home Planners

Quote One®
Cost to build? See page 684
to order complete cost estimate
to build this house in your area!

Here's a traditional farmhouse design that's made for down-home hospitality, casual conversation and the good grace of pleasant company. The star attractions are the large covered porch and terrace, which are perfectly relaxing gathering points for family and friends. The hardworking interior offers separate living and family rooms, each with its own fireplace, and a formal dining room with separate access to the terrace. The U-shaped kitchen shares natural light from a bayed breakfast nook and offers a sizable pantry and lots of counter space. The mudroom and laundry offer access from the garage and from the rear terrace, while the adjoining workshop enjoys its own entries. The second floor contains a spacious master suite with twin closets and three family bedrooms that share a full bath. The two-car garage connects at the laundry.

DESIGN 2946
First Floor: 1,581 square feet
Second Floor: 1,344 square feet
Total: 2,925 square feet
L D

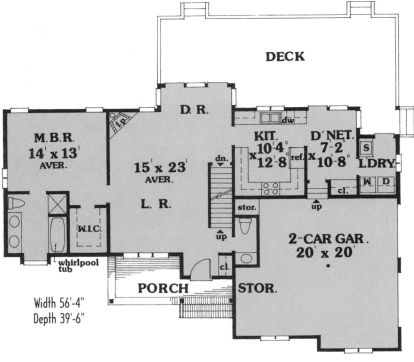

DECK

Design by
© Perfect Home Plans, Inc.

M.B.R.
14' x 13'
AVER.

D. R.

KIT.
10'-4"
x
12'-8"

D'NET.
7'-2"
x
10'-8"

LDRY.

15' x 23'
AVER.

L. R.

W.I.C.

whirlpool
tub

stor.

2-CAR GAR.
20' x 20'

PORCH

STOR.

cl.

Width 56'-4"
Depth 39'-6"

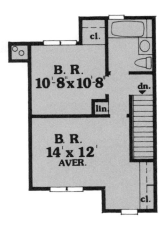

B. R.
10'-8"x 10'-8"

lin.

B. R.
14' x 12'
AVER.

**DESIGN
N114**
First Floor: 1,110 square feet
Second Floor: 441 square feet
Total: 1,551 square feet

Economical to build through the use of open planning for family spaces, this roomy 1½-story, three-bedroom country farmhouse exudes plenty of charm. The entry foyer with closet and adjacent powder room flows into the living and dining rooms, which feature a corner fireplace and double doors open to the rear deck. The U-shaped kitchen opens to the well-lighted dinette with doors leading to the deck. The private master suite at the opposite side of the house features a five-fixture bath and large walk-in closet. Two additional bedrooms and full bath are on the second floor. Note the storage space in the garage. Please specify basement or slab foundation when ordering.

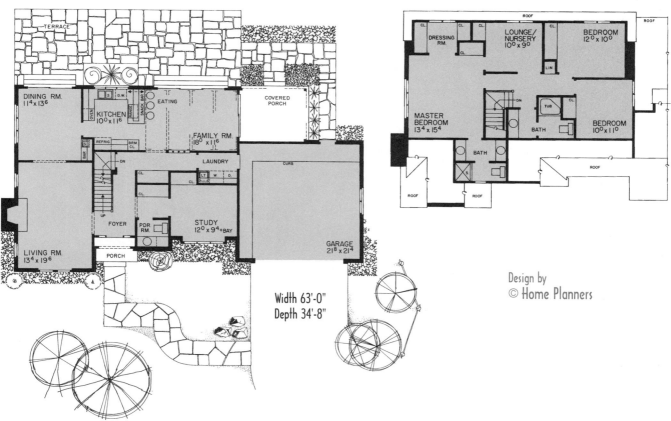

DINING RM.
11⁴ x 13⁶

KITCHEN
10⁰ x 11⁶

EATING

COVERED PORCH

FAMILY RM.
18⁰ x 11⁶

LAUNDRY

CURB

LIVING RM.
13⁴ x 19⁶

PORCH

FOYER

PDR. RM.

STUDY
12⁰ x 9⁴ +BAY

GARAGE
21⁸ x 21⁴

Width 63'-0"
Depth 34'-8"

TERRACE

DRESSING RM.

LOUNGE/ NURSERY
10⁰ x 9⁰

BEDROOM
12⁰ x 10⁰

MASTER BEDROOM
13⁴ x 15⁴

BATH

TUB

BATH

BEDROOM
10⁰ x 11⁰

ROOF

Design by
© Home Planners

T his charming Tudor-style home truly demonstrates a person's home is their castle. Though technically a story and a half, the second floor offers so much livability, it's more like a two-story plan. The first floor is solidly designed for efficiency and contains a living room with fireplace, a large formal dining room, a beam-ceilinged family room, an efficient U-shaped kitchen, a study with sunny bay window and a covered porch. In addition to a large master suite, two family bedrooms and a second full bath, the second floor includes a cozy spot that could serve as a home office, a nursery or a play area.

DESIGN 2854
First Floor: 1,261 square feet
Second Floor: 950 square feet
Total: 2,211 square feet

TUDOR & VICTORIAN HOMES

DESIGN 2802
Square Footage: 1,729

L D

This attractive plan displays an effective use of half-timbered stucco and brick as well as an authentic bay window to create an elegant Tudor elevation. The gathering room will be a favorite place for friends and family with its rustic appeal and rear terrace doors. A full-sized kitchen with snack bar and breakfast room is well suited for the gourmet. The master bedroom has a large walk-in closet, private bath and doors to the terrace. Two additional bedrooms share a hall bath.

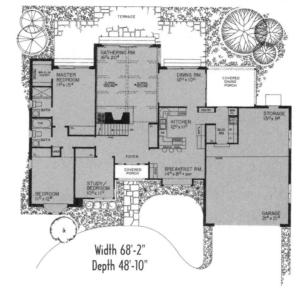

Width 68'-2"
Depth 48'-10"

Design by
© Home Planners

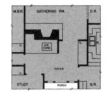

OPTIONAL NON-BASEMENT

QUOTE ONE®
Cost to build? See page 684 to order complete cost estimate to build this house in your area!

Design by
© Home Planners

DESIGN 2929
Square Footage: 1,608

This cozy Tudor features a very contemporary interior for convenience and practicality. The floor plan features a strategically located kitchen handy to the garage, dining room and dining terrace. The spacious living area has a dramatic fireplace that functions with the rear terrace. A favorite spot is the media room with space for a TV, VCR and stereo system. The master bedroom is large and has plenty of wardrobe storage. The extra guest room, or nursery, has a full bath.

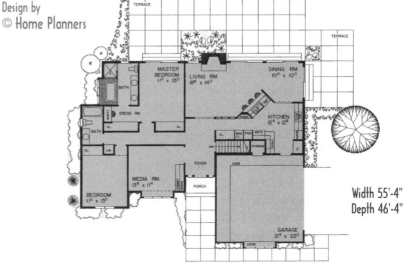

Width 55'-4"
Depth 46'-4"

TUDOR & VICTORIAN HOMES

This home's English Tudor exterior houses a contemporary, well-planned interior. Each of the three main living areas—sleeping, living and working—are but steps from the foyer. Open planning, a sloped ceiling and plenty of glass create a nice environment for the living-dining area. Its appeal is further enhanced by the open staircase to the lower level recreation/hobby area. The L-shaped kitchen with its island range and work surface opens to the large, sunny breakfast room. The sleeping area has the flexibility of functioning as a two-or three-bedroom plan.

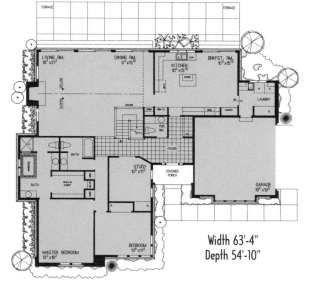

Design by
© Home Planners

Quote One®
Cost to build? See page 684
to order complete cost estimate
to build this house in your area!

Width 63'-4"
Depth 54'-10"

This modest-sized house could hardly offer more in the way of exterior charm and interior livability. Measuring only 60 feet in width means it will not require a huge, expensive piece of property. The orientation of the garage and the front drive court are features that promote an economical use of property. In addition to the formal living and dining rooms, there is the informal kitchen/family room area. Note the beamed ceiling, the fireplace, the sliding glass doors and the eating area in the family room.

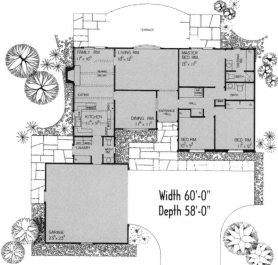

OPTIONAL
BASEMENT

Design by
© Home Planners

Quote One®
Cost to build? See page 684
to order complete cost estimate
to build this house in your area!

Width 60'-0"
Depth 58'-0"

TUDOR & VICTORIAN HOMES

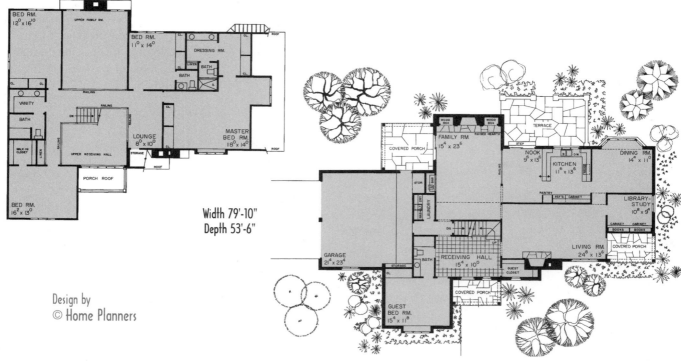

Width 79'-10"
Depth 53'-6"

Design by
© Home Planners

DESIGN 2356
First Floor: 1,969 square feet
Second Floor: 1,702 square feet
Total: 3,671 square feet
L D

Here is truly an exquisite Tudor adaptation. The exterior, with its interesting rooflines, window treatment, stately chimney and its appealing use of brick and stucco, could hardly be more dramatic. Inside, the delightfully large receiving hall has a two-story ceiling and controls the flexible traffic patterns. The living and dining rooms, with the library nearby, will cater to formal living pursuits. The guest room offers another haven for the enjoyment of peace and quiet. Observe the adjacent full bath. For the family's informal activities, there are the interactions of the family room/ covered porch/nook/kitchen zone. Notice the raised-hearth fireplace, the wood boxes, the sliding glass doors, built-in bar and the kitchen pass-through. Adding to the charm of the family room is its high ceiling. The second floor offers three family bedrooms, a lounge and a deluxe master suite. The two-car garage opens to the laundry room and the covered porch.

Design by
© Home Planners

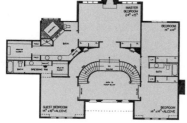

Width 97'-4"
Depth 53'-0"

DESIGN
2957

First Floor: 2,557 square feet
Second Floor: 1,939 square feet
Total: 4,496 square feet

L D

The decorative half-timbers and stone wall-cladding on this manor are stately examples of Tudor architecture. A grand double staircase is the highlight of the elegant, two-story foyer that opens to each of the main living areas. The living and gathering rooms are anchored by impressive central fireplaces. Filled with amenities, the island kitchen has a nearby breakfast room for casual meals. The outstanding master suite features a bedroom fireplace, whirlpool bath and convenient walk-in closet.

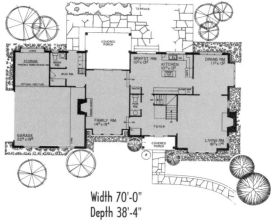

Design by
© Home Planners

Width 70'-0"
Depth 38'-4"

Quote One®

Cost to build? See page 684
to order complete cost estimate
to build this house in your area!

DESIGN
2855

First Floor: 1,372 square feet
Second Floor: 1,245 square feet
Total: 2,617 square feet

L D

This elegant Tudor house is perfect for the family who wants to move-up in living area, style and luxury. As you enter this home you will find a large living room with a fireplace on your right. Adjacent, the formal dining room provides easy access to the kitchen. The kitchen/breakfast room includes access to the rear terrace. Sunken a few steps, the spacious family room is highlighted with a fireplace and access to the rear covered porch. Upstairs, are three family bedrooms and a spacious master bedroom suite.

Classic capstones and arched windows complement rectangular shutters and pillars on this traditional facade. The family room offsets a formal dining room and shares a see-through fireplace with the keeping room. Upstairs, the master suite has a tray ceiling and a vaulted bath with a whirlpool spa. Please specify basement or crawlspace foundation when ordering.

Design by
© Frank Betz Associates, Inc.

Width 50'-0"
Depth 46'-0"

This new country home features a fresh face and a dash of Victoriana. The two-story foyer leads to an elegant dining room and a spacious living room. The heart of the home is a two-story family room with an eye-catching fireplace. The breakfast room offers a walk-in pantry and shares a snack bar with the kitchen. Please specify basement or crawlspace foundation when ordering.

Width 60'-0"
Depth 46'-4"

Design by
© Frank Betz Associates, Inc.

TUDOR & VICTORIAN HOMES

www.homeplanners.com

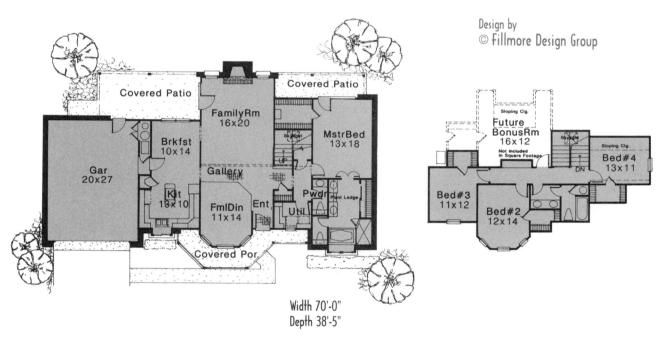

Design by
© Fillmore Design Group

Covered Patio

Covered Patio

FamilyRm
16x20

Brkfst
10x14

MstrBed
13x18

Gar
20x27

Gallery

Kit
13x10

FmlDin
11x14

Ent

Pwdr

Util

Plant Ledge

Covered Por.

Width 70'-0"
Depth 38'-5"

Sloping Clg.

Future
BonusRm
16x12
Not Included
In Square Footage

Bed#4
13x11

Bed#3
11x12

Bed#2
12x14

DN

Sloping Clg.

A charming porch wraps the front of this comfortable four-bedroom farmhouse, providing a warm welcome to all who enter. Inside, the entry opens to a formal dining room sized to accommodate special occasions and holiday festivities. The efficient U-shaped island kitchen and sun-filled breakfast area are located nearby. Large enough to house a family reunion, the family room is warmed by a welcoming fireplace flanked by windows. Here, access to the rear covered patio allows you to linger over morning coffee or do a little star gazing in the evening. Located for privacy, the first-floor master bedroom features its own covered patio and a master bath designed for relaxation. The second floor contains three family bedrooms—each with a walk-in closet—a full bath and a bonus room for future development.

DESIGN M115
First Floor: 1,572 square feet
Second Floor: 700 square feet
Total: 2,272 square feet
Bonus Room: 212 square feet

TUDOR & VICTORIAN HOMES

DESIGN Q406

First Floor: 1,205 square feet
Second Floor: 1,254 square feet
Total: 2,459 square feet

With details reminiscent of Victorian design, this home is graced by a covered veranda wrapping on three sides. The vaulted foyer introduces an octagonal staircase and an archway to the living room and adjoining dining room. A country kitchen offers a spacious walk-in pantry, center prep island and breakfast bay with porch access. The upstairs master bedroom is graced by a bayed sitting area and bath with private deck. Plans include details for both a basement and a crawlspace foundation.

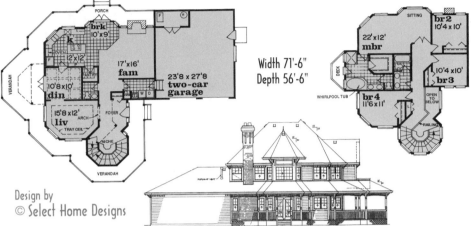

Width 71'-6"
Depth 56'-6"

Design by
© Select Home Designs

REAR VIEW

DESIGN Z020

First Floor: 1,358 square feet
Second Floor: 894 square feet
Total: 2,252 square feet
Bonus Room: 300 square feet

This charming country traditional home provides a well-lit home office, harbored in a beautiful bay with three windows. The second-floor bay brightens a bedroom. The living room has a fireplace. The first-floor master suite features a walk-in closet. The gourmet kitchen enjoys a window sink and outdoor views through sliding glass doors in the breakfast area. This home is designed with a basement foundation.

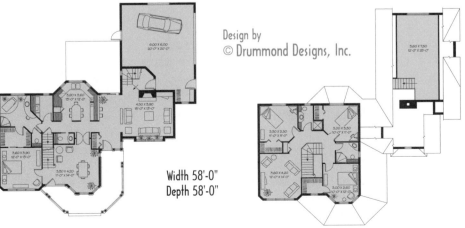

Design by
© Drummond Designs, Inc.

Width 58'-0"
Depth 58'-0"

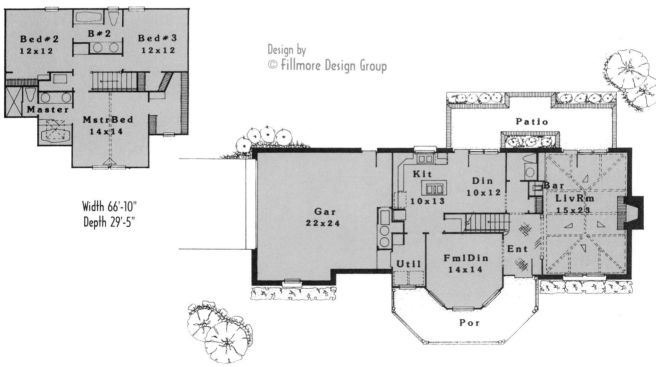

Design by
© Fillmore Design Group

Width 66'-10"
Depth 29'-5"

Bed #2 12x12
B #2
Bed #3 12x12
Master
MstrBed 14x14

Patio
Kit 10x13
Din 10x12
Bar
LivRm 15x23
Gar 22x24
Util
FmlDin 14x14
Ent
Por

TUDOR & VICTORIAN HOMES

Farmhouse fresh with a touch of Victorian style best describes this charming home. A covered front porch wraps around the dining room's bay window and leads the way to the entrance. To the right of the entry is a living room that features a wet bar and a warming fireplace. At the rear of the plan, an L-shaped kitchen is equipped with an island cooktop, making meal preparation a breeze. Casual meals can be enjoyed in a dining area, which merges with the kitchen and accesses the rear patio. A powder room and utility room complete the first floor. Sleeping quarters contained on the second floor include a relaxing master suite with a large walk-in closet, two family bedrooms and a connecting bath. A two-car garage connects to the main house at the utility room.

DESIGN M114
First Floor: 1,082 square feet
Second Floor: 838 square feet
Total: 1,920 square feet

DESIGN 2973

First Floor: 1,269 square feet
Second Floor: 1,227 square feet
Total: 2,496 square feet

L

A most popular feature of the Victorian house has always been its covered porches. However, in addition to its wonderful Victorian facade, this home provides a myriad of interior features that cater to the active, growing family. Living and dining areas include a formal living room and dining room, a family room with a fireplace, a study and a kitchen with an attached breakfast nook. The second floor has three family bedrooms and a luxurious master bedroom with whirlpool tub and His and Hers walk-in closets.

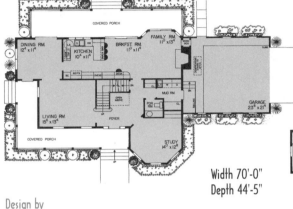

QUOTE ONE®
Cost to build? See page 684
to order complete cost estimate
to build this house in your area!

Width 70'-0"
Depth 44'-5"

Design by
© Home Planners

TUDOR & VICTORIAN HOMES

DESIGN 2971

First Floor: 1,766 square feet
Second Floor: 1,519 square feet
Total: 3,285 square feet

L

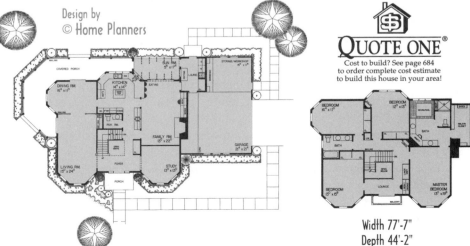

The stately proportions and exquisite Victorian detailing of this home are exciting indeed. Like so many Victorian houses, interesting rooflines set the character of this design. Inside is a very livable plan. The kitchen features a center island cooktop and shares a wide counter for casual dining with the adjoining family room. A bayed dining room with access to the rear porch is available for more formal occasions. Upstairs, each of the four bedrooms features a bay area and plenty of closet space.

Design by
© Home Planners

QUOTE ONE®
Cost to build? See page 684
to order complete cost estimate
to build this house in your area!

Width 77'-7"
Depth 44'-2"

The home, as shown in the photograph, may differ from the actual blueprints. For more detailed information, please check the floor plans carefully.

Photo by Bob Greenspan

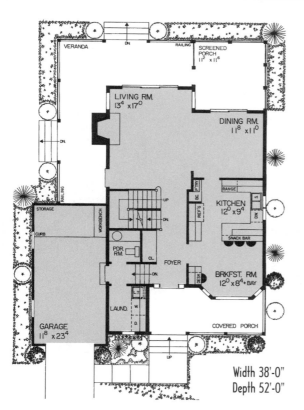

Width 38'-0"
Depth 52'-0"

QUOTE ONE ®
Cost to build? See page 684 to order complete cost estimate to build this house in your area!

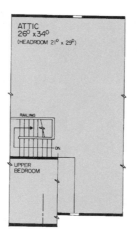

Design by
© Home Planners

V ictorian houses are well known for their orientation on narrow building sites. This house is 38 feet wide, but the livability is tremendous. From the front covered porch, the foyer directs traffic all the way to the back of the house with its open living and dining rooms. The U-shaped kitchen conveniently services both the dining room and the front breakfast room. The rear living area contains a veranda and a screened porch that both highlight the outdoor livability presented in this design. Three bedrooms account for the second floor.

DESIGN 2974
First Floor: 911 square feet
Second Floor: 861 square feet
Total: 1,772 square feet

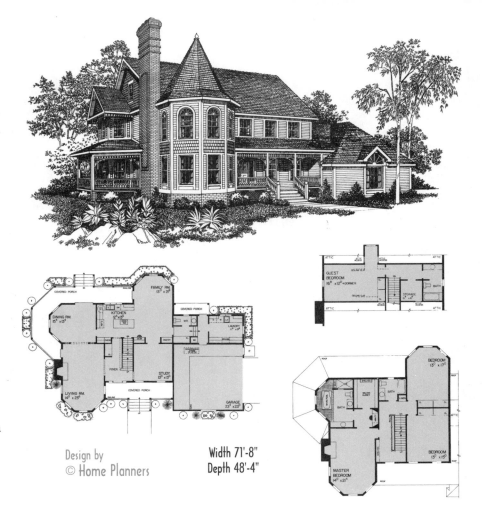

DESIGN 2969

First Floor: 1,618 square feet
Second Floor: 1,315 square feet
Third Floor: 477 square feet
Total: 3,410 square feet

L D

What could beat the charm of a turreted Victorian with covered porches to the front, side and rear? Projecting bays make their contribution to the exterior styling and provide an extra measure of livability. The efficient kitchen, with its island cooking station, functions well with the dining and family rooms. A study provides a quiet first-floor haven. Upstairs, there are three big bedrooms and a fine master bath. The third floor provides a guest suite.

Design by
© Home Planners

Width 71'-8"
Depth 48'-4"

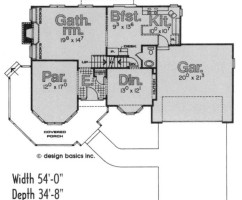

DESIGN 7395

First Floor: 1,054 square feet
Second Floor: 1,262 square feet
Total: 2,316 square feet

A two-story bay, a turret and a wraparound porch create an eye-catching Victorian exterior. Inside, the parlor and the dining room are ideally situated for easy entertaining. Family and guests will delight in the gathering room, with its fireplace and built-in bookcases. The breakfast room offers sliding glass doors to the backyard as well as a pantry, desk and a nearby powder room. The skylit master suite pampers with a walk-in closet, whirlpool tub and dual sinks. Three family bedrooms share a large bath.

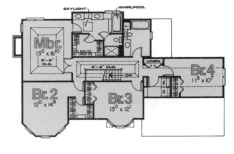

© design basics inc.

Width 54'-0"
Depth 34'-8"

Design by
© Design Basics, Inc.

TUDOR & VICTORIAN HOMES

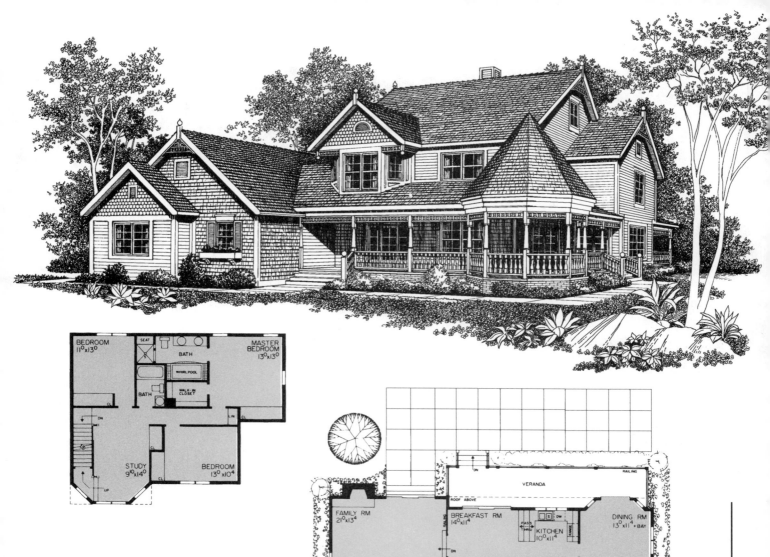

Design by
© Home Planners

Quote One®

Cost to build? See page 684
to order complete cost estimate
to build this house in your area!

Width 62'-7"
Depth 54'-0"

Covered porches, front and back, are a fine preview to the livable nature of this Victorian design. Living areas are defined in a family room with a fireplace, formal living and dining rooms and a kitchen with a breakfast room. An ample laundry room, garage with storage area and a powder room round out the first floor. Three second-floor bedrooms are joined by a study and two full baths. The master suite on this floor has two closets, including an ample walk-in, as well as a relaxing bath with a tile-rimmed whirlpool tub and a separate shower with a seat. Note the storage space in the two-car garage.

DESIGN 3309
First Floor: 1,375 square feet
Second Floor: 1,016 square feet
Total: 2,391 square feet

L

DESIGN 9251

First Floor: 1,653 square feet
Second Floor: 700 square feet
Total: 2,353 square feet

Beautiful arches and elaborate detail give the elevation of this four-bedroom, one-story home an unmistakable elegance. Inside, the floor plan is equally appealing. Note the formal dining room with bay window, visible from the entrance hall. The large great room has a fireplace and a wall of windows out the back. A hearth room, with bookcase, adjoins the kitchen area with a walk-in pantry. The private, first-floor master suite features a pampering bath.

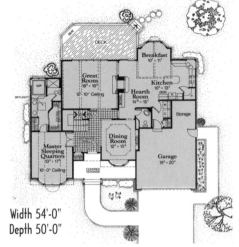

Width 54'-0"
Depth 50'-0"

Design by
© Design Basics, Inc.

QUOTE ONE®
Cost to build? See page 684
to order complete cost estimate
to build this house in your area!

DESIGN 9252

First Floor: 1,113 square feet
Second Floor: 965 square feet
Total: 2,078 square feet

Elegant detail, a charming veranda and a tall brick chimney make a pleasing facade on this four-bedroom, two-story Victorian home. From the large bayed parlor with a sloped ceiling to the sunken gathering room with a fireplace, there's plenty to appreciate about the floor plan. The formal dining room opens to the parlor for convenient entertaining. Second-floor quarters include a master suite, with private dressing area and whirlpool tub, and three family bedrooms.

Design by
© Design Basics, Inc.

Width 46'-0"
Depth 41'-5"

QUOTE ONE®
Cost to build? See page 684
to order complete cost estimate
to build this house in your area!

TUDOR & VICTORIAN HOMES

www.homeplanners.com

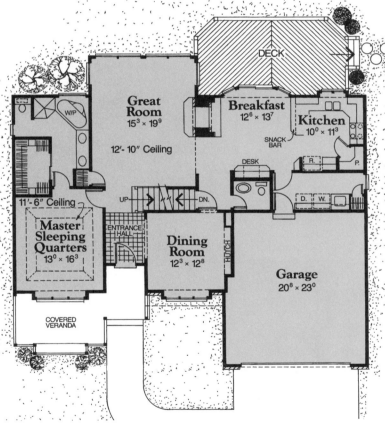

DECK

Great Room
15³ × 19⁹

12'-10" Ceiling

Breakfast
12⁶ × 13⁷

Kitchen
10⁰ × 11³

SNACK BAR

W/P

11'-6" Ceiling

Master Sleeping Quarters
13⁰ × 16³

ENTRANCE HALL

UP

DESK

DN.

R.

P.

D. W.

HUTCH

Dining Room
12³ × 12⁸

Garage
20⁸ × 23⁰

COVERED VERANDA

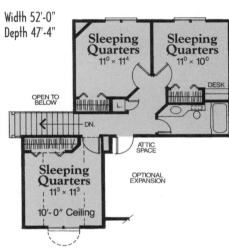

Width 52'-0"
Depth 47'-4"

Sleeping Quarters
11⁰ × 11⁴

Sleeping Quarters
11⁰ × 10⁰

DESK

OPEN TO BELOW

DN.

ATTIC SPACE

OPTIONAL EXPANSION

Sleeping Quarters
11³ × 11³

10'-0" Ceiling

Design by
© Design Basics, Inc.

Victorian details and a covered veranda lend a peaceful flavor to the elevation of this popular home. A volume entry hall views the formal dining room and luxurious great room. Imagine the comfort of relaxing in the great room that features a 12'-10" ceiling and abundant windows. The kitchen and breakfast area include a through-fireplace, snack bar, walk-in pantry and wrapping counters. The secluded master suite features a vaulted ceiling, luxurious dressing/bath area and corner whirlpool tub. Upstairs, the family sleeping quarters feature special amenities unique to each. Note the optional expansion area.

DESIGN 9288
First Floor: 1,421 square feet
Second Floor: 587 square feet
Total: 1,999 square feet

TUDOR & VICTORIAN HOMES

Design by
© Select Home Designs

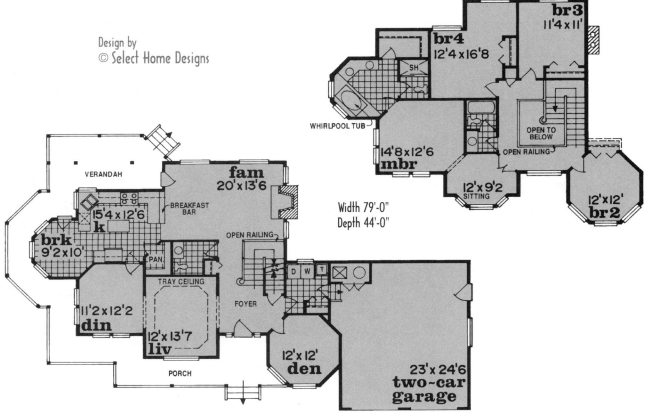

Width 79'-0"
Depth 44'-0"

DESIGN Q416
First Floor: 1,362 square feet
Second Floor: 1,270 square feet
Total: 2,632 square feet

Rich with Victorian details—scalloped shingles, a wraparound veranda and turrets—this beautiful facade conceals a modern floor plan. Archways announce a distinctive living room with a lovely tray ceiling and also help to define the dining room. An octagonal den across the foyer is a private spot for reading or studying. The U-shaped island kitchen holds an octagonal breakfast bay and a pass-through breakfast bar to the family room, which offers a fireplace and access to the veranda. Second-floor sleeping quarters include a master suite and three family bedrooms that share a full bath.

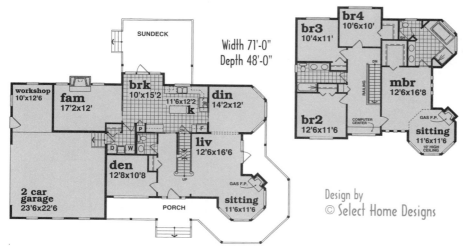

SUNDECK

Width 71'-0"
Depth 48'-0"

workshop 10'x12'6

fam 17'2x12'

brk 10'x15'2

11'6x12'2

k

din 14'2x12'

br4 10'6x10'

br3 10'4x11'

mbr 12'6x16'8

br2 12'6x11'6

COMPUTER CENTER

GAS F.P.

sitting 11'6x11'6
10' HIGH CEILING

2 car garage 23'6x22'6

den 12'8x10'8

liv 12'6x16'6

UP

GAS F.P.

PORCH

sitting 11'6x11'6

Design by
© Select Home Designs

This distinctive country design features a polygonal tower surrounded by a wraparound porch. The center-hall entry introduces formal living areas—a living room with hearth-warmed sitting room—and casual space—a family room with fireplace and island kitchen with attached break-fast nook. A den is privately tucked into a corner off the entry. Three family bedrooms and a full bath share the second floor with a mas-ter suite that includes a sitting room with fireplace, a walk-in clos-et and a bath with corner whirlpool tub. Plans include both a basement and a crawlspace foundation.

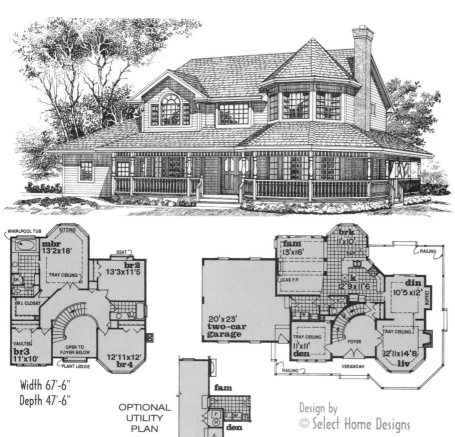

whirlpool tub

SITTING

mbr 13'2x18'

TRAY CLNG

SEAT

br2 13'3x11'5

W.I. CLOSET

brk 11'x10'

fam 13'x16'

BAR

GAS F.P.

k 12'9x11'6

din 10'5x12'

BUFFET

VAULTED

br3 11'x10'

OPEN TO FOYER BELOW

PLANT LEDGE

12'11x12'

br4

20'x23' two-car garage

TRAY CLNG 11'x11'

den

FOYER

TRAY CEILING

12'11x14'8

liv

RAILING

VERANDAH

Width 67'-6"
Depth 47'-6"

OPTIONAL UTILITY PLAN

fam

den

Design by
© Select Home Designs

A turret, wood detailing and a wraparound veranda signal Victorian style for this home. The double-door entry opens to a foyer with a love-ly curved staircase. The living room has a fireplace, and the for-mal dining room features a buffet alcove and access to the veranda. The family room includes a fire-place and sliding glass doors to the rear yard. A tray ceiling highlights the master suite. Plans include both a basement and a crawlspace foundation

TUDOR & VICTORIAN HOMES

DESIGN Q331

First Floor: 1,290 square feet
Second Floor: 1,239 square feet
Total: 2,529 square feet
Bonus Room: 256 square feet

Turrets fascinate us with their hint of Old World romance. This one houses the living room on the first floor and the master bedroom on the second floor. The living room is especially attractive with its bay window and three-way fireplace shared by the dining room. The sunken family room shares a two-way fireplace with the breakfast room and kitchen. The master suite opens through French doors and has a walk-in closet and a deluxe bath.

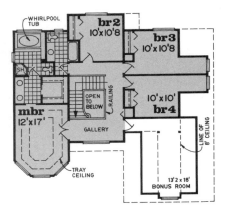

Design by
© Select Home Designs

Width 47'-0"
Depth 50'-6"

DESIGN Q388

First Floor: 1,360 square feet
Second Floor: 734 square feet
Total: 2,094 square feet
Bonus Room: 378 square feet

Traditional accents and a covered porch lend charm to the exterior of this Victorian home. The entry opens directly to the formal rooms with bay windows. The U-shaped kitchen provides an attached breakfast bay, which is open to the family room. A fireplace and sliding glass doors to the rear yard are highlights of the family room. The first-floor master bedroom is appointed with a vaulted ceiling and a private bath with whirlpool tub. Three secondary bedrooms on the second floor share a full bath.

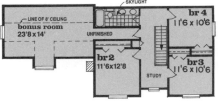

Width 56'-0"
Depth 48'-0"

Design by
© Select Home Designs

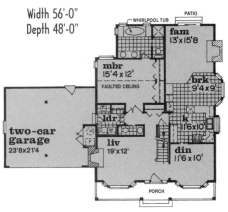

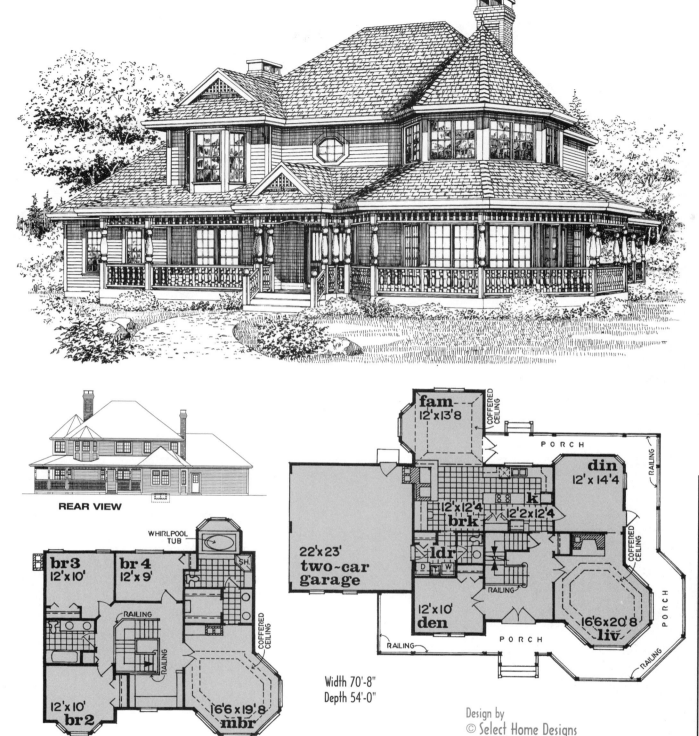

REAR VIEW

WHIRLPOOL TUB

br3 12'x10'
br 4 12'x9'
SH.

RAILING

COFFERED CEILING

12'x10' br2

16'6 x 19'8 mbr

fam 12'x13'8
COFFERED CEILING

PORCH

RAILING

din 12'x14'4

12'x12'4
brk
k
12'2x12'4

22'x23' two-car garage

ldr
D W

RAILING

COFFERED CEILING

12'x10' den

RAILING

PORCH

16'6x20'8 liv

RAILING PORCH

Width 70'-8"
Depth 54'-0"

Design by
© Select Home Designs

TUDOR & VICTORIAN HOMES

A touch of Victoria enhances the facade of this home: a turret roof over a covered railed porch (note the turned wood spindles). The porch wraps around three sides of the home and is accessed from the foyer, the dining room and the family room. Special attractions on the first floor include a tray ceiling in the octagonal living room, fire-places in the country kitchen and the living room, a coffered ceiling in the family room and double-door access to the cozy den. The master suite sits on the second floor and boasts a coffered ceiling, walk-in closet and bath with whirlpool tub, double vanities and separate shower. Three family bedrooms share a full bath that has double vanities.

DESIGN Q300
First Floor: 1,462 square feet
Second Floor: 1,288 square feet
Total: 2,750 square feet

Design by
© Home Planners

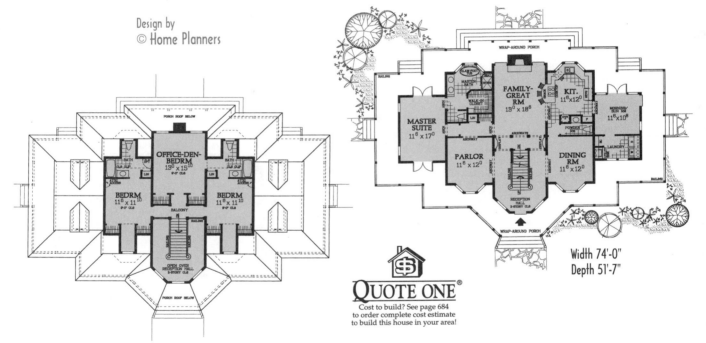

PORCH ROOF BELOW

OFFICE-DEN-
BEDRM
19⁰ x 15¹⁰

BEDRM
11⁵ x 11

BEDRM
11⁵ x 11¹⁰

BALCONY

RAILING

OPEN OVER
RECEPTION HALL

PORCH ROOF BELOW

WRAP-AROUND PORCH

MASTER
SUITE
11⁸ x 17⁰

FAMILY-
GREAT
RM
19⁰ x 18⁶

KIT.
11⁸ x 12⁰

PARLOR
11⁸ x 12⁰

DINING
RM
11⁸ x 12⁰

RECEPTION
HALL

WRAP-AROUND PORCH

Width 74'-0"
Depth 51'-7"

QUOTE ONE®
Cost to build? See page 684
to order complete cost estimate
to build this house in your area!

**DESIGN
3621**

First Floor: 1,752 square feet
Second Floor: 906 square feet
Total: 2,658 square feet

L D

D elightfully proportioned and perfectly symmetrical, this Victorian farmhouse has lots of curb appeal. The wraparound porch offers rustic columns and railings, and broad steps present easy access to the front, rear and side yards. Archways, display niches and columns catch the eye on the way to the large family/great room with a fireplace. The kitchen offers a snack bar to this room. The formal parlor and the dining room flank the reception hall. The left wing of the plan is devoted to the master suite. French doors provide direct access to the front and rear porches. The compartmented master bath enjoys a bay with a claw-foot tub, twin lavatories, a walk-in closet and a stall shower with a seat. Upstairs, a perfectly symmetrical layout presents a big office/den (or make it a bedroom) flanked by two bedrooms, each with a full bath.

TUDOR & VICTORIAN HOMES

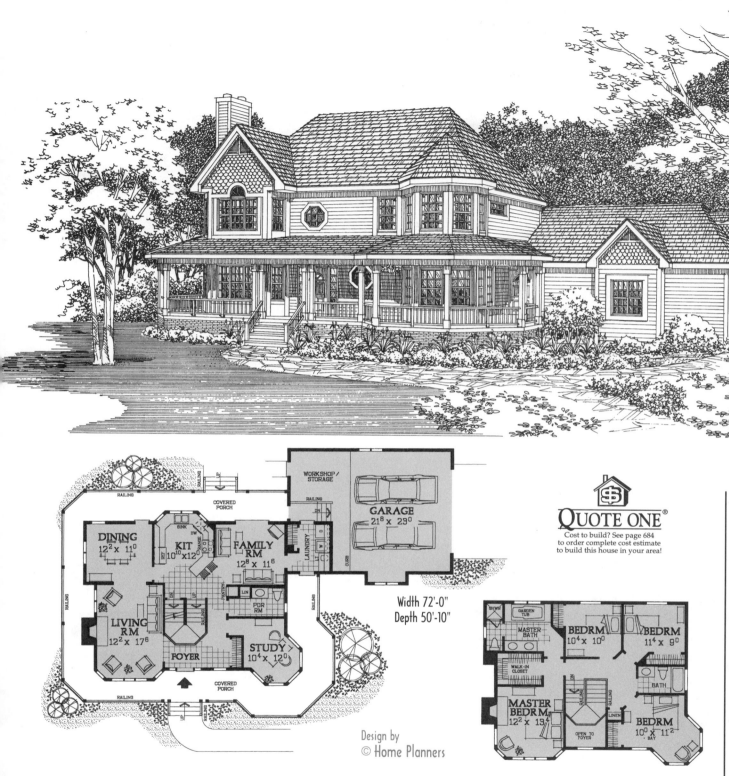

Design by
© Home Planners

Width 72'-0"
Depth 50'-10"

Victorian style is highly evident on this beautiful four-bedroom, two-story home. With fish-scale trim, a turret skirted by an octagonal porch and varied window treatments, this home is a true winner. The interior continues with a cozy octagonal study, a spacious living room complete with a warming fireplace, a formal dining room that offers access to the rear porch, and a large and efficient kitchen that shares a snack bar with the comfortable family room. The sleeping zone upstairs consists of three secondary bedrooms—one in the top of the tower—that share a full hall bath, and a lavish master suite. This suite pampers with a fireplace, large walk-in closet and sumptuous bath.

DESIGN 3696
First Floor: 1,186 square feet
Second Floor: 988 square feet
Total: 2,174 square feet

TUDOR & VICTORIAN HOMES

This distinctive Victorian exterior conceals an open, contemporary floor plan. The entrance foyer with round columns offers visual excitement. The octagonal great room contains a high tray ceiling and a fireplace. A generous kitchen with an angular island counter is centrally located, providing efficient service to the dining room, breakfast room and deck. The luxurious master bedroom suite features a large walk-in closet and a compartmented bath. Two additional bedrooms—one that would make a lovely study—and a full hall bath round out this favorite plan.

© 1991 Donald A. Gardner Architects, Inc.

© 1991 Donald A. Gardner Architects, Inc.

Width 61'-6"
Depth 74'-8"

Design by
Donald A. Gardner
Architects, Inc.

A wrapping veranda introduces the entry of this Victorian home and opens to a vaulted foyer lit by a transom window. The living room features a tray ceiling and is just across the hall from the dining room with box-bay window. Note the fireplace and French-door access to the veranda in the family room. A gourmet kitchen, with bayed breakfast nook, includes a walk-in pantry, built-in desk and center cooking island. The master bedroom includes access to the veranda, a walk-in closet and lavish bath with whirlpool tub.

Design by
© Select Home Designs

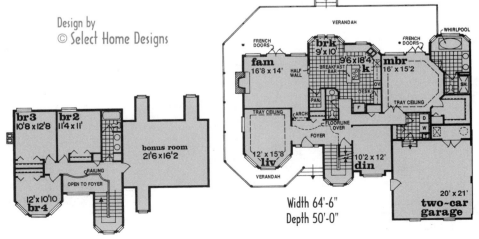

Width 64'-6"
Depth 50'-0"

TUDOR & VICTORIAN HOMES

www.homeplanners.com

Design by
© Chatham Home Planning, Inc.

Width 39'-6"
Depth 78'-3"

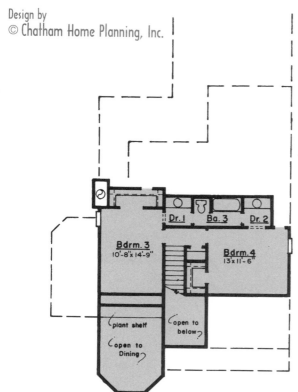

Bdrm. 3
10'-8"x14'-9"

Dr. 1   Ba. 3   Dr. 2

Bdrm. 4
13'x11'-6"

plant shelf

open to below

open to Dining

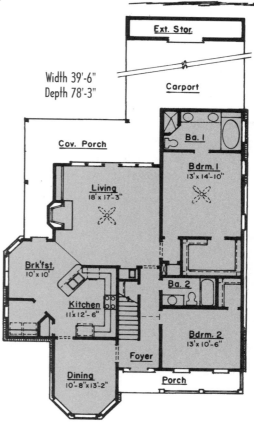

Ext. Stor.

Carport

Cov. Porch

Ba. 1

Bdrm. 1
13'x 14'-10"

Living
18' x 17'-3"

Brk'fst
10'x 10'

Kitchen
11'x12'-6"

Ba. 2

Bdrm. 2
13'x 10'-6"

Foyer

Dining
10'-8"x13'-2"

Porch

TUDOR & VICTORIAN HOMES

Covered porches in front and back soften the natural light flooding in through the many windows in this design, while a dramatic bayed dining area with pretty, arch-topped windows lets the sun shine in full force. Adjacent to the dining room, the kitchen and breakfast room adjoin the living room with fireplace and built-in shelves. The bedroom to the right of the foyer might be converted handily to an office. To the rear is the master suite, featuring a walk-in closet, dual lavatory and oval tub. Each of the two bedrooms upstairs has its own vanity and walk-in closet, while they share a bath.

**DESIGN
E143**

First Floor: 1,505 square feet
Second Floor: 555 square feet
Total: 2,060 square feet

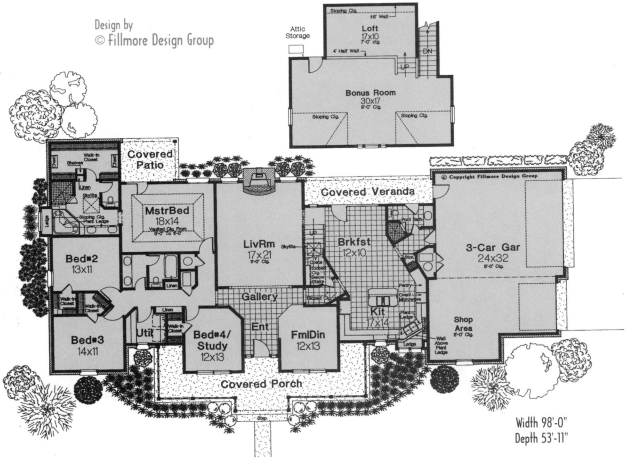

Design by
© Fillmore Design Group

Attic Storage

Loft
17x10
7'-0" Clg.

Sloping Clg.
±6' Wall

DN

4' Half Wall

UP

Bonus Room
30x17
9'-0" Clg.

Sloping Clg.

Sloping Clg.

Covered Patio

Walk-In Closet

Shelves

Linen

Skylite

Ledge

MstrBed
18x14
Vaulted Clg. From
9'-0" To 11'-0"

Covered Veranda

© Copyright Fillmore Design Group

Bed#2
13x11

LivRm
17x21
11'-0" Clg.

Skylite

Brkfst
12x10

Pool Bath

3-Car Gar
24x32
8'-0" Clg.

Linen

Gallery

Sloped Clg.

Pantry

Over/Microwave

Kit
17x14

Shop Area
8'-0" Clg.

Walk-In Closet

Walk-In Closet

Bed#3
14x11

Utit

Linen

Walk-In Closet

Bed#4/
Study
12x13

Ent

FmlDin
12x13

Ledge

Wall Above Plant Ledge

Covered Porch

Step

Width 98'-0"
Depth 53'-11"

DESIGN M111
First Floor: 2,539 square feet
Second Floor: 639 square feet
Total: 3,178 square feet

Classic country character complements this one-story home complete with rustic stone corners, a
covered front porch and interesting
gables. The entry opens to formal living
areas that include a large dining room to
the right, and straight ahead, a spacious
living room warmed by a fireplace. A
gallery leads the way into the efficient
kitchen enhanced with a snack bar and
large pantry. Casual meals can be enjoyed
overlooking the covered veranda and rear
grounds from the connecting breakfast
room. The other side of the gallery
accesses the luxurious master suite and
three second bedrooms all with walk-in
closets. A pool bath and a shop area in the
three-car garage are welcome amenities to
the first floor. The bonus room is available for future development.

www.homeplanners.com

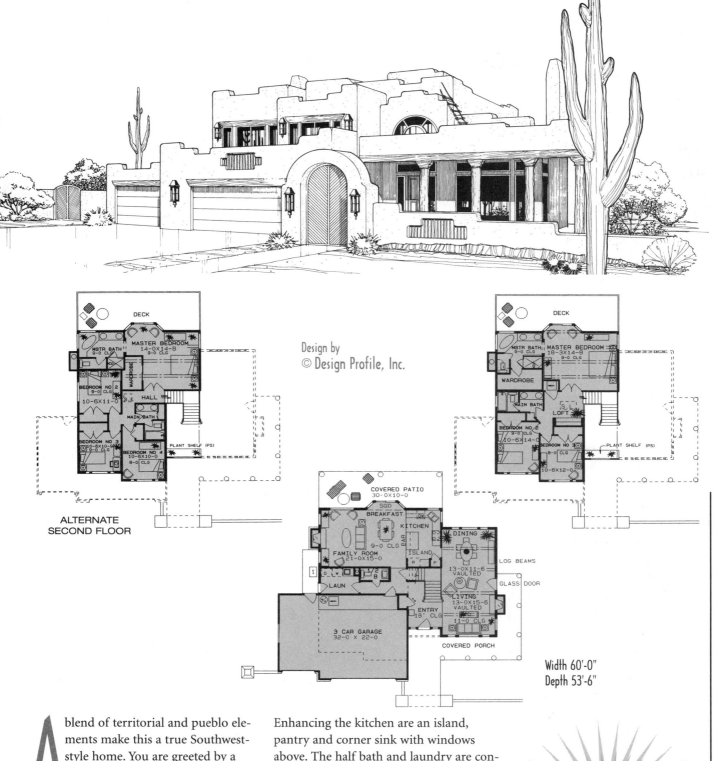

DECK

MASTER BEDROOM
14-0X14-8
9-0 CLG

MSTR BATH
9-0 CLG

BEDROOM NO 2
9-0 CLG
10-6X11-0

HALL

MAIN BATH

BEDROOM NO 3
10-6X10-9
9-0 CLG

BEDROOM NO 4
10-6X10-0
8-0 CLG

PLANT SHELF (PS)

**ALTERNATE
SECOND FLOOR**

Design by
© Design Profile, Inc.

DECK

MASTER BEDROOM
18-3X14-8
9-0 CLG

MSTR BATH
9-0 CLG

WARDROBE

MAIN BATH

LOFT

BEDROOM NO 2
9-0 CLG
10-6X14-0

BEDROOM NO 3
8-0 CLG
10-6X12-0

PLANT SHELF (PS)

COVERED PATIO
30-0X10-0

SGD

BREAKFAST

KITCHEN

FAMILY ROOM
21-0X15-0
9-0 CLG

ISLAND

BAR

LAUN

DINING
13-0X11-6
VAULTED

LOG BEAMS

GLASS DOOR

LIVING
13-0X15-6
VAULTED
11-0 CLG

ENTRY
18' CLG

3 CAR GARAGE
32-0 X 22-0

COVERED PORCH

Width 60'-0"
Depth 53'-6"

A blend of territorial and pueblo elements make this a true Southwest-style home. You are greeted by a thick, gated archway leading to the front courtyard and a wraparound covered porch. Formal dining and living rooms have eleven-foot ceilings with log vigas and access to the covered patio. The entry showcases an eighteen-foot ceiling and a wood-railing staircase to the second floor. The rear family room is open to the kitchen and a breakfast bay that includes a glass door to the large covered patio.

Enhancing the kitchen are an island, pantry and corner sink with windows above. The half bath and laundry are conveniently located with access directly out from the laundry room. The three-car garage offers extra storage space or room for a boat. This plan comes with either a three-bedroom or four-bedroom option! The master features a double-door entry, log-viga ceiling beams, and a glass bay with door to a private view deck for lounging. Please specify basement or slab foundation when ordering.

**DESIGN
K116**
First Floor: 1,166 square feet
Second Floor: 995 square feet
Total: 2,161 square feet

SOUTHWEST & FLORIDA HOMES

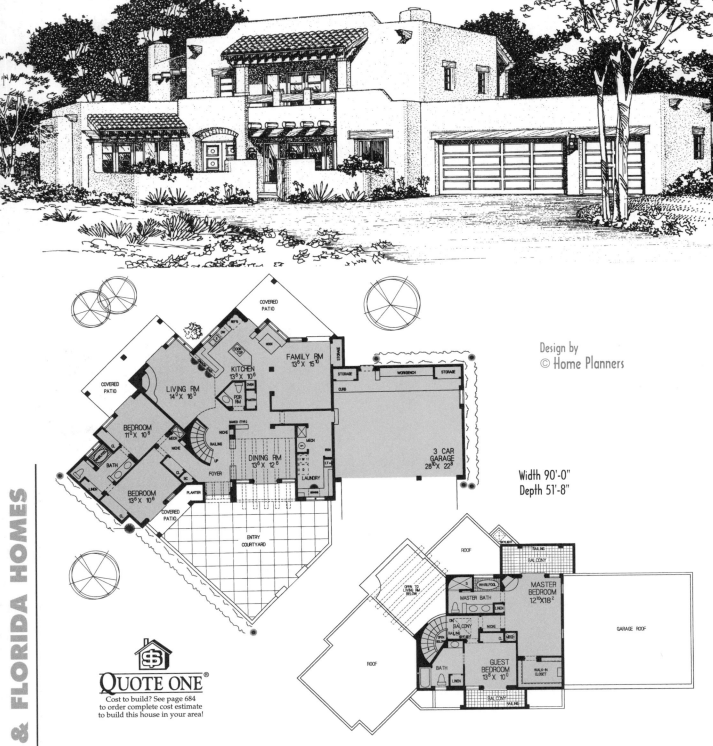

Design by
© Home Planners

Width 90'-0"
Depth 51'-8"

Quote One®

Cost to build? See page 684
to order complete cost estimate
to build this house in your area!

DESIGN 3432

First Floor: 1,966 square feet
Second Floor: 831 square feet
Total: 2,797 square feet

L

Unique in nature, this two-story Santa Fe-style home is as practical as it is lovely. The entry foyer leads past a curving staircase to living areas at the back of the plan. These include a living room with a corner fireplace and a family room connected to the kitchen via a built-in eating nook. The kitchen furthers its appeal with an island cooktop and a snack bar. Two family bedrooms on this level include one with a private covered patio. They share a full bath that has dual lavatories and a whirlpool tub. Upstairs, the master suite features a grand bath, corner fireplace, large walk-in closet and private balcony. A guest bedroom accesses a full bath. Every room in this home has its own outdoor area.

Design by
© Home Planners

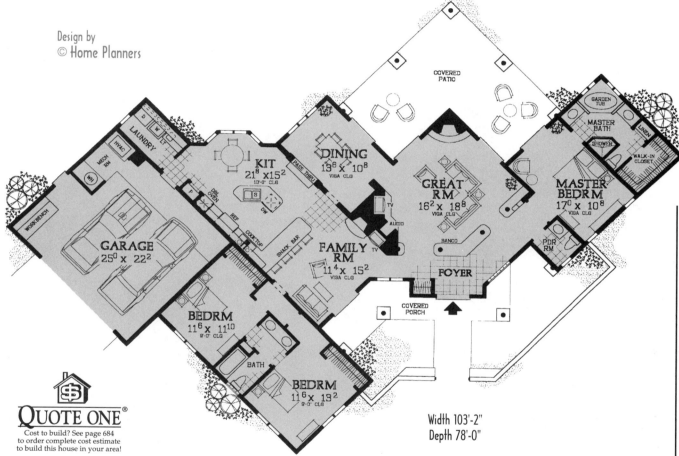

LAUNDRY

MECH RM

HVAC

WH

WORK BENCH

GARAGE
25⁰ x 22²

KIT
21⁸ x 15²
12'-0" CLG

DINING
13⁶ x 10⁸
VIGA CLG

COVERED PATIO

GARDEN TUB

MASTER BATH

LINEN

SHOWER

WALK-IN CLOSET

GREAT RM
16² x 18⁸
VIGA CLG

MASTER BEDRM
17⁰ x 10⁸
VIGA CLG

TV

AUDIO

BANCO

PDR RM

PASS-THRU

SNACK BAR

FAMILY RM
11⁴ x 15²
VIGA CLG

TV

FOYER

BEDRM
11⁶ x 11¹⁰
9'-0" CLG

BATH

BEDRM
11⁶ x 13²
9'-0" CLG

COVERED PORCH

Width 103'-2"
Depth 78'-0"

Quote One®
Cost to build? See page 684
to order complete cost estimate
to build this house in your area!

The impressive, double-door entry to the walled courtyard sets the tone for this Santa Fe masterpiece home. The expansive living room shows off its casual style with a centerpiece fireplace and abundant windows overlooking the patio. Joining the living room is the formal dining room, again graced with windows and patio doors. The large gourmet kitchen has an eat-in snack bar and joins the family room to create a warm atmosphere for casual entertaining. Family room extras include a fireplace, entertainment built-ins and double doors to the front courtyard. Just off the family room are the two large family bedrooms, which share a private bath. The relaxing master suite is privately located off the living room and provides double doors to the back patio.

DESIGN
3694
Square Footage: 2,226
L

SOUTHWEST & FLORIDA HOMES

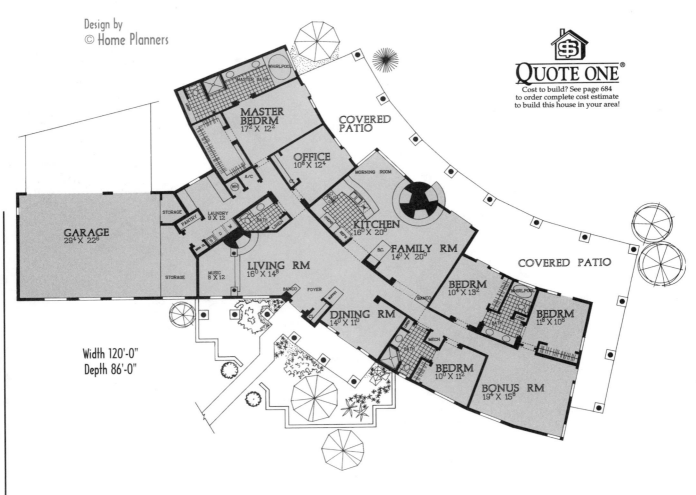

Design by
© Home Planners

GARAGE
29⁴ X 22⁶

MASTER
BEDRM
17² X 12²

MASTER BATH

WHIRLPOOL

COVERED
PATIO

OFFICE
10⁸ X 12⁴

MORNING ROOM

STORAGE

LAUNDRY
9 X 12

PANTRY

BATH

LINEN

KITCHEN
16⁰ X 20⁰

FAMILY RM
14⁰ X 20⁰

COVERED PATIO

STORAGE

MUSIC
8 X 12

LIVING RM
16⁰ X 14⁸

BANCO

FOYER

DINING RM
14⁰ X 11⁰

BANCO

BEDRM
10⁴ X 13²

WHIRLPOOL

BEDRM
11⁸ X 10⁸

BATH

MECH

BEDRM
10⁰ X 11²

BONUS RM
19⁴ X 15⁸

Width 120'-0"
Depth 86'-0"

SOUTHWEST & FLORIDA HOMES

DESIGN
3434
Square Footage: 3,428
L

An in-line floor plan follows the tradition of the original Santa Fe-style
homes. The slight curve to the
overall configuration lends an
interesting touch. From the front courtyard, the plan opens to a formal living
room and dining room complemented by
a family room and a kitchen with an

adjoining morning room. The master
bedroom is found to one side of the plan
while family bedrooms share space at the
opposite end. There's also a huge office
and a bonus/study area for private times.
With 3½ baths, a workshop garage, full
laundry/sewing area and three courtyards,
this plan adds up to great livability.

www.homeplanners.com

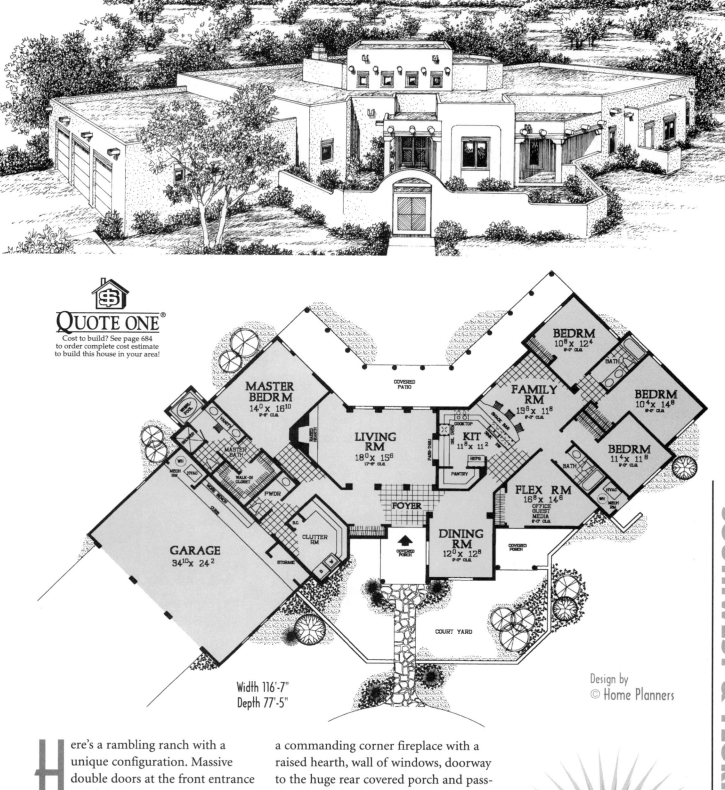

Cost to build? See page 684 to order complete cost estimate to build this house in your area!

QUOTE ONE®

MASTER BEDRM
14⁰ x 16¹⁰

MASTER BATH

WALK-IN CLOSET

PWDR

GARAGE
34¹⁰ x 24²

CLUTTER RM

STORAGE

LIVING RM
18⁰ x 15⁶

FOYER

COVERED PORCH

DINING RM
12⁰ x 12⁸

COVERED PATIO

KIT
11⁸ x 11²

PANTRY

FAMILY RM
19⁸ x 11⁸

FLEX RM
16⁸ x 14⁶
OFFICE
GUEST
MEDIA

BEDRM
10⁸ x 12⁴

BATH

BEDRM
10⁴ x 14⁸

BEDRM
11⁴ x 11⁸

COVERED PORCH

COURT YARD

Width 116'-7"
Depth 77'-5"

Design by
© Home Planners

DESIGN 3646
Square Footage: 2,966

L

SOUTHWEST & FLORIDA HOMES

Here's a rambling ranch with a unique configuration. Massive double doors at the front entrance are sheltered by a covered porch. This well-zoned plan offers exceptional one-story livability for the active family. The central foyer routes traffic effectively while featuring a feeling of spaciousness. Note the dramatic columns that accentuate the big living room with its two-story ceiling. This interesting, angular room has a commanding corner fireplace with a raised hearth, wall of windows, doorway to the huge rear covered porch and pass-through to the kitchen. The informal family room offers direct access to the rear porch and is handy to the three family bedrooms. At the opposite end of the plan, and guaranteed its full measure of privacy, is the master suite. The master bedroom, with its high ceiling, enjoys direct access to the rear porch.

DESIGN
3431
Square Footage: 1,907

Graceful curves welcome you into the courtyard of this Santa Fe home. Inside, a gallery directs traffic to the work zone on the left or the sleeping zone on the right. Straight ahead lies a sunken gathering room with a beamed ceiling and a raised-hearth fireplace. The covered rear porch is accessible from the dining room, gathering room and secluded master bedroom. Luxury describes the master bath, with a whirlpool tub, separate shower, double vanity and closet space. Two family bedrooms share a compartmented bath.

QUOTE ONE®
Cost to build? See page 684 to order complete cost estimate to build this house in your area!

Design by
© Home Planners

Width 61'-6"
Depth 67'-4"

DESIGN
3433
Square Footage: 2,350
L

Santa Fe styling creates interesting angles in this one-story home. A grand entrance leads through a courtyard into the foyer with a circular skylight, closet space, niches and a convenient powder room. Fireplaces in the living room, dining room and on the covered porch create a warming heart of the home. Make note of the island range in the kitchen and the cozy breakfast room adjacent. The master suite offers a deluxe bath and a study close at hand. Two more family bedrooms are placed quietly in the far wing of the house near a segmented family room.

Design by
© Home Planners

Width 92'-7"
Depth 79'-0"

QUOTE ONE®
Cost to build? See page 684 to order complete cost estimate to build this house in your area!

SOUTHWEST & FLORIDA HOMES

www.homeplanners.com

Design by
© Home Planners

PATIO RETREAT

MASTER SUITE 13² x 15⁶ 9'-2" CLG

GREAT RM 13⁰ x 16⁰ T&G/VIGA CLG 10'-2" CLG

KIT 11⁶ x 13⁴ 9'-0" CLG

NOOK 10⁰ x 12⁶ 9'-0" CLG

MASTER BATH 9'-8" CLG

WALK-IN CLOSET

PANTRY

BEDRM 10⁰ x 11²

THREE CAR GARAGE 25⁴ x 33¹⁰

NICHE

DINING RM 11¹⁰ x 10² 10'-6" CLG

FOYER 9'-0" CLG

PDR

BEDRM 10⁰ x 11²

BATH

HVAC

LAUNDRY

SINK

COVERED PORCH

Width 96'-5"
Depth 54'-9"

Quote One®
Cost to build? See page 684
to order complete cost estimate
to build this house in your area!

DESIGN 3644
Square Footage: 2,015

This Santa Fe-style home is as warm as a desert breeze and just as comfortable. Outside details are reminiscent of old-style adobe homes, while the interior caters to convenient living. The front covered porch leads to an open foyer. Columns define the formal dining room and the giant great room. The kitchen has an enormous pantry, a snack bar and is connected to a breakfast nook with rear-patio access. Two family bedrooms are found on the right side of the plan. They share a full bathroom that includes twin vanities. The master suite is on the left side of the plan and has a sizable walk-in closet and a bath with spa tub and separate shower. Note the angled three-car garage.

SOUTHWEST & FLORIDA HOMES

Design by
© Home Planners

Width 126'-7"
Depth 60'-10"

Quote One®
Cost to build? See page 684
to order complete cost estimate
to build this house in your area!

**DESIGN
3693**
Square Footage: 3,838

This diamond in the desert gives new meaning to old style. Though reminiscent of old Pueblo-type dwellings of the Southwest, the floor plan is anything but ancient history. A cozy courtyard gives way to a long covered porch with nooks for sitting and open-air dining at the front. The double-door entry opens on the right to a gracious living room highlighted by a corner fireplace. Just beyond is the formal dining room with adjacent butler's pantry and access to the porch dining area. To the left of the foyer is a private office with convenient built-ins and attached powder room. The kitchen, family room and morning room separate family bedrooms from the master suite. Both sleeping areas are luxurious with whirlpool spas and separate showers. The master suite also boasts its own exercise room. Though connected to the main house, the guest suite has a private entrance as well, and includes another corner fireplace. Maintain the family fleet in the spacious three-car garage.

www.homeplanners.com

The home, as shown in the photograph, may differ from the actual blueprints. For more detailed information, please check the floor plans carefully.

Photo by Allen Maertz Photography

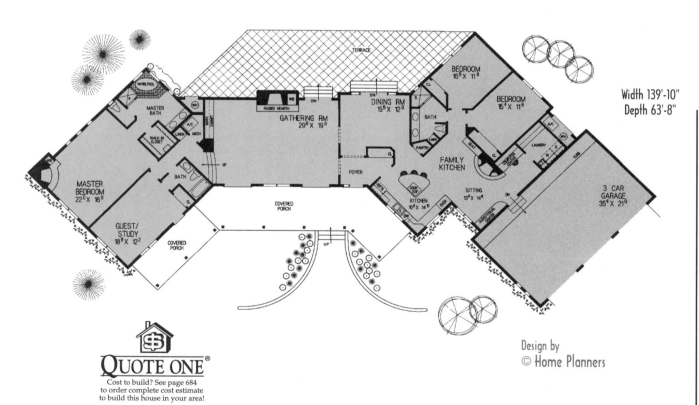

Width 139'-10"
Depth 63'-8"

Design by
© Home Planners

QUOTE ONE®
Cost to build? See page 684
to order complete cost estimate
to build this house in your area!

I n classic Santa Fe style, this home strikes a beautiful combination of historic exterior detailing and open floor planning on the inside. A covered porch running the width of the facade leads to an entry foyer that connects to a huge gathering room with a fireplace and a formal dining room. The family kitchen allows special space for casual gatherings. The right wing of the home holds two family bedrooms and a full bath. The left wing is devoted to the master suite and a guest room or study. The laundry area and computer center complete the plan.

DESIGN 3405
Square Footage: 3,144
L

MASTER SUITE
12⁶ x 16⁴
17'-6" CLG

RETREAT
8⁶ x 8⁰
10'-0" CLG

GREAT ROOM
22⁴ x 15⁶
17'-6" CLG

OFFICE-GUEST
12⁶ x 10⁰
9'-0" CLG

KITCHEN
12⁰ x 19⁰
9'-0" CLG

DINING RM
11⁰ x 10⁰
17'-6" CLG

BEDRM
10⁶ x 10⁰
9'-0" CLG

BEDRM
10² x 11²
9'-0" CLG

BEDRM
11⁴ x 11⁴
9'-0" CLG

2-CAR GARAGE
22⁰ x 22⁰

PATIO RETREAT

ENTRY GALLERY
17'-6" CLG

COVERED PORCH

BREAKFAST NOOK

LAUNDRY ROOM

COVERED PATIO

PRIVATE GARDEN

Width 76'-6"
Depth 77'-4"

Design by
© Home Planners

Quote One®
Cost to build? See page 684
to order complete cost estimate
to build this house in your area!

DESIGN 3665
Square Footage: 2,678
L

A vaulted entry and tall muntin windows complement a classic stucco exterior on this Floridian-style home. An entry gallery opens to the great room, with generous views to the rear property and columned access to a patio retreat. Niches, built-ins and half walls decorate and help define this area. The island kitchen serves a convenient snack bar, while the nearby formal dining room offers privacy and natural light from a bay window. A secluded master wing soothes the homeowner with a sumptuous bath, a walk-in closet and an inner retreat with access to a covered patio. The wing also features an office with triple windows—this room could accommodate a guest.

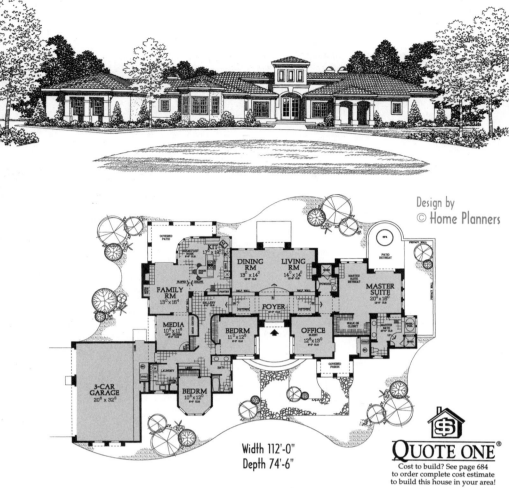

**DESIGN
3630**

Square Footage: 3,034

L

A grand entry enhances the exterior of this elegant stucco home. The office located at the front of the plan makes this design ideal for a home-based business. Formal areas combine to provide lots of space for entertaining. The kitchen, complete with a snack bar and a breakfast nook, opens to the family room, which connects to the media room. The private master suite includes a multi-windowed sitting area, its private patio contains a spa for outdoor enjoyment. A walk-in closet and a luxurious bath complete this area.

Design by
© Home Planners

Width 112'-0"
Depth 74'-6"

QUOTE ONE®
Cost to build? See page 684
to order complete cost estimate
to build this house in your area!

**DESIGN
3667**

Square Footage: 2,085

From the stylish tiled entry, the spacious great room extends an invitation to relax with a fireplace and wide views of the outdoors. The nearby gourmet kitchen serves all occasions, with an eating nook nearby. A rambling master suite enjoys its own wing with lavish amenities. On the opposite side of the plan, two family bedrooms—or make one a study—share a full bath that has two vanities.

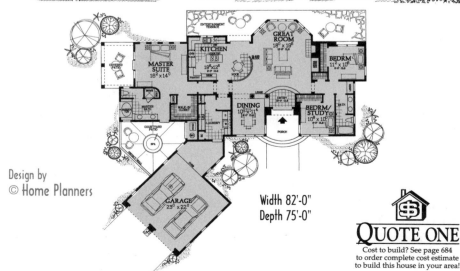

Design by
© Home Planners

Width 82'-0"
Depth 75'-0"

QUOTE ONE®
Cost to build? See page 684
to order complete cost estimate
to build this house in your area!

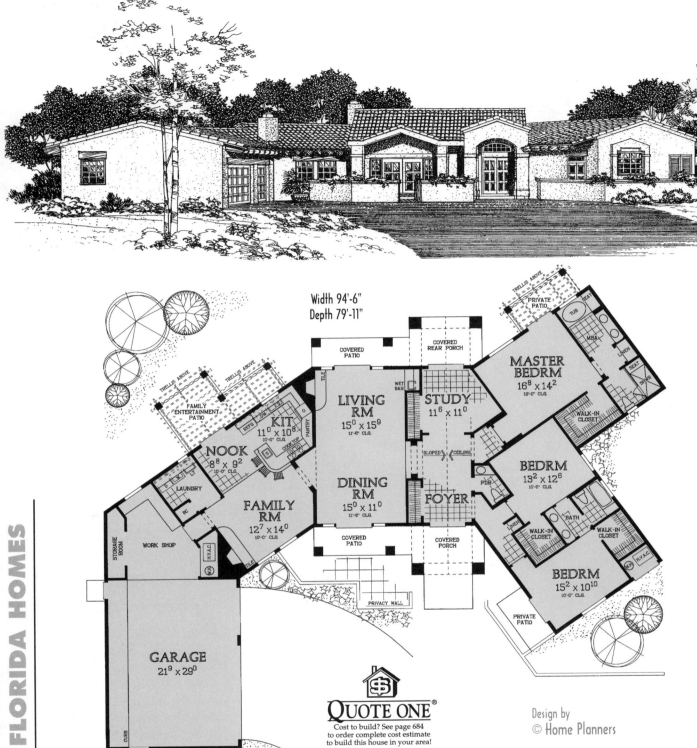

Width 94'-6"
Depth 79'-11"

QUOTE ONE®
Cost to build? See page 684
to order complete cost estimate
to build this house in your area!

Design by
© Home Planners

DESIGN 3436
Square Footage: 2,573
L

Oversized, double wood doors and an elegant tile foyer set the impressive tone of this Southwestern classic home. The grand living room and adjoining dining room are the perfect backdrop for entertaining, with a fireplace and access to both the front and rear covered patios. Casual living is just as inviting in the family room with a snack bar and its own fireplace with an extended bench. The large, gourmet kitchen has a breakfast nook that opens to the family entertainment patio. The sleeping zone features two family bedrooms with walk-in closets and private entrances to the compartmented bath. The master suite has a private patio, huge walk-in closet and a master bath with luxe appointments such as a spa tub, dual vanity and an oversized, walk-in shower.

www.homeplanners.com

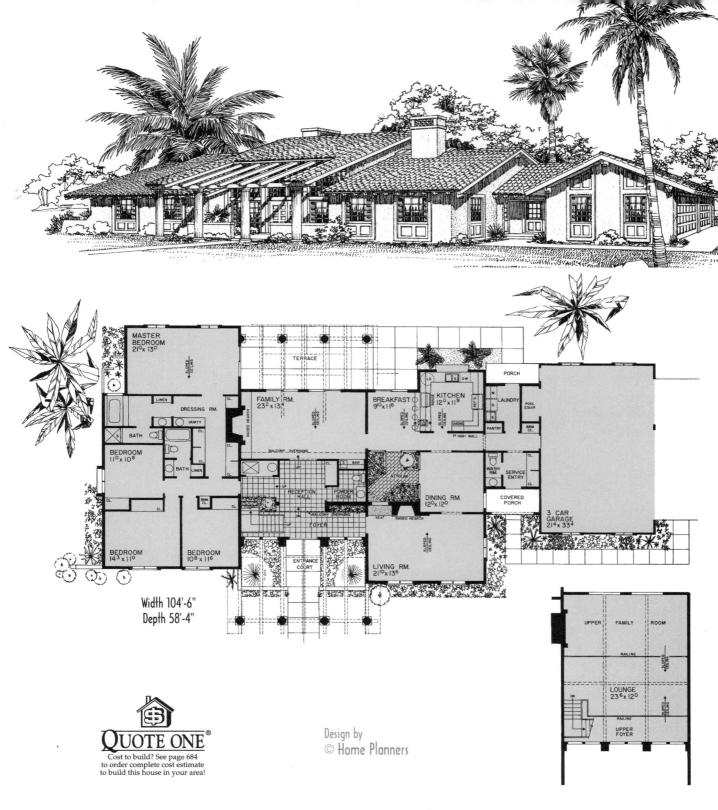

MASTER BEDROOM 21⁰ x 13⁰

SLOPED CEILING

LINEN

DRESSING RM.

VANITY

BATH

BEDROOM 11⁰ x 10⁸

BATH LINEN

TERRACE

FAMILY RM. 23² x 13⁴

SLOPED CEILING

RAISED HEARTH

BALCONY OVERHANG

RECEPTION HALL

POWDER ROOM

UP

BALCONY OVERHANG

FOYER

ATRIUM

SEAT RAISED HEARTH

BREAKFAST 9⁰ x 11⁶

SLOPED CEILING

KITCHEN 12⁰ x 11⁹

RANGE

OVEN THRU

OVENS

7' HIGH WALL

PORCH

LAUNDRY

POOL EQUIP.

PANTRY

BRM. CL.

WASH RM.

SERVICE ENTRY

DINING RM. 12⁰ x 12⁰

COVERED PORCH

BEDROOM 14³ x 11⁰

BEDROOM 10⁸ x 11⁶

ENTRANCE COURT

LIVING RM. 21¹⁰ x 13⁶

SLOPED CEILING

3 CAR GARAGE 21⁴ x 33⁴

Width 104'-6"
Depth 58'-4"

UPPER   FAMILY   ROOM

RAILING

LOUNGE 23⁶ x 12⁰

DN

RAILING

UPPER FOYER

QUOTE ONE®

Cost to build? See page 684
to order complete cost estimate
to build this house in your area!

Design by
© Home Planners

A centrally located interior atrium is just one of the interesting features of this Spanish design. The atrium has a built-in seat and will bring light to the adjacent living room, dining room and breakfast room. Beyond the foyer, down one step, is a tiled reception hall that includes a powder room. This area leads to the sleeping wing and up one step to the family room with its raised-hearth fireplace and sliding glass doors to the rear terrace. Overlooking the family room is a railed lounge that can be used for various activities. Sleeping areas include a deluxe master suite and three family bedrooms.

DESIGN 2670
Square Footage: 3,058
Lounge: 279 square feet

SOUTHWEST & FLORIDA HOMES

DESIGN 3660

Square Footage: 2,086

L

Design by
© Home Planners

This home exhibits wonderful dual-use space in the sunken sitting room and media area. Anchoring each end of this spacious living zone is the raised-hearth fireplace and the entertainment center. The outstanding kitchen has an informal breakfast bay and looks over the snack bar to the family area. Through the archway are two family bedrooms and a bath with twin vanities. At the far end of the plan is the master suite with a sitting area. A few steps away, French doors open to the covered master patio.

QUOTE ONE®
Cost to build? See page 684
to order complete cost estimate
to build this house in your area!

Width 82'-0"
Depth 58'-4"

DESIGN 2922

Square Footage: 3,505

Loaded with custom features, this plan is designed to delight the imagination. The foyer enters directly into the commanding sunken gathering room. Framed by an elegant railing, this centerpiece for entertaining is open to both the study and the formal dining room, and has sliding glass doors to the terrace and a full bar. The country-style kitchen contains an efficient work area, as well as a morning room and sitting area. The grand master suite includes a private terrace, fireplace alcove with built-in seats and a huge spa-style bath.

Design by
© Home Planners

Width 110'-7"
Depth 66'-11"

QUOTE ONE®
Cost to build? See page 684
to order complete cost estimate
to build this house in your area!

www.homeplanners.com

DESIGN 2875
Square Footage: 1,913

L D

Design by
© Home Planners

Width 77'-10"
Depth 46'-4"

Quote One®
Cost to build? See page 684
to order complete cost estimate
to build this house in your area!

This elegant Spanish design incorporates excellent indoor/outdoor living relationships for modern families who enjoy the sun. Note the overhead openings for rain and sun to fall upon a front garden, while a twin-arched entry leads to the front porch and foyer. Inside, the floor plan features an efficient kitchen with pass-through to a large gathering room with fireplace. Other features include a dining room, laundry room, a study off the foyer, plus three bedrooms including a master bedroom with its own whirlpool tub.

DESIGN 3640
Square Footage: 2,612

L

Design by
© Home Planners

Width 93'-7"
Depth 74'-10"

Quote One®
Cost to build? See page 684
to order complete cost estimate
to build this house in your area!

Dramatic interior angles provide for an immensely livable plan. The open passage to the formal rooms from the foyer is perfect for entertaining, while casual areas are positioned to the rear of the plan. The spacious kitchen, with extra storage at every turn, has an eat-in nook and a door to the rear patio. Two family bedrooms share a hall bath to complete this wing. The master bedroom can easily accommodate a sitting area and has a luxurious bath, walk-in closet and sliding doors to a private patio.

SOUTHWEST & FLORIDA HOMES

DESIGN
2950
Square Footage: 2,559

A natural desert dweller, this stucco, tile-roofed beauty is comfortable in any clime. Common living areas—gathering room, formal dining room and breakfast room—are offset by a quiet study that could be used as a bedroom or guest room. A master suite features two walk-in closets, a double vanity and whirlpool spa. The two-car garage provides a service entrance; close by is an adequate laundry area and a pantry. A lovely hearth warms the gathering room and complements the snack bar.

Width 74'-0"
Depth 66'-10"

Design by
© Home Planners

Quote One®
Cost to build? See page 684
to order complete cost estimate
to build this house in your area!

DESIGN
3423
Square Footage: 2,577

This spacious Southwestern home will be a pleasure to come home to. Immediately off the foyer are the dining room and step-down living room with bay window. The highlight of the four-bedroom sleeping area is the master suite with porch access and a whirlpool tub for soaking away the day's worries. The informal living area features an enormous family room with fireplace and bay-windowed kitchen and breakfast room. Notice the snack-bar pass-through to the family room.

Design by
© Home Planners

Quote One®
Cost to build? See page 684
to order complete cost estimate
to build this house in your area!

Width 72'-0"
Depth 57'-4"

SOUTHWEST & FLORIDA HOMES

www.homeplanners.com

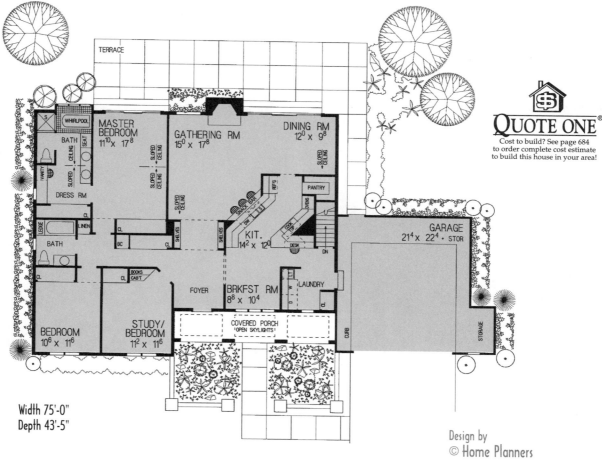

TERRACE

WHIRLPOOL

MASTER BEDROOM
11¹⁰ x 17⁸

BATH

SEAT

DRESS RM

VANITY

GATHERING RM
15⁰ x 17⁸

SLOPED CEILING

SLOPED CEILING

SLOPED CEILING

DINING RM
12⁰ x 9⁸

SLOPED CEILING

REFG

PANTRY

LEDGE

LINEN

CL

CL

BC

CL

SHELVES

SHELVES

DW

SNACK BAR

OVENS

COOK

DN

STAIRS

BATH

KIT.
14² x 12⁰

DESK

GARAGE
21⁴ x 22⁴ + STOR

DN

CL

BOOKS CAB'T

CL

FOYER

BRKFST RM
8⁸ x 10⁴

W D

LAUNDRY

CL

CURB

STORAGE

BEDROOM
10⁶ x 11⁶

STUDY/ BEDROOM
11² x 11⁶

COVERED PORCH
'OPEN SKYLIGHTS'

Width 75'-0"
Depth 43'-5"

Quote One®
Cost to build? See page 684
to order complete cost estimate
to build this house in your area!

Design by
© Home Planners

S tyled for Southwest living, this home is a good choice in many areas. Among its many highlights are a gathering room/dining room combination that includes a fireplace, a snack-bar pass-through and sliding glass doors to the rear terrace. The kitchen is uniquely shaped and sports a walk-in pantry plus a breakfast room with windows to the front covered porch. Bedrooms include a master suite with a sloped ceiling, access to the rear terrace, a whirlpool spa and a double vanity. Two additional bedrooms share a full bath. One of these bedrooms makes a fine study and features built-in book shelves and cabinet.

DESIGN 2948
Square Footage: 1,830

SOUTHWEST & FLORIDA HOMES

DESIGN 3631
Square Footage: 2,831
L

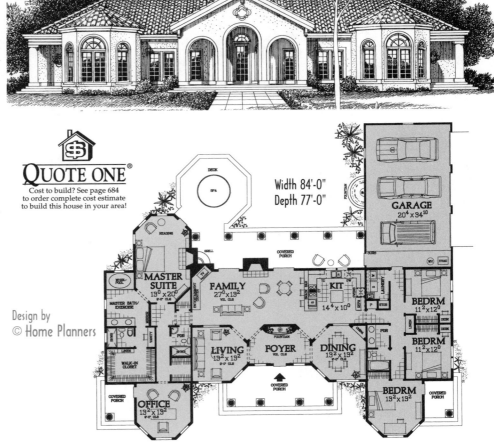

Besides great curb appeal, this home has a wonderful floor plan. The foyer features a fountain and leads to a formal dining room on the right and a living room on the left. A large family room at the rear has a built-in entertainment center and a fireplace. To the right of the plan, three family bedrooms share a full bath. On the left side, the master suite has a large sitting area, an office and an amenity-filled bath. Outside the master suite is a deck with a spa.

QUOTE ONE®
Cost to build? See page 684 to order complete cost estimate to build this house in your area!

Width 84'-0"
Depth 77'-0"

Design by
© Home Planners

DESIGN 3633
Square Footage: 3,163
L

An open courtyard provides a happy marriage of indoor comfort and outdoor style on this lovely Mediterranean plan. A gallery hall enhances the entry. The formal dining room accommodates planned events, while the nearby country kitchen provides a snack bar for easy meals. At the heart of the home, the great room features a raised-hearth fireplace flanked by a built-in media center. The master suite offers a sitting room and a pampering private bath.

Design by
© Home Planners

Width 75'-2"
Depth 68'-8"

QUOTE ONE®
Cost to build? See page 684 to order complete cost estimate to build this house in your area!

SOUTHWEST & FLORIDA HOMES

www.homeplanners.com

© 1997 Donald A. Gardner Architects, Inc.

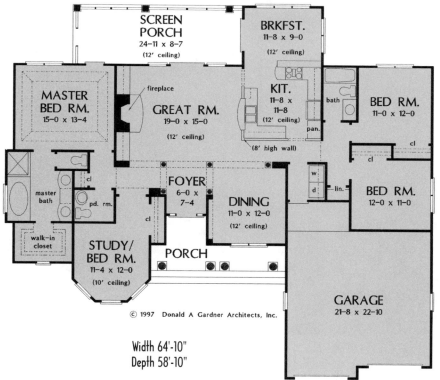

SCREEN PORCH
24-11 x 8-7
(12' ceiling)

BRKFST.
11-8 x 9-0
(12' ceiling)

MASTER BED RM.
15-0 x 13-4

fireplace

GREAT RM.
19-0 x 15-0
(12' ceiling)

KIT.
11-8 x 11-8
(12' ceiling)

bath

BED RM.
11-0 x 12-0

(8' high wall)

pan.

cl

master bath

pd. rm.

cl

FOYER
6-0 x 7-4

DINING
11-0 x 12-0
(12' ceiling)

w
d

lin.

cl

BED RM.
12-0 x 11-0

walk-in closet

STUDY/ BED RM.
11-4 x 12-0
(10' ceiling)

PORCH

GARAGE
21-8 x 22-10

© 1997   Donald A Gardner Architects, Inc.

Width 64'-10"
Depth 58'-10"

Design by
Donald A. Gardner
Architects, Inc.

cl

(optional full bath)

Direct from the Mediterranean, this Spanish-style one-story home is not only decorous, it also offers a very practical floor plan. The façade features arch-top, multi-pane windows, a columned front porch, tall chimney stack and a tiled roof. The interior has a wealth of livability. What you'll appreciate first is the juxtaposition of the great room and the formal dining room—both defined by columns. A more casual eating area is attached to the L-shaped kitchen and has access to a screened porch, as does the great room. Three bedrooms mean abundant sleeping space. The study could be a fourth bedroom—choose the full bath option in this case. A tray ceiling decorates the master bedroom, which is further enhanced by a bath with separate shower and tub, a walk-in closet and double sinks. You can also access the porch from the master bedroom. Please specify crawlspace or slab foundation when ordering.

DESIGN
7659
Square Footage: 1,954

DESIGN 8653
Square Footage: 2,962

Enter the formal foyer of this home and you are greeted with a traditional split living and dining room layout. The family room is where the real living takes place—whether gathered around the fireplace or expanding the space with the help of sliding glass, to include the outside patio and summer kitchen. The ultimate master suite contains coffered ceilings, a "boomerang" vanity and angular mirrors that reflect the bayed soaking tub and shower. Two family bedrooms are situated to share a hall bath. Another bedroom has a semi-private bath.

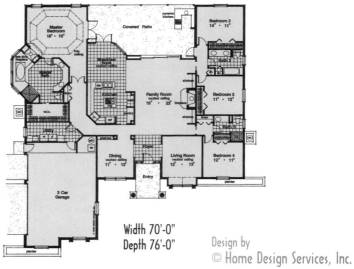

Width 70'-0"
Depth 76'-0"

Design by
© Home Design Services, Inc.

DESIGN 8692
Square Footage: 4,222
Bonus Room: 590 square feet

The striking façade of this magnificent estate is just the beginning. The entry foyer passes the formal dining room to the columned gallery. The living room opens to the rear patio and the showpiece pool. Expanding the entertaining options, a sunken wet bar serves the living room and the pool via a swim-up bar. The family room includes extras such as a built-in media center, fireplace and a breakfast nook with doors to the covered patio. The covered patio is fully equipped with a summer kitchen and dramatic steps to the pool and spa.

Width 83'-10"
Depth 112'-0"

Design by
© Home Design Services, Inc.

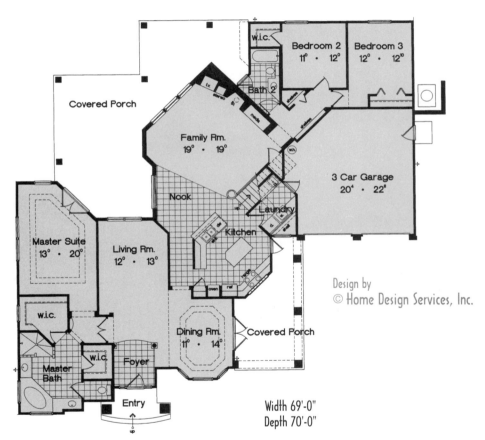

Covered Porch

Family Rm.
19⁰ · 19⁰

Nook

w.i.c.

Bath 2

Bedroom 2
11⁰ · 12⁰

Bedroom 3
12⁰ · 12⁰

3 Car Garage
20⁴ · 22⁸

Master Suite
13⁰ · 20⁰

Living Rm.
12⁰ · 13⁰

Laundry

Kitchen

w.i.c.

Master
Bath

w.i.c.

Foyer

Dining Rm.
11⁰ · 14⁰

Covered Porch

Entry

Design by
© Home Design Services, Inc.

Width 69'-0"
Depth 70'-0"

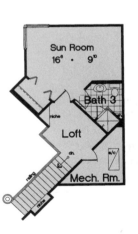

Sun Room
16⁸ · 9¹⁰

Bath 3

Loft

Mech. Rm.

The columned foyer welcomes you into a series of spaces that reach out in all directions. The living room has a spectacular view of the huge covered patio that's perfect for summer entertaining. The dining room has a tray ceiling and French doors that lead to a covered porch. A secluded master suite affords great views of the pool through French doors. The master bath is complete with His and Hers walk-in closets and a soaking tub. The family wing combines an island kitchen, nook and family gathering space, with the built-in media/fireplace wall being the focal point. While two secondary bedrooms share the versatile pool bath, a staircase overlooking the family room takes you up to the sun room complete with a bath, making this a very desirable kid's space.

DESIGN 8705

First Floor: 2,365 square feet
Second Floor: 364 square feet
Total: 2,729 square feet

DESIGN 8644
Square Footage: 1,831

A two-story entry, varying rooflines and multi-pane windows add to the spectacular street appeal of this three-bedroom home. Off the foyer, to the right, is the dining room surrounded by elegant columns. Adjacent is the angular kitchen, which opens to the bayed breakfast nook. The family room includes plans for an optional fireplace and accesses the covered porch. The secluded master bedroom features a walk-in closet and full bath with a dual vanity, spa tub and oversized shower. Two additional bedrooms share a full bath.

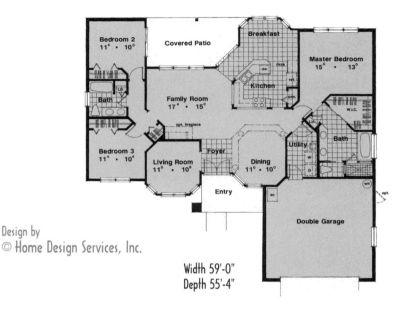

Design by
© Home Design Services, Inc.

Width 59'-0"
Depth 55'-4"

DESIGN 8669
Square Footage: 2,287

Low-pitched roofs and a grand, columned entry introduce a floor plan designed to carry over into the next millennium. Ceramic tiles lead from the foyer to the breakfast area and roomy kitchen, which offers an angled wrapping counter and overlooks the family room. French doors open off the foyer to a secluded den or guest suite, which complements the nearby master suite. A gallery hall off the breakfast nook leads to family sleeping quarters, which share a full bath.

Design by
© Home Design Services, Inc.

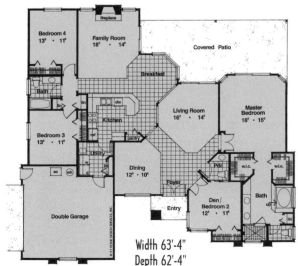

Width 63'-4"
Depth 62'-4"

DESIGN
8601

Square Footage: 2,125

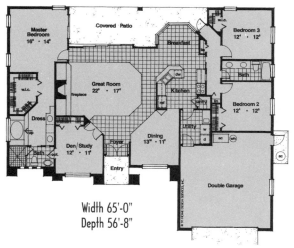

Design by
© Home Design Services, Inc.

Width 65'-0"
Depth 56'-8"

A luxurious master suite is yours with this lovely plan—and it comes with two different options—one has a wet bar and fireplace. An oversized great room with a grand fireplace is the heart of casual living in this relaxed plan. A formal dining room lies just off the foyer and offers easy access to the gourmet kitchen. Family bedrooms are split from the living area, perfect for a guest's comfort and privacy. A hall bath is shared by the two bedrooms as is a private door to the covered patio.

DESIGN
8646

Square Footage: 2,352

Design by
© Home Design Services, Inc.

Width 61'-8"
Depth 64'-8"

ALTERNATE
VIEW

An array of varied, arched windows sets off this striking Italianate home. The foyer, announces the living room accented by a wet bar, niche and patio access. The coffered dining room combines with the living room to create a perfect space for formal entertaining. A pass-through kitchen comes with a deep pantry and informal eating bar. Double doors open to the coffered master bedroom. The sumptuous master bath enjoys two walk-in closets, a dual vanity and spa tub. Blueprints include an alternate elevation.

SOUTHWEST & FLORIDA HOMES

Italianate lines add finesse to the formal facade of this home. Strong symmetry, a soaring portico and gentle rooflines are the prized hallmarks of this relaxed, yet formal design. To the right of the foyer, columns and a stepped ceiling offset the dining room. A plant shelf heralds the living room, which also has a twelve-foot ceiling. An angled cooktop counter adds flair to the kitchen, which also has a desk and walk-in pantry. A corner fireplace, high ceiling and patio enhance the family room.

Design by
© Home Design Services, Inc.

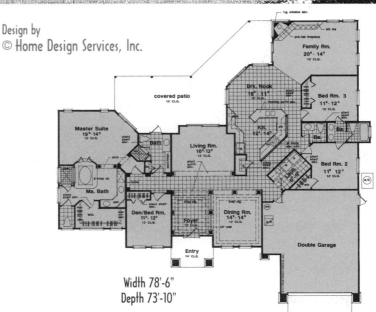

Width 78'-6"
Depth 73'-10"

The playful use of Palladian and other window shapes, and massive columns, set the stage for this elegant one-story home. Inside, columns and floating soffits create an open, airy design. Formal living areas flank the foyer, while the rear of the plan is occupied by the more casual family room with its welcoming corner fireplace. The secluded master bedroom opens to the rear patio and features an opulent master bath complete with a corner tub. Secondary bedrooms share a unique pool bath. Bedroom 2 is ideally situated for use as a den or home office.

Design by
© Home Design Services, Inc.

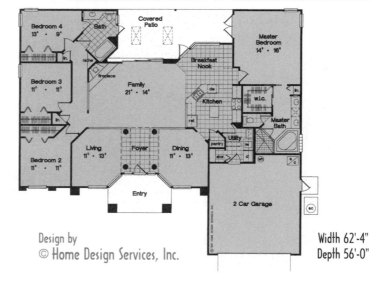

Width 62'-4"
Depth 56'-0"

DESIGN 8600
Square Footage: 2,041

The striking facade of this house is only the beginning to a very livable design. A dramatic foyer with columns branches off into the living room on one side and the dining room on the other. A spacious family room graces the center of the house—a true focal point. Beyond the kitchen and breakfast nook you'll find the master suite with private access to the covered patio. The bath here is grand with a corner whirlpool tub, large shower, dual sinks and walk-in closet. Three family bedrooms occupy the other side of the house.

Design by
© Home Design Services, Inc.

Width 60'-0"
Depth 56'-0"

Design by
© Home Design Services, Inc.

DESIGN 8682
Square Footage: 2,551
Bonus Room: 287 square feet

Shutters and multi-pane windows dress up the exterior of this lovely stucco home. Formal and informal areas flow easily, beginning with the dining room and the adjacent living room. A gourmet kitchen is complete with a walk-in pantry and a cozy breakfast nook. Double doors lead to the spacious master suite. The lavish master bath features His and Hers walk-in closets, a tub framed by a columned archway and an oversized shower. Off the angular hallway are two bedrooms that share a pullman-style bath and a study desk.

Width 69'-8"
Depth 71'-4"

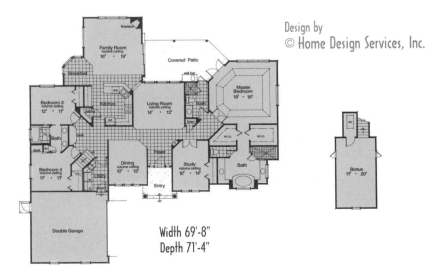

SOUTHWEST & FLORIDA HOMES

**DESIGN
8687**

Square Footage: 2,278

The grand entrance of this one-story home offers a fine introduction to an open, spacious interior. A delightful formal living and dining room extends from the foyer. To the left, a short hall accented with a decorator's niche precedes the master suite, which includes a sitting area, two walk-in closets and a spa-style bath. Family living centers in the kitchen where wrapping counters, a walk-in pantry and an angular snack bar balance out the spacious family room and breakfast nook.

Design by
© Home Design Services, Inc.

Width 57'-9"
Depth 71'-8"

**DESIGN
8688**

Square Footage: 2,636

A towering entry welcomes all into the foyer of this soaring contemporary design with a multitude of elegant volume ceilings. The open dining room and living rooms each have sunny bay windows and built-in features. The spacious family room features a charming corner fireplace, plenty of windows and a breakfast nook easily in reach of the roomy kitchen. Three family bedrooms sit just off the family room. The master suite contains a sitting area, twin closets and an oversized bath designed for relaxing.

Design by
© Home Design Services, Inc.

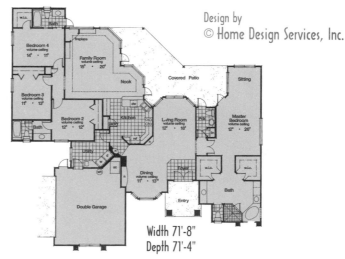

Width 71'-8"
Depth 71'-4"

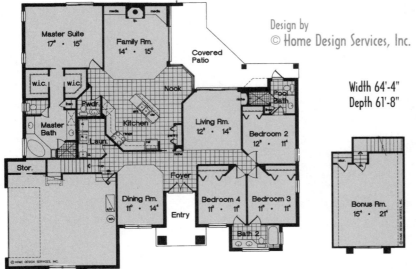

Design by
© Home Design Services, Inc.

Master Suite
17⁴ · 15⁰

Family Rm.
14⁴ · 15⁰

Covered Patio

w.i.c. w.i.c.

pwdr

Nook

Pool Bath

Master Bath

Kitchen

Laun.

Living Rm.
12⁰ · 14⁰

Bedroom 2
12⁰ · 11⁰

Stor.

Foyer

Dining Rm.
11⁰ · 14⁴

Entry

Bedroom 4
11⁰ · 11⁰

Bedroom 3
11⁰ · 11⁰

Bath 2

© HOME DESIGN SERVICES, INC.

Width 64'-4"
Depth 61'-8"

Bonus Rm.
15⁴ · 21⁴

DESIGN 8732

Square Footage: 2,311
Bonus Room: 279 square feet

A niche becomes the focal point as the tiled foyer flows to the heart of the home. The gourmet kitchen invites all occasions—planned events and casual gatherings—with an island counter, a sizable pantry and angled counters. A wall of sliding glass doors in the living room offers wide views of the back property. Two walk-in closets introduce a spacious bath in the master suite. Three family bedrooms are placed at the opposite end of the plan with a full bath. A cabana bath serves traffic from the back covered patio.

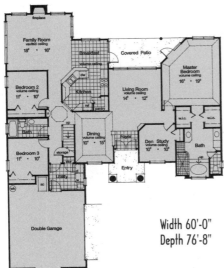

fireplace

Family Room
vaulted ceiling
16⁰ · 16⁰

Breakfast
volume ceiling

Covered Patio

Bedroom 2
volume ceiling
11⁰ · 10⁰

Kitchen

Living Room
volume ceiling
14⁰ · 12⁰

Master Bedroom
volume ceiling
16⁰ · 19⁰

pantry

Bath

w.i.c. w.i.c.

Bedroom 3
11⁰ · 10⁰

storage

Dining
10⁰ · 15⁰

Foyer

Den / Study
volume ceiling
10⁰ · 10⁰

Bath

Utility

Entry

Double Garage

Bonus Room
15⁰ · 23⁰

down

up

Width 60'-0"
Depth 76'-8"

Design by
© Home Design Services, Inc.

DESIGN 8681

Square Footage: 2,322
Bonus Room: 370 square feet

G rand Palladian windows create a classic look for this sensational stucco home. A magnificent view from the living room provides unlimited vistas of the rear grounds through a wall of glass. The nearby dining room completes the formal area. The kitchen, breakfast nook and family room comprise the family wing. Two secondary bedrooms share a bath and provide complete privacy to the master suite. The master bedroom sets the mood for relaxation and the lavish master bath pampers with a soaking tub flanked by a step-down shower and a compartmented toilet.

SOUTHWEST & FLORIDA HOMES

DESIGN 6663
Square Footage: 2,978

This gracious home features a series of arched windows and a deep hip roof that are reminiscent of historical styles, yet have the flavor of a contemporary sun-country home. The high entry porch opens to the gallery foyer and the living room and dining area—both offer sliding glass doors to the veranda. Casual living is simply elegant in the demonstration kitchen with a breakfast nook and adjoining leisure room. Two family bedrooms share a full hall bath. The master suite is well appointed, with a private garden, spa-style bath and twin closets.

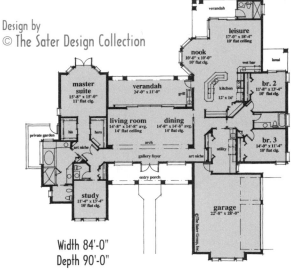

Design by
© The Sater Design Collection

Width 84'-0"
Depth 90'-0"

DESIGN 6641
Square Footage: 3,896
L

This elegant exterior blends a classical look with a contemporary feel. Corner quoins and round columns highlight the front elevation. The formal living room, complete with a fireplace and a wet bar, and the formal dining room access the lanai through three pairs of French doors. The well-appointed kitchen features an island prep sink, walk-in pantry and a desk. The secondary bedrooms are full guest suites. The master suite enjoys enormous His and Hers closets, built-ins, a wet bar and a three-sided fireplace that separates the sitting room and the bedroom.

Width 90'-0"
Depth 120'-8"

Design by
© The Sater Design Collection

© The Sater Group, Inc.

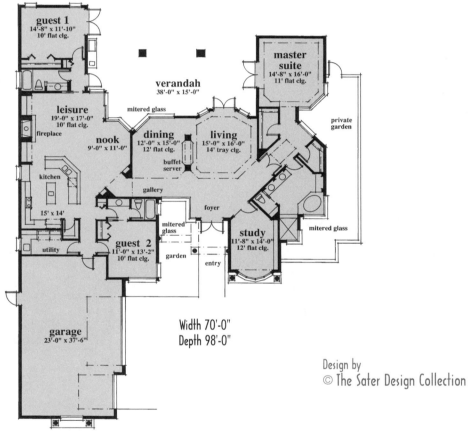

guest 1
14'-8" x 11'-10"
10' flat clg.

master suite
14'-8" x 16'-0"
11' flat clg.

verandah
38'-0" x 15'-0"

private garden

mitered glass

leisure
19'-0" x 17'-0"
10' flat clg.

fireplace

nook
9'-0" x 11'-0"

dining
12'-0" x 15'-0"
12' flat clg.

living
15'-0" x 16'-0"
14' tray clg.

buffet server

kitchen

15' x 14'

gallery

mitered glass

foyer

utility

guest 2
11'-0" x 13'-2"
10' flat clg.

mitered glass

garden

entry

study
11'-8" x 14'-0"
12' flat clg.

mitered glass

garage
23'-0" x 37'-6"

Width 70'-0"
Depth 98'-0"

Design by
© The Sater Design Collection

Classic columns, circle-head windows and a bay-windowed study give this stucco home a wonderful street presence. The foyer leads into the formal living and dining areas. An arched buffet server separates these rooms and contributes an open feeling. The kitchen, nook and leisure room are grouped for informal living. A desk/message center in the island kitchen, art niches in the nook and a fireplace with an entertainment center and shelves add custom touches. Two additional suites have private baths and offer full privacy from the master wing. The master suite hosts a private garden area, while the master bath features a walk-in shower that overlooks the garden, and a water-closet room with space for books or a television. Large His and Hers walk-in closets complete these private quarters. Note the spacious three-car garage.

DESIGN 6602
Square Footage: 2,794

L

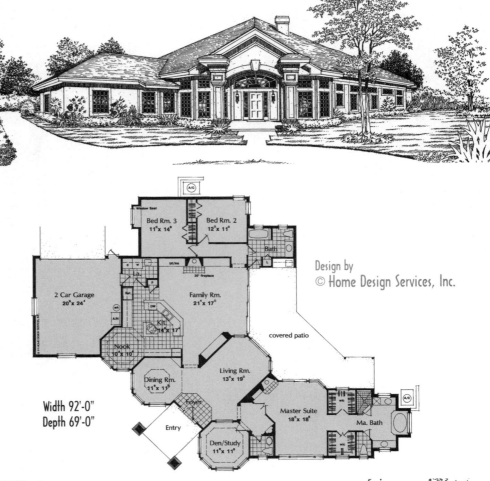

DESIGN 8603
Square Footage: 2,656

A graceful design sets this charming home apart from the ordinary and transcends the commonplace. From the foyer, the dining room branches off the sunny living room, setting a lovely backdrop for entertaining. Casual living is the focus in the oversized family room, where sliding doors open to the patio and the eat-in, gourmet kitchen is open for easy conversation. Two family bedrooms and a cabana bath are just off the family room. The master suite boasts a cozy fireplace in the sitting area, twin closets and a compartmented bath.

Width 92'-0"
Depth 69'-0"

DESIGN 8645
Square Footage: 2,224

Arches crowned by a gentle, hipped roof provide Italianate charm in this bright, spacious, family-oriented plan. A covered entry leads to the foyer that presents the angular, vaulted living and dining rooms. A kitchen with V-shape counter includes a walk-in pantry and looks out over the breakfast nook and family room with fireplace. The master suite features a sitting area, two walk-in closets and a full bath with garden tub. A roomy bedroom, with an adjacent cabana bath, opens off the family room and works perfectly as a guest room.

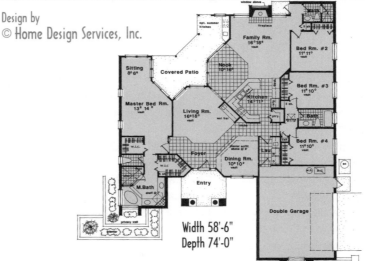

Width 58'-6"
Depth 74'-0"

www.homeplanners.com

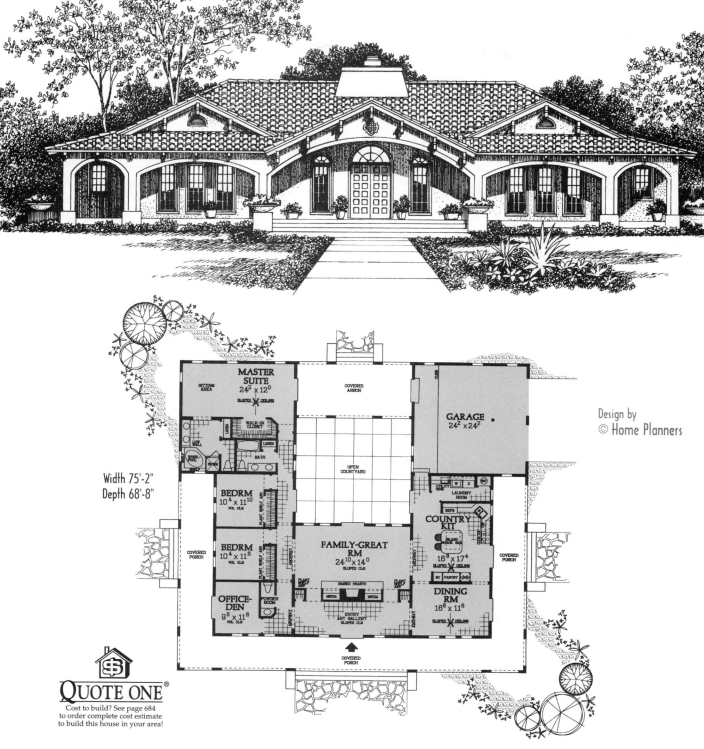

MASTER
SUITE
24² x 12⁰
SITTING AREA
SLOPED CEILING

COVERED ARBOR

GARAGE
24² x 24²

Design by
© Home Planners

WALK-IN CLOSET

LINEN

BATH

OPEN COURTYARD

Width 75'-2"
Depth 68'-8"

LAUNDRY ROOM

BEDRM
10⁴ x 11¹⁰
VOL CLG

PLANT SHELF ABV

COVERED PORCH

COUNTRY KIT
16⁸ x 17⁴
SLOPED CEILING

COVERED PORCH

BEDRM
10⁴ x 11⁸
VOL CLG

PLANT SHELF ABV

FAMILY-GREAT RM
24¹⁰ x 14⁰
SLOPED CLG

OFFICE-DEN
9⁸ x 11⁸
VOL CLG

POWDER ROOM

RAISED HEARTH

DINING RM
16⁸ x 11⁸
SLOPED CEILING

ENTRY ART GALLERY
SLOPED CLG

COVERED PORCH

Quote One®
Cost to build? See page 684
to order complete cost estimate
to build this house in your area!

E xposed rafter tails, arched porch detailing, massive paneled front doors and stucco exterior walls enhance the western character of this U-shaped ranch house. Double doors open to a spacious, slope-ceilinged art gallery. The quiet sleeping zone is comprised of an entire wing. The extra room at the front of this wing may be used for a den or an office. The family dining and

kitchen activities are located at the opposite end of the plan. Indoor-outdoor living relationships are outstanding. The large open courtyard is akin to the fabled Greek atrium. It is accessible from each of the zones and functions with a covered arbor that looks out over the rear landscape. The master suite offers a generous sitting area, walk-in closet, twin lavatories, a whirlpool tub and a stall shower.

DESIGN 3632
Square Footage: 2,539
L

SOUTHWEST & FLORIDA HOMES

DESIGN 6684

Main Level: 2,385 square feet
Lower Level: 80 square feet
Total: 2,465 square feet

Adapted from styles of the tropics and the Caribbean, this cottage plan creates a tremendous first impression. The lower level includes two rooms that could serve many purposes. Upstairs, the great room will be the focus of family activities, offering an entertainment center, built-in shelves and a nearby breakfast nook. Enjoy outdoor living on the delightful porch, reached through sliding doors from both of these rooms as well as the deluxe master suite. Two family bedrooms share a bath to complete the plan.

Design by
© The Sater Design Collection

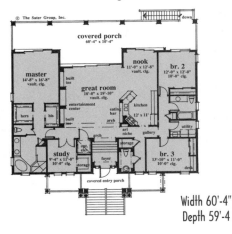

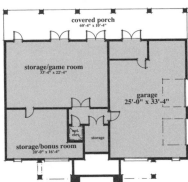

Width 60'-4"
Depth 59'-4

REAR VIEW

DESIGN 6692

Square Footage: 2,190

The dramatic arched entry of this Southampton-style cottage borrows freely from its Southern coastal past. The foyer and central hall open to the grand room. The kitchen is flanked by the dining room and morning nook, which opens to the lanai. On the left side of the plan, the master suite also accesses the lanai. Two walk-in closets, a compartmented bath with separate tub and shower and a double-bowl vanity complete the homeowners opulent retreat. The right side of the plan includes two secondary bedrooms and a full bath.

Design by
© The Sater Design Collection

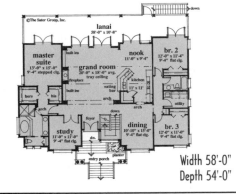

Width 58'-0"
Depth 54'-0"

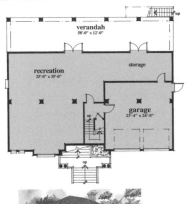

REAR VIEW

SOUTHWEST & FLORIDA HOMES

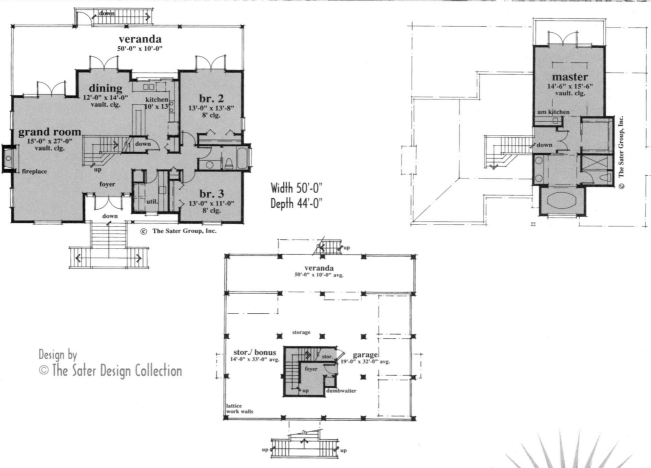

veranda
50'-0" x 10'-0"

dining
12'-0" x 14'-0"
vault. clg.

kitchen
10' x 13'

br. 2
13'-0" x 13'-8"
8' clg.

grand room
15'-0" x 27'-0"
vault. clg.

fireplace

down

up

foyer

util.

br. 3
13'-0" x 11'-0"
8' clg.

down

© The Sater Group, Inc.

Width 50'-0"
Depth 44'-0"

master
14'-6" x 15'-6"
vault. clg.

am kitchen

down

© The Sater Group, Inc.

Design by
© The Sater Design Collection

veranda
50'-0" x 10'-0" avg.

storage

stor./ bonus
14'-0" x 33'-0" avg.

stor.

garage
19'-0" x 32'-0" avg.

foyer

dumbwaiter

up

lattice
work walls

up   up

L attice walls, pickets and horizontal siding complement a relaxed Key West design that's perfect for water-front properties. The grand room, with a fireplace, the dining room and Bedroom 2 open through French doors to the veranda. The master suite occupies the entire second floor and includes a morning kitchen, private bath and French doors to the balcony. Enclosed storage plus bonus space is on the lower level, along with the three-car garage.

DESIGN 6655
First Floor: 1,586 square feet
Second Floor: 601 square feet
Total: 2,187 square feet

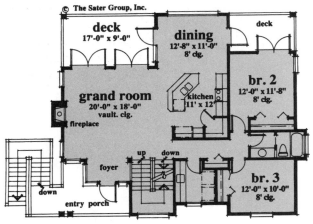

© The Sater Group, Inc.

deck 17'-0" x 9'-0"

dining 12'-8" x 11'-0" 8' clg.

deck

grand room 20'-0" x 18'-0" vault. clg.

fireplace

kitchen 11' x 12'

br. 2 12'-0" x 11'-8" 8' clg.

up   down

foyer

down

entry porch

br. 3 12'-0" x 10'-0" 8' clg.

Width 44'-0"
Depth 40'-0"

Design by
© The Sater Design Collection

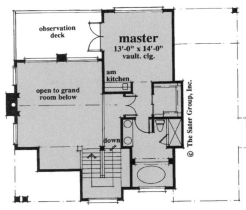

observation deck

master 13'-0" x 14'-0" vault. clg.

open to grand room below

am kitchen

down

© The Sater Group, Inc.

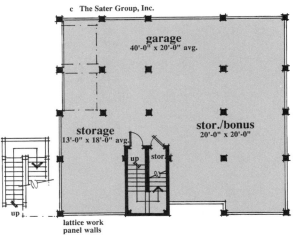

c   The Sater Group, Inc.

garage 40'-0" x 20'-0" avg.

storage 13'-0" x 18'-0" avg.

stor./bonus 20'-0" x 20'-0"

up   stor.

up

lattice work
panel walls

DESIGN 6654
First Floor: 1,342 square feet
Second Floor: 511 square feet
Total: 1,853 square feet

With influences from homes of the Caribbean, this island home is a perfect seaside residence or primary residence. The main living area is comprised of a grand room with a fireplace and access to a deck. The dining space also accesses this deck plus another that it shares with a secondary bedroom. An L-shaped kitchen with a prep island is open to the living areas. Two bedrooms on this level share a full bath. The master suite dominates the upper level with an observation deck and a bath with dual vanities and a whirlpool tub.

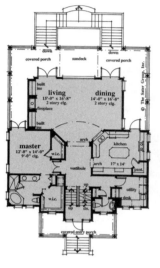

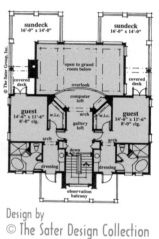

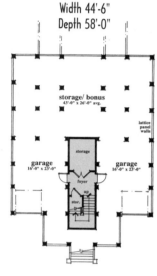

Width 44'-6"
Depth 58'-0"

DESIGN 6693

Main Level: 1,642 square feet
Upper Level: 1,165 square feet
Lower Level: 150 square feet
Total: 2,957 square feet

A faux widow's walk creates a stunning complement to the observation balcony and two sun decks. Inside, the open living and dining area is defined by two pairs of French doors that frame a two-story wall of glass while built-ins flank the fireplace. The efficient kitchen features a walk-in pantry, a work island and a door to the covered porch. Upstairs, two guest suites provide private baths. A gallery loft includes a built-in desk and a balcony overlook.

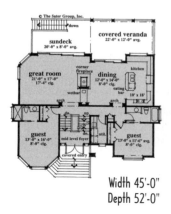

DESIGN 6698

First Floor: 1,684 square feet
Second Floor: 1,195 square feet
Total: 2,879 square feet
Bonus Room: 674 square feet

A symmetrical rooflines set off a grand turret and a two-story bay that allow glorious views from the front of the home. Arch-top clerestory windows bring natural light into the great room, which shares a corner fireplace and a wet bar with the dining room. A winding staircase leads to a master suite that shares a fireplace with the bath and includes a morning kitchen, French doors to the balcony, a double walk-in closet and—down the hall—a study and a balcony that overlooks the great room.

Width 45'-0"
Depth 52'-0"

SOUTHWEST & FLORIDA HOMES

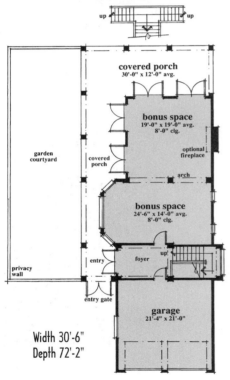

covered porch
30'-0" x 12'-0" avg.

bonus space
19'-0" x 19'-0" avg.
8'-0" clg.

garden courtyard

covered porch

optional fireplace

arch

bonus space
24'-6" x 14'-0" avg.
8'-0" clg.

privacy wall

entry

foyer

up!

entry gate

garage
21'-4" x 21'-0"

Width 30'-6"
Depth 72'-2"

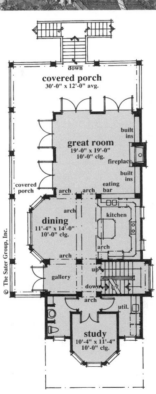

covered porch
30'-0" x 12'-0" avg.

down

great room
19'-0" x 19'-0"
10'-0" clg.

built ins

fireplace

built ins

covered porch

arch   arch

eating bar

arch

dining
11'-4" x 14'-0"
10'-0" clg.

kitchen

arch

arch

gallery

up!

down

arch

util.

study
10'-4" x 11'-4"
10'-0" clg.

© The Sater Group, Inc.

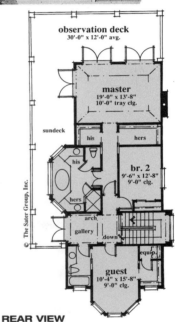

observation deck
30'-0" x 12'-0" avg.

master
19'-0" x 13'-8"
10'-0" tray clg.

sundeck

his   hers

his

br. 2
9'-6" x 12'-8"
9'-0" clg.

hers

arch

gallery

down

equip.

guest
10'-4" x 15'-8"
9'-0" clg.

© The Sater Group, Inc.

REAR VIEW

Design by
© The Sater Design Collection

Louvered shutters, balustered railings and a slate-style roof complement a stucco-and-siding blend on this narrow design. Entry stairs lead up to the living areas, defined by arches and columns. A wall of built-ins and a fireplace highlight the contemporary great room, while four sets of French doors expand the living area to the wraparound porch. Second-floor sleeping quarters include a guest suite with a bayed sitting area, an additional bedroom and a full bath. The master suite features two walk-in closets, separate vanities and French doors to a private observation deck. The lower level offers bonus space for future use, another porch and the two-car garage.

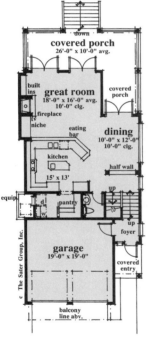

covered porch
26'-0" x 10'-0" avg.

down

built ins

great room
18'-0" x 16'-0" avg.
10'-0" clg.

covered porch

fireplace

tv niche

eating bar

dining
10'-0" x 12'-0"
10'-0" clg.

kitchen
15' x 13'

half wall

equip.

d w

pantry

up

up

foyer

garage
19'-0" x 19'-0"

covered entry

balcony line abv.

c The Sater Group, Inc.

sundeck
26'-0" x 10'-0" avg.

master
16'-6" x 15'-0"
vault. clg.

sundeck

w.i.c.

art

study/br.
12'-0" x 10'-0"
9'-0" clg.

w.i.c.

landing

dn.

up

art

br. 2
9'-8" x 11'-0"
9'-0" clg.

br. 3
9'-8" x 11'-0"
9'-0" clg.

Width 27'-6"
Depth 64'-0"

Design by
© The Sater Design Collection

REAR VIEW

© The Sater Design Collection

SOUTHWEST & FLORIDA HOMES

Key West Conch style blends Old World charm with New World comfort in this picturesque design. A glass-paneled entry lends a warm welcome and complements a captivating front balcony. The narrow floor plan works well—reminiscent of the Caribbean "shotgun" houses. Two sets of French doors open the great room to wide views and extend the living areas to the back covered porch. A gourmet kitchen is prepared for any occasion with a prep sink, plenty of counter space, an ample pantry and an eating bar. The mid-level landing leads to two additional bedrooms, a full bath and a windowed art niche. Double French doors open the upper-level master suite to a sun deck. Circle-head windows and a vaulted ceiling maintain a light and airy atmosphere. The master bath has a windowed soaking tub and a glass-enclosed walk-in shower. The plan offers the option of a fourth bedroom.

DESIGN 6701
First Floor: 876 square feet
Second Floor: 1,245 square feet
Total: 2,121 square feet

DESIGN 8706
Square Footage: 2,636

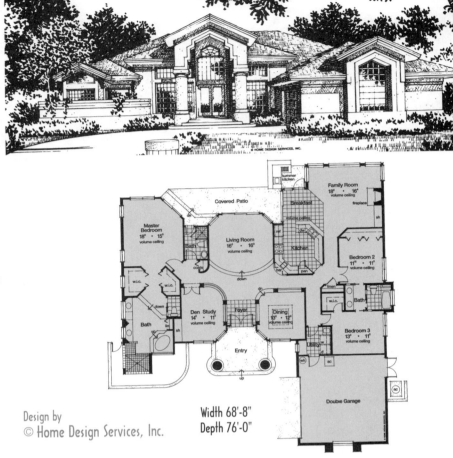

A towering entry welcomes you in the foyer of this soaring contemporary design. Interior glass walls give openness to the den/study and mirror the arches to the formal dining room. The sunken living room has a bayed window wall, which views the patio. Sliding glass doors in the master suite access the patio. The master bath features dual closets, a sunken vanity/bath area and a doorless shower. The family wing holds the gourmet kitchen, nook and family room with fireplace.

Design by
© Home Design Services, Inc.

Width 68'-8"
Depth 76'-0"

DESIGN 8702
Square Footage: 2,397

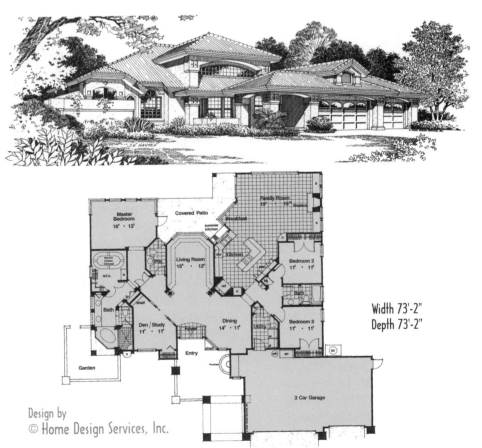

Dramatic rooflines and a unique entrance set the mood of this contemporary home. Double doors lead into the foyer, which opens directly to the formal rooms. An adjacent den/study offers a quiet retreat. The spacious kitchen provides a large cooktop island, plenty of counter and cabinet space and an adjoining breakfast nook. The spacious family room expands this area and features a wall of windows and a warming fireplace. Included in the master suite is a lavish bath and a deluxe walk-in closet, as well as access to the covered patio.

Design by
© Home Design Services, Inc.

Width 73'-2"
Depth 73'-2"

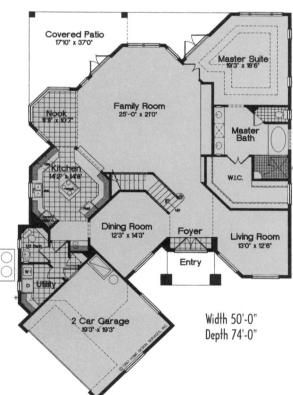

Covered Patio
17'10" x 37'0"

Master Suite
19'3" x 18'6"

Family Room
25'0" x 21'0"

Nook
11'1" x 10'7"

Master Bath

Kitchen
14'2" x 14'8"

W.I.C.

1/2 Bath

Dining Room
12'3" x 14'3"

Foyer

Living Room
13'0" x 12'6"

Entry

Utility

2 Car Garage
19'3" x 19'3"

Width 50'-0"
Depth 74'-0"

Design by
© Home Design Services, Inc.

Deck

Loft

open to below

down

W.I.C.

Bath 2

Bedroom 2
14'3" x 10'11"

Closet

open to below

Bedroom 3
17'6" x 16'7"

At only 50 feet in width, this fabulous design will fit anywhere! From the moment you enter the home from the foyer, this floor plan explodes in every direction with huge living spaces. Flanking the foyer are the living and dining rooms, and the visual impact of the staircase is breathtaking. Two-story ceilings adorn the huge family room with double stacked glass walls. Sunlight floods the breakfast nook, and the kitchen is a gourmet's dream, complete with cooking island and loads of overhead cabinets. A half bath and utility area are nearby. Tray ceilings grace the master suite, which also offers a well-designed master bath. Here, a large soaking tub, doorless shower, private toilet chamber and huge walk-in closet are sure to please. Upstairs, two oversized bedrooms and a loft space—perfect for the home computer—share a full bath.

**DESIGN
8698**
First Floor: 2,051 square feet
Second Floor: 749 square feet
Total: 2,800 square feet

DESIGN 3441

First Floor: 2,022 square feet
Second Floor: 845 square feet
Total: 2,867 square feet

Special details make the difference between a house and a home. A snack bar, an audio-visual center and a fireplace make the family room a favorite place for informal gatherings. A desk, an island cooktop, a bay and skylights enhance the kitchen area. The dining room features two columns and a plant ledge. The first-floor master suite includes His and Hers walk-in closets, a spacious bath and a bay window. On the second floor, one bedroom features a walk-in closet and private bath, while two additional bedrooms share a full bath.

Design by
© Home Planners

Width 63'-8"
Depth 56'-2"

QUOTE ONE®
Cost to build? See page 684
to order complete cost estimate
to build this house in your area!

DESIGN 3425

First Floor: 1,776 square feet
Second Floor: 1,035 square feet
Total: 2,811 square feet

Here's a two-story Spanish design with an appealing, angled exterior. Formal areas are to the right of the entry tower: a sunken living room with a fireplace and a large dining room with access to the rear porch. The kitchen has loads of counter space and is complemented by a bumped-out breakfast room. Note the second fireplace in the family room and the first-floor guest suite. Three second-floor bedrooms radiate around the upper foyer, including the deluxe master suite.

Design by
© Home Planners

Width 52'-0"
Depth 64'-4"

QUOTE ONE®
Cost to build? See page 684
to order complete cost estimate
to build this house in your area!

The home, as shown in the photograph, may differ from the actual blueprints. For more detailed information, please check the floor plans carefully.

Photo by Andrew D. Lautman

FIRST FLOOR

- WHIRLPOOL
- MASTER BATH
- HER WALK-IN CLOSET
- HIS WALK-IN CLOSET
- FAMILY RM 19⁸ x 18⁶
- COVERED PORCH
- BREAKFAST 12⁰ x 9⁶
- MASTER BEDROOM 14² x 20⁴
- SLOPED CEILING
- SNACK BAR
- KITCHEN 11⁸ x 12⁶
- PANTRY
- REF'G
- DINING 16⁴ x 8⁸
- MECH RM
- LAUNDRY
- PDR RM
- CL
- DN
- UP
- RAILING
- CURB
- FOYER
- DN
- SLOPED CEILING
- COVERED PORCH
- LIVING RM 16⁰ x 13¹⁰
- WH
- FURN
- GARAGE 29⁰ x 19⁶

Width 57'-0"
Depth 64'-0"

SECOND FLOOR

- GUEST BEDROOM 14⁰ x 17⁴
- DECK
- UPPER FAMILY ROOM
- BATH
- CL
- BEDROOM 10⁴ x 12⁰
- RAILING
- DN
- MECH WH FURN
- CL
- BATH
- WALK-IN CLOSET
- CL
- UPPER FOYER
- BEDROOM 12⁴ x 11⁸
- BEDROOM 12⁴ x 10⁵

Design by
© Home Planners

Quote One®

Cost to build? See page 684 to order complete cost estimate to build this house in your area!

Though seemingly compact from the exterior, this home gives a definite feeling of spaciousness inside. The two-story entry connects directly to a formal living/dining area, a fitting complement to the more casual family room and cozy, bayed breakfast room. Located on the first floor for privacy, the master suite is luxury defined. A bayed sitting area, His and Hers walk-in closets, a whirlpool tub and twin vanities all combine to provide a lavish retreat. Upstairs, three family bedrooms share a full hall bath, while a large guest room awaits to pamper with its private bath and access to its own deck. A three-car garage will protect both the family fleet and visitor's vehicles.

DESIGN 3414

First Floor: 2,024 square feet
Second Floor: 1,144 square feet
Total: 3,168 square feet

SOUTHWEST & FLORIDA HOMES

DESIGN
8672
Square Footage: 2,397

Low-slung, hipped rooflines and an abundance of glass enhance the unique exterior of this sunny, one-story home. Inside, the use of soffits and tray ceilings heighten the distinctive style of the floor plan. To the left, double doors lead to the private master suite, which enjoys a garden setting from the corner tub. Convenient planning of the gourmet kitchen places everything at minimum distances and serves the outdoor summer kitchen, breakfast nook and family room with equal ease.

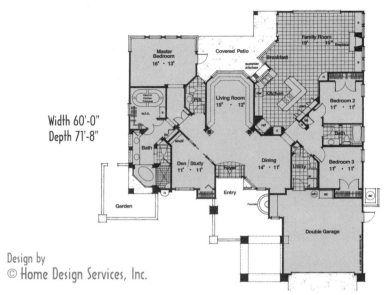

Width 60'-0"
Depth 71'-8"

Design by
© Home Design Services, Inc.

DESIGN
8683
First Floor: 2,254 square feet
Second Floor: 608 square feet
Total: 2,862 square feet

Indoor/outdoor relationships are enhanced by the beautiful courtyard that decorates the center of this home. A gallery provides views of the courtyard and leads to a kitchen featuring a center work island and an adjacent breakfast room. The secluded master bedroom features a tray ceiling and double doors that lead to a covered patio. Retreat to the master bath, that includes a relaxing tub. The second floor contains a full bath shared by Bedrooms 3 and 4 and a loft with its own balcony that provides flexible space for an additional bedroom.

Width 66'-0"
Depth 78'-10"

OPTIONAL BEDROOM

Design by
© Home Design Services, Inc.

© '91 HOME DESIGN SERVICES, INC.

J. V. HANSEN P.T.L.

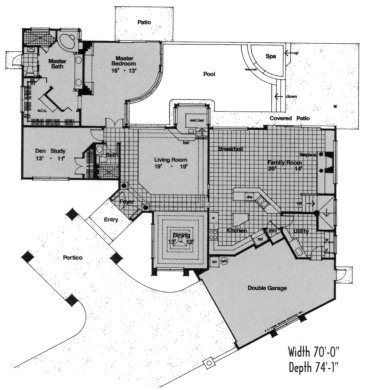

Width 70'-0"
Depth 74'-1"

Design by
© Home Design Services, Inc.

A s you drive up to the porte-cochere entry of this home, the visual movement of the elevation is breathtaking. The multi-roofed spaces bring excitement the moment you walk through the double-doored entry. The foyer leads into the wide glass-walled living room. To the right, the formal dining room features a tiered pedestal ceiling. To the left is the guest and master suite wing of the home. The master suite, with its sweeping, curved glass wall, has access to the patio area and overlooks the pool. The master bath, with its huge walk-in closet, comes complete with a columned vanity area, soaking tub and shower for two. Two large bedrooms on the second floor—one with a bay window and one with a walk-in closet—share a sun deck, full bath and activity area.

DESIGN 8652
First Floor: 2,212 square feet
Second Floor: 675 square feet
Total: 2,887 square feet

SOUTHWEST & FLORIDA HOMES

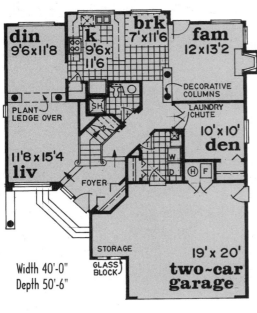

din
9'6x11'8

k
9'6x 11'6

brk
7'x11'6

fam
12x13'2

DECORATIVE COLUMNS

LAUNDRY CHUTE

PLANT LEDGE OVER

liv
11'8 x 15'4

FOYER

10' x 10'
den

STORAGE

GLASS BLOCK

19' x 20'
two-car garage

Width 40'-0"
Depth 50'-6"

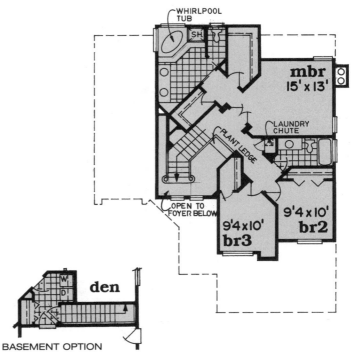

WHIRLPOOL TUB

SH.

mbr
15' x 13'

LAUNDRY CHUTE

PLANT LEDGE

OPEN TO FOYER BELOW

9'4 x10'
br3

9'4 x 10'
br2

den

BASEMENT OPTION

Design by
© Select Home Designs

⸎ DESIGN
Q329
First Floor: 1,199 square feet
Second Floor: 921 square feet
Total: 2,120 square feet

A n angled entry gives a new slant to this cool California design. The two-story foyer is lighted by a multi-paned window and leads down two steps to a sunken foyer. A pair of decorative columns separates the living room and formal dining room. A U-shaped kitchen, with walk-in pantry, serves the breakfast room. Just beyond is the family room with fireplace and rear-

yard access. A den is tucked in between the laundry room and two-car garage (note the storage space). On the second floor, the master suite holds a walk-in closet and a private bath with a corner whirlpool tub and separate shower. Two additional bedrooms share a full bath. A laundry chute in the hall sends clothes to the laundry room, which offers convenient access to the two-car garage.

www.homeplanners.com

Width 37'-0"
Depth 30'-8"

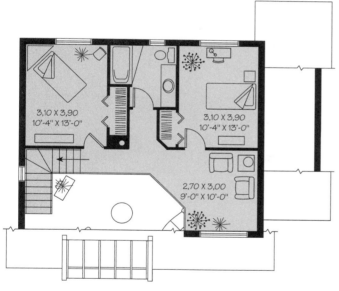

Design by
© Drummond Designs, Inc.

This contemporary four-season cottage offers plenty of windows to take in great views. The living room offers a cathedral ceiling with a balcony overlook and a fireplace. The compartmented entry features a coat closet. An L-shaped kitchen provides access to a side porch. The first-floor master suite includes direct access to the laundry area. Upstairs, two additional bedrooms share a hall bath. A balcony hall leads to a sitting area with views of the front property. This home is designed with a basement foundation.

DESIGN Z035
First Floor: 946 square feet
Second Floor: 604 square feet
Total: 1,550 square feet

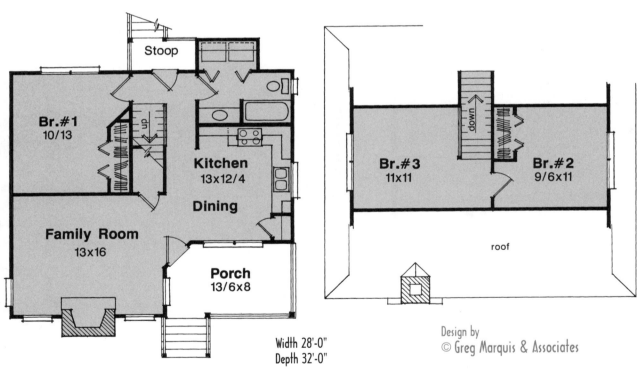

Stoop

Br.#1
10/13

Kitchen
13x12/4

Dining

Family Room
13x16

Porch
13/6x8

Br.#3
11x11

down

Br.#2
9/6x11

roof

Width 28'-0"
Depth 32'-0"

Design by
© Greg Marquis & Associates

DESIGN
B139

First Floor: 728 square feet
Second Floor: 300 square feet
Total: 1,028 square feet

From its inviting front porch to the old-fashioned back stoop, this is a home designed for relaxation. The angled front door opens into a spacious family room, complete with a cheerful fireplace. A good-sized kitchen/dining area lets the cook socialize with family or guests while preparing the meal. The kitchen offers a double sink with a window and a pantry. A large bedroom and nearby full bath with laundry area attached complete the first floor. Either of the two upstairs bedrooms could also serve as a study or a recreation room.

www.homeplanners.com

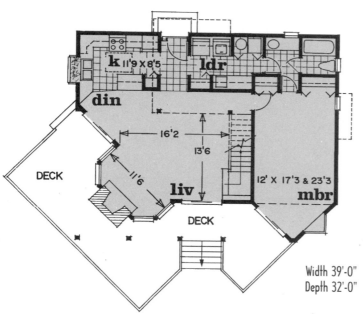

Width 39'-0"
Depth 32'-0"

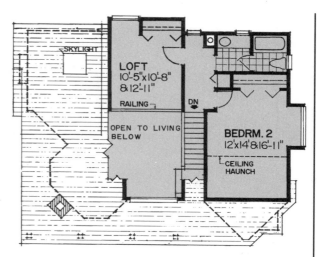

This quaint cottage works equally well in the mountains or at the lake. Its entry is sliding glass and opens to a vaulted living room with a fireplace tucked into a wide windowed bay. The dining room has sliding glass access to the deck. The skylit kitchen features a green-house window over the sink and is just across from a handy laundry room. The master bedroom captures views through sliding glass doors and a triangular fea-ture window. It has the use of a full bath. The second floor holds another bedroom, a full bath and a loft area.

DESIGN Q204
First Floor: 1,022 square feet
Second Floor: 551 square feet
Total: 1,573 square feet

VACATION HOMES

DESIGN 9697

First Floor: 1,039 square feet
Second Floor: 583 square feet
Total: 1,622 square feet

Charming and compact, this delightful two-story cabin is perfect for the small family or empty-nester. Designed with casual living in mind, the two-story great room is completely open to the dining area and the spacious island kitchen. The master suite is on the first floor for privacy and convenience. It features a roomy bath and a walk-in closet. Upstairs, two comfortable bedrooms—one includes a dormer window, the other features a balcony overlooking the great room—share a full hall bath.

© 1992 Donald A. Gardner Architects, Inc.

PORCH 34-6 × 8-0
KIT./DINING 10-10 × 17-8
walk-in closet
MASTER BED RM. 12-0 × 17-0
w d
bedroom above
sto.
GREAT RM. 17-4 × 17-2
fireplace
up cl
master bath
PORCH 34-6 × 8-0

BED RM. 12-6 × 13-8
bath
walk-in closet
closet
railing
down
great room below
BED RM. 12-0 × 15-8

Width 37'-9"
Depth 44'-8"

Design by
Donald A. Gardner
Architects, Inc.

DESIGN 9666

First Floor: 1,027 square feet
Second Floor: 580 square feet
Total: 1,607 square feet

This economical, rustic three-bedroom plan sports a relaxing country image with both front and back covered porches. The openness of the expansive great room to the kitchen/dining area and loft/study area is reinforced with a shared cathedral ceiling for impressive space. The first level allows for two bedrooms, a full bath and a utility area. The master suite on the second level contains a walk-in closet and a master bath with whirlpool tub, shower and double-bowl vanity. A basement or crawlspace foundation is available.

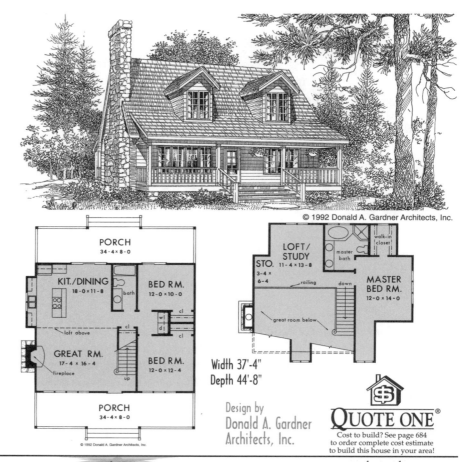

© 1992 Donald A. Gardner Architects, Inc.

PORCH 34-4 × 8-0
KIT./DINING 18-0 × 11-8
bath
BED RM. 12-0 × 10-0
loft above
w d
cl
cl
cl
GREAT RM. 17-4 × 16-4
fireplace
up
BED RM. 12-0 × 12-4
PORCH 34-4 × 8-0

LOFT/STUDY 11-4 × 13-8
STO. 3-4 × 6-4
master bath
walk-in closet
railing
down
great room below
MASTER BED RM. 12-0 × 14-0

Width 37'-4"
Depth 44'-8"

Design by
Donald A. Gardner
Architects, Inc.

© 1992 Donald A. Gardner Architects, Inc.

Quote One®
Cost to build? See page 684 to order complete cost estimate to build this house in your area!

www.homeplanners.com

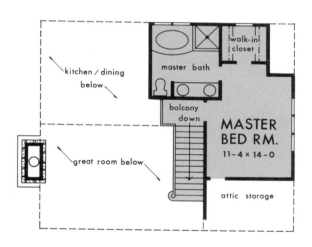

kitchen / dining below

master bath

walk-in closet

balcony down

MASTER BED RM.
11-4 × 14-0

great room below

attic storage

Width 36'-8"
Depth 44'-8"

Design by
Donald A. Gardner
Architects, Inc.

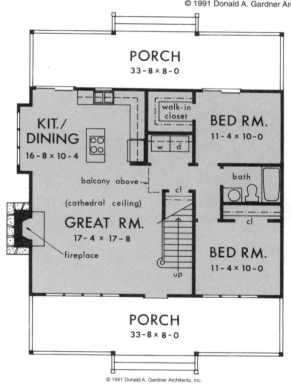

PORCH
33-8 × 8-0

walk-in closet

KIT./ DINING
16-8 × 10-4

BED RM.
11-4 × 10-0

w   d

balcony above

cl

(cathedral ceiling)

bath

GREAT RM.
17-4 × 17-8

cl

fireplace

BED RM.
11-4 × 10-0

up

PORCH
33-8 × 8-0

A mountain retreat, this rustic home features covered porches front and rear. Open living is enjoyed in a great room and kitchen/dining room combination. Here, a fireplace provides the focal point and a warm welcome that continues into the L-shaped island kitchen. The cathedral ceiling that graces the great room gives an open, inviting sense of space. Two bedrooms—one with a walk-in closet—and a full bath on the first level are complemented by a master suite on the second level that includes a walk-in closet and deluxe bath. A basement or crawlspace foundation is available.

DESIGN 9663
First Floor: 1,002 square feet
Second Floor: 336 square feet
Total: 1,338 square feet

VACATION HOMES

DESIGN 4061

First Floor: 1,036 square feet
Second Floor: 273 square feet
Total: 1,309 square feet

D

This charming farmhouse design will be economical to build and a pleasure to occupy. Like most vacation homes, this design features an open plan. The large living area includes a living room, dining room and massive stone fireplace. A partition separates the kitchen from the living room. The first floor also holds a bedroom, full bath and laundry room. Upstairs, a spacious sleeping loft overlooks the living room. Don't miss the large front porch—this will be a favorite spot for relaxing.

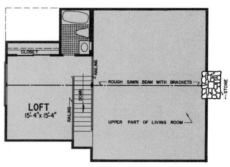

Width 39'-0"
Depth 38'-0"

Design by
© Home Planners

Quote One®
Cost to build? See page 684 to order complete cost estimate to build this house in your area!

Design by
© Home Planners

DESIGN 3680

First Floor: 1,093 square feet
Second Floor: 580 square feet
Total: 1,673 square feet

L D

Designed with relaxation in mind, this home opens from the foyer to a great room warmed by the glowing embers of a cheerful fire. Nearby, meal preparation is easy, with a U-shaped kitchen designed to serve the snack bar and nook area. When weather permits, outdoor dining may be enjoyed on the rear covered porch. Two secondary bedrooms on this level share a full bath. The second floor holds the master bedroom with a private bath and lots of closet space. A loft/study, perfect for reflective moments, completes this floor.

Width 36'-0"
Depth 52'-0"

Quote One®
Cost to build? See page 684 to order complete cost estimate to build this house in your area!

Photo by Andrew D. Lautman

The home, as shown in the photograph, may differ from the actual blueprints. For more detailed information, please check the floor plans carefully.

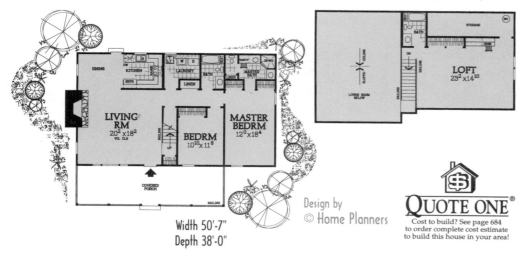

Width 50'-7"
Depth 38'-0"

Design by
© Home Planners

Quote One®
Cost to build? See page 684
to order complete cost estimate
to build this house in your area!

DESIGN 3699

First Floor: 1,356 square feet
Second Floor: 490 square feet
Total: 1,846 square feet

L D

Split-log siding and a rustic balustrade create country charm with this farmhouse-style retreat. An open living area features a natural stone fireplace and a cathedral ceiling with exposed rough-sawn beam and brackets. A generous kitchen and dining area complement the living room and share the warmth of its fireplace. A master suite and a nearby family bedroom with a hall bath complete the main floor. Upstairs, a spacious loft affords extra sleeping space—or provides a hobby/recreation area—and offers a full bath.

© 1987 Donald A. Gardner Architects, Inc.

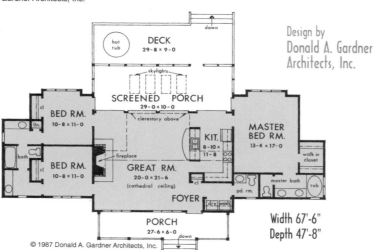

Design by
Donald A. Gardner
Architects, Inc.

Width 67'-6"
Depth 47'-8"

© 1987 Donald A. Gardner Architects, Inc.

DESIGN 9609

Square Footage: 1,426

Rustic charm abounds in this amenity-filled three-bedroom plan. From the central living area with cathedral ceiling and fireplace to the sumptuous master suite, there are few features omitted. Be sure to notice the large walk-in closet in the master bedroom, the pampering whirlpool tub, and the separate water-closet compartment. Two other bedrooms have a connecting bath with a single-bowl vanity for each. The house wraps around a screened porch with skylights—a grand place for eating and entertaining.

VACATION HOMES

DESIGN
1425
Square Footage: 1,152

L D

Here is a vacation home that can easily be built within any budget and in stages. The sloped ceilings contribute to the feeling of spaciousness. The basic unit features the kitchen, bath, a bedroom and the living room. Add on additional bedrooms or a screened porch in the second stage. The screened porch can be modified to be built as a family room that permits year-round living.

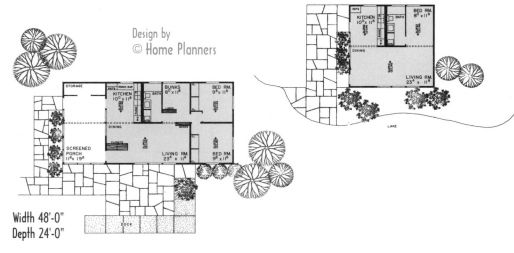

Design by
© Home Planners

Width 48'-0"
Depth 24'-0"

DESIGN
1486
Square Footage: 480

For that prime piece of property, this little vacation house will delight all vacationers. Two sets of sliding glass doors open to the living and dining area. A kitchen with a double sink, closet and porch door is just a step away. Two bedrooms share the same dimensions while utilizing a full hall bath. Whether you decide to build this house on your own or with the aid of a professional, you will not have to wait long for its completion.

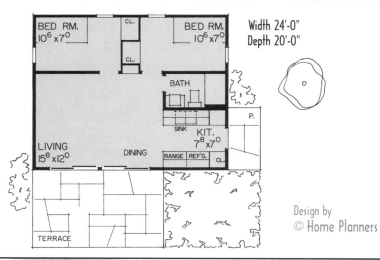

Width 24'-0"
Depth 20'-0"

Design by
© Home Planners

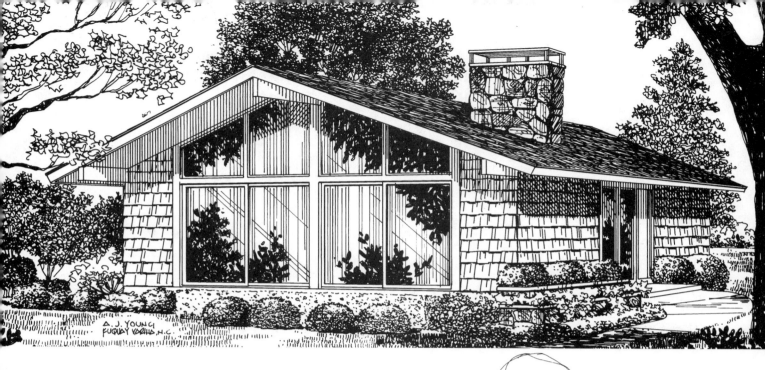

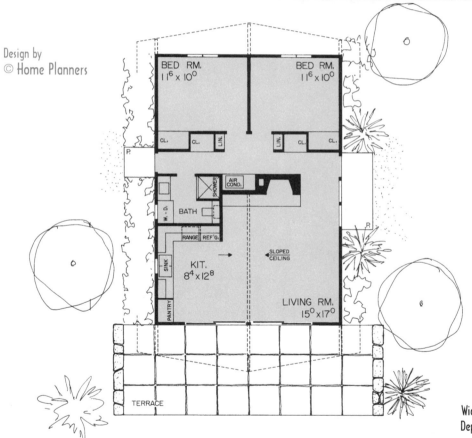

Design by
© Home Planners

BED RM.
$11^6 \times 10^0$

BED RM.
$11^6 \times 10^0$

CL. CL. LIN.   LIN. CL. CL.

P.

SHOWER AIR COND.

W.·D. BATH

RANGE REF'G.

SINK

KIT.
$8^4 \times 12^8$

SLOPED CEILING

LIVING RM.
$15^0 \times 17^0$

P.

PANTRY

TERRACE

Width 34'-8"
Depth 48'-0"

DESIGN
2423
Square Footage: 864

A true vacationer's delight, this two-bedroom home extends the finest contemporary livability. Two sets of sliding glass doors open off the kitchen and living room where a sloped ceiling lends added dimension. In the kitchen, full counter space and cabinetry assure ease in meal preparation. A pantry stores all of your canned and boxed goods. In the living room, a fireplace serves as a nice design as well as a practical feature. The rear of the plan is comprised of two bedrooms of identical size. A nearby full bath holds a washer/dryer unit. Two additional closets, as well as two linen closets, add to storage capabilities.

DESIGN
Q202

Square Footage: 680
Unfinished Loft: 419 square feet

Full window walls flood the living and dining rooms of this rustic vacation home with natural light. A full sun deck with built-in barbecue sits just outside the living area and is accessed by sliding glass doors. The entire large living space has a vaulted ceiling to gain spaciousness and to allow for the full-height windows. The efficient U-shaped kitchen has a pass-through counter to the dining area and a corner sink with windows over. A vaulted loft on the second floor overlooks the living room.

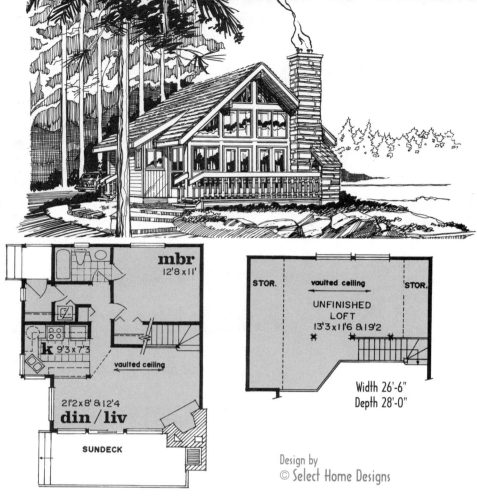

mbr
12'8 x 11'

k 9'3 x 7'3

vaulted ceiling

21'2 x 8' & 12'4

din / liv

SUNDECK

STOR.   vaulted ceiling   STOR.

UNFINISHED
LOFT
13'3 x 11'6 & 19'2

Width 26'-6"
Depth 28'-0"

Design by
© Select Home Designs

DESIGN
Q205

First Floor: 1,185 square feet
Second Floor: 497 square feet
Total: 1,682 square feet

A full-length multi-paned window wall adorns the living room of this cottage and is topped by a gabled roof. The vaulted living room provides a masonry fireplace and wood storage bin. Double doors open to the covered patio. The L-shaped kitchen is open to the dining room. The rear covered veranda opens to a storage laundry room, with the entrance to the single-car garage nearby. The first-floor master suite features a walk-through closet to a private bath with a corner tub and separate shower. Second-floor bedrooms share a full bath.

Design by
© Select Home Designs

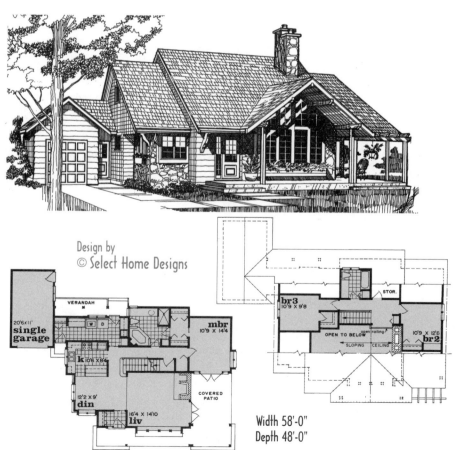

VERANDAH

20'6 x 11'
single garage

k 10'6 x 8'4

mbr
10'9 x 14'4

12'2 x 9'
din

16'4 x 14'10
liv

COVERED
PATIO

br3
10'9 x 9'8

STOR.

OPEN TO BELOW   open railing

SLOPING CEILING

10'9 x 12'6
br2

Width 58'-0"
Depth 48'-0"

mbr
12'x14'2

DECK

Design by
© Select Home Designs

SH.

k
13'7x11'

D

W

br2
10'x10'6

br3
10'x14'
VAULTED

COUNTER

BENCH
FOYER

WOOD
COLUMNS

din
8'x13'
VAULTED

VAULTED

15'x17'8
liv

RAILING

OPEN TO BELOW

RAILING

VAULTED
LOFT

PLANT
LEDGE

SUNKEN
SPA

DECK

Width 36'-0"
Depth 40'-0"

OPEN TO
BELOW

This leisure home is perfect for outdoor living with French doors opening to a large sun deck and sunken spa. The open-beam, vaulted ceiling and high window wall provide views for the living and dining rooms, which are decorated with wood columns and warmed by a fireplace. The step-saving U-shaped kitchen has ample counter space and a bar counter to the dining room. The master bedroom on the first floor features a walk-in closet and bath with twin vanity, shower and soaking tub. A convenient mudroom with adjoining laundry accesses a rear deck. Two bedrooms on the second floor share a full bath. Plans include both a basement and a crawlspace foundation.

**DESIGN
Q499**

First Floor: 1,157 square feet
Second Floor: 638 square feet
Total: 1,795 square feet

VACATION HOMES

DESIGN Q439

First Floor: 1,042 square feet
Second Floor: 456 square feet
Total: 1,498 square feet

With a deck to the front, this vacation home won't miss out on any outdoor fun. The living and dining rooms are dominated by a window wall to take advantage of the view. A high vaulted ceiling and wood-burning fireplace create a warm atmosphere. The U-shaped kitchen, with adjoining laundry room, is open to the dining room with a pass-through counter. Note the deck beyond the kitchen. The master bedroom to the rear offers a full bath with large linen closet. Two family bedrooms upstairs share a full bath with skylight.

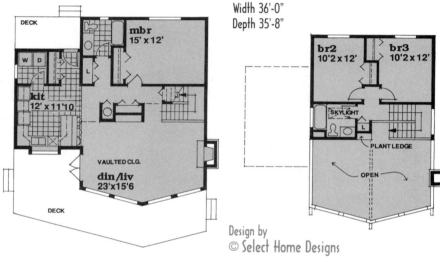

Width 36'-0"
Depth 35'-8"

DECK

mbr
15' x 12'

W D

kit
12' x 11'10

VAULTED CLG.

din/liv
23'x15'6

DECK

br2
10'2 x 12'

br3
10'2 x 12'

SKYLIGHT

PLANT LEDGE

OPEN

Design by
© Select Home Designs

DESIGN Q430

First Floor: 1,061 square feet
Second Floor: 482 square feet
Total: 1,543 square feet

A sun deck makes this design popular, but it is enhanced by views through an expansive wall of glass in the living and dining rooms. They are warmed by a wood stove and enjoy vaulted ceilings, as well. The kitchen is also vaulted and includes a prep island and breakfast bar. Behind the kitchen is a laundry room with side access. Two bedrooms and a full bath are found on the first floor. A skylit staircase leads up to the master bedroom and its walk-in closet and private bath on the second floor.

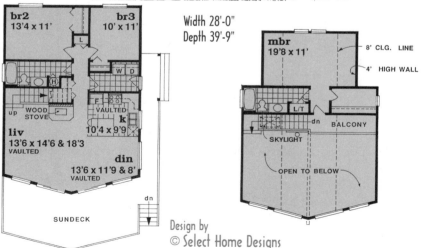

br2
13'4 x 11'

br3
10' x 11'

up WOOD STOVE

VAULTED

W D

liv
13'6 x 14'6 & 18'3
VAULTED

k
10'4 x 9'9

din
13'6 x 11'9 & 8'
VAULTED

SUNDECK

dn

Width 28'-0"
Depth 39'-9"

mbr
19'8 x 11'

8' CLG. LINE
4' HIGH WALL

L/T

dn BALCONY

SKYLIGHT

OPEN TO BELOW

Design by
© Select Home Designs

Design by
© Select Home Designs

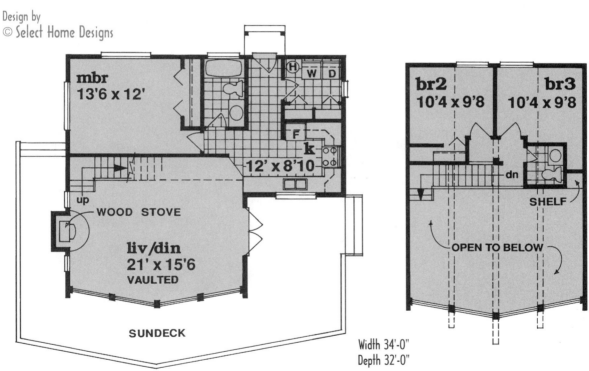

mbr
13'6 x 12'

H W D

F

k
12' x 8'10

up

WOOD STOVE

liv/din
21' x 15'6
VAULTED

SUNDECK

br2
10'4 x 9'8

br3
10'4 x 9'8

dn

SHELF

OPEN TO BELOW

Width 34'-0"
Depth 32'-0"

A surrounding sun deck and expansive window wall capitalize on vacation-home views in this design. The full-height windows flood the living and dining rooms with abundant natural light and bring attention to the high vaulted ceilings. A wood stove in the living area warms cold winter nights. The efficient U-shaped kitchen has ample counter and cupboard space. Behind it is a laundry room and rear entrance. The master bedroom sits on this floor with a large wall closet and full bath. Two family bedrooms on the second floor use a half bath.

**DESIGN
Q424**
First Floor: 898 square feet
Second Floor: 358 square feet
Total: 1,256 square feet

VACATION HOMES

DESIGN 3331

First Floor: 1,115 square feet
Second Floor: 690 square feet
Total: 1,805 square feet

This quaint Tudor cottage holds an open floor plan that is designed for easy living. The gathering room is accented with a cathedral ceiling and a full Palladian window. The dining room is joined to the efficient kitchen with extra entertaining space available on the deck. The first-floor master suite boasts a large compartmented bath and bumped-out windows. Upstairs, a lounge overlooks the gathering room. Two additional bedrooms and a full hall bath complete the second floor.

Design by
© Home Planners

Width 43'-0"
Depth 32'-0"

Quote One®
Cost to build? See page 684
to order complete cost estimate
to build this house in your area!

DESIGN 2488

First Floor: 1,113 square feet
Second Floor: 543 square feet
Total: 1,656 square feet

D

This winsome design performs equally well serving active families as a leisure-time retreat or a retirement cottage that provides a quiet haven. As a year-round home, it provides the second floor with its two sizable bedrooms, full bath and lounge area overlooking the gathering room, to comfortably hold family and guests. The second floor may also be used to accommodate a home office, study, sewing room, music area or hobby room. No matter what the lifestyle, this design functions well.

The home, as shown in the photograph, may differ from the actual blueprints. For more detailed information, please check the floor plans carefully.

Photo by Laszlo Regos

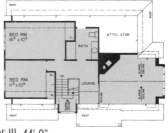

Width 44'-0"
Depth 32'-0"

Design by
© Home Planners

Quote One®
Cost to build? See page 684
to order complete cost estimate
to build this house in your area!

VACATION HOMES

www.homeplanners.com

Photos by Andrew D. Lautman

The home, as shown in the photograph, may differ from the actual blueprints. For more detailed information, please check the floor plans carefully.

REAR VIEW

QUOTE ONE®

Cost to build? See page 684
to order complete cost estimate
to build this house in your area!

Width 30'-0"
Depth 51'-8"

Design by
© Home Planners

Perfect for a narrow lot, this shingle-and-stone Nantucket Cape design caters to casual lifestyles. The side entrance gives direct access to the wonderfully open living areas: gathering room with fireplace; kitchen with angled, pass-through snack bar; and dining area with sliding glass doors to a covered eating area. Note also the large deck that further extends the living potential. Also on this floor is a large master suite. Upstairs is a convenient guest suite with a private deck. Two additional bedrooms share a full bath on this floor.

DESIGN 2493
First Floor: 1,387 square feet
Second Floor: 929 square feet
Total: 2,316 square feet

DESIGN 3658

First Floor: 784 square feet
Second Floor: 275 square feet
Total: 1,059 square feet

L D

This chalet-type vacation home with its steep, overhanging roof, will catch the eye of even the most casual onlooker. It is designed to be completely livable whether the season be for swimming or skiing. The dormitory on the upper level will sleep many vacationers, while the two bedrooms on the first floor provide the more convenient and conventional sleeping facilities. The upper level overlooks the beam-ceilinged living and dining area. With a wraparound terrace and plenty of storage space, what more could you ask for?

Design by
© Home Planners

Width 32'-0"
Depth 30'-0"

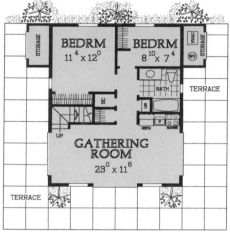

Cost to build? See page 684
to order complete cost estimate
to build this house in your area!

DESIGN 3842

Main Level: 1,328 square feet
Upper Level: 503 square feet
Lower Level: 403 square feet
Total: 2,234 square feet

Expansive views enhance the floor plan of this fine retreat or second home. Thoughtful planning creates open, flowing spaces on the main level. Here, a living room warmed by a fireplace shares space with an efficient eating nook and kitchen. Two bedrooms—one a master suite—complete this level. The upper level contains two family bedrooms, a full bath and an open loft that overlooks the main-level living room. The lower level includes a large basement area, full bath and covered patio.

Design by
© Home Planners

Width 44'-0"
Depth 52'-0"

Cost to build? See page 684
to order complete cost estimate
to build this house in your area!

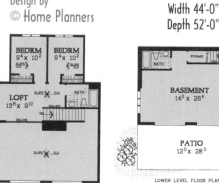

LOWER LEVEL FLOOR PLAN

VACATION HOMES

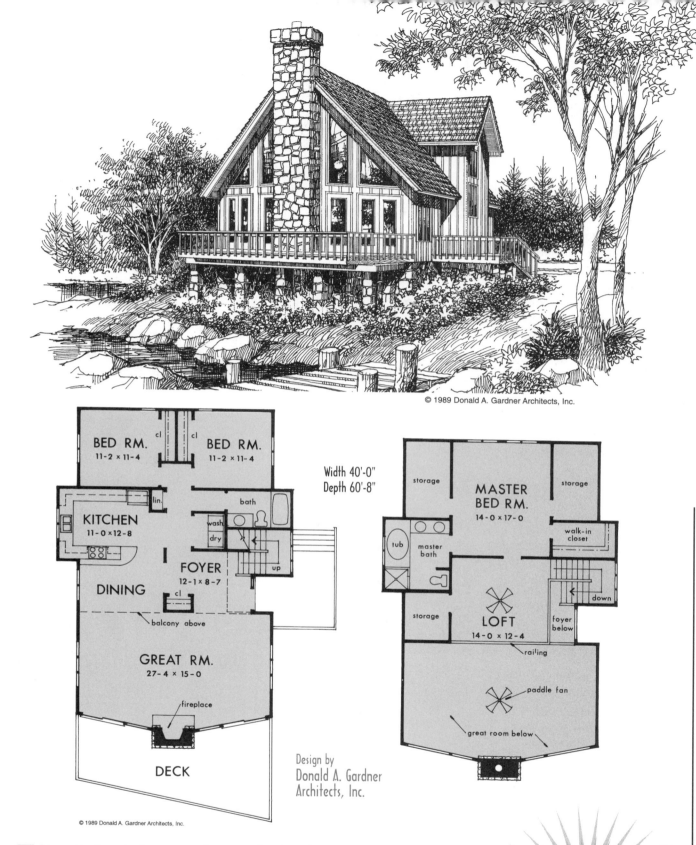

© 1989 Donald A. Gardner Architects, Inc.

BED RM.
11-2 x 11-4

cl   cl

BED RM.
11-2 x 11-4

lin.

bath

KITCHEN
11-0 x 12-8

wash   dry

FOYER
12-1 x 8-7

up

DINING

cl

balcony above

GREAT RM.
27-4 x 15-0

fireplace

DECK

© 1989 Donald A. Gardner Architects, Inc.

Width 40'-0"
Depth 60'-8"

storage

MASTER BED RM.
14-0 x 17-0

storage

tub   master bath

walk-in closet

down

storage

LOFT
14-0 x 12-4

foyer below

railing

paddle fan

great room below

Design by
Donald A. Gardner
Architects, Inc.

This rustic three-bedroom vacation home allows for casual living both inside and out. The two-story great room offers dramatic space for entertaining with windows to the roof that maximize the outdoor view. A stone fireplace dominates this room. Bedrooms on the first floor share a full bath. The second floor holds the master bedroom with spacious master bath and walk-in closet. A large loft area overlooks the great room and entrance foyer.

DESIGN 9630
First Floor: 1,374 square feet
Second Floor: 608 square feet
Total: 1,982 square feet

VACATION HOMES

DESIGN 1482

First Floor: 1,008 square feet
Second Floor: 637 square feet
Total: 1,645 square feet

Here is a chalet right from the pages of travel folders! In addition to the big bedrooms on the first floor, there are three more upstairs. The large master bedroom offers a balcony that overlooks the lower wood deck. There are two full baths. The first-floor bath is directly accessible from the outdoors. Note the snack bar and the pantry in the kitchen. A laundry area is adjacent to the side door.

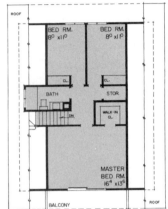

Width 28'-0"
Depth 48'-0"

Design by
© Home Planners

DESIGN 2427

First Floor: 784 square feet
Second Floor: 504 square feet
Total: 1,288 square feet

Make your vacation dreams a reality with this fabulous chalet. The most carefree characteristic is the second-floor master balcony that looks down to the wood deck. Also on the second floor is the three-bunk dormitory. Panels through the knee walls give access to an abundant storage area—perfect for all of your seasonal storage needs. Downstairs, the kitchen utilizes a dining area and an efficient layout and offers direct access outside. A large living room provides a grand view to a fantastic deck and includes a warming fireplace.

Width 44'-0"
Depth 28'-0"

Design by
© Home Planners

VACATION HOMES

www.homeplanners.com

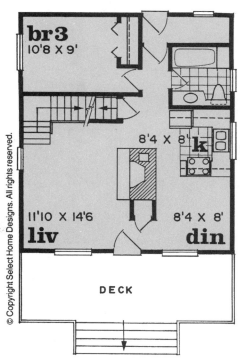

br3
10'8 X 9'

8'4 X 8' **k**

11'10 X 14'6   8'4 X 8'

liv   **din**

DECK

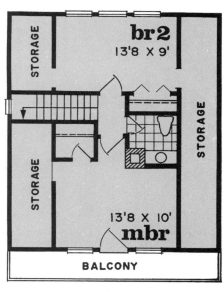

STORAGE

br2
13'8 X 9'

STORAGE

STORAGE

13'8 X 10'
mbr

BALCONY

Width 24'-0"
Depth 36'-0"

REAR VIEW

Design by
© Select Home Designs

This chalet plan is enhanced by a steep gable roof, scalloped fascia boards and fieldstone chimney detail. The front-facing deck and covered balcony add to outdoor living spaces. The fireplace is the main focus in the living room. It separates it from the dining room, which is near the U-shaped kitchen. One bedroom on the first floor has the use of a full hall bath. A storage/mudroom is at the back for keeping skis and boots. Two additional bedrooms and a full bath are upstairs. The master bedroom holds a full bath and walk-in closet. Three large storage areas are also found on the second floor.

VACATION HOMES

**DESIGN
Q207**
First Floor: 672 square feet
Second Floor: 401 square feet
Total: 1,073 square feet

Order Blueprints Toll Free 1-800-521-6797

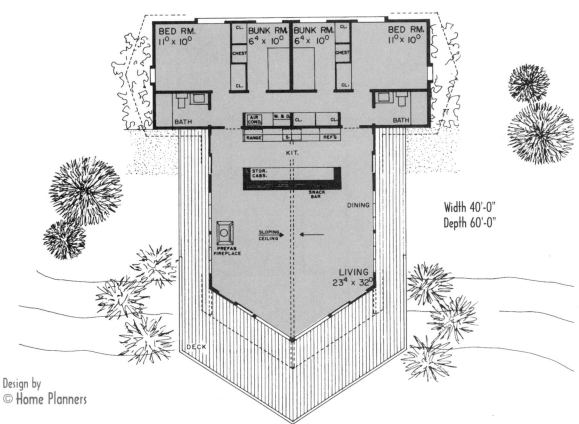

Width 40'-0"
Depth 60'-0"

VACATION HOMES

DESIGN 2439
Square Footage: 1,312

Here is a wonderfully organized plan with an exterior that will command the attention of each and every passerby. The rooflines and the pointed glass gable-end wall will be noticed immediately—the delightful deck will be quickly noticed, too. Inside, visitors will be thrilled by the spaciousness of the huge living room. The ceilings slope upward to the exposed ridge beam. A free-standing fireplace will make its contribution to a cheerful atmosphere. The kitchen offers a snack bar to this area. The sleeping zone has two bedrooms, two bunk rooms, two full baths, two built-in chests and fine closet space.

DESIGN 1451

First Floor: 1,224 square feet
Second Floor: 464 square feet
Total: 1,688 square feet

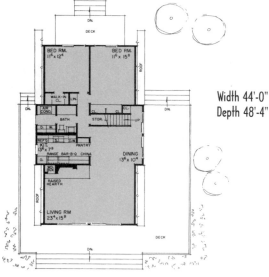

Design by
© Home Planners

Width 44'-0"
Depth 48'-4"

This dramatic A-frame design will surely command its share of attention wherever located. Its soaring roof and large glass areas put this design in a class all on its own. Raised wood decks on all sides provide delightful outdoor living areas. In addition, there is a balcony outside the second-floor master bedroom. The attractive raised-hearth fireplace is a favorite feature of the living room. Another favored highlight is the lounge area overlooking the living room. The kitchen work center has all the conveniences of home. Note the barbecue unit, pantry and china cabinet.

DESIGN 2431

First Floor: 1,057 square feet
Second Floor: 406 square feet
Total: 1,463 square feet

Dramatic use of glass and sweeping lines characterize a classic favorite—the A-frame. The sloped ceiling and exposed beams in the living room are gorgeous touches complemented by a wide deck for enjoying fresh air. The convenience of the central bath with attached powder room is accentuated by space here for washer and dryer. The truly outstanding feature of this plan, however, is its magnificent master suite. There's a private balcony outside and a balcony lounge inside—the scenery is splendid from every angle.

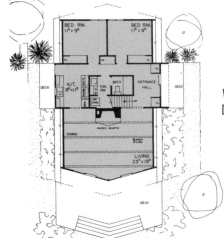

Width 28'-0"
Depth 60'-0"

Design by
© Home Planners

VACATION HOMES

Design by
© Home Planners

Main level floor plan:
- STOR.
- BATH
- CL.
- BED RM. 9⁰ x 12⁰
- RANGE REF'G
- KIT. 11⁸ x 8⁰
- SINK
- CL.
- DN.
- UP
- DN.
- SNACKS
- DINING
- ROOF
- ROOF
- DN.
- LIVING 23⁰ x 15⁴
- DECK

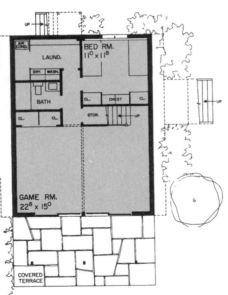

Lower level floor plan:
- UP
- AIR COND.
- LAUND.
- BED RM. 11⁰ x 11⁸
- DRY. WASH.
- BATH
- CL.
- CHEST
- CL.
- CL.
- CL.
- STOR.
- UP
- GAME RM. 22⁸ x 15⁰
- COVERED TERRACE

Width 28'-0"
Depth 32'-0"

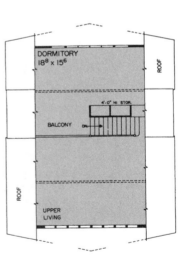

Upper level floor plan:
- DORMITORY 18⁸ x 15⁶
- ROOF
- 4'-0" HI STOR.
- BALCONY
- DN.
- ROOF
- UPPER LIVING

VACATION HOMES

DESIGN 1499

Main Level: 896 square feet
Upper Level: 298 square feet
Lower Level: 896 square feet
Total: 2,090 square feet

Three-level living results in family living patterns that will foster a delightful feeling of informality. Upon arrival at this charming second home, each family member will enthusiastically welcome the change in environmen—both indoors and out. Whether looking down into the the living room from the dormitory balcony, walking through the sliding doors to the huge deck, or participating in some family activity in the game room, everyone will count the hours spent here as relaxing ones. Study the plan carefully. Note the sleeping facilities on each of the three levels. Two bedrooms and a dormitory all keep the family and friends comfortably. There are two full baths, a separate laundry room and plenty of storage. Don't miss the efficient U-shaped kitchen.

Design by
© Home Planners

Width 35'-0"
Depth 52'-0"

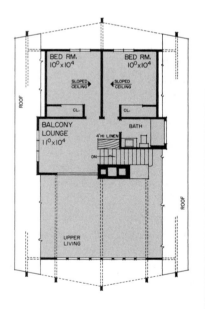

If ever a design had "vacation home" written all over it, this one does. Built to accomadate the slopes, this hillside design with an exposed lower level meets winter vacation needs without a second thought. The covered lower terrace is the ideal ski storage area. A ski lounge with a raised hearth highlights this level. The main floor holds slope-ceilinged dining and living areas (with raised-hearth fireplace), a kitchen with a patio, two bedrooms and a full bath. The most carefree characteristic is the second-floor balcony that looks down to the living room. Also on the second floor are two additional bedrooms and a bath.

DESIGN 1475
Main Level: 1,120 square feet
Upper Level: 522 square feet
Lower Level: 616 square feet
Total: 2,258 square feet

VACATION HOMES

DESIGN 1437

First Floor: 592 square feet
Second Floor: 592 square feet
Total: 1,184 square feet

This design is a compact leisure-time home with plenty of livability and a refreshing exterior. Whether overlooking the lake shore, or perched deep in the woods, the view of the surrounding outdoors will be enjoyed to the fullest. The expanses of glass will permit those inside to be delightfully conscious of nature's beaty. The deck, which envelops the cottage on three sides, will become the favorite spot to enjoy outdoor relaxation.

Design by
© Home Planners

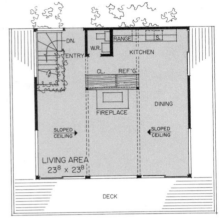

Width 32'-0"
Depth 30'-2"

DESIGN 2420

Main Level: 768 square feet
Lower Level: 768 square feet
Total: 1,536 square feet

Two-level living can be fun anytime. When it comes to two levels by the lake, at the seashore or in the woods, the experience will be positively delightful. Two huge living areas include a lower game room filled with natural light from two sets of sliding glass doors, with two bedrooms and a bath nearby, and an upper-level living room, also with a set of sliding glass doors and a dining area at one end.

Design by
© Home Planners

Width 40'-0"
Depth 44'-0"

Design by
© Home Planners

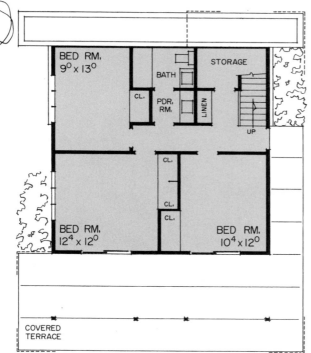

BED RM.
9⁰ x 13⁰

BATH

STORAGE

CL.

PDR. RM.

LINEN

UP

CL.

CL.

CL.

BED RM.
12⁴ x 12⁰

BED RM.
10⁴ x 12⁰

COVERED TERRACE

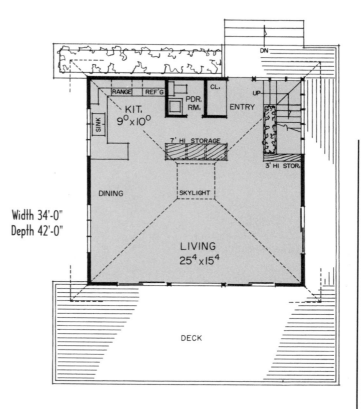

Width 34'-0"
Depth 42'-0"

DN

RANGE   REF'G   PDR. RM.   CL.   ENTRY   UP

KIT.
9⁰ x 10⁰

SINK

7' HI STORAGE

3' HI STOR.

DINING

SKYLIGHT

LIVING
25⁴ x 15⁴

DECK

Vacation living patterns, because of the very nature of things, are different than the everyday living of the city or suburban America. However, they can be made to be even more delightfully so, when called upon to function in harmony with such a distinctive two-level design as this. The upper level is the pleasently open and spacious living level. The ceilings are sloped and converge at the skylight. Outside the glass sliding doors is the large deck that looks down to the surrounding countryside. The lower level contains three bedrooms, a full bath, a linen closet and a large storage area.

**DESIGN
1468**
Main Level: 676 square feet
Lower Level: 676 square feet
Total: 1,352 square feet

VACATION HOMES

I f you have the urge to make your vacation home one that has a distinctive flair of individuality, definite consideration should be given to the design illustrated here. Not only does this plan present a unique exterior, but it also offers an exceptional living pattern. The basic living area is a hexagon. To this space, conscious geometric shape is incorporated with the sleeping wings and baths. The center of the living area enjoys a warming fireplace as its focal point.

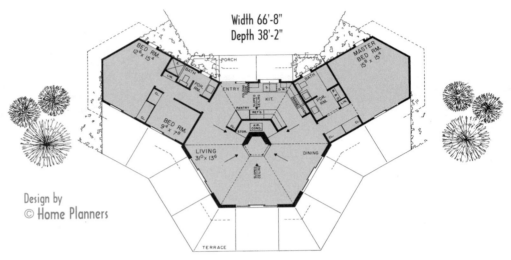

Width 66'-8"
Depth 38'-2"

Design by
© Home Planners

DESIGN 1404
Square Footage: 1,336

T his design, with its frame exterior and large glass areas, has as its dramatic focal point a hexagonal living area that gives way to interesting angles. The spacious living area features sliding glass doors through which traffic may pass to the terrace stretching across the entire length of the house. The wide overhanging roofs project over the terraces, thus providing partial protection from the weather. The sloping ceilings converge above the unique, open fireplace. The sleeping areas are located in each wing from the hexagonal center.

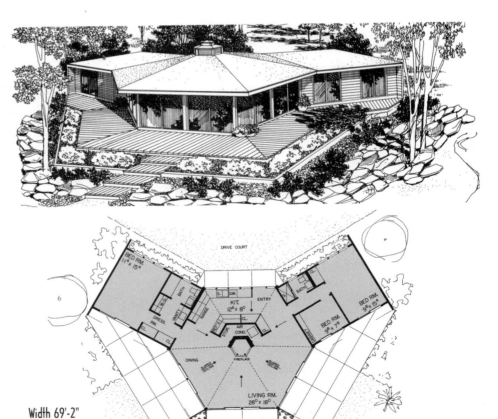

Width 69'-2"
Depth 39'-11"

Design by
© Home Planners

VACATION HOMES

www.homeplanners.com

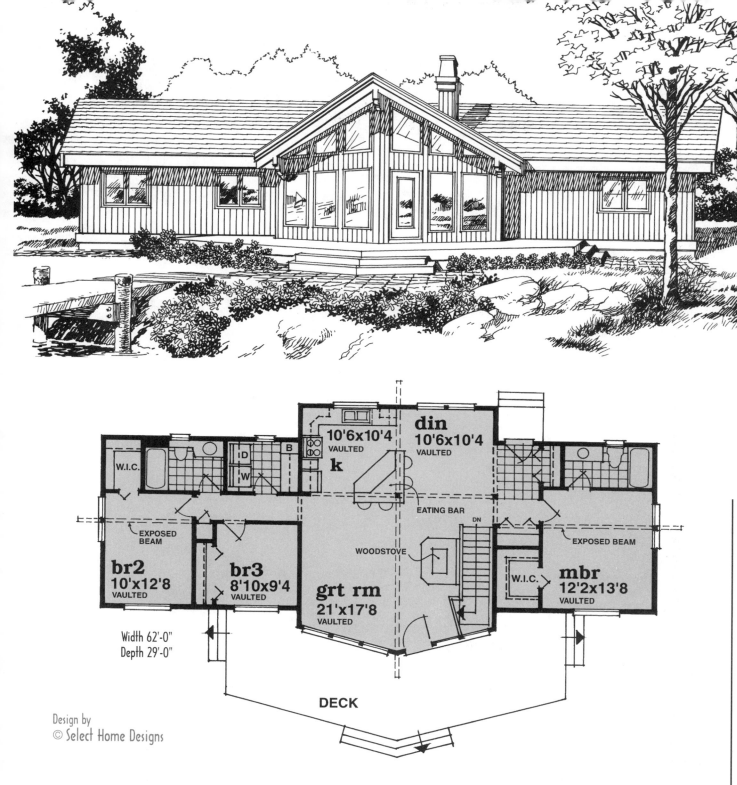

din
10'6x10'4
VAULTED

10'6x10'4
VAULTED

k

W.I.C.

ID
W
B

EATING BAR

DN

WOODSTOVE

EXPOSED BEAM

EXPOSED BEAM

br2
10'x12'8
VAULTED

br3
8'10x9'4
VAULTED

grt rm
21'x17'8
VAULTED

W.I.C.

mbr
12'2x13'8
VAULTED

Width 62'-0"
Depth 29'-0"

DECK

Design by
© Select Home Designs

This three-bedroom leisure home is perfect for the family that spends casual time out of doors. An expansive wall of glass gives a spectacular view to the great room and accentuates the high vaulted ceilings throughout the design. The great room is also warmed by a hearth and is open to the dining room and L-shaped kitchen. A triangular snack bar graces the kitchen and provides space for casual meals. Bedrooms are split, with the master bedroom on the right side of the plan and family bedrooms on the left. The master suite contains exposed beams in the ceiling, a walk-in closet and a full bath with soaking tub. Family bedrooms share a full bath; Bedroom 2 features a walk-in closet.

**DESIGN
Q516**
Square Footage: 1,405

VACATION HOMES

DESIGN
Q438
Square Footage: 1,495

This three-bedroom cottage has just the right rustic mix of vertical wood siding and stone accents. High vaulted ceilings are featured throughout the living room and master bedroom. The living room also includes a fireplace and full-height windows overlooking the deck. The dining room provides double-door access to the deck. A convenient kitchen has a U-shaped work area with a large storage space beyond. Two family bedrooms share a bath between them. The master suite features a walk-in closet, private bath and access to the deck.

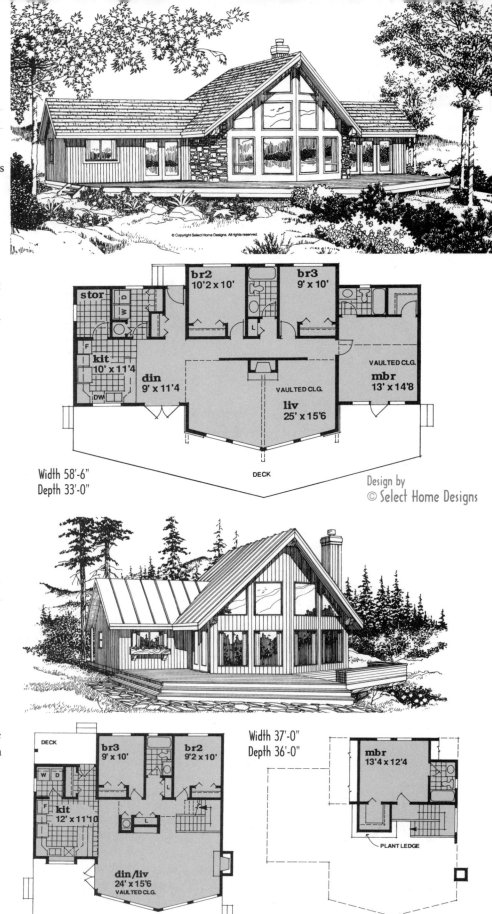

Width 58'-6"
Depth 33'-0"

Design by
© Select Home Designs

DESIGN
Q437
First Floor: 1,084 square feet
Second Floor: 343 square feet
Total: 1,427 square feet

Vertical siding and a wide deck grace the exterior of this plan. Inside, the floor plan features a secluded second-floor master suite with private bath and walk-in closet. Extra-high vaulted ceilings and a wall of windows make the living/dining room a comfortable gathering area. It is warmed by a fireplace and open to the U-shaped kitchen. A laundry room is just beyond. The back entrance has a closet and opens to a rear deck. Two family bedrooms on the first floor share a full bath.

Width 37'-0"
Depth 36'-0"

Design by
© Select Home Designs

VACATION HOMES

www.homeplanners.com

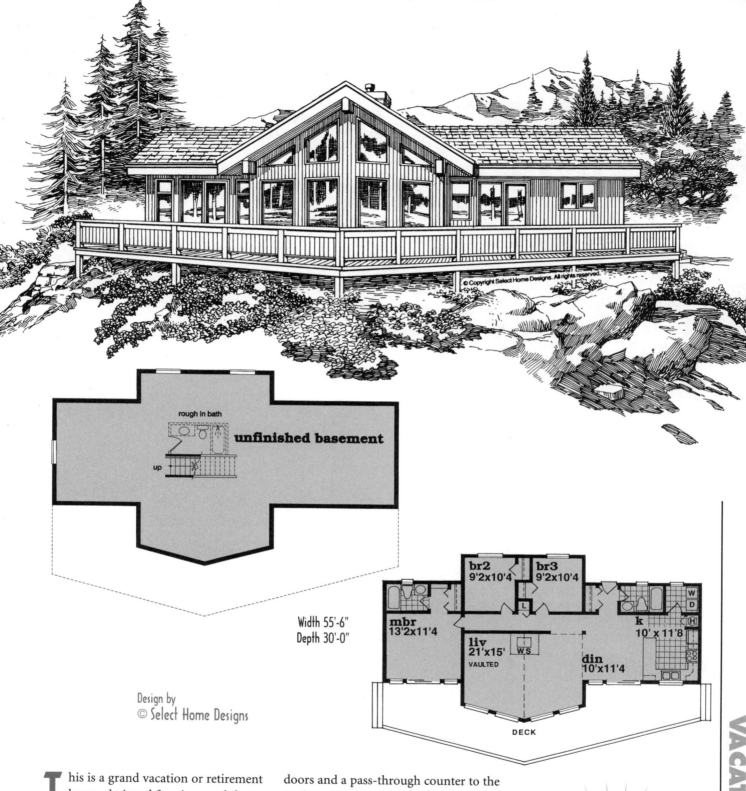

rough in bath

unfinished basement

up

Width 55'-6"
Depth 30'-0"

Design by
© Select Home Designs

br2
9'2x10'4

br3
9'2x10'4

L

mbr
13'2x11'4

liv
21'x15'
VAULTED

W S

din
10'x11'4

k
10' x 11'8

W
D
H

DECK

This is a grand vacation or retirement home, designed for views and the outdoor lifestyle. The full-width deck complements the abundant windows in rooms facing its way. The living room is made for gathering. It features a vaulted ceiling, a fireplace and full-height windows overlooking the deck. Open to this living space is the dining room with sliding glass doors to the out-doors and a pass-through counter to the U-shaped kitchen. The kitchen connects to a laundry area and has a window over the sink for more outdoor views. Two family bedrooms sit in the middle of the plan. They share a full bath. The master suite has a private bath and deck views. The basement option for this plan adds 1,296 square feet to its total and extends the depth to 33 feet.

DESIGN Q429
Square Footage: 1,230

VACATION HOMES

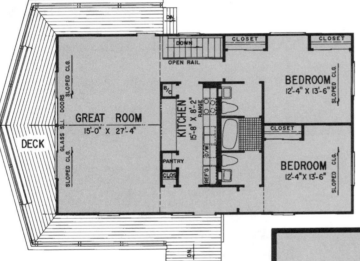

GREAT ROOM
15'-0" X 27'-4"

DECK

KITCHEN
15'-8" X 8'-2"

BEDROOM
12'-4" X 13'-6"

BEDROOM
12'-4" X 13'-6"

CLOSET

CLOSET

CLOSET

DOWN

OPEN RAIL

PANTRY

SLOPED CLG.

GLASS SLI. DOORS

SLOPED CLG.

SLOPED CLG.

SLOPED CLG.

RANGE

REF'G

D/W

DN.

Width 52'-0"
Depth 36'-0"

QUOTE ONE®
Cost to build? See page 684
to order complete cost estimate
to build this house in your area!

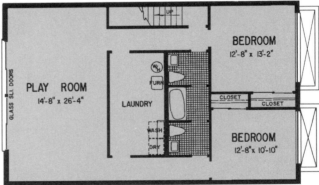

PLAY ROOM
14'-8" X 26'-4"

LAUNDRY

BEDROOM
12'-8" x 13'-2"

BEDROOM
12'-8" x 10'-10"

CLOSET

CLOSET

GLASS SLI. DOORS

W.H.

FURN.

WASH

DRY

UP

Design by
© Home Planners

DESIGN
4027
Square Footage: 1,320

VACATION HOMES

Good things come in small packages! The size and shape of this design will help hold down construction costs without sacrificing livability. The enormous great room is a multi-purpose living space with room for a dining area and several seating areas. Also notice the sloped ceilings. Sliding glass doors provide access to the wraparound deck and sweeping views of the outdoors. The well-equipped kitchen includes a pass-through and pantry. Two bedrooms, each with sloped ceilings and compartmented bath, and a play room round out the plan. Develop space in the basement as needs arise.

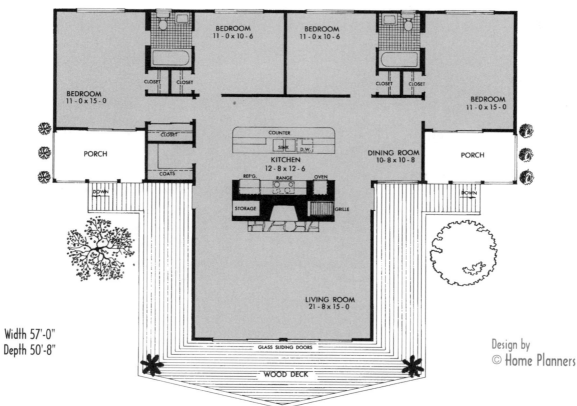

Width 57'-0"
Depth 50'-8"

Design by
© Home Planners

The perfect vacation home combines open, informal living spaces with lots of sleeping space. The spacious living room has a warming fireplace and sliding glass doors to the deck. Convenient to the dining room, the efficient kitchen is carefully placed so as not to interfere with the living room. Notice the four spacious bedrooms—there's plenty of room for accommodating guests. Two of the bedrooms boast private porches.

DESIGN
4015
Square Footage: 1,420

DESIGN Z042

First Floor: 895 square feet
Second Floor: 576 square feet
Total: 1,471 square feet

The four-season Cape Cod cottage features a lovely sun room that opens from the dining room and allows great views. An angled hearth warms the living and dining areas. The gourmet kitchen has an island counter with a snack bar. The main-level master bedroom enjoys a walk-in closet and a nearby bath. A daylight basement allows a lower-level portico.

Width 26'-0"
Depth 36'-0"

Design by
© Drummond Designs, Inc.

DESIGN Z054

First Floor: 576 square feet
Second Floor: 480 square feet
Total: 1,056 square feet

If you have a site with beautiful views, this is the perfect plan for you! Windows abound, from the front-facing sun room to the wall of windows off the dining/living area with sliding doors opening to an expansive veranda. A rounded-hearth fireplace is a focal point of the living area. Two bedrooms and a full bath are located on the upper level. The master bedroom provides room for a private sitting area. This home is designed with a basement foundation.

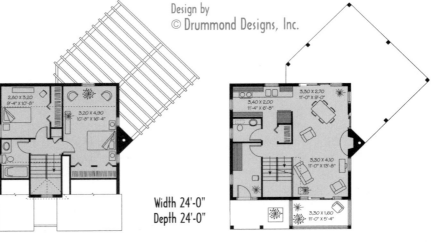

Design by
© Drummond Designs, Inc.

Width 24'-0"
Depth 24'-0"

VACATION HOMES

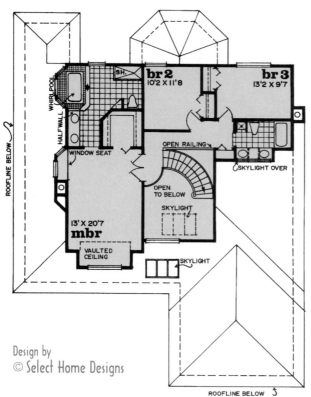

SH.

br 2
10'2 X 11'8

br 3
13'2 X 9'7

WHIRLPOOL

HALFWALL

WINDOW SEAT

OPEN RAILING

SKYLIGHT OVER

ROOFLINE BELOW

OPEN TO BELOW

SKYLIGHT

13' X 20'7

mbr

VAULTED CEILING

SKYLIGHT

Design by
© Select Home Designs

ROOFLINE BELOW

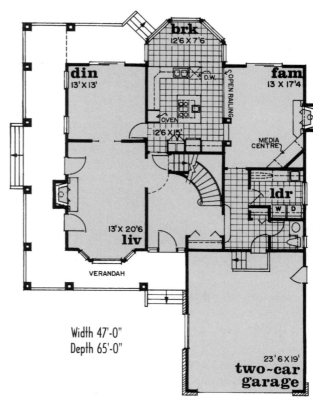

brk
12'6 X 7'6

din
13' X 13'

fam
13 X 17'4

OPEN RAILING

OVEN

12'6 X 15'

D.W.

MEDIA CENTRE

ldr

W   D

13' X 20'6

liv

VERANDAH

Width 47'-0"
Depth 65'-0"

23' 6 X 19'

two~car
garage

This unique design is bedecked with a veranda that wraps around two sides of the design. The skylit foyer contains a curved staircase to the second floor. On the left are the living room with fireplace and bay window and dining room with sliding glass doors to the veranda. The living room accesses the veranda through double doors. A family room at the other end of the plan holds a corner media center and a fireplace. Sliding glass doors open to the rear yard. In between is an island kitchen with breakfast bay. The bedrooms upstairs include a master suite with walk-in closet, vaulted alcove and private bath with whirlpool tub. Family bedrooms share a full bath that includes a double vanity.

DESIGN Q260
First Floor: 1,446 square feet
Second Floor: 1,047 square feet
Total: 2,493 square feet

When You're Ready To Order . . .

Let Us Show You Our Home Blueprint Package.

Building a home? Planning a home? Our Blueprint Package has nearly everything you need to get the job done right, whether you're working on your own or with help from an architect, designer, builder or subcontractors. Each Blueprint Package is the result of many hours of work by licensed architects or professional designers.

QUALITY

Hundreds of hours of painstaking effort have gone into the development of your blueprint set. Each home has been quality-checked by professionals to insure accuracy and buildability.

VALUE

Because we sell in volume, you can buy professional-quality blueprints at a fraction of their development cost. With our plans, your dream home design costs only a few hundred dollars, not the thousands of dollars that custom architects charge.

SERVICE

Once you've chosen your favorite home plan, you'll receive fast, efficient service whether you choose to mail or fax your order to us or call us toll free at 1-800-521-6797. For customer service, call toll free 1-888-690-1116.

SATISFACTION

Over 50 years of service to satisfied home plan buyers provide us unparalleled experience and knowledge in producing quality blueprints. What this means to you is satisfaction with our product and performance.

ORDER TOLL FREE 1-800-521-6797

After you've looked over our Blueprint Package and Important Extras on the following pages, simply mail the order form on page 701 or call toll free on our Blueprint Hotline: 1-800-521-6797. We're ready and eager to serve you. For customer service, call toll free 1-888-690-1116.

Each set of blueprints is an interrelated collection of detail sheets which includes components such as floor plans, interior and exterior elevations, dimensions, cross-sections, diagrams and notations. These sheets show exactly how your house is to be built.

Among the sheets included may be:

Frontal Sheet
This artist's sketch of the exterior of the house gives you an idea of how the house will look when built and landscaped. Large ink-line floor plans show all levels of the house and provide an overview of your new home's livability, as well as a handy reference for deciding on furniture placement.

Foundation Plan
This sheet shows the foundation layout

SAMPLE PACKAGE

including support walls, excavated and unexcavated areas, if any, and foundation notes. If slab construction rather than basement, the plan shows footings and details for a monolithic slab. This page, or another in the set, may include a sample plot plan for locating your house on a building site.

Detailed Floor Plans
These plans show the layout of each floor of the house. Rooms and interior spaces are carefully dimensioned and keys are given for cross-section details provided later in the plans. The positions of electrical outlets and switches are shown.

House Cross-Sections
Large-scale views show sections or cut-aways of the foundation, interior walls, exterior walls, floors, stairways and roof details. Additional cross-sections may show important changes in floor, ceiling or roof heights or the relationship of one level to another. Extremely valuable for construction, these sections show exactly how the various parts of the house fit together.

Interior Elevations
Many of our drawings show the design and placement of kitchen and bathroom cabinets, laundry areas, fireplaces, bookcases and other built-ins. Little "extras," such as mantelpiece and wainscoting drawings, plus moulding sections, provide details that give your home that custom touch.

Exterior Elevations
These drawings show the front, rear and sides of your house and give necessary notes on exterior materials and finishes. Particular attention is given to cornice detail, brick and stone accents or other finish items that make your home unique.

Note: Because of the diversity of local building codes, our blueprints may not include Electrical, Plumbing or Mechanical plans or layouts.

Frontal Sheet

Foundation Plans

Detailed Floor Plans

Exterior Elevations

Interior Elevations

House Cross-Sections

*I*mportant Extras To Do The Job Right!

Introducing eight important planning and construction aids developed by our professionals to help you succeed in your home-building project.

MATERIALS LIST

(Note: Because of the diversity of local building codes, our Materials List does not include mechanical materials.)

For many of the designs in our portfolio, we offer a customized materials take-off that is invaluable in planning and estimating the cost of your new home. This Materials List outlines the quantity, type and size of materials needed to build your house (with the exception of mechanical system items). Included are framing lumber, windows and doors, kitchen and bath cabinetry, rough and finish hardware, and much more. This handy list helps you or your builder cost out materials and serves as a reference sheet when you're compiling bids. A Materials List cannot be ordered before blueprints are ordered.

SPECIFICATION OUTLINE

This valuable 16-page document is critical to building your house correctly. Designed to be filled in by you or your builder, this book lists 166 stages or items crucial to the building process. It provides a comprehensive review of the construction process and helps in making choices of materials. When combined with the blueprints, a signed contract, and a schedule, it becomes a legal document and record for the building of your home.

QUOTE ONE®

Summary Cost Report / Materials Cost Report

A new service for estimating the cost of building select designs, the Quote One® system is available in two separate stages: The Summary Cost Report and the Materials Cost Report.

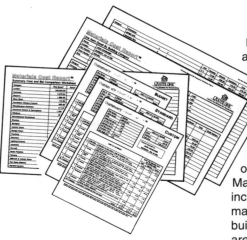

The Summary Cost report is the first stage in the package and shows the total cost per square foot for your chosen home in your zip-code area and then breaks that cost down into various categories showing the costs for building materials, labor and installation. The total cost for the report (which includes three grades: Budget, Standard and Custom) is just $29.95 for one home, and additionals are only $14.95. These reports allow you to evaluate your building budget and compare the costs of building a variety of homes in your area.

Make even more informed decisions about your home-building project with the second phase of our package, our Materials Cost Report. This tool is invaluable in planning and estimating the cost of your new home. The material and installation (labor and equipment) cost is shown for each of over 1,000 line items provided in the Materials List (Standard grade) which is included when you purchase this estimating tool. It allows you to determine building costs for your specific zip-code area and for your chosen home design. Space is allowed for additional estimates from contractors and subcontractors. This invaluable tool is available for a price of $120 ($130 for a Schedule C4–L4 plan) which includes a Materials List. A Materials Cost Report cannot be ordered before blueprints are ordered.

The Quote One® program is continually updated with new plans. If you are interested in a plan that is not indicated as Quote One®, please call and ask our sales reps, they will be happy to verify the status for you. To order these invaluable reports, use the order form on page 701 or call 1-800-521-6797.

Plan-A-Home®

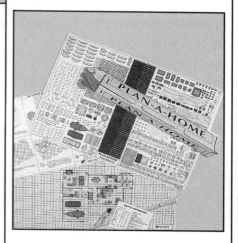

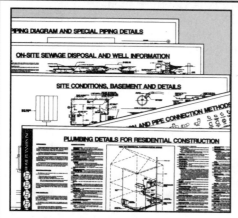

PLUMBING

The Blueprint Package includes locations for all the plumbing fixtures in your new house, including sinks, lavatories, tubs, showers, toilets, laundry trays and water heaters. However, if you want to know more about the complete plumbing system, these 24x36-inch detail sheets will prove very useful. Prepared to meet requirements of the National Plumbing Code, these six fact-filled sheets give general information on pipe schedules, fittings, sump-pump details, water-softener hookups, septic system details and much more. Color-coded sheets include a glossary of terms.

ELECTRICAL

The locations for every electrical switch, plug and outlet are shown in your Blueprint Package. However, these Electrical Details go further to take the mystery out of household electrical systems. Prepared to meet requirements of the National Electrical Code, these comprehensive 24x36-inch drawings come packed with helpful information, including wire sizing, switch-installation schematics, cable-routing details, appliance wattage, door-bell hookups, typical service panel circuitry and much more. Six sheets are bound together and color-coded for easy reference. A glossary of terms is also included.

Plan-A-Home® is an easy-to-use tool that helps you design a new home, arrange furniture in a new or existing home, or plan a remodeling project. Each package contains:

- **More than 700 reusable peel-off planning symbols** on a self-stick vinyl sheet, including walls, windows, doors, all types of furniture, kitchen components, bath fixtures and many more.

- **A reusable, transparent, ¼-inch scale planning grid** that matches the scale of actual working drawings (¼-inch equals one foot). This grid provides the basis for house layouts of up to 140x92 feet.

- **Tracing paper** and a protective sheet for copying or transferring your completed plan.

- **A felt-tip pen,** with water-soluble ink that wipes away quickly.

Plan-A-Home® lets you lay out areas as large as a 7,500 square foot, six-bedroom, seven-bath house.

CONSTRUCTION

The Blueprint Package contains everything an experienced builder needs to construct a particular house. However, it doesn't show all the ways that houses can be built, nor does it explain alternate construction methods. To help you understand how your house will be built—and offer additional techniques—this set of drawings depicts the materials and methods used to build foundations, fireplaces, walls, floors and roofs. Where appropriate, the drawings show acceptable alternatives. These six sheets will answer questions for the advanced do-it-yourselfer or home planner.

MECHANICAL

This package contains fundamental principles and useful data that will help you make informed decisions and communicate with subcontractors about heating and cooling systems. The 24x36-inch drawings contain instructions and samples that allow you to make simple load calculations and preliminary sizing and costing analysis. Covered are today's most commonly used systems from heat pumps to solar fuel systems. The package is packed full of illustrations and diagrams to help you visualize components and how they relate to one another.

To Order, Call Toll Free 1-800-521-6797

To add these important extras to your Blueprint Package, simply indicate your choices on the order form on page 701 or call us Toll Free 1-800-521-6797 and we'll tell you more about these exciting products. For customer service, call toll free 1-888-690-1116.

D *The Deck Blueprint Package*

Many of the homes in this book can be enhanced with a professionally designed Home Planners' Deck Plan. Those home plans highlighted with a **D** have a matching or corresponding deck plan available which includes a Deck Plan Frontal Sheet, Deck Framing and Floor Plans, Deck Elevations and a Deck Materials List. A Standard Deck Details Package, also available, provides all the how-to information necessary for building *any* deck. Our Complete Deck Building Package contains 1 set of Custom Deck Plans of your choice, plus 1 set of Standard Deck Building Details all for one low price. Our plans and details are carefully prepared in an easy-to-understand format that will guide you through every stage of your deck-building project. This page contains a sampling of 12 of the 25 different Deck layouts to match your favorite house. See page 688 for prices and ordering information.

SPLIT-LEVEL SUN DECK
Deck Plan D100

BI-LEVEL DECK WITH COVERED DINING
Deck Plan D101

WRAP-AROUND FAMILY DECK
Deck Plan D104

DECK FOR DINING AND VIEWS
Deck Plan D107

TREND SETTER DECK
Deck Plan D110

TURN-OF-THE-CENTURY DECK
Deck Plan D111

WEEKEND ENTERTAINER DECK
Deck Plan D112

CENTER-VIEW DECK
Deck Plan D114

KITCHEN-EXTENDER DECK
Deck Plan D115

SPLIT-LEVEL ACTIVITY DECK
Deck Plan D117

TRI-LEVEL DECK WITH GRILL
Deck Plan D119

CONTEMPORARY LEISURE DECK
Deck Plan D120

L The Landscape Blueprint Package

For the homes marked with an L in this book, Home Planners has created a front-yard landscape plan that matches or is complementary in design to the house plan. These comprehensive blueprint packages include a Frontal Sheet, Plan View, Regionalized Plant & Materials List, a sheet on Planting and Maintaining Your Landscape, Zone Maps and Plant Size and Description Guide. These plans will help you achieve professional results, adding value and enjoyment to your property for years to come. Each set of blueprints is a full 18" x 24" in size with clear, complete instructions and easy-to-read type. Six of the forty front-yard Landscape Plans to match your favorite house are shown below.

Regional Order Map

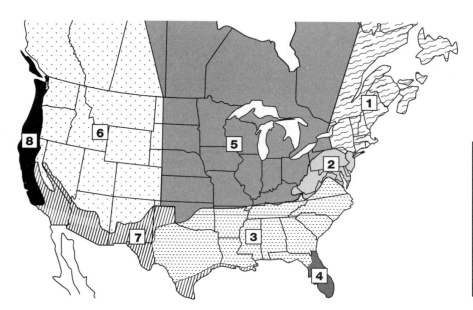

Most of the Landscape Plans shown on these pages are available with a Plant & Materials List adapted by horticultural experts to 8 different regions of the country. Please specify Geographic Region when ordering your plan. See page 688 for prices, ordering information and regional availability.

Region	1	Northeast
Region	2	Mid-Atlantic
Region	3	Deep South
Region	4	Florida & Gulf Coast
Region	5	Midwest
Region	6	Rocky Mountains
Region	7	Southern California & Desert Southwest
Region	8	Northern California & Pacific Northwest

CAPE COD COTTAGE
Landscape Plan L202

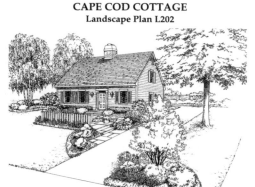

GAMBREL-ROOF COLONIAL
Landscape Plan L203

CENTER-HALL COLONIAL
Landscape Plan L204

CLASSIC NEW ENGLAND COLONIAL
Landscape Plan L205

COUNTRY-STYLE FARMHOUSE
Landscape Plan L207

TRADITIONAL SPLIT-LEVEL
Landscape Plan L228

Price Schedule & Plans Index

Blueprint Price Schedule
(Prices guaranteed through December 31, 2000)

Tiers	1-set Study Package	4-set Building Package	8-set Building Package	1-set Reproducible Sepias	Home Customizer® Package
P1	$20	$50	$90	N/A	N/A
P2	$40	$70	$110	N/A	N/A
P3	$60	$90	$130	N/A	N/A
P4	$80	$110	$150	N/A	N/A
P5	$100	$130	$170	N/A	N/A
P6	$120	$150	$190	N/A	N/A
A1	$400	$440	$500	$600	$650
A2	$440	$480	$540	$660	$710
A3	$480	$520	$580	$720	$770
A4	$520	$560	$620	$780	$830
C1	$560	$600	$660	$840	$890
C2	$600	$640	$700	$900	$950
C3	$650	$690	$750	$950	$1000
C4	$700	$740	$800	$1000	$1050
L1	$750	$790	$850	$1050	$1100
L2	$800	$840	$900	$1100	$1150
L3	$900	$940	$1000	$1200	$1250
L4	$1000	$1040	$1100	$1300	$1350

Options for plans in Tiers A1–A4
Additional Identical Blueprints in same order for
"A1–L4" price plans......................................$50 per set
Reverse Blueprints (mirror image) with 4- or 8-set
order for "A1–L4" price plans............$50 fee per order
Specification Outlines..$10 each
Materials Lists for "A1–C3" price plans..........$60 each
Materials Lists for "C4–L4" price plans...........$70 each

Options for plans in Tiers P1–P6
Additional Identical Blueprints in same order for
"P1–P6" price plans......................................$10 per set
Reverse Blueprints (mirror image) for "P1–P6"
price plans...$10 per set
1 Set of Deck Construction Details...............$14.95 each
Deck Construction Package............add $10 to Building
Package price
    (1 set of "P1–P6" price plans, plus 1 set Standard
    Deck Construction Details)
1 Set of Gazebo Construction Details..........$14.95 each
Gazebo Construction Package.......add $10 to Building
Package price
    (1 set of "P1–P6" price plans, plus 1 set Standard
    Gazebo Construction Details)

IMPORTANT NOTES
The 1-set study package is marked "not for construction."
Prices for 4- or 8-set Building Packages honored only at time
of original order.

Index

To use the Index below, refer to the design number listed in numerical order (a helpful page reference is also given). Note the price index letter and refer to the House Blueprint Price Schedule above for the cost of one, four or eight sets of blueprints or the cost of a reproducible sepia. Additional prices are shown for identical and reverse blueprint sets, as well as a very useful Materials List for some of the plans. Also note in the Index below those plans that have matching or complementary Deck Plans or Landscape Plans. Refer to the schedules above for prices of these plans. All Home Planners' plans can be customized with Home Planners' Home Customizer® Package. These plans are indicated below with this symbol: 🏠. See page 701 for information. Some plans are also part of our Quote One® estimating service and are indicated by this symbol: 🏛. See page 684 for more information.

To Order: Fill in and send the order form on page 701—or call toll free 1-800-521-6797 or 520-297-8200. Fax: 1-800-224-6699 or 520-544-3086

DESIGN	PRICE	PAGE	MATERIALS LIST	CUSTOMIZABLE	QUOTE ONE®	DECK	DECK PRICE	LANDSCAPE	LANDSCAPE PRICE	REGIONS
1113	A3	111	✓	🏠	🏛	D113	R	L202	X	1-3,5,6,8
1191	A3	110	✓	🏠		D114	R	L225	X	1-3,5,6,8
1311	A3	112	✓	🏠				L225	X	1-3,5,6,8
1318	A4	220	✓	🏠						
1323	A3	122	✓	🏠	🏛	D117	S	L225	X	1-3,5,6,8
1325	A4	113	✓	🏠		D106	S	L225	X	1-3,5,6,8
1361	A4	223	✓	🏠		D117	S	L225	X	1-3,5,6,8
1364	A3	113	✓	🏠		D117	S			
1394	A2	177	✓	🏠		D105	R	L202	X	1-3,5,6,8
1404	A3	674	✓	🏠						
1425	A3	656	✓	🏠						
1437	A2	672	✓	🏠						
1451	A4	669	✓	🏠						
1468	A3	673	✓	🏠						
1475	C1	671	✓	🏠						
1482	A4	666	✓	🏠						
1486	A2	656	✓	🏠						
1499	C1	670	✓	🏠						
1791	A4	173	✓	🏠	🏛	D114	R	L205	Y	1-3,5,6,8
1829	A4	120	✓	🏠		D113	R	L226	X	1-8
1850	C1	359	✓	🏠	🏛					
1858	L1	405	✓	🏠		D101	R			
1868	A4	224	✓	🏠						
1890	A3	117	✓	🏠						

DESIGN	PRICE	PAGE	MATERIALS LIST	CUSTOMIZABLE	QUOTE ONE®	DECK	DECK PRICE	LANDSCAPE	LANDSCAPE PRICE	REGIONS
1892	A4	116	✓	✓		D106	S	L225	X	1-3,5,6,8
1896	A3	116	✓	✓						
1956	A3	225	✓	✓	✓	D117	S			
1957	A4	223	✓	✓	✓	D100	Q	L228	Y	1-8
1974	C2	372	✓	✓						
2145	A3	176	✓	✓	✓			L209	Y	1-6,8
2146	A3	175	✓	✓		D114	R	L203	Y	1-3,5,6,8
2192	C2	207	✓	✓		D117	S	L218	Z	1-6,8
2356	C3	584	✓	✓		D119	S	L219	Z	1-3,5,6,8
2420	A4	672	✓	✓						
2423	A1	657	✓	✓						
2427	A3	666	✓	✓						
2431	A3	669	✓	✓						
2439	A3	668	✓	✓						
2461	A3	674	✓	✓						
2488	A4	662	✓	✓	✓	D102	Q			
2490	C2	343	✓	✓	✓					
2493	A4	663	✓	✓	✓					
2511	C1	356	✓	✓	✓	D108	R	L229	Y	1-8
2534	C2	330	✓	✓	✓			L227	Z	1-8
2538	C1	209	✓	✓		D113	R	L201	Y	1-3,5,6,8
2540	C1	221	✓	✓		D113	R	L205	Y	1-3,5,6,8
2543	L1	415	✓	✓		D107	S	L218	Z	1-6,8
2563	C1	172	✓	✓	✓	D114	R	L201	Y	1-3,5,6,8
2571	A3	179	✓	✓		D114	R	L202	X	1-3,5,6,8
2596	A4	178	✓	✓		D114	R	L201	Y	1-3,5,6,8
2603	A4	115	✓	✓	✓	D106	S	L220	Y	1-3,5,6,8
2606	A3	583	✓	✓	✓			L221	X	1-3,5,6,8
2608	A4	358	✓	✓	✓	D112	R	L228	Y	1-8
2610	C2	215	✓	✓	✓	D114	R	L204	Y	1-3,5,6,8
2622	A3	222	✓	✓	✓	D103	R	L200	X	1-3,5,6,8
2623	A4	209	✓	✓		D100	Q	L205	Y	1-3,5,6,8
2639	C1	210	✓	✓		D114	R	L215	Z	1-6,8
2654	A3	208	✓	✓						
2657	A4	175	✓	✓	✓			L200	X	1-3,5,6,8
2659	C2	202	✓	✓	✓	D113	R	L205	Y	1-3,5,6,8
2660	C4	403	✓	✓						
2661	A4	177	✓	✓	✓	D113	R	L202	X	1-3,5,6,8
2662	C3	22	✓	✓	✓			L216	Y	1-3,5,6,8
2665	C3	402	✓	✓						
2667	C2	219	✓	✓				L216	Y	1-3,5,6,8
2668	C1	218	✓	✓	✓			L214	Z	1-3,5,6,8
2670	C2	617	✓	✓	✓			L236	Z	3,4,7
2671	A4	121	✓	✓	✓	D114	R	L234	Y	1-8
2672	A3	130	✓	✓	✓	D112	R	L226	X	1-8
2679	C3	354	✓	✓						

DESIGN	PRICE	PAGE	MATERIALS LIST	CUSTOMIZABLE	QUOTE ONE®	DECK	DECK PRICE	LANDSCAPE	LANDSCAPE PRICE	REGIONS
2682	A4	174	✓	✓	✓	D115	Q	L200	X	1-3,5,6,8
2683	L1	23	✓	✓	✓	D101	R	L214	Z	1-3,5,6,8
2684	C2	178	✓	✓		D114	R	L204	Y	1-3,5,6,8
2686	C2	381	✓	✓		D112	R	L209	Y	1-6,8
2690	C2	403	✓	✓						
2693	C3	409	✓	✓						
2694	C3	390	✓	✓	✓			L209	Y	1-6,8
2699	C3	170	✓	✓				L211	Y	1-8
2707	A3	87	✓	✓	✓	D117	S	L226	X	1-8
2711	A4	342	✓	✓	✓	D105		L229	Y	1-8
2729	C1	350	✓	✓				L234	Y	1-8
2731	A4	211	✓	✓		D114	R	L205	Y	1-3,5,6,8
2733	A4	221	✓	✓	✓	D100	Q	L205	Y	1-3,5,6,8
2756	C2	335	✓	✓		D101	R	L234	Y	1-8
2761	C1	373	✓	✓				L229	Y	1-8
2774	C1	8	✓	✓	✓	D100	Q	L207	Z	1-6,8
2776	A4	535	✓	✓		D113	R	L207	Z	1-6,8
2777	A4	162	✓	✓		D101	R	L221	X	1-3,5,6,8
2781	C3	340	✓	✓	✓	D121	S	L230	Z	1-8
2789	C1	378	✓	✓		D117	S	L228	Y	1-8
2802	A3	582	✓	✓	✓	D118	R	L220	Y	1-3,5,6,8
2805	A4	87	✓	✓	✓	D113	R	L220	Y	1-3,5,6,8
2806	A3	87	✓	✓		D113	R	L220	Y	1-3,5,6,8
2810	A4	120	✓	✓	✓	D112	R	L204	Y	1-3,5,6,8
2818	A3	332	✓	✓	✓	D101	R	L234	Y	1-8
2826	A4	341	✓	✓	✓	D116	R			
2832	C1	339	✓	✓		D113	R			
2843	C2	17	✓	✓				L228	Y	1-8
2851	C2	114	✓	✓	✓			L217	Y	1-8
2854	C1	581	✓	✓		D112	R	L220	Y	1-3,5,6,8
2855	C2	585	✓	✓	✓	D103	R	L219	Z	1-3,5,6,8
2858	A4	338	✓	✓						
2864	A3	107	✓	✓	✓	D100	Q	L225	X	1-3,5,6,8
2870	A3	214	✓	✓						
2871	A4	334	✓	✓	✓	D117	S			
2875	A4	619	✓	✓	✓	D113	R	L236	Z	3,4,7
2878	A4	97	✓	✓	✓	D112	R	L200	X	1-3,5,6,8
2879	C3	331	✓	✓	✓					
2889	L1	406	✓	✓	✓	D107	S	L215	Z	1-6,8
2902	A4	12	✓	✓	✓			L234	Y	1-8
2905	A4	13	✓	✓	✓	D121	S	L229	Y	1-8
2908	C2	574	✓	✓	✓	D117	S	L205	Y	1-3,5,6,8
2913	A4	333	✓	✓		D124	S			
2915	C2	333	✓	✓	✓	D114	R	L212	Z	1-8
2918	A4	334	✓	✓	✓	D124	S			
2920	C4	19	✓	✓	✓	D104	S	L212	Z	1-8

Left section:

DESIGN	PRICE	PAGE	MATERIALS LIST	CUSTOMIZABLE	QUOTE ONE®	DECK	DECK PRICE	LANDSCAPE	LANDSCAPE PRICE	REGIONS
2921	C4	172	✓	●	🏠	D104	S	L212	Z	1-8
2922	C4	618	✓	●	🏠					
2925	A3	342	✓	●						
2926	C3	346	✓	●						
2929	A3	582	✓	●						
2937	C3	377		●	🏠			L229	Y	1-8
2940	L3	463	✓	●	🏠	D114	R	L230	Z	1-8
2941	A3	86	✓	●		D112	R			
2945	C1	576	✓	●	🏠					
2946	C2	579	✓	●	🏠	D114	R	L207	Z	1-6,8
2947	A4	3	✓	●	🏠	D112	R	L200	X	1-3,5,6,8
2948	A4	621	✓	●	🏠					
2950	C2	620	✓	●	🏠					
2951	L2	420	✓	●						
2953	C4	394	✓	●	🏠	D111	S	L223	Z	1-3,5,6,8
2955	L3	421	✓	●	🏠					
2957	C4	585	✓	●		D107	S	L218	Z	1-6,8
2962	C1	583	✓	●	🏠					
2966	C3	420	✓	●						
2968	L2	416	✓	●	🏠			L227	Z	1-8
2969	C2	592	✓	●		D110	R	L223	Z	1-3,5,6,8
2970	C3	9	✓	●	🏠			L223	Z	1-3,5,6,8
2971	C2	590	✓	●	🏠			L223	Z	1-3,5,6,8
2973	A4	590	✓	●				L223	Z	1-3,5,6,8
2974	A4	591	✓	●				L223	Z	1-3,5,6,8
2977	L1	478	✓	●				L214	Z	1-3,5,6,8
2979	C1	210	✓	●						
2981	L1	201	✓	●				L224	Y	1-3,5,6,8
2984	L2	409	✓	●	🏠			L214	Z	1-3,5,6,8
2991	C4	380	✓	●	🏠	D111	S	L215	Z	1-6,8
2995	C3	170	✓	●	🏠	D106	S	L217	Y	1-8
3305	L1	416	✓	●						
3309	C1	593	✓	●	🏠			L209	Y	1-6,8
3310	C1	30	✓	●	🏠	D111	S	L227	Z	1-8
3311	C4	16	✓	●	🏠	D109	S	L220	Y	1-3,5,6,8
3314	A4	164	✓	●	🏠			L200	X	1-3,5,6,8
3316	A3	180	✓	●	🏠			L202	X	1-3,5,6,8
3325	C2	578	✓	●	🏠	D100	Q	L238	Y	3,4,7,8
3327	C1	94	✓	●	🏠	D110	R	L217	Y	1-8
3328	C2	536	✓	●	🏠					
3331	A3	662	✓	●	🏠			L203	Y	1-3,5,6,8
3332	C1	115	✓	●	🏠			L200	X	1-3,5,6,8
3337	C4	408	✓	●	🏠			L214	Z	1-3,5,6,8
3349	C4	404	✓	●	🏠	D107	S	L216	Y	1-3,5,6,8
3355	A2	119	✓	●	🏠	D117	S	L220	Y	1-3,5,6,8
3357	C1	332	✓	●	🏠	D115	Q	L211	Y	1-8

Right section:

DESIGN	PRICE	PAGE	MATERIALS LIST	CUSTOMIZABLE	QUOTE ONE®	DECK	DECK PRICE	LANDSCAPE	LANDSCAPE PRICE	REGIONS
3360	L1	374	✓	●	🏠			L207	Z	1-6,8
3368	C1	18	✓	●	🏠	D104	S	L220	Y	1-3,5,6,8
3380	L1	415	✓	●	🏠					
3397	C2	536	✓	●	🏠	D110	R	L209	Y	1-6,8
3405	C3	613	✓	●	🏠			L236	Z	3,4,7
3414	C3	645	✓	●	🏠			L233	Y	3,4,7
3423	C1	620	✓	●	🏠					
3425	C2	644	✓	●	🏠					
3431	A4	610	✓	●	🏠					
3432	C2	606	✓	●	🏠			L233	Y	3,4,7
3434	C2	608	✓	●	🏠			L233	Y	3,4,7
3435	C3	610	✓	●	🏠			L227	Z	1-8
3436	C1	616	✓	●	🏠			L227	Z	1-8
3441	C1	644	✓	●	🏠			L239	Z	1-8
3442	A3	133	✓	●	🏠	D115	Q	L200	X	1-3,5,6,8
3454	A3	336	✓	●	🏠	D110	R	L220	Y	1-3,5,6,8
3460	A3	4	✓	●				L200	X	1-3,5,6,8
3461	C1	540	✓	●	🏠			L204	Y	1-3,5,6,8
3466	A3	510	✓	●	🏠	D110	R	L207	Z	1-6,8
3471	L1	399	✓	●	🏠			L236	Z	3,4,7
3486	A3	15	✓	●	🏠					
3487	A4	109	✓	●	🏠			L209	Y	1-6,8
3491	A4	101	✓	●	🏠	D111	S	L215	Z	1-6,8
3500	C3	412	✓	●	🏠	D111	S	L214	Z	1-3,5,6,8
3508	C3	200	✓	●	🏠			L206	Z	1-6,8
3515	C3	380	✓	●	🏠	D111	S	L214	Z	1-3,5,6,8
3521	A4	200	✓	●	🏠			L282	X	1-8
3527	C4	412	✓	●	🏠					
3558	C2	293	✓	●	🏠	D105	R	L203	Y	1-3,5,6,8
3559	C2	139	✓	●	🏠	D111	S	L217	Y	1-8
3560	C1	336	✓	●	🏠			L234	Y	1-8
3562	A4	26	✓	●	🏠	D110	R	L238	Y	3,4,7,8
3563	A3	346	✓	●	🏠	D115	Q	L233	Y	3,4,7
3569	A3	139	✓	●	🏠	D105	R	L238	Y	3,4,7,8
3606	C2	171	✓	●	🏠	D110	R	L224	Y	1-3,5,6,8
3608	C3	515	✓	●	🏠			L223	Z	1-3,5,6,8
3609	A4	553	✓	●	🏠	D100	Q	L224	Y	1-3,5,6,8
3612	C2	148	✓	●	🏠			L206	Z	1-6,8
3615	A3	247	✓	●	🏠			L200	X	1-3,5,6,8
3619	A4	555	✓	●	🏠	D111	S	L207	Z	1-6,8
3621	C2	600	✓	●	🏠	D111	S	L223	Z	1-3,5,6,8
3622	C1	169	✓	●	🏠			L224	Y	1-3,5,6,8
3630	C3	615	✓	●	🏠			L209	Y	1-6,8
3631	C2	622	✓	●	🏠			L214	Z	1-3,5,6,8
3632	C2	635	✓	●	🏠			L237	Y	7
3633	C3	622	✓	●	🏠			L237	Y	7

DESIGN	PRICE	PAGE	MATERIALS LIST	CUSTOMIZABLE	QUOTE ONE®	DECK	DECK PRICE	LANDSCAPE	LANDSCAPE PRICE	REGIONS
3635	C2	552	✓	🏠	🏠			L283	X	1-8
3636	C2	349	✓	🏠	🏠			L238	Y	3,4,7,8
3637	C3	349	✓	🏠	🏠			L235	Z	1-3,5,6,8
3638	C3	148	✓	🏠	🏠			L215	Z	1-6,8
3639	C2	14	✓	🏠	🏠			L217	Y	1-8
3640	C2	619	✓	🏠	🏠			L286	Z	1-8
3644	C1	611	✓	🏠	🏠					
3646	C1	609	✓	🏠	🏠			L237	Y	7
3652	C1	103	✓	🏠	🏠	D105	R	L220	Y	1-3,5,6,8
3653	C1	556	✓	🏠	🏠	D111	S	L209	Y	1-6,8
3654	C1	573	✓	🏠	🏠			L292	X	1-8
3655	A3	118	✓	🏠	🏠			L205	Y	1-3,5,6,8
3656	A2	118	✓	🏠	🏠			L205	Y	1-3,5,6,8
3657	C1	149	✓	🏠	🏠					
3658	A3	664	✓	🏠	🏠	D102	Q	L202	X	1-3,5,6,8
3659	A3	126	✓	🏠	🏠			L290	Y	1-8
3660	C1	618	✓	🏠	🏠			L236	Z	3,4,7
3662	A4	5	✓	🏠	🏠			L287	Z	1-8
3665	C1	614	✓	🏠	🏠			L288	Z	1-8
3667	C1	615	✓	🏠	🏠					
3672	C1	479	✓	🏠	🏠	D111	S	L209	Y	1-6,8
3675	A4	533	✓	🏠	🏠	D110	R	L223	Z	1-3,5,6,8
3677	C1	532	✓	🏠	🏠	D110	R	L222	Y	1-3,5,6,8
3679	A4	533	✓	🏠	🏠	D111	S	L282	X	1-8
3680	A4	654	✓	🏠	🏠	D111	S	L282	X	1-8
3681	A4	525	✓	🏠	🏠	D111	S	L282	X	1-8
3682	A4	524	✓	🏠	🏠	D111	S	L282	X	1-8
3683	A4	525	✓	🏠	🏠	D111	S	L292	X	1-8
3687	A4	552	✓	🏠	🏠	D110	R	L282	X	1-8
3688	A4	132	✓	🏠	🏠			L200	X	1-3,5,6,8
3689	A3	488	✓	🏠	🏠	D124	S	L284	Y	1-8
3693	C4	612	✓	🏠	🏠					
3694	C1	607	✓	🏠	🏠			L237	Y	7
3696	C1	601	✓	🏠	🏠	D110	R	L287	Z	1-8
3697	A4	524	✓	🏠	🏠					
3699	A4	655	✓	🏠	🏠	D115	Q	L292	X	1-8
3700	A3	124	✓	🏠						
3701	A3	106	✓	🏠						
3704	A3	131	✓	🏠						
3705	A3	106	✓	🏠						
3708	A3	96	✓	🏠						
3713	A3	359	✓	🏠						
3715	A4	551	✓	🏠						
3718	A2	489	✓	🏠						
3721	A3	489	✓	🏠						
3725	A2	111	✓	🏠						
3842	C2	664	✓	🏠	🏠					
4015	A3	679	✓	🏠						
4027	A3	678	✓	🏠	🏠					
4061	A3	654	✓	🏠	🏠	D115	Q			
4115	A4	376		🏠						
4308	C2	376		🏠				L231	Z	1-8
5503	C1	256	✓	🏠	🏠					
5507	A4	132	✓	🏠	🏠					
5511	C1	573	✓	🏠	🏠					
5512	C1	237	✓	🏠	🏠					
5517	C1	256	✓	🏠	🏠					
5519	C1	257	✓	🏠	🏠					
5527	C2	272	✓	🏠	🏠					
5538	A2	230	✓	🏠						
5541	C1	224	✓	🏠	🏠					
5548	C1	556	✓	🏠	🏠					
5555	C2	272	✓	🏠	🏠					
6602	C2	633								
6635	L4	468	✓		🏠					
6641	C4	632								
6651	L2	466								
6652	C2	275								
6654	A4	638								
6655	A4	637								
6656	L1	466								
6660	C3	468								
6661	C3	471								
6663	C2	632								
6684	C1	636								
6689	C1	32								
6692	A4	636								
6693	C1	639								
6698	C1	639								
6700	C1	640								
6701	A4	641								
6721	C3	275								
7019	C4	291	✓							
7023	C1	270	✓							
7036	C2	424	✓							
7204	C3	424	✓							
7222	C2	383	✓							
7229	A3	368	✓							
7232	C1	56	✓		🏠					
7233	C1	79	✓							
7240	C1	274	✓							

DESIGN	PRICE	PAGE	MATERIALS LIST	CUSTOMIZABLE	QUOTE ONE®	DECK	DECK PRICE	LANDSCAPE	LANDSCAPE PRICE	REGIONS
9369	C1	276	✓							
9370	C1	280	✓							
9375	C1	33	✓		🏠					
9395	C1	279	✓							
9478	C1	293	✓							
9504	C1	279	✓							
9509	A3	351	✓							
9537	C1	370	✓							
9601	A3	509	✓							
9605	A4	531	✓							
9606	A3	529	✓		🏠					
9609	A2	655	✓							
9616	C1	558	✓							
9619	A4	137	✓							
9620	A2	504	✓							
9621	A3	531	✓		🏠					
9622	A3	508	✓							
9623	A4	516	✓		🏠					
9625	A4	544	✓							
9626	A3	529	✓		🏠					
9630	A3	665	✓							
9632	A4	7	✓		🏠					
9634	A4	74	✓							
9638	A3	602	✓							
9639	A3	504	✓							
9644	A3	562	✓							
9645	A3	516	✓		🏠					
9654	A4	528	✓							
9655	A4	136	✓							
9656	A4	61	✓							
9660	A4	56	✓							
9661	A3	185	✓		🏠					
9662	A3	560	✓		🏠					
9663	A2	653	✓							
9664	A2	493	✓		🏠					
9666	A3	652	✓		🏠					
9667	C1	560	✓		🏠					
9669	C1	519	✓							
9671	C1	513	✓							
9673	A4	527	✓		🏠					
9679	A3	505	✓							
9687	A3	557	✓							
9688	A4	566	✓							
9690	A3	539	✓		🏠					
9692	A3	541	✓							
9693	A3	490	✓							
9694	A4	520	✓		🏠					
9696	A3	492	✓							
9697	A3	652	✓							
9702	A4	518	✓		🏠					
9703	A4	512	✓							
9705	A4	197	✓							
9706	A4	518	✓							
9707	A4	538	✓		🏠					
9709	C1	11	✓							
9711	A3	540	✓							
9712	A4	6	✓		🏠					
9713	A3	503	✓							
9717	A4	568	✓							
9721	C3	526	✓		🏠					
9723	C1	523	✓		🏠					
9725	A4	559	✓							
9726	A2	506	✓							
9727	A2	506	✓							
9728	A3	76	✓							
9729	C3	539	✓							
9730	C1	563	✓							
9732	A4	521	✓							
9733	C1	520	✓							
9734	A3	57	✓		🏠					
9736	A4	184	✓							
9738	A4	480	✓		🏠					
9742	A3	482	✓		🏠					
9743	C3	389	✓							
9745	C1	522	✓							
9746	C1	522	✓							
9747	A3	545	✓		🏠					
9748	A3	488	✓							
9749	A3	501	✓		🏠					
9750	A3	502	✓							
9751	C1	512	✓							
9752	A4	538	✓							
9753	A2	495	✓		🏠					
9756	A4	501	✓		🏠					
9757	A4	194	✓		🏠					
9759	A3	549	✓		🏠					
9760	A2	76	✓							
9761	C1	511	✓							
9763	A3	502	✓		🏠					
9764	A3	494	✓		🏠					
9766	C1	547	✓							

DESIGN	PRICE	PAGE	MATERIALS LIST	CUSTOMIZABLE	QUOTE ONE®	DECK	DECK PRICE	LANDSCAPE	LANDSCAPE PRICE	REGIONS
T126	L4	411								
T127	L3	413								
T165	C4	384								
T201	C3	197								
T203	C2	323								
T209	C2	141								
T240	C3	39								
T241	C2	78								
U104	C1	295								
U107	A3	337								
U109	A3	352								
U112	C1	65								
U114	C2	400								
U171	C2	387								
U188	A3	357								
U207	C1	82								
U208	C1	82								
U257	A3	64								
U279	L1	422								
V012	C3	444	✓							
W006	A4	534								
W008	A4	126								
W300	A3	183	✓							
W311	C4	397								
X003	A3	366								
X012	A3	162	✓							
X013	A3	372	✓							

DESIGN	PRICE	PAGE	MATERIALS LIST	CUSTOMIZABLE	QUOTE ONE®	DECK	DECK PRICE	LANDSCAPE	LANDSCAPE PRICE	REGIONS
X016	A4	535								
X022	C1	301								
X025	A3	254								
X031	C1	294								
X033	C1	145								
X041	C1	300								
Y007	A4	46								
Y009	C1	193								
Y013	A4	50	✓							
Y015	C1	90								
Z007	C3	288	✓							
Z010	C1	555	✓							
Z011	C2	347	✓							
Z012	C1	287	✓							
Z015	C2	571	✓							
Z016	A4	289	✓							
Z017	A4	571	✓							
Z018	C3	570	✓							
Z020	C3	588	✓							
Z023	A3	248	✓							
Z033	C1	283	✓							
Z035	A3	649								
Z042	A3	680	✓							
Z047	A3	134	✓							
Z050	A1	486	✓							
Z054	A3	680	✓							

Before You Order . . .

Before filling out the coupon at right or calling us on our Toll-Free Blueprint Hotline, you may want to learn more about our services and products. Here's some information you will find helpful.

Quick Turnaround

We process and ship every blueprint order from our office within two business days. Because of this quick turnaround, we won't send a formal notice acknowledging receipt of your order.

Our Exchange Policy

Since blueprints are printed in response to your order, we cannot honor requests for refunds. However, we will exchange your entire first order for an equal number of blueprints at a price of $50 for the first set and $10 for each additional set; $70 total exchange fee for 4 sets; $100 total exchange fee for 8 sets . . . *plus* the difference in cost if exchanging for a design in a higher price bracket or *less* the difference in cost if exchanging for a design in lower price bracket. One exchange is allowed within a year of purchase date. **(Sepias and reproducibles are not refundable, returnable or exchangeable.)** All sets from the first order must be returned before the exchange can take place. Please add $18 for postage and handling via Regular Service; $30 via Priority Service; $40 via Express Service. Returns and cancellations are subject to a 20% restocking fee; shipping and handling charges are not refundable.

About Reverse Blueprints

If you want to build in reverse of the plan as shown, we will include an extra set of reverse blueprints (mirror image) for an additional fee of $50. Although lettering and dimensions will appear backward, reverses will be a useful aid if you decide to flop the plan.

Revising, Modifying and Customizing Plans

The wide variety of designs available in this publication allows you to select ideas and concepts to fit your building site and match your family's needs, wants and budget. Like many homeowners who buy these plans, you and your builder, architect or engineer may want to make changes to them. Some minor changes may be made by your builder, but we recommend that most changes be made by a licensed architect or engineer. If you need to make alterations to a design that is customizable, you need only order our Home Customizer® Package to get you started. As set forth below, we cannot assume any responsibility for blueprints which have been changed, whether by you, your builder or by professionals selected by you or referred to you by us, because such individuals are outside our supervision and control.

Architectural and Engineering Seals

Some cities and states are now requiring that a licensed architect or engineer review and "seal" a blueprint, or officially approve it, prior to construction due to concerns over energy costs, safety and other factors. Prior to application for a building permit or the start of actual construction, we strongly advise that you consult your local building official who can tell you if such a review is required.

About the Designers

The architects and designers whose work appears in this publication are among America's leading residential designers. Each plan was designed to meet the requirements of a nationally recognized model building code in effect at the time and place the plan was drawn. Because national building codes change from time to time, plans may not comply with any such code at the time they are sold to a customer. In addition, building officials may not accept these plans as final construction documents of record as the plans may need to be modified and additional drawings and details added to suit local conditions and requirements. We strongly advise that purchasers consult a licensed architect or engineer, and their local building official, before starting any construction related to these plans.

Local Building Codes and Zoning Requirements

At the time of creation, our plans are drawn to specifications published by the Building Officials and Code Administrators (BOCA) International, Inc.; the Southern Building Code Congress (SBCCI) International, Inc.; the International Conference of Building Officials; or the Council of American Building Officials (CABO). Our plans are designed to meet or exceed national building standards. Because of the great differences in geography and climate throughout the United States and Canada, each state, county and municipality has its own building codes, zone requirements, ordinances and building regulations. Your plan may need to be modified to comply with local requirements regarding snow loads, energy codes, soil and seismic conditions and a wide range of other matters. In addition, you may need to obtain permits or inspections from local governments before and in the course of construction. Prior to using blueprints ordered from us, we strongly advise that you consult a licensed architect or engineer—and speak with your local building official—before applying for any permit or beginning construction. We authorize the use of our blueprints on the express condition that you strictly comply with all local building codes, zoning requirements and other applicable laws, regulations, ordinances and requirements. **Notice: Plans for homes to be built in Nevada must be re-drawn by a Nevada-registered professional. Consult your building official for more information on this subject.**

Foundation and Exterior Wall Changes

Most of our plans are drawn with either a full or partial basement foundation. Depending on your specific climate or regional building practices, you may wish to change this basement to a slab or crawlspace. Most professional contractors and builders can easily adapt your plans to alternate foundation types. Likewise, most can easily change 2x4 wall construction to 2x6, or vice versa.

Disclaimer

We and the designers we work with have put substantial care and effort into the creation of our blueprints. However, because we cannot provide on-site consultation, supervision and control over actual construction, and because of the great variance in local building requirements, building practices and soil, seismic, weather and other conditions, WE CANNOT MAKE ANY WARRANTY, EXPRESS OR IMPLIED, WITH RESPECT TO THE CONTENT OR USE OF OUR BLUEPRINTS, INCLUDING BUT NOT LIMITED TO ANY WARRANTY OF MERCHANTABILITY OR OF FITNESS FOR A PARTICULAR PURPOSE.

Terms and Conditions

These designs are protected under the terms of United States Copyright Law and may not be copied or reproduced in any way, by any means, unless you have purchased Sepias or Reproducibles which clearly indicate your right to copy or reproduce. We authorize the use of your chosen design as an aid in the construction of one single family home only. You may not use this design to build a second or multiple dwellings without purchasing another blueprint or blueprints or paying additional design fees.

How Many Blueprints Do You Need?

A single set of blueprints is sufficient to study a home in greater detail. However, if you are planning to obtain cost estimates from a contractor or subcontractors—or if you are planning to build immediately—you will need more sets. Because additional sets are cheaper when ordered in quantity with the original order, make sure you order enough blueprints to satisfy all requirements. The following checklist will help you determine how many you need:

____ Owner

____ Builder (generally requires at least three sets; one as a legal document, one to use during inspections, and at least one to give to subcontractors)

____ Local Building Department (often requires two sets)

____ Mortgage Lender (usually one set for a conventional loan; three sets for FHA or VA loans)

____ TOTAL NUMBER OF SETS

The Home Customizer®

"This house is perfect...if only the family room were two feet wider." Sound familiar? In response to the numerous requests for this type of modification, Home Planners has developed **The Home Customizer® Package**. This exclusive package offers our top-of-the-line materials to make it easy for anyone, anywhere to customize any Home Planners design to fit their needs. Check the index on pages 688-699 for those plans which are customizable.

Some of the changes you can make to any of our plans include:

- exterior elevation changes
- kitchen and bath modifications
- roof, wall and foundation changes
- room additions and more!

The Home Customizer® Package includes everything you'll need to make the necessary changes to your favorite Home Planners design. The package includes:

- instruction book with examples
- architectural scale and clear work film
- erasable red marker and removable correction tape
- ¼"-scale furniture cutouts
- 1 set reproducible, erasable Sepias
- 1 set study blueprints for communicating changes to your design professional
- a copyright release letter so you can make copies as you need them
- referral letter with the name, address and telephone number of the professional in your region who is trained in modifying Home Planners designs efficiently and inexpensively.

The price of the **Home Customizer® Package** ranges from $650 to $1350, depending on the price schedule of the design you have chosen. **The Home Customizer® Package** will not only save you 25% to 75% of the cost of drawing the plans from scratch with a custom architect or engineer, it will also give you the flexibility to have your changes and modifications made by our referral network or by the professional of your choice. Now it's even easier and more affordable to have the custom home you've always wanted.

 ORDER TOLL FREE!
For information about any of our services or to order call 1-800-521-6797 or 520-297-8200 Browse our website: www.homeplanners.com

BLUEPRINTS ARE NOT RETURNABLE EXCHANGES ONLY

For Customer Service, call toll free 1-888-690-1116.

O R D E R   F O R M

HOME PLANNERS, LLC
Wholly owned by Hanley-Wood, LLC
3275 WEST INA ROAD, SUITE 110
TUCSON, ARIZONA 85741

THE BASIC BLUEPRINT PACKAGE
Rush me the following (please refer to the Plans Index and Price Schedule in this section):

_____	Set(s) of blueprints for plan number(s) _____.	$_____
_____	Set(s) of sepias for plan number(s) _____.	$_____
_____	Home Customizer® Package for plan(s)_____.	$_____
_____	Additional identical blueprints in same order @ $50 per set.	$_____
_____	Reverse blueprints @ $50 per set.	$_____

IMPORTANT EXTRAS
Rush me the following:

_____ Materials List: $50 (Must be purchased with Blueprint set.)
$75 Design Basics. Add $10 for a Schedule C4–L4 plan. $_____
_____ **Quote One®** Summary Cost Report @ $29.95 for one, $14.95 for
each additional, for plans _____ $_____
Building location: City _____ Zip Code _____
_____ **Quote One®** Materials Cost Report @ $120 Schedule P1–C3; $130
Schedule C4–L4 for plan _____ $_____
(Must be purchased with Blueprints set.)
Building location: City _____ Zip Code _____
_____ Specification Outlines @ $10 each. $_____
_____ Detail Sets @ $14.95 each; any two for $22.95; any three
for $29.95; all four for $39.95 (save $19.85). $_____
❑ Plumbing ❑ Electrical ❑ Construction ❑ Mechanical
(These helpful details provide general construction
advice and are not specific to any single plan.)
_____ Plan-A-Home® @ $29.95 each. $_____

DECK BLUEPRINTS
_____ Set(s) of Deck Plan _____. $_____
_____ Additional identical blueprints in same order @ $10 per set. $_____
_____ Reverse blueprints @ $10 per set. $_____
_____ Set of Standard Deck Details @ $14.95 per set. $_____
_____ Set of Complete Building Package (Best Buy!)
Includes Custom Deck Plan _____.
(See Index and Price Schedule)
Plus Standard Deck Details $_____

LANDSCAPE BLUEPRINTS
_____ Set(s) of Landscape Plan _____. $_____
_____ Additional identical blueprints in same order @ $10 per set. $_____
_____ Reverse blueprints @ $10 per set. $_____

Please indicate the appropriate region of the country for
Plant & Material List. (See Map on page 687): Region _____

POSTAGE AND HANDLING	1-3 sets	4+ sets
Signature is required for all deliveries.		
DELIVERY NO CODS (Requires street address - No P.O. Boxes)		
•Regular Service (Allow 7-10 business days delivery)	❑ $15.00	❑ $18.00
•Priority (Allow 4-5 business days delivery)	❑ $20.00	❑ $30.00
•Express (Allow 3 business days delivery)	❑ $30.00	❑ $40.00
CERTIFIED MAIL		
If no street address available. (Allow 7-10 days delivery)	❑ $20.00	❑ $30.00
OVERSEAS DELIVERY Note: All delivery times are from date Blueprint Package is shipped.	fax, phone or mail for quote	

POSTAGE (From box above) $_____
SUBTOTAL $_____
SALES TAX (AZ, MI, WA residents, please add appropriate state and local sales tax.) $_____
TOTAL (Subtotal and tax) $_____

YOUR ADDRESS (please print)
Name _____
Street _____
City _____ State _____ Zip _____
Daytime telephone number (_____) _____

FOR CREDIT CARD ORDERS ONLY
Please fill in the information below:
Credit card number _____
Exp. Date: Month/Year _____
Check one ❑ Visa ❑ MasterCard ❑ Discover Card ❑ American Express

Signature _____

Please check appropriate box: ❑ Licensed Builder-Contractor
❑ Homeowner

 **ORDER TOLL FREE!**
1-800-521-6797 or 520-297-8200

Order Form Key
TB78

Helpful Books & Software

Home Planners wants your building experience to be as pleasant and trouble-free as possible. That's why we've expanded our library of Do-It-Yourself titles to help you along. In addition to our beautiful plans books, we've added books to guide you through specific projects as well as the construction process. In fact, these are titles that will be as useful after your dream home is built as they are right now.

ONE-STORY

1 448 designs for all lifestyles. 860 to 5,400 square feet. 384 pages $9.95

TWO-STORY

2 460 designs for one-and-a-half and two stories. 1,245 to 7,275 square feet. 384 pages $9.95

VACATION

3 345 designs for recreation, retirement and leisure. 312 pages $8.95

MULTI-LEVEL

4 214 designs for split-levels, bi-levels, multi-levels and walkouts. 224 pages $8.95

COUNTRY

5 200 country designs from classic to contemporary by 7 winning designers. 224 pages $8.95

MOVE-UP

6 200 stylish designs for today's growing families from 9 hot designers. 224 pages $8.95

NARROW-LOT

7 200 unique homes less than 60' wide from 7 designers. Up to 3,000 square feet. 224 pages $8.95

SMALL HOUSE

8 200 beautiful designs chosen for versatility and affordability. 224 pages $8.95

BUDGET-SMART

9 200 efficient plans from 7 top designers, that you can really afford to build! 224 pages $8.95

EXPANDABLES

10 200 flexible plans that expand with your needs from 7 top designers. 240 pages $8.95

ENCYCLOPEDIA

11 500 exceptional plans for all styles and budgets—the best book of its kind! 352 pages $9.95

AFFORDABLE

12 Completely revised and updated, featuring 300 designs for modest budgets. 256 pages $9.95

ENCYCLOPEDIA 2

13 500 completely new plans. Spacious and stylish designs for every budget and taste. 352 pages $9.95

VICTORIAN

14 160 striking Victorian and Farmhouse designs from three leading designers. 192 pages $12.95

ESTATE

15 Dream big! Twenty-one designers showcase their biggest and best plans. 208 pages. $15.95

LUXURY

16 154 fine luxury plans-loaded with luscious amenities! 192 pages $14.95

COTTAGES

17 25 fresh new designs that are as warm as a tropical breeze. A blend of the best aspects of many coastal styles. 64 pages. $19.95

BEST SELLERS

18 Our 50th Anniversary book with 200 of our very best designs in full color! 224 pages $12.95

SPECIAL COLLECTION

19 70 romantic house plans that capture the classic tradition of home design. 160 pages $17.95

COUNTRY HOUSES

20 208 unique home plans that combine traditional style and modern livability. 224 pages $9.95

CLASSIC

21 Timeless, elegant designs that always feel like home. Gorgeous plans that are as flexible and up-to-date as their occupants. 240 pages. $9.95

CONTEMPORARY

22 The most complete and imaginative collection of contemporary designs available anywhere. 240 pages. $9.95

EASY-LIVING

23 200 efficient and sophisticated plans that are small in size, but big on livability. 224 pages $8.95

SOUTHERN

24 207 homes rich in Southern styling and comfort. 240 pages $8.95

SUNBELT

25 215 designs that capture the spirit of the Southwest. 208 pages $10.95

WESTERN

26 215 designs that capture the spirit and diversity of the Western lifestyle. 208 pages $9.95

ENERGY GUIDE

27 The most comprehensive energy efficiency and conservation guide available. 280 pages $35.00

Design Software

BOOK & CD-ROM

28 Both the Home Planners Gold book and matching Windows™ CD-ROM with 3D floorplans. $24.95

3D DESIGN SUITE

29 Home design made easy! View designs in 3D, take a virtual reality tour, add decorating details and more. $59.95

Outdoor Projects

OUTDOOR

30 42 unique outdoor projects. Gazebos, strombellas, bridges, sheds, playsets and more! 96 pages $7.95

GARAGES & MORE
31 101 multi-use garages and outdoor structures to enhance any home. 96 pages $7.95

DECKS

32 25 outstanding single-, double- and multi-level decks you can build. 112 pages $7.95

Landscape Designs

| EASY CARE | FRONT & BACK | BACKYARDS | BEDS & BORDERS | BATHROOMS | KITCHENS | HOUSE CONTRACTING | WINDOWS & DOORS |

   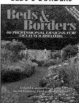    

33 41 special landscapes designed for beauty and low maintenance. 160 pages $14.95

34 The first book of do-it-yourself landscapes. 40 front, 15 backyards. 208 pages $14.95

35 40 designs focused solely on creating your own specially themed backyard oasis. 160 pages $14.95

36 Practical advice and maintenance techniques for a wide variety of yard projects. 160 pages. $14.95

37 An innovative guide to organizing, remodeling and decorating your bathroom. 96 pages $10.95

38 An imaginative guide to designing the perfect kitchen. Chock full of bright ideas to make your job easier. 176 pages $14.95

39 Everything you need to know to act as your own general contractor...and save up to 25% off building costs. 134 pages $14.95

40 Installation techniques and tips that make your project easier and more professional looking. 80 pages $7.95

| ROOFING | FRAMING | VISUAL HANDBOOK | BASIC WIRING | PATIOS & WALKS | TILE | TRIM & MOLDING |

41 Information on the latest tools, materials and techniques for roof installation or repair. 80 pages $7.95

42 For those who want to take a more-hands on approach to their dream. 319 pages $19.95

43 A plain-talk guide to the construction process; financing to final walk-through, this book covers it all. 498 pages $19.95

44 A straightforward guide to one of the most misunderstood systems in the home. 160 pages $12.95

45 Clear step-by-step instructions take you from the basic design stages to the finished project. 80 pages $7.95

46 Every kind of tile for every kind of application. Includes tips on use installation and repair. 176 pages $12.95

47 Step-by-step instructions for installing baseboards, window and door casings and more. 80 pages $7.95

Additional Books Order Form

To order your books, just check the box of the book numbered below and complete the coupon. We will process your order and ship it from our office within two business days. Send coupon and check (in U.S. funds).

YES! Please send me the books I've indicated:

☐ 1:VO . . . $9.95	☐ 25:SW . . . $10.95	
☐ 2:VT . . . $9.95	☐ 26:WH . . . $9.95	
☐ 3:VH . . . $8.95	☐ 27:RES . . . $35.00	
☐ 4:VS . . . $8.95	☐ 28:HPGC . . . $24.95	
☐ 5:FH . . . $8.95	☐ 29:PLANSUITE . . $59.95	
☐ 6:MU . . . $8.95	☐ 30:YG . . . $7.95	
☐ 7:NL . . . $8.95	☐ 31:GG . . . $7.95	
☐ 8:SM . . . $8.95	☐ 32:DP . . . $7.95	
☐ 9:BS . . . $8.95	☐ 33:ECL . . . $14.95	
☐ 10:EX . . . $8.95	☐ 34:HL . . . $14.95	
☐ 11:EN . . . $9.95	☐ 35:BYL . . . $14.95	
☐ 12:AF . . . $9.95	☐ 36:BB . . . $14.95	
☐ 13:E2 . . . $9.95	☐ 37:CDB . . . $10.95	
☐ 14:VDH . . . $12.95	☐ 38:CKI . . . $14.95	
☐ 15:EDH . . . $15.95	☐ 39:SBC . . . $14.95	
☐ 16:LD2 . . . $14.95	☐ 40:CGD . . . $7.95	
☐ 17:CTG . . . $19.95	☐ 41:CGR . . . $7.95	
☐ 18:HPG . . . $12.95	☐ 42:SRF . . . $19.95	
☐ 19:WEP . . . $17.95	☐ 43:RVH . . . $19.95	
☐ 20:CN . . . $9.95	☐ 44:CBW . . . $12.95	
☐ 21:CS . . . $9.95	☐ 45:CGW . . . $7.95	
☐ 22:CM . . . $9.95	☐ 46:CWT . . . $12.95	
☐ 23:EL . . . $8.95	☐ 47:CGT . . . $7.95	
☐ 24:SH . . . $8.95		

Additional Books Sub-Total $_____
ADD Postage and Handling $ 4.00
Sales Tax: (AZ, MI, WA residents, please add appropriate state and local sales tax.) $_____
YOUR TOTAL (Sub Total, Postage/Handling, Tax) $_____

YOUR ADDRESS (Please print)

Name _____
Street _____
City ....State ..Zip ......
Phone (_____) _____ — _____

YOUR PAYMENT
Check one: ☐ Check ☐ Visa ☐ MasterCard ☐ Discover Card ☐ American Express
Required credit card information:
Credit Card Number _____
Expiration Date (Month/Year) _____/_____
Signature Required _____

 Home Planners, LLC
Wholly owned by Hanley-Wood, LLC
3275 W. Ina Road, Suite 110, Dept. BK, Tucson, AZ 85741

TB78

Canadian Customers
Order Toll-Free 1-877-223-6389

Design 3608, page 515

OVER 3 MILLION BLUEPRINTS SOLD

"We instructed our builder to follow the plans including all of the many details which make this house so elegant…Our home is a fine example of the results one can achieve by purchasing and following the plans which you offer…Everyone who has seen it has assured us that it belongs in 'a picture book.' I truly mean it when I say that my home 'is a DREAM HOUSE.'"

> S.P.
> Anderson, SC

"We have had a steady stream of visitors, many of whom tell us this is the most beautiful home they've seen. Everyone is amazed at the layout and remarks on how unique it is. Our real estate attorney, who is a Chicago dweller and who deals with highly valued properties, told me this is the only suburban home he has seen that he would want to live in."

> W. & P.S.
> Flossmoor, IL

"Your blueprints saved us a great deal of money. I acted as the general contractor and we did a lot of the work ourselves. We probably built it for half the cost! We are thinking about more plans for another home. I purchased a competitor's book but my husband wants only your plans!"

> K.M.
> Grovetown, GA

"We are very happy with the product of our efforts. The neighbors and passersby appreciate what we have created. We have had many people stop by to discuss our house and kindly praise it as being the nicest house in our area of new construction. We have even had one person stop and make us an unsolicited offer to buy the house for much more than we have invested in it."

> K. & L.S.
> Bolingbrook, IL

"The traffic going past our house is unbelievable. On several occasions, we have heard that it is the 'prettiest house in Batavia.' Also, when meeting someone new and mentioning what street we live on, quite often we're told, 'Oh, you're the one in the yellow house with the wrap-around porch! I love it!'"

> A.W.
> Batavia, NY

"I have been involved in the building trades my entire life…Since building our home we have built two other homes for other families. Their plans from local professional architects were not nearly as good as yours. For that reason we are ordering additional plan books from you."

> T.F.
> Kingston, WA

"The blueprints we received from you were of excellent quality and provided us with exactly what we needed to get our successful home-building project underway. We appreciate your invaluable role in our home-building effort."

> T.A.
> Concord, TN